Colección Támesis
SERIE A: MONOGRAFÍAS, 243

A COMPANION TO
LATIN AMERICAN LITERATURE

*Tamesis*

*Founding Editor*
J. E. Varey

*General Editor*
Stephen M. Hart

*Editorial Board*
Alan Deyermond
Julian Weiss
Charles Davis

STEPHEN M. HART

# A COMPANION TO
# LATIN AMERICAN LITERATURE

TAMESIS

© Stephen M. Hart 1999, 2007

*All Rights Reserved*. Except as permitted under current legislation no part
of this work may be photocopied, stored in a retrieval system,
published, performed in public, adapted, broadcast,
transmitted, recorded or reproduced in any form or by any means,
without the prior permission of the copyright owner

The right of Stephen M. Hart to be identified as
the author of this work has been asserted in accordance with
sections 77 and 78 of the Copyright, Designs and Patents Act 1988

First published 1999
Reprinted in paperback 2001
New edition 2007
Paperback edition 2010

Transferred to digital printing

ISBN 978-1-85566-065-6 (1999)
ISBN 978-1-85566-076-2 (2001)
ISBN 978-1-85566-147-9 (2007)
ISBN 978-1-85566-211-7 (2010)

Tamesis is an imprint of Boydell & Brewer Ltd
PO Box 9, Woodbridge, Suffolk IP12 3DF, UK
and of Boydell & Brewer Inc.
668 Mt Hope Avenue, Rochester, NY 14620, USA
website: www.boydellandbrewer.com

A CiP catalogue record for this book is available
from the British Library

This publication is printed on acid-free paper

## CONTENTS

| | |
|---|---|
| Foreword | vii |
| Introduction: Unpacking the Canon | ix |
| 1  The Amerindian Legacy, and the Literature of Discovery and Conquest | 1 |
| 2  Colonial and Viceregal Literature | 35 |
| 3  Early Nineteenth-Century Literature | 67 |
| 4  Late Nineteenth-Century Literature | 106 |
| 5  Early Twentieth-Century Literature | 140 |
| 6  Late Twentieth-Century Literature | 191 |
| 7  Some Postmodern Developments | 250 |
| Postlude | 289 |
| Suggestions for Further Reading | 291 |
| Bibliography | 303 |
| Index | 331 |

For Jordan

# FOREWORD

I take this opportunity to thank the librarians at the libraries I visited while conducting the research on which this book is based, at the Fondo Reservado, in the Biblioteca Nacional, Mexico City, the Biblioteca Nacional in Bogotá, Colombia, the Bodleian, Oxford, the University Library, Cambridge, the British Library, London (and particularly Barry Taylor), the Stetson Collection in the University of Florida Library, and the National Libraries in Buenos Aires, Lima and Rio de Janeiro. Special thanks to my former colleagues in the Department of Spanish and Italian, University of Kentucky, whose willingness to discuss some of the concepts explored in the first edition of this book helped me to make fewer errors than would otherwise have been the case, and allowed me to appreciate the value of Colonial literature which, by and large, is not studied in Britain. I also express my gratitude here to those scholars who guided me in the preparation of this second edition. Thanks are due to Jason Wilson for advice about recent developments in Latin American literature, to João Cezar de Castro Rocha, John Gledson, David Treece, Claire Williams, Aquiles Alencar Brayner and Else Vieira, for their advice on trends in contemporary Brazilian literature, and especially to Maria Aparecida Ferreira de Andrade Salgueiro for her hospitality during my research trip to Rio de Janeiro in the spring of 2006. I am grateful to the Museu Nacional de Belas Artes, Rio de Janeiro, and to João Candido Portinari, President of the Portinari Project for permission to reproduce Portinari's *Coffee* as the jacket illustration. I gratefully acknowledge the support of my research trip to work in the archives of the National Library in Rio provided by the University of London Central Fund, the UCL Graduate School, the Arts and Humanities Dean's Fund and the Department of Spanish and Latin American Studies. Thanks too are in order for the generous assistance of the editorial team at Boydell and Brewer, especially Ellie Ferguson. Lastly, I thank the anonymous reviewers of the manuscript whose wisdom saved me from many an error; the others, of course, are mine.

S.M.H.

INTRODUCTION
# Unpacking the Canon

This book is designed for the moderately specialised reader of Spanish and Portuguese who wants an introduction to the main works of the Latin American literary canon. It takes its point of departure from an historical coincidence, namely that the discovery and colonisation of the area of the earth now called Latin America largely coincided with the birth of a new technology for the transmission of knowledge, namely, printing. The world has never been quite the same since Johann Gensfleisch zum Gutenberg printed his forty-two-line Bible in Mainz, Germany, in 1452–56 (Steinberg 21). Gutenberg's discovery of movable type spread like wildfire in the Europe of his day; as Steinberg suggests, '[w]ithin fifteen years after Gutenberg's death in 1468 printing presses had been set up in every country of western Christendom from Sweden to Sicily and from Spain to Poland and Hungary' (Steinberg 27). Twenty-five years after Gutenberg's death, the American continent was discovered and it is no exaggeration to state that the discovery, conquest and colonisation of that land took on a unique quality in the imagination of the West precisely because of the recent discovery of print. The newly-created presses of Europe printed copies of Christopher Columbus's letters to the Catholic Monarchs, they circulated printed versions of Hernán Cortés's letters, as well as Theodor de Bry's images of Brazilian cannibals, which were eagerly bought by the new mercantile classes then emerging in Europe. An earlier age had to be content with the Bayeux Tapestry. As this work hopes to show, the printed word was a crucial component in the cultural configuration that Latin America would gradually create over the next five centuries.

The present study is different from previous studies in three main ways. The typical survey of Latin American literature published in the last twenty-five years fails to address two issues which recent research in adjacent disciplines has discovered to be central to the notion of canon formation that underpins, consciously or not, any literary survey. The first issue concerns the treatment given to pre-1900 literature and, in particular, the indigenous cultural tradition in a study of the Latin American literary canon. For example, in her important study, *An Introduction to Spanish-American Literature* (1969), Jean Franco devotes her introduction to literature of Spanish America written between the conquest and c.1750 (Franco 1–27), and, within that, gives barely four out of 390 pages to the treatment of indigenous literature (Franco 5–8). Most critics agree that, in its ability to combine general sweep with detailed discussion, Franco's study is unmatched. Since the publication of *Spanish-American*

*Literature*, however, our notion of the Spanish-American literary canon has drastically altered and the importance of colonial and indigenous literature has increased accordingly. The present study reflects that trend and gives more space to literature written before the nineteenth century and, in particular, before the conquest. It also attempts to integrate a discussion of a period of literature (the post-Boom novel, poetry and theatre in the 1970s and 1980s) which was not treated in Franco's book simply because of its time of publication, as well as giving more space to significant women writers, especially in the modern period.

The second point of difference between the present study and previous works concerns the issue of evaluation. In this study I have not been exhaustive in selecting works for inclusion. Enrique Anderson-Imbert, in the introduction to his major study, *Historia de la literatura hispanoamericana* (1954, 1966, and 1982) has identified two of the main dangers which an historian of literature risks, namely, of writing on the one hand 'a history of literature containing very little history' or, on the other, 'a history of literature containing very little literature' (Anderson-Imbert, vol. 2, 441). Especially in the modern period, Anderson-Imbert, in his desire to be all-inclusive, discusses writers whose work is of minimal literary value; he mentions, after all, in his introduction that he has included a 'farrago' of secondary writers. I have decided not to follow that path in the present study, preferring to limit the number of writers included in order to give them the space they deserve. For the benefit of the general reader, I have also included a very brief plot summary of the novels discussed in order to clarify the subsequent analysis. The list of canonical authors studied here is based on a survey conducted in 1995 of the main literary works taught in departments of Spanish in United States research institutions.

The third point of difference between my analysis and previous studies concerns the social value of the literary work, the way in which it functioned within the society which gave it life, and (to the extent that it is possible) the role that the writer played in that society. What the present study attempts to do is provide a continuous, brief narrative about the main writers and works of the Latin American canon, and frame that historical narrative in the context of literary print culture (for further discussion see Stephen Hart, 'Literary Print Culture in the Spanish Colonies', 'Literary Print Culture in Spanish America 1880–1910', and '"El oficio de escribir"'). Footnotes and reference to the criticism have been kept to a minimum, while some indication of the main bibliographical trends has been made in the Suggestions for Further Reading. It is hoped that this overview of Latin American literature will be useful as a refresher course for the student preparing for masters and doctoral exams in Spanish – especially if he or she also minors in Portuguese – as well as the general reader.

Some words here about the term 'literature' as used in this study are necessary. A number of manuals do tremendous injustice to the proper understanding of the term 'literature' when they define it in universal, anti-historical terms. The entry on literature in the *Enciclopedia Universal Ilustrada Europea-Americana*, for example, begins by stating that literature is a work of art written for aesthetic effect only ('Género de producciones del entendimiento humano, que tienen por fin próximo o remoto expresar lo bello por medio de la palabra'; 1076), but then contradicts itself by giving space in the same article to ecclesiastical literature, judicial literature, and even military literature (1076–87). Through its recurrence to universalisms (for example, literature is a 'medio universal de expresión de todas las ideas'; 1077), the article in effect remains blind to the premise on which its argument is built. A more historicised approach to the meaning attached to the term literature clearly becomes necessary. In effect, the idea of literature changed during the Romantic period in Europe as much as in South America and, as a result, the term itself came more and more to signify a literary work written for aesthetic effect, a meaning which has remained with us until the present day. As Terry Eagleton has pointed out, literature, before the nineteenth century, meant 'the whole body of valued writing in society: philosophy, history, essays and letters as well as poems' (Eagleton 17). However, 'by the time of the Romantic period, literature was becoming virtually synonymous with the "imaginative"; to write about what did not exist was somehow more soul-stirring and valuable than to pen an account of Birmingham or the circulation of the blood' (Eagleton 18). The first recorded example of literature used in this sense in English was in 1812, although the term itself was in existence by at least the fourteenth century.[1] A similar situation exists for Spanish and Portuguese. Though 'literatura' is recorded as in use by 1490, it was in the nineteenth century that its more narrow, specialised sense of 'literary work written for aesthetic effect' came to replace the earlier more inclusive meaning of 'something written'.[2]

The three main differences mentioned above – reference to pre-Columbian literature, emphasis upon representativeness at the expense of all-inclusiveness, and the use of literary print culture as a paradigm to contextualise individual works – should not detract from the fact that the present book is offered as a complement to other studies (in particular the *Cambridge History of Latin*

---

[1] The *Oxford English Dictionary* defines literature as 'writing which has claim for consideration on the ground of beauty of form or emotional affect', noting that this sense is 'of very recent emergence both in English and French' (VIII, 1029). The older original meaning of literature as 'acquaintance with letters or books' is recorded as early as c. 1375 (VIII, 1029).

[2] 'Literatura' appears in Alonso Fernández de Palencia's *Universal Vocabulario en latín y en romance* (1490); see Corominas and Pascual, III 636. 'Letras' to mean 'carta misiva' is recorded in Spanish as early as 1250, and 'letrado' is already found in medieval texts by Berceo (1220–50) (Corominas and Pascual, III 636); a similar development is evident in Portuguese. This more narrow notion of literature emerged during the nineteenth century as a direct consequence of the specialisation of other fields of knowledge; the social sciences, for example, were born in the nineteenth century and, as a result of their mapping out their territory, literature was forced to retreat into a smaller, more cramped, domain. The term most frequently used in Spain, Portugal and Latin America during the pre-Romantic period ('letras') meant anything printed and included what we now understand by the term literature (i.e. writing normally published and written for aesthetic effect), as well as other disciplines such as law, history, religion and science.

*American Literature*, in three volumes, edited by Enrique Pupo-Walker and Roberto González Echeverría, and published in 1996, and the *Encyclopedia of Latin American Literature*, edited by Verity Smith and published in 1997) on that complex protean creature, Latin American literature.

The aim of this second edition has in the main been to supplement the original narrative of the history of Spanish American literature with an analysis of the most significant works of Brazilian literature. The sections as arranged in the first edition have largely been retained, but – as a result of the synergy produced by juxtaposing the analysis of certain key authors – the arrangement of the sections changed. In a number of sections the decision was taken to include discussion of important Spanish American works which, for reasons of space, could not be addressed in the first edition. Many of these additions were based on recommendations which surfaced in the various reviews that the first edition received. My hope is that the new sections will persuade the reader of the wealth and beauty of the best works of Brazilian literature. If it inspires future scholars to take up and critically test some of the ideas expounded here, in the classroom or elsewhere, its purpose will have been well served.

# 1
# The Amerindian Legacy
# and the Literature of Discovery and Conquest

Christopher Columbus, on behalf of the Spanish monarchy, landed in the Bahamas on 12 October 1492, and Pedro Álvares Cabral, on a charge from the Portuguese throne and with plans drawn up by Vasco da Gama, sighted the eastern coastline of mainland South America on 22 April 1500; thus began the discovery and conquest of the New World. While neither man was aware of the nature and extent of the land they had discovered – they were both seeking the spices of the East – their respective governments were quick to claim these territories. Since the land discovered by Álvares Cabral was well within the zone assigned to Portugal by the papal Treaty of Tordesillas of 1494, it was claimed for Portugal and baptised Vera Cruz, a name which was soon abandoned in favour of Brazil, after the red dyewood (*pau-brasil*) which grew abundantly there. The first descriptions of these new lands appear in Columbus's famous letter of 1493 to Luis de Santangel and Vaz de Caminha's equally famous letter of 1500 (both of which are discussed in more detail below), and it is striking how similar their accounts are, particularly with regard to the notion of the primitiveness of the inhabitants of this newly discovered world. Both Columbus and Vaz de Caminha comment on their lack of clothing, their docility and the facility with which they might be Christianised (itself predicated on the notion of their cultural bereftness). While the suggestion that the Amerindians were somehow bereft of human culture would be revised substantially in the case of the later Spanish discoverers and conquistadors – particularly when they came into contact in the 1520s and 1530s with the Mayas, the Aztecs and the Incas whose cultures were highly developed (in terms of cultural memory, social organisation and scientific knowledge [i.e. of astronomy]) – it remained a hermeneutic benchmark in Brazil. Indeed there was one feature of Amerindian culture which appeared to many of the European observers who came to the New World to confirm its 'primitive' condition, and this was the prevalence within the New World – from the Tupi Indians of the east to the Incas of the west – of cannibalism.

The most substantial difference between the various ethnic groups of Amerindia concerned their level of competence in the area of cultural memory which, in Europe at least, was epitomised by the book. While none of the Amerindian cultures possessed an alphabetic script some did have cultural artifacts that resembled the European book in some respects. The codices of the Mayas and the Aztecs, for example, were sacred books which dealt with the ritual calendar, divination and the actions of the gods; their notation was a combination of pictography, ideograms and phonetic symbols. They were kept in temples and used by the priestly caste in their divine ceremonies. Some indication of the hermetic nature of the knowledge they encapsulated is suggested by the following passage in the *Cantares mexicanos*:

> Yo canto las pinturas del libro
> lo voy desplegando
> cual florido papagayo,
> hago hablar a los códices.
> (quoted in Oviedo, *Historia*, vol. 1, 35)

Because of their religious content only a small number of the codices escaped destruction by the Spanish. In 1562, for example, Bishop Diego de Landa held a triumphalist *auto-da-fé* in Maní, Yucatan, in which he burned all the Maya books with hieroglyphic writing that he was able to capture. As Landa recalled in chapter LXI of his *Relación de las cosas de Yucatán*: 'Hallámosles gran número de libros de estas sus letras [hieroglyphs], y porque no tenían cosa en que no hubiese superstición y falsedades del demonio, se los quemamos todos, lo cual sintieron a maravilla y les dio mucha pena' (Diego de Landa 117–18). There are only three Maya codices and a handful of pre-Columbian Aztec codices now in existence (for more information see 'The Codices' below). As a result of the brutal rupture brought about by the conquest, many of these repositories of cultural knowledge – ranging from the *quipus* (Incan accounting tools made of rope) to Maya texts – remain undeciphered to this day.

Much of what we now know about Amerindian culture comes down to us filtered through a vast enterprise of transliteration by the Portuguese and Spanish invaders. This process can be compared to that of the last will and testament taken from a dying man whose language is imperfectly understood by the scribe: the testimony is meant to summarize the whole of the individual's previous life and, given the circumstances, it is inevitably characterized by gaps. Add to this the role of the scribe who transliterates the testimony and who – unconsciously or not – moulds the narrative to fit his own view of the world, and we can see how difficult it becomes to separate out the various strands within this process of transculturation. When considering the texts below, we must bear in mind that all were created in the process of transliteration which occurred after the conquest and produced what might be described as a 'negative transparency' of Amerindian culture. Even the sacred verbal texts, such as the *Popol Vuh*, were transliterated *after* the conquest, though their textualisation was based on an oral account which had been passed down through the generations.

The best example of this transliteration process is the work of Bernadino de Sahagún (1499–1590) who was one of the first Franciscans to arrive in New Spain. Soon after his arrival there in 1529 he quickly learned Nahuatl, the language of the Aztecs, and, with the help of twelve chieftains from the town of Tepulco and four interpreters, he began to write the *Historia general de las cosas de Nueva España* (1569). The chieftains provided him with a verbal as well as a pictographic account of the history of their people; Sahagún incorporated the images into his text, transliterated the Nahuatl account and provided a translation into Spanish in an adjacent column. A vast encyclopedia about the history and customs of the Aztecs, the *Historia general de las cosas de Nueva España* is particularly valuable since, in the final chapter, it describes the conquest of Tenochtitlan from the Aztec point of view, and it has been used by León-Portilla to good effect in his compilation *Visión de los vencidos* (see 'The Amerindian View of the Conquest' below). Given its hybrid nature – it is a chronicle since it has an historical narrative, and a codex since it has illustrations (thus it is also known as the *Codex Florentino*) – the *Historia general de las cosas de Nueva España* offers an unparalleled glimpse into the transculturation process which occurred in Spanish America after the conquest.

## The *Popol Vuh*

The most important of the Amerindian sacred verbal texts is the *Popol Vuh*, literally 'Book of the Community', but customarily known as the Sacred Book of the Quiché Maya. The original Quiché manuscript of the *Popol Vuh* had been transliterated probably by one Diego Reynoso, a member of the Maya priestly caste, possibly between 1554 and 1558, and was discovered by Father Francisco Ximénez in the late seventeenth century while he was serving as parish priest of the village of Santo Tomás Chichicastenango in the highlands of Guatemala. He copied it and then produced his own dual-language version (Quiché original with Spanish translation) of the original manuscript. From that point Ximénez's manuscript lay dormant in the library of the university of San Carlos in the city of Guatemala until discovered by Carl Scherzer, a Viennese doctor, who published the Spanish text in Vienna in 1857. This book was followed four years later by the publication in Paris of the original Quiché text together with a French version, introduction and notes by Abbé Brasseur de Bourbourg entitled *Popol Vuh, Le Livre Sacré et les mythes de l'antiquité américaine, avec les livres héroïques et historiques des Quichués* (1861).[1] Any hope that the *Popol Vuh* might be a completely pre-Columbian text is dispelled in the introduction in which the (unknown) author refers to writing 'under the Law of God and Christianity' (*Popol Vuh* 79–80). The text has, since Abbé Brasseur de Bourbourg's suggestion, been divided up into four parts and, although there is nothing in the text to indicate that this is necessary, this

---

[1] The original copy of the manuscript – i.e. that probably transcribed by Diego Reynoso – has been lost but Father Ximénez's original handwritten text is now held in the Edward E. Ayer collection in the Newberry Library of Chicago.

division clarifies its structure. Part I begins like the Old Testament book of Genesis with the creation of the human race, although in the *Popol Vuh* this is only successful on the third attempt; the first two attempts, with mud and wood respectively, do not produce the desired result, and it is only when ears of corn are used that the creation is to the satisfaction of the gods (I, i–iii, 81–93; III, i–ii, 165–69). As with Genesis, the *Popol Vuh* stresses the continuity between the first examples of mankind, in this case the four men Balam-Quitzé, Balam-Acab, Macutah and Iqui-Balam, and the Quiché people of which the author is a member, mainly through the genealogy lists given in III, iii, 170–73, and IV, xii, 228–35. These creation stories are mixed freely with stories from individuals of the principal houses of the Quiché peoples such that the empirical and the supernatural, history and religion, are merged to form one narrative. The world of the Quiché is presented as coming to an end with the invasion of the Spaniards. The arrival of Pedro de Alvarado, called Donadiú, the sun, by the Quiché since he burned their kings (IV, xii, 230), coincided with the twelfth generation and, as the narrative concludes,

> this was the life of the Quiché, because no longer can be seen [the book of the *Popol Vuh*] which the kings had in olden times, for it has disappeared. In this manner, then, all the people of the Quiché, which is called Santa Cruz, came to an end. (IV, xii, 234–35)

As the penultimate sentence makes quite clear, the *Popol Vuh* is not to be understood simply as a symbolic transcription of the laws of the Quiché people but rather as an outward sign of the inter-generational continuity of a living community. Though we have the book (*Vuh*), the community (*Popol*) to which it testifies is no more.

## The Codices

The codices are a unique Latin American art-form; they were often made of deer-skin, covered with a chalk-like varnish to preserve them, and, typically, folded like a screen (*leporello*). Some were drawn on *amatl*, a native paper made from the inner bark of trees belonging to the genus *Ficus*, and they are normally read from right to left, backwards and forwards in a zig-zag motion (Caso 10). The codices, as mentioned above, are partly ideographic, partly phonetic. They are normally divided into three distinct types: those which focus on the annals of a people and/or their gods and divine rituals; the Techialoyan books, that is, petitionary documents used to defend lands and communities against changes in the law; and the Testerian manuscripts whose main purpose was Christian instruction (Brotherston, *Mexican Painted Books*, 3). What follows will concentrate in the main on the first category of codex (both the Mayan and the Mexican), although some mention will be made of the second type. It would, of course, be a mistake to see the codices as offering unmediated access to the truth about Amerindian culture since, ironically enough, many owe their very existence to the Spanish invasion and, for that reason, demonstrate a hybrid character.

There are only three known Mayan codices in existence, the *Codex Dresden*, the *Codex Pérez* and the *Codex Madrid*, all named after the city in which they are now held. The *Codex Pérez* is exemplary; it was named after the Yucatecan Don Juan Pío Pérez (1798–1859) who collected, collated and copied a number of Maya manuscripts which he came across in Ticul (Craine and Reindorp xv–xvi). It is a compilation of various 'books' authored by different Jaguar priests, but it does have a unified focus; the Maya notion of time (with its combination of the 365-day 'vague' year and the 260-day ritual almanac) around which all else orbited in the thought-universe of the Mayas. It also contains a version of the important sacred text *The Book of Chilam Balam of Maní* (literally, 'The Book of the Jaguar Priest of Maní'), and a charming short narrative entitled 'The Maiden Teodora', which recounts how a young beautiful girl enchants the court of the King Almanzor with her unrivalled intelligence and good looks (*Codex Pérez* 59–62). A close reading of the *Codex Pérez* suggests that the narrative which predicted the return of the Mayan culture-hero, Kukulcán, was tampered with to produce a text which predicted 'the coming of the Spaniards and Christianity, both of which should be welcomed with enthusiasm' (*Codex Pérez* 69, n. 21).

The Aztec codices, many more of which survived, reveal similar evidence of transculturation. One of the most famous of these, the *Codex Mendoza*, which derives its name from the first Viceroy of Spain, Antonio de Mendoza, who commissioned it, is divided into three parts: the first concerns the Mexican annals from the founding of Mexico (1324) until Moctezuma II's death (1520) (fols. 1–18r); the second describes the tributes paid to the Mexican lords (fols. 18v–71v), and the third part concentrates on the social and political life of Mexico (fols. 56v–71v) (Madan and Craster, entry 3134). It was compiled some twenty years after the conquest by native scribes under the supervision of missionary priests; while it appears that the document as a whole was prepared for the Spanish crown, there is little doubt that Parts 1 and 2 were copied from earlier pictorials dating from pre-contact times (Berdan and Anawalt vol. 1, xiii). Some of the codices are clearly revisionist, post-conquest documents. The *Codex Aubin* (or *Codex 1575*), for example, portrays the Mexican gods as devils ('salieron llevando al diablo a quien adoraban como un dios'; *Códice de 1576* 5); it is significant that the only Castilian word to appear consistently in the Nahuatl portion of the text is 'diablo'.

There are also a number of codices which were composed some time after the conquest and which document the harshness of colonial rule. The *Codex Kingsborough*, for example, drawn in the middle of the sixteenth century in watercolours and accompanied by a narrative in Spanish, was first published by Lord Kingsborough (1795–1837) in a volume entitled *Various Papers* (1831); the original of the *Codex Kingsborough*, now separated into two separate codices, is held in the British Museum.² In this codex the Spaniards are depicted as malevolent, almost out of place in the mental universe of the Tepetlaoztoc Indians with its abundance of natural symbols (fish, frogs, etc.). The scene on page 250 is typical, showing two Spaniards standing on top of two reclining figures wrapped in funereal robes, and a severed head on top; the symbolism could not be more brutal. One of the most intriguing of these later more politicised codices is the *Codex Osuna* which documents the early municipal life of the indigenous population of Mexico City. Originally published in 1878 from the library of the Duque de Osuna as a forty-page document, it is now known to be part of a longer document of over four hundred folios which is, in essence, a lawsuit dated 2 March 1564, brought by the Indian governor, mayors and chieftains against the Viceroy and *oidores* (judges) of New Spain on the occasion of Don Gerónimo de Valderrama's visit to New Spain as official *visitador* of the crown (1563–66). The document accuses the Viceroy and others of legal malpractice, greed, cheating, and immorality (frolicking naked with naked women in the steam baths in full sight and knowledge of all and sundry). The first folio, for example, accuses the Viceroy Luis de Velasco, with drawings as evidence, of having received 215 'cargas' of lime to repair his residence but without returning just recompense (Chávez Orozco 264); it also records how the *Oidor* Doctor Vasco Puga was given lime for which he did not pay, as did the *Oidor* Villalobos (fols. 465–3v; fol. 466–4r). It was usual for legal documents of this kind to contain drawings since Indians during trial proceedings often needed interpreters and relied on pictography to present their case. The *Codex Osuna* therefore offers invaluable insight into the conflict between Spanish and Amerindian culture, as well as the interplay between written text and pictography during this period.

## Quechua Runasimi

Any expression of Amerindian culture was expressly prohibited during the colonial era by viceregal decree. Thus a council in Lima in 1583 ordered that all *quipus* be destroyed, and, in 1613, Father Arriaga rejoiced at the destruction of musical instruments and religious icons; the following year festivals and indigenous dances were prohibited, especially those in which Quechua was spoken or sung. After the 1780 rebellion of Tupac Amaru, Quechua was outlawed in the viceroyalty of Peru; a good example of the excessiveness of this prohibition is that even Garcilaso de la Vega's *Comentarios Reales*, which in the final analysis supported Catholicism, was banned (Aybar xxvii–xxviii).

---

² Its original reference was MS Add. 13964. The *Codex Kingsborough* has subsequently been disbound, since it was seen to contain two different texts, the Tepetlaoztoc Codex and a Cochineal Treatise (*Relación de lo que toca a la Grana Cochinilla*), which, in the exhibition 'Mexican Painted Books before and after the Spanish Conquest', held in the British Museum 4 June to 6 September 1992, were listed separately; see Brotherston, *Mexican Painted Books* 29.

It comes as no surprise, therefore, to learn that Quechua literature was not 'discovered' until the nineteenth century and then by foreign scholars such as Markham, Tschudi, Middendorf and Trimborn (Aybar xxviii).

Referring to a body of knowledge passed on from generation to generation by oral means – as happened with Quechua, its language and its culture – in terms of 'literature' is, of course, problematic. Literature was understood as *runasimi* by the Incas, that is, verbal art, rather than 'literature' in the Western sense of the term (written, normally printed, designed to have an aesthetic effect). *Runasimi* was used by the Incas in their religious ceremonies of communication with the Sun God, Inti, in a ceremony called Inti Raymi. Edmundo Bendezú Aybar mentions a number of ways in which the *runasimi* could be expressed: the *hayllis* (a joyful war song), the *hauri* (a mournful, nostalgic song), a theatrical performance in a public space called a *mellquis*, and the recitation of short songs or stories of a fabulous nature and usually told to children (Aybar xxiii). During the colonial period, Quechua literature went into a state of what Aybar calls *ukupacha* (the underground world), although some works emerged during this period, such as *Yauri Tito Inca*, *Usca Páucar* and, most famous of all, *Ollantay*. Some of these texts expressed a terrible vision of the collapse of Incan civilisation, such as *La Tragedia del Fin de Atahuallpa*, discovered in Bolivia by Jesús Lara. The two genres which survived during the colonial era and, indeed, surfaced, were poetry and short narrative.

Some of the most interesting material is the poetry. It is difficult to tell of those poems which have survived from the Incan period whether they are truly untouched by the influence of the Spanish. Certainly those poems which express non-Christian sentiments ('Beberemos en el cráneo del enemigo / haremos un collar de sus dientes / haremos flauta de sus huesos / de su piel haremos tambores / y así cantaremos'; Aybar 18) may be safely seen as pre-Columbian. Those which emphasise the Christian notion of sin and penance ('Tú, el que previene y manda / ¿lejos estás o cerca / del pecador? / Sálvame de esta cárcel, / tú, gobierno del hombre, dios'; Aybar 21) appear to be post-Columbian. Although it would be foolish to discount the role of acculturation (some of the poems we know of come, after all, from Garcilaso de la Vega), the poems collected by Aybar constitute a good collection, and offer a fair indication of the main themes of Quechuan verse. The first thing that needs to be underlined is that the typical Incan poem is performative, not only in the sense that it exists in performance in a social context with an audience in attendance, but also in the sense of being an enactment of the community's desire, rather than the description of a personal emotion. Many of the poems, after all, ask Viracocha for his guidance (normally in the form of advice), and for his protection from want and from war. A good example is the poem 'Wiraqocha', perhaps the oldest of the Incan hymns, which opens as follows:

> Es Wiraqocha
> señor del origen,
> 'sea esto hombre',

>'sea esto mujer'.
>De la fuente sacra
>supremo juez,
>de todo cuanto hay
>enorme creador.
>¿Dónde estás?
>¿No te veré acaso? (Aybar 5)

One other characteristic of these poems, evident in this hymn, is their emphasis on the separation of the sexes. Viracocha created man and woman deliberately, and this sense of separation is very distinctly carried over in the communal songs in which the men and women of the community recite their lines antiphonally and sequentially. In '¡Ea, el triunfo!' for example, the men speak of their work in the fields ('¡He aquí el arado y el surco! ¡He aquí el sudor y la mano!') while the women spur them on in recalling their prowess. The penultimate 'estribillo' ('¡He aquí la infanta, la hermosa!') brings to mind the notion of the commerce of love after the work has been done. Other poems which emphasise the commerce of love ('Morena mía ...' 20–21, 'Canción amorosa' 28 and 'Canción' 31) likewise underline that these poems were written for specific social ends such as building a sense of community and expressing the religious urge to petition Viracocha's protection. The language of love and courtship here becomes pragmatic and performative.[3]

## Aztec Poetry

The corpus of extant Aztec poetry is based on four main sources, which are (i) the twenty sacred hymns collected by Bernardino de Sahagún, (ii) the songs scattered in various testimonies of the 'ancient word' or *huehuehtlahtolli*, (iii) the *Cantares mexicanos* held in the National Library in Mexico, and (iv) the *Romances de los señores de Nueva España* housed in the Nettie Lee Benson Latin American collection, University of Texas Library at Austin (León-Portilla, *Fifteen* 18).[4] The major bulk of these songs were transcribed alphabetically in Nahuatl soon after the conquest from oral performances given by indigenous singers or poets, which were inspired by pictoglyphic books. As one singer put it: 'I sing the pictures of the books, / and see them widely known, / I am a precious bird / for I make the books speak, / there in the house of the painted books' (quoted in León-Portilla, *Fifteen* 5). These poems fall into a number of genres which are as follows: *xopancuicatl* (songs of springtime), *xochicuicatl* (flowery songs), *totocuicatl* (songs of birds), *michcuicatl* (songs of fish),

---

[3] For a brief discussion of literature written in Guaraní, see Oviedo, *Historia*, vol. 1, 69–70.

[4] I have focused in this section on Aztec poetry since it is the genre of Aztec literature about which most is known; for a discussion of pre-Columbian drama, see the Theatre section of this chapter.

*icnocuicatl* (songs of orphanhood), *cozcacuicatl* (necklace songs), *teuccuicatl* (songs of the lords), *tlaocolcuicatl* (songs of suffering), *cuauhcuicatl* (songs of eagles), *yaocuicatl* (songs of war), *atequilizcuicatl* (songs of pouring water), *cihuacuicatl* (songs of women), *cococuicatl* (songs of doves), *cuecuechcuicatl* (provocative songs), and *huehuehcuicatl* (songs of old people) (*Fifteen* 28). León-Portilla has identified and named fifteen Aztec poets, reconstructing their biographies and works painstakingly, based on the scant evidence available. While their work clearly demonstrates individual features, the similarity of the themes treated in their poetry is overwhelming. Perhaps most noticeable is the obsessive preoccupation with the brevity of life. A good example is the 'Song of the Flight' by Nezahualcoyotl of Tezcoco (1402–72) which begins as follows: 'In vain was I born, in vain have I come forth / to earth from the house of the Lord' (*Fifteen* 90). The gloominess of the poetic emotion expressed is reinforced by the parallelism. 'Sad Song of Cuacuauhtzin' by Cuacuahtzin of Tepechpan (mid-fifteenth century) offers a similar lesson in fatalism: 'Where would we go / that we never have to die?' (*Fifteen* 109). A striking feature of these poems is their sense of metaphysical uncertainty, for example in the 'Song of Axayacatl, Lord of Mexico' by Axayacatl (1449–81): 'Will there perhaps be an end to pain? / Perhaps they will come again? / Who can teach me about this?' (*Fifteen* 169). At times this metaphysical uncertainty is borne out of distressing historical events such as the loss of material power. In the 'Song of Axayacatl' quoted above, for example, the loss of leaders is expressed in terms of orphanhood (*Fifteen* 168). Yet, at other times, this uncertainty is transformed into an eerie sense of loss of identity: 'Am I perchance a shield of turquoise, / will I as a mosaic be embedded once more in existence? Will I come again to the earth?' (*Fifteen* 145), and also of life being no more than a dream: 'We only rise from sleep, / we come only to dream, / it is not true, it is not true, / that we come on earth to live' (*Fifteen* 153).

In terms of style, the overriding feature of Aztec verse is its consistent use of an interlocking mesh of images, as when one image is related to another, painted books to song, song to music, music to birds, birds to flowers, flowers to intoxication, intoxication to spring, spring to earth, and earth to (fleeting) life. Typically these images are constructed paratactically (which is to be expected, perhaps, given the grammar of Nahuatl which works 'by the process of compounding and derivation' [Campbell and Kartunnen vol. 1, 10]), and are treated as a woven artifact to be offered as a sacrificial offering to God the Giver of Life. A good example of this is the 'Song of Springtime' by Nezahualcoyotl of Tezcoco which progresses through a series of images (painting–singing– music–flowers–birds–intoxication), and yet does so by weaving backwards and forwards in a gentle see-saw motion in which 'singing' becomes the axial image.

One other striking feature of Aztec poetry is its ludic, sexual side, the best example of which is 'The Song of the Women of Chalco' by Aquiauhtzin of Ayapanco (*c*. 1430–*c*. 1500). This poem teases its addressee, Axayacotl, challenging him to make love to its female author, sometimes bluntly ('Do it in my warm vessel, much / light on fire./ Come, put it in, put it in'; *Fifteen* 274) and sometimes poetically ('Look on my flowering painting: my breasts./ Will it fall in vain, / your heart, / little man, Axayacatl? / Here are your small hands, / now take me with your hands. Let us take pleasure'; *Fifteen* 279).[5] The sexual explicitness of this female Aztec writer offers a vivid contrast with the displaced, polite rhetoric used by colonial poets such as Bernardo de Balbuena who were writing at around this time.

## The Legacy

As is clear from the analysis above, the legacy of Amerindian culture, though rich, comes down to us in chequered form. Linguistic-oral culture such as the *Popol Vuh*, the 'Song of Springtime' by Nezahualcoyotl of Tezcoco, and the Inca poem dedicated to Viracocha, show us a world in which oral culture and religious ritual are mutually porous. The codices, for their part, offer a fascinating glimpse into the Amerindian world. They range from the ritualistic (namely, a pictorial, non-linguistic representation of the activities of the gods of the Mayan and Aztec pantheon), to part-illustration, part-verbal description of the history of a particular people, to an account – from the Indian's point of view – of the excesses of Spanish colonial administration; they are immeasurably valuable in providing insight into the vitality of Amerindian culture. While it is only right to discuss them before analysing the literature of discovery and conquest, it is important to remember that these texts were not historically evident to the Spaniards who arrived in the New World from 1492 onwards. They were, indeed, deliberately ignored or, in the case of Bishop Diego de Landa, wilfully destroyed. (It is naive to assume any other type of reaction from a colonizing culture, perhaps.) It was only in the era of independence, and particularly the middle of the nineteenth century, that a receptivity to these texts emerged. As already noted, Juan Pío Pérez began collecting Maya manuscripts in about 1835, the *Popul Vuh* was rediscovered in the 1850s, and many of the Mexican codices were discovered and published for the first time in the nineteenth century, often by French and British scholars. The ideology of the discoverer as much as of the conquistador, was one which required the New World to be a blank page on which they would write their exploits and their destiny.

The Amerindian legacy in Brazil is at first glance distinctly unimpressive when compared to that found in Spanish-speaking America. Most of what we know about the cultural customs of the sixteenth-century Tupi Indians, for example, comes to us via the writings of Jesuits such as José de Anchieta, Manoel da Nóbrega and Fernão Cardim (see discussion below, pp. 20–2); Brazil

---

[5] There are some similarities between Aztec verse and Mayan verse, particularly in the choice of imagery; see Oviedo's discussion of *Libro de los Cantares de Dzitbalché* (Oviedo, *Historia*, vol. 1, 59–60).

lacks an independent Amerindian archive equivalent to the codices discovered in Spain's American colonies discussed above. Indeed, knowledge about their community narratives is also patchy; Nóbrega, for example, drew attention to the fact that the Tupi Indians appeared to have knowledge of the flood described in the Book of Genesis, although the individual who escaped was not Noah but an old woman who climbed up a tree. As a result of their cannibalism and their polygamy the Indians were accused by the early Jesuits of being savages, and this view proved to be remarkably resilient over time – despite Montaigne's remarkably prescient essay on cannibalism, 'Des cannibales', published in his *Essais* (1595) – even underpinning the hostile sociology of an influential essayist such as Gilberto Freyre in the 1930s, as we shall see (pp. 186–7). It was only with the advent of artists and writers associated with Modernism in the first half of the twentieth century that the view of the Amerindian as monstrous was upturned; for writers such as Oswald de Andrade, whose 'Manifesto Antropófago' called for the rejection of Father Vieira as well as an emotional identification with cannibalism, a new assessment of the value of Amerindian culture was paramount. Perhaps curiously it was the anthropological research of a foreigner which ignited an interest in the Brazilian Amerindians' world-view. Claude Lévi-Strauss, a French anthropologist, worked as a visiting professor at the University of São Paolo from 1935 until 1939, and during this period he carried out fieldwork in the Matto Grosso and the Amazon Rainforest. In a series of brilliant studies – including *Les Structures élémentaires de la parenté* (1949), *Tristes Tropiques* (1955) and *La Pensée sauvage* (1962) – Lévi-Strauss revolutionised not only the world's awareness of the Brazilian Amerindians' world-view but also the field of anthropology itself. Indeed it is possible to argue that it was in Lévi-Strauss's work that for the first time the voice of the Brazilian Amerindian subaltern was audible (for further discussion of Lévi-Strauss's work in Brazil, see Pace).

## Discovery and Conquest

The conquest of the Americas by the Spanish and the Portuguese was first and foremost a military event, but it was accompanied by a massive intellectual conquest through the written word. Literacy and military conquest, indeed, went hand in hand during this period since, as C. M. Cipolla has pointed out, 'after the fifteenth century, technological progress in warfare required, and at the same time was based on, an adequate supply of literate soldiers ... Societies which produced an increasing number of literate soldiers had a decisive advantage over those that failed to do so' (quoted in Cruickshank 812). We have already noted that New World culture was seen by the European invaders as a 'blank page' on which they would write their own exploits, and the book played an important role in this process given the authority and power invested in print during the fifteenth and sixteenth centuries. Printing came to Spain in the early 1470s (Cruickshank 800) and to Portugal in 1487 (the first book published in Portugal, specifically in Faro, was the Pentateuch translated by Samuel Porteiro), and as we shall see, the printed word was used by the conquistadors and their accomplices as a means of asserting ownership of land in the New World.⁶ The literature examined in this section consists in the main of chronicles, treatises and letters which focus on the conquest and discovery of the New World; some of these texts were published in Spain or Portugal soon after composition, but many only came into the public domain many years later (following in the footsteps of Vaz de Caminha's letter which lay undiscovered for nearly 320 years). No work, religious or otherwise, was published in the New World before 1535, and the book, or intellectual, industry, was heavily dependent on Spain and Portugal for many years after that date. Intellectual traffic was, like trade, minimal between the viceroyalties and was normally one-way from Europe; the average edition of this period, the fifteenth century and the first half of the sixteenth century, involved a print-run of about two hundred copies (Steinberg 140).

Some of the texts examined in this section could arguably be seen as examples of Spanish or Portuguese rather than Latin American literature, but given precedent and the undeniable logic of analysing these texts, they are here presented as an integral part of the roots of Latin American literature. These works specifically mark themselves as part of the print-language of Spanish and Portuguese, in contradistinction to the oral-vernacular diversity of the Indian languages, which Nebrija refers to in his *Gramática castellana* as 'peregrinas lenguas' as opposed to the 'language of empire' of, for example, Spanish ('siempre la lengua fue compañera del imperio', he notes in his opening words of justification to the Catholic Monarchs; Nebrija 11, 5). Much of the writing of the early chronicles is based on the European medieval tradition of recording historic events for the benefit of the national collective memory. The mood of many of the authors of these early texts has been aptly described by Greenblatt (9):

> The Europeans who ventured to the New World in the first decades after Columbus's discovery shared a complex, well-developed, and, above all, mobile technology of power: writing, navigational instruments, ships, warhorses, attack dogs, effective armor, and highly lethal weapons, including gunpowder. Their culture was characterised by immense confidence in its own centrality, by a political organisation based on practices of command and submission, [and] by a willingness to use coercive violence on both

---

⁶ In the sixteenth and seventeenth centuries in Spain, the printed word was held to possess great authority. This is suggested by an exchange in Lope de Vega's play, *La octava maravilla*, written in about 1609, in which a master and servant are discussing printed ephemera. As Cruickshank elucidates: 'The servant has come across a pamphlet which states that in Granada a man has given birth. The master is scornful. The servant, surprised, asks: "¿Está de molde, y te burlas?" (roughly translated as 'It's in print, and you still mock the idea')' (Cruickshank 808). Though treated ironically in Lope's play, this incident suggests the power of print in the early seventeenth century (and presumably before) in Spain and, one must assume, in the Spanish colonies in the New World.

strangers and fellow countrymen ... Such was the confidence of this culture that it expected perfect strangers – the Arawaks of the Caribbean, for example – to abandon their own beliefs, preferably immediately, and embrace those of Europe as luminously and self-evidently true. A failure to do provoked impatience, contempt, and even murderous rage.

It is ironic that the first published text in Spanish focusing on the reality of the New World should have been written by an individual who was a non-Spaniard with a defective knowledge of Castilian and who was unaware of what he had witnessed, namely, Cristóval Colón (as his name is printed in his *Diario*). What we know about the discovery of the New World by Christopher Columbus (1451–1506) is contained within the log-book journal he kept of his four voyages to the New World (1492–93; 1493–96; 1498–1500; 1502–4), as well as the famous letter dated 15 February 1493 which he sent to Luis de Santangel, the Catholic Monarchs' scribe, in which he announced the discovery of a New World. Columbus also wrote other letters to the sovereigns based on his subsequent voyages, namely, a memorial in April 1493 proposing that trading posts be established in Hispaniola, a letter to the same on 18 October 1498 and a letter to Doña Juana Torres, Isabella's confidante, in 1500 giving details of his third voyage, and the Lettera Rarissima to Philip II on 7 July 1503 (Murray 38–54). The *Carta a Luis de Santangel* (1493) is in effect, if not in intention, a proclamation of the discovery of a New World. While still labouring under the misapprehension that he was visiting islands off the coast of China, Columbus described the Caribbean islands he had visited in such terms that would lead to further investment by the Catholic Monarchs, enticing them with the hope of possession of foreign lands. The mountains are so enormous they reach the sky, the trees never lose their leaves, there is evidence of abundant spices and the rivers flow with gold ('traen oro'). The rest of the letter takes care in pointing out that the people encountered there are docile and would be easy to Christianise; they have neither iron or arms, and are 'temerosos a maravilla'. Columbus's concluding paragraph gives to understand that the islands he has visited are an abundant source of commodity, mineral and human capital: 'pueden ver sus Altezas que yo les daré oro cuanto hubieran menester con muy poquita ayuda que Sus Altezas me darán ahora' (Chang-Rodríguez and Malva E. Filer 13–14). It was a letter which would fire the imagination of the West for many years to come but it simultaneously spelt death for the inhabitants of the Caribbean whose lands and domestic environment would soon be savagely destroyed by the arrival of Spaniards hungry for gold.

The Brazilian counterpart to Columbus's discovery-letter is Pêro Vaz de Caminha's *A carta de Pêro Vaz de Caminha*, which was sent to Manuel I, the King of Portugal, on 1 May 1500, proclaiming the discovery of Brazil (at that time known as the Ilha de Vera Cruz; Caminha thought it was an island) by Pedro Álvares Cabral on 22 April 1500. Oddly enough, the letter lay undiscovered for 317 years in the Torre do Tombo archive in Lisbon; once discovered it was published (in 1817) (Menezes 2). Seen as the baptismal certificate of

Brazil, Vaz de Caminha's letter narrates the act of discovery and proposes future action. It begins with the customary laudatory introit, fitting for the time given its addressee, and also makes the crucial point that its content was based on events actually witnessed: 'aqui não há de pôr mais do que aquilo que vi e me pareceu' (9). Leaving Belem on 9 March 1500, according to the letter they passed by the Canary Islands, then the Cabo Verde Islands, until finally land was sighted on 22 April, and they set down anchor the following day at ten o'clock in the morning (11). The Indians they see are described thus: 'Pardos, nus, sem coisa alguma que lhes cobrisse suas vergonhas. Traziam arcos nas mãos' (12). Caminha describes the various hand movements used to communicate, the gifts exchanged, and how impressed the men were by the uncovered women, in a section called 'O encanto das vergonhas' (20–21), the nudity of the women being set off by their red paint. It describes a humorous event when the Indian chieftain attempts to put a green stone into the captain's mouth, and the captain was annoyed, though the crew laughed (28). Vaz de Caminha concludes, after a number of interactions, that 'é gente bestial e de pouco saber, e por isso tão esquiva' (30). The captain sends Afonso Ribeiro and two others to visit the Indian village consisting of nine or ten wood and straw houses (33). Vaz de Caminha also makes an important observation that, given the lack of culture or belief, the Indians would be easily Christianised: 'Parece-me gente de tal inocência que, se nós entendêssemos a sua fala e eles a nossa, seriam logo cristãoes, visto que não têm nem entendem crença alguma, segundo as aparências' (39). His letter concludes with the notion that the salvation of the indigenous inhabitants' souls is a more worthy prize than the silver and gold that these lands might possess, but it is important to recognise that even in the realm of the spiritual the notion of possession is central.

The connection between ownership and writing is also played out in the letters of the greatest of the conquistadors, Hernán Cortés (1485–1547), conqueror of Mexico, Governor and Captain-General of New Spain and later Marquis of the Valley of Oaxaca. His letters, like Columbus's before him, were written to the Catholic Monarchs during the years of conquest (1519–26) to inform them of current developments but also to persuade them that this venture was worth further monetary investment. Their importance is based on two things: they provided Spanish and other Europeans 'with their first great paradigm for European encounters with an organised native state' and, 'through their swift publication in several European languages' reached a wide audience in the Old World (Clendinnen 87).[7] Cortés's letters, however, also had the purely pragmatic aim of ensuring that his own land privileges were retained; thus he is at great pains to record the various acts of treachery carried out by others (such as Diego Velázquez and Pánfilo de Narváez, fellow conquistadors whom

---

[7] The publication of these letters and their wide circulation was an indication of a paradigm-shift which occurred in the sixteenth century as a result of the creation of print. As Cruickshank has pointed out, while manuscript transmission involved a slow process, '[t]he press could make an author famous overnight' (Cruickshank 800), and this is essentially what happened in the case of Cortés's letters.

Cortés casts as villains of the piece in the first and second letters). The value of the letters nowadays is more to be found in what they show us about the process of transculturation. Cortés tells an unconsciously amusing anecdote: when the first conquistadors arrived on the Mexican mainland they understood the indigenous population to say that the land they had arrived in was called Yucatán, although the words pronounced actually meant 'we do not understand your words' (Cortés 3). The scene epitomises the drama of the conquest: on the one hand we have a native population which finds the words and actions of the European incomprehensible, while, on the other, we have the European coloniser mapping out a new world based on a misreading.

## The Chroniclers

There were a great number of chronicles published in Spain, Portugal and Spanish America soon after the conquest (the Portuguese throne was able to keep a tighter grip on printing in its colonies than the Spanish monarchy; see below, p. 35), and still more have emerged into print in more recent years, such that it would be impossible to give an account of all or even some of them in an introductory study of this kind. What I propose to do therefore is to take a few chronicles as representative texts and discuss their information value and techniques of persuasion. It is important to recall that the works of this period were not necessarily written for the benefit of posterity. As the letters by Columbus and Vaz de Caminha already alert us, texts written during the early years of the aftermath of conquest were more concerned to persuade their audience of the justice of their claim to wealth, position or land. A good example is the manuscript, 'Nueva obra y breve en metro y prosa sobre la muerte del adelantado Don Diego de Almagro, hecha por un testigo de vista – por los años de 1550' held in the Biblioteca Nacional in Lima (Sala de Investigaciones A124, 5ff.). This work, which was notarised by Fray Félix Ponce de León (fol. 5v), seeks to restore the reputation of Diego de Almagro who, as this manuscript suggests, as a result of the foul deeds of 'Don Francisco y sus hermanos', was deprived of 'honra, vida y hazienda' (fol. 1v). This work crosses between the realms of literature (in the sense of a work written for aesthetic effect), history (understood as a chronicle), and legal document (in the sense of claiming the right to property, etc.). Typical of its era, 'Nueva obra y breve ...' conflates various discourses for the purely pragmatic end of persuading the addressee of its truth-value.

Among the body of chronicles, two divergent trends can be identified. On the one hand were the official accounts of the conquest, such as *Historia general y natural de las Indias* (1526) authored by Gonzalo Fernández de Oviedo y Valdés (1478–1557), which were either commissioned by the Catholic Monarchs or received the royal seal at some stage during their composition. The official nature of Oviedo's text is underlined by his claim that members of the Council of the Indies saw and corrected the manuscript; it is dedicated to Cardinal Fray García Jofre de Loaysa, President of the Royal Council of the Indies. Oviedo's work won fame in Europe, and justly so, for being the first ever description of the sub-continent's flora and fauna (Brading 43). In contrast to the official chronicles were those accounts which reported the first-hand experience of an individual's life (normally of a traumatic kind), such as Alvar Núñez Cabeza de Vaca's *Naufragios* (1542). Núñez accompanied Pánfilo de Narváez on his expedition to colonise the provinces of Florida, occupying the position of treasurer and *alguacil mayor*. The expedition set out from Spain on 27 June 1527. Núñez's *Naufragios* covers the voyage with Narváez, the fate of the expedition and specifically his adventures with a contingent of Spanish sailors shipwrecked on the coast of North America. They wandered through the mainland of the northern continent, gaining the friendship of the Indian tribes through their apparent ability to heal sick people, living on nuts, berries and tuna fish, until they met up with some Spaniards from the settlement of San Miguel, and were finally transported to Mexico City, where they arrived in July 1536. To this day, Núñez's route is disputed, and there are at least eight different hypotheses concerning which route he took (Hellenbeck 243–306). With a matter-of-factness which at times seems unsuited to the events described, Núñez recounts the various misadventures which befell him over a period of nine years. Particularly gripping is his description of the plight on the island which the Spaniards named Malhado, given their experience there. Again its identity is a matter of dispute, although Hellenbeck advances Galverston Island as the most likely (Hellenbeck 119–27). Having beached on this island on or around 6 November 1528, after being separated from the other barges and lost at sea with no knowledge of where they were for nine days, Núñez and his companions had a spell of good luck, since they were fed by the Indians they encountered there, although this was probably as much due to Cabeza de Vaca's 'skill as a cultural negotiator' (Ahern 225). When they had sufficiently recovered they put to sea once more on the barge which promptly capsized because of an enormous wave and three of the crew were drowned. Núñez Cabeza de Vaca's account of the perils of sea voyages is the matrix text of a rich autobiographical tradition in Spanish America; Carlos de Sigüenza y Góngora's *Infortunios de Alonso Ramírez*, for example, provides an important stepping-stone between these narratives and the first fully-fledged novel in Spanish America, *Periquillo Sarniento*.

A Brazilian text which may usefully be compared to Núñez Cabeza de Vaca's expeditionary text is the diary of the journey of Martim Afonso de Souza which was written by his brother Pêro Lopes de Souza. The expedition, which consisted of three ships and two caravels, was commissioned by King João III to ward off French designs on the newly discovered territories of Brazil, and set off from Lisbon on 3 December 1530; the subsequent adventures, described in *Diário da navegação da armada, que foi à terra de Brasil em 1530 sob a capitania-mor de Martin Affonso de Souza, escripto por seu irmão Pêro Lopes de Souza*, lasted for a period of almost two years (the last entry is for 23 November 1532); the first edition was published in 1839, a symptom of the zeal with which the intellectuals of the newly independent Brazil sought to recover their past. The diary consists of a series of short entries for each day. The explicit aim of the expedition was to demarcate territory; thus on 28 December 1530 a Spanish ship was seen off, a French ship found near the Brazilian coast on 31 January 1531 was fired upon, and subsequently requisitioned (Lopes de Souza 38). The Indians met in the Bay of Todos los Santos are described as comely, especially the women: 'A gente desta terra é toda alva, os homens mui bem dispostos e as mólheres mui fermosas, que nom ham nenhua enveja às da Rua Nova de Lisboa' (48). The narrator subsequently describes a war the Indians had with a neighbouring tribe, how they captured, roasted and ate their prisoners, while appearing to ignore the Portuguese, clearly not seeing them as a threat (48). With hindsight this was indeed an ironic moment: Indians waging war on each other in a land which had already been claimed by another nation in a series of agreements made on another continent, and about which they had not the slightest inkling. It is noticeable how, from October 1531 onwards, the log entries become longer, the nautical details less prominent, with the emphasis switching to a description of the flora and fauna of the land: 'A terra é mais fermosa e aprazível que eu jamais cuider de ver: nom havia homen que fartasse de oulhar os campos e a fermosura deles' (77). The narrator gets caught up in the enthusiasm of naming the islands and lands he discovers. He describes the bizarre Indian custom of cutting off a finger every time a family member dies (96–97) and, perhaps most significant of all, the act of founding São Vicente on 22 January 1532; the captain 'repartio a gente nestas duas vilas e fez nelas oficiaes e pôs tudo em bõa obra de justiça, de que a gente tomou muita consolação com verem povoar vilas e ter leis e sacrifícios e celebrar matrimónios e viverem em comunicação das artes' (101), Brazil's prototype of the *Mayflower* experience (Lívio Ferreira 20).

Most of the accounts of military action in the New World, following in the vein of Cortés's letters, took the bias of the invading forces. Such was certainly the case with the *Historia general de las Indias* (1552) by Francisco López de Gómara (1511–64), and this is not surprising since he was for four years Cortés's chaplain (1541–45) and subsequently resided in the conquistador's house. Gómara's account of the Amerindian population is harsh to say the least: of the inhabitants of the Caribbean he charged that their god is the devil (XXVII, 45), the women are lascivious and the men are sodomisers, lazy, deceitful, ungrateful, capricious and uncultured (XXVIII, 47). Unlike Gómara's account, which was penned by someone who had never set foot in the New World, Bernal Díaz del Castillo's *Verdadera historia de la conquista de la Nueva España* is concerned with the daily grind of the conquest. His is an eyewitness account; he was a 'testigo de vista' (Bernal Díaz, vol. 1, 65). It is for his emphasis on ocular evidence and his lack of interest in annotation that Bernal Díaz is favoured by the modern historian.

In the *Chronica del Peru* (1554) by Pedro Cieza de León (1518?–60), the author depicts himself as a soldier-writer, and in this he establishes a precedent which later writers such as Ercilla y Zúñiga would emulate; his two professions are 'escreuir, y seguir a mi vandera y Capitan' (fol. 3r). Cieza de León's approach to the Incas is that of a Christian seigneurial colonist; like other chroniclers he has no hesitation in calling the Incas' god the 'devil' (the solemn feast of Hatum Raimi is described as 'witchcraft'; Book II, Chap. xxx), but unlike some hardliners such as José de Acosta, he is willing to cede that the Spanish have some blame to bear for their treatment of the Indians. At the end of Book II, Chap. xxv, for example, Cieza de León implores God to give the Spanish the grace necessary to repay the Incas the enormous human debt they owe them as a result of the conquest. Without a doubt the most skilled of all the chroniclers was El Inca Garcilaso de la Vega (1539–1616), according to one critic, 'the first New World native and the first person of Amerindian descent to be published and read widely throughout Europe' (Zamora 3). He was the son of a leading conquistador and the descendant of a highly literate family which included among its ancestors the Marqués de Santillana, Jorge Manrique and Garcilaso de la Vega, and of the Inca princess, Isabel Chimpu Occlo, a grand-daughter of the Emperor Tupac Inca Yupanqui. Like earlier chronicles such as Cieza de León's *Chronica del Peru*, Garcilaso's *Comentarios Reales* (1609) shows a keen awareness of transculturation; as Garcilaso points out in the first chapter, it was as a result of the clash between the print-based culture of the Spaniards and the oral-based culture of the Incas that he decided to write down the history of the Incas. His knowledge had been culled from the conversations he had with his family while a young man and offers a remarkable insight into the Inca way of life which, in effect, makes the commentaries not only historiographical but also autobiographical.

Apart from the military chroniclers there was also a group of religious who wrote accounts of their experiences in the New World. An important early chronicler was Fray Toribio de Paredes o Benavente (1490?–1568), also known as Motolinía, a name based on the Yucatec word for poverty which he adopted for himself; his major work was *Historia de los indios de la Nueva España* (1541). Motilinía saw the New World as the work of the devil; thus he translated the Yucatec word for temple, *teocalli*, as 'templo del demonio' (Motolinía 24). A similar desire to depict Amerindian culture in satanic terms underlies *Historia natural y moral de las Indias* (1590) by José de Acosta (1540–1600), who described the New World as a giant parody of the Christian world created by the devil (V, xxx; Acosta 181). His view of Aztec hieroglyphics was also uncompromising: 'la pintura es libro para los idiotas que no saben leer' (VI, iv; 185). Similar in tone and intention to Acosta's *Historia natural* is the *Relación de las Cosas de Yucatán* by Fray Diego de Landa. Diego de Landa's chronicle, though, throws light on the ambiguous space inhabited by the religious in the middle of the sixteenth century in the New World. On the one hand they were enemies of the conquistadors and the *encomenderos* (see Diego de Landa, chap. XVII, 36–7); on the other hand, they were hostile to the Amerindian culture and especially its religious precepts as embodied by the Jaguar priests. Thus, he calls the Yucatecans' priests 'idolatrous' and describes their social function as 'dar al pueblo las respuestas de los demonios' (XXVII, 55).

Though written by a man of the cloth like Motilinía, José de Acosta and Diego de Landa, the version of the conquest found in the chronicles of Bartolomé de las Casas (1484–1566) could not be more different. His most celebrated pamphlet is the *Brevísima historia de la destrucción de las Indias* (1552), which, in one fell swoop, established the so-called Black Legend which would plague the Hispanic world for centuries to come. Las Casas's text was eagerly taken up by Spain's imperial rivals – the Dutch, French and English – in order to discredit the methods whereby the Spanish established their overseas empire. It describes the recently colonised empire region by region, beginning with Hispaniola and ending with Río de la Plata, and describes the initial peaceful overtures made by the Indians, followed by the treachery of the Spaniards (torture, forced slavery, rape, murder, etc.). Las Casas's main point in this essay is to underline the irony of the Spanish purporting to be ambassadors of Jesus Christ while acting like devils.

There were some chronicles which, like the *Codex Osuna*, highlighted the evils of conquest from the Indian perspective. Such is the case of *Nueva corónica y buen gobierno* by Felipe Guaman Poma de Ayala (*c*. 1535–*c*. 1615), a sixteenth-century Quechua-speaking *ladino* Indian from the Ayacucho region. His text did not have a sympathetic hearing in the era in which it was written and languished in manuscript form for nearly three hundred years before it was finally discovered in the National Library in Copenhagen in 1908 by Richard Pietschmann and published in facsimile form in 1936. Guaman Poma de Ayala's basic point – the West imposed on the inhabitants of newly discovered lands a creed they did not live up to themselves – has had a sympathetic hearing in our anti-colonialist times.

The most sophisticated and searching religious discourse produced about Latin America was that created by the Jesuits in Brazil. Father José de Anchieta (1534–97) is the lynchpin of that extraordinary flowering of Jesuit culture which occurred in the Portuguese colony of the New World from its discovery in 1500 until the unceremonious expulsion of the Jesuit order in 1759 by Marquis Pombal. The main reason for the success of the Jesuits in Brazil – and, indeed, the cause of their eventual discomfiture – was that they literally accepted no jurisdiction other than that of God or of the Pope, and as a consequence often rebelled against temporal authority. That independence of mind was epitomised by Anchieta, co-founder of São Paolo, Christian proselytiser, first linguistician of the Indian languages and, in the words of one of Brazil's most important literary critics, Afrânio Peixoto, the 'initiator' of Brazilian literature (he wrote a number of essays, poems and plays discussed below; see pp. 32–4) (Peixoto 34). Anchieta's father was Spanish but, at the age of seventeen, Anchieta went to study as a novice at the Society of Jesus in Coimbra, and on 8 May 1553, he set off for Bahia on the third Jesuit mission, and stayed in the New World until his death. Anchieta's letters offer a fascinating insight into the early stages of colonisation in Brazil. His 1554 Piratininga letter (it covers the events from May to September of that year) describes the various small communities set up by the religious along the coast of Brazil, how they attempted to gain the trust of the Indians living there, the problems they had with the Portuguese laity who were establishing families with the Indian women, and their attempts to force the Indians to desist from consuming human flesh: 'Indios que usiam todos comer em seus banquetes carne humana, no que mostram achar tanto prazer e doçura, de modo que comummente caminhan mais de 300 milhas para a guerra' (Anchieta, *Cartas*, 55). Anchieta at times found the Indians difficult: 'são indomitos e ferozes, e nem se contêm bastante pela razão' (46). His letters, written to the various members of the Jesuit community scattered in different parts of Brazil, have the hybrid feel of St Paul's letters in the Bible – they interweave news of what is going on in the various communities with information about his progress in the Tupi language (he later published the first grammar of the Tupi language, *Arte de Grammatica da lingoa mais usada na costa do Brasil* in 1595, an extraordinary feat), prayers and Christocentric thoughts. In one letter of June 1554 to the head of the order, Ignacio de Loyola, he recalls how two of the priests had run off with Indian women; the temptation was too much for them in Brazil 'onde as mulheres andam nuas e não sabem se negar a ninguém, mas até elas mesmas cometem e importunam os homens, jogando-se com eles nas redes porque têm por honra dormir com os Cristãos' (78). His May 1560 letter to the São Vicente community describes the various snakes, scorpions, panthers, and other animals, birds and trees found in the region – using their Indian names to do so, and thereby providing one of the first detailed descriptions of the flora and fauna of the New World; he even provides some description of the various malignant spirits which the Indians held to live in the forests and rivers (113–39). The letter are sprinkled with accounts of the various wars that the Indian tribes wage on each other, and on the Christians (letter of 16 April 1563 to General Diogo Lainez, 191–203, esp. 194–6), as well as valuable accounts of important historical events such as the founding of Rio de Janeiro (letter to Father Diogo Mirão of 9 June 1565, 255–64), the attack on São Vicente by English pirates (letter of 7 September 1594 to Father Claudio Aquaviva, 300–2). Anchieta's 'Informacões', as they came to be known, in which he gives succinct summaries of significant landmarks in Brazil's colonial history, including the discovery, the first settlements, the captaincies and governorships, bishops and priests elected to office, with – as might be expected – particular reference to the Society of Jesus, provide valuable historical vignettes of Brazil's early days as a fledgling nation (309–470; for the sermons see 503–41).

Called 'o Cavalheiro da Triste-Fala' (Lívio Ferreira 29, 40–1), Padre Manoel da Nóbrega, Brazil's first apostle (Lívio Ferreira 37) entered the Society of Jesus at the age of twenty-seven on 24 November 1544 (Lívio Ferreira 41). His letters offer a great deal of insight into the early days of colonisation. A letter to Padre Mestre Simão Rodrigues de Azevedo (1549), for example, tells of his efforts at proselytising. One of the chiefs 'diz que quer ser cristão e não comer carne humana, nem ter mais de uma mulher e outras cosas, sómente que ha de ir à guerra' (Nóbrega 72), which suggests that proselytisation at an early stage involved advice about cultural behaviour. Another letter to Padre Mestre Simão, written in the same year, tells of the difficulties for the recent settlers produced by the lack of women:

> Todos se me escusam que não têm mulheres com que casem, e conheço eu que casariam si achassem con quem, em tanto que uma mulher, ama de um homem casado que veiu nesta armada, pelejavam sobre ella a quem a haveria por mulher. (Nóbrega 79–80)

He provides some first-hand experience of the cannibalism practised by the Indians on war prisoners:

> Si acontece aprisionarem um contrario na guerra, conservam-o por algum tempo, dão-lhe por mulheres suas filhas, para que o sirvam e guardam, depois de que o matam com grande festa e ajuntamento dos amigos e dos que moram por alli perto, e si delles ficam filhos, os comem, ainda que sejam seus sobrinhos e irmãos, declarando ás vezes as proprias mães que só os paes e não a mãe, têm parte nelles. (letter to Dr Navarro, Nóbrega 88–96 at p. 90)

Information on habits such as eating one's own niece quickly stirred up a view in Europe that the Indians of Brazil were no more than dreadful savages. In the same letter Nóbrega speaks of how the Indians appear to know something about what the Bible refers to as Noah's flood, although in their version, the individual who survived was an old woman who climbed up a tree and waited for the water to recede: 'Sabem do diluvio de Noé, bem que não conforme a verdadeira historia, pois dizem que todos morreram, excepto uma velha que escapou em uma arvore' (Nóbrega 91). This same letter has a memorable account of Nóbrega berating in raised voice and at great length, with the aid of a translator, a *feiticeiro*, which finally leads to the latter – no doubt completely browbeaten – expressing a wish to be baptised (95–6). On a number of occasions, in order to put a stop to the illegal couplings taking place, he asks for white women, particularly orphans, to be shipped to the New World (letter of 9 August 1599 to Padre Mestre Simão 79–87 at p. 80; letter to King João III of 14 September 1551, 123–7 at p. 126; letter to King João III, no precise date but 1552, 133–6 at p. 133). It is noticeable how Nóbrega's letters, as the decade of the 1550s progresses, become less anthropological (as, for example, his letter of 1549 to Padre Mestre Simão, 71–6), and more Pauline, that is, drawing on Paul of Tarsus's experiences and using a similar rhetoric to encourage Christian living in the various communities over which he now watches (see, for example, the letter 'Aos moradores de S. Vicente' of 1557, probably written between 23 April and 27 May of that year, 163–8; for discussion of Nóbrega's interest in St Paul, see Lívio Ferreira 35–7).

Padre Fernão Cardim, born at some point between 1540 and 1550 in Évora, Portugal, went to Brazil as a Jesuit missionary in 1583, working in Rio and Bahia. Apart from one notorious trip, he remained in Brazil until his death in 1625. In 1601 the ship on which he was travelling was attacked by English pirates, and he was taken to England and imprisoned there. The manuscript Cardim was working on at the time, 'Do princípio e origem dos Indios do Brasil e de seus costumes, adoração e ceremonias', was taken from him and published in English in 1625 under the title, *A Treatise of Brazil written by a Portuguese which had long lived there*, under the false attribution of Irmão Manuel Tristão. It was only in the 1880s that Capistrano de Abreu proved that this work was actually written by Cardim, and the latter's works are now customarily studied in a group of essays brought together under the title of *Tratados da terra e gente do Brasil*. Cardim's essays range widely over the climate, geography, people, flora and fauna of Brazil. His essay, 'Do clima e terra do Brasil', is a detailed description of the flora and fauna of Brazil, among which there is a chapter on the sea monsters which by all accounts kill human beings by kissing them to death: 'O modo que têm en matar he: abração-se com a pessoa tão fortemente beijando-a, e apertando-a comsigo que a deixão feita toda en pedaços' (Cardim 57). The essay 'Do princípio e origem das Indias do Brasil' describes the customs of the Indians, their lack of knowledge of God, their manner of eating, drinking, sleeping, dressing, their abodes, their burial ceremonies, and also includes a rather long description of the cannibalistic feasts in which they appear to take an inordinate delight (113–20). Finally Cardim's *Narrativa epistolar de uma viagem e missão jesuística*, first published in 1847, is of the three texts mentioned the one with the most authentic Jesuit feel to it in that it describes his arrival in the Jesuit College at Bahia and his impressions of daily life in the New World, although focused more specifically on the Catholic rituals whereby the Indians were converted to Christianity. Though he sees the Indians as infidels Cardim is clearly struck by the gentle manner in which the parents treat their children, and the happiness which exudes from the children's games: 'Nenhum genero de castigo têm para os filhos; nem ha pai nem mãe que em toda a vida castigue nem toque em filho, tanto os trazem nos olhos' (187). He offers at one stage a valuable early (1584) description of a sugar mill ('O serviço é insoffrivel, sempre os serventes andam correndo, e por isso morrem muitos escravos', 193), as well as a portrait of the enormous wealth created by this emerging industry, such that there is more vanity in Pernambuco than in Lisbon (202). Cardim's entertaining account of his visit to the various settlements of Brazil from 1582 to 1585 (it offers a charming picture of Rio de Janeiro, for example, where 'parece estão os corpos bebendo vida', 29), before returning to Bahia, makes of this text a Jesuit version of Souza's *Diário de navegação*.

Brazil, like the Spanish viceroyalties, had its secular chroniclers and, of these, three deserve special mention: Pêro de Magalhães de Gândavo, Gabriel Soares de Sousa (*c.* 1540–91) and Ambrósio Fernandes Brandão. Seen as one of the great stylists of the Brazilian colonial period, Pêro de Magalhães de Gândavo in his *Tratado da Terra do Brasil*, offers the reader a panoramic overview (in a synchronic as well as a diachronic sense) of Brazilian culture in a style which is balanced and erudite, lively and informed. When first published in Lisbon this book had the title of *Historia da provincia de Santa*

*Cruz, a que vulgarmente chamamos Brasil* (1576), and, because of its scarcity, a second edition was brought out ('Livro que já hoje he sumamente raro, não tendo nunca tido outra Edição mais a primeira em 1576', see 'Introdução', *Tratado da Terra do Brasil* 186). The second edition also prints the dedication to Dom Anrrique, Cardenal, Infante de Portugal; the aim of the publication, he says, is 'para que nestes Reinos se divulgue sua fertilidade, e provoque a muitas pessoas pobres que se vão viver a esta provincia, que nisso consiste a felicidade' (185). In Chapter II of the second book, Magalhães de Gândavo spells out the recipe for success in the New World:

> As pessoas que no Brazil querem viver, tanto que se fazem moradores da terra, por pobres que sejão, se cada hum alcançar dous pares ou meia duzia de escravos, que póde hum por outro cusstar, pouco mais ou menos, até dez cruzados, logo tem remedio para sua susstentação; porque huns lhe pescão e cação, outros lhe fazem mantimentos, e fazenda; e assi pouco a pouco enriquecem os homens, e vivem honradamente na terra com mais descanço que neste Reino. (198; Rare Books Collection, Biblioteca Nacional, 67, 6, 30)

Gândavo offers a very attractive picture of Brazil, a land where there is a great abundance of food, especially meat and fish (190–2), no beggars such as can be found in Portugal (199), where people live longer and are healthier (200), and where the food is tastier (202–5).

Magalhães de Gândavo mentions that the main reason the Portuguese were able to colonise Brazil is because the Indians were always warring among themselves (205). And he is able to use the material available to him in a witty way, thus insuring that the point will be made effectively. When alluding to the Indians' language, he makes the following point: 'A lingoa destes gentios toda pela Costa he huma, carece de tres letras, silicet [*sic*], não se acha nela = F = nem = L = nem = R, cousa digna despanto, porque assi não tem Fé, nem Ley, nem Rey' (II, vii, 205). It also provides a description of the cannibalistic rituals associated with warfare (II, vii, 206–9), and Treatise 2 concludes with a short narrative about the discovery of precious metals, and a further encouragement to the Portuguese to emigrate to Brazil, and there to find prosperity. Gândavo's style is the nearest to that of the chroniclers of Spanish America such as El Inca Garcilaso de la Vega; not tarrying too much on descriptions of the flora and fauna, it picks its details carefully, providing thereby the most balanced account of all the Brazilian chroniclers. It is also distinctive in that it is dedicated to Cardenal Dom Anrrique – it is clearly placed within the maecenal system, and has a very precise aim, that of encouraging immigration – and it uses its rhetorical weapons carefully and expertly to do so.

The *Tratado descritivo do Brasil em 1587* by Gabriel Soares de Sousa followed on just eleven years after Gândavo's *Historia da provincia de Santa Cruz, a que vulgarmente chamamos Brasil* (1576), and very much attempts to improve on the original. The prologue is directed to João III's successor, to remind him of the importance of Brazil, and to draw his attention to the increasing interest on the part of corsairs along the Brazilian coast, 'porque se os estrangeiros se apoderarem desta terra custará muito lançá-los fora dela' (Soares de Sousa 2). It offers the 'official version' of the process of colonisation. Part I is careful to specify – no doubt in order to gain the edge over the Spanish in any future boundary dispute – the lines of demarcation for each of the provinces. Soares's text is written from the point of view of the Portuguese, noting, for example, when 'armadas' were sent out to relieve various coastal cities in 1550 (II, iv, 92), the number of inhabitants in each settlement, their fortifications, and so on and so forth. There is mention of the English hovering ready to strike at Bahia (II, xiv, 107). The wealth that each of the districts possesses (in industrial terms, as in the sugar mills) as well as the fertility of those plants and trees transported to Bahia from Spain (II, xxxiii–xxvi, 124–33), are intended as a pleasing reminder that the Portuguese now have access to Spanish produce without the intermediary of Spain. There are lengthy descriptions of other plants and fruit-bearing trees in Brazil (II, xxxvii–lxxvii, 133–87), as well as its fauna (II, lxxvi-cxxiv, 185–235), followed by a cluster of chapters on the fish in the seas around Brazil (cxxvi-cxlvi, 235–58), which contains a description of the mysterious *homens marinhos*, an unnatural combination of man and fish (II, cxxvii, 237–8), concluding with a section on the Indian communities (II, cxlvii-clxxxvi, 259–300). Though essentially a revamping of Gândavo's treatise, the *Tratado descritivo do Brasil em 1587* provides more details – on, for example, the Tupinambas' sexual customs (they commit incest, the old women seduce the young boys, the men put insects on their penises to make them swell and thereby increase their sexual prowess despite the pain this evidently produces, the wives often bring women home to their husbands for sex, and there is a general predilection for sodomy; 268–9). Soares de Sousa's text also contains an intriguing account of a number of young Frenchmen who were left with the Tupinambas to learn their language, but, when recalled, refused to return, preferring to stay with their women, and their children called 'mamelucos' (II, clxxvii, 291–92). The treatise strikes very much a coloniser's note at its conclusion in its description of the various metals (iron, steel, copper, gold and silver) as well as the precious stones (emeralds, sapphires) which are there for the taking in Brazil (II, cxciii-cxcvi, 307–11).

*Diálogos das Grandezas do Brasil*, composed by Ambrósio Fernandes Brandão in 1618, only saw the light of day many years later, sporadically in academic journals during the nineteenth century, and then in an accessible edition drawn up by Afrânio Peixoto in the early decades of the twentieth. It is an engaging text, a dialogue between two fictitious people (and here there is a similarity with Francisco Javier Eugenio de Santa Cruz y Espejo's essays, see pp. 55–6 below), one Alviano, who has recently arrived in Brazil and is sceptical about the advantages of the country compared to Portugal, the other Brandônio, now residing in Brazil and intent on persuading his friend about the benefits of the New World. It offers a snapshot of life in Brazil at the beginning of the seventeenth century. In the first dialogue Alviano does not allow himself to be persuaded that Portugal's colony has more to offer than Spain's, but Brandônio sets out to prove that Brazil was destined for greatness, and is already showing signs of its 'grandeza': 'a terra novamente descoberta havia de ser uma opulenta província, refúgio e abrigo da gente portuguêsa, pôsto que a isto não devemos dar crédito, são sinais da grandeza em que cada dia se vai pondo' (Fernandes Brandão 55). Clearly some of Alviano's questions are designed as prompts for a brief history and geography lesson on Brazil (the description of each captaincy especially has much in common with the accounts in the letters of the Jesuits of the previous century), for the arguments are carefully juxtaposed in order to give the impression that Alviano's resistance is gradually being worn down. Dialogue 2 sounds a slightly more philosophical note in attempting to solve the hoary chestnut that haunted the sixteenth and seventeenth centuries – did the ancients have any knowledge of this newly-discovered land? Brandônio brings the discussion around to an appreciation of the superiority of the weather in Brazil, and the curative powers of some of the New World's flora. Brandônio's observation that there are no fleas in Brazil (148) has the desired effect, and Alviano's resistance begins to buckle under the weight of positive evidence. Indeed, by Dialogue 3, confronted with a barrage of information about the wealth created, inter alia, by sugar, wood and cotton, Alviano is beginning to accept everything he is told, often offering no more than a 'Nem isso nego' (165). In Dialogue 4, Alviano attempts to argue that Brazilian food is not as tasty as Portugal's, but this is soon dismissed when Brandônio discusses Brazil's fruit. In Dialogue 5 Brandônio rams his advantage home by listing the great variety of birds, fish and wild animals found in the New World, and in the final and sixth dialogue he brings the cycle of argumentation to a close. Alviano has no option but to admit his error: 'Estou já bem arrependido do meu engano' (328). Brandônio is now so confident that he has won the argument that he does not recoil from telling Alviano about the Indians' predilection for cannibalism which, he says, is based on their desire for revenge on their enemies. Despite the gruesome accounts, Alviano is happy to conclude that the grandeur of Brazil does, indeed, merit praise (361). Though he takes a leaf out of the Jesuits' book – they are continually praising Brazil in their letters – Fernandes Brandão does so with more wit since he shows an unconvinced interlocutor from Portugal gradually becoming persuaded of Brazil's greatness.

## The Amerindian View of the Conquest

Though fragmented by a colonial power not overkeen on hearing the story of the conquest as seen through Amerindian eyes, the other version of the conquest described in the previous section has gradually emerged. By Miguel León-Portilla's computation, there are twelve surviving documents, in written or pictographic form, which describe the conquest from the Amerindian point of view (*The Broken Spears* 129). One very important source is Fray Bernadino de Sahagún's history of New Spain based on oral accounts of the conquest given to him by Indian informants as described above, the *Historia general de las cosas de Nueva España*, also known as the *Codex Florentino*. Other important extant Amerindian accounts of the conquest are: *Anonymous Manuscript of Tlaletolco* (1528), *Codice Aubin* (or *Codex 1576*), *Codice Ramírez* (probably compiled from the data assembled before 1580 by Fray Diego de Duran, and published in 1944), Fernando de Alva Ixtilxochitl, *XIII relación* and *Historia chichimeca* (written in Spanish and based on Nahuatl sources no longer extant), *Lienzo de Tlaxcala* (dating from the middle of the sixteenth century and published in 1892), Diego Muñoz Camargo, *Historia de Tlaxcala* (written in Spanish during the second half of the sixteenth century and published in 1892), Fernando Alvarado Tezozomac, *Cronica mexicana* (1944) and *Cronica mexicayotl* (1975), and the *VII relación* by the historian of Chalco, Domingo Francisco de San Anton Munon Chimalpain Cuauhtlehuanitzin. Though centred on different geographical areas, these texts were collected by authors concerned to keep this history alive, and were based on information given by oral informants in Nahuatl which was then transcribed phonetically and recorded in written form; many of these original manuscripts are now scattered in libraries around the world and have been published. A highly influential collection of these texts was published by León-Portilla, translated into Spanish as *Visión de los vencidos* (1959).

The passages of the *Codex Florentino* relating to the conquest are the most dramatic. They present a picture of the Aztecs whom Cortés faced as riven by internal political tensions, caught in an uneasy truce with the various Mesoamerican peoples surrounding them, and led by a leader, Moctezuma, who was paralysed by indecision and submitted to the invasion with a fatalistic resignation. All of these factors Cortés was able to exploit cleverly to his own advantage. The *Codex Florentino* presents an internally and chronologically coherent version of the events leading up to the destruction of Tenochtitlan; it begins with the eight bad omens (the most incredible of which was the appearance of *tlacantzolli*, or men with two heads, symbolizing, perhaps, the *mestizo* race soon to emerge),[8] the first sightings of the Spanish galleons, the alliance of the peoples hostile to the Aztecs, and leading to the description of the Spaniards' relentless march on Tenochtitlan, the capture of Moctezuma, the massacre of the Aztec warriors during the Feast of Toxcatl on the orders of Diego de Alvarado (seen as an example of the most perverse treachery by the Aztecs), the subsequent expulsion of the Spanish army, and concludes with their return to Tenochtitlan which they vengefully razed to the ground (1519–22). One of the most striking features of the *Codex Florentino* are the illustrations which accompany the narrative. Examples are the description of Cortés firing a gun at which the Indians faint (fol. 9r), La Malinche speaking from a rooftop to an Indian on behalf of Cortés (fol. 29r), the carnage during the Feast of Toxcatl (fol. 33r-v, fol. 34r), and the Spaniards escaping from

---

[8] The most miraculous of the signs is the captured bird with a mirror on its head ('tenya esta ave, en medio de la cabeça, un espejo redondo, donde se parecia el cielo') in which Moctezuma saw a 'muchedumbre de gente iunta que venyan todos, armados encima de cavallos'; fol. 3r.

Tenochtitlan (fol. 43r). Certain symbols are used to tell the story over and above the words. While the war has not been lost by the Aztecs, the figures show a triumphant eagle (fol. 54r, fig. 2, and fig. 3 in which a cactus takes the place of the eagle, and later on fol. 50r, figs. 2 and 3). But when the war is nearing its conclusion, the eagle is depicted as cowering in fear, its wings held close to its body (fol. 50v, fig. 3). The eagle is absent from the last twenty-two illustrations as if to suggest that the Aztec empire has now fallen (fols. 63r–69v). It is surely not insignificant that the last pages of the text (fols. 70r–87r) bear no drawings, as if to suggest the reality was too painful to illustrate in visual terms.

Other Nahuatl documents can in the main be used to support this basic narrative; Tezozomac's *Cronica mexicana*, for example, contains the first detailed eyewitness account by a poor *macehual* (common man) of the Spanish in their ships, described as 'two towers or small mountains floating on the waves of the sea' (*The Broken Spears* 16), and expanded in the following account:

> Our lord and king, it is true that strange people have come to the shores of the great sea. They were fishing from a small boat, some with rods and others with a net. They fished until late and then they went back to their two great towers and climbed up into them. There were about fifteen of these people, some with blue jackets, others with red, others with black or green, and still others with jackets of a soiled colour, very ugly, like our *ictilmatli*. There were also a few without jackets. On their heads they wore red kerchiefs, or bonnets of a fine scarlet color, and some wore large round hats like small *comales*, which must have been sunshades. They have very light skin, much lighter than ours. They all have long beards, and their hair comes only to their ears. (*The Broken Spears* 17)

The beauty of this passage is that it reveals the unfamiliarity of the sight of the Europeans for the Amerindian mind (the ships' masts become 'mountains' or 'towers'), in contrast to the account of the Spanish chroniclers who see the Amerindian world as strange and barbaric. A similar defamiliarisation technique is evident in the description provided by the *Codex Florentino* of the Spanish in their military garb. With regard to the cannons, we hear 'de los truenos que quyebran las orejas, y del hedor de la polvora, que parece cosa infernal, y del huego que echan por la boca, y del golpe de la pelota, que desmenuza un arbol de golpe' (Chap. 7; fol. 11r). As for the Spaniards, their swords are iron; their bows are iron; their shields are iron; their spears are iron, and 'tenyan las caras blancas, y los ojos garços, y los cabellos rojos, y las barbas largas' (Chap. 7; fol. 11v). Their horses are called 'deer' which 'carry them on their backs wherever they wish to go' and are 'as tall as the roof of a house', and they have dogs which have 'burning yellow' eyes which 'flash fire and shoot off sparks' (*The Broken Spears* 30–1). To judge by descriptions such as these it is no wonder the Aztecs were terrified by the arrival of the Spanish.

It would be naive, however, on the basis of the above, to assume that all the extant Amerindian versions of the conquest are univocal. There are, indeed, differences in emphasis between the texts and, at times, disagreements about the course of events due to political considerations (as is the case with the Spanish chronicles, a good example being the contestatory versions of Cortés's achievement found in Gómara and Díaz Bernal del Castillo, respectively). There is a notable gap between the versions of the massacre of Cholula as they appear in the *Codex Florentino* and in Camargo's *Historia de Tlaxcala*. In Sahagún's version the Tlaxcaltecans, a neighbouring tribe of the people of Cholula, used the presence of the new invaders to settle old scores, whereas according to Muñoz Camargo, the Cholultecans provoked their own demise by callously flaying an envoy sent by the Tlaxcaltecans advising them to surrender to the Spanish (*The Broken Spears* 37–49).

An important feature of these Amerindian texts is that they testify not to a culture which was suppressed in the early fifteenth century, but rather to a living though repressed community. Not only the texts mentioned above but later Nahuatl texts such as *An Eighteenth-Century Nahua Testimony* and *The Manifestos of Emiliano Zapata of April 1918* (the latter written in Nahuatl to mobilise the Mexican peasantry; *The Broken Spears* 158–68) testify to the strength and continuity of the Amerindian cultural tradition, as indeed do more recent texts such as Mário de Andrade's novel, *Macunaíma* (1925), Miguel Ángel Asturias's *Hombres de maíz* (1948), and Menchú's testimonial text *Me llamo Rigoberta Menchú* (1982) (see below, Chapters 4 and 5).

**Theatre**

The branch of Amerindian drama about which most is known is Aztec drama. As Miguel León-Portilla has pointed out, Nahuatl drama can be divided into four basic forms, which are (i) hymns in the form of a dialogue, (ii) comic acting and entertainment, (iii) representations of significant myths, and (iv) themes related to family and society (*Teatro*). The important point here is the preeminence of ritual, because of this drama's continued connection to its origins in religion and magic; the 'presentation of cosmic balance remains one of the chief functions of drama' at this time (Weiss 28). In the Aztec culture, where human sacrifice was most prevalent, the prisoner or volunteer was coached in the dialogue and the ritual acts that he would perform as he was taken up to the place of sacrifice. It is perhaps best to see pre-Columbian drama, if it can be so called, as an offshoot of religious ritual. Certainly the many descriptions of human sacrifice which appear in Book II of Sahagún's *Historia general de las cosas de la Nueva España* follow a similar pattern. The captives, whether they be children, slaves, or war prisoners from another tribe, are adorned with feathers and flowers, and then the people sing and dance in front of them, after which they are led away for sacrifice; sometimes, as in the festival of Tlacaipeoaliztli, the prisoners were flayed and various ceremonies were performed by soldiers wearing their skins (Sahagún, *History* 52). The songs could involve ritual dances and the wearing of masks, and dramatic dialogues could be performed, normally emphasizing the continuity of family lineage. These details give a sense of what should be meant by the term drama used here. Three elements common to these practices should be mentioned as related to the symbolic language of drama; all have to do with identification through performance. The first is that the sacrificee 'becomes' the god as a result of the ritual; in the festival of Toxcatl, for example, a youth was treated regally for one year and, in the ritual twenty-day month immediately before the sacrifice, he becomes Tezcatlipoca and is revered as such (Sahagún, *History* 54–5). The second element involving identification concerns the flaying of the sacrificial victim, based on the notion of becoming that person in his or her newly gained divine identity. Thirdly, the flesh of the victim was often consumed, and this action again emblematised identification through the ritual of drama: the victim becomes the god, the actor becomes the person.[9] It is as a result of this element of identification that we can describe the practices described above as drama.

The only extant pre-Columbian play is the Mayan drama, *Rabinal Achí*, an anonymous work which dates from fifteenth-century Guatemala. It was first heard by the French scholar, Charles Etienne Brasseur de Bourbourg, from the lips of a Guatemalan Indian, one Bartolo Ziz; Brasseur de Bourbourg subsequently published the original Mayan text, accompanied by a French translation, in Paris in 1862. *Rabinal Achí* is a ritualistic text which focuses on the dialogue between the chief of one tribe – the Rabinal – who 'captures' the chief from another tribe – the Quiché – (the capture is enacted in the first scene). The bulk of the drama is taken up with an elaborately rhetorical exchange between captor and prisoner in which the former attempts to establish the virility, or lack thereof, of the latter, with the natural world acting at once as backdrop and jury of this process, which reaches its climactic finale with the sacrificial death of the Varón de Quiché. It has been suggested that the sacrificial element of these Amerindian practices 'was taken up in the sacramental auto, which with its sacrifical substitution of Jesus Christ, was imported and adapted by Catholic missionaries from Mexico to Brazil' (Weiss 33). While this may be true with hindsight, it is important to recognise that, apart from the obvious difference that a human being is not literally sacrificed during the *auto sacramental*, there is also the difference that the Amerindian drama is not marked off as a symbolic space separate from everyday life, as was the case with theatre in contemporary Europe, in the sense of being entertainment for which an entrance fee is paid. In this, the analogy cited at the beginning of this chapter ought to be recalled. For just as the Mexican codex had no legend to explain its symbolic meaning (unlike the European map which bears a legend which explains the code of the represented territory), so Amerindian drama needed no symbolic space marked off from the discourse of everyday life.

---

[9] In special ceremonies the identification through drama reached the audience as well; in the feast of Atmalqualilitzi, for example, the people dressed in costumes, impersonated birds, butterflies and beetles, and even carried on their backs a sleeping man whom they called sleep (Sahagún, *History* 146).

The first examples of theatre brought by the Spanish were related to Franciscan missionary activity, of which the earliest were the auto (the Iberian version of the miracle play), the 'Pastores' (Shepherds' Play), and the 'Moros y Cristianos' (legendary-ritual play). Four more genres were added over time: the *paso*, the *entremés*, the *loa* and the *coloquio*. There were some examples of secular drama (by the late 1500s, the *comedias* of the Spanish Golden Age were gaining popularity in the colonies and Conquistador Pizarro had ordered some *comedias* to be performed for the entertainment of his troops) but most drama was related to proselytisation. Missionary drama notably took the form of the presentation of the fundamentals of the Christian gospel in the church-sponsored Corpus Christi celebrations. The earliest reference to any form of dramatic performance involves the Corpus Christi festivities held in Mexico City cathedral in 1525. Noticing that dance and song were integral parts of the Aztec ceremonies of worship, Pedro de Gante composed songs for worship at the nativity scene. When the chiefs of Texcoco, Tlatelolco, Clalco and Huejotzinjo heard native Americans singing in their own language, they were greatly impressed and agreed to be baptised and to let their children attend the school the Franciscans had built (Weiss 47). Amerindian-language plays followed in Tlalolco, by Father Andrés de Olmos, a Spanish auto in Nahuatl translation in 1533, and in Tlaxcala a Corpus Christi festivity arranged by Fray Toribio de Benavente. In Tlaxcala on Easter Wednesday 1539 an impressive version of 'The Fall of Adam and Eve' was presented; Fray Jerónimo de Mendieta said of this ceremony that it was 'la cosa más agradable a la vista que en mi vida he visto' (Mendieta, vol. 2, 50).

A good example of early missionary drama is the anonymous *Coloquio de Nueua conberción Y bautismo delos quatro Vltimos Reyes de Tlaxcala en la Nueua España*, written and performed at the end of the sixteenth or beginning of the seventeenth century (some give the date of performance as 1619). The manuscript of this play was discovered in the 1920s in a collection in the University of Texas Library. It was subsequently published by the man who discovered it, Carlos E. Castañeda, in the *Revista Mexicana de Estudios Históricos* in 1928, and attributed to Gutiérrez de Luna; this attribution has been questioned by José Rojas Garcidueñas (*Tres piezas* 151–81). The play focuses on the conquest of Tlaxcala by Hernán Cortés in 1519, an event which played a crucial role in the subsequent subjugation of the Aztec kingdom. Contemporary indigenous texts, such as those included in *The Broken Spears* (see above), suggest that the reason why the Tlaxcaltecans sided with Cortés was in order to settle old scores with the Cholultecans. The *Coloquio*, however, could not be more different. The four kings of Tlaxcala are presented in the opening scene as wrestling with the dilemma posed by the arrival of the Spanish. They are first visited by their god, called Hongol and later revealed to be none other than the devil, then by an angel of the Lord, who manages to persuade them to convert instantly to Christianity. Cortés and la Malinche subsequently pay them a visit, the kings are baptised and the play concludes with the partaking of mass. Though called a *coloquio*, the play is essentially an *auto sacramental*. That this is an early colonizing text is suggested by the naivety involved in the naming of the Indians' god; as Angel María Garibay points out, Nahuatl does not have the 'g' sound (*Tres piezas* 163); the name of the Tlaxtaltecan god is probably a version of the name of one of the prominent leaders of the Araucanian Indians who appears in Ercilla's *La Araucana*, namely Ongol (*Tres piezas* 168). Whatever its source – it may even have come from Lope de Vega's *El nuevo mundo descubierto por Cristóbal Colón* – the use of the word Ongol betrays an historically inaccurate but convenient shorthand notation for denoting cultural otherness.

The important point to be retained from the above is that the early missionary activity as expressed through drama was profoundly assimilationist and synchretistic. Mendieta, for example, has commented on the great ability with which the Mexicans learned to write Spanish and Latin, to sing in choirs, to play instruments and to learn grammar (vol. 2, 38–40). They were so successful, indeed, that their compositions were indistinguishable from Spanish compositions:

> Yo, lo que más es, que pocos años después que aprendieron el canto, comenzaron ellos a componer de su ingenio villancicos en canto de órgano a cuatro voces y algunas misas y otras obras, que mostrados a diestros cantores españoles, decían ser escogidos juicios, y no creían que pudiesen ser de indios. (Mendieta, vol. 2, 40)

The Mexicans were also able to enclose Christian ceremony within their own culture-specific religious ceremonies: 'Acabados los maitines a las dos o a las tres de la mañana, ya están aparejados en el patio de la iglesia los que han de comenzar el baile a su modo antiguo, con cánticos aplicados a la nueva fiesta' (Mendieta, vol. 2, 50). The vogue of religious dramas floreció until the 1550s in Mexico and Central America, and until the 1560s in South America (Weiss 42). The Dominicans and the Jesuits, who were later on the scene, copied the Franciscans in the use of drama for proselytisation. But this was not without its problems; in 1586, in Etla, near Oaxaca, during a performance arranged by the Dominican friar Andrés de Moguer, the balcony of the convent collapsed, killing many people, including a friar (Weiss 55).

The most significant play of the early colonial era was the *Tragedia intitvlada triuvmpho de los sanctos en qve se representa la persecucion de Diocleciano, y la prosperidad que se siguio con el Imperio de Constantino* (1579), probably written by two Jesuits, Vincencio Lanuchi and Juan Sánchez Baquero, and published by Antonio Ricardo in Mexico City. The play is medieval in design in that it contains characters who are emblems of abstract concepts, such as Iglesia, Fe, Idolatría, Crueldad, etc., and Senecan in pedigree in that the enunciation of long-winded morality-based speeches by the characters is the norm. The theme, as suggested by the title, is a comparison between the vice of the Roman emperor Diocletian (245–316 A.D.) who, during his reign (284–305 A.D.), was responsible for the persecution of Christians, and the virtue of Constantine I (280?–337 A.D.), the first Roman emperor attested to have become a Christian. Just as interesting as the play itself is the social ritual which accompanied its performance, for it was part of a week-long celebration in Mexico City in November 1578 in which some holy relics donated by Pope Gregorius XIII were officially transmitted to the Jesuits. On All Saints Day, a procession of great pomp and ceremony attended by every significant state and ecclesiastical dignitary took place in which the relics were transported from the cathedral where they had been deposited to the Colegio Máximo de San Pedro y San Pablo. On the following day, 2 November 1578, the *Tragedia* was staged in the Jesuit College; the performance was four hours long and was attended by the Viceroy, the members of the Real Audiencia, the Inquisition, as well as other state and ecclesiastic officials (*Tres piezas* 3–10). At the conclusion of the play, the character Iglesia addresses the 'amado pueblo mío MEXICANO' exhorting it to follow Constantine's example and embrace Christianity (line 666; *Tres piezas* 146). The play, intriguingly enough, also has a post-Tridentine political edge in that the character Fe subsequently exhorts the Mexican people to accept the sacred treasure of the relics 'a pesar del engaño luterano' (line 681; *Tres piezas* 146). Some critics have criticised this play for its turgid style, with Seneca mentioned as the culprit (notably H. L. Johnson, quoted. in *Tres piezas* 22–6), but it is surely more important to observe that the intended audience for the *Tragedia* – essentially the executive elite of society, both secular and ecclesiastic – may well have enjoyed, and even expected, a type of drama in which characters on a stage before them pronounced decrees ratifying executive decisions intended to guide the future direction of Christendom; they would have felt 'at home', so to speak.

The most significant drama produced in Brazil during the early colonial period were the plays composed by the Jesuit José de Anchieta, whose essays have already been discussed above (pp. 19–20; for an overview of the main theatrical works performed in the latter half of the sixteenth century, see Galante de Sousa 86–115). Similar in purpose and scope to the missionary drama produced by the religious in the Spanish colonies, Anchieta's plays set out to instruct the Tupi Indians about the basics of the Christian faith, and to persuade them to give up their beliefs and customs in order to embrace Christianity. His theatre embodies the drama of Christianity by re-enacting scenes from the Bible, though these are often given a relevance to the contemporary situation, by having Indian warriors of the past acting as a negative foil to the Christian heroes. Anchieta wrote some of his plays in Tupi. *Dia da assunção, cuando levaram sua imagem a Reritibia*, for example, was performed in Tupi in Reritibia, now called Anchieta, possibly on 15 August 1579 (Martins 563). It opens with a short dialogue between a devil and an angel on the way to visit the town of Reritibia. The devil is at first confident ('Aáni, erejú teñe / tába suí xe peábo'; Não vens debalde / afastar-me da aldeia; Martins 567), but when he realises that he is no match for the Virgin Mary who is coming to save the town, he and his fellow devils decide to flee (568). This is followed by a number of dancers who sing stanzas honouring the Virgin Mary. In one section, the 'Tupána Kuápa' (576–7), Anchieta transposes the refrain into a Tupi chant:

> Akoeýme, guimanómo,
> añanga esapyá
> xe ánga ajusá
> pecado irumóno.
> Aé reroyrómo,
> > *koí, asausú,*
> > *xe jára, Iesu.* (576)

There are five more stanzas, each ending with the refrain, in italics here for ease of reference. Notice that the only two words left in Portugese are 'Iesu' and 'pecado', suggesting that the Christian notion of sin was foreign to the Tupi Indians. The various other plays – which were only printed in 1954 – follow basically the same form, namely enacting the drama of the acceptance of Christ. Apart from their obvious differences (some of the plays were written in Tupi, some in a mixture of Tupi and Portuguese, as in *Recebimento que fizeram os índios de Guaraparim ao padre provincial Marçal Beliarte* [663–78], some in Tupi, Portuguese and Spanish, for example, *Na festa de são Lourenço* [681–746]), some of the plays have distinct thematic emphases. *Na Aldea de Guaraparim*, for example, gives the devils the names of Indian tribe leaders of the recent past, and focuses on the sexual improprieties committed during their rule (618–19, 629), while *Recebimento que fizeram os índios de Guaraparim ao padre provincial Marçal Beliarte*, in its climatic conclusion of the struggle between Amerindian devils and the Christian angel, has one of the Indians turn upon another and break his head open ('Quebra-lhe a cabeça', as the stage directions explain; 676), thereby, curiously enough, echoing the conclusion of the Amerindian cannibalistic ritual which Anchieta, like the other Jesuits, was attempting to stamp out. No doubt intended as an act of inauguration of a new spiritual context, it bears witness nevertheless to the fundamentally transculturated nature of the regime which the Jesuits were establishing in Brazil. *Na festa de são Lourenço*, performed probably on 10 August 1583, and the most sophisticated in dramatic terms of Anchieta's plays, has recourse to the usual repertoire of angels reproving devils, but does so in the contemporary context of the alliance of the French and the Tameroy Indians (they joined forces in July 1566 in an attempt to overcome Rio de Janeiro). The devils gleefully recount what they persuade the Indians to do:

> Jemoyró, morapiti,
> joú, tapúia rára,
> aguasá, moropotára,
> mañána, syguarajý
> naipotán abá sejará.

> (enfurecer-se, andar matando,
> comer um ao outro, prender tapuias,
> amancebar-se, ser deshonesto,
> espião, adúltero
> – não quero que o gentio deixe.) (686)

St Sebastian, who was believed to have aided the relief of Rio against the French–Tameroy invasion (684, n. 2), takes on the devils in the play, and they are eventually consigned to the fires of hell (707), as are other enemies of Christianity such as Décio and Valeriano (731). The concluding scenes of Act III become increasingly tense and dramatically effective, as the characters gradually describe the flames of hell approaching (722–32). Anchieta's plays provide a vivid sense of the vibrancy of culture in Brazil towards the close of the seventeenth century, a world in which Portuguese, Spanish, Tupi, and Latin jostled shoulders and in which the Amerindian and the Christian cultures clashed radically. The Tupi Indians were not given a choice. Either they accepted Christianity immediately or they would be burned in the fires of hell, and Anchieta's plays reveal this poignantly.

2

# Colonial and Viceregal Literature

The second generation of settlers in the New World used print where their predecessors had used military exploits for, as one commentator points out, the 'sword was yielding to the quill as an instrument of material advancement, and a familiarity with letters and learning was becoming a surer guarantee of social preferance than military skill' (Leonard, *Books* 198). From its inception, printing in Latin America was associated with royal privilege and, throughout the colonial era, permission in the form of a licence from the sovereign was necessary before a printing press could be set up. During the early days of the colony in Brazil, indeed, a printing industry proved to be neither administratively necessary nor economically viable. As a result of Pope Alexander VI's recommendation in 1501 that a system be devised whereby printed works could be regulated by the state, the Portuguese authorities in 1508 required that all works dealing with matters of religion be submitted for royal approval, and this decree was re-affirmed in 1537 soon after the re-establishment of the Inquisition in Portugal, and then spectacularly enforced by a royal decree of 4 December 1576 which prohibited the publication of any work without royal sanction (Hallewell 77–8). This was a prohibition that had teeth; Antonil's *Cultura e Opulência do Brasil* was banned for fear that the description therein of Brazil's material wealth would lead to unwelcome interest on the part of rival European nations (Hallewell 78). As a result of a combination of factors the development of a printing industry was forestalled in Brazil.

The situation was somewhat different in the Spanish colonies where printing was allowed, though only under certain conditions. The connection between the crown and print was, however, a constant one; the establishment of printing in New Spain coincided almost exactly with the establishment of the first viceroyalty. Don Antonio de Mendoza's viceroyalty began in 1535 and a printing press may have been operational in Mexico City in that year (if we subscribe to José Toribio Medina's notion that one Esteban Martín was at work in the capital of New Spain from 1535 to 1538), or at least by 1539 when a native of Brescia, Giovanni Paoli, or Juan Pablos as he came to be known, worked as a printer in Mexico City on behalf of the leading Seville printer, Juan Cromberger, in the service of Archbishop Zumárraga under a contract negotiated with Antonio de Mendoza (Thompson 12–13). In a contract drawn up between Cromberger and Pablos on 12 June 1539 Pablos agreed to go to Mexico with his wife and stay there for at least ten years; he was to be manager-cum-compositor and, demand permitting, given power to contract labour and print 3,000 sheets a day (Griffin, *The Crombergers* 85). It was not long before New Spain became pre-eminent for book publishing in the Spanish colonies; during the seventeenth century, New Spain was able to contribute to other parts of the empire not only textiles, clothes, jewelry and leather goods, but also books (Adrien 35).

Early on in the colonial era printing was in the main restricted to the publication of works for missionary purposes (catechisms and the like).[1] From its beginnings in New Spain, the art of printing gradually spread to the rest of the Spanish empire, reaching La Ciudad de los Reyes, or Lima, by 1584, Old Paraguay by 1700, Cuba by 1723, New Granada (specifically Bogotá) by 1738, the Río de la Plata region by 1766, and Chile by 1776 (Thompson 34, 47, 94, 76, 87). A quick survey of some of the books published early on in the colonial era gives some insight into the culture of the period, based as it was on a view of print as performative rather than descriptive, law-enforcing rather than politically mediational. The first work published in the New World of which reliable information exists is Bishop Zumárraga's *Breve y mas compendiosa doctrina christiana*, published in 1539 on Juan Pablos's press, and of which no copy is now extant (Menéndez Pidal viii–ix). During the second half of the sixteenth century print diversified to include theology (notably Fray Alonso de la Vera Cruz's *Recognitio Summularum* published by Juan Pablos in 1554), medicine (the first medicinal text was Francisco Bravo's *Opera medicinalia* published by Pedro Ocharte in 1570), philology (the first dictionary of an Indian language was Alonso de Molina's *Vocabulario en la lengua Castellana y Mexicana* [1555]), and navigation (such as Diego García de Palacio's *Instrvcion nauthica para el bven Vso y regimiento de las Naos* [1587]). Unlike the missionary publications, these works were dedicated to and funded by prominent individuals, typically the Viceroy; the catechisms were simply dedicated to God and funded by the Church. The bulk of the early literary works were published in Latin, such as Francisco Cervantes de Salazar's six dialogues in Latin (1554), and the Jesuits' edition of Ovid and some *Emblemata* by Alciato (1577). But some original literary works were published in Spanish, such as Bartolomé de las Casas's *Cancionero Espiritual* (1546), and Cervantes de Salazar's *Túmulo Imperial* (1560), inspired by the funeral honours for Charles V in Mexico City. But we have to wait until the seventeenth century for a major original literary work to be published in the New World: Balbuena's *Grandeza Mexicana* (1604) closely followed by Mateo Alemán's *Ortografía* (1609).[2]

By comparison the situation of printing in the Lusophone colonies was much less advanced, and Brazil had to wait more than a century before it published its first book, let alone a literary work. Given the more advanced state of the

---

[1] This is largely to be expected of the time since, as Steinberg has pointed out, the 'great publishing successes of the sixteenth century were achieved in the realm of theology' (Steinberg 142).

[2] It is important to recall in this context that, as far as printed books were concerned, Spain was one of only two countries (the other being England) in which 'vernacular books outnumbered Latin ones from the beginning' (Steinberg 118).

printing industry in the Spanish colonies, it is perhaps not surprising that the first book published in Portuguese in the Americas, *D.O.M. Luzeiro Evangelico, que mostra à todos os Christãos das Indias orientais o caminho unico seguro & certo da recta Fé, para chegarem ao porto de salvação eterna* (1710) by João Morelli de Castelnovo, was printed not in the Portuguese colony but in New Spain (Hallewell 84). The Dutch had attempted to set up a press in Pernambuco during their occupancy of that region in the period 1630–55, but the typographer chosen for the task, Pieter Janszoon, died before he began work (Hallewell 85–6). During the colonial period Brazilian writers routinely sent their works to be published in Portugal, as occurred, for example, with Anchieta's *Arte de Grammatica* (1595), Teixeira's *A Proposopéia* (1601), and Antônio Vieira's sermons. Despite the royal embargo on printing in the New World there were sporadic attempts by the Jesuits in the early eighteenth century in Recife to publish pamphlets (Hallewell 88), but the first verifiable work published in Brazil came out on 7 February 1747, the *Relação da Entrada Que Fez o Excellentissimo e Reverendissimo Senhor D. F. Antonio do Desterro Malhevro*..., authored by Luis Antonio Rosado de Cunha, and published by Antonio Isidora de Fonseca in Rio de Janeiro (there is a copy in the Obras Raras section of the National Library in Rio, 595-JAM). In order to print this work Rosado de Cunha obtained the permission of the bishop and neither was aware that royal permission was also needed for publication to take place legally. As soon as news of the print reached royal ears, the authorities in Lisbon demanded that the printing shop be closed down (Hallewell 93–4). As far as printing was concerned, Portugal maintained an iron grip on Brazil – in marked contrast to Spain's more liberal approach to printing in the New World – although this draconian situation would change dramatically in Brazil with the advent of independence, as we shall see (see pp. 67–8).

Before passing to a discussion of the three main genres of literature of this period, it is important to emphasise that its sources were European. During the pre-independence period the intellectual in the Spanish and Portuguese colonies saw Europe as the source of ideas, statecraft, money and power, and America as an inferior replica of the European model. This is clear from three book orders which survive from the early colonial period, two from Mexico City (21 July 1576 and 22 December 1576), and one from Lima (22 February 1583). The promissory note of 21 July 1576 orders from Spain 341 volumes, of which half are theological; the creative literature ordered is mostly by Latin authors (Lucan, Martial, Seneca, Terence, Horace, Suetonius and Ovid) (Leonard, *Books* 200–4). In the promissory note of 22 December 1576, which orders 1,190 books, a preference for Latin authors in the literature section is evident (Vergil, Ovid, Cicero), although original works by Castilian authors Marqués de Santillana and Jorge Manrique, and the *Celestina* are also requested; the most popular work, of which twenty-six copies were ordered, was Nebrija's *Arte de la lengua* (Leonard, *Books* 205–6). The book order made by the *limeño* bookseller, Juan Jiménez del Río, on 22 February 1583, with one Francisco de la Hoz, lists a little under 2,000 books, of which 44 per cent are ecclesiastical,

32 per cent non-fiction, and 24 per cent for belles-lettres (Leonard, *Books* 220). All three of the book orders show a Eurocentric bias; as Leonard suggests, '[t]his apparent indifference to local themes and preoccupation with Spanish and European literature characterise the entire colonial period and illustrate the complete spiritual and literary as well as political and economic subordination of the colonies to the mother country' (*Books* 224). This helps to explain why the first texts studied here – namely, Ercilla's, Balbuena's and Teixeira's – were published in Spain and Portugal respectively rather than in the New World.

## Poetry

The social experience of poetry in this period was more likely to be in the form of a public reading than what we normally understand by reading poetry nowadays, given, *inter alia*, the exorbitant material cost of printed volumes during this period. Very common during the colonial period, especially in the large viceregal capitals of Mexico and Peru, were poetic contests in which aspiring poets of the day read their verses before an audience. The *certamen poético* would typically take as its theme an important historical event – the arrival of a new viceroy or archbishop, the celebration of a martial victory, the reiteration of an article of faith – and would be underwritten by a generous patron, normally a member of the aristocracy. Often the requirements of the tournament were quite specific; one organised by the University of Mexico in 1683 required that the subject be the Immaculate Conception and stated that the metrical model to be imitated would be lines 71 to 98 of the third book of Vergil's *Aeneid*. The rules circulated for the occasion also mentioned that authors should avoid 'a false playing on words of double meaning' and that 'words shall be kept in all their proper meanings' (Leonard, *Baroque* 136–8). To win one of these contests was a sure way of achieving literary visibility. Bernardo de Balbuena, for example, whose work is discussed below, won a poetic contest held in Mexico City in 1685, against 300 other contestants (Leonard, *Baroque* 132), and later proved to be one of the most significant poets of his day in new Spain.

*La Araucana*, three volumes of which were published successively in 1569, 1578, and 1589 by Alonso de Ercilla y Zúñiga (1533–94), is the most significant epic poem treating the theme of the conquest. The high respect which it gained in its day is suggested by an incident described in Cervantes's *El Ingenioso Hidalgo Don Quijote de la Mancha*; it is one of the few books in Don Quijote's library which is not consigned to the flames by the barber and the priest.[3] The

---

[3] In Part I, Chap. 6 of the *Quijote* the priest comes across *La Araucana*, as well as Juan Rufo's *La Austríada* and Cristóbal de Virus's *El Montserrate*, and makes the following comment: '– Todos esos tres libros – dijo el cura – son los mejores que, en verso heroico, en lengua castellana están escritos; y pueden competir con los más famosos de Italia: guárdense como las más ricas prendas de poesía que tiene España –' (Cervantes vol. 2, 126–7).

documents which precede the text of the epic proper, most of which are not reproduced in modern editions, and which include the letter by the scribe, Pedro del Marmol, the *imprimatur* by Antonio de Eraso on the king's behalf, the author's prologue and declaration, and two sonnets which praise Ercilla's martial valour, all bespeak the patronage system of publication customary throughout the colonial era (*La Araucana*, facsimile copy, 1967). For the last two volumes at least, Ercilla drew on first-hand experience of warfare in Chile from 1577 to 1579; his work provides a surprisingly favourable depiction of the enemy of the Spanish army, the Araucanian Indians. Apart from empiric experience, it is generally acknowledged that the single most important literary source for his work was *Orlando Furioso* (1510–32), which was one of the best-sellers of the period (Steinberg 144–5). Ercilla echoes Ariosto's playful control of his subject matter, and specifically borrowed the Italian's technique of interjecting his poetic persona into the story at certain crucial junctures, leaving the warriors in the middle of the battle to create suspense, for example (Bautista Avalle-Arce). But there are some significant differences between Ercilla and Ariosto. For example, while the Italian was celebrating events set in a mythic past, Ercilla's subject matter is drawn from contemporary events (the wars with the Araucanian Indians were raging during the years when Ercilla's volumes were published).

*La Araucana* is typical of the heroic verse poems published in the pre-Tassesque period in which we encounter 'Aeneas-like heroes who stand for national tradition and endeavour' (Pierce xii) before the Counter-Reformation required more catholic subject matter (an example being Diego de Hojeda's post-Tridentine *La Christiada* [1611]). Given the leisurely pace of its publication (Cantos I–XV, 1569; Cantos XVI–XXIX, 1578; Cantos XXX–XXXVII, 1589), it is not surprising that the poem becomes gradually more sprawling and more disorganised in form as it proceeds, such that the third volume contains much material which is extraneous to Ercilla's specific purpose, namely, describing the war between the Spanish and the Araucanians; in Cantos XXXII–XXIII, for example, we hear about Dido's life, and in Canto XXXVII we are treated to a fulsome defence of Phillip II's right to the kingdom of Portugal. In this he is typical of his age; Ercilla could not resist various digressions into areas not obviously germane to his subject, such as the Spanish triumph at San Quentin, or the naval battle of Lepanto, or, still less relevant, the discussion towards the end of the poem of Philip II's right to the throne of Portugal. The poem is written in the octava real, or octava rima verse form, in stanzas of eight hendecasyllables with alternating rhyme (ABABABCC), a form originally introduced in the Spanish lyric from the Italian tradition by Boscán (Navarro Tomás 206). The most common stress pattern used throughout the poem, not surprisingly given its subject-matter, is the heroic hendecasyllable, that is with stress on the second and sixth syllables (Navarro Tomás 263). Each stanza constitutes a separate sense-unit (there is very rarely any semantic run-on between stanzas), and, very often, the stanzas themselves are split into two sense-units of four lines each. This leads to an impression of severe regularity that at times makes the poem monotonous, especially in some of the long, turgid speeches made by the Araucanian Indians and the Spaniards.

*Arauco domado* (1596) by Pedro de Oña (1570–1643) consciously imitated Ercilla's masterpiece, in theme but not in political bias. Like Ercilla before him, Oña had first-hand experience of warfare, having participated in an expedition to quell an uprising in Quito, Ecuador. His description of these events in Cantos XIV–XVI of *Arauco domado* was thought so offensive by members of the Audiencia of Quito that their protests caused the first edition to be withdrawn. It was only with the publication of the second edition in 1605 that Oña achieved fame for his poem. Oña's aim in writing, following established practice of the day, was to secure a high government post. In this he was successful since, soon after its publication, the by-then Viceroy of Peru, García Hurtado de Mendoza, whom he had extolled in his poem, rewarded him with the post of Corregidor of Jaén de Bracamoros in Peru. *Arauco domado* could not be called a well-constructed poem; it spends too much time on elaborate digressions, such as the description of the Quito rebellion which Oña had helped to suppress and his description of the defeat of the English pirate, Richard Hawkins, none of which are related to the body of the narrative. To make matters worse, Oña fails to find time to describe the subsequent capture of the Araucanian chieftain, Caupolicán, surely the main historical event encapsulating the meaning of the title of Oña's poem. Despite his first-hand experience of warfare, Oña's description of clashes between Spaniards and the Araucanian Indians is awkward, and has none of the verve of Ercilla's narrative.

Bento Teixeira's *Prosopopéia* (1601), which consists of ninety-four hendecasyllabic 'octavas' with the rhyme scheme ABABABCC, is Brazil's first literary work. Dedicated to Jorge Dalbuquerque Coelho, a captain and governor of Pernambuco, it functions very much within the patronage system of the period (a literary work extolling the deeds of a powerful man could bring rich dividends for the author). But it was not an immediate success. As the prologue to the 1873 edition published in Rio de Janeiro by the Typographia do Imperial Instituto Artistico points out, the discovery of a copy of the *Prosopopéia* in Lisbon led to the unearthing of a copy in the Biblioteca Nacional in Rio by Benjamin Franklin Remiz Galvão, which was then printed in facsimile (copy in the Biblioteca Nacional, Rio, III–319, 4, 16, n.14). The poems need to be read in the context of the narrative which accompanied the *editio princeps*, that is, the narrative describing the miraculous survival by Jorge de Albuquerque from the shipwreck of a vessel on its way to Lisbon from Pernambuco in 1565 which (the frontispiece appears to suggest) Teixeira wrote up. The narrative, entitled *Naufragio que passou Jorge de Albuquerque Coelho Vindo do Brazil para este Reyno no anno de 1565*, is a thrilling tale which recounts how Albuquerque set off from Pernambuco with a small crew. The ship was attacked by a French ship, then commandeered, then – after a storm which destroyed the ship, ripping off its sails and masts – abandoned to its fate but, by dint of strength of will and many prayers, finally made its way back to Portugal, half of its crew already dead from exhaustion or hunger. Teixeira's *Prosopopéia* is intriguing because it ignores the reality of the events which made the Albuquerque family name famous and, instead of referring to the God which – in his very post-Tridentine way – Albuquerque clung to (such that he cannot bear to sit down to eat with the French since he regards them all as Lutheran heretics, as described in the *Naufragio* 20), Teixeira follows the literary spirit of the day and envelops the hero of his poem in a classical garb. Thus while he is happy to extol Albuquerque as a man of great faith ('Que eu canto hu Albuquerque soberano / Da fé, da cara Patria firme muro' (stanza 1, ll. 5–6, f. 2v), nevertheless the gods whose agency is described are classical. We hear Neptune 'gemer no Mar profundo' (stanza 13, l. 8, f. 4v), we see Zeus in his 'Carro Triunphal' (stanza 14, l. 2, f. 4v), as well as Proteus 'que vaticina' (stanza 15, l. 1, f. 4r). Teixeira maintains that

> Vereys emfin o garbo, & alto brio,
> Do famoso Albuquerque vosso Tio. (stanza 4, ll. 7–8, f. 2r)

the reference here being in all likelihood to the Albuquerque uncle who survived the shipwreck described in the *Naufragio*. The difficulty with Teixeira's poem is that the vehicle (the Homeric struggle between the Greeks and the Trojans) overwhelms the tenor (the Brazilian garrison under attack from various European forces, especially the French), such that the final result is a poem about classical antiquity more than the contemporary situation. Thus, the formula so successfully implemented by Camões in *Os Lusíadas* of bringing the classical backdrop into play in a description of Portugal's overseas adventures, is not in evidence in Teixeira's poem. Teixeira, a new Christian, was twice tried by the Inquisition, once in 1589 and again in 1599, the first occasion as a result of his wife's denunciation of his Judaic views, the second as a result of the murder of his wife whom he accused of adultery, and it is likely that the poem was an attempt to ingratiate himself with the civil authorities. The fact that the poem was published after Teixeira's death (in fact one year later) may explain some of the contradictions which scholars have pointed to; though the account of the shipwreck mentions on the frontispiece that Teixeira was actually in the shipwreck, his name is not listed among the survivors in the text. It is certain that Teixeira was the author of the poem, but not likely that he was author of, or had much to do with, the account contained in the *Naufragio*, as suggested by the frontispiece. If this is the case then the two works may have been juxtaposed by a zealous publisher wishing to kill two birds with one stone, and drawing a connection as regards authorship which was at best tenuous. Conveniently for the publisher, being already dead, Teixeira would have had no say in the matter. In many ways, Teixeira's *Prosopopéia* is more interesting for what it does not say than for what it says.

*Grandeza Mexicana* (1604) by New Spain's Bernardo de Balbuena (1568–1627) is arguably one of the finest poems written in the colonial period. Given his occupation – Balbuena was a priest for most of his life – and the sedentary way in which he fulfilled his duties, Balbuena's work does not have the cut-

and-thrust adventure characteristic of the epic poem. *Grandeza Mexicana* describes a colonial city set in the heart of the Spanish empire, confident of its position in the world, not involved in costly wars subjugating foreign tribes, and not split by internal dissension. Some years before publishing *Grandeza Mexicana*, Balbuena had written *Siglo de oro en las selvas de Erfile* (though it was only published in 1608), which sharpened his skills in composing eclogues. Like the earlier work, *Grandeza Mexicana* is essentially a bucolic poem but it focuses not on the countryside, as do the eclogues of the most famous contemporary practitioner of the genre, the Spaniard Garcilaso de la Vega (1503–36), but rather on the urban environment of Mexico City, except possibly in chapter VI of the poem, which devotes some time to the countryside. *Grandeza Mexicana* consists of an eight-line *argumento* followed by eight chapters, the titles and themes of which are taken successively from the eight lines of the *argumento*. The poem thus functions as a three-tiered structure with the empirical world of Mexico City encapsulated within the eight chapters of the poem, which in turn are encapsulated within the *argumento*. Balbuena's poem is therefore not simply a (medievalising) gloss but involves a playful exploration of the notion of perspective and, in particular, miniaturism. Balbuena's poem is introduced as a missive to an illustrious Mexican lady, Doña Isabel de Tovar y Guzmán, which emphasizes the aristocratic social framework of patronage into which the poem inserts its discourse. The whole of the *Grandeza Mexicana*, apart from the *argumento*, is written in hendecasyllabic tercets, which are interconnected in the sense that the second line of each stanza rhymes with the first and third lines of the subsequent stanza, and so on throughout the entire length of the poem. The tercet was traditionally used, at least in the sonnet with which it is normally associated, with the point of semantic summation of the poem. The form of *Grandeza Mexicana* thus gives it an almost breathless feel as if its wonders could only be described in hyperbolic terms.

*La Christiada* (1611) by Diego de Hojeda (1571?–1615) is an epic poem which tells, in twelve cantos, the story of Christ's Passion from the Last Supper to the Resurrection. Like many of the works published at this time, its author was well connected in religious and political circles; Hojeda had founded a Dominican convent in Lima in 1606 and had been made a Master of Theology in appreciation, and his poem was dedicated to the then Viceroy of Peru, the Marqués de Montesclaros (almost de rigueur as a custom in the early colonial period, as we have seen). The verse form is identical to that used in Ercilla's *La Araucana*, namely, the Italianate octava real which had stanzas of eight hendecasyllables with alternating rhyme (ABABABCC). One of the problems faced by the poem (one that has led to its being less popular with modern audiences) is the disjunction between its poetic form, which suggests the epic with all its contemporary associations with nation-building, hero worship, warfare and a swift-moving narrative, and its subject matter. The historical events which took place from a Thursday night (the Last Supper) to a Friday afternoon (the Crucifixion) and, indeed, their written account in the synoptic gospels does not lend itself as obviously to epic treatment as do Ercilla's. *La Christiada* is a devotional poem which consciously diverts attention away from action understood in a canonic epic sense to digressionary material which leads to contemplation and which includes the psychological (in the form of the agonised thoughts running through Christ's mind), the doctrinal (mainly in allusions to the mystery of Christ's incarnation as man and God), and what for lack of a better term might be called the 'Baroque imaginary'. All three of these types of digressionary material tend to slow up the poem's forward propulsion, and it is in the third type that Hojeda's skill is most apparent. A good example of the latter occurs in canto I when the New Testament account of Christ carrying the sins of mankind in the Garden of Gethsemane is transformed into a fifty-stanza Baroque exposé detailing the sins of mankind as etched on Christ's clothes (Pierce 99–110).

The authors mentioned thus far were well connected. In order to publish it was important to know personally either the Viceroy or a member of his court or somebody influential in the church hierarchy. If a writer openly criticised a figure of authority, his chances of being published and of achieving a position in the state hierarchy were, for obvious reasons, small. Such was the fate of two writers who were writing at the end of the sixteenth century, Fernán González de Eslava (1533?–1601?) and Francisco de Terrazas (1525?–1600?). González de Eslava wrote some satirical *entremeses* criticizing the recently imposed *alcabala* (sales tax) which appeared within a play of his (*Coloquios III*) staged in Mexico City in 1574 during Archbishop Pedro Moya de Contreras's inauguration: some satiric *pasquines* which attacked the King appeared on the wall of the cathedral ten days later, and González de Eslava, suspected of being the author, was imprisoned (along with Francisco de Terrazas) for seventeen days on the orders of the Viceroy of New Spain, Martín Enríquez de Almaza. Those works which have survived show a finely honed use of irony and a trained eye for the vicissitudes of everyday life. His 'Entremés del ahorcado' for example, is a funny skit about a ruffian who pretends he has been hanged when he sees one of his enemies approaching, and has to restrain himself when hearing the insults poured on his head; the 'Entremés de Diego Moreno y Teresa' depicts a hilarious argument between a wife who complains to her husband about their poverty and suggests they go to China, and the husband who is unwilling to go (Luzuriaga and Reeve 54–59).

## Satiric Verse

As the seventeenth century progressed and publishing activity began gradually to extricate itself from royal influence, satire emerged much more clearly as a vibrant social energy. As Julie Greer Johnson has shown in her important study, *Satire in Colonial Spanish America: Turning the New World Upside Down*, there were a number of writers who turned to satire to express their vision of New World society; three names stand out and these are Mateo Rosas de

Oquendo (1559?–1612?), Juan del Valle y Caviedes (1651?–97?) and Gregório de Matos Guerra (1623–96). *Sátira hecha por Mateo Rosas de Oquendo a las cosas que pasan en el Pirú, año de 1598*, to give the text its full name, by Rosas de Oquendo, though written in 1598, was not published until it was discovered in the Biblioteca Nacional in Madrid at the beginning of the twentieth century; it first emerged in excerpts prepared and published by Antonio Paz y Melia in the *Bulletin Hispanique* in 1906. As Pedro Lasarte has pointed out, however, the manuscript clearly made an impact in the seventeenth century, being cited in at least two contemporary documents: Baltasar Dorantes de Carranza's *Sumaria relación de las cosas de la Nueva España*, of 1604, and a satirical ballad known to have been circulating in Lima in 1621 (Rosas de Oquendo xv n. 1). The *Sátira*, which consists of 2,120 octosyllabic lines, provides a fascinating insight into viceregal society at the turn of the seventeenth century and, though vindictive (Rosas de Oquendo's outlook was soured by his inability to make much headway socially during his stay in Peru, as suggested by the unsuccessful period he spent in the service of the Viceroy of Peru, Don García Hurtado de Mendoza), may contain much that was true. The *Sátira* is a well-structured work; it begins with an exhortation to all and sundry, from white men to black women, to come and listen to his tale since it deals with a theme which is relevant to everyone, 'propio onor', or social reputation (l. 47; Rosas de Oquendo 2). It then provides some background information about the author himself (ll. 59–110), which is followed by the introduction proper which argues that Peru is a topsy-turvy world in which the rich are poor, and the poor rich, the guilty walk the streets, and the innocent are in prison (ll. 111–289). After this introduction the poem proper begins, and roughly the first half is concerned with describing the multifarious venal sins of the population of Lima, and particularly the female residents. In this section, in which no woman seems to be spared satire (included are married women whose husbands are away, married women looking to bring extra money into the household, old lascivious toothless women, young women not yet married but who know how to feign virginity later on, and so on), Rosas de Oquendo shows his poetic ingenuity through elaborate metaphors of sexual commerce; the technical language of sewing, that of journeys (particularly sea journeys), the action of entering and leaving an abode, the language of war, of tutoring, even the language of the rites of Christian penitence, all are grist to Rosas de Oquendo's mill in his search for elaborate means of describing by innuendo the sexual act. Perhaps most striking about the poem is its ability to expose the lies beneath the official version of events. Thus, in his account of the military conquest of the southern region of the viceroyalty of Peru, in which he had participated, Rosas de Oquendo contrasts the written report sent to the Viceroy, which described how they had founded a city after fighting three days with 200 enemy Indians, with what actually happened (they built four yards, and were welcomed by the Indians who, to boot, offered them food; Rosas de Oquendo 42–43). Though clearly suffering from its own type of bias – that of a *peninsular* expecting to succeed in the colonies and being sorely disappointed when this does not happen – Rosas de Oquendo's *Sátira* offers an entertainingly sardonic picture of the carryings-on of viceregal society, only surpassed in its wit by Caviedes.

Juan del Valle y Caviedes is, with the exception of Sor Juana, the most significant writer of this period. Although he also wrote religious and didactic poetry his fame largely rests on his *Diente del Parnaso* (c. 1689), in which Caviedes, in a style reminiscent of the Spanish poet, Francisco de Quevedo, directs mordant satire at the doctors of his day. At least twelve of the doctors mentioned have been identified as real individuals practising medicine in Lima in the second half of the seventeenth century (Reedy 66). Only three of his poems were published in his own lifetime, in 1687, 1689 and 1694; for this reason his work mainly circulated in manuscript form (Caviedes x).[4] The butt of his mordant satire can vary, ranging from a hunchback (whom he advises to cure himself by piercing his hump with a sharp instrument, 'Receta que el poeta le dio a Liseras que sanase de la giba'; Caviedes 72–4), to a mulatto who believes he is marrying a white girl but is mistaken ('Al casamiento de Pedro de Utrilla' 141–2), to a contemporary poet whose work Caviedes compares to excrement ('pues son tus letras tan sucias / que me parecen letrinas', 'Un poeta que de hacer versos le dieron cursos', Caviedes 200–1 [p. 201]). Singled out for particularly ribald treatment are those whose lives are ruined by the misfortunes engendered by lust. Thus, he recounts in meticulous and sordid detail the agonies suffered by a prostitute named as Anarda who is attempting to recuperate from syphilis in a hospital. This situation provides Caviedes with the opportunity to make a *conceptista* pun based on sweat. The laxatives she is being given make her sweat as much as she used to make others sweat in the past: 'Vivirá de su sudor / si viviere de hoy ve más / la que de ajenos sudores / vivía antes de enfermar' (Caviedes 159). A pimp from Cuzco, likewise, is satirised for selling her daughters 'in pieces' as a result of her business:

> Una mestiza consejos
> estaba dando a sus hijas,
> que hay de mestizas consejos
> como hay el Consejo de Indias.
> Al diablo se estaban dando
> todas en cosas distintas: la vieja se da por tercios,
> por cuartos se dan las niñas. (Caviedes 252)

Caviedes's wittiest and most sardonic poems are reserved for doctors. 'Fe de erratas', for example, uses the analogy of editorial amendment to emphasise the connection between doctors and death: 'En cuantas partes dijere / *doctor*,

---

[4] At the present time there are ten manuscripts of Caviedes's poetry whose whereabouts are known, according to María Leticia Cáceres Sánchez ('Don Juan del Valle y Caviedes, foco de interés en el quehacer de la crítica hispanoamericana', paper given on 4 September 1996 at the I Encuentro de Peruanistas held at the Universidad de Lima).

el libro está atento; / por allí has de leer *verdugo*, / aunque éste es un poco menos' (Caviedes 6–7). As a general rule, Caviedes's poetry tends to function in terms of the repetition of the underlying motif rather than by amplification of a given theme. 'Coloquio que tuvo con la muerte un médico estando enfermo de riesgo', one of Caviedes's most famous poems, with great humour presents a doctor trying to persuade Death to let him live since that will bring him a greater yield in time. One of his best poems, 'A un doctor que curaba las cataratas y los cegaba peor de los que estaba' draws out an analogy between the literal blindness that the doctor visits upon his patients ('Cupido de medicina, / pues ciegas a los que curas', Caviedes 136) as well as the metaphorical, spiritual blindness engendered by delusion ('Mucho más que la primera/ es la ceguedad segunda,/ porque se viene a los ojos/ que hace ciencia de la astucia', Caviedes 138). For his mordant satire, and his inventive word-play, rather than his versatility, Caviedes will be remembered as one of the most significant poets of the colonial era.[5]

One Brazilian writer whose work has often compared to Caviedes's is Gregório de Matos Guerra; he is mainly remembered for his strikingly satirical poems in which he attacked all walks of life including corrupt priests, the *reinóis* (those of Portuguese blood born in the New World), governors, the *arrivistes* and the newly rich. From a wealthy Brazilian family, Matos Guerra was sent to Coimbra where he studied law, returning to Brazil in 1681. The satires he wrote earned him the wrath of the Bahia elite who managed to have him deported to Africa; he was eventually allowed to return to Pernambuco where he died. Writing during a period when printing was still prohibited in Brazil (we should recall that printing only came to Brazil with the declaration of the Republic), his satires circulated – like those of Caviedes in Peru – in manuscript form. There are four extant collections of Gregório de Matos's poems in the Biblioteca Nacional, Rio, Sala de Manuscritos ('Poesias', 388 pp., 50, 59, 59,-A; 'Sonetos do Doutor Gregório de Matos Guerra', 363 pp., 50, 61; 'Obras de Gregório de Matos', 511 pp. 50, 65; and 'Obras do Doutor Gregório de Matos "Guerra"', 363 pp. 50, 64/65). The first published edition of his work was Alfredo do Valle Cabral's edition which came out in 1881, which was followed in the early twentieth century by the scholarly editions of his work prepared by Afrânio Peixoto (the lyric poems in 1923, the sacred poems in 1929 and the satiric and humorous works in 1930; see Buarque de Holanda). D. João de Alencastre, then Governor of Bahia, was a great fan of Matos Guerra's and had copies of the poems transcribed. He even asked Matos to write a satire about him, which he did (it may be consulted in Valle Cabral's 1881 edition, in the section *Satyricas* 185–7). One of the specialties of his satirical poetry consisted in insulting the physical attributes of his victims. His

---

[5] Other poets whose work, for reasons of space, cannot be treated here are Juan Bautista Aguirre (1725–86), Miguel de Guevara (1585–1646), Hernando Domínguez Camargo (1606–56), Jacinto de Evia (1629–?) and Luis de Sandoval y Zapata (1645–83). For an excellent discussion of the minor poets of this period, see Oviedo, *Historia*, vol. 1, 151–7, 178–81.

satire 'Retrato do Governador Antonio de Sousa de Menezio', describes the governor's body as like a 'sack of melons', his head is bald, his moustache patchy (155), he is blind, has a flat nose and bad breath (Valle Cabral 155–6). He accuses the Archbishop João de Mestre de Deus of being unconcerned about the thieves whose sins he absolves willy-nilly (Valle Cabral 159–63). His poem dedicated to Father Danoso de Silvia homes in on how large he is, concluding that the bones of his feet could provide enough relics for the whole of Christendom (Valle Cabral 170). It is no wonder that the rich and powerful of Bahia banded together and got him expelled! Matos Guerra saw satire as having a special type of knowledge ('Noutras obras de talento / só eu sou o asnerão; / Mas, sendo sátiro, então, Só eu tenho entendimento'; Guerra 10), and not all of his satires simply poke fun at the ugliness of others. An important part of his ironic vision involves stripping the pomp and pageantry from everyday life, thereby allowing us to see life for what it is:

> Faço versos mal limados
> A uma moça como un brinco,
> Que ontem foi alvo dos olhos,
> E hoje é negro dos sentidos. (Alvaro Guerra 38)

A metaphor enhancing a young beauty ('black of the eyes') has been turned deftly into a pejorative reference ('black in the senses') to the girl's moral blackness. Matos Guerra was as keen to break the myth of poetic conceit (particularly the Gongorine) as he was to undermine the facade of social propriety. The beauty of his work is in its wit. On one occasion he sent a relative a gift of sweets on a silver tray, and was displeased to find that the tray was not returned to him. When he next came across his relative he gave his reaction in verse:

> As almas de outro mundo
> Dizem que vão e não vêm,
> E a minha bandejinha
> Será alma também? (Álvaro Guerra 17)

## The Brazilian Enlightened Epic

The eighteenth century can be seen as the century in which a number of discourses vying for pre-eminence in Brazil's political future clashed irrevocably. It was a time when the *ancien régime*, epitomised by the Jesuits, found itself overwhelmed by a succession of new ideas emanating from Europe, ranging from the Reason promulgated by the English rationalists to the new value attached to scientific enquiry epitomised by d'Alembert and the French *encyclopédistes*. A number of academies sprang up, places where men of letters and scientists could gather and discuss the latest intellectual innovations, such as the Academy of the Esquecidos (1724), the Felizes (1736–40), the Selectos (1752), and the Renascidos (1759). The Arcádia Lusitana was founded by Antônio Dinis and other poets in 1757; the Duque de Lafões founded the Academia Real das Ciências in Lisbon, and a number of academies were established in the colonies based on the European template. Poetry came under attack from various sides; the rationalist Luís Antônio Verney, in the seventh letter of his *Verdadeiro Método de Estudar Para ser Util à Republica e à Igreja* (1746), argued that poetry was not necessary for the Republic since it is an arbitary faculty and designed for entertainment only (quoted in Camarinha da Silva 6), and Francisco José Freire, in response, wrote an *Arte poética ou Regras da Verdadeira Poesia* (1748) in which he argued that poetry was useful since poetic beauty is based on truth and 'um conceito que não é justo, sem fundamento sôbre a natureza das coisas, não pode ser bello' (quoted in Camarinha da Silva 7). Domingos Caldas Barbosa founded the Nova Arcádia soon afterwards. Marquis Pombal, the powerful first minister of Dom José I, was a force for change in Brazil and, as a result of the attempted assassination of the King on 3 September 1758 for which the Jesuits were blamed, he issued an expulsion order of all Jesuits from Brazilian soil. The poetics of the seventeenth century were underwritten by the political discourse installed by Marquis Pombal, echoing some of the main ideas of the period (moral philosophy, reason, nature, clarity and common sense), such that poetry and politics became coterminous, as Ivan Teixeira has convincingly argued. Basílio da Gama (1741–1795), one of the best known writers of the time, was very much involved in this introduction of a brusque wind of change; his epic poem *O Uraguai* (1769) was dedicated to Pombal, whose title at the time was that of Conde de Oeiras. Da Gama went as far as to treat Pombal's brother, Minister Mendonça Furtado, as the hero of the poem since he had headed the commission which defined the boundary between the Portuguese and Spanish empires, according to the Madrid treaty of 1750. In his poem Da Gama uses the decasyllable, a traditional verse scheme, though he uses enjambement in places and he avoids the over-wrought Baroque rhetoric of Teixeira's *A Prosopopéia*. Focusing on the wars between Gomes Freire de Andrade (1688–1763), then Governor of Rio de Janeiro, and the Indian warrior, Cacambo (based on an Indian called José Tyarayú, *O Uraguai* 58, n. 46), it balances the description of the actual conflict with a report of their conversation about the real owner of the piece of land called Uruguay. Freire de Andrade lays the blame for the Indian insurrection firmly at the door of the Jesuits who offered the Indians their freedom without possessing the authority to do so, and then scolds Cacambo with a coloniser's logic:

> O rei é vosso pai; quer-vos felices.
> Sois livres, como eu sou; e sereis livres,
> Não sendo aqui, em outra qualquer parte.

Mas deveis entregar-nos estas terras.
Ao bem público cede o bem privado. (*O Uraguai*, II, ll. 133–7, 43–4)

The hypocrisy of it all beggars belief to the modern era, but these lines are entirely consistent with the imperial policy of eighteenth-century Europe: freedom for all when the 'all' was European. When the showdown occurs and the Indians are slaughtered, the Jesuit missions are presented negatively; like cowards they leave the Indians to their fate once they are threatened with arms (V, ll. 110–11, 96; for a more objective account of the forcible removal of the Jesuits from Latin America, see Louis Antoine de Bougainville).

*Caramuru: poema épico do descobrimento da Bahia* (1781)[6] by José de Santa Rita Durão (1722–84) is similar in theme (conflict between the Europeans and the Indians) to Da Gama's *O Uraguai* but it illustrates this via the meeting between civilians rather than military personnel. Like Da Gama, Santa Rita Durão was a member of the anti-Jesuit claque forming in Brazil in the 1750s. On 9 February 1759 he preached a sermon against the Jesuits, and a pastoral letter written by him accusing the Jesuits of involvement in the failed assassination attempt on the King was published later that month. In the poem he published more than twenty years later, however, the focus has moved to the conquest of Bahia by Diogo Alvares Correia, who was called Caramuru (the name of a fish) by the Tupi Indians as a result of his escaping death from a shipwreck by swimming ashore (in 1510). Unlike *O Uraguai* which keeps the Tupi Indians at the other end of a sword, *Caramuru* attempts to bring the reader into an appreciation of their world. By the end of Canto II (Santa Rita Durão used Camões's *Os Lusíadas* as a structural model) we see Diogo falling in love with a young Indian woman called Paraguaçu whom he promises to marry (*Caramuru*, II, lxxviii–xci, 75–80). Canto III introduces the reader to the Indians' knowledge of God and, although we may surmise that much of this information is based quite heavily on the anthropological work of Jesuits such as Father Nóbrega, it is valuable since it is the first inkling in Brazilian literature of what would later be known as Indianism, a literary movement which, despite its idealism, attempted to express sympathy for the Amerindian world. Just as Diogo has evolved into Caramuru so Paraguaçu develops into Catarina; the latter's Catholicization is completed when she experiences a vision of the Virgin Mary. By showing the daughter of an Indian chief not only baptised but also having a vision of the mother of God, the poem in effect underwrites the necessity of conquest and acculturation, though it is important to recall that this conquest occurs via a love affair and via religion, rather than military conquest (the bald truth as enunciated in *O Uraguai*). Something of a hybrid text in that it allows a variety of idiolects ranging from Camõens' epic style to Gongorine imagery to a nascent Romantic Indianism, *Caramuru* offers an

---

[6] There is a first edition in the Biblioteca Nacional in Rio, but it fell apart in my hands when I consulted it; Obras Raras, IV–42, 1, 21.

important counterbalance to the martial rigour of *O Uraguai* as a result of its ability to draw the reader into the mind of the Indian Other.

## Prose in Spanish America

During this period, as a result of a number of royal decrees (the first of which was promulgated in 1531), the publication, circulation and reading of novels in the New World was prohibited because, it was believed, their fantastic contents could induce immorality, especially among the young, women and Indians. This prohibition, nevertheless, was consistently violated during the colonial period in the sense that novels found their way to the colonies from Spain (see Oviedo, *Historia*, vol. 1, 210–12), but it did have its effect on the works produced in the Spanish American viceroyalties in that the prose works of this period were often hybrid and, as we shall see, had recourse to the ploy of mixing the genres of history, autobiography and fiction in order to escape the dull hand of censorship.

One of the most significant prose writers of the colonial period is Juan Rodríguez Freile (1566–1640), son of a first-generation immigrant who made his wealth in farming. He is remembered above all for his *El Carnero*, which he began writing at the age of seventy, in 1636, and finished in 1638, and which was first published in 1859; two manuscript copies of the work are held in the Sección de Raros y Curiosos in the National Library in Bogotá, Colombia (Rodríguez Torres 6). *El Carnero* is written within the chronicle tradition; as its sub-title suggests, it will tell the story of the conquest and discovery of New Granada (now Colombia and Venezuela). It is different from the early chronicles in that it also sets out to record the details of early colonial administration, with emphasis on the military and ecclesiastical figures who played important roles in that process; the Real Audiencia of Bogotá is, according to the foreword, a privileged place in Rodríguez Freile's account ('Los generales, capitanes y soldados que vinieron a su conquista, con todos los presidentes, oidores y visitadores que han sido de la Real Audiencia'; Rodríguez Freile vi). One could be forgiven for assuming, on the basis of the foreword with its pious stance and the de rigueur letter to the King of Spain, in this case Philip IV, that *El Carnero* will be a dry, academic account of the early years of the colonisation of New Granada. This expectation is confirmed by the first few chapters; Chapters I–VII concentrate on the discovery and conquest and are detailed on the names of the participants, especially Chapter VI, while Chapter VIII is concerned with the founding of the Audiencia Real and various religious orders in New Granada. The nearer the narrative comes to the days in which Rodríguez was writing, however, the more the narrative veers away from canonical, official history towards the personal, everyday spheres of the inhabitants of the New World, especially the uppers echelons of society (usually the clergy, the military and members of the *Audiencia Real*). The second half of *El Carnero* consists of self-contained narratives which, while purporting to be moral tales, have an air of the fable about them, and take a keen delight in recounting the various skullduggeries of witches, rogues, murderers, whores, outlaws, priests and judges. Given the importance at the time of expressing allegiance to Christian doctrine, the scenes of roguery are interspersed with long, rather dull sermonizing passages which fulfil the function of an *excursus* which the modern reader is likely to find of little interest (Martinengo). Indeed, they fulfil no more than a lip-service function, since the central part of the tales is the depiction of evil in all its nakedness. *El Carnero* exhibits a tension between the canonised history of the *oidores*, *visitadores*, and the clergy and an array of micro-narratives based on hearsay, gossip and legend.

*Historia de la Villa Imperial de Potosí* by Bartolomé Arzáns de Orsúa y Vela (1676–1736), like *El Carnero*, offers a series of vignettes of life in the colonies, although it is based on one city, that of Potosí, the source of the greatest wealth in silver that the world had ever seen. It is annalistic and recounts the main events of each year, starting with the year of its foundation (1545) and ending in the year of the author's death (1736). Arzáns's work was not published in his lifetime and this was no doubt because of its satiric nature, and the fact that it names the perpetrators of ignominious deeds; in this sense it is closer in spirit to Caviedes than to the chronicles discussed in Chapter 1. During its heyday Potosí was not only the richest city in the New World, but, according to Arzáns's account, the most violent as well. Arzáns claims that his *Historia de la Villa Imperial de Potosí* is historical and factual, based on real individuals, and derived from a number of printed sources. The picture of Potosí that emerges changes little during the 150 or so years covered; consistently, we hear details of family, tribal and racial feuds (typically between the *criollos* and the *peninsular* groups), all of which end in death, adultery, murder, theft, treachery and corruption. The most salient feature of the world depicted in the *Historia de la Villa Imperial de Postosí* is violence. A struggle between the Basques and the *criollos* in 1602 leads to a process of tit-for-tat actions, until there are seventy-nine dead and sixty wounded; in 1657, when a mother finds out that her daughter is with child, she tortures her by stripping her naked, hanging her up by her hair and thrusting a red-hot iron into her private parts until she dies; in 1661 a wife who is so disappointed with her husband's reluctance to carry out her wishes that she kills him, tears his heart out of his chest and then, according to one version, eats it (Arzáns 13–19, 81–86, 103–15). Another important feature of these tales is their use of the supernatural: in 1616 eight Indians and a boy emerged from a mine having been trapped for sixteen days, claiming to have been given water and bread and led out of the cave by the Virgin Mary; in 1658 some souls of purgatory appeared in the bedroom of a woman whose lover was under the bed and therefore stilled her husband's suspicions; and in the same year a criminal being pursued by the Corregidor was transformed into a blessed corpse at the convent of Santo Domingo (Arzáns 33–6, 86–90, 91–3). Though purporting to be historical, Arzáns's tales freely combine the real and the fantastic, and are typical of the hybrid nature of much of the prose writing of this period.

*El gobierno eclesiástico-pacífico* (1656–57) by Gaspar Villarroel (*c.* 1587–1665), also known as *Los dos cuchillos*, like Rodríguez Freile's *El Carnero* is a collection of vignettes of contemporary life in the Spanish colonies, although in Freile's work the setting as well as the theoretical edifice is ecclesiastic. Villarroel's tone and touch are lighter, giving a humorous twist to stories of ill-doing, such as the vignettes entitled 'Como los obispos recobran la salud' in which Villarroel tells anecdotes of how bishops are miraculously revived on their death-beds by servants intent on robbing them and who inadvertently puncture abcesses and thus revive them (Flores 29–30). Others tell tales of saintly intervention in the lives of men (such as 'San Luis ayuda a los cazadores', Flores 32). *El gobierno eclesiástico-pacífico* also contains a less colourful version of the story of the misdeeds of Mesa, the Oidor of the Audiencia who was driven to murder through his lust. Villarroel's version, however, does not involve a third party, but simply recounts how Mesa killed the husband of a woman he desired; no third party, such as we saw in Rodríguez Freile's version, is in evidence. Though designed to explicate the rules of ecclesiastical government in colonial New Spain, Villarroel's text offers a down-to-earth insight into the customs of everyday life in the Spanish colonies of the late seventeenth century.

An example of first-person narrative recounting personal adventure was *Cautiverio feliz* by Francisco Núñez de Pineda y Bascuñán (1607–82?), which recalls the author's experience as a 'happy captive' of the Araucanian chieftain Maulicán by whom he was held from May to November of 1629. This work, like Alonso de Ercilla's, shows immense respect for the Araucanian Indians. By the end of the narrative, the author and his enemy, Maulicán, are the best of friends. Núñez de Pineda eventually feels a degree of allegiance to his captor that stretches verisimilitude; when an opportunity to escape presents itself, such as in Part II, when he crosses a turbulent river and is separated from the rest of the tribe, he refuses to flee and returns to his captor. This loyalty is clearly mutual, since Maulicán is prepared to endanger his own life and that of his tribesmen in order to protect Núñez de Pineda from hostile Araucanian tribes. But the greatest danger, as Núñez de Pineda sees it, came not from outside but rather from inside in the guise of the young nubile bodies of the Indian girls who repeatedly offer him their sexual favours. With great strength of will, Núñez de Pineda refuses them all, even Maulicán's daughter, the sight of whom used to make Núñez de Pineda's knees tremble; his respectful distance could not be more at variance with the devil-may-care attitude of the *conquistadores* who came a century earlier. Núñez de Pineda's text stands as an important stepping-stone between the artless earthiness of the chronicles which preceded it and the artful grace of the novel which came later.

Another important example of the stirrings of the genre of narrative was *Infortunios de Alonso Ramírez* (1690) by Carlos de Sigüenza y Góngora (1645–1700), nephew of the Spanish poet Luis de Góngora (1561–1627), holder of the Chair of Mathematics and Astrology at the University of Mexico, and Chief Cosmographer of the Realm. This text has sometimes been referred to as the first novel of Latin America, but it is perhaps best described as a more sophisticated version of the type of personal adventure chronicle typified by Cabeza de Vaca's *Naufragios*. It is not coincidental that the first true precursor of the realist novel was written by a scholar who favoured the new scientific method of empirical observation rather than the hide-bound scholasticism which still held sway at the time. *Infortunios de Alonso Ramírez* describes the misadventures of a young Puerto Rican boy, Alonso Ramírez, who ran away from home before his thirteenth birthday for a life at sea. His search for personal wealth leads him around the Caribbean, Cuba, to New Spain, the Philippines (where he is captured by English pirates), Guadalupe Island, and finally back to Mexico. During his travels he suffers shipwreck, hardship, illness and hunger. His story has all the verve of Cabeza de Vaca's *Naufragios*; he experiences the same kind of fears but the historical frame has changed. Now the enemies are not the Amerindians; they are the English who roam the Caribbean looking for plunder. The story has a type of happy ending, in that the Viceroy of New Spain orders that the boy's adventures be compiled by none other than Carlos de Sigüenza y Góngora, in recognition of services rendered. The ending of *Infortunios de Alonso Ramírez* may seem no more than a naive ploy to bring the narrative full circle back to the author's direct remit, but it is an early indication of the self-reflexive and ludic route that the novel would subsequently take in Latin America (Lagmanovich 411–12).

One other significant prose writer of this period who deserves mention is Francisca Josefa de la Concepción de Castillo (1671–1742), the 'Colombian Santa Teresa' as she is sometimes known, famous for her *Afectos espirituales* (written between *c.* 1694 and *c.* 1716). Sor Francisca took the veil in 1693 after two years as a novice, and became a nun the following year, when she was twenty-three years old (Castillo 48). The *Afectos espirituales* consist of forty-four prose passages followed by one poem, all of which have a mystic intent, and are best understood as a record of the trials of Sor Francisca's personal pilgrimage to God. They fall roughly into two groups. The first half of the 'Afectos' concentrate on the nun's emotional affliction and remorse caused by a sense of separation from God, and the tone bears much similarity with the Old Testament Psalms in their anguished petitions to God (roughly 'Afectos' 1–20). The remainder ('Afectos' 21–45) speak with more confidence and authority of God and His will in the world, suggested by the frequent use of verbs of knowing such as *entendí* and *conocí*. Taken as a whole, the 'Afectos' evolve, gain in spiritual depth and insight, and reach their culmination in 'Afecto 37', an extraordinary text with numerous similes (including comparisons to clouds, iron, musical instruments, streams of water and a golden ring) which build up a sense of the difference between the soul who turns to God and the damned. It is clear from the *Afectos espirituales* that Sor Francisca hung on every word of her male confessor, P. Francisco de Herrera, to such an extent that she is emotionally distraught when she finds out that he will no longer be visiting her, as suggested by 'Afecto 5' (Castillo 46–7). The original manuscript of 'Afecto 41' contains a written note to her confessor which describes her affliction and concludes with the following sentence: 'Esto es darle cuenta de lo que me pasa, para que vea si será bueno quemar estos papeles; pues, mientras más me esfuerzo a tomar sus consejos, es más la guerra' (Castillo 353, n. 1). What the *Afectos espirituales* reveal is not only a seventeenth-century Colombian nun's struggle with God but also her struggle with the authority of her male confessor. What their relationship reveals is the overpowering control the Church had, not only over publishing but also over writing and, indeed, thought itself during this period.

The most significant prose work of the colonial period was *El lazarillo de ciegos caminantes* (1775 or 1776) by Concolocorvo, alias Alonso Carrió de la Vandera (1715?–83). Born in Gijón, he went to New Spain at the age of twenty, where he worked for ten years as a merchant. He worked as a corregidor in the 1750s and simultaneously as Captain General, General Mayor of Mines and Subdelegate of the Goods of the Deceased. In 1771 he was promoted to Second Commissioner of the postal system between Montevideo, Buenos Aires and Lima; José Antonio Pando, one of his rivals, was nominated Administrador de Correos; this antagonism would be one of the motives behind Carrió de la Vandera's decision to write and publish his travelogue, *El lazarillo de ciegos caminantes*, copies of which were sent to the head office of the postal service in Madrid (Lorente Medina xii). The journey from Buenos Aires to Montevideo to Lima on which he based his travelogue took place between May 1771 and June 1773. *El lazarillo de ciegos caminantes* is an intriguing, hybrid work, halfway between personal account and public census, between autobiography and novel. In some ways it fits the mould of those works commissioned by the Viceroy on subjects such as description of the land, description of the mine industry, or a census of a particular city, of which there are many examples throughout the colonial period. If these works were to the Viceroy's satisfaction they were sometimes published and often led to public office, sometimes even a sinecure. Thus, Carrió de la Vandera has separate sections on the cities of Montevideo and Buenos Aires, their population, the customs of their inhabitants, the important families who reside there (Carrió de la Vandera 20–3, 25–9); he describes minutely the vagaries of transport by cart between Buenos Aires and Carcarañal (33–6). The subsequent sections on Córdoba, Santiago del Estero, San Miguel de Tucumán, Salta, Jujuy, Porco, Potosí, Chuquisaca, and Cuzco, for example, all follow a similar pattern in that they describe the topography of each region, the highlights of the main cities and towns there, as well as the customs and commerce of their inhabitants. All of these elements make *El lazarillo de ciegos caminantes* like an *informe* commissioned by the office of the Viceroy. But there are others which reveal to what extent Carrió de la Vandera's work is transitional and deviates from the state sponsorship pattern of publication normal during the colonial era. Most notably the author is introduced in section XI of Part II by the outlandish name of Concolorcorvo: 'Ya, señor Concolorcorvo, me dijo el visitador, está Vm. en sus tierras' (Carrió de la Vandera 109), and the work is dedicated not to 'hombres sabios, prudentes y piadosos' but rather to those 'de la Hampa o Cáscara amarga, ya sean de espada, carabina y pistolas, ya de bolas, guampar y lazo'. The importance of *El lazarillo de ciegos caminantes* lies not only in the invaluable insight it offers into cultural customs of colonial Spanish America but also in its place as a transitional text between viceregal patronage and the republican energy of print capitalism.[7]

**Essay**

The most important essayist of the colonial period was the Peruvian Francisco Javier Eugenio de Santa Cruz y Espejo (1747–95). He published three significant essays, all of which are expressed in dialogue form: *El Nuevo Luciano de Quito* (1779), *Marco Porcio Catón* (1780), and *El Nuevo Luciano de Quito o Despertador de Ingenios Quiteños (Ciencia Blancardina)* (1780). The first dialogue sets the blueprint for what is to follow; *El Nuevo Luciano* consists of nine dialogues between Dr Murillo, a doctor of the old school much enamoured of Thomism, and Dr Mera, clearly a projection of the author Santa Cruz y Espejo, who argues against the rhetorical excesses of scholasticism and shows awareness and admiration for the knowledge and scientific method of the Enlightenment. The nine conversations ostensibly focus on different themes – the first explains how the dialogue itself was inspired by Dr Mera's disappointment at a recent sermon given by one Dr D. Sancho de Escobar, the second discusses the use of Latin in church, the third deals with rhetoric and poetry, the fourth with good taste, the fifth with philosophy, etc. – but the same pattern emerges during each conversation: Dr Murillo is wedded, with some misgivings, to the status quo, while Dr Mera attacks the educational system as well as the deplorable state of science and philosophy of his day in Ecuador. For example, Mera rejects the blandly over-formalistic citation of classical texts such as those of the Church Fathers, instead arguing for a more critical treatment of the text. He champions the deductive method of the scholars of the Enlightenment, and challenges the usefulness of an education system which does not teach the theory of ethics, which looks to Spain as its paragon even though Spain is so backward, where lawyers learn their trade by rote and have no historical knowledge of their discipline, and where churchmen cease to study once they have graduated from college (Santa Cruz y Espejo 53, 54–5). Santa Cruz y Espejo's use of the dialogue form in his essays is, indeed, itself an example of an inductive rather than a by-rote attitude towards knowledge and learning. Rather like the Spanish philosopher Feijóo, with whom he has much in common, Santa Cruz y Espejo deplores the dangers caused by an intransigent scholasticism, as typified by speculative theology, and respects the scientific method of the Enlightenment as epitomised by the work of scientist/philosophers such as René Descartes and Isaac Newton; he is, however, not prepared to

---

[7] For a good background discussion of other prose writers of the colonial period which emphasises the porousness of fiction and history during this period, see Pupo-Walker, 'El relato virreinal'.

embrace the atheism which some of the *encyclopédistes* proclaimed to be a necessary ingredient of the new science.

## Theatre

During the colonial period the viceregal court was a centre of artistic, musical and dramatic activity (Weiss 92). Theatrical culture had gradually moved out of the Church into the opera house; the Nuevo Coliseo of Lima, built at the height of the Baroque period, with the latest in stage machinery and sets, was inaugurated in 1662 by the departing Viceroy Guzmán, who had made its construction possible. Many guilds were directed by executive fiat to commission plays; in 1630 in Lima, for example, the birth of Prince Baltasar Carlos was celebrated with a series of plays sponsored by various guilds: the candymakers (6 November), the *pulperos* (grocers or tavern-keepers; 8 and 9 November), the blacksmiths (22 November), and the meat suppliers (10 December) (Weiss 101). Most coliseums, opera houses, and playhouses were built in the eighteenth century, under the enlightened Bourbon monarchs, but largely by private capital (Weiss 97).

Indeed, it is the genre of theatre which reveals most clearly the cultural dependence the Spanish colonies experienced with regard to the mother country. The playhouses (*corrales*) in Mexico City were modelled on those in Spain, and the playwrights, plays and troupes came from Spain. Their popularity is suggested by Balbuena's observation in his *Grandeza mexicana* at the beginning of the seventeenth century that Mexico City enjoys new plays and *entremeses* every day: 'fiestas y comedias nuevas cada día, / de varios entremeses y primores / gusto, entretenimiento y alegría' (Balbuena 41). The most popular dramatists whose works were staged in Mexico during the colonial era were, as in Spain, Lope de Vega, Calderón de la Barca (1600–81), and Pérez de Montalbán (1602–38). The latter's play, *La monja-alférez*, based on the bizarre adventures of Catalina de Erauso who escaped as a young girl from a nunnery in Spain and fled to the New World, dressed as a man, was a great local success.[8] The case of Juan Ruiz de Alarcón (1581?–1639) is symptomatic. Though born in New Spain he sought fame and fortune in the mother country; his plays were staged, and often set, there as well. His masterpiece is *La verdad sospechosa* (1634), which tells the story of a young man, Don García, whose mendaciousness eventually leads to his own discomfiture. The tale is very skilfully told, and its staging shows a well-attuned sensitivity to the opportunity for humour arising from mutual misunderstanding, particularly in the use of the aside.

There was, however, some homegrown dramatic talent in the colonies. One play which enjoyed some success during the early colonial period ought to be

---

[8] The Inquisition was, as always, alert to any hint of blasphemy or irreverence expressed in the public space of theatre. Montalbán's play, *El valor perseguido y traición vengada*, was banished from the Mexican stage in 1682 (Leonard, *Baroque* 109–16).

mentioned here, the *Comedia de San Francisco de Borja* (1641) by the Jesuit Mathias de Bocanegra (1612–88). A lively, witty drama, it was written to commemorate the arrival of Viceroy Marqués de Villena in Mexico City. The first act is a wonderful piece of art, showing a good sense of the dramatic potential of events on the stage, such as when Flora and Belisa, unbeknownst to each other, both approach Borja at exactly the same time (*Tres piezas* 263–65), as well as a masterful use of the omen (the Emperatriz's dream that she is going to die proves to be a true prediction), and, finally, a lively use of the poetic joust *topos* when Borja, Carlos V and Sansón compete with each other in order to see who can best express the dilemma as to whether man is easier to control than a beast (*Tres piezas* 247–50). The second and third acts, however, which describe how Borja gradually disentangles himself from the world and achieves sainthood, are wooden by comparison.

As might be expected with a genre as socially sensitive as drama, the plays of this period, which were mainly from Spain, had a profound effect on the culture of the times; *sueltas* (single plays in pamphlet form) and *partes* (collections of plays) were imported from Spain and purchased in surprisingly high quantities. Irving gives two examples of how influential this literature was on the creation of a culture of love; he quotes a contemporary observer who notes that 'the reading of books of plays was so general in ladies' drawing rooms and in maidens' chambers that women could only feel sophisticated when they talked about a love affair, an amorous difficulty, the vanquishing of male indifference, or the humble devotion of a swain'. The other example concerns the indifference of a woman who impassively carried on reading a volume of plays while the two men who had fought for her love were hanged on the other side of the street (Leonard 106–7). While the works of Spanish dramatists were the main feature in any dramatic performance, those of native-born Spanish Americans were performed as the *entremés*. By the end of the seventeenth century, however, it appears that drama had fallen on bad times. An Italian traveller, Gemelli Careri, commented, after seeing a local performance of *La dicha y desdicha del nombre*, that '[i]t was so badly played that I would gladly have given the two *reales* it cost me to go in and take a seat not to have seen it' (quoted in Leonard, *Baroque* 106).

The late colonial period presents a slightly different picture, in the sense that the models used were not Spanish (they were often French or Italian), but the same sense of derivativeness remains. Of the three plays known to have been in Peralta y Barnuevo's repertoire, all had European models. *La Rodoguna* (1708) was an adapted translation of Corneille's play, *Rodogune*, *Triunfos de amor y poder* (1711) was a Baroque-mythological piece, and *Afectos vencen finezas* (1720) was a play of impeccable Calderonian pedigree. Peralta y Barnuevo also translated an Italian play, *Bersabé* by Ferrante Pallavicino (1616–44) (Núñez 22–3), as well as a number of other short occasional pieces to accompany these works (Tamayo Vargas).

Another important dramatist of this period is Pablo Olavide y Jáuregui (1725–1803); his contribution can be seen mainly in his translations of French plays which served to revitalize the theatre of his day. Though born in Peru, Olavide spent much of his adult life in Spain and there established his reputation as a dramatist. His translations included works by Racine (*Phèdre*, *Mithrydate*) and by Voltaire (*Zayre*, *Cassandre et Olympie*, and *Merope*), although his best work in translation is probably *El desertor* (1775), based on the French dramatist Mercier's *Le déserteur* (1769) which, in elegant octosyllabic verse, tells the story of a young couple in love whose marriage is ruined by the discovery that the prospective groom is an army deserter, but which, by virtue of a happy *deus ex machina* event, ends happily. Olavide's sensitivity to the social and particularly national value of theatre is evident in the only play known to be an original work composed by him, *El zeloso burlado* (1764), a lively one-act *zarzuela*. Set in the Paseo del Prado, Madrid, on the evening of a much-anticipated firework display to be held nearby in the Parque del Retiro, this play is very much a circumstantial piece. The opening scene alludes in glowing terms to the royal members of the audience, including Queen Luisa, who is described as 'pasmo / De talento y discreción' (Olavide, *Obras dramáticas* 2), as well as to the sovereigns ('Dichosos Pueblos, que tienen / Tan amables Soberanos'; 3), and other members of the royal family (Fernando, Gabriel, Antonio and Xavier; 3). The plot focuses on the comical aspects of the jealous possessiveness of an older man for a young woman, and is similar in terms of comic wit to Cervantes's short story, *El celoso extremeño*. It is important to note that the overriding ethos of theatrical production during this period centred on the imitation of foreign models which, while serving an important purpose, also ultimately stunted any possible growth of an intrinsically national theatrical tradition.

Some Amerindian language plays were also written and performed during this period. In Cuzco the cleric Gabriel Centeno de Osma is credited as the author of the Quechua-language adaptation of a parable of spiritual versus earthly riches, *Yauri Tito Inca o El rico más pobre* (manuscript dated 1701). But the first truly major native-language work is *Ollantay* (anonymous, dating from end of the eighteenth century), which is based on a pre-conquest legend, embroidered with the addition of a romantic intrigue between the hero and his beloved, a vestal virgin (Weiss 117). The manuscript of the play, in Quechua, was found among the papers of a *mestizo* priest, Antonio Valdes, on his death (Guzuriaga and Reeve 167). Although some critics have argued that the mixture of a romantic love narrative with the story of a struggle for political power is incongruous, what is notable about *Ollantay* is the way in which the discourse of love and the narrative of nation-building are projected as intimately connected (for more discussion of this idea, see Sommer). Ollantay's desire to marry Estrella, the daughter of Pachacutic, King of Cuzco, is also, in effect, a desire to ascend to the throne. Likewise the period when Estrella is locked away in a cave in a vestal virgin nunnery coincides with the time that Ollantay becomes a rebel fighting against the state, now in the person of King Yupanqui, Pachacutic's son. Pointing in a similar direction, the denouement of the play – in which, contrary to all expectations, Yupanqui elevates Ollantay to the throne and offers him Estrella to be his wife – underlines how successful statehood and blossoming love are interlocking discourses. The distinctive characteristic of the play, which makes it so different from the Mayan play, *Rabinal Achí*, which concludes with the sacrifice of the enemy, is that it ends on a note of political harmony within the Incan state; brother and brother-in-law share the kingdom. The projection of a harmonious state is, of course, in direct contradistinction to what actually happened some 250 years before when the two sons of Huayna-Capac, Huáscar and Atahualpa, were engaged in a civil war (Hemming), and therefore were conquered by Pizarro. *Ollantay* should thus be interpreted as an important political gesture bodying forth the dream of an Incan state united against Spanish oppression and using the metaphorical symmetry of love to do so.[9]

Jesuit theatre went into decline in Brazil in the seventeenth century, and the information about theatrical performance during this era is patchy. From poems that Gregório de Matos wrote, such as 'A uma comedia que fizeram os pardos confrades de Nossa Senhora de Amparo' (referred to by Galante de Sousa 117), it is clear that works were being performed. There are references to *Autos Sacramentais* written by Gonçalo Ravasco Cavalcânti de Albuquerque (1639–1725), a work entitled *A Constância com Triunfo* by José Borges de Barros (1657–1719), and a work *Santa Felicidade e seus Filhos* by Frei Francisco Xavier de Santa Teresa (1686–1737); these works have now all been lost (Galante de Sousa 117–18). There are also references to a *Comédia* performed in Rio de Janeiro on 4 April 1641 to commemorate the *aclamação* of Dom João IV, and an *Auto de S. Francisco Xavier* performed in the College of Jesuits in Maranhao in 1668 (Galante de Sousa 119), but once more the texts have not survived. The only two plays written by a Brazilian of which there are extant copies are by Manuel Botelho de Oliveira (1636–1711), and these, ironically, were published in Spanish, *Hay Amigo Para Amigo* and *Amor, Engaños y Celos* (Galante de Sousa 118). Oliveira's *Música do Parnaso* (1705) published these two plays as well as a number of poems in Portuguese, Spanish, Italian and Latin, written in the Gongorine style. Both *Hay Amigo Para Amigo* and *Amor, Engaños y Celos* are written in a rather austere Calderonian style, although there are flashes of humour in the former play when *cultista* style and its predilection for hyperbaton is mocked (Botelho de Oliveira 7).

Brazilian theatre gradually became more secularised in the eighteenth century but it struggled to find its feet. At the beginning of the eighteenth century churches and convents were still being used to put on plays but this practice ended soon afterwards. In a pastoral letter of 13 March 1726, the Bishop of Pernambuco, D. José Fialho, prohibited the performance of plays in churches and in another pastoral letter of 1734, he banned them completely (Galante de Sousa 121). Gradually, as the eighteenth century wore on, new secular spaces for opera and theatre were created. As a result of the boom created by the discovery of precious metals and stone in Ouro Prêto, for example, a theatre

---

[9] For a discussion of other dramatists of this period, such as 'El Ciego de la Merced', see Oviedo, *Historia*, vol. 1, 291–2.

was in operation there from 1753 to 1811 putting on works such as *Encantos de Medéia*, *Porfiar amando* and *Pelo Amor de Deus* (Galante de Sousa 124). In São Paolo an opera house was built (1793–95) to cater for a growth of interest in the performing arts, though most of the works performed were foreign (if not from Portugal, then from Spain or France). Given the low social esteem in which acting was held (in Portugal in the eighteenth century, for example, actors were denied a sacred burial because of their profession; Galante de Sousa 133), most of the actors were mulattoes (see letter 5 of the *Cartas chilenas*, quoted by Galante de Sousa 131). Since women, for moral reasons, were prohibited from acting, as a contemporary observer noted, this led to some rather strange scenes in which shepherdesses appeared on the stage sporting unkempt beards (quoted in Sousa Bastos, *Carteira de artista* 672). It was only in the nineteenth century that Brazilian theatre found a life of its own, dominated as it was during this period by works such as *El Monstruo de los jardines* by the Spaniard Calderón de la Barca put on in Bahia in 1729, *Comédia* by the Italian Metastasio in Rio de Janeiro in 1750, and *Amor Mal Correspondido* by the Portuguese Luís Alves Pinto in 1780 (Galante de Sousa 146, 148, 151).

## Antônio Vieira versus Sor Juana Inés de la Cruz

The Luso-Brazilian Jesuit Father Antônio Vieira (1608–97) has often appeared in Spanish American colonial studies as the unwitting cause of the downfall of New Spain's greatest writer, Sor Juana Inés de la Cruz (1651–95), and his reputation has suffered as a result, but his work deserves analysis in its own right. Vieira, of all the Brazilian Jesuits, was clearly the most sophisticated and urbane. As C. R. Boxer has pointed out, he was recognised as 'the greatest master of Portuguese prose in his day and generation', and the twentieth-century Portuguese poet Fernando Pessoa called him 'O Imperador da língua portuguesa' (Boxer 3). His work has none of that anthropological ambiance evident in the letters of his predecessors such as José de Anchieta and Manoel de Nóbrega (see discussion of their work above, pp. 19–20) and gives an indication of how, in the space of fifty or so years, Brazil had been transformed from an outpost of the empire into a flourishing colony. Vieira accompanied his parents from Portugal to Brazil when he was six years old in 1614, and remained there for twenty-five years, taking his first vows as a novice in the Jesuit order in 1625 (Boxer 5). He soon made a name for himself as a preacher and, as noted by the English consul at Lisbon, Thomas Maynard, in 1666, his sermons were printed immediately after they were given 'and sent for out of all parts of Spain, Italy and France' (Boxer 4, n. 1). Dom João IV fell under his spell, regarding him as 'o primeiro homem do mundo' (quoted in Boxer 9). Vieira was scathing in his condemnation of the Portuguese mistreatment of the Amerindians in Brazil, stating that this had resulted in the death of over two million Indians in forty years (surely an exaggeration). He also criticised the governance of the colony; when asked by Dom João, for example, whether Brazil should be governed by two captain-majors or by one governor, Vieira answered that a single governor was better since one thief was a lesser evil than two (Boxer 21). It was in his preaching, though, that Vieira's influence was unquestioned; his sermons were as intellectually challenging as they were theologically imaginative, and he did not shy away from dealing with contemporary events. In his 'Sermão pelo bom sucesso das armas de Portugal contra as de Holanda' (1640), for example, he implores God not to give up the land of Brazil to the Dutch heretic (Vieira 66–111). At times his satire becomes almost Swiftian such as in his 'Sermão de Santo Antônio' (112–68) in which he argues, in an extraordinarily imaginative way, that fish seem to have more reason than men.

In the 'Sermão de Sexagésima' (Vieira 11–65), perhaps his most famous sermon, preached in the Royal Chapel in 1655, Vieira delivers a no-holds-barred attack on those who would proselytise while never leaving the comfort of their native land. He had in his sights the rival religious order of Frei Domingos de S. Tomaz, whose members were content to preach in Portugal (Vieira 12, n. 2), but he managed to ruffle a few feathers elsewhere, including Sor Juana's (of which more later). In the same sermon he also turned his attention to the 'estilo violento e tirânico que hoje se usa' (34), particularly by the Spanish poet, Luis de Góngora, and his followers. Vieira accused the Gongorists of using unnaturally complicated metaphors, and opposites (34–6); he went as far as to argue that their word-play was as deceitful as the words of temptation used by the Devil to Jesus when he was on top of the temple: 'as mesmas palavras, que tomadas em verdadeiro sentido são palavras de Deus, tomadas em sentido alheio são armas do Diabo' (53).

Although Sor Juana does not refer to this sermon in her own discussion of Vieira's work, it is highly likely, given that it was his most famous essay, that she would have read it, and one can imagine that she might have felt implicated by Vieira's words, since he had attacked those people who, like her, had a sedentary-religious life-style (she was a nun in a Dominican convent in Mexico) as well as those who, like her, had a predilection for the Gongorine style. As it was, however, Sor Juana chose to attack another of Vieira's sermons, his Maundy Thursday sermon delivered in 1650 in the Royal Chapel (the text of the 'Sermão do mandato' is included among Marcelo Baches's 1999 edition of *Os melhores sermões*, and the text appears in the Spanish translation which Sor Juana may have read, in *Obras completas de Sor Juana Inés de la Cruz*, vol. 4, 673–94). There is some controversy about which edition of Vieira's work Sor Juana used (see Ricard; Sor Juana, *Obras*, vol. 4, 637; Boxer 29; Cohen 86–90), and the wealth of editions of Vieira's sermons in the National Library in Rio suggests that it will be difficult to pin this one down.[10]

In his 1650 Maundy Sermon – which was not his best sermon by any stretch

---

[10] There were two Spanish translations of sermons published in Madrid in 1675 and 1678, before the Portuguese edition published in 1679 (Cohen 87), and there were numerous other editions such as *Aprovechar Deleytando. Nueva Idea de Pulpito Christiano Politica; Delineada en Cinco Sermones Varios, y otros Discursos*. Zaragoza: Pedro Alfay, 1661, 160 pp., BN, Rio, Sala João Antônio Marquês, 64, 2, 22.

– Vieira had attempted to answer the question as to which is the most refined manifestation of Christ's love for mankind, and he proceeded to demolish St Augustine's argument (who argued that this occurred when He gave up His life on the cross), St Thomas Aquinas's view (this was when Christ remained with us despite His departure) and St John Chrysostom's opinion (it was most manifest when Christ washed His disciples' feet), by suggesting that Christ's love was more evident firstly (*pace* St Augustine) in the act of absenting Himself, secondly (*pace* St Thomas Aquinas) in the act of covering himself, and thirdly (*pace* St John Chrysostom) by not excluding Judas from the washing of feet. The modern reader (*pace* Vieira) might be forgiven for believing this to be simply word-play since the theological understanding produced by Vieira's punctiliousness is not particularly profound. Be that as it may, what Sor Juana did in her essay, the *Carta Atenagórica* (1690), was to question whether Vieira's propositions were any more convincing than those of the Church Fathers: 'Mi asunto es defenderme con las razones de los tres Santos Padres' (Sor Juana, *Obras completas*, vol. 4, 413). She questions the validity of each of Vieira's propositions in turn by deconstructing their rhetoric, thereby in effect vindicating the original ideas of St Augustine, St Thomas Aquinas and St John Chrysostom. Sor Juana concludes by rejecting Vieira's view that the highest manifestation of Christ's love was 'amar sin correspondencia' by referring to the biblical story of Abraham's love for his son Isaac (Sor Juana, *Obras completas*, vol. 4, 424–8). Although it is clear that Sor Juana was unaware of the specific cultural context of Vieira's sermon (Cohen, for example, argues that Sor Juana misunderstood the pastoral purpose which lay behind this sermon; Cohen 88–9), her *Carta Atenagórica* is a lucid piece of robust theological exposition which – and here is the irony – adopts a more conservative approach than Vieira, in the sense of echoing rather than rejecting the *sententiae* of the Church Fathers. Yet it would land her in so much trouble that it can be described as the opening gambit of the chess game which would end in her own death.

The publication of her *Carta Atenagórica* in November 1690 embroiled her in an intrigue for which she was ill-prepared, as Octavio Paz has shown. Born of a poor but honourable family in Nepantla, learning had become Sor Juana's passion. She was barred from attending the university in Mexico City because she was a woman, and her plan to attend dressed as a man failed. In 1669 she took vows as a nun and entered the Convent of San Jerónimo where, for a number of years, she had been writing various literary works. Indeed, Sor Juana felt protected since she enjoyed the confidence of the Viceroys. Nevertheless, by publishing a rebuttal of Vieira's ideas, Sor Juana was attacking the Jesuit clique in Mexico, and particularly the Archbishop of Mexico, Francisco de Aguiar y Seijas, who was closely allied with the Jesuits; this is clear because the two Spanish-language editions of Vieira's work (*Las cinco piedras de la Honda de David en cinco discursos morales predicados a la serenísima reina de Suecia, Cristina Alejandra, en lengua italiana. Por el reverendisimo padre Antonio de Vieyra*, and *Sermones varios del padre de Vieyra de la Compañía de Jesús*, published in Madrid in 1675 and 1678 respectively), were both dedicated to Aguiar y Seijas (Paz, *Obras completas*, vol. 5, 479). Sor Juana had been encouraged in this act of defiance by the Bishop of Puebla, Manuel Fernández de Santa Cruz y Sahagún, who was a mortal enemy of Aguiar y Seijas's. However, she was subsequently reprimanded by the Bishop, who used a feminine *nom de plume*, Sor Filotea de la Cruz, to do so but, rather than back down, Sor Juana wrote a response, her famous *Respuesta de la poetisa a la muy ilustre Sor Filotea de la Cruz*, dated 1 March 1691, but only published posthumously in 1700 (Paz, *Obras completas*, vol. 5, 490, 502). As a result of this latter work – which circulated in manuscript – Aguiar y Seijas had her silenced, and she was forced to sell her library (Paz, *Obras completas*, vol. 5, 540), which for the time was an extremely rich one, having over 4,000 books; she distributed the profits to the poor; Sor Juana later died while tending the sick in Mexico City during an outbreak of plague.

Her essay, *Respuesta de la poetisa a la muy ilustre Sor Filotea de la Cruz*, is an exercise in ingenuity. It opens with an elaborate modesty *topos* and then proceeds to a devastating attack of her opponent's argument. In this essay she made the famous declaration that she joined the nunnery in order to avoid marriage (Sor Juana, *Obras completas* 446). The aim of Sor Juana's argument is to turn the tables on her phallocentric audience; this is evident on one level in that she retains the feminine pseudonym of her interlocutor in the title of her essay, but, more importantly, she continually underlines the injustice of the roles ascribed to men and women.

Much of Sor Juana's poetry makes more sense when put in the context of her *Respuesta* since it invokes the rhetoric of the day but recasts it in an iconoclastic way. Her poetry is normally described as Baroque, in the sense of being marked by complexity and elaborate form, calculatedly ambiguous imagery, and a penchant for the creation of dynamic intellectual oppositions and contrasts. Like many poets of her age, Sor Juana felt the influence of the great contemporary Spanish Baroque poets, Francisco de Quevedo and Luis de Góngora.[11] Her most famous work, *Inundación castálida* (1689), gives a good indication of the type of literary work published at the end of the seventeenth century in Spain and the colonies. It was dedicated to Vicereine Luisa Gonzaga Manrique de Lara (whose full title made her also Countess of Paredes and Marchioness de la Laguna), who was so impressed by its contents that she took it upon herself to take the manuscript to Madrid to have it printed. The contents of *Inundación castálida* can be divided into four categories, the *loas* (introits, or mini plays which acted as a preface to a play), the *villancicos* (roughly equivalent to Christmas carols), the lengthy poem *Neptuno* (an allegorical description of the triumphal arch built for the Viceroys de la Laguna on their arrival in

---

[11] The *Encyclopedia Britannica* mentions two possible sources for the term Baroque, both of which are apposite descriptors of Sor Juana's work. The first is the Italian *barroco*, a term 'used by philosophers during the Middle Ages to describe an obstacle in schematic logic', while another source is that of the Portuguese word *barroco* which is used to describe 'an irregular or imperfectly shaped pearl' (vol. 1, 910).

Mexico in 1680), and the lyrical poems with a personal focus. Whereas the first three categories of work were commissioned and fit the Maecenal model, the fourth was not; it is not coincidental that it is for her poems with a personal focus that Sor Juana is now remembered.[12] Some of her most witty poems, written it must be assumed before she took her vows, expose herself as caught in an unbearable love-triangle. Using a device called *encontradas correspondencias* the poems express how she loves a man who does not love her, and is loved by another man whom she does not love. The first stanza of 'Al que ingrato me deja, busco amante' is a fine example of the Baroque conceit:

> Al que ingrato me deja, busco amante;
> al que amante me sigue, dejo ingrata;
> constante adoro a quien mi amor maltrata;
> maltrato a quien mi amor busca constante. (Campa & Rodríguez 261)

The repetition of words, such as 'ingrato/ingrata', 'busco/busca', and 'constante' serves to underline how she is at once dishing out and at the receiving end of spurned love. 'Feliciano me adora y le aborrezco' treats the same theme and shows the same skill in producing opposing semantic units expressed by phonetically identical words in the last tercet of the poem: 'pues ambos atormentan mi sentido: / aquéste, con pedir lo que no tengo; / y aquél, con no tener lo que le pido' (Campa and Rodríguez 260–1). Sor Juana's most famous poem is the *redondilla* entitled 'Hombres necios que acusáis' in which she uses the rhetorical baggage of the Baroque to express the double values attached to the sexes in the Mexico of her time. The sixth stanza of this poem, for example, refers to the irony of the man who breathes on a mirror (by which we are to understand takes a woman's virginity) and then complains he cannot see (by which we are to understand he complains that her honour is besmirched):

> ¿Qué humor puede ser más raro
> que el que, falto de consejo,
> él mismo empaña el espejo,
> y siente que no esté claro? (Campa and Rodríguez 254)

Sor Juana's most significant single poem is her *Primero sueño*. It is a 950-line self-averred imitation of Góngora's poetry written in honour of Don Gaspar de Sandoval Cerda Silva y Mendoza, the Viceroy of Mexico and Count of

---

[12] This is part of the funnelling process whereby over time the notion of literature has been refined, so that *letras* (which once included creative literary works as well as philosophical, historical, scientific, legal and medicinal works) has been replaced by *literatura* which in turn came to mean, largely as a result of the paradigm shift brought about by the Romantic movement, imaginative writing written for aesthetic effect. Terry Eagleton has argued that this paradigm shift was accompanied by a change in the patronage system; thus, during the Romantic movement, Art became its own patron (Eagleton 27; for further discussion see Introduction). Quite clearly, the sonnets in *Inundación castálida* are closer to the post-Romantic sense of literature than the commissioned poem, *Neptuno*, is.

Galve, on whose orders French forces attempting to invade the Spanish part of Hispaniola were defeated at the mouth of the Guarico, Hispaniola, on 21 January 1691 by an expeditionary force sent from New Spain. It is written in the poetic form of the *silva*, perhaps as a witty reference to the Viceroy's third surname. Like Góngora's verse, the *Primero sueño* makes liberal use of hyperbaton, mythological culturalism and a Latinate syntax and vocabulary. However, Sor Juana's poem is unlike Góngora's *Soledades* in that it describes an ontological enquiry into the nature and function of the universe.[13] The poem opens with a description of nightfall, and how the world, including the human body gradually falls asleep (ll. 1–265). The second part of the poem, which is the most substantial, describes how Fantasy begins to copy the things of the phenomenal world showing them to the soul ('las representaba / y al alma las mostraba'; ll. 290–1), and includes a section on two pyramids used as figures of the human soul (Sabat de Rivers 105–9), a disquisition on the great chain of being and an anguished awareness of the limits of human understanding as compounded by the proliferation of diverse human languages and diverse species (ll. 266–826). The final section describes the human mind waking up and returning to the world of everyday life (ll. 827–975). *Primero sueño* is a poetic *tour de force* without equal in the literary scene of the colonial period. The conclusion of the poem, in particular, is remarkable in that it suggests that, through the dream knowledge engendered by her poem, the world has become brighter and she more awake (ll. 967–75).

Sor Juana was not only the foremost poet of her day but also an outstanding dramatist. Her play *El Divino Narciso* is a Calderonian *auto sacramental* which, as Alexander Parker has pointed out, takes the idea of applying a Christian dogmatic principle to a mythological story from Calderón's *El Divino Orfeo* (Parker). The central part of *El Divino Narciso* follows the classical story of Narcissus closely: spurning all women and even the loveliest of nymphs, Echo, Narcissus is punished by falling in love with his own image, at which point Echo becomes unable to say anything other than repeat what has been said to her, a technique adopted with some verve in the play (Act IV, Scene XI; ll. 1480–691; Sor Juana, *Obras completas* 66–78). Other characters are added, such as Naturaleza Humana, Soberbia, Amor Propio and Gracia, who serve to turn the play into a Christian allegory play. Narciso's last words ('Este es Mi cuerpo y Mi Sangre / que entregué a tantos martirios / por vosotros. En memoria / de Mi Muerte, repetidlo' (ll. 2187–90; 95) echo Christ's words at the Last Supper. At this point of transfiguration of human nature, Eco, Amor Propio and Soberbia die, allowing Naturaleza Humana and Gracia to embrace. Lest one should see this as simply a rewriting of the Calderonian code, attention is focused on Eco's feminine plight, which is seen as more serious than that of

---

[13] Octavio Paz describes the difference between the two poets effectively: 'Por genio natural, sor Juana tiende más al concepto agudo que a la metáfora brillante; Góngora, poeta sensual, sobresale en la descripción – casi siempre verdera recreación – de cosas, figuras, seres y paisajes, mientras que las metáforas de sor Juana son más para ser pensadas que vistas' (Paz, *Sor Juana* 470).

the others. Amor Propio and Soberbia simply commit suicide (l. 2201; l. 2204), while Eco is condemned to eternal torment: 'Y yo, ¡ay de mí!, que lo he visto, / enmudezca, viva sólo / al dolor, muerta al alivio' (ll. 2196–98; 95). Eco will continue to 'live' to pain, which tends to suggest perhaps a feminised consciousness barred from the patriarchal economy of death and sacrifice. In Sor Juana's world vision, thus, a harmonious relationship between the sexes is impossible and can only be transcended through the transfiguring role of Christianity's redemptionism.

# 3
# Early Nineteenth-Century Literature

The nineteenth century in Latin America is remembered as the century of independence. Forces for political change had been building up in Brazil as much as in Spain's colonies throughout the latter half of the eighteenth century. Thus there is an undeniable symmetry between the actions of Tupac Amaru II (José Gabriel Condorcanqui) who fought against the Spanish colonial regime in Peru only to be executed (May 1781) and Tiradentes (Joaquim José da Silva Xavier) who took on the colonial regime in Brazil and suffered the same fate (April 1792), but the way in which independence eventually came about in the two colonies in the 1820s proved to be very different. Napoleon's invasion of the Iberian peninsula in November 1807 had an impact in Caracas as much as in Rio de Janeiro, persuading Simón Bolívar to take up arms against the Spanish monarchy (in June 1808 Napoleon's elder brother, Joseph 'Pepe Botellas' was to be installed on the Spanish throne), and forcing the entire Portuguese court to leave Lisbon and sail, escorted by the British Navy, to Brazil, where it arrived in early 1808. Spain's war with its colonies – declared as a result of the insubordination of Bolívar and San Martín – proved to be a costly and bloody affair which was only resolved by the final rout of royalist troops in 1824. Brazil's transition to independence was, by contrast, relatively smooth. When Napoleon's troops were driven from the Iberian peninsula in late 1808, the King Dom João VI returned to Portugal, leaving his son, Dom Pedro, in charge as Prince Regent. When ordered home in 1822, Dom Pedro refused to return to Portugal, thereby in effect bringing about Brazilian independence, though it was an independence which retained the political structure of the monarchy. Unlike the Spanish colonies, Brazil had not needed to go to war with Europe to achieve independence.

There were differences too in the way that the printed word interacted with the independence movement in the two colonies. In terms of technology the turn of the eighteenth to the nineteenth century was, as Steinberg argues, 'not a break but rather a sudden leap forward' (Steinberg 275). As he goes on:

> Technical progress, rationalised organisation, and compulsory education interacted one upon another. New inventions lowered the cost of production; mass literacy created further demands, the national and international organisation of the trade widened the channels and eased the flow of books from the publishers' stock departments to the retailers' shelves. (Steinberg 275)

But this was played out in different ways in Brazil and the Spanish colonies. Even at the end of the eighteenth century, Brazil was still very dependent on Portugal for intellectual commerce, but this changed dramatically in 1808. The transfer of political power symbolised by Dom João VI's residence in Rio de Janeiro had implications for what might be called the 'power of attorney' associated with printing. A royal press was immediately established, and its first publication, *Relação dos despachos publicados na Corte pelo Expediente da Secretaria de Estado dos Negocios Estrangeiros* rolled off the press in Rio on 13 May 1808 (Hallewell 110). The royal library, consisting of 60,000 books which had been transported by ship from Lisbon, was used to found the Biblioteca Real (later Nacional). Book culture as a result took off exponentially. The book trade was transformed overnight; from two booksellers in 1808, their number grew to five in 1809, seven in 1812, and twelve in 1816 (Hallewell 106–8). The Royal Print flourished in Rio, monopolising printing in both Portugal and Brazil, although it cut its ties with Portugal in 1822 when Dom Pedro declared Brazil's independence. A number of French publishers opened premises in Rio during the course of the nineteenth century – such as Plancher, Villeneuve and the Frères Garnier (Hallewell 147–9, 198–203) – and they were to have a decisive influence on the evolution of printing in Brazil, endowing it with a more international flavour than in the Spanish-speaking countries of Latin America.

In Spanish America the creation of an independent literary print culture was more of an internal affair. The two areas where the independence grew most virulently, the viceroyalty of New Granada (Bolívar) and that of Río de la Plata (San Martín), were also regions which enjoyed a relative degree of freedom from external pressure as far as printing was concerned. Thus, by the time printing came to these two areas – situated as they were outside the capitals of the two pre-eminent viceroyalties, Mexico City and Lima – the time was ripe for its use to fan the flames of independence which would sweep across the sub-continent in the first two decades of the nineteenth century.[1] By the end of the eighteenth century, for example, the need to seek royal permission for the establishment of a printing press seemed less urgent. Thus Vertiz, Viceroy of the Río de la Plata region from 1778 to 1784, gave permission for a press to be set up in Buenos Aires in 1779, and the crown gave formal approval in 1782, after some 150 items had already been printed (Thompson 61).

It is furthermore clear that there was a direct causal link between the establishment of the newspaper press at the end of the eighteenth century in Spanish America and the growth of the emancipation movements in the major cities of the various viceroyalties. In Bogotá towards the end of the seventeenth century, for example, the printing press served the political objectives of the

[1] In what follows I follow broadly the categories suggested by Pierce and Kent to describe the growth of the press in Latin America: Pre-Journalism, 1539–1790; Founding Period, 1790–1820; Factional Press, 1820–1900; Transition to Modernism, 1900–60; and the Modern Period, since 1960 (Pierce and Kent 230).

revolutionaries; in 1793 Antonio Nariño set up a printing shop named La Patriótica in which he published the pro-independence essay, *Derechos del hombre* (based on the seventeen articles of the new French constitution) (Foreno Benavides 21–38); printing flourished in Colombia during the revolutionary decades and the new presses were typically allied with the pro-independence movement (Thompson 77). In almost all of the urban centres in Spanish America gazettes were established by the newly-independent governments to promote the intellectual ideals underpinning independence, such as the *Gaceta del Gobierno de Mexico* in Mexico City (established 2 January 1810), the *Gazeta de Buenos Ayres* in Buenos Aires (7 June 1810), the *Gaceta del Gobierno* in Lima (13 October 1810), and the *Gazeta del supremo gobierno de Chile* in Santiago (26 February 1817) (Charno 348, 14, 533, 127). In some cases, as for example in Upper Peru and Chile, the first newspaper printed coincides almost exactly with the proclamation of independence. Thus, the University of Chuquisaca began to publish the newspaper *La Gaceta de Chuquisaca* on 30 July 1823, and on 8 August of the same year published the Act of Independence of Upper Peru (Quesada 85). Likewise, the newly-independent government of Chile purchased a technologically advanced printing press from the United States in 1811 specifically in order to promulgate the advantages of independent government (Quesada 88–9).

In terms of emerging ideology as well as mode of production (a specific example of which was the new gazette), the new era ushered in by the nineteenth century was one in which the previous indissoluble link between the published word and royal privilege was actively challenged. The new era was one in which the democratisation of the written word through the newspaper press was accompanied by a burgeoning capital-based democracy based on individual freedom. In particular, the growth of newsprint was directly linked to the growth of nationalism for the newspaper, as Benedict Anderson suggests, like the novel, 'provided the technical means for "re-presenting" the *kind* of imagined community that is the nation' (Anderson 30). This new print-capitalism allowed the notion of nationhood to flourish since it made it possible for growing numbers of people to think about themselves in new ways, particularly in terms of a new cross-national simultaneity. While it is true, as Checa Godoy points out, that the nineteenth century was dominated by politically-driven rather than literature-driven newspapers (Checa Godoy 11), the literature produced during this period, as Ángel Rama rightly says, needs to be seen as foundational texts which build identity for the newly emergent nations of Latin America: 'la literatura se formula inicialmente como una parte, pequeña aunque distinguida, de la construcción de la nacionalidad' (Rama, *Crítica* 67). As Thomas Carlyle succinctly put it, and his words are as applicable to Mexico's Fernández de Lizardi as they are to Brazil's Antônio de Almeida: 'Literature is our Parliament too' (Carlyle 219).

## Romanticism

Arguably the most important literary movement of the nineteenth century in Europe and the Americas, Romanticism had an important role to play in the evolution of Latin American literature. Romanticism is a literary movement which swept through Europe in the last half of the eighteenth century and the first half of the nineteenth, originating in Germany and spreading thence to England, France, Spain, Italy and the Americas. It is a literary movement which emphasises the transcendence, necessity and centrality of love, which sees the individual as more important than the society in which (s)he lives, which valorises the imagination and the emotions at the expense of logic and reason, and which values nature rather than culture or the urban environment. Other features which recur in Romantic literature are: subjectivism, uncertainty about identity, the religious instinct (often associated with pantheism), forbidden love (especially incest), medievalism, nationalism, religion and superstition, liberalism and literary devices such as melodrama, fantastic coincidence and the *deus ex machina* technique.

Romanticism came to Spanish America in the 1830s; Río de la Plata was more influenced by French Romanticism while Mexico, Peru and Colombia fell under the influence of Spanish Romantic writers (Carilla, vol. 1, 42–5).[2] The first authentic Romantic work is normally given as Echeverría's *Elvira o la novia del Plata* (1832), and the most significant Romantic works were centred in the genre of poetry. The European writers who made the greatest impact in Spanish America were Hugo, Byron, Chateaubriand, Walter Scott, Larra, and Espronceda (Carilla, vol. 1, 59). The more colourful polemics about Romanticism were centred in the Southern Cone, particularly in the Buenos Aires Salón Literario (1837), the Montevidean Certamen de Mayo (1841), that expressed in the local press, in Santiago de Chile in 1842 and especially the articles of Vicente Fidel López and Sarmiento (Carilla, vol. 1, 134–41). Jotabeche, for example, was scabrous about the facile imitation of Hugo's work (quoted in Carilla, vol. 1, 141). There were also those writers who may be grouped in terms of part of a social Romanticism movement, such as Alberdi and Sarmiento; as Alberdi wrote: 'Queremos una literatura profética del porvenir, y no llorona de lo pasado' (quoted in Carilla, vol. 1, 155).

Romanticism is said to have begun in Brazil with the publication of *Suspiros poéticos e saudades* (1836) by Gonçalves de Magalhães (1811–82), along with his Romantic manifesto, 'Discurso sobre a história da literatura no Brasil' in which he calls for freedom, feeling and an authentic (namely Romantic) type of literature. In his poem about Napoleon, Gonçalves de Magalhães chooses not to focus on the latter's triumphs in Egypt but rather his defeat at Waterloo: 'Ah! todo el perdeu! a esposa, o filho, / A pátria, o mundo, o seus fiéis soldados'

---

[2] A French traveller, Xavier Marmier, who visited Buenos Aires in the mid-nineteenth century, was struck by its French ambiance. Booksellers stocked Dumas and Musset but not Garcilaso de la Vega (Carilla, vol. 1, 62–3).

(Bandeira 19). This gloomy obsession with death and failed illusions was a recurrent *topos* of the time; one sonnet by José Maria do Amaral (1813–85) provides a very biting sense of the remembrance of things past by having every line conclude with a past participle (Bandeira 34). A favoured image was that of darkness standing for melancholia, as in 'A melancholia' by Antônio Francisco Dutra e Melo (1823–46):

> A lua, que já brilhava,
> Pouco a pouco se escurece,
> E meu coração aperta,
> E minha alma se entristece. (Bandeira 38)

These ideas and images are, of course, fairly standard stage props in the Romantic imaginary. It was Antônio Gonçalves Dias (1823–64) who managed to breathe new life into these *topoi*, by using popular verse structures which add a spring to the rhythm ('Olhos verdes' and 'Não me deixes' are good examples; Bandeira 45, 48), as well as making a serious intellectual attempt to confront Brazil's Amerindian past, so much so, indeed, that he was called 'o cantor dos meus guerreros' by Machado de Assis. Gonçalves Dias's poem 'I-Juca-Pirama' takes as its point of departure one of the set pieces of Jesuit historiography, namely, the captive waiting for his death as part of the cannibalistic rite (see above pp. 20–1):

> O prisioneiro, cuja morte anseiam,
> Sentado está,
> O prisioneiro, que outro sol no ocaso
> Jamais verá! (Bandeira 83)

We hear his death song (Bandeira 86–9), and, as a result of the captive's tearful address, the chieftain (surely a piece of poetic licence) decides to free him. The prisoner's father is horrified, and persuades his son to return to battle and immolate himself; Gonçalves Dias thereby gives a fresh, Amerindian twist to the European Romantic fascination with death. Love, when it appears in the work of Brazil's Romantic poets, is often a *Liebestod*; as Francisco Otaviano (1825–89) puts it rather succinctly: 'Ela fugiu, morro eu' (Bandeira 108). Another Romantic theme which had a good innings in Brazil is that of the interchangeability of the female beloved and nature. In 'Hino a Aurora' and 'Hino a tarde' by Bernardo Guimarães (1825–84), for example, it is difficult to separate them out. In another poem the poet, in rather grandiose style, asks the universe what it all means, and then simply hears one word echoing back: 'dúvida!' (Bandeira 128). One poet whose work continues to elicit interest is Manuel Antônio Alvares de Azevedo (1831–52); his poem 'Teresa' (Bandeira 178–80), directed at a fifteen-year-old virgin, is emotionally tortured in a Byronian sense (not for nothing does it have an epigraph by Clément Marot the French medieval poet, 'Je l'ayme tant que je n'ose l'aymer'). The work of Antônio de Castro Alves (1847–71) strikes a harsher note within this chorus of plaintive, lovesick voices. His 'Cantiga de escrava' contrasts the loss that the bourgeois experience with the radical dispossession a slave feels: 'eu não tenho mãe nem filhos, / Nem irmão, nem lar, nem flores' (Bandeira 354). His 'Vozes d'Africa' is now something of an anthology piece; it addresses God directly as someone who has forsaken the African race: 'Deus, ó Deus! onde estás que não respondes?' (Bandeira 356). His powerful poem, about the plight of captives on a slaver, 'Tragédia no Mar (O Navio Negreiro)', uses a similar technique, in that it describes the horrors of death, and then turns it face upwards to the sky to beg for God's reaction:

> Senhor Deus dos desgraçados!
> Dizei-me vós, Senhor Deus!
> Se é loucura, se é verdade
> Tanto horror perante os céus. (Bandeira 365)

## 'Criollo' Civic Poetry (1820–30)

The three poets studied in this section, José Joaquín de Olmedo (1780–1847), Andrés Bello (1781–1865), and José María Heredia (1803–1839), called 'transition poets' by one critic (Carilla, vol. 1, 53), have been placed together since their work demonstrates, firstly, the links that existed at this period between art and politics and, secondly, the differing ways in which the components of a *criollo* national consciousness were arranged in post-independence Spanish America.[3] All three men moved in a tight circle of powerful men who were the intellectual engineers of independence and avid supporters of nationalism. The nationalism that they experienced and expressed was necessarily hybrid given the recent emergence of nationhood in Spanish America. David Lloyd has described the problems confronted by intellectuals of the post colonial nation with the term 'perpetually split consciousness' (Lloyd 112), which is eminently applicable to this trio of writers, the first generation of *criollo* intellectuals. Olmedo, Bello and Heredia, as their works and their biographical itineraries show, were gripped by a nationalist fervour which used the language of the oppressor, both literally and in terms of its institutional culture, to find expression.

In Olmedo's 'La victoria de Junín' (1825) we have the first poem which celebrates the independence of Spanish America. Like the many examples of civic verse designed to commemorate this event it had its ideological inconsistencies. The most significant of these was one identified by Simón Bolívar in his *Carta de Jamaica* (1815), that the *criollos* have as little right to the land they inherit as the Spaniards who arrived some three hundred years before:

---

[3] In this context Ricardo Palma's words are telling: 'Casi no hay en toda la cadena de repúblicas que baña el Pacífico un solo nombre literario que no sea al mismo tiempo un nombre político' (quoted in Carilla, vol. 1, 20).

no somos indios ni europeos, sino una especie media entre los legítimos proprietarios del país y los usurpadores españoles: en suma, siendo nosotros americanos por nacimiento y nuestros derechos los de Europa, tenemos que disputar éstos a los del país y que mantenerse en él contra la invasión de los invasores; así nos hallamos en el caso más extraordinario y complicado. (Bolívar 46)

It was the elements within this 'most extraordinary and complicated case' that the poets writing about the independence movement attempted to reconcile. It is important to note that the notion of Spanish as language-of-state was never questioned by the *criollo* writers; it was only many years later, particularly in Fernández Retamar's *Calibán* (1971), that the language itself would be seen as the bedrock of the post colonial dilemma rather than an unpleasant side-effect. Spanish as language-of-state was, in those years immediately after independence, not seen as problematical, but a political unease was, nevertheless, evident in the work of *criollo* writers. Olmedo responded to this dilemma by having much of the narrative of his poem spoken by an Incan emperor, Huayna-Capac, thereby giving greater authority to the sense of justice involved in emancipation from Spanish rule. Olmedo's poem is, thus, a good example of the Indianist mode.[4] In a review of Olmedo's poem, Bello referred to the Incan emperor's speech as 'la parte más espléndida y animada de su canto' (Bello 267), since it was an ingenious way of resolving the contradiction between on the one hand the desire of presenting Bolívar as the author of independence in Peru and on the other hand the historical fact that Bolívar was absent from the decisive battle which sealed independence, namely, the battle of Ayacucho (1824). Bolívar was present at the battle of Junín which took place earlier that year; to solve this problem, as Bello points out, in a *leger-de-main*, Olmedo fuses the two battles together (Bello 268). Yet, despite the favouritism this rhetorical gesture accorded Bolívar, the latter was not impressed. Having read the copy which Olmedo sent him, Bolívar replied in a letter to the author that he found the Inca in the poem 'un poco hablador y embrollón' (Espinosa Pólit 538). As the above quote suggests, Bolívar knew that to view his great deeds as somehow justifying the Amerindian heritage of South America was a distortion. In his reply to Bolívar, Olmedo basically defended his poem in terms of poetic licence, while skirting around ideological matters (Espinosa Pólit 538-39).

Nevertheless, and despite Bolívar's own quibbles, Olmedo chose not to revise his poem; thus Bolívar is hailed by the Incan emperor in the following terms: '¡Oh predilecto / Hijo y Amigo y Vengador del Inca!' (Olmedo 136). The Spaniards, predictably enough, are seen as cruel usurpers and, through Bolívar's and Sucre's efforts, the Incas have finally been justified: 'Esta es la hora feliz. Desde aquí empieza / la nueva edad al Inca prometida / de libertad,

---

[4] Carilla makes a further helpful distinction between 'indianismo' and 'indigenismo': 'Indianismo, como evocación, idealización, proyección hacia el pasado; indigenismo, como realidad concreta e inmediata, como realidad social' (Carilla, vol. 2, 19).

de paz y de grandeza' (Olmedo). Echoing Bolívar's dream of a united Spanish American republic, Olmedo naturalises its proportions by tying it to the geography of Latin America, and specifically the Andes. Like much of the civic verse of its day, thus, Olmedo's poem predicates its political dream for the future on an organicist faith in the interchangeability of nature and culture, a *topos* which, as we shall see, played an even more significant role in Andrés Bello's civic verse.

Both 'Alocución a la poesía' (1823) and 'La agricultura de la zona tórrida' (1826) by Andrés Bello, despite their non-political titles, are what might be called civil poems which extol the American way of life, its culture and its flora and fauna. Like Olmedo's poetry, they speak on behalf of an educated elite; his poems were certainly not literature for the masses. In a letter to Fray Servando Teresa de Mier, Bello reproached him for having sent 750 copies of one of his books to Buenos Aires; as he suggested, '50 ejemplares hubiera sido un exceso y estoy seguro de que no se habrán vendido 20' (quoted in Rama, *Crítica*, 69). Though not having a massive popular impact, however, Bello's work, and particularly his poems, are noteworthy in that they demonstrate the ideals about nationhood epitomised by the new elite *criollo* intelligentsia produced after the Wars of Independence. In its markedly inclusivist way, Bello's poetry defines culture as nature and vice versa, and reveals an impeccable Rousseauesque pedigree. It could be argued that this use of nature as the pointer to cultural identity in Latin America is an ideological cul-de-sac since it belies a facile organicism (to use Terry Eagleton's term) which does not face the challenge of history squarely.

'La agricultura de la zona tórrida' is written in *silvas*, that is, a mixture of seven-syllable and eleven-syllable lines, a traditionally appropriate *culto* verse form for the epic description of nature. Part I of the poem stresses the unbounding creativity of the natural world, while Part II extends this theme, and underlines in particular the different ways in which nature *clothes* the earth (an important metaphor in this context since it stresses culturalism; 'Tú vistes de jazmines / el arbusto sabeo'; ll. 16-17; Bello 41). In Part III the *locus amoenus* is given a political edge, as Bello rejects 'el ocio pestilente ciudadano' (line 11), in favour of the blissful peace of the farm-labourer's lot. City dwellers are goaded, so Bello suggests, by greed, ambition and patriotism:

> y en el ciego tumulto se aprisionan
> de míseras ciudades,
> do la ambición proterva
> sopla la llama de civiles bandos,
> al patriotismo la desidia enerva. (ll. 81–5; Bello 42)

It is intriguing that patriotism should be included in the bag of many ills contingent upon urban life which suggests, on the face of it, that Bello's discourse is anti-political. Given that the poem was written and published in the midst of the Wars of Independence, it may indicate that Bello was tired of political violence. True liberty, as Bello suggests in Part IV of the poem, inhabits the countryside:

> ¿Amáis la libertad? El campo habita:
> no allá donde el magnate
> entre armados satélites se mueve,
> y de la moda, universal señora,
> ve la razón al triunfal carro atada. (ll. 148–52; Bello 44)

The 'magnate' referred to here who moves 'between armed satellites' exposes Bello's notion of what Spanish colonial rule essentially meant for the people of New Spain, since 'satellite' itself suggests how the pockets of Spanish power were simply supervising from afar. This type of government, as Bello suggests, is part of the political trend ('moda'), not based on reason. Part V of the poem reiterates this idea, and calls upon the natural world to heal the political wounds that the fratricidal war with Spain created:

> Abrigo den los valles
> a la sediente caña:
> la manzana y la pera
> en la fresca montaña
> el cielo olviden de su madre España. (ll. 213–17; Bello 45)

It becomes clear in Part VI that Bello is speaking from a specifically *criollo* perspective in that he neither speaks on behalf of the Spaniard nor of the Amerindian: 'Asaz de nuestros padres malhadados / expiamos la bárbara conquista' (ll. 302–4; Bello 47). The emperors of the Incas and the Aztecs are recalled as mere shadows put to rest by the Spanish: 'Saciadas duermen ya de sangre ibera / las sombras de Atahulpa y Moctezuma' (ll. 311–12; Bello 47). Unlike the Spanish 'fathers', or the Amerindian 'shades', the *criollo* 'sons' hold the key to the future (ll. 366–73; Bello 49). As the conclusion of the poem makes quite clear, the new culture which is destined to emerge from the slaying of Spanish imperialism will be based on the laws of the natural world.

José María Heredia's poetry, like Olmedo's and Bello's, combines the personal with the civic levels. By far his most famous poem is 'En el teocalli de Cholula' (1820), written when Heredia was only seventeen years old, and acknowledged to be one of the finest nineteenth-century poems of Spanish America. Like many of the poems of the time celebrating independence from Spain, Heredia's poem takes its point of reference from the Amerindian world, in this case the Aztecs and specifically the impressive Great Pyramid of Cholula, which, at 425 metres square and 60 metres high, ranks as the largest ancient pyramid in the Americas. But Heredia takes a different approach to Olmedo, for example, since he uses Aztec culture as a lesson from which the future republics of Spanish America need to learn. He describes the 'teocalli', the main temple at Cholula, as an immense structure which 'vio a la superstición más inhumana / en ella entronizarse' (ii, 134–5; Flores 160). Superstition is a key word in the poem, since it is associated in Heredia's personal conceptual network with war, and specifically the internecine war which had gripped the sub-continent. The present silence of the scene as the poet sits looking at the ruins contrasts with these visions of war:

> ¡Qué silencio! ¡Qué paz! ¡Oh! ¿Quién diría
> que en estos bellos campos reina alzada
> la bárbara opresión ...? (ll. 42–51)

Heredia is thus writing a type of palimpsest in which the violence of the War of Independence is superimposed on the violence and superstition of the Aztec rite of human sacrifice. The Aztec rite and war are linked terms in an equation of something Heredia specifically rejects. As in Bello's 'La agricultura de la zona tórrida', Heredia's poem places its faith in nature, as the opening stanza eloquently suggests (ll. 1–23; Flores 158), for which Heredia felt a deep affinity, as his poems 'En una tempestad', 'A la estrella de Venus' and 'Niágara' in particular show. Like the other poems studied in this section, 'En el teocalli de Cholula' is a poem which strives to promote a notion of *criollo* nationalism through an uneasy balance mediated on the one hand by a rejection of the external accoutrements of Spanish culture and on the other by an ambivalent evocation of the grandeur of pre-Columbian culture.

## Post-Independence Poetry: Melgar and 'Plácido'

The work of two poets stands out in this era, that of the Peruvian Mariano Melgar (1790–1815), and the Cuban 'Plácido', Gabriel de la Concepción Valdés (1809–44). Mariano Melgar is mainly remembered for his *Yaravíes*, Quechuan lyrics translated into Spanish. They describe the author's pangs of unrequited love for María Santos Corrales, who is provided with the pseudonym Silvia in the poems (Melgar 19–23), and their use of a refrain as well as a simple idiom assured them instant popularity. The *Yaravíes* are sparse in the use of metaphor and simile, and they possess as a result a transparency which verges on the colloquial. But the apparent simplicity of these poems is deceptive. The use of one-word lines, introducing a staccato effect, shows skill in the use of rhythm which is refreshing when compared to the turgid formalism of much poetry of the early nineteenth century in Spanish America. 'Lágrimas que no pudieron', for instance, is a powerful five-stanza poem built around the comparison between the salt of the sea and the saltiness of the tears of unrequited love:

> Lágrimas que no pudieron
> Tanta dureza ablandar,
> Yo las volveré a la mar,
> Porque de la mar salieron. (Melgar 101)

The use of the octosyllabic metre here, in its brevity, an impression heightened by the use of *acento agudo* in the infinitives ending the two internal lines of the stanza, shows Melgar at his best, a master of the short line. Melgar was a fervent Republican (he was captured and executed while fighting against the Spaniards at the battle of Humachiri, Peru, in 1814), and this is clearly evident in his earnest poem, 'A la libertad'. Given his pro-Indian sympathies, it is perhaps not surprising that he takes the side of the Amerindian populace in his depiction of the struggle for independence in this poem (Oda II, ll. 7–12; Melgar 124). Unlike Heredia, who simply used the Amerindian heritage as a negative point of reference, Melgar saw independence as ushering in a new era of Inca culture, although it is presided over by Spain's spirit in the form of Iberia. Political independence, of course, led to no such thing in an empiric sense (the indigenous populations were as bad if not worse off after the Wars of Independence), but the fact that poets continued to visualize independence in these terms suggests a groundswell of (theoretical) support for the idea.

'Plácido' (1809–44), the son of a Spanish barber and a mulatto woman, was put to death on the orders of the Captain General of Cuba, Leopoldo O'Donnell, in 1844 for his involvement in the anti-slavery movement in Matanzas. Called 'the Strauss of Havana' by the Countess of Merlin (Meyer 15), Plácido has since become an icon of Afro-Cuban culture. The vicissitudes of his life have inspired a number of literary works: two novels, Cirilo Villaverde's *La peineta caleda* (1843), and Joaquín de Lemoine's *El mulato Plácido* (1875), as well as a play, Diego Vicente Tejera's *La muerte de Plácido* (1875) (Plácido 10, n. 2). Plácido wrote many different types of verse, ranging from historical poems such as 'Jicotencal' based on the Tlascalan chief who first fought against Cortés and then fought on the latter's side, to political poems such as '¡Habaneros, libertad!', religious verse such as 'Muerte de Jesucristo', and fable-type poems such as 'Los dos perros' (Plácido 85–7, 112–13, 123, 68–9), but his fame rests now with his satirical verse and, especially, his 'flora cubana' poems. The association made throughout these latter poems is that between womanhood and flowers. Again, like Melgar, the 'flora cubana' poems have a poetic transparency which verges on the colloquial. As 'La flor del café' opens:

> Prendado estoy de una
>   Hermosa
> Por quien la vida daré
> Si me acoge cariñosa;
> Porque es cándida y hermosa
> Como la flor del café. (Plácido 34)

Each of the following eleven stanzas ends with the refrain 'Como la flor del café' and builds on the poetic association between coffee blossom and the object of the poet's desire. One of Plácido's most elegant pieces is 'La flor de la caña', a poem of nine verses each with twelve sin-syllable lines, the twelfth containing the refrain 'flor de la caña'. One important feature of Plácido's verse, evident in this poem, is its re-moulding of the tradition of amatory verse, the object of which was normally a white woman with blond hair. Plácido's beloved, however, is a mulatto ('Veguera preciosa / De la tez tostada'; Plácido 39). Some of the poems have a ribald tone. 'La calentura no está en la ropa', for example, is an ironic, humorous poem about a local prostitute, which is redolent of the caustic wit of Caviedes (Plácido 55).

**Narrative Poetry**

While a number of writers have composed and written fables, such as Fray Matías de Córdova, Antonio José de Irisarri, Simón Bergaño y Villegas and Luis Andrés Zúñiga, one name in Spanish America is naturally linked to the fable form, and that is Rafael García Goyena (1766–1823).[5] His *Fábulas y poesías varias* (1825) were published posthumously, and this was undoubtedly due to their political content, specifically, their pro-independence ideological stance. The aim of Goyena's fables, like Aesop's before him, was to expose human folly through reference to events, which occur to normally two or three animals. Thus, in 'La mosca, la hormiga y la palomilla nocturna', for example, Goyena depicts some scenes from the lives of a fly, an ant and a moth, and then concludes with the following moralistic axiom:

> La mosca en la miel que gusta
> muere; y a la hormiga arrasa
> por su hacienda tropa injusta;
> la palomilla se abrasa
> en la que ama luz augusta.
>
> Así, lector erudito,
> quien la razón avasalla
> por seguir el apetito,
> en su misma pasión halla
> quién castigue su delito. (García Goyena 59)

Excessive desire leads to human ruin. Other of Goyena's fables use the Aesopian format, rather like La Fontaine's fables, to expose the ills of contemporary society. Fable XIII, 'La araña y el mosquito', for example, uses the example of the ensnarement of the mosquito in the spider's web as an image of legal corruption: 'en los procesos escritos / jamás se prueban delitos / de una araña enredadora' (García Goyena 48). Fable XXI, 'La mariposa y la abeja', uses the difference between the butterfly's flitting between flowers and the bee's

---

[5] For a discussion of these and other minor poets of this period, see Oviedo, *Historia*, vol. 1, 367–71, and Franco, 74–7.

attentiveness to one flower as a means of differentiating between frivolous literature and serious literary creation:

> Si unas con otras cotejas
> las obras de los autores,
> verás que liban las flores
> más mariposas que abejas. (García Goyena 69)

Goyena's fables not only recreate Aesopian wisdom, however, they also extend it by applying it specifically to the Latin American context. Thus, Goyena will introduce animals into his fables which are only found on the sub-continent; Fable XXVII, for example, has as one of its protagonists a Guatemalan forest bird, the guarda. Goyena's fables are most interesting when they take on a political meaning, Fable IX being a good example of this. It begins with a reference to the political slant given to some events:

> Hoy fui testigo de un caso
> que, aunque común y trivial,
> bajo un político aspecto
> tiene algo de novedad. (García Goyena 37)

It then proceeds to tell the story of a cook who stole some baby pigeons with impunity, but was unable to steal any baby chickens because of the alarm sounded by the chickens and the roosters, and concludes with the following statement:

> Ciudadanos españoles,
> los que en Guatemala estáis,
> las gallinas os enseñan
> cuál es la acción popular.
>
> Quien agravia al individuo
> ofende a la sociedad,
> y da motivo a la queja
> y clamor universal. (García Goyena 38)

Some of Goyena's more successful fables operate in this way. Indeed, even when they do not ostensibly possess a political message, this can sometimes be detected. Fable XXX, 'Las golondrinas y los barqueros', for example, tells the story of some swallows who haughtily refuse the help of some sailors when it is first offered to them, only to die at sea later on in the voyage. As the fable ends:

> Y apenas dos leguas
> llevaban andadas,
> cuando ven llegar
> las aves cansadas.

> Con súplicas mil
> todas desmayadas,
> amparo pedían
> a los de las barcas.
>
> Mas ellos entonces
> riendo a carcajadas,
> sólo les decían: -
> -¿Pues no tenéis alas?-
>
> Al fin perecieron
> nuestras camaradas,
> y así los barqueros
> tomaron venganza.
>
> Esta fabulilla
> se llama la capa,
> vístela el lector
> si acaso le entalla. (García Goyena 110)

On one level this is a fable which exposes and satirises the foibles of the human race in the manner of Aesop's Fables. But the fact that the poem was written during the turbulent times of the independence movement, and that the destination of the swallows was Spain, suggests that the poem can also be read as an anti-colonialist satire. The impact of this particular fable, which is often anthologised, is reinforced by the use of a regular rhythm throughout (four-line hexasyllabic stanzas). While Goyena's fables clearly do not have the sophistication of La Fontaine's work, their politicization of the Aesopian model gives them more than a playful significance. The continuing appeal of Goyena's work is suggested by its being republished in the 'Clásicos del Istmo' collection in 1950 in Guatemala, as part of a nationalist redefinition of cultural property. On 18 October 1946, a commission chaired by Rafael Arrévolo Martínez, short story writer and then president of Guatemala, issued a decree asserting the importance of works like Goyena's as being a 'precioso aporte a la cultura nacional centroamericana' as produced 'durante los 125 años de independencia política de Centroamérica' (García Goyena iii).

Another significant writer of narrative poetry during this period was José Batres Montúfar (1809–44). Author of a number of lyric poems and dedicatorial pieces, he is now remembered for his *Tradiciones de Guatemala*, and especially 'Don Pablo' which, in a light-hearted, mock-ironic way, tells the story of a failed love affair. Its intended audience is female ('Amables damas, que leéis gustosas / Alguna u otra alegre anecdotilla / de aventuras galantes y amorosas'; Batres Montúfar 47). In a brisk narrative, with a number of excursions which serve to heighten the suspense, it tells how Pablo, a licentious young man, falls in love with a young woman, Isabel. But, as soon as he meets her, he is banished to a monastery and she to a convent, and he is admonished to repent. To frighten

Pablo into leading a good life, a monk shows him the skull of a once beautiful woman:

> Aquel fragmento había sido parte
> De una bella mujer muy disoluta,
> Que de Venus seguía el estandarte
> De hombres haciendo amplísima recluta;
> Pues de enganchar sabía a fondo el arte:
> Erase el hueso de una rica fruta
> En cuya dulce pulpa, en cien lugares
> Habían caído moscas a millares. ('Don Pablo', ll. 217–24; Batres Montúfar 69–70)

In the following stanza Batres Montúfar cannot resist an aside suggesting that the female members of his audience would never do such things:

> No son así mis jóvenes lectoras
> Que no pierden a nadie, ni se envidian,
> Ni lanzan miradillas seductoras,
> Ni tiene redes, ni al amor conviden. (ll. 225–8; Batres Montúfar 70)

The metaphor of the female body as fruit is echoed in Pedro's response to the priest's admonition in the play on the double meaning of 'hueso' as 'bone' and 'pit':

> – Conque ha dispuesto la fortuna avara
> Hacer de tanto hechizo y embeleso,
> Que a los otros la carne les tocara
> Y a mí tan sólo me tocara el hueso! (ll. 241–4; Batres Montúfar 70)

As a result of his blasphemy, a piece of the building falls on his head and kills him. To crown the melodrama the devil carts his body off to hell. Batres Montúfar cleverly avoids ending his *tradición* with a moral axiom, in the manner of Goyena's *Fábulas*, by arguing that his delicate readers do not need one:

> Mas ¿a qué me lleva el pensamiento? ¡A predicar a mis lectoras bellas
> Un poco de moral al fin del cuento!
> ¿Acaso, pues, lo necesitan ellas? (Batres Montúfar 72)

A playful narrative poem, skilfully told and with a good ear for its audience, 'Don Pablo' is a delightful example of the art of storytelling. It is unique in the early nineteenth century in that it specifies its intended audience as female.

## The Novel

It is often said that the Spanish American novelists of the nineteenth century do not compare well with some of the European masters such as Tolstoy and Balzac, Stendhal and Dickens. One reason that has been adduced is the lack of large cities in Spanish America in the nineteenth century; as Sarmiento argued, it was in the large city that the artist had at his disposition 'esa multitud de acontecimientos de las grandes y poderosas ciudades, donde la especie humana aglomerada, oprimida, despedazada, deja oír a cada momento gritos tan terribles de desesperación, de dolor' (quoted in Carilla, vol. 2, 72). But probably more compelling is the role of the intellectual influence that Europe exerted throughout the nineteenth century on Spanish American writers. The artistic dilemma for the nineteenth-century novelist centred around the tension between describing a reality (the new post-independence reality) with an artistic medium (the Realist novel form) designed and implemented elsewhere (Europe).[6] The results, predictably enough, were mixed in success.

*El Periquillo Sarniento* (1816) by José Joaquín Fernández de Lizardi (1776–1827) is generally credited with being the first Spanish American novel. The novel echoes the structure of the picaresque novel, as epitomised by *Vida de Lazarillo de Tormes*, in that it describes the misadventures of a young man, Periquillo, driven by hunger and poverty to make a way in the world in which he must cheat to survive, and has a liberal amount of slapstick humour (good examples of which occur during his residency as a doctor's assistant in Tula, and the episode when he attempts to steal jewellery from a corpse). Like the protagonist of *Lazarillo de Tormes*, Periquillo experiences a series of apprenticeships – in a ranch, a monastery, a barber's shop, a pharmacy – thereby learning a variety of trades which range from the socially prestigious (doctor's assistant, sacristan's assistant) to the dubious (croupier, cardsman) to the illegal (thief). The important part of these learning experiences is that they are all based on deception. The novel also describes Periquillo's marriage to Mariana and his discussion, which takes up most of the third volume of the novel, with a Chinese chieftain, as a result of which he decides to give up the error of his former ways. These elements, which *El Periquillo Sarniento* shares with the great Spanish classic, are effective. But, unlike *Lazarillo de Tormes*, Fernández de Lizardi's

---

[6] I am using Realism here to mean a literary work which aspires to create 'the objective representation of contemporary social reality' (Wellek 241–2), and which shows man as embedded within a specific social fabric (Auerbach 431). There are a number of accompanying characteristics associated with the Realist style which (summarised from Ian Watt) are: (i) the use of non-traditional plots, either wholly invented or based in part on a contemporary incident, (ii) the plot as acted out by particular people in particular circumstances, (iii) characterisation and presentation of background become essential elements, (iv) characters have ordinary contemporary proper names, (v) characters are rooted in the temporal dimension, (vi) the action takes place in an actual physical environment, (vii) the novel works by exhaustive presentation rather than by elegant concentration, and (viii) the novel's mode of imitating reality is similar to that of the jury in a court of law (Watt 15–31).

novel inserts long, moralising passages which expatiate on the moral meaning of the events described and, for the modern reader at least, reduce their impact. Another important influence, evident to good effect in the prologue to the second volume is Cervantes; like *Don Quijote*, the second volume opens with a discussion between the editor and a personage called Conocimiento about the reputation that Periquillo now has as a result of the publication of the first volume, as if to underscore that Periquillo is a real person.

The society which *El Periquillo Sarniento* describes is one which is in flux, particularly as far as the professional classes were concerned. The growing production for export made possible by expanding metropolitan markets and the faster ships employed in ocean trade in the eighteenth century led to new needs for intermediaries, credit facilities, and suppliers in urban centres, which was accompanied by the growth of a new class made up of doctors, lawyers and merchants. Especially the second half of the seventeenth century in the Spanish colonies saw a displacement of power from the hands of the Church, the monarchy, and the landowning elite to this new self-aware professional class. A key date is 1778 when Charles III's Decree of Free Trade allowed the twenty-four ports of Spanish America to trade between themselves directly without any need for Spain as an intermediary. *El Periquillo Sarniento* is sensitive to these changing social phenomena and gives a vivid picture of a society under the Bourbons (whose family succeeded to the throne in 1713) which gradually was becoming more economically and politically independent from Spain. An indication of this change of ambience is evident in the opening pages of the novel. Illustrating the growth of a capital-based democracy which accompanied the democratisation of the written word at the turn of the eighteenth century (see pp. 67–9 above), the novel's prologue describes an imaginary conversation between the author and a friend. The friend tries at first to persuade the author to dedicate his work to a wealthy patron, preferably a count, but then advises him to dedicate it to his readers since 'ellos son los que costean la impresión, y por lo mismo sus mecenas más seguros' (Fernández de Lizardi 3). In *El Periquillo Sarniento* we see at work what Anderson calls the 'national imagination' as encapsulated by 'the movement of a solitary hero through a sociological landscape of a fixity that fuses the world inside the novel with the world outside' (Anderson 35). It is not by chance that the first Spanish American novel should refer to a new mode of production (capital-based entrepreneurial book production) and, by implication, to the new class from which it sprang, since the nineteenth-century novel is an outgrowth of the bourgeoisie. In Spanish America, as elsewhere, the growth of the new professional classes, including doctors, lawyers, merchants, suppliers, and, indeed, printers, was accompanied by a parasitical group of unqualified and dishonest professionals; it is these latter that *El Periquillo Sarniento* sets out to satirise.[7]

---

[7] Other writers whose works can broadly be characterised as Realist during this period but which cannot be treated here are Alberto Blest Gana (1830–1920) and Ignacio Manuel Altamirano (1834–93). For discussion of these and other minor Realists of this era, see Franco, 70–3, 113–15.

José Mármol (1817–71), like Echeverría (see below, pp. 91–3), was unfortunate enough to experience first hand Manuel Rosas's dictatorship in Argentina. In more senses than one, his work can profitably be studied in parallel with Echeverría's *El matadero*. Mármol's claim to fame largely rests on his novel, *Amalia* (1851), which is normally remembered as the first Spanish American dictator novel, being based on the life and regime of Juan Manuel Rosas who ruled Argentina with an iron fist for more than twenty years in the early nineteenth century. But perhaps more remarkable is the novel's uneasy mix between the fictional and the purportedly real, since it brings together within its covers an historically real individual, Rosas, and the conspicuously fictional, Eduardo and Amalia (the romantic heroine and Eduardo's lover). The text strives to blur the distinction; at the beginning of Chapter X, for example, the omniscient narrator refers to 'escenas de que la imaginación duda, y de que la historia responde' (Mármol 107). History is the guarantor of the events which appear in the novel. The whole of the political struggle between the *federales* and the *unitarios* which tore Argentina apart in the civil unrest of the first few decades of the nineteenth century is focused on the competing wills of Rosas and the archetypal *unitario*, Eduardo, who is wounded badly in a street brawl early on, nursed back to health by Amalia (who promptly falls in love with him), and forced into exile at the conclusion of the novel; the ideology of the struggle is thus scaled down to a more manageable scale, focusing on the competing wills of two men, and a love affair is added to spice up the ingredients. *Amalia* is very much a thesis novel in that we are left in no doubt whom to love and whom to hate; the *unitarios*, Eduardo and Amalia, are struggling to fall in love in a world hostile to them, while the *federales* are variously described as sadistic (Rosas who forces his daughter to kiss the priest against her wishes in Chapter IV, and his sister-in-law, Doña María Josefa Ezcurra, who in the course of a surprise visit deliberately leans on Eduardo's injured thigh in order to cause him as much pain as possible, in Chapter XII) and physically repulsive (Mármol 122). Perhaps most tellingly of all, the threat of the *federales* is presented as an invasion of the domestic sphere; one of the results of Rosas's violence was that 'El hogar doméstico era invadido' (Mármol 126). Pointing in a similar direction, the title of the novel, which focuses on Amalia and her associations with receptive domesticity, shows where Mármol's ideological affiliations ultimately lay.

*Memórias de um Sargento de Milícias* by Manuel Antônio de Almeida (1831–61) was published in the liberal-leaning Rio de Janeiro newspaper, *Correo mercantil*, in instalments in the Sunday 'Pacotilha' section from 27 June 1852 until 31 June 1853, a *folhetim*, and thus in the French style (Jarouche 27). *Memórias* focuses on a crucial moment of Brazil's history, the royal period when Dom João VI had removed his royal court from Portugal to Brazil (see above p. 67). As such the novel had a political edge to it, and was clearly a liberal dig at the pro-Old World leanings of the conservatives who, in the 1850s, were trying to restore Brazil's broken links with Portugal. Almeida, indeed, was not adverse to works of literature having a political subtext since, as he pointed out in 1856, 'a nossa literatura é filha da política' (quoted in Jarouche 39–40). Perhaps not surprisingly, given the candid force of its critique, the novel was first published under the nom de plume of 'Um Brasileiro', and it remained an anonymous work in the subsequent editions of 1854 and 1855; it was only in 1863 that the author's real name was publicly divulged. The *Memórias* strikes a markedly different note from those Romantic classics of the nineteenth century such as *Iracema* and *A Escrava Isaura* (see below, pp. 118–19) for it uses humour and satire to make its point. Defined as a 'romance de costumes brasileiros' in the definitive edition published in 1876, if offers a vivid series of vignettes of the royal period which are tied to historical events and people. Miguel Nunes Vidigal, the head of police in Rio known for his brutal methods, appears as himself in the novel (see especially Part I, Chapter V, Almeida 91–6), and the King referred to in the novel can only be King João VI; intriguingly though, Almeida took out the harsh critique of the King which had appeared in the first edition of the work from the later editions (Jarouche 45–6) and, as a result, the latter are more polished but less raw, less engaging.

The novel tells the story of Leonardo Pataca and his son, Leonardo; the narrator is omniscient and comments on the action from the sidelines, almost as if he were a spectator watching the events unfold before his eyes. Some critics have seen the novel as a direct descendant of the Spanish picaresque novel, particularly *Vida de Lazarillo de Tormes*, whereas others, such as Antônio Candido in his essay 'Dialética da Malandragem', have seen it as a 'romance malandro' (quoted in Jarouche 57). The political swipes at the Portuguese are dropped innocently enough into the narrative; in Part I, Chapter VI, for example, we hear about the Portuguese community in Brazil, how they are bone-idle and seem to have left any remnant of civilisation they once had back in Portugal (Almeida 98). The novel moves effortlessly between episodes, and the reader is addressed in such a way as to whet his appetite for what comes next: 'Entretanto vamos satisfazer ao leitor, que há de talvez ter curiosidade de saber onde se meteu o pequeno' (Almeida 98). Humour is often elicited as a result of the inappropriateness of an individual's behaviour as driven by a fortuitous set of events, the best example of which occurs when Leonardo is discovered by the local constabulary prancing around in the nude at the local fortune-teller's (Part I, Chapter V), or when the priest is told the wrong time to give his sermon, and an Italian priest takes his place so that nobody understands a word of what is going on (Part I, Chapter XIV). The humour is very much of the slapstick kind. True to its picaresque roots, the narrative darts around: for example the plot, in Part I, Chapter XVII, jumps unexpectedly to an occasion when Doña Maria is introduced to readers via a visit she makes to church, and hears the life-history of the young boy Leonardo (Almeida 163–70), which allows for some *costumbrista* description of the clothes worn by the black woman of Bahia (Almeida 165).

Rather a hybrid text, the *Memórias* begins as a picaresque novel, gradually turns into a novel depicting the social manners of the period, before becoming a romantic tale of impossible love, and concluding with a description of

Leonardo's experience in the military. But there is a common thread bringing this sequence of disparate events together, and it is the overwhelming sense of Leonardo as a star-crossed individual. Beginning with the moment his father boots him out of the family home as a young lad, to his various periods of incarceration, his doomed love affair with Luisinha (here he is outwitted by an older man, José Manuel), then with Vidinha (her two cousins are jealous of her), he just does not seem to be able to get things right. As Doña Maria puts it: 'aquel rapaz não nasceu em bom dia' (Almeida 318). The book is also set up as a response to the received ideas of the day, one of them being the Romantic notion that only the first love is true love, to which the narrator responds: 'o verdadeiro amor [...] não é o primeiro, é o último' (Almeida 319). Perhaps the most engaging aspect of the story is the way in which the women are depicted as working things out behind the scenes – the *comadre* who tries to engineer the marriage between Luisinha and Leonardo, Doña Maria who manages to get one of Major Vidigal's former lovers to influence him, and thereby secures Leonardo's early release from prison (Part II, Chapter XXII, 319–20). As only to be expected in a *folhetim*, the plot is not averse to using the *deus ex machina* device, principally in José Manuel's unbelievably fortuitous death in the penultimate chapter of the novel (Part II, xxiv), along with Leonardo's extraordinarily swift promotion to the rank of seargent in the same chapter. The last chapter brings the events to a happy close; Leonard applies for a transfer to the post of sergeant of the Militias which will allow him to marry Luisinha. The moral of the story appears to be that God works in mysterious ways: 'Deus é assim, escreve direito por linhas tortas' (Almeida 331).

## Two Romantic Novels: *Iracema* and *María*

*Iracema* (1865) by José de Alencar (1829–77), one of the classics of the nineteenth-century Romantic Brazilian novel, is based on the early seventeenth-century expedition to the uncharted territory near the Jaguaribe Falls by Martim Soares Moreno from Rio Grande do Norte, which led to the founding of the fort of Nossa Senhora do Amparo in 1611. It was the first Brazilian novel to be translated into English; soon after publication it caught the attention of the then British consul in Santos, Sir Richard Burton, and his wife Isabel, who translated it into English, and it was published by Bicher and Son in 1886 (Hallewell 212). Alencar takes the narrative of that historical event to create an allegory of the founding of Brazil which struck a chord with his readers in the nineteenth century (see Sommer 138–71), preoccupied as they were with the re-visioning of the Brazilian nation caught in the throes of a painful transition towards republicanism. (Independence was almost a family affair in nineteenth-century Brazil; Dom Pedro I had broken allegiance from Portugal and his father, Dom João VI, to declare independence for Brazil in 1822; he then left Brazil in the hands of his son, Dom Pedro II, in 1831; the latter ascended to the throne in 1840, and the republic was only declared forty-nine years later, in 1889, after a protracted struggle.) While Alencar was writing the novel, as he points out in his letter to Dr Jauaribe which concludes the novel, he found himself in a nation characterized by 'o estado da prática entorpecida pela indiferença' (*Iracema* 134).

Like many nineteenth-century novels the drama of Brazil's founding is portrayed through the union of a white Christian, Martim, and the beautiful daughter of an Indian chief (Araquém) called Iracema. Although Alencar's notes provide an Amerindian etymology for Iracema's name ('Iracema em guarani significa lábios de mel – de ira, e tembe – lábios'; *Iracema* 125), she is clearly a symbol of the New World in that her name is an anagram of America. Indeed the allegory of the conquest of the New World, and the metaphors associated with that conquest, overpower the novel, so that it is very un-novel-like compared to the typical novel of nineteenth-century Europe. Iracema has little plot to speak of, the characters are not rounded or psychologically convincing, and it provides a minimal sense of historical verisimilitude. The opening chapter of the novel describes the arrival of Martim's boat in the cove where Iracema lives, but any hint of realism is submerged beneath the burden of the poetic and the metaphorical:

> Verdes mares bravios de minha terra natal, onde canta a jandaia nas frondes da carnaúba! Verdes mares que brilhas como líquida esmeralda aos raios do sol nascente, perlongando as alvas praias ensombradas de coqueiros! (*Iracema*, Chapter I, 9)

It comes at no surprise therefore to learn that, as Alencar pointed out in his 'Carta Ao Dr Jauaribe' (a conventional pseudo-letter designed to explain the genesis of the work to its readers), the novel began life as a poem (*Iracema* 134), what we might call an epic poem, written in the style of the indigenous language, and based on the 'as idéias, embora rudes e grosseiras, dos indios' (*Iracema* 134); only later did Alencar hit upon the idea of trying an experiment in prose (*Iracema* 138). This poetic, even epic, quality of Alencar's novel is evident not only in the imagery but also in the depiction of the characters. When Iracema is first introduced, for example, her presence is fused to such a degree with the natural landscape that she loses her human identity: 'A lufada intermitente traz da praia um eco vibrante, que ressoa entre o marulho das vagas: "Iracema!"' (*Iracema*, Chapter I, 9). Though she at first attempts to wound the white foreigner, Martim, she then feels sorry for him and takes him under her wing (Chapter II). She is shown subsequently as prepared to kill her own brother in order to keep Martim's love (Chapter XVIII). Finally, when she gives birth to Martim's child, she is overwhelmed by sadness (in the sense that this birth spells the end of Tupa culture), and – rather too conveniently, one might think – dies and leaves the future open for Martim's progeny. The final chapter proclaims the birth of a new European culture in the New World: 'A mairi que Martim erguera à margem do rio, nas praias do Ceará, medrou.

Germinou a palavra de Deus verdadeiro na terra selvagem; e o bronze sagrado ressoou nos vales onde rugia o maracá' (*Iracema*, Chapter XXXIII, 121). Iracema at the end of the novel is not even given the consolation prize of being heard in the breeze: 'A jandaia cantava ainda no ôlho do coqueiro; mas não repetia já o mavioso nome de Iracema' (*Iracema*, Chapter XXXIII, 122).

*Iracema* is an ambiguous text, seeming to pull in different semantic directions at once; its imagery and poetry are drawn from Amerindian sources, the God whose voice is heard throughout the narrative is that of Tupa, and yet the final dénouement of the novel is, ideologically speaking, a pro-Conquest statement. The story has some magical-real elements. Thus Iracema's father, Araquém, is able stamp his foot on the ground, produce a parting of the earth, and allow Tupa's voice to be heard:

> Araquém, proferindo essa palavra terrível, avançou até o meio da cabana; ali ergueu a grande pedra e calcou o pé com fôrça no chão; súbito, abriu-se a terra. Do antro profundo saiu um medondho gemido que parecia arrancado das entranhas do rochedo. (*Iracema*, Chapter XI, 43)

Because of his love for Iracema Martim is shown, later on, to be able to participate in this magic of the earth: 'Iracema cerra a mão do guerreiro e o leva à borda do antro. Somem-se ambos nas entranhas da terra' (*Iracema*, Chapter XIII, 52). This image of the opening of the earth is crucial to the novel since Martim's conquest of Iracema is related to the opening of her heart ('Que o guerreiro branco venha, e o seio de Iracema se abra para o vencedor'; *Iracema*, Chapter VII, 29) and, by extension, her womb for Martim. The implication is that Iracema's bearing of Martim's child entails not only the first step of the creation of a new race in the New World, but also the seizure of a new land and the capture of its magic and its gods (specifically the God of Thunder, Tupa, who is depicted in the novel as inhabiting – like the majority of the gods of Amerindia – the subterranean realms of the Earth).

Jorge Isaacs (1837–95) is celebrated in Colombia and elsewhere in Spanish America as an icon of the Romantic movement. His novel *María* (1867), the most famous of the nineteenth-century Romantic novels published in the subcontinent, certainly helps to foster this image. As a result of political instability, Isaacs's father lost his estate, which reduced his family to penury. His son, Jorge, was part of a formerly moneyed generation forced to earn a living in the newly emerging capitalist society of his day as a result of circumstances beyond his control. In effect, it was that world of inherited rather than independently created wealth that Isaacs would look back to nostalgically, and would form the emotional matrix of the nostalgia which coloured the literature he wrote. It is for *María*, of course, that Isaacs is now remembered; essentially a Romantic novel set in rural Colombia, it describes in poignant detail the ill-starred love between the protagonist and first-person narrator, Efraín, and María.[8] Typical of many

---

[8] Numerous editions of the novel abounded throughout Spanish America in the second half of the nineteenth century. A play based on the novel, written by E. O. Palencia, was

nineteenth-century Romantic novels, the protagonists spend much of their time not in earning a living, marrying and raising children but in being in love and, particularly evident in this novel, breaking down into tears at the slightest provocation. The plot is skimpy; Efraín for as long as he can remember has been in love with María who has lived in the family home since the age of three when she was adopted by Efraín's father from a close friend, Salomón, whose wife had recently died. María is diagnosed as suffering from epilepsy but, despite this, Efraín's parents agree to the couple's desire to marry, although Efraín is sent away to London to finish his studies and launch his career before the marriage takes place. In the two years that Efraín is away María gradually wilts and dies before he returns. The emphasis in the novel is on what Freud identified as 'obstacle-love', that is, a sexual love which is characterised by repeated deferral and, eventually, non-consummation (Tanner 88). The love as projected in the novel is quiveringly platonic. The parting scene epitomises this; there is no verbal language, much body language and many tears. María is sitting praying in the oratory and utters a 'weak cry' when she hears Efraín approach (Chap. LIII; Isaacs 131). Efraín subsequently kisses María's forehead and the three suspension points which follow this statement ('Mis labios descansaron sobre su frente ...') underline how momentous the occasion is felt to be. Also important in this scene is the religious motif; details such as Efraín's kneeling posture, María's parting gesture in which she points towards the altar ('extendió uno de los brazos para señalarme el altar') make very clear, if the name were not enough, that María is being explicitly conflated with the Mother of Christ (an image that occurs later on when María, already dead, is described as wearing 'un delantal azul como si hubiera sido formado de un jirón de cielo' (Chap. LXIX; Isaacs 153). This becomes a highly-charged image given that the motif of incest occurs not only in the son–mother but the brother–sister paradigm; by the time María is nine years old, for example, she is seen as indistinguishable from Efraín's sisters (Chap. VII; Isaacs 12). On one level this incestuous pattern in *María* is to be understood as an allusion to the fascination with incest which characterised Romantic literature; we may recall here Byron's contention that 'great is their love who live in sin and fear' (quoted in Praz 73). It is also a specific allusion to Chateaubriand's *Le Génie du Christianisme* which describes the socially impossible love between a brother and sister and which Efraín and María read together ecstatically and mournfully (Chaps. XII–XIII).

The structure of Isaacs's novel is striking since it gives less the impression of being a polished work and has that disregard for form which is the hallmark of the epic. Thus, the novel is constructed around a series of interludes which fill out the resonance of the main action (Efraín's love for María), such as the hunting expedition during which Efraín shoots a tiger (Chap. XXI), and the

staged in the Teatro Baranquilla on 21 January 1892, and published the same year. *María: leyenda dramática tomada de la novela del mismo bombre, de don Jorge Isaacs*. Baranquilla: Imprenta Americana, The Old Reliable, E. P. Pellet, Proprietario, 1892. Miscelánea, No. 90, Biblioteca Nacional, Santafe de Bogotá. A movie version of the novel was made and shown in Bogotá in 1922; unfortunately the film has been lost.

story of how Feliciana came to America from Africa (Chaps. XL–XLIII). Even the *post facto* blow-by-blow description of María's death is introduced as a transcription of the account given to Efraín by his sister, Emma (Chap. LXII). This, indeed, underlines the future perfect atmosphere of the novel, its insistence on the importance of memory. The continuity of the love theme and the use of recurrent symbols, however, manage to ensure that *María* is a unified work of art. The two most significant examples of symbolism are the flowers which María repeatedly places in Efraín's bedroom as a sign of her love (the devotional resonances are clear here too), and the sinister blackbird which appears in the narrative on three crucial occasions – when the first clear sign of María's illness appears (Chap. XV; Isaacs 20), when the fatal letter arrives which announces the bankruptcy of Efraín's father's business (Chap. XXXIV; Isaacs 74), and at the end of the novel as an emblem of María's death when it lands on her tombstone (Chap. LXV; Isaacs 154).

## Short Narrative

The nineteenth century was the century in which the subaltern gradually but painfully threw off the yoke of his oppression. In 1817 Spain signed a treaty with Britain agreeing to abolish the slave trade in 1820, although the trade continued to flourish in the remaining Spanish colonies until late on in the century; thus, while Mexico and Peru abolished slavery in 1829 and 1854 respectively, it was not until 1880 that Cuba finally rid itself of the white man's curse. There was, indeed, little incentive to abolish slavery in the circum-Caribbean during the nineteenth century. Although the sugar plantations were not as profitable in the nineteenth century as they had once been (during the seventeenth and eighteenth centuries, the sugar plantations were among the contemporary world's largest and most profitable enterprises, paying about 10 per cent on invested capital), they were still capable of producing enormous profits, particularly in Cuba. Juan Francisco Manzano's *Autobiografía de un esclavo* (1840) is a unique text in that it is the only autobiographical text written in Spanish by a slave. Juan Francisco Manzano was the son of Toribio Castro and María Pilar Manzano, born in 1797. From birth until the age of twelve he lived with his parents who were servants to the Marquesa de Santa Ana. When the latter died, the family passed into the service of the Marquesa de Prado Ameno, a cruel woman, from whom Manzano fled. He taught himself to read and write while serving as a page in the home of Nicolás de Cárdenas y Manzano (1773–1863), where he went in 1818. After escaping from the Marquesa he worked independently in Havana, and married a mulatto pianist, Delia, in 1835. The prominent Cuban abolitionist, Domingo del Monte, urged Manzano to write up his autobiography, offering him his liberty in exchange for the manuscript, and, in a letter dated June 1835, Manzano expressed his reluctance to do so since me abochorna el contarlo, y no se como demostrar los hechos dejando la parte mas terrible en el tintero, y ojala tubiera otros hechos con que llenar la historia de mi vida sin recorder el esesivo rigor con que me ah tratado mi Antigua ama, obligandome o poniendome en la forsosa nesesidad a apelar a una ariesgada fugar para aliviar mi triste cuerpo de las continuas mortifcasiones que no podria ya sufrir mas. (Moliner 85–6)

But Manzano finally acceded to Domingo del Monte's request and eventually completed his autobiography in 1839.

The *Autobiografía de un esclavo* was first published in English translation by R. R. Madden, the British abolitionist, in London the following year, and it was used as ammunition in the abolitionist movement of the time. The 1840 edition contains the autobiography, some poems dealing with the life of a slave in nineteenth-century Cuba, as well as some other documents relating to slavery, which are used to introduce the English reader to some of the horrors of slavery. The autobiography recalls the happy time Manzano spent at the home of the Marquesa of Santa Ana, his discomfiture when placed at the age of ten into the household (in Matanzas) of the Marquesa de Prado Ameno who had him beaten constantly, especially between the ages of thirteen and fourteen. He was locked in the charcoal room for twenty-four hours as punishment for 'crimes' such as not hearing the first time she called, or complaining about his food. On one occasion, Don Sylvester whipped Francisco's mother, and he attacked him, and as a result both mother and son ended up in the stocks, stripped and whipped. A pattern emerges in the text of a punishment far outweighing the 'crime'. For picking a flower, for example, Francisco was sentenced to a night in the stocks. When accused of stealing a capon, he fled – since he knew he would not be believed – and was viciously attacked by some dogs. Though put in the stocks and lashed until he admitted his guilt – he had to admit to it – it was subsequently discovered that the steward had eaten the capon. Because he did not give a peseta to the beggar as instructed, he was punished and then sent away to the Ingenio San Miguel where he was lashed fifty times a day for nine days. A tragic detail, Franciso falls in love and, for having a bath, he is hit by his mistress, and told to carry the barrel of water on his shoulders around the house. He slips while carrying it, and smashes the barrel. Don Saturnino is called. At midnight Francisco decides to make his escape for Havana, and here the narrative ends. A brutally honest text, it is instructive to compare the view of a slave's lot which emerges from *Autobiografía de un esclavo* with the vision found in Gómez de Avellaneda's *Sab* (discussed below, pp. 103–4).

With *El matadero* (written 1838; published 1871) by Esteban Echeverría (1805–51) came the birth of the short story in Latin America. It is an effective if at times over-obvious allegory of the struggle between the unitarians and the federalists in Argentina in the second quarter of the nineteenth century. In an essay 'Ojeada retrospectiva' written in exile in Montevideo in 1848, Echeverría described Argentina during those years as characterised by 'dos facciones irreconcilables por sus odios' (Echeverría 155). *El matadero* employs the slaughter-house as a symbol of Argentine society under Rosas's despotic rule, and the allegory works on two levels, local and universalist. The local level – the image of the slaughter-house – refers to the greatest source of capital over which the federalists, a loose federation of ranch-owners and Rosas's die-hard supporters, had direct control: beef livestock. Echeverría also manages to use this image to poke fun at the Catholic Church, stressing the Church's connivance with the federalists in forcing beef prices up when prohibiting the consumption of meat during Lent (Echeverría 427–8). The Church is projected as a restrictive organisation better suited, in Echeverría's eyes, to pre-independence days (Echeverría 432). Throughout the story the connections between the slaughter-house and Rosas's regime are underlined, sometimes unsubtly. When the slaughter-house workers turn on a bull, as if the political metaphor were not clear enough already, one of them remarks: 'Es emperrado y arisco como un unitario' (Echeverría 436). Some details are a little more subtle. When the workers chase the bull, the symbol of the unitarian cause, there are two casualties; the first is a child who is decapitated (destruction of innocence) and the second is a *gringo* who is knocked down in the rush (destruction of the goodwill of foreign investors). Though a seemingly insignificant detail, the allegory is written from a unitarian perspective. The unitarians espoused the doctrine of free trade based on the harbour of Buenos Aires, and were bitterly opposed to what they saw as the Federalists' closed-market philosophy and use of high protectionist tariffs which frightened foreign investors away. This much is hinted at in the detail.

*El matadero* is curious in that the use of allegory (sacrifice of the bull) then leads into a stretch of Realist narrative (an actual unitarian appears on the scene). Rather than being killed by the federalists, however, as might have been expected giving the allegorical playing-out of a federalist execution just before, the unitarian explodes in a torrent of blood caused by the outrage of being stripped of his clothes, which is probably to be understood as denoting allegorically the divestment of his unitarian culture: 'Entonces un torrente de sangre brotó borbolloneando de la boca y las narices del joven y extendiéndose empezó a caer a chorros por entreambos lados de la mesa' (Echeverría 442). The final image is one of political defiance on the part of the unitarian in the face of inevitable destruction by the federalists: suicide is preferable to defeat, the metaphor suggests. The image of the body is crucial here since it acts as an allegory mediating between the national and the personal drama. Although bodily violation (either in the form of castration or rape) is not explicitly mentioned in the second scene in which the unitarian has his clothes pulled off, its potency is evoked through associative juxtaposition with the earlier scene in which the testicles are cut out of the dead bull's body ('¡Aquí están los huevos!'; Echeverría 438), and details of the scene which operate as displaced images of rape (scissors are mentioned repeatedly, the federalists cut off the unitarian's sideburns, they expose his buttocks for punishment, etc.). This adds a further level of association which helps to explain the artistic logic behind the image of the unitarian's exploding body. Just as the body politic is violated and confined by Rosas's dictatorship, both of which ideas are suggested in the slaughter-house image, so the only appropriate image of escape is one of bodily explosion which defies the confinements of forced bondage.[9]

## Theatre

Nineteenth-century Spanish American drama has little of the vigour of its European counterparts. There were flourishing theatre houses in the major Spanish American cities, but most of the works put on derived from Spain and France. The most popular works staged were by Alexandre Dumas, Victor Hugo, Larra, García Gutiérrez, Ventura de la Vega, Zorrilla, Bretón de los Herreros, Hartzenbusch, Ducange; other works included those by Shakespeare, Schiller, Martínez de la Rosa and Moratín (Carilla, vol. 2, 40–1). The three most memorable dramatists of the mid-nineteenth century were the Mexican, Manuel Eduardo de Gorostiza (1789–1851), born in Veracruz, and the two Peruvians, Felipe Pardo y Aliaga (1806–68), and Manuel Ascensio Segura (1805–71). The work of these dramatists concentrates on the nodal point of the middle-class way of life in the nineteenth century, namely, the family. In the nineteenth century, as Tony Tanner has pointed out, middle-class society viewed marriage as sacrosanct, the 'all-subsuming, all-organizing, all-containing contract' (Tanner 15). The best-known plays by these three authors focus, indeed, on the centrality of marriage, and specifically on the struggle, common in Spanish Romantic drama, between the will of the parents and the will of the daughter as to the latter's marriage partner. What makes these plays different from their Spanish counterparts – plays such as Duque de Rivas's *Don Álvaro o la fuerza del sino* (1835), Antonio García Gutiérrez's *El Trovador* (1836) and José de Zorrilla's *Don Juan Tenorio* (1844) – is that the Spanish plays typically end in death for one or both of the lovers, while the Spanish American plays tend to express more pragmatism with regard to the dilemma of choice between a marriage based on romantic love or one based on social pedigree; they often conclude by voting on the side of happiness rooted in domesticity.

Gorostiza's play, *Contigo pan y cebolla* (1833), for example, has all the classic ingredients of a Romantic play: Doña Matilde is in love with Don Eduardo de Contreras and, against the wishes of her father, Don Pedro de Lara, she plans to elope with her lover. The play is careful to point out that Doña Matilde's views about love have been created by her literary readings. In the opening scene of the play, the servant, Bruno, scolds her for staying up too late reading (Luzuriaga and Reeve 204). And when Matilde first sees Eduardo,

---

[9] Another significant short-story writer of this period whose work is not discussed here is the Chilean Daniel Riquelme (1857–1912).

it becomes clear that she is dramatising the events of her own life and attempting to fit them into a preconceived literary stereotype; Eduardo says he is late because he had to shave and she replies that she would have expected him to arrive without having shaved if he had travelled non-stop for three or four days to see her, but, since he only lives down the street, then his shaven face seems reasonable (Act I, Scene ii; Luzuriaga and Reeve 206). The amusing interface between Matilde's expectations about her future elopement and reality continues throughout the play; one of the most comical scenes occurs when she refuses to leave the house through the door, but insists on squeezing through the window instead. Attempting to compress her life into the shape of a Romantic cliché, she refuses Eduardo's offer of marriage once it becomes clear that her father is in favour of such a union (Act I, Scene viii). Bruno subsequently comments that women have changed:

> las nuestras pasaban sus días y sus noches haciendo caleta [...] Pero las de ahora, como todas leen la *Gaceta* y saben dónde está Pekín, ¿qué sucede? Que se le va el tiempo en averiguar lo que no les importa [...] y ni cuidan de casarse, ni saben cómo se espuma el puchero. (Luzuriaga and Reeve 216)

It is noteworthy that reading the *Gaceta de México* should be seen as the cause of a paradigm shift in the social behaviour of women. Indeed, Matilde only decides to run off with Eduardo once she 'discovers' (it is, in fact, an elaborate trick) that he has been disinherited. And, when she does elope, she is very much disillusioned by her meagre life in a garret, and is humiliated when one of her friends, the marchioness, comes to visit her and lord it over her. As soon as her father asks her to come home, Matilde agrees to do so, much to her lover's chagrin; Eduardo comments wryly that the pleasures of indigence which Matilde is now giving up still have merit in the eyes of 'las jóvenes de diecisiete años que leen novelas' (Act IV, Scene xi; Luzuriaga and Reeve 250).

*Frutos de la educación*, by Felipe Pardo y Aliaga, which was first staged in the Teatro de Lima on 6 August 1829, also focuses on the generational conflict over the value of marriage. Don Feliciano, because of some business losses, is keen to marry off his daughter, Pepita, to Bernardo, a young man who is soon to inherit a great deal of wealth. The mother, Doña Juana, aided and abetted by her brother-in-law, Don Manuel, favours an English businessman, Don Eduardo, as a better candidate. The struggle between the husband and wife, which also appears (and virulently so) in *Ña Catita* (see below), is intensified by the question of cultural difference; Don Eduardo is English and therefore assumed to be a heretic by Don Feliciano (Act II, Scene iv; Pardo y Aliaga 81). The play has many scenes, such as the marchioness's ball, which are essentially *costumbrista* pieces which slow the play down. It does not really possess a *desenlace* since, by the final act of the play, Pepita is left with no suitor in sight; Don Eduardo goes back on his word to marry her because he saw her dancing an Afro-Peruvian dance, the *zamacueca*, in an over-suggestive way, while Bernardo decides to marry somebody else. The significance given to subaltern culture as a result of this appears not to be accidental. The play ends with a speech given by Don Feliciano ostensibly to advise his daughter, but which at the same time serves as an assessment of the moral health of the (Peruvian) nation; he advises her, as a *criolla*, to avoid mixing with the lower classes by, for example, dancing the *zamacueca* (Act III, Scene xi; Pardo y Aliaga 164). This echoes the white-aesthetic ideology of the play taken as a whole in the sense that the one Negro who appears, Perico, is treated as a caricature; he is called a savage by Don Manuel and a devil by Doña Juana (Pardo y Aliaga 130, 161). Yet, more than simply a part of a process of grotesque caricaturing, Africanness seems to exist in *Los frutos de la educación* as the skeleton in the cupboard; it is, after all, Perico who brings news of the identity of Bernardo's intended; she is a *mulatiya* (Pardo y Aliaga 160), whom he met, presumably, in one of his secret nocturnal sallies to the other side of town, and on account of which he lost his reputation in Doña Juana's eyes. These elements, when placed together, point to the prickly nature of the issue of race in the play. Pepita loses one (upper-class) man because she is associated with the lower classes, and loses another man to a woman of a lower class; her intermediary position at the conclusion of the play, stuck in the middle of two social/racial options, portrays perhaps the ideological unease of the middle class of the time with regard to citizens of African descent who are perceived to be encroaching on the 'sacrosanct' space occupied by the social institution of marriage. If anything, thus, Pardo y Aliaga's play speaks out against the social validity of the notion of Romantic love, since the latter involves the risk of racially dangerous liaisons.

A similar type of distance with regard to the Romantic ideal of love expressed so fervently in a play like Duque de Rivas's *Don Álvaro o la fuerza del sino*, is evident in Ascensio Segura's delightfully well-written play *Ña Catita* (1856). This play again begins with all the ingredients of a Romantic drama: two lovers, Manuel and Juliana, who desire to get married but are thwarted in this by Juliana's mother, Doña Rufina, and her dastardly accomplice, Ña Catita, a hypocritical old maid who will stop at nothing to ruin other people's happiness. Instead they propose a young man, Alejo, a pompous pedant who appears to be wealthy. Their plans are dashed, however, when one of Alejo's friends arrives and hands Alejo a letter from his wife (Act IV, Scene xiv). After this *deus ex machina* device the play only has one place to go, and the marriage of Manuel and Juliana is assured. The play concludes on a note of moralism:

> Desconfía, en adelante,
> del que ostenta beatitud,
> y de todo hombre pedante,
> que nunca fue la virtud
> ficciosa ni petulante. (Luzuriaga and Reeve 354)

It is quite clear that Ascensio is satirizing in this play the middle class's acquisitive and capitalist attitude towards the choice of marriage partners. The moral of *Ña Catita* is that arranged marriages are misguided and that unions based on mutual consent and Romantic love are necessary for the well-being of society.

By European standards Brazilian theatre at the beginning of the nineteenth century was still rather rudimentary. As Saint-Hilaire noted in his *Viajem Pelas Provincias de Rio de Janeiro e Minas Gerais*, 'os atôres eram todos operários, a maior parte mulatos, as atrizes, mulheres públicas. O talante destas últimas corria parelhas como a sua moralidade: dir-se-iam fantoches movidos por um fio' (quoted in Galante de Sousa 131). But the arrival of the King and his entourage released a new energy into theatre; and a royal decree of 28 May 1819 by Dom João VI declared the need for 'um teatro decente, e proporcionado à população e ao maior grau da elevação e grandeza em que hoje se acha pela minha residência nela' (quoted in Galante de Sousa 159–60). The Royal Theatre was inaugurated in 1813, and three years later the French Artistic Mission arrived in Rio at the King's invitation, bringing a number of internationally acclaimed plays to be performed in Brazil. In 1833 the first Brazilian drama troupe was founded, and the première of Gonçalves de Magalhães's *Antonio José* on 13 March 1838 is normally given as the date when national theatre was born in Brazil (Galante de Sousa 194).

Some of the revolutionary fervour of the times can be guessed at in *O Juiz do Paz da Roça* by Luis Carlos Martins Pena (1815–48). This is ostensibly a one-act play about one Manuel João, who is charged with taking a man to prison by the local justice of the peace. The prisoner escapes and ends up marrying Manuel João's daughter, and all ends happily. It is clear, however – after digging beneath the surface a little – that the play is an allegory of the corruption of power in Brazil: the audience is encouraged to sympathise with the discomfiture of the justice of the peace and to sympathise with the plight of the socially oppressed. Martins Pena's *O Noviço* is similar in that it encourages rebellion against the *ancien régime*, here symbolised by the Church which attempts to force Emilia and Carlos to take vows. After a sequence of slapstick scenes in which the rich and powerful are discomfited, the plays concludes with a happy marriage between Carlos and Emilia, thereby speaking on behalf of a new Brazil, no longer weighed down by the social laws which force children to marry whom their parents want, a new world in which personal freedom, social freedom and the love of literature are valued.

Gonçalves Dias is mainly known for his poetry (see above pp. 71–2), but he also wrote plays and his best-known work is *Leonor de Mendonça* (1846) which was based on a Portuguese chronicle which recounted the murder in Vila Viçosa in 1512 of Leonor de Mendonça by her husband, Dom Jaime, since he suspected her of adultery. The play is based on the notion of fatality, not divine but human. As Gonçalves Dias points out in his prologue to the play: 'É a fatalidade cá de terra a que eu quis descrever, aquela fatalidade que nada tem de Deus e tudo dos homens, que é filha das circunstâncias e que dimana toda dos nossos hábitos de civilização' (Gonçalves Dias 61). He goes on to explain how this is relevant to the play since it is women's subjection to man's law that makes the tragedy inevitable: 'Se a mulher não fosse escrava, como é de fato, D. Jaime não mataria sua mulher' (61). *Leonor de Mendonça* differs from the standard Romantic play in which the love between a young man and woman is forbidden by the woman's father (the classic example being *Don Alvaro o la fuerza del sino*), for here the forbidden passion involves the suspicion of adultery, and thus leads the work to have more parallels with Calderón's wife-murder plays which, as we have seen (above, p. 59), were popular in Brazil's colonial days. But the overwhelming tone of the work is Romantic, particularly in terms of the foreboding of death (Alcaforado in his love-speech to the Duquesa says he is prepared to go to the scaffold for her [Act I, Scene iv; Gonçalves Dias 77], which turns out to be premonitory; the Duke is obsessed by the memory of his father's death; the Duquesa is almost killed by a wild boar [Act I, Scene i, 85–6]) and, in its emotional restlessness, it is clear that this play expresses a powerful desire for liberation from patriarchal tyranny and, as such, encapsulated the Romantic *Zeitgeist*.

Like Gonçalves Dias, the novelist José de Alencar (already mentioned for his novel, *Iracema*, see pp. 85–8) also wrote plays. His *Verso e Reverso* (1857), like many other dramas of the period, focuses on love but it does so in a lighthearted rather than a *Sturm und Drang* way; the happy ending in which the two cousins, Ernesto and Julia, are allowed to allow confirms that this is a comedy of manners rather than a Romantic drama. *Os Miseravéis* (1863) by Agrário de Sousa Meneses has as its theme the Machievellian techniques of the various suitors who are courting a rich widow, Fausta. It is a world in which true love can have no part since money is 'o maravilhoso eixo em que gira este mundo' (Sousa Meneses 23). Fausta attempts to ruin the pure love which exists between Eugenio and Christina by spreading malicious rumours, and a note of social critique is brought into play: 'Não é o povo que anima os miseravéis; são os miseravéis que abusão do povo' (Sousa Meneses 178). As the conclusion of the play makes clear, it is the rich Fausta who is the 'wretched' villain of the piece not the poor.

Occasionally the Romantic formula was given a harder political edge, as was the case with *Sangue limpo* by Paulo Eiró, first performed in São Paolo on 2 December 1861, and published two years later. In the prologue to the play Eiró describes his work as the antithesis of the 'nódoa negra da escrivadão' (Eiró 26). The play is set in São Paulo on the eve of the declaration of independence (25 August–7 September 1822), and the plot revolves around the ill-fated love between a young man, Aires, from a wealthy family and Luísa, a descendant of slaves. Their lack of freedom to love – because of society's prejudice (as Luísa exclaims: 'Meu sangue não é puro ... ferve, queima-me! E quando lhe ouço falar em sernos felizes ... Não! nunca o seremos!' [Act I, Scene viii, 58]) – becomes a paradigm of the oppression experienced by Brazilians under colonial rule. As Rafael suggests in Act II, Scene xii:

O Brasil é uma terra do cativerio. Sim, todos aqui são escravos. O negro que trabalha seminu, cantando aos raios do sol; o índio que por um miserável salário é empregado na feitura de estradas e capelas; o salvagem, que, fugindo às bandeiras, vaga de mata em mata; o pardo a quem apenas se reconhece o direito de viver esquecido: o branco enfim, o branco orgulloso, que sofre de má cara a insolência das Cortes e o desdém dos europeus. Oh! quando cairem tôdas estas cadeias, quando êstes cativos todos se resgatarem, há de ser um belo e glorioso dia! (Eiró 79)

Like much Romantic drama, *Sangue limpo* is full of unexpected events, as Act III, Scene vii certainly illustrates. A liberated slave bursts into a social gathering, demands a drink and, when challenged by soldiers, confesses that he has killed Dom José, Aires's father, then stabs himself and dies (Eiró 93). The way is now open for Aires and Luisa to marry, a scene set against the shouts of 'Independência, ou morte!' (Act III, Scene x; Eiró 98) which are echoing in the streets outside. The play thus concludes on a strong note of reconciliation between high- and lower-class Brazilians, now united against the common enemy of the Portuguese. When *Sangue limpo* was performed, slavery was still in existence in Brazil and the ideology of the play appears to be pro-independence, pro-liberty, while at the same time expressing the inwardly-turning anger of the slaves whose time has not quite yet come.

## Essay

Perhaps the single most important post-independence essay is the *Carta de Jamaica* (1815) by Simón Bolívar (1783–1830). Bolívar is arguably one of the most important, if not the most important, icon of Latin America. According to a recent survey published in *The Guardian* which used the number of books about an individual as an indication of their world-wide fame, Bolívar emerges as the most famous Latin American ever to have lived. In a table of world icons Christ came first with 17,239 books, Shakespeare second with 9,801, and Bolívar 26th with 1,467 books, just pipped at the post by Beethoven (Kettle). Statues of Bolívar adorn the main squares of almost all the major cities of Spanish America – including, of course, Caracas (where he is admired so much that Venezuela has a city, a mountain, its international airport, its currency, its main university, main square, hospitals, streets, and even the country itself named after him – it is now the Bolivarian Republic of Venezuela), Bogotá, Lima, Quito, where he lived for a number of years during a crucial phase of his career, and La Paz (Bolivia, of course, was named after him). It is difficult to think of a figure who is more closely associated in the popular mind with the heroic feats of the independence movement in Spanish America (for further discussion see Hart, 'Blood, Ink and Pigment'). Bolívar's *Carta de Jamaica* is now revered as a classic. The letter is dated 6 September 1815, when Bolívar was gathering his strength and troops in preparation for his counter-attack from

Jamaica on Royalist forces in Venezuela and New Granada. Though written in response to a letter of enquiry from a sympathiser ('Contestación de un americano meridional a un caballero de esta isla'), the letter is in effect an independence manifesto. It begins by stating that the paths of Spain and its American colonies are now distinct; Spain is no longer the mother country but a 'desnaturalizada madrastra' (Bolívar 38). Bolívar then describes the population of the main political blocks of Spanish America, including Río de la Plata, Chile, Perú, Nueva Granada, Venezuela, New Spain, and the Caribbean (Puerto Rico and Cuba). That his letter is directed to Europe is suggested by his rhetorical question: '¿Y la Europa civilizada, comerciante y amante de la libertad, permite que una vieja serpiente, por sólo satisfacer su saña envenenada, devore la más bella parte de nuestro globo?' (Bolívar 41). Much of the rest of the letter is designed to persuade the Western powers to intervene in the struggle for independence then in full swing. Bolívar complains that Spain is sucking its colonies dry of wealth and, as a representative *criollo*, complains that his people have been excluded from office and power, 'ausentes del universo en cuanto es relativo a la ciencia del gobierno y administración del estado' (Bolívar 48). The political position that Bolívar subsequently fleshes out is intriguing; he argues that neither federalism nor democracy are entirely suitable for the newly-independent nations of Spanish America (Bolívar 53), and also argues against the notion of a republic (Bolívar 55). He concludes his essay by suggesting that Spanish America will achieve independence but different parts will do so in different ways (some democratic, some federal, some monarchical). It is clear from his concluding statements that his own political ideal is a strong, unified republic ('una sola nación con un solo vínculo que ligue sus partes entre sí y con el todo'; Bolívar 61). This, however, was not to be and twenty years later Spanish America was already well along the path of division. This letter was by no means the only one that Bolívar wrote during the turbulent years of independence; he wrote eighty-three letters to his allies in the independence movement during the period 1812–29 (Bolívar, *Documentos*) and most repeat his ideological repertoire: war against Spain, bring the European powers, especially England, into the conflict, and conserve unity after independence. But no letter puts these main points over as forcefully as the *Carta de Jamaica*.

One essayist whose work demonstrates some interesting points of overlap with Bolívar's is José Bonifácio de Andrade e Silva (1763–1838). Like Bolívar, Bonifácio de Andrade e Silva was intimately involved in the process whereby his native land achieved independence, so much so that he soon came to be known as the Patriarch of the Independence in Brazil. He also, like his Venezuelan counterpart, wrestled with issues such as slavery, the direction that the newly-independent state should take, and how power should used in the state for the good of all. No military man, Silva was a scientist, and one of the best of his age. Born into a wealthy family in Santos, São Paulo, Silva – like many of his contemporaries from well-to-do backgrounds (indeed like Bolívar) – went to Europe for his education. He studied mathematics, natural philosophy and the sciences at the University of Coimbra in Portugal and showed such aptitude, particularly in chemistry and mineralogy, that, in 1800, he was appointed professor of geology there. He went on to publish a series of essays and *memórias* on subjects as diverse as mineralogy, chemistry, horticulture and economics – his first essay, *Sobre as minas de caravão-de-pedra em Portugual,* was published in 1813 – and he is credited with being the discoverer of Petalite, a lithium-based mineral, while on a mining expedition in Sweden in the late 1790s.

Silva cuts more of a profile nowadays for his political views; he was personally involved in the independence of Brazil – in 1819 he urged Dom Pedro I to resist the political pressures emanating from Lisbon and, when independence was secured, he was awarded the high-ranking post of minister of interior and foreign affairs. He was a fully-fledged constitutionalist and this finally led to his downfall; as a result of his views (he argued that a constitution which simply exists on paper is worthless, and that 'a Constituição deve estar arraigada en nossas leis, establecimentos e costumes'; Silva, *Projetos*, 235), he came into opposition with Dom Pedro I over the issue of the role of the National Constituent Assembly of which he was president, and he was subsequently relieved of his post, and later exiled to France from 1823 until 1829. Silva was a passionate abolitionist, arguing that the slave trade was a crime against the eternal laws of justice and religion (Silva, *Projetos* 51), and, indeed, contrary to natural law (Silva, *Projetos* 60). What was the point, he argued, of forcing twenty slaves to ferry bags of sugar around when a cart or so could do the trick just as well (57)? Yet his support of the rights of the African slave led to a curious reversal of the argument used by Bartolomé de las Casas in the sixteenth century (see above p. 19) which had originally disadvantaged Africans; Silva argued that Indians were 'prejuiçosos, dorminhocos, pesados e voluptuosos' (Silva, *Projetos* 133), and, furthermore, that they were lazy and detested work (144), this despite his arguments in favour of equality for all in Brazil: 'Brasil é uma terra de igualdade. Igualdade no exercício dos direitos, igualdade nas pretensões legais, igualdade perante à justiça, igualdade nos impostos, igualdade no modo de adquirir, possuir e transmitir na propriedade' (Silva, *Projetos* 189). Clearly some portions of the populace were more equal than others! It was for this reason that he argued for national unity; the greatest impediment to the creation of that aim was not the Portuguese but the racial heterogeneity which characterised Brazil, and it was here that his knowledge of chemistry came into play:

> É da maior necessidade ir acabando tanta heterogeneidade física e civil; cuidemos, pois, desde já, em combinar sabiamente tantos elementos discordes e contrários e em amalgamar tantos metais diversos, para que saia um todo homogêneo e compacto, que se não esfacele ao pequeno toque de qualquer nova convulsão política. Mas que ciência química e que desteridade não são precisas aos operadores de tão grande e difícil manipulação? (Silva, *Memórias* 63)

This led him to propose the mulatto as the race of the future: 'O mulato deve ser a raça mais ativa e empreendedora; pois reúne a vivacidade impetuosa e a robustez do negro com a mobilidade e sensibilidade do europeu; o índio e naturalmente melancólico e apático' (Silva, *Projetos* 126). But a good mix would be black male with Indian female since the child would have his father's energy and his mother's good temperament (Silva, *Projetos* 156). Clearly Silva's metallurgical frame of mind meant that he was lacking in an awareness of the cultural determinants within the formation of national character, but his works continue to be of interest to later generations because of the ways in which he attempted to deal with notions such as race, character formation and national identity.

The most celebrated prose work written in Latin America in the nineteenth century was undoubtedly *Facundo o civilización y barbarie* (1845) by Domingo Faustino Sarmiento (1811–88). Like Echeverría and Mármol mentioned above, Sarmiento fell foul of Rosas's regime; after the unitarian defeat at the battle of Chañón in 1831, he was forced to flee to Chile, and he was to remain in exile throughout Rosas's dictatorship. *Facundo o civilización y barbarie*, as the title suggests, is primarily about the Argentine gaucho *caudillo*, Juan Facundo Quiroga (1793–1835), but also about the dichotomy in contemporary Argentina between civilisation and barbarism. Sarmiento's thesis is that Western culture was the only way forward and that the main problem with Argentina was its savage, untamed land. An important after-effect of Sarmiento's text was the policy in the last two decades of the nineteenth century in Argentina of 'gobernar es poblar' which led to the massive immigration of Italian and Spanish workers along with the ruthless decimation of the remaining Indian tribes in the Argentine hinterland, while simultaneously 'whitening' the population. Even though Sarmiento's text promotes Europe and the rapidly emerging United States as the paragons of the social model to be followed by Argentina, it also expresses a sneaking admiration for the 'natural savage' prototype (and here Sarmiento shows his Romantic credentials), typified by ruthless individuals such as Quiroga, known for his ability to trick individuals into confessing their guilt and for confronting man-eating tigers and winning (Chapter V, 1; Flores 203–4). It is precisely, Sarmiento argues, the struggle between civilization and barbarism that will define Argentina's literary culture:

> Si un destello de literatura nacional puede brillar momentáneamente en las nuevas sociedades americanas, es el que resultara de la descripción de las grandiosas escenas naturales y, sobre todo, de la lucha entre la civilización europea y la barbarie indígena, entre la inteligencia y la material; lucha imponente en América y que da lugar a escenas tan peculiares, tan características y tan fuera del círculo de ideas en que se ha educado el espíritu europeo, porque los resortes dramáticos se vuelven desconocidos fuera del país donde se toman, los usos sorprendentes y originales los caracteres. (Sarmiento 55–6)

Sarmiento goes on to repeat all the anecdotes which led to the creation of Quiroga's 'reputación misteriosa' (Chapter V, 2; Flores 206) which in effect does nothing to dampen its power:

> ¡Sombra terrible de Facundo, voy a evocarte, para que sacudiendo el ensangrentado polvo que cubre tus cenizas te levantes a explicarnos la vida secreta y las convulsiones internas que desgarran las entrañas de un noble pueblo! Tú posees el secreto: ¡revélanoslo! (Sarmiento 21)

Though the gaucho is a negative influence on Argentina's social progress, his mystery is clearly good for literature.


## The Multi-genre Writer

Gertrudis Gómez de Avellaneda (1814–73), although born in Cuba, spent much of her life in Spain. Avellaneda left Cuba for Spain in 1836 and, apart from a five-year period when she returned (1859–64), she resided for the remainder of her days in Spain, and, indeed, established her literary career there. She is without doubt one of the most significant women writers of the nineteenth century, and she wrote in the three main genres. Despite this, her candidacy in 1853 for membership in the Spanish Royal Academy of Letters was denied. Avellaneda's poetry typifies the Romantic mentality, is defiantly related to biographical events, and focuses above all on the themes of death and love and their interconnectedness. For this, in her view, she had a unique perspective as a woman since her gender provided her with the 'title of sovereignty in the immense sphere of the emotions', as she put it (Meyer 25). A frequently anthologised poem, 'Al partir', written, if we accept the poetic convention, on the boat as she left Cuba for Spain, emphasises the sense of fragmentation and loss associated with (self-imposed) exile. Typical of the Romantics, Avellaneda's view of love is of an all-powerful, chaotic and often malevolent force. Her two poems with the same title, 'A él', both dedicated to Ignacio de Cepeda y Alcalde with whom she had a stormy love affair soon after her arrival in Spain, abound in metaphors of nature and transcendance. The first shows the 'él' of the title as produced idealistically within nature before she meets her lover, and compares the fascination that her lover holds for her to that of the serpent for the bird, an animal with whom she often compares herself when in love (Gómez de Avellaneda 69). The second treats their love affair, now over, as guided by divine forces: 'No era tuyo el poder que irresistible / Postró ante ti mis fuerzas vencedoras / Quísolo Dios' (Gómez de Avellaneda 147). The metaphors used in the poem give an indication of the class-value of the backdrop against which their love affair is measured. The sixth stanza opens with the line, 'Cayó tu cetro, se embotó tu espada' (Gómez de Avellaneda 147), which points to the aristocratic/tragic nature of the love projected in the poem. Avellaneda's most famous poem, however, is 'A la muerte del célebre poeta cubano Don José

María de Heredia' dedicated to one of the many Latin American poets who died in their mid-thirties (Heredia [thirty-five], Plácido [thirty-five], Batres Montúfar [thirty-five]; Melgar was only twenty-five years old at death). Avellaneda uses the well-known *topos* of the death of a loved one to inquire into metaphysical matters. As we have already noted, Heredia was a fierce 'independentista' who was condemned to death for his political beliefs; little of this, however, surfaces in Avellaneda's elegy to him. Heredia is remembered as 'el férvido patriota' (l. 10; Gómez de Avellaneda 71), and the ideal for which he fought, his 'patria', is described as '¡Idolo puro de las nobles almas!' (l. 28), but the main emphasis of the poem diverts attention away from the political towards the transcendance of his ideal achieved through death. 'A la muerte del célebre poeta cubano Don José María de Heredia', thus, is an important statement of her own political position during the post-independence epoch. While Heredia was forced into exile from his country, Avellaneda accepted the colonial structure which underlay the Spanish monarchy (she wrote a poem of homage to Queen Isabel II, and the Spanish monarchs were godparents at her wedding to Domingo Verdugo y Massieu in 1855; Gómez de Avellaneda 134–38, 11), and appeared to place her faith in the dispensation of true justice in the next world.

Avellaneda's *Sab* (1841) is often remembered for its historical, anti-abolitionist content but there is more to *Sab* than first meets the eye. Set in Cuba in the early years of the nineteenth century when the Caribbean island was still a Spanish colony, this novel tells the story of a mulatto slave's love for his master's daughter, Carlota, with whom he spent most of his childhood. When Carlota finally decides to marry the son of a rich English privateer, Enrique son of Jorge Otway, the slave, Sab, dies heartbroken, leaving evidence of his love in a long, passionate letter he writes to Teresa, Carlota's maid. This letter, whose contents Carlota finally becomes aware of five years after Sab's death, is the finale to the novel. Though the story is verisimilar enough, the author is not eager to stress the realistic qualities of the plot, showing a fondness for the *deus ex machina* device so dear to the heart of the Romantics. Sab's brother, Luis, for example, dies soon after he is visited by Sab; Sab dies soon after his brother's death and, to underline the supernatural coincidence, at the precise time that Carlota and Enrique are pronouncing their marriage vows: 'Sab expiró a las seis de la mañana; en esa misma hora Enrique y Carlota recibían la bendición nupcial' (199). The characters, in a way which is reminiscent of the Romantic rather than the Realist mode, are larger than life: Enrique Otway, the English villain, only marries Carlota because of her money; Carlota is a mindless *criolla* who thinks only of love; Teresa, her long-suffering maid, is in denial; Sab, the noble savage, dies of love. Indeed, the stereotyping at times goes awry. This is clearest in the case of Sab, the enigma of this text. Sab bears little resemblance to the historical mulatto; he is more like a *criollo* disguised as a mulatto. This is made plain when he begins speaking to Enrique Otway in the dramatically charged opening chapter of the novel; Enrique is so impressed by Sab's speech, clothes and demeanour that he assumes he is a landowner. These signals of social, reinforced by spiritual, nobility continue throughout the novel, so that we almost forget that Sab is a mulatto. In this sense we can agree with Richard Jackson's conclusion about the novel:

> [t]hough camouflaged by [...] her antislavery pronouncements, Gómez de Avellaneda's false tears are nevertheless manifest in her apologetic descriptions of other slaves and in her penchant for portraying them as being tranquil, docile, and happy with their lot, indeed, even unaware of their misfortune. (*Black Image* 27)

If we look more closely at Sab as the symptom of a dilemma, his role becomes clearer. On one level the novel projects the personal anguish the author felt as a result of unrequited love but, on another level, it allegorises the national dilemma. Cuba, throughout the nineteenth century, was torn between two power factions, the *criollos* who wanted independence from Spain and the *peninsulares* who opposed such an idea. We only find reference to this historical dilemma in the novel if we assume that the veiling process has gone one step further to include the main characters, so that Sab stands for the *criollo* option just as Enrique stands for the *peninsular* option (in this scenario Carlota, standing for Cuba, would be the prize to be won as a result of this historical struggle). What makes this allegory stronger in the novel is that Sab's testament appears in the form of a letter; 'Carta de Sab' is the title of the last chapter of the novel. This letter reads like a reworking of Bolívar's *Carta de Jamaica*, since there are manifold references to Sab's desire to die for his country, although this theme has not been raised in the rest of the novel, and it strikes the reader as oddly inopportune. The veiling argument also works here, since Avellaneda was in the unusual situation of being a Cuban émigré living in Spain, and therefore not in a position to bite the hand that fed her. If we see the novel as an example of veiled self-expression, as it undoubtedly is, then the kernel of its meaning lies in its promotion of the female desire for sexual, political and emotional liberation even at the same time that the validity of this desire is negated. *Sab* the novel is itself a kind of post-factum linguistic event, like Sab's letter within its covers, since it is the only means whereby the desire for liberation could be expressed. In a sense, therefore, Avellaneda pronounces a death sentence on herself, since she places herself in a similar position to Sab's, the difference being that Sab dies when he speaks his truth, and Avellaneda distorts the ingredients of her personal narrative in order to avoid the kernel of her desire being openly expressed. *Sab* is, therefore, anything but a transparent anti-slavist novel; it is rather a subtly veiled document which expresses a feminist desire for liberation even while, simultaneously, debunking its validity.

Among Avellaneda's more famous plays are *Saúl* (1846) and *Baltasar* (1858). *Saúl* (completed 1846; first performed 1849) recounts in dramatic form the story of Saul, King of Israel who, despite being consecrated by Yahweh, later turns from Him and commits a number of evil deeds, including plotting to kill his son-in-law, David, because of jealousy of his fame and military valour (I Samuel 10–31). *Saúl* follows the biblical text in its main outline and even in some of the small details, such as Saul's visit to the medium at Endor and the resuscitation in bodily form of Samuel's spirit (I Samuel 28; Act IV, Scene vii). The few changes made to the plot, such as the suppression of the fact that David had other wives apart from Michal (Abigail and Ahinoam; I Samuel 25: 39–44) and the addition of the murder of Jonathan by his father, Saul (Act IV, Scene xiv; the Old Testament suggests that Jonathan committed suicide after his father; I Samuel 31: 3–4), streamline the play and emphasise the motif, in effect converting a narrative concerned with succession in the Royal House of Israel into a Romantic love story between David and Saul's daughter, who is hardly mentioned in the Bible. The biblical story, however, lends itself very well to this treatment since it includes a 'family romance', namely a generational conflict compounded by sexual love, which is one of the mainstays of the Romantic plot (Hart, *Other*, 7–18). Other devices in the play emphasise its Romantic pedigree. Act IV, for example, opens with a scene in which David and Jonathan dramatically reveal their identities by taking their masks off. There are abundant references to a malevolent fate, one example being Jonathan's question to his father (which will be proved correct): '¿La fatal dolencia/ Se anuncia ya con tétricos amagos?' (Gómez de Avellaneda 168), as well as to the supernatural world (Samuel's dramatic appearance as a ghost at the end of Act IV, Scene vii is reminiscent of the appearance of the statue in Zorrilla's *Don Juan Tenorio* [1844].) Yet, despite these Romantic elements, Avellaneda's play is distinct in that it does not exclude the possibility of a happy ending, something which typically Romantic plays could not have countenanced. *Saúl* indeed ends with the suggestion that, now Saul has died, David and Micol will ascend to the throne and live happily ever after. Unlike others of Avellaneda's dramas, there is no third party in a love triangle to mar the happiness of David and Micol (Harter 97). This is the reason why the play is called a 'biblical tragedy' by Avellaneda in her prologue (Gómez de Avellaneda 141), which we must assume to mean 'a play with a happy ending'. But, more important for our purposes, *Saúl* refocuses the biblical story from a personal and feminine rather than a social and male perspective; in effect Micol gets what she wants and her dream comes true. Avellaneda's play therefore contains glimpses of a feminine perspective in that, unlike the Book of Samuel which tells the story from the point of view of David and Jonathan, the main drama of *Saúl* is focused from the point of view of Micol and her maidservant Sela (Act I, Scenes ii–iii; Act I, Scene xii; Act II, Scene v; Act III, Scene i).

# 4
# Late Nineteenth-Century Literature

The last few decades of the nineteenth century were a crucial period in which the social role of the writer in Latin America was radically transformed. For the first time in history the Latin American writer was able to make a career as a writer. No longer at the beck and call of a Maecenal figure, he could make a living directly from the investment of his readers in his published work. The Argentine Eduardo Gutiérrez, for example, sold so many copies of his newspaper serial novel, *Juan Moreira* (1879) – it was serialized in *La Patria Argentina* from 28 November 1879 until 8 January 1880 and then re-issued as a book – that he managed to purchase a country estate in San Juan de Flores from the royalties (Hart, 'Public Execution' 675). Some writers of this period made a conscious decision to tailor their writing based on what their readers wanted; the Brazilian Bernardo Guimarães deliberately began to write potboilers since he knew he could make a living out them (see the discussion of *A escrava Isaura* below, pp. 118–19). This was the time when the novel, as the Mexican essayist, Ignacio Altamirano, suggested, 'dejando sus antiguos límites, ha invadido todos los terrenos y ha dado su forma a todas las ideas y a todos los asuntos' (quoted in Rama, *Crítica* 77), It was not only the novel which benefited from the enormous rise in readership; José Hernández's epic poem, *Martín Fierro* (Part I, 1872; Part II, 1879), was published in eleven editions in barely six years and sold 48,000 copies (Hart, 'Print Culture' 166). But there was a cost involved since this pandering to public taste inevitably involved a gear-shift down from the pedestal previously occupied by the writer as genius (in the sense of Shelley's 'unacknowledged legislator of mankind'); now the writer was rubbing shoulders with the *hoi polloi* as a journalist. Many writers of this period resented what was happening to art as a result. As the Colombian poet, Julián del Casal, put it:

> Journalism can be, in spite of its intrinsic hatred of literature, the benefactor that puts money in our pockets, bread on our table, and wine in our cup, but, alas, it will never be the tutelary deity that encircles our brow with a crown of laurel leaves. (quoted in González 86)

The main difference in terms of the writer's role in society during this period, compared with the previous century, was the absence of an explicit connection between print and state power (normally in the form of a position sponsored by the Viceroy) and the emergence of a new type of social value attached to print in the form of the newspaper article. If there is one thing which characterises the writers of the late nineteenth century it is their social position as a relayer of information about decisions taken by others. Many of the *modernistas*, for example, were journalists or diplomats, and some were both. This is, indeed, what journalists and diplomats have in common; one step removed from the decision-making process associated with statecraft, they relay that information on to other members of the society in which they live. The writers of this period, especially the *modernistas*, might be seen as 'diplomats' of the literary Word, using smooth words to relay truths dictated to them from on high.[1]

*Modernismo*, which should not be confused with its English cognate Modernism, or indeed the Brazilian movement *Modernismo* (see discussion in Chapter 5, pp. 142–5), is the first example of a genuinely Latin American literary movement, 'strong' enough in Bloom's phrase, to produce ripples in the Old World. With *modernismo*, and particularly the work of Rubén Darío, Latin America was no longer simply an echo chamber of bigger events happening elsewhere, but was now at the centre of its creative movement. While this is undeniable in artistic terms we would do well to heed Ángel Rama when he argues convincingly that *modernismo* was the cultural equivalent of the imperial expansion of capitalism which characterised the relationship between Latin America and Europe at the turn of the century (*Crítica* 19–33), the prototype being the export–import growth of Argentina's economy during the last two decades of the nineteenth century (Skidmore and Smith 44–38). *Modernismo* was an intrinsically literary movement spearheaded by the Nicaraguan poet, Rubén Darío (1867–1916), and its dates are normally given as emerging in 1888 (with the publication of Darío's *Azul...*) and disappearing off the literary horizon by 1916 (the year of Darío's death), including a period of decline from 1910 until 1916. *Modernismo*'s gradual movement of crescendo followed by a diminuendo after the apex around the turn of the century is best understood in visual terms (see Figure 1).

The main sources of inspiration for the *modernistas* were not Spanish but French poets, particularly the Parnassians and the Symbolists. The main themes were aestheticism, exoticism, cosmopolitanism, escapism, scepticism, indifference to moral issues, fascination with death, pessimism and melancholy. The metaphors and symbols of the *modernistas* typically refer to an ideal realm of regal splendour; their favorite symbols of elegance are the swan, the peacock, the lily, precious gems, and the nocturne.

Many writers, and particularly the *modernistas*, however, were not content with their new social role. While they were protective of their freedom to say what they wanted, they were disgruntled by the lack of stable employment

---

[1] For a short description of the careers of the *modernistas*, see Schulman and Picon Garfield which has a very helpful short biography for each poet included in the anthology. It is striking how similar the careers of the writers of this period are. It is important to note that there is a perceptible paradigm-shift from the role of the writer in the Romantic era – epitomised by Bello the legislator – to the *modernista*, typically a journalist/diplomat.

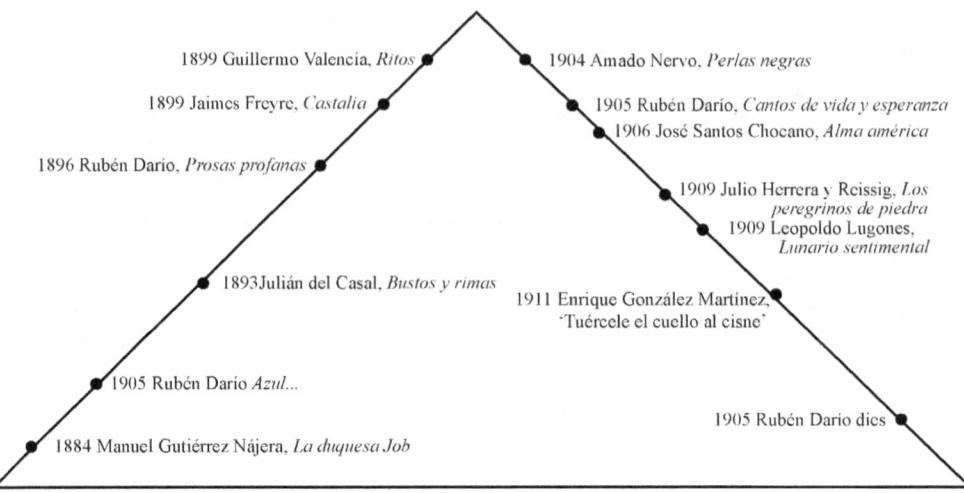

based on that ability. Manuel Gutiérrez Nájera, in particular, was depressed by what he saw as the social demeaning of the writer. Even brilliant writers such as the Greek dramatists Aristophanes and Aeschylus, he argued, would have ended up as third-rate hacks in the nineteenth century (quoted in Rama, *Crítica* 85). For many of the writers of the period, literature was, in Lafleur's word, a 'pretext', a prelude to greater things (Lafleur 14). This period was also accompanied by an unprecedented growth of literary societies whose aim was to provide a forum for the reading and discussion of literature. One of the most successful of these literary societies was the Ateneo de Buenos Aires, officially inaugurated on 26 April 1893, presided over by Carlos Guido Spano, and which met in a house on the calle Florida, no. 783 (Lafleur 15).

Important precursors of the *modernista* movement were Salvador Díaz Mirón (1853–1928), Manuel Gutiérrez Nájera (1859–95), Julián del Casal (1863–93) and José Asunción Silva (1865–96); the one thing linking these poets is their attention to the technical art of poetic composition. Díaz Mirón's striking poem, 'Ejemplo', for instance, inspired by the sight of a dead man hanging from a tree, is written in alexandrines which have three *esdrújulo* rhymes ('patíbulo', l. 10; 'turíbulo', l. 12; 'Tíbulo', l. 14). Despite the stench of the man's corpse, as the poem concludes, the countryside around him is worthy of an elegiac poem by the Latin poet, Tibullus (59–19 BC) (Schulman and Picón Garfield 53–5). Gutiérrez Nájera's best poem, 'Mis enlutadas', has sixteen five-line stanzas, each stanza combining different metrical patterns, with the normal pattern being hendecasyllables (ll. 1 and 3), heptasyllables (l. 2), and pentasyllables (l. 5); this descending pyramidal metric structure echoes formally the semantic movement of the poem which searches out the sadness contained within the poet's subconscious, employing a confessional cadre. One of Julián del Casal's best poems, 'Crepuscular', focuses on a seascape at dusk in which images of violence and disharmony abound; the sunset is compared to the sun dripping from a 'split open stomach' (l. 1), the noise of seagulls becomes a 'chirrido agudo' (l. 6), and the seaweed is described as covered with 'infecto lodo' (l. 14). This dissonance is echoed on a formal level by the metric structure of the poem; the five quatrains are dodecasyllables except for the fifth line ('Alzan sus moles húmedas los arrecifes') which has thirteen syllables and introduces a note of barely audible dissymmetry into the poem. Asunción Silva, for his part, in his most famous poem, 'Nocturno' (1894), written to express his anguish at the death of his sister, evinces a bold desire to reformulate the stanzaic structures which had traditionally modelled the expression of poetic thought until then, combining long with short lines and repeating phrases as if they were refrains. Also striking about this poem is its refusal to retreat to the world of Greek mythology or Christian symbolism; its point of reference is the quotidian, itself suggested by the recourse to a conversational tone in opposition to the abstract dignity of rhymed verse. In this, Silva was more prescient than Darío about the direction that twentieth-century poetry would follow.

Rubén Darío (1867–1916) dominated the literary horizon of Spanish America at the turn of the twentieth century. The narrative of his life – born an orphan, perpetually travelling either as a correspondent for *La Nación* or in search for new experiences, a string of unhappy and passionate love affairs on different continents – suggests perpetual displacement and, indeed, centrelessness. This is a motif that binds together what are normally seen as the three stages of his work, which centre around *Azul...* (1888), *Prosas profanas* (1896) and *Cantos de vida y esperanza* (1905). *Azul...* combines short prose poems in the Baudelairean style with fifteen poems dedicated, in the main, to weather, seasons, legendary Greek figures and famous contemporary poets. The opening prose poem, 'El rey burgués', sets the tone for the whole collection in its affirmation of a non-bourgeois, aristocratic type of art which rejects the dictates of commercialism. The most striking characteristic of *Prosas profanas* was, certainly for readers of the time, its innovatory versification. In the collection of poems, Darío mixed half-conventional forms – sonnets whose rhyme was orthodox but which had more than the traditional eleven-syllable lines (most were French-inspired alexandrines such as 'El cisne'; Darío 587–88) – with unconventional forms such as the elegy to Paul Verlaine, 'Responso', which followed a syllabic pattern of 14–14–7 throughout (a sort of inflated 'copla de pie quebrado'), the 'Elogio de la seguidilla' (Darío 586) which resurrected an irregular Castilian metre not used since the Renaissance, and 'La página blanca' which combines assonant rhyme with a gradually increasing ametricality (Darío 588–89), among many other variations. Dario's 'galicismo mental', as Juan Valera called it, led him to seek an ethnically white poetic ideal; as he suggested in the prologue to *Prosas profanas*:

¿Hay en mi sangre alguna gota de sangre de África, o de indio chorotega o nagrandano? Pudiera ser, a despecho de mis manos de marqués; mas he aquí que veréis en mis versos princesas, reyes, cosas imperiales, visiones de países lejanos o imposibles: ¡qué queréis!, yo detesto la vida y el tiempo en que me tocó nacer. (Darío 546)

Indeed, many of the poems explicitly follow the blueprint set out here. 'Era un aire suave', for example, describes a utopian social gathering hosted by Eulalia the marchioness and attended by Greek gods and goddesses such as Terminus (Pluto), Diana, Eros, and Philomela. 'Divagación' likewise invites ('¿Vienes?') the reader to accompany him on his travels to a utopian land which is defiantly cosmopolitan: stanzas 1–14 situate us in ancient Greece and France (though the former is refracted through the latter: 'Amo más que la Grecia de los griegos / la Grecia de la Francia'; Darío 553); stanzas 15–22 turn to Italy and Germany, while stanzas 23–31 turn to the Far East, China, Japan and India. Throughout these visits to far-off places, the emphasis is on exotic love; as stanza 25 begins, 'Ámame en chino' (Darío 555). The poet's lover, as the comparison suggests, will feel attracted to the poet because of his wisdom, although the reference to 'mi unicornio cuerno de oro' also points to a sexual latency in the poet's gesture. 'Sonatina' follows a similar line of reasoning, although it is now the poet who arrives from afar to awaken the imprisoned princess of his dreams, like Sleeping Beauty, with a kiss: 'el feliz caballero que te adora sin verte, / y que llega de lejos, vencedor de la Muerte, / a encenderte los labios con su beso de amor' (Darío 557). What is important about these poems is the connection they assert between the death implied in the statues which embody culture and the penned-in nature of the female beloved as projected in Darío's dreams, a theme which occurs repeatedly in *Prosas profanas*. In 'Yo persigo una forma', for example, we find a combination of dreamscapes which include an impossible embrace between the poet and the Venus of Milo statue (l. 4), and between the poet and Sleeping Beauty (l. 12). The swan in the poem operates not only as a symbol of the aristocratic ideal but also as a sign of the ambiguous nature of the poetic universe created by the poet himself. The poem concludes with an image of 'el cuello del gran cisne blanco que me interroga' (Darío 622), indicating a point of crisis in the poet's symbol-creating process.

Three poets – Ricardo Jaimes Freyre (1868–1933), Amado Nervo (1870–1919), and Guillermo Valencia (1873–1943) – are normally considered to be part of the *modernista* inner circle, suggesting their proximity in poetic terms to an ideal epitomised by Darío's poetry. While seeming at first quaint, it is perhaps logical that Freyre should have lighted upon a Nordic environment for his poetic projections since the country in which he grew up – Bolivia – especially in its northern regions such as Lake Titicaca, has cold, hostile weather. But, at the same time, Freyre's rhetorical gesture shows how other-culture-orientated the *modernistas* were. His poem 'El camino de los cisnes' from *Castalia bárbara* (1899), for example, re-focuses Darío's swan within the framework of a Viking burial (Schulman and Picón Garfield 179). Amado

Nervo's poem, 'Como blanca teoría por el desierto' from *Los jardines interiores* (1905), in its emphasis on the comparison between his spiritual/writerly emptiness and the vastness of the desert, is ostensibly a re-writing of Darío's poem, 'La página blanca' from *Prosas profanas* (1896) (Darío 588–89) in neo-Catholic terms. Valencia's best poem, 'Cigüeñas blancas', from *Ritos* (1899) is a long, meditative piece of forty-seven cross-rhyme, hendecasyllabic quatrains and one five-line concluding stanza which takes its point of departure from a phrase from Petronius's *Satyricon* 'ciconia pietatis cultrix'; a group of storks are evoked in a stanza which periodically recurs as 'la augusta calma de mejores días' (line 36; Schulman and Picón Garfield 204). The poem is *modernista* in its evocation of *topoi* such as the pictorial, the melancholic, the musical, cosmopolitanism and the conflict between religion and sex, but striking in its evocation of a Latin culturalist backdrop (of which the *Satyricon* is the centrepiece), and its exchange of Darío's swan for the stork.

The decline of *modernismo* was decisively signalled in 1911 by the publication of 'Tuércele el cuello al cisne' by Enrique González Martínez (1871–1952); as the first line went: 'Tuércele el cuello al cisne de engañoso plumaje' (Schulman and Picón Garfield 197). Two poets whose names are associated with the latter phase of *modernismo* are Julio Herrera y Reissig (1875–1910) and Leopoldo Lugones (1874–1938). In the work of both poets, which ranks among some of the best written by the *modernistas*, the *modernista* ideal is taken to such an extreme that the cracks in its ideological superstructure begin to appear. Herrera y Reissig's 'La vida' (written in 1903 but published in *Las pascuas del tiempo* in 1920), for example, demonstrates precisely a dissonant figure; the poem begins as a fairy-tale narrative about the poet chasing his beloved and ends unexpectedly as the poet's beloved turns into a man and pierces his heart with a sword blow. Likewise 'Solo verde-amarillo para flauta: llave de U' (1901) turns the *modernista* pursuit of musicality into a hodgepodge of sound written in the 'key of U' (Schulman and Picón Garfield 250). Like Herrera y Reissig, though more ostentatiously than his compatriot, Lugones mercilessly unravelled the poetic threads of *modernismo*. In *Lunario sentimental* (1909), for example, Lugones builds upon the ironic and parodic vein of *Los crepúsculos*; the opening poem of that collection, 'A mis cretinos', effectively sets the tone. The moon is lauded as the inspiration of his verse, but rather than the wistful poetry of the early *modernistas* we meet an aggressive voice which brings all those notions crashing to earth; for greater effect, Lugones shortens the lines of his poetry, making them punchier:

> A ella da en obra pingüe
> poéticos tributos
> por sus dobles cañutos
> mi zampoña bilingüe.

Rather than Orpheus's lyre, Lugones projects himself as paying tribute to the moon with a rustic flute; his *zampoña* is 'bilingual', perhaps, since his verse will be using Spanish to refer to an American reality. Lugones's later experiments with free verse, such as in 'La blanca soledad', *El libro fiel*, are important indicators of the mood of the literary times which, within the next decade, would discard the heritage of *modernismo* and, to quote González Martínez's words, give the final 'twist' to the swan's neck.[2]

**Postmodernismo**

There is an intriguing group of poets writing at the turn of the century who were not included in the *modernista* group, and were not quite part of the avant-garde movement, and who have, for want of a better title, been labelled members of the *postmodernismo* movement. Ramón López Velarde (1888–1921) is normally listed as a member, and the distinctive feature of his work is its private perspective. In particular, his poetry has a *fin de siècle* feel about it in that Catholicism and sin form the ideological backdrop for the anguished investigation of sexual feelings. Many of the key images – the projection of womanhood as purity, mixing up of the codes of sex and religion, melancholy, the nocturne as backdrop – are culled from the *modernistas*.

While the male poets of this period were busily setting up genealogies for themselves, the female poets of this period, such as Delmira Agustini (1886–1914), Gabriela Mistral (1889–1957), Alfonsina Storni (1892–1938) and Juana Ibarbourou (1895–1938) found themselves ostracised from the literary establishment. Agustini's work is, indeed, an intriguing example of the halfway house of women's writing at the turn of the century, for it is a type of writing in which two ideologies – one female-specific and one male-specific – are vying for supremacy in her discourse. An analysis of the image-universe of her poetry, for example, shows that she rewrites – and in the process feminises – the image-universe of the *modernistas*. 'El cisne', for example, opens with a typical dreamy *modernista* landscape in which an aristocratic swan is pictured swimming around a lake. From the fourth stanza on, however, the swan's sexual nature is emphasised, and, as the final two lines of the poem read: 'el cisne asusta de rojo, / y yo de blanca doy miedo!' (Agustini 57).

Mistral, for her part, is something of an enigma. The first Spanish American writer to receive the Nobel Prize (1945), schoolteacher and cultural educator (she was invited to work with José Vasconcelos in his cultural enterprise in Mexico in 1922), her poetry at first glance tends to confirm the traditional notion of her as a female poet frustrated by her lack of luck in love, and her consequent inability to have children.[3] Poems such as 'El niño solo' and 'La mujer estéril'

---

[2] One other significant poet of this period not discussed in this section is José Santos Chocano (1875–1935); for a good overview of his work, see Franco 165–67.

[3] This image of Mistral was enhanced by a tragic incident which occurred in her personal life. While a young woman living in Monterde, Chile, Mistral fell in love with a young office worker, Romelio Ureta; although they were in love, they did not marry, and, tragically, for reasons which have never been satisfactorily explained, Ureta took his own life in 1909.

from *Desolación*, 'Sueño grande' and 'Piececitos' from *Ternura*, tend to underline the traditional image of Mistral as a loving, maternal figure. But there is another side of Mistral's poetry which is much more disturbing. 'Los sonetos de la muerte', for example, opens with an image of Mistral imagining how she will cradle the body of the young man she has lost within the earth (an association common throughout her work between femaleness and nature). The poem specifically contrasts the togetherness that she and her dead lover will share and the death that is presented as if instituted by 'los hombres'. The final tercet of this sonnet underlines this point even more graphically: 'Me alejaré cantando mis venganzas hermosas, / ¡porque a ese honor recóndito la mano de ninguna / bajará a disputarme tu puñado de huesos!' (Chang-Rodríguez 343). There is almost a smug satisfaction in these lines; no woman can take her man from her now, since she is able to hold his bones in her hand. The notion of possession outlined here – one which not even death can dispute – is one which contradicts the homely image of Mistral we derive from other poems.

Storni's poetry, for its part, provides a stark contrast with Mistral's; it contains a feminist structure of feeling in that it turns away from Mistral's maternalism and focuses instead on the writer's identity as a new woman of the modern world. Her view of feminism has a suffragette-like wisdom about it; beginning with the premise that 'life is not an equation perceivable by the eyes of men', Storni reasoned that feminism 'is nothing more than man's managerial failure to achieve by legal means the necessary equilibrium of human happiness' ('An Old Story', in Meyer 102). Storni's most famous poem, 'Tú me quieres blanca', turns the tables abruptly on the male stereotype of womanhood. If the man wants his woman to be so perfect then he must be perfect too; she advises him, with tongue in cheek, to go to the mountains, clean his mouth, live in a cabin, eat bitter roots, sleep on the hoarfrost, talk to the birds and get up at dawn. Then, only then, as the poem finishes: 'preténdeme blanca, / preténdeme nívea, / preténdeme casta' (Chang-Rodríguez 352). The short verse form Storni uses for this poem – the hexasyllable – emphasises its jocularity.

## Brazilian Parnassianism and Symbolism

In seeming to find a literary idiom in the second half of the nineteenth century which would allow for some intellectual independence from its former colonial master, Brazil – and in this it was similar to Spanish-speaking republics in the New World – looked to France for inspiration. This mental Gallicism became gradually more pronounced as the century wore on, reaching its zenith in the work of the three poets who were most influenced by Parnassianism, Olavo Bilac (1865–1918), Alberto de Oliveira (1857–1937) and Raimundo Correia

---

A legend thereby grew that much of the poetry Mistral was subsequently to write was inspired by the abrupt (and undeserved) loss of Ureta's love and of the children that she would have borne him had they married.

(1860–1911), and the two who fell under the spell of Symbolism, namely João de Cruz e Sousa (1861–98) and Afonso Henriques da Costa Guimarães (1870–1921).

Théophile Gautier, the pope of French Parnassianism, emphasised formal perfection as the golden key to poetic beauty, comparing writing poetry to the chiselling of words, and we find some of this obsession with formal perfection in Alberto de Oliveira's poetry. His 'Fantástica', for example, consists of seven hendecasyllabic quartets each rhyming ABAB describing a beautiful princess in rigor mortis:

> E inda ornada de gemas e vestida
> De tiros de matiz de ardentes côres,
> Uma bela princesa está sem vida
> Sôbre um toro fantástico de flôres. (Cândido, *Presença*, vol. 2, 227)

The rigidity of the verse scheme is clearly intended to echo the rigidity of its subject. 'Vaso Grego' asks us to imagine a poet (no doubt Oliveira himself) drinking from a Greek vase, thereby stressing the connection between classical and contemporary culture in a way which is redolent of Rubén Darío's poetry (see above pp. 109–10). His 'O Lírio intangível' draws attention to the deep psychological frustration underlying the desire for art for art's sake which is at the heart of the Parnassian creed. It opens with a description of the poet's dream in which he is drowning in a swamp:

> Vi-me em sohno a nadar por um pantâno escuro,
> Inteiramente escuro.
> A água era grossa e infecta, o ar adensado e impuro;
> E eu, agitado e aflito, a submerger-me hondo. (Cândido, *Presença*, vol. 2, 233)

It soon becomes clear that this 'dark swamp' is a metaphor for the world in which we live, from which the poet desperately wants to escape; this escape is offered to him via a 'grande lírio branco', an obvious metaphor for death. Despite his frantic search for the lily, however, the poem ends with a vision of the poet drowning in the 'água [...] grossa e infecta' (Cândido, *Presença*, vol. 2, 233).

Raimundo Correia's poetry, like Oliveira's, has recourse to classical motifs which he patches together to form a backdrop to his thoughts about life; intriguingly, though, he often tropicalises Mount Olympus so that Zeus's nymphs suddenly find themselves in the jungle. As the third stanza of the sonnet 'Tristeza de Momo' suggests: 'Fauno o indigita; a Náide o caçoa; / Sátiros vis, da mais indigna laia, / Zomban. Não há quem dêle se condoa!' (Cândido, *Presença*, vol. 2, 236). Likewise his 'Banzo', a hexasyllabic sonnet, begins to break down under the strain of its distressed vision of the continuing effect of slavery in Brazil; the dislocation of the images, the breaking up of the lines, the use of suspension points – all indicate the dismantling of the cold objectivity of Gautier's sculptured poetry (Cândido, *Presença*, vol. 2, 239–40). Whether or not we agree that Correia's poety is 'without genius' and 'superficial' as Cândido argues (*Presença*, vol. 2, 124–5), it is certainly the case that the final impression derived of Correia's poetry is of a transculturated, Brazilian form of Parnassianism which some would find jarring.

The most accomplished of the Brazilian Parnassians was Olavo Bilac. In his hands the sonnet form becomes graceful and the semantic flow is not hindered. Poem XXXI of *Via Lactea* describes the pain the poet feels when his lover's name is uttered by others, and concludes:

> Porque teu nome é para mim o nome
> De uma pátria distante e idolotrada,
> Cuja saudade ardente me consome:
> E ouvi-lo é ver a eterna primavera
> E a eterna lua da terra abençoada,
> Onde, entre flôres, teu amor me espera. (Cândido, *Presença*, vol. 2, 249–50)

His poem 'In extremis' is a powerful expression of the vision of himself on his death bed, his fingers frozen, his heart going cold, watching his beloved writhing in agony at the sight of his death. It is in many ways a typically Romantic poem in that it visualises death from 'the other side' in that post-corporeal state to which the Romantics were irresistibly drawn ('E eu morrendo! e eu morrendo, vendo-te, e vendo o sol'; Cândido, *Presença*, vol. 2, 255), and yet it is able to retain a verse structure despite the emotional urgency; the result is not a displeasing one. His most Parnassian and possibly his most famous poem, however, is 'A um poeta' in which he admonishes a younger poet, Beneditino, in the sacred labour of composing poetry. Away from the madding crowds, the poet is instructed: 'Trabalha, e teima, e lima, e sofre, e sua!' (Cândido, *Presença*, vol. 2, 256), the verb 'limar' having been lifted directly from Gautier's image system. The end result of such labour will be that 'a imagem figue nua, / Rica, mas sóbria, como um templo grego' (Cândido, *Presença*, vol. 2, 256), the Greek temple being an icon of sober and measured beauty to which poetry aspires. The last three lines of the poem, in their simplicity and beauty, are an appropriate testimony to Bilac's classical ideal: 'Porque a Beleza, gêmea da Verdade, / Arte pura, inimiga do artifício, / É a fôrça e a graça na simplicidade' (Cândido, *Presença*, vol. 2, 256).

Symbolism was based on the need for poetry to possess a suggestive vagueness; as Stéphane Mallarmé, the leading light of the Symbolists in France put it: 'Évoquer, dans une ombre exprès, l'objet tu, par des mots allusifs, jamais directs, se réduisant à du silence égal, comporte tentative proche de créer' (Mallarmé 304). Many of João de Cruz e Sousa's poems seem painted with precisely this type of brush; it is quite possible to read his poems and then wonder afterwards what they were about. The opening stanza of 'Antífona' provides some notion of what is at stake here:

> O Formas alvas, brancas, Formas claras
> de luares, de neves, de neblinas!
> O Formas vagas, fluidas, cristalinas ...
> Incensos dos turíbulos das aras ... (Cândido, *Presença*, vol. 2, 295)

Many of the nouns are abstract ('formas') or are fluid and gaseous ('luares', 'neves', 'neblinas'), and even the adjectives ('vagas', 'fluidas') contrive to make the referent of the poem difficult to define; this gives the poem a sense of a shimmering, sensorial experience which is not visually defined, the equivalent perhaps of what the Impressionists were attempting to do at the time in their paintings. Afonso de Guimarães's poetry points in a similar direction, though he often gives a Christian mystical twist to the evocation of formless forms, as evident in his poem 'Ária do luar' (Cândido, *Presença*, vol. 2, 310).

## Narrative Poetry

The most significant narrative poem of the latter half of the nineteenth century was *Martín Fierro* (Part I, 1872; Part II, 1879) by José Hernández (1834–86). This grand poem, seen by some as the epic of the *gauchos*, faithfully represents the speech, life-style and world-view of the *gauchos* who were soon to be brushed aside by the new urban-based Argentina which mushroomed in the last two decades of the nineteenth century. Unlike many of the works considered so far in this chapter, *Martín Fierro* was an extremely popular work, so popular in fact that Hernández was obliged to write a second instalment of the poem, *La vuelta de Martín Fierro* (1879) because of public demand:

> Entrego a la benevolencia pública, con el título de *La vuelta de Martín Fierro*, la segunda parte de una obra que ha tenido una acogida tan generosa que en seis años se han repetido once ediciones con un total de cuarenta y ocho mil ejemplares. (quoted in Rama, *Crítica* 74)

A far cry, indeed, from the early days of the century when Bello berated a colleague for sending 750 copies of his book to Buenos Aires, thinking that twenty would be sufficient. Hernández had some first-hand experience of the *gaucho* way of life, although he was not one himself; as a young man he was sent to the southern frontier and participated in the warfare which the *gauchos* were waging on the Indians. *Martín Fierro* is perhaps best read as a counter-response to Sarmiento's *Civilización y barbarie* (see below pp. 101–2) in which the odds are firmly stacked against the *gaucho* way of life. Hernández was a supporter of the federalists and, when they were defeated in 1872, was forced to flee to Brazil. His text is thus to be seen not only in terms of a literary creation but also as a political statement which, through the *gauchos*, offers justification for the rough-and-tumble of the federalist way of life.

In *Martín Fierro* Hernández presents the *gauchos* as a misunderstood, misrepresented group of individuals forced to fight a war against the Indians in which they have no special advantage to gain. Martín Fierro's story is presented as a typical life history; wrenched from the domestic bliss of his home life on the *pampas* he is sent to the frontier to fight against savage Indians, for which he receives no monetary recompense, suffers hunger and inclement weather and lives in perpetual fear of death. To cap it all, when he finally decides to desert and return home, he finds his wife and children have disappeared; Martín's life from this point onwards becomes a monotonous ritual of drinking, tavern fights, murder and perpetual fleeing from the law. In Cantos X–XII we hear Cruz's life story which bears a striking resemblance to Martín's. The poem is written throughout in six-line octosyllabic stanzas and in such a way as to echo the spoken style of the *gaucho*. Because of the violence of the *gauchos'* actions (the tavern scene when Martín crudely insults a black woman and then stabs her husband to death outside is particularly notable; Part I, Canto VII), they are presented as human enough. Martín's repentant feelings after his wrongdoings and his grief at finding his family scattered (Part I, Canto IX) give all appearances of sincerity. The destruction of his family home led to a restless life, a fact he often laments: 'Soy un gaucho desgraciado, / no tengo dónde ampararme, / ni un palo donde rascarme' (Part I, Canto IX, ll. 285–90; Flores 240). The mixture here of sorrow at loneliness coupled with defiance of social convention is at the heart of the *gauchos'* troubled world-vision. In *Martín Fierro* Hernández expresses the cultural dilemma underlying the gaucho's world-view with a freshness of vision which countless imitations have failed to surpass.

## The Novel by Instalments

The novel of the second half of the nineteenth century was dominated by arguably Latin America's most important novelist, Joaquim Maria Machado de Assis (1839–1908) (for discussion of his work, see below pp. 131–7), but there were a number of novels published in Latin America during this period, some of them serialized, which are nowadays seen as of secondary status. According to the teleological reading of the nineteenth-century novel already sketched in Chapter 3, the Spanish American novel comes of age in *El Periquillo Sarniento* after a succession of early premonitory drafts stretching back to the personal-experience chronicles of writers such as Núñez Cabeza de la Vaca's *Naufragios* and with an important transition phase expressed in texts such as Carlos Sigüenza y Góngora's *Infortunios de Alonso Ramírez* (1690). But while a teleological reading has its advantages, we should avoid seeing the text which initiates the Spanish American novel as solely produced by antecedent classics and see it rather in the context of popular narrative discourse. As we have seen, the newspaper press in Spanish America burgeoned at the turn of the nineteenth century and with this came, as the century progressed, a new beast, the novel published in instalments. The apogee of the *folletín* occurred roughly in the period 1880–1910, and all over Spanish America, though most clearly in

Buenos Aires, its growth coincided with the expansion of a literate urban proletariat. As has been pointed out, it 'served as a mediation between literature, consumed only by a small educated elite, and the masses'; its *criollista* ideology served a public 'in transition between the country and the city or who had recently entered Argentina as immigrants' (Rowe and Schelling 98). Print-runs were huge compared to those normal for works of literature of the same period; while less than 1,000 copies was usual for what we normally call a work of literature, the *folletín* would be published in tens of thousands of copies, and theatrical versions could also aid circulation.[4] This was the era when the Latin American writer was beginning to make a living out of writing, but to do so he had to take account of what his readers wanted. Indeed, the works he was most likely to be commissioned to write were Romantic page-turners, the distant forebears of the Mills and Boon novels which populate bookshops in today's airports.

The Brazilian writer, Bernardo Guimarães (1825–84), offers an interesting example of this phenomenon. As David T. Haberly has pointed out:

> Bernardo Guimarães, unlike almost all other Brazilian writers of the 19th century, published substantial amounts of both poetry and prose. This division of labour, in part, reflects his constant desire for popularity; Guimarães did not begin publishing fiction until after other writers had established the Brazilian novel and created a market for national fiction. (Haberly 395)

His work has normally been seen as having those defects we now associate with a writer-on-demand: 'a certain technical and intellectual laziness'; 'writing simple narratives designed for unsophisticated readers'; 'secondary status' (Haberly 395). Cândido, furthermore, has mentioned the following defects: 'idealização descabida, ênfase psicológica e verbal, banalidade e excesso dos adjetivos, caracterização mecânica dos personagens' (Cândido, *Formação*, vol. 2, 239). Despite some of its technical flaws, however, Guimarães's work is significant in the ways in which it addresses key contemporary social issues. His novel, *A escrava Isaura* (1875), for example, a classic abolitionist novel, is similar to many other novels published during this period in Spanish America in that it uses a love story in order to allegorise the injustice of slavery. A marked departure from the poetic style of *Iracema*, *A escrava Isaura* has a fast-moving plot set in real places (Rio de Janeiro, the municipality of Campos de Goitacases) and verisimilar though somewhat stereotypical people (Isaura the beautiful slave, Leôncio the manipulative and lascivious *fazendeiro*, Malvina the jealous wife, Alvaro the knight in shining armour, and Belchior the ugly gardener), and it downplays description in favour of lively dialogue. The plot is simple enough. Despite his recent marriage to Malvina, Leôncio has his eye on a slave he owns, Isaura, famous not only for her good looks but also for her education (she was

---

[4] This is essentially what happened with *Juan Moreira*; the first theatrical version was put on in the Politeama Theater in Buenos Aires in 1884 (Dauster 29), and many others followed; for further discussion, see the Theatre section.

educated by Leôncio's mother who took great care in bringing her up). His evil exploitation of her becomes a metaphor for the injustices of the slave trade (the novel came out in the decade before slavery was banned in Brazil and offers a barometric reading of the growing resentment about slavery which prevailed in the society of the time). Intriguingly enough, Isaura – given her beauty and the different bloods coursing through her veins – comes to symbolise the national archetype in its most perfect form; 'é uma perfeita brasileira', as Malvina's brother, Henrique, comments (Guimarães 20). Isaura's misfortunes are presented via the imagery of Romanticism rather than, say, the detailed description of the drudgery of menial labour; she feels 'persecuted', 'martyred', her life is 'made bitter' by those around her, and – most important of all – she suffers 'a desgraça de nascer cativa' (Guimarães 43). When her life becomes intolerable she escapes with her father, Miguel, and they settle in Recife. A rich landowner there, Alvaro, falls in love with her and this love is couched in the standard imagery we associate with Romanticism; Isaura becomes more than simply a woman: 'Não é uma mulher; é uma fada, é um anjo, é uma deusa' (*A escrava Isaura* 57). Yet – and again in order to fulfil, it would appear, the Romantic stereotype – their love is doomed; just as it seems that Isaura will find love with Alvaro, she is revealed at a ball to be nothing more than a runaway slave, and returned to her rightful owner, Leôncio. He, overcome with jealousy and desiring revenge since Isaura will not give in to his advances, decides to humiliate her by forcing her to marry the ugly gardener. So far so Romantic. But then the Gordean knot of Romanticism is broken by an unforeseen turn of events which gives the impression of being more of a *deus ex machina* than a logical working-out of the basic plot. Alvaro returns, just as Isaura is about to be married off, reveals that Leôncio is a debtor and that he now in effect owns all of Leôncio's possessions – including of course Isaura – and offers her his hand in marriage. A melodramatic last touch, Leôncio, overcome with despair, shoots his brains out. A rather curious mix of Realism and Romanticism, the final dénouement of the novel gives to understand that true love can conquer all, that slavery is an unlawful and abhorrent practice, and that a union between the beautiful, mixed-blood woman and the honest, chivalrous landowner holds the key to Brazil's future success. *A escrava Isaura* is, of course, very different from Machado de Assis's paradigm-changing masterpiece, *Memórias Póstumas de Brás Cúbas* (1880), which was published only five years later than Guimarães's novel, and does not have the literary quality of the latter, but it is significant in terms of its market penetration (illustrated by the fact that there have been two very popular soap opera versions of the novel – the Rede Globo 1976 version which had 167 episodes, and the Rede Record 2004 version which still today commands a prime-time TV spot in Brazil).

In Spanish America a similar picture emerges for this period. Such was the thirst for new material that not only were original *folletines* published but old classics were re-vamped and turned into *folletines*, such as Sarmiento's own *Facundo*, Echeverría's *Dogma socialista*, Renan's *La vida de Jesús*, Bartolomé Mitre's *Soledad*, Vicente Fidel López's *La novia del hereje*, and Alberto Blest

Gana's *Martín Rivas*. There were a number of *folletín* writers in the nineteenth century among whom should be mentioned the Mexicans Justo Sierra, Manuel Payno and Vicente Riva Palacio; the Colombians Eladio Vergara y Vergara, Bernardino Torres Torrente, and Mercedes Gómez Victoria; the Chileans Martín Palma, José Antonio Torres and Daniel Barros Grez (for a discussion of his theatre see below); and the Argentinian Eduardo Gutiérrez (Carilla, vol. 2, 106–8).

Set in the appropiately named Matanzas, Argentina, Gutiérrez's *Juan Moreira*, published in the 'Dramas policiales' series, has all the ingredients of the *folletín* genre. The eponymous hero is presented as an honest, hard-working *gaucho* driven to crime by the corruption of the society in which he lives, epitomised by Francisco, the local judge, who covets and eventually steals from him his beautiful wife, Vicenta. In this way sympathy is engineered for Moreira, a sympathy which occurs even at those potentially most alienating points in the narrative when Moreira hacks his adversaries to pieces. Invariably, Moreira's action is justified as an example of honourable reprisal. The novel is structured chapter by chapter around the knife fights which are their climax and which normally show the same pattern: Moreira is threatened, he is persuaded to fight, he suffers a knife wound, and then quickly polishes off his assailant, a scene which the spectators watch with a mixture of horror and admiration. Though Gutiérrez's is an embellished account, it is based on a real individual; thus, the narrator feels confident enough to state in chapter V: 'No hacemos novela, narramos los hechos …' (Gutiérrez 68). In order to emphasise its veracity there are references to contemporary newspaper reports of Moreira's deeds, with which at one point the *folletín* takes issue (Chapter XIV; Gutiérrez 178–80), and a letter addressed to the author dated 20 March 1880, from one Julio Llanos, describing other of Moreira's marvellous feats (Gutiérrez 222–23). The main aim of this *folletín* is to give a positive portrayal of the *gaucho*'s way of life and his sense of honour as evidenced during the knife fight, and to emphasise that the responsibility for the waywardness of his life path lies ultimately with the society in which he lives. It is written for an urban audience which was no doubt fascinated in the abstract by life on the wild side but would have found it repugnant if it interrupted everyday life in Buenos Aires in a concrete sense. Following in the *folletín* tradition, *Juan Moreira* specializes in melodrama, a good example of this being when Vicenta and Juan meet, one stormy winter night, many years after Vicenta had given him up for dead (Chapter X; Gutiérrez 136–38); it also consciously alludes to the Romantic literary tradition of the hero pursued by malignant fortune; in Chapter XVI, for example, Moreira is described as

> uno de estos seres llenos de hermosas cualidades, con un espíritu noble e inquebrantable y dotados de un carácter hidalgo, lanzados al camino del crimen y empujados a una muerte horrible, por la maldad de uno de esos tenientes alcaldes de campaña a quienes desgraciadamente está librado el honor y la vida del humilde y noble gaucho porteño. (Gutiérrez 211)

The reader's sympathies could not be more overtly directed. Moreira is finally killed by a posse from Buenos Aires although it is clear, given the pointers throughout the novel, that he accepts death of his own volition. In finishing the book thus, Juan Moreira in effect lays to rest the myth of the *gaucho* in the national psyche, thereby allowing Argentina more elbow room to build the skyscrapers which adorn Buenos Aires's skyline today.[5]

*Cecilia Valdés o la Loma del Angel: novela de costumbres cubanas* (1882) by the Cuban novelist Cirilo Villaverde, though a novel in the traditional sense of the term, does demonstrate some features normally associated with the *folletín*. Published while the author was in exile in New York, the novel opens with a portrayal of the childhood and adolescence of Cecilia Valdés, a beautiful mulatto woman who is a celebrated dancing singer in the bars of Havana at the beginning of the nineteenth century. Her origins are a mystery (specifically nobody knows who her father was) and, gradually, the reader is able to piece together the story. Many years before, a rich landowner in Havana, Don Cándido Gamboa, had fathered an illegitimate child and arranged for that child to be looked after via the services of his doctor friend. Gamboa's legitimate son, Leonardo, from his wife Doña Rosa, falls in love with Cecilia, and despite his father's admonitions, determines to marry her. This eventually leads to tragedy when a musician who plays in the same bar as Cecilia, José Dolores Pimienta, out of spite since he is in love with Cecilia, kills Leonardo during the wedding ceremony. The novel's sub-title ('novela de costumbres cubanas') indicates its *costumbrista* pedigree, but it is best to see the novel not as a late example of the *costumbrista* style in the Caribbean, but rather as an early example of the confluence of various discourses, such as Romanticism, *costumbrismo* and Realism. The first part of the novel was published in 1839, and the second, third and fourth parts, though written in the 1870s, follow the earlier formula – so much so that they constitute a re-writing of a pre-established formula rather than a venture into pastures new. *Cecilia Valdés* has Romantic elements such as the focus on socially forbidden love (Cecilia and Leonardo, in effect, commit incest since they are half-brother and sister), *costumbrista* elements such as the description of the clothes worn, and the use of these clothes as a pointer to social class (Part I, Chap. V), and Realist elements such as the stress upon the *empiric* nature of the events described (the novel is twice described as a 'verídica historia'; Part I, Chap. X; Part II, Chap. I).

The novel is very blunt about race, and characters are consistently typified according to their racial origin. Cecilia becomes a Caucasian-African Venus (Part I, Chap. III), blacks are routinely described as savages (Part II, Chap. II), Don Cándido refers to Negroes as 'sacks of coal' (Part II, Chap. VI), blacks are described by one character as born for slavery (Part III, Chap. III). Oppression of the African races is so intense that suicide seems an almost

---

[5] For further discussion of this novel, see Hart, 'Public Execution'. A similar sense of the tug-of-war between *gaucho* and *porteño* culture in Argentina, this time expressed via the competition between two women, is expressed in Eugenio Cambaceres's *Sin rumbo* (1885). For further discussion see Hart, '"La boca asfixiada"'.

inevitable result; in one particularly grotesque episode we learn of how a black slave killed himself by swallowing his own tongue, a vivid metaphorical image of political unvoicing (Part III, Chap. VII); in the same chapter slaves' bodies are found hanging from trees, ripped apart by passing vultures. As if to confirm that blackness is a projection of social class, the narrator at one point refers to how money corrects the impurity of blood and even the lack of virtue (Part I, Chap. X). As with *Sab*, it is clear that there is a discontinuity between the author's self-avowed antislavery stance and the ideology that the events and imagery of *Cecilia Valdés* betoken. As Richard Jackson argues, in this novel

> Villaverde describes excessively the ethnic differences in people and the various stratifications and divisions of Cuban society. But his accepting them as a *fait accompli* suggests that his antislavery argument is built on a false premise, or at least one that does not attempt to contradict the hierarchy of color. (*Black Image* 30)

The most striking feature of *Cecilia Valdés* is its use of mystery. Consistently, the narrator introduces a character, describes his/her actions, and only later reveals his/her identity. Thus, Cecilia is introduced on two separate occasions, as a young eleven- or twelve-year-old girl in Part I, Chap. II, and as a cabaret singer in Part I, Chap. V, and her identity is revealed subsequently. The opening chapter of the novel describes the visit by a rich man to a shady part of town in Havana, but it is only later that we realize that this was Don Cándido visiting the mother who bore his illegitimate child. Likewise, we are not told who the Negro is who enters the ball and wishes to dance with Cecilia and then causes a scene when she refuses to do so; it is only later on that we realize it was Dionisio, María la Regla's long-lost husband. In this sense we can talk about the novel as echoing, in terms of its style of presentation, the thematic core of the novel, namely, the unspeakability and unknowability of incest within the family unit. Incest is, indeed, the ghost in the family wardrobe which finally emerges at the end of the novel. What is intriguing about this is that the sexual and the political plots are shown to interlope in the novel. For, just as the lower classes at first collude in keeping the family secret – the sexual crime – which, however, finally emerges, so the political crime of slavery, in which the lower classes collude, is finally revealed in all its horror in the closing stages of the novel. José Dolores Pimienta's act of murder, which concludes the novel, thus can be seen as at once an act of sexual vengeance, but also an action with political resonance, since it is also a lower-class individual killing a member of the upper classes. Leonardo's family, it should be pointed out, are to be understood as typifying the *criollo* and patrician class; they exploit the Negroes on La Tinaja, yet they feel aggrieved by the presence of the Spanish; at least this is what emerges from Leonardo's nationalistic discomfiture when he discovers that his sister, Adela, is being courted by a Spanish soldier.

One of the most significant novels published at the end of the nineteenth century was *Aves sin nido* (1899) by Clorinda Matto de Turner (1852–1909).

This novel describes, with a Realism that verges on Naturalism, the plight of the Indians in a town called Killac (meaning in Quechua 'of the moon' [Quillac] and based on Tinta, the Andean town where the author spent much of her life after marriage). The Indians are exploited by an unholy trinity of landowners, priests and lawyers. *Aves sin nido* may be described as a Naturalist novel in the sense that it emphasises a purely materialist view of human actions and the motives that underlie them. In particular, it focuses on the wrongful killing of Marcela and Juan Yupanqui; Marcela and Juan ask for relief from the debt they owe jointly to the priest (Pascual Vargas) and the governor (Sebastián), at which point they are judged to be seditious and subsequently murdered. Between the Indians, represented by the Yupanquis in Part I of the novel and the Chumpis in Part II, and the evil elite, are Lucía and Fernando, a happily married *criollo* couple. They attempt to mediate between the two political camps, but eventually give up and move back to Lima. Luis Alberto Sánchez has argued that *Aves sin nido* breaks with previous idealised descriptions of Indian life since the Indians are no longer used for decoration but are studied as exploited human beings (Sánchez 35). The reader's sympathy is directed towards Lucía and Fernando, who symbolize a new emerging class in Peru in the second half of the nineteenth century, that is, the entrepreneurial middle class which was urban and Eurocentric in taste. (The economic boom of the second half of the nineteenth century in Peru, we may recall, was based on the industrial use of 'guano' found off the coastline of Peru and transformed into artificial fertiliser for export to Europe.) The other main characters in the story, Don Sebastián the governor, the priest Pascual Vargas, the colonel Paredes, and the lawyer, are wedded to the ethos of the *ancien régime* of the landowning oligarchy. Despite the apparent pessimism of *Aves sin nido* (the new middle classes represented by Lucía and Fernando are defeated by the old oligarchy), there is another level in which Lucía and Fernando win out in the end. Manuel, the son of Sebastián and Doña Petronila (at least we think so until the end of the novel), in effect turns against his parents by seeking advice from his father's political enemy, Fernando; this advice has to do not only with a life-decision such as going to university, but also with future investments in the stock market. To make this distancing even more striking the novel also presents Manuel falling in love with one of the Yupanqui daughters, Margarita, who was taken in by Lucía after her parents, Juan and Marcela, were brutally murdered (hence the title 'aves sin nido' which refers to the two daughters).

There are two other significant points about the novel which ought to be mentioned and these are the incest theme and its feminist ideology. Incest is, of course, a very common theme in Romantic literature ranging from Lord Byron's poetry to Jorge Isaacs's *María*, and it has in *Aves sin nido* the same significance, namely, the cult of socially forbidden love as a metaphor of the primacy of individual desire. In Matto de Turner's novel, the theme of incest is revealed in the last paragraph of the novel when Margarita and Manuel discover that they share a father, Bishop Claro y Miranda, mentioned (with what irony) in the opening section of the novel as the cornerstone of the Killac community. This revelation has all the high intensity of a Romantic melodrama of the 1830s. The feminist ideology is evident in this novel in the way in which certain motifs common in the work of her male contemporaries are given a new feminocentric focus. Incest plays its role here since it alludes not only to the cult of individualism in Romantic literature, but also has a feminist edge in that it specifically underlines the brutality of men against women: the priest Vargas, for example, is just as lascivious as Bishop Claro, co-habits with a woman despite his vows, and dies tormented by starkly lascivious visions. Also tending to underline the feminist import of the novel is the fact that all of the positive human beings in the narrative are female; Marcela initiates the action, Lucía acts as the mediator, and even Margarita is more self-possessed than her beau, Manuel. *Aves sin nido* has been criticized for being badly structured and badly written, but this is not true; it is a subtle, complex novel which repays further attention and which hollows out the patriarchalism of Realism from within to hint at a world of feminine social harmony in which sacrifice is unnecessary and in which social sharing can take place.

## Prose

The Peruvian Ricardo Palma (1833–1919) is famous for his *Tradiciones peruanas*, which rank among the wittiest period pieces of the nineteenth century. The *tradiciones* were published by Palma in eleven series, without any particular chronological order. They border on the short story and are not quite *cuadros de costumbres* understood in a strictly generic sense, and indeed succeed in creating a genre all of their own; as one critic suggests, '[l]a tradición es un género típicamente americano, un producto del romanticismo americano' (Carilla, vol. 2, 91). Normally the *tradición* is a short story based on an historical event – which is normally rooted in the colonial era – told in a witty manner. Many of the *tradiciones* begin with a reference to a saying which Palma claims to have heard said in Lima, such as 'esto es más caro que la camisa de Margarita Pareja', or 'esto vale tanto como el alacrán de fray Gómez', but, as soon becomes clear, this is simply a convenient pretext which introduces the story and whets the reader's appetite for what is to come. Thus in one *tradición*, 'Capa colorada, caballo blanco y caja turún-tun-tun', popular culture in the form of gossip is used as a source rather than the written word: 'Muchas, pero desgraciadamente ineficaces, diligencias he hecho para obtener copia de la respuesta del monarca, y tengo que conformarme con repetir lo que corre en boca de todos los vecinos de Puno' (Palma, vol. 1, 120). Typically, the *tradición* is set in the era of the viceroyalty, and the references to the Viceroy of the time, and even the most important personages to appear in the story, are historically based. Once the historical stage is set, Palma then proceeds to create his plot, employing various techniques to contrive a sense of verisimilitude, namely, the reference to historical individuals, the reference to written records which the author has (normally with great difficulty) consulted, and allusion to common proverbs.

Many of the *tradiciones* focus on the power struggles of the colonial period. 'Las orejas del alcalde', for example, narrates the story of one Don Diego de Esquivel, a gentleman who lived in Potosí in the middle of the sixteenth century and who was so affronted by the indignity of his treatment at the hands of the mayor that he vowed to cut off the latter's ears exactly one year after he was publicly flogged; Don Diego kept his word (Palma, vol. 1, 26).

As this suggests, the *tradiciones* portray a world in which the laws of custom, especially as far as honour is concerned, are inflexible. Some of the *tradiciones* begin and end with the proverb being cited. 'Carta canta' relates the humorous story of two Indians who are taking ten melons to their owner in Lima; they decide to eat two of them and they attempt to keep this a secret by hiding the letter under a stone and behind a wall (Palma, vol. 1, 46). Needless to say, their ruse is unsuccessful, and the explanation given by Don Antonio as to how he knew that the Indians were lying is 'Canta carta'; the *tradición* goes full circle and concludes with a reference to the proverb that initiated the narrative.

## Theatre

As earlier on in the century, this period was one in which theatrical productivity was heavily influenced by European and, especially, Spanish models. The *género chico* was imported to Argentina from Spain in the second half of the nineteenth century (the first recorded performance occurred in Buenos Aires in 1878) and caught on extremely well. A local imitation of the genre, the *género chico criollo*, soon followed. Mini-plays such as *De paso por aquí* by Miguel Ocampo, *De paseo por Buenos Aires* by Justo López de Gómara (both of 1890), and *Chin-Chun-Chan* (1904) by José F. Elizondo played well with the Buenos Aires middle-class theatre-going public (Dauster 40). *Chin-Chun-Chan*, astonishly, was perfomed over a thousand times (Dauster 45). One of the most popular theatrical works, however, was undoubtedly *Juan Moreira*, a pantomime version of Eduardo Gutiérrez's *folletín* of the same name (see discussion in 'Novel' section of this chapter above). Created by José J. Podestá (1858–1936), it was first staged in Chivilcoy in April 1886 (Luzuriaga and Reeve 406). The theatrical version more or less follows the *folletín* version in its depiction of Juan Moreira's various escapades, always careful to retain the audience's sympathy for the outlaw. The first scene sets the stage for what is to follow; Moreira is in court asking for the return of some money he paid to one Sardetti (Luzuriaga and Reeve 408–9), and, for his impudence, he is flogged. Moreira subsequently kills Sardetti for this treachery and, from this point onwards, becomes an outlaw. As in the *folletín*, and in this he recalls the prototypical Romantic hero, Moreira blames fate for his misfortune:

> Yo era feliz al lao de mi mujer y de mi hijo y jamás hice a un hombre ninguna maldad. Pero yo habré nacido con algún sino fatal porque la suerte se me

dio güelta y de repente me vi perseguido al extremo de pelear pa defender mi cabeza. (Luzuriaga and Reeve 418)

Following the *gaucho* version of his predetermined fate, also apparent in Hernández's *Martín Fierro* (see above), Juan Moreira loses his wife after others spread the rumour that he has died (Luzuriaga and Reeve 419–21). It is clear that this pantomime version of *Juan Moreira* left much up to the individual ingenuity of the director; the last scene, for example, offers few stage directions other than to say that Moreira is killed (Luzuriaga and Reeve 423).

Alongside those works more appropriately classified under popular culture were those dramas in which the central issues perturbing the *criollo* middle to upper classes of the time were expressed. One of the best works of this period is *Como en Santiago* (1875) by the Chilean dramatist, Daniel Barros Grez (1834–1904). It focuses, like Ascensio Segura's *Ña Catita* of the previous decade (discussed in Chapter 3), on the conflict involved in the choice of a marriage partner within a family. A contrast is drawn up from the very beginning of the play between Dorotea, the priggish, self-important daughter of Don Victoriano and Doña Ruperta, and Victoriano's adopted niece, Inés, who is in love with Dorotea's betrothed, Silverio. Dorotea, aided by her mother, Ruperta, callously drops Silverio once a better candidate appears – a member of parliament, Don Faustino – and much of the drama, from that point onwards, focuses on the difference between Dorotea's materialistic, capitalist and power-based view of love and her cousin's Romantic 'true' love (she loves Silverio for who he is, not for what he can buy her). The plot is rather skimpy – it revolves around a false legal document created by Manuel, Silverio's father, in order to demonstrate that Faustino is only interested in money, and, as soon as he 'discovers' that marriage to Dorotea will not bring him the expected award (a handsome dowry). There is also a capital versus provinces theme in the play which surfaces in Faustino's exclamation which concludes the play: '!Pícaros provincianos, me quitaron un negocio de las manos!' (Luzuriaga and Reeve 405).

Arguably the best play of this period is *Barranca abajo* (1905) by Florencio Sánchez; it is a bleak play about an old man, Zoilo, who loses his money and, as a result, is driven to suicide (at least in the second and final version of the play). The play may have some bearing on Sánchez's own life since he was known to prefer poverty rather than sell his talents (Dauster 33). A remarkable feature of *Barranca abajo* is the oblique way in which its subject matter is introduced; the tragedy of poverty is presented as experienced above all by the women of the family, Zoilo's wife (Misia Dolores), who is simply bewildered by the situation, his daughters Robusta and Prudiencia, who are desperate to marry and discover pastures new, and his sister, Rudelinda, whose inheritance he cynically squanders. The opening scene of the play, for example, simply shows the women of the family squabbling over domestic chores, and it is only gradually that the full extent of their financial ruin emerges. A hint appears in Act I, Scene vi; Rudelinda asks Zoilo if he did the errands she asked of him, and he is evasive about the money she gave him (Florencio Sánchez 117–18). She presses him later on, and he finally admits her inheritance no longer exists in Act I, Scene xiv (Florencio Sánchez 126–27). The drama of the play, thus, occurs off-stage, as it were; the events we see only refer obliquely to that reality, as if the truth were too painful to talk about. Even the discussion between Zoilo, Butiérrez and the former's creditor, Juan Luis (Act I, Scenes xvii–xxi) proceeds in an angular fashion, rather like the conversations in Chekhov's *The Cherry Orchard*. Butiérrez's thrice-repeated refrain 'Qué embromar con las cosas', rather like Misia Dolores's interjections to the Virgin Mary, seems almost a deliberate ploy to avoid the truth. As the play continues, the women get ready to abandon a sinking ship, which finally leads to Zoilo's suicide. In the first version of the play, the ending was more open in the sense that the possibility is left open that Zoilo took Anicito's advice and did not commit suicide. In the revised version, however, which Florencio Sánchez wrote as a result of the reviews of the opening night's performance, the ending is disambiguated. Despite Anicit's remonstrations, Zoilo puts his neck in the noose, with the words: 'Se deshace más fácilmente el nido de un hombre que el nido de un pájaro' (Florencio Sánchez 175). The importance of *Barranca abajo* lies in its modern, capitalist ethos. The tragedy no longer lies in the malevolence of the gods, but arises as a result of poverty and the destruction of the bourgeois home, as the last lines of the play quoted above suggest. The significance of Florencio Sánchez's play rests on this. While it is clearly a product of its era in the sense of the techniques it employs – namely, the Realism of the characters' speech, the Naturalism which surrounds the daughters' dilemma (in the sense of their situation being created by deterministic invariables) – the importance of the play is grasped when we compare it to the typical play of the Romantic era. For whereas there the heroine and/or heroine would typically die as a result of the pangs of unrequited love, here the emphasis is on poverty, and particularly the loss of the family fortune, as the cause which triggers the tragedy. In that sense it is a very apt voicing of the society in which it was created; the Southern Cone at the end of the nineteenth century and the beginning of the twentieth was caught up in an almost frenzied social programme of modernisation and urbanisation, which was hastened by the large-scale immigration of Europeans which characterised especially cities such as Montevideo and Buenos Aires. It is legitimate, thus, to interpret *Barranca abajo* as bidding farewell to the *gaucho* (the gradual demise of their lifestyle was inevitable) while simultaneously lamenting that same demise. (For a discussion of Brazilian theatre, see the section on Machado de Assis's work below, pp. 136–7.)

**Essay**

Two minor essayists of this period ought to be mentioned: the Ecuadorian Juan Montalvo (1832–89) and the Puerto Rican Eugenio María de Hostos (1839–

1903). Montalvo was an ardent opponent of dictatorship and a fervent admirer of Simón Bolívar, and his essays, collected in the *Siete tratados* (1882), ooze a republican zeal. His essay comparing Napoleon and Bolívar demonstrates a recurring theme in his thought, namely, that political power without vision is as limiting as political power with vision is liberating ('Napoleón y Bolívar'; Flores 244–6). He was acutely aware of the political problems facing the newly-independent republics of Spanish America. In 'La República de América', for example, he states:

> no tienen de ella [i.e. the republic] sino el nombre, y muchas veces las constituciones, las leyes y los procedimientos escritos; pero en realidad son despotismos, porque el dictador llamado presidente se ríe de los códigos donde está campando al formar de gobierno más liberal y sensata del mundo. (Montalvo 51)

Hostos, like Montalvo, was, broadly speaking, a liberal thinker; his special interest was in arguing for the autonomy of his home country, Puerto Rico. His essays demonstrate that he often used the lens provided by the concept of race to analyse the political problematics of Latin America. His essay 'El cholo', published in *La Sociedad* in Lima on 24 December 1870, is typical in this respect:

> no concibo el triunfo de la justicia en el Nuevo Continente sino mediante la rehabilitación de la raza abrumada por la conquista, envilecida por el coloniaje, desamparada por la independencia, y esa rehabilitación me parece imposible en tanto que la fusión no dé por resultado una raza que, poseedora de la inteligencia de los conquistadores, tenga también la sensibilidad de los conquistados y aquella voluntad intermedia, enérgica para el bien, pasiva para el mal, productor de una gran inteligencia y una gran sensibilidad que puede darse por la fusión de los caracteres definitivos de las razas europea y la americana. (Flores 248)

Hostos's focus on miscegenation, and its implications for political power, is one which would dominate Latin American thought for years to come, and was certainly still current during the first three decades of the twentieth century, as we shall see.

By far the most significant essay of this period was Enrique Rodó's *Ariel* (1900), the 'founding essay in the modern Latin American essayistic tradition' in the words of one critic (González Echeverría 16). This essay proposed a character from Shakespeare's *The Tempest* as a model of Latin American culture in contradistinction to the utilitarian and spiritless culture of North America. It is important to recall that this text was written at the end of a decade in which the United States had been flexing its military muscles in Central America and the Caribbean; the United States's military superiority was shown when Spain's navy was blown out of the water in a matter of weeks in the summer of 1898, causing Puerto Rico, Cuba and the Philippines to be annexed to the United States. Shakespeare's Ariel is, in fact, only a front for the image of Graeco-Roman civilisation which Rodó idealises in almost maudlin fashion, in a way that is paralleled by the poetry of the *modernistas*. In effect, this was the swan song of a culture which Western civilisation had idealised since the Renaissance, admittedly in a book-based sense. In Rodó's work, Greece and Rome function as a synecdoche of a pre-Edenic cultural plenitude subsequently destroyed by the Fall of the Industrial Revolution, mechanism and materialism. A series of image associations is set up in *Ariel* according to which Ariel stands for the future, youth, energy, the spirit, nature, the inner life, classical 'otium', the imagination, literature, nobility, and contemplative life, specifically 'pensar, soñar, admirar' (Rodó 40). As might be guessed from the above, when Rodó comes to discuss the cultural alternative – the United States – all of the positive adjectives have been used up; in quick succession, in the second part of the essay, Rodó rejects the work ethic, utilitarianism, Puritanism and the cult of mediocrity which he sees as characteristic of North American culture. The English too are to blame: 'Si ha podido decirse del utilitarismo, que es el verbo del espíritu inglés, los Estados Unidos pueden ser considerados la encarnación del verbo utilitario' (Rodó 69). The essay concludes with a call to the youth of Spanish America to throw off the yoke of 'nordomanía', since it hints at the possibility of 'una América *deslatinizada* por propia voluntad' (Rodó 70), an idea which causes him to shudder, in order to embrace their Latin heritage (Rodó 97). In the final pages of the book Rodó returns to the image of Ariel, described as 'la razón y el sentimiento superior' and 'este sublime instinto de perfectibilidad' (Rodó 101); the very last sentence ends with an evocation of Ariel as straddling, like some mythical Colossus, the mountain ranges of South America (Rodó 103). Rodó, like his contemporaries in Spain such as Ángel Ganivet and Miguel de Unamuno, was loath to focus on mundane matters such as his nation's economy or its industrial base; instead he pondered his vision of the future, ideas. While Rodó may seem dated to the modern reader, his work is important as a turn-of-the-century statement of distrust towards North American culture and, by implication, the symptom of an urgent re-evaluation of Latin American culture. Rodó's view of culture is aristocratic and, at times, rabidly anti-democratic (Rodó 54–5). His sense of protectionism towards high culture is reinforced by the authors he quotes most frequently – Compte, Taine, Renan and Carlyle – whose broad sweep of the materialism of modern urban life lends itself to a negative portrayal of that reality. His cultural elitism reveals itself equally when he rewrites Alberdi's famous dictum 'gobernar es poblar' to read: 'Gobernar es poblar, asimilando y en primer término: educando y seleccionando, después' (Rodó 56). Quality is more important, he goes on to say, than numbers. Rodó's use of Ariel as a symbol of all that Latin America should strive for perfectly evokes the Eurocentric decade in which it was written. Like the *modernistas*, Rodó idealised Graeco-Latin antiquity and its aura of aristocracy; the importance of *Ariel* is confirmed when we consider that one of the major essayists of the second half of the twentieth century, Fernández Retamar, saw fit to break Rodó's Colossus into pieces, promoting instead the image of Ariel's oppositional double in Shakespeare's play, Caliban (see Chapter 6).

## Two National Icons: Machado de Assis and Martí

There are writers whose work comes to achieve such importance with the passing of time that it takes on a mythic grandeur, and such is the case with Joaquim Maria Machado de Assis (1839–1908) in Brazil and José Martí (1853–95) in Cuba. Machado de Assis is seen as a writer years ahead of his time (it is as if only now we are beginning to understand him) while Martí died a hero fighting for his country, and has been invoked by Fidel Castro as the intellectual architect of the event which radically transformed the political climate of Latin America in the second half of the twentieth century, the Cuban Revolution.

Machado de Assis towers above his Latin American contemporaries of this era, not only in terms of the brilliance of his fiction but also because of the versatility of his literary output. He excelled in the genres of short fiction, the novel and theatre, and his work in each of these areas will be discussed separately. His collection of short stories, *Contos fluminenses* (1870), provides some early indication of the themes and preoccupations which would come to fruition in the novels, a genre in which he is universally acclaimed as a master. Starting from an apparently insignificant event (such as the fortuitous rescue of a dog) the stories broaden out into an analysis of the human heart (a bachelor's love for a young widow) which is expanded in significance by subtle allusions to literary masterpieces often drawn from Greek mythology but including works such as La Rochefoucauld's *Maximes*. Typically they conclude on a note of ironic wisdom about the mystery of human motive (accepting an offer of marriage only then in order to live separately). This applies most obviously to the opening short story of the collection, 'Miss Dollar'; it is not only Margarida's heart which remains a mystery to Dr Mendonça who has fallen in love with her, but the reader too, for this story, like much of Machado's fiction, has a sting in its tail. It is not only about the mystery of one particular woman's motives, it is also about the mystery of language. As the opening section of the story points out, Miss Dollar is 'uma inglesa pálida e delgada' (Machado de Assis, *Contos fluminenses* 11), or 'uma robusta americana' (11), or a 'brasileira rica' (12), but none of these is right since she is in fact a dog. Indeed this jolt into reality will prove to be a characteristic feature of Machado de Assis's fiction, a Cervantine irony allowing the reader to tilt at windmills, encouraging him to do so, in order to bring him crashing back down to earth. In the process we find out more about the contours of our imaginative faculties. 'Luis Soares' is the story of the discomfiture of a young man who spends his inheritance, then tries to win the heart of the cousin whom once he scorned. It has almost a biblical side to it, except that, unlike the prodigal son of the Bible who repents and is forgiven, in Machado de Assis's story the prodigal son is rejected. Luis is humiliated by Adelaide; on his knees before her, she simply smiles and says 'Trezentos contos! E muito dinheiro para comprar um miserável' (*Contos fluminenses* 51). Typically of the *mal de siècle*, the short story ends with Luis's suicide (53).

'A mulher de preto' offers once more a story with an unexpected dénouement. In a clear rewriting of Cervantes's *El celoso extremeño*, Estevão becomes the unwitting go-between for two individuals, Meneses and Madalena, who have become estranged; Madalena has been attempting to use Estevão as a means of proving her fidelity, and that fact that Estevão falls in love with her is bitterly ironic. 'O Segredo de Augusta' focuses on the interaction between love and money, and treats the problem of debts (as when Vasconcelos is visited by his creditor, *Contos fluminenses* 92) in a manner which is reminiscent of the social vision we find in the novels of Balzac and Pérez Galdós, though Machado de Assis's touch is lighter. Augusta's secret is that she does not want her daughter to marry in case she becomes a grandmother – vanity is at the heart of the story. 'Confisões de uma Viúva Moça' tells the story in epistolary form of a woman's adulterous love affair; she is abandoned by her lover once her husband dies. At first she finds this mysterious, but now years later she concludes: 'Emilio era um sedutor vulgar e só se diferençava dos outros em ter um pouco mais de habilidade que eles' (*Contos fluminenses* 128–9). The fact that she first saw him at the theatre is not coincidental. Being successful in love, Machado de Assis seems to be saying, is as much about one's ability to act as it is about deep feelings. As 'Linha reta e linha curva' suggests, love is a fame in which sincerity, revealing one's true feelings, if done at the wrong time, can lead to failure, while playing with the fires of love can often be fatal. As Emilia puts it: 'quis fazer fogo e queimei-me nas mesmas chamas' (*Contos fluminenses* 172).

But it was in the novel genre that Machado de Assis really made an impact. His *Memórias Póstumas de Brás Cúbas* (1880) has been identified by Judith Payne and Earl Fitz as the single most important novel to change completely the horizon of narrative in Latin America; it was only in Argentina in the 1940s, they argue, that a figure emerged who could rival Machado de Assis, namely Jorge Luis Borges and his *Ficciones* (1944) (Payne and Fitz 1–24). Machado de Assis's *Memórias Póstumas* was a paradigm-shift not only for Latin American narrative but also for his own work. Even his contemporaries were surprised by the novel; Mário de Alencar, for example, asked Machado de Assis how he could have written *Memórias Póstumas* after writing *Helena*, to which Machado replied that he had changed his writing style as a result of losing all faith in mankind ('explicou o romancista que se modificara porque perdera todas as ilusões sôbre os homens'; quoted by Meyer 29). The novelty of *Memórias Póstumas* was that it thrust at the very heart of Realism, in effect, dealing it a death blow, when Realism was still very much in vogue in Brazil and Spanish America, in Spain, even in France. Though written in the matter-of-fact, objective, chronologically-governed discourse associated with the Realism of the time (true, it was written in the first person and Realism in the Balzacian mode necessitated a third-person narrative, but this at first glance appears a tweak rather than a revolution of the system), the narrative is told from beyond the grave. As the narrator points out in the first page of the novel proper, 'eu não sou própiamente um autor defunto, mas um defunto autor' (*Memórias Póstumas* 39), that is, he is not a deceased author, but someone who has died and is now writing, a curious notion more redolent of the oddness of twentieth-century fiction (Joyce or Kafka, perhaps) than the standard author of Realism (Balzac or Pérez Galdós). He tells us he died in his home in Catumbi on a Saturday in August 1869 (*Memórias Póstumas* 39), then describes his funeral (40), in a very matter-of-fact way, and then turns swiftly to the narrative of his life, beginning with his family name (42), but framed by an extraordinary chapter 'O delirio' (48–54) in which he is allowed to go back in time and witness the early history of man, aided by a hippopotamus who turns out to be his cat (54). He is born on 20 October 1805 (55), he describes his experience at school, his first love, how he subsequently falls in love with Virgília, how she is stolen from him by one Lôbo Neves (110), and how he finally succeeds in seducing her despite her marriage to another ('Amo-te, é a vontade do céu', as she says to him; 127). Their love survives a number of years – despite nearly being caught out by an anonymous letter sent to the husband denouncing their dangerous liaisons (175–7), and despite their secret love-nest being almost discovered (it is Virgília's quickness of wits which saves the day; 184–5). Indeed their love remains 'true' if such a word can be used of an adulterous passion. For their passion, despite its ups and downs, survives until Brás Cúbas's death (the woman who is not initially named at the beginning of the narrative and who is completely distraught at Brás Cúbas's death is Virgília (*Memórias Póstumas* 40), as we later discover). Yet this is anything but the portrayal of a love which is beautiful despite not being condoned by society's laws, as we find in a Romantic literary work such as Zorilla's *Don Juan Tenorio* (1844), for example, where there is no distance between the lovers, Ana and Juan; their hearts, as it were, beat with the same beat. But in Machado de Assis's novel, the love between Brás Cúbas and Virgília is based on the deception of others (such as her husband, Lôbo Neves, who suspects but never knows the truth), and is also itself shot through with deception. On a number of occasions, Brás Cúbas believes that Virgília is deceiving him. Thus on one occasion she asks him why he did not attend a social function, and he explains himself to her; as readers we are not privy to his explanation, and are therefore unable to determine whether or not he is telling her the truth. He then asks the same of her; she gives her excuse, at which he laughs and then comments wryly: 'Era claro que me enganara' (153).

In a tale in which the main relationship is based on concealment, it should not perhaps surprise us that deceit should also appear in the context of their love, and, indeed, there are many occasions when Brás Cúbas feels that he is not only the deceiver but also the deceived, but what is remarkable about this novel is that this deceit should also filter into the contract between reader and writer. In Chapter 3, the narrator mentions that the strange manner in which his death is being recounted may lead some readers to have doubts, but he challenges them that it is all true: 'a causa da minha morte, e possível que o leitor não me creia, e todavia é verdade. Vou expor-lhe sumáriamente o caso. Julgue-o por si mesmo' (*Memórias Póstumas* 41). Indeed, as time goes on, the reader becomes gradually less inclined to take the narrator's words at face value, not least because of the liberties he takes with the narration, asking the reader to take it all on trust, yet leaving the door open for his words to be questioned. Thus, in Chapter 75, he says that the reader may, on reflection, want to know what he said in the previous chapter, so he quotes the words he used on that occasion (150). Another time he refers to how he is unable to understand the emotions elicited by a particular event, saying that the reader also will not comprehend them, thereby in effect drawing a veil of secrecy over the whole episode; as he concludes: 'Suponhamos que não disse nada' (188). Furthermore, he asks rather bizarrely for Chapter 130 to be placed before the first and second sentence of the previous chapter (210). Chapter 138 is addressed 'To a critic', and it draws attention to a sentence in Chapter 134 which the critic may find incomprehensible, which he then begins to elaborate on (210). It happens that this is precisely the chapter in which he makes the point that these fifty years of his life, though the best, were also characterised by duplicity: 'Era portanto a minha vida que descia pela escada abaixo, – ou a melhor parte, ao menos, uma parte cheia de prazeres, de agitacões, de sustos – capeada de dissimulacões e duplicidade, – mas enfim a melhor, se devemos falar a linguagem usual' (213). It is difficult to see the narrative as remaining immune from this dissimulation and even thereby undercutting the reference to the 'linguagem usual' in this sentence, for the novel undercuts not only the language of the novel, and the language of social custom, but also the language of life and death, the validity of Christianity.

It was the novel published nineteen years later, however, *Dom Casmurro* (1899), that established Machado de Assis's reputation as the greatest writer of nineteenth-century Latin American fiction. The plot is easily dispensed with: Bento, aka Dom Casmurro, provides the story of his life: how he acquired the nickname of Dom Casmurro, how he was first intent on becoming a priest, how he then fell in love with a young girl called Capitu whom he married (in March 1865) (*Dom Casmurro* 120). They have a child, Ezequiel, and Bento begins to notice that he has the same gestures and look as his friend Escobar (136). After Escobar dies by drowning in the Glória bay (140–41), Bento becomes obsessed that the child is not his, which leads him to break up with Capitu (154) and disown his son, though he sees him briefly before he sets off for an archaeological expedition to Greece, Egypt and Palestine, where he dies of typhoid (161).

For many years the novel was taken at face value as a classic tale of adultery and betrayal, but in 1970 a critic raised the idea that it was likely that Dom Casmurro was an unreliable narrator, that Ezequiel was very likely to be his son, and that this was a story about self-deception rather than adultery (Caldwell). A careful reading of the novel suggests, indeed, that the evidence is finely balanced and that both hypotheses are possible interpretations of the novel. The evidence provided by the text itself to the effect that Ezequiel is not Dom Casmurro's son is that he looks like the deceased friend, Escobar, and that he has his gestures. When Dom Casmurro and Capitu see a photograph of Escobar as a child, he believes that his wife's facial expression is an admission of guilt (*Dom Casmurro* 155). A number of years after their separation he sees Ezequiel again and is confirmed in his view that he has 'o mesmo rosto do meu amigo' (159). The other important piece of evidence – although the text is not crystal-clear about this – is that, given that Capitu and Dom Casmurro, Sancha and Escobar, were very good friends, and often did things as a foursome, the opportunity for adultery would have been available. And – perhaps the most important point – we are accustomed to taking the author of first-person narrative as a trustworthy person, and are more likely to give credence to his version of events, as opposed to that of any other individual. The genre of first-person narrative, we might say, inclines us to trust the narrator. But there are a number of factors which oblige us to question Dom Casmurro's account. Firstly, Escobar made no confession before his death and is (rather conveniently) safely out of the picture; secondly, Capitu makes no confession and, indeed, when confronted with the accusation, reacts indignantly (*Dom Casmurro* 154). Thirdly, her explanation ('é a casualidade de semelhança', 155) is as believable as Dom Casmurro's reasoning which, indeed, at this point becomes deliberately obscurantist ('Ri-se? É natural; apesar do seminário, não credita em Deus; eu creio ... Mas não falemos nisto; não nos fica bem dizer mais nada'; 153); fourthly, Capitu's reaction to the whole affair, as relayed in the text later on (she simply accepts his decison: 'atou às suas ordens' 155; and, as reported by Ezequiel: 'A mãe falava muito em mim, louvendo-me extraordinariamente, como o homem mais puro do mundo, o mais digno de ser querido', 160), appears to be the reaction of a woman whose heart has been broken by an unjust separation rather than the contrition of an adulteress; and fifthly, there is hint in the text that, after his friend's death, Dom Casmurro began to harbour adulterous thoughts himself for Sancha, especially after she squeezes his fingers (138), an idea given further weight by his suggestion that, one day, he and Sancha will go to heaven's gate: 'Um dia, vamos daqui até à porta do céu, onde nos encontraremos renovados, como as plantas novas, como piante novelle, "Rinovellate di novelle fronde". O resto em Dante' (146). It is very difficult to read these lines and not conclude that Dom Casmurro had fallen in love with Sancha; it is even possible that the whole text is an elaborate lie to cover up for the fact that he was the adulterous party, and that he forced the separation in order to cover his tracks. This is, of course, pure speculation, and cannot be proved, but it does demonstrate that there are so many holes in Dom Casmurro's story, so many things that do not add up, that a whole range of hypotheses become possible. Perhaps the most logical explanation is that, as a result of an awareness of adulterous thoughts within himself, and given his theological training, Dom Casmurro transferred his sense of guilt onto his wife, thereby finding a psychological remission of his sins. The true tragedy of the novel, thus, would not be Dom Casmurro's but Capitu's, since she has been unjustly rejected by the only man she ever loved, and also the son's, for Ezequiel, whose love for Dom Casmurro knows no bounds as the text is careful to point out, will have found that rejection very painful indeed, though of this matter this (as ever) enigmatic text gives us no clue.

In Machado de Assis's eighth novel, *Esaú e Jacó*, published in 1902, and called by Earl E. Fitz a 'complex and often overlooked novel' (Fitz, *Machado de Assis*, 59), some of the twisting of the novel's screw evident in *Dom Casmurro* is applied still further. This is a story narrated by an older man, Counselor Aires, about two brothers, Pedro and Paulo, from a powerful nineteenth-century Rio family, who are at odds over their affections for a beautiful young woman, Flora, though they are both eventually frustrated since she dies prematurely. The reader will be forgiven for concluding that *Esaú e Jacó* is therefore a novel in which nothing happens. On one level, of course, this is true yet, as we find so often in Machado de Assis's fiction, appearances can be deceptive. At one point the narrator, Aires, compares the relationship between the author and his attentive reader to that of a cow's rumination of its food in its four stomachs: 'O leitor atento, verdadeiramente ruminante, tem quatro estômagos no cérebro, e por eles faz passar e repasar os atos e os fatos, até que deduz a verdade, que estava, ou parecia estar escondida' (*Esaú e Jacó* 149). This unusual metaphor alerts us to the fact that the Brazilian novelist is not simply alluding to the four levels of significance traditionally ascribed by medieval rhetoric to the literary text – the literal, the allegorical, the moral and the anagogic – but rather hints at the possibility that this novel is a *roman à clé*. But what is its secret? It is possible, indeed, to posit four levels within the novel, which might be (i) the mythic-religious level (i.e. that the lives of the two boys, Paolo and Pedro, re-enact the biblical narrative of Jacob and Esau in the Old Testament as well as Peter and Paul in the New Testament); (ii) the national-allegory level (namely, that Paolo and Pedro's lives encapsulate the drama of Brazilian nationalism, its progression from monarchy to republic during the course of the nineteenth century); (iii) the ironic-sceptical level (i.e. that the narrator, Aires, keeps a safe distance from these very mythic-religious and national-allegory interpretations); and (iv) the novel is a *roman à clé* about the concealed love affair between Flora and the narrator Aires. A number of critics have pointed to the existence of the mythic-religious (Gomes), national-allegory (Fitz), and sceptical (Maia Neto) levels in the text, but there are a number of pieces of internal evidence which suggest that there is more going on in this novel than first meets the eye. For example, we never find out who Flora's third lover is, one person who is mentioned so mysteriously in Chapter XCV, and, though we do not know what Flora died of, the possibility is raised that Flora died of love: 'mas que crime teria cometido aquela moça, além do de viver, e porventura o de amar, não se sabe a quem, mas amar?' (*Esaú e Jacó* 227). There are also some worrying signs of the narrator's behaviour which likewise suggest that he is not all he seems: on numerous occasions he seems jealous of Paulo and Pedro, he is mortified by Flora's death, and no secret of his ability to conceal the truth is made: 'Aires fora diplomata excelente, apesar da aventura de Caracas, se não e que essa mesma lhe aguçou a vocação de descobrir e encobrir. Toda a diplomacia está nestes dois verbos parentes' (*Esaú e Jacó* 214). *Esaú e Jacó* is an intellectual teaser which – unlike the detective novel which reveals all in the last pages of the work – takes its ultimate meaning with it to its metaphorical 'grave' (for further discussion of this novel, see Hart, 'Four Stomachs').

Machado de Assis's plays may, in his friend Quinto Bocaiúva's words, be 'para serem leidas e não representadas' (Assis, *Obra completa*, vol. 2, 1099) but they still count as some of the best theatrical works of the late nineteenth century in Brazil. *Desencantos* (1861) is a two-act play centring on the rivalry of two men, Luiz and Pedro, for the love of one woman, in the process putting a number of notions to the test, including the idea that women mediate between men and angels (*Desencantos*, Act I, Scene i, 5); sincerity and passion are rarely found together (Act I, Scene iii, 14); fantasy, though ultimately deceptive, can make human society appear better than it really is (Act I, Scene v, 26); a trip is a good way of getting over a bad experience in love (Act II, Scene v, 54). All these ideas are discussed rather than implemented dramatically.

His play *Os deuses de Casaca* was performed on 28 December 1865 in Rio and it takes one of the ideas which is touched upon (fantasy versus reality) and, as the prologue suggests, builds this up to form the main structural buttress of the play: 'O poeta que fez? Tomou um terrão medio; E deu, para fazer uma dualidade, / A dextra á phantasia, a sestra á realidade' (*Os deuses de Casaca* 4). The characters are all drawn from classical mythology (Jupiter, Mars, Apollo, Proteus, Cupid, Vulcan, Mercury) and the play, written in alexandrines, is a witty disquisition on the disjunction between the gods and men. Cupid is attempting to persuade the gods to leave Mount Olympus, escape Jupiter's control and become men like him, and gradually, one by one, he succeeds in enticing them to earth. Recalling Dom Pedro's famous performative phrase in which he celebrated his staying in Brazil, Cupid says: 'eu fico!' (*Os deuses de Casaca* 24). Finally, overwhelmed by his ranks moving to earth, Jupiter decides to become human and, in a humorous reference to the class which held power in Brazil at the turn of the century, Jupiter, when asks what he will he do on earth, replies: 'Vou ser banqueiro!' (*Os deuses de Casaca* 9).

*Tu Só, Tu, Puro Amor*, first performed in Rio on 10 June 1880, takes advantage of the fact that little is known about Luis de Camões's life in order to construct a fast-moving one-act play about a love affair between Camões and Caterina, the daughter of Antonio de Lima. The latter is displeased, and Camões is unceremoniously banished to the East. The historical event which is more likely to have caused Camões's dismissal into exile (he was pardoned for taking part in a street brawl in 1553 by King John III on the condition that he would go to India in the King's service) is downplayed in order to allow the play to create an entertaining investigation of the ways in which elevated poetic verse jars with the language of everyday life. This is evident not only in the humorous ditty about the Duke of Alveiro which Camões writes (Scene i, *Obra Completa*, vol. 2, 104) which delights the King but riles his court rivals, but also in the use of *culto* imagery and verse to delineate the delicate love which Camões and Caterina feel for each other (Scene viii, 1108–11), and in the convincingly drawn portrait of how jealousy (both in terms of love and social preferment) can lead individuals to destroy the careers of others for personal gain.

*Não Consultes Médico* (1906), first published posthumously in *Reliquias de Casa Velha* by H. Garnier, focuses on the miseries of unrequited love. A lighthearted comedy of manners, this play is most remarkable for its humour (a good example of which occurs when Dr Cavalcante gets his turkey mixed up with the country Peru (the word in Brazil means both things; Scene ii, *Obra Completa*, vol. 2, 1125), and the way it explores the awkwardness of strangers talking to each other about their emotions (Scene vii, 1128–31; Scene xii, 1132–5). *Lição de Botânica*, which was also published posthumously in 1906, is likewise a living-room drama, with reminiscences of Ibsen in that everyday conversation often slips into the depths of emotional trauma. It is built around a conceit – the study of flowers (botany) cannot be confused with the study of (human) flowers, namely, women. Barão Segismundo de Kernoberg goes to see Helena and requests that the growing love affair between his nephew, Henrique, and her daughter, Cecília, be curtailed, since it will hinder Henrique's studies in botany. The baron, though celibate himself, is finally persuaded – by Helena's words – not only to allow his nephew to ask for Cecília's hand but also to ask for Helena's hand in marriage himself. Skilfully drawn in terms of character, Machado de Assis's plays have a witty, humorous dialogue, reminiscent in some ways of Pérez Galdós's plays, but deserving of greater critical attention. (For a discussion of Machado de Assis's poetry, see Murilo Leal.)

Typical of his century, José Martí (1853–95) was a writer with more than one occupation; he combined the various fields of political activity, essay writing and poetic composition. Though both his parents were Spanish, he soon became identified with the Cuban independence movement; in 1892 he took over leadership of the Partido Revolucionario Cubano, and, in 1895 he was killed in action by Spanish soldiers while attempting to launch a pro-independence raid on Cuba from the United States. Martí – very much like Che Guevara – casts a long shadow in modern-day Cuba: his statue dominates the Plaza de la Revolución in Havana and the house he lived in is revered as a shrine of Cubanness (at least in this he had better fortune than Machado de Assis, whose house in Corcovado in Rio has unfortunately been destroyed). Martí's poetry is striking in its ability to bring the political and the personal to bear in one poem. Some of his poems, such as 'Yo soy un hombre sincero' and 'Quiero a la sombra de una ala', the celebrated poem about the Guatemalan girl who fell in love with him and died broken-hearted when he returned to Guatemala, now married, have become popular classics, put to music on innumerable occasions. But the collection of poems to which he owes his fame as a poet, *Versos sencillos* (1891), contains some poems which are intellectually complex. In some ways, Martí's poetry is closer to Andrés Bello's than it is to

Rubén Darío's. He is at great pains, for example, to underline the ways in which his poetry differs from that of the *modernistas*. In 'Mi poesía' Martí likewise differentiates himself from the *modernistas*: 'No la [la poesía] pinto de gualda y amaranto / como aquesos poetas' (Martí, *Versos Libres* 128). The preferred object of comparison for his poetry is nature: 'la vierto al mundo / A que cree y fecunde, y ruede y crezca / Libre cual las semillas por el viento' (Martí, *Versos* 128). Nature, as a number of other poems suggest, is, indeed, the central metaphor of *Versos sencillos*, and is used to signify all that is good and positive about human existence. This attention to the civic sphere makes his poetry redolent comparable to Andrés Bello's, but there is one crucial difference. While Bello was writing in the early decades of the nineteenth century, his poetry essentially spoke on behalf of the new political regime which had recently won its independence from Spain; Martí, however, was speaking on behalf of a dream that was not then a political reality. His ideological stance towards the state is thus much more aggressive, as 'Banquete de tiranos' clearly suggests. Martí was keenly aware of his new role as a writer which resulted from his subalternity. In the insightful poem, 'Hierro', Martí begins by stating that poetry is something to be written after his daily bread has been earned: 'Ganado tengo el pan: hágase el verso' (Martí, *Versos* 65). This will obviate the need to find a Maecenas, an idea he greets with Olympic scorn: 'póstrate, calle cede, lame / manos de potentado, ensalza, excusa / defectos, tenlos' (65). If the sycophant decides to do this, he will find his 'bare poorman's plate' turned into a 'plate of fine gold' but, as Martí goes on to point out, that gold is 'pawned' ('empañado'); here the suggestion is that the colonial power is paying for its cultural capital with money it does not own, but has 'borrowed' from the colonized people. Much better than gold, Martí suggests, is iron, since that metal can produce the weapons which are need to overcome political slavery ('las armas son de hierro!' Martí, *Versos* 66). Martí thereby turns the value image system of the poetaster upside down, and in its place proposes a poetry which reveals injustice and fights for liberty.

The overriding theme of Martí's essays, which comes as no surprise after reading his poetry, is the Spanish American independence movement; his view, for which he suffered imprisonment and, subsequently, exile, is that Cuba should have followed the example of the rest of the sub-continent in cutting its political ties with Spain. The last stanza of the poem of independence, to use his own analogy, still needed to be written (Martí, *Prosas* 62). Martí's most influential essay on this topic was 'Nuestra América' published in the Mexican journal, *El Partido Liberal*, on 30 January 1891. The main idea advanced in this essay is that Latin America would be better off in future adopting its own systems of government, education and philosophy, which would grow out of its own culture rather than being simply adopted from Europe or the United States. For too long, he argued, the Latin American people had simply been a heterogeneous mix of other cultures: 'Eramos unas máscaras, con los calzones de Inglaterra, el chaleco parisiense, el chaquetón de Norteamérica y la montera de España' (Martí, *Prosa escogida* 152). Echoing Sarmiento's dualistic distinction between the natural and the cultural, which Martí here projects using the metaphor of clothes, the Cuban writer reverses the privileged element in the analogy; it is now America, rather than Europe, which is foregrounded as important: 'La historia de América, de los incas a acá, ha de enseñarse de dedillo, aunque no se enseñe la de los arcontes de Grecia. Nuestra Grecia es preferible a la Grecia que no es nuestra' (Martí, *Prosa escogida* 149). Only once they have taken off their Yankee or French spectacles ('antiparras yanquis o francesas', 149) will the youth of South America truly be able to create an independent political system. As the quotation makes clear, the future identity of Latin America must rely, in Martí's view, to a great degree in taking account of the Indian and Negro elements. As his essay concludes, the seed of the new America will spring from the nature god of the pre-Columbian Indians of the Antilles.

The afterlife of Martí has been an extremely intriguing one in cultural-political terms, since he has been claimed as an icon by both revolutionary Cubans and Cubans in exile. Fidel Castro claimed that Martí was the 'intellectual author' of the attack he carried out on 26 July 1953 on the Moncada barracks, which was planned to coincide with the hundredth anniversary of Martí's birth (Judson 236). For their part, Cubans living in exile in the United States also claim cultural ownership over Martí. In the early 1980s, for example, a broadcasting station, Radio Antorcha Martiana, operated by the Movimiento Insurreccional Martiana, began to broadcast anti-Castro political messages from Miami which reached the whole Caribbean; as their name suggested they sought to reclaim the cultural capital of Martí's work for their own use. This was followed by the founding of Radio Martí, the official United States government propaganda service to Cuba, which began transmitting anti-revolutionary messages to Cuba in 1985 (Soley and Nichols 188–89). The posthumous history of Martí's work is a good litmus test of the value of literature as cultural capital employed for political purposes.

# 5
# Early Twentieth-Century Literature

We have already noted in previous chapters the shifts in emphasis in the publication industry which occurred at the beginning and end of the colonial era in Latin America; from a state industry strictly controlled by regal or viceregal patronage it became an enterprise largely dominated by pro-independence factions. Another shift of emphasis is evident at the beginning of the twentieth century; the book industry now becomes part of a new print capitalism. The axiom of new events calling for new news is certainly relevant to the turbulent years of the Mexican Revolution; hundreds of new newspaper titles were generated throughout Mexico during the period 1910–17. This print explosion of the dailies occurred all over Latin America – Mexico was not the exception – and was accompanied in the literary field by new avant-garde journals from Europe which were exploring the language of colours, the calligram, and the visual image. Certainly, many more specifically literary journals were published; in Argentina, for example, Lafleur lists sixty-four literary reviews for the period 1893–1914 compared to 188 for the period 1915–39 (Lafleur 49–57, 156–75). One new feature of the literary world in the first few decades of the twentieth century was the growth, alongside the literary reviews, of inexpensive and accessible editions of works by contemporary authors. An example in Buenos Aires in the first decade of the century was the series Ediciones mínimas, which came out monthly, edited by Ernesto Morales and Leopoldo Durán, and which specialized in short stories and novels. With their low price, (10 centavos a copy), and higher than usual print-runs, these series were highly successful, and led to spin-off series such as La novela sentimental (1917), La novela para todos (1918), La novela cordobesa (1919), La novela universitaria (1921), La novela femenina (1920), La novela porteña (1922), to name but a few (Lafleur 68).

The publishing industry in Brazil followed a similar route to that traced in Spanish America though, if anything, it was even more abrupt. Crucial was the role in the early twentieth century played by an imaginative entrepreneur and writer, José Bento Monteiro Lobato (1882–1948). He changed the look of literary works (including illustrations, designing attractive covers) and, most importantly, opened up the circulation of books, bringing vendors other than simply booksellers into the distribution stream. In 1918 he sent out the following circular to stationer's shops, grocery shops, even chemists:

> Vossa Senhoria tem o seu negócio montado, e quanto mais coisas vende, mais será o lucro. Quer vender também uma coisa chamada 'livros'? Vossa

Senhoria não precisa inteirar-se do que essa coisa é. Trata-se de um artigo comercial como qualquer outro: batata, querosene ou bacalhau. (Quoted in Hallewell 320)

Amazingly, the strategy worked, and now Lobato had almost 2,000 distributors scattered around Brazil; sales of literary works he published grew exponentially as a result. Whereas before, the outlet base consisted of thirty or so booksellers with print-runs of typically 300 copies (Hallewell 319), now the number of copies sold could be ten times as much. Lobato's edition of *Sacri-Pererê-Resultado de um Inquérito* was published on 26 June 1918, and had sold 1,000 copies within a month. He brought out a second edition which went through a further 1,800 copies by 3 October, and by June 1919, the work had sold 11,500 copies. In 1920 Lobato brought out a print-run of 8,000 copies, an almost unheard-of figure for a work of fiction at the time. By 1923, there had been nine impressions of *Sacri-Pererê* and 30,000 copies had been sold (Hallewell 315–16). The irony is that the success of *Sacri-Pererê* was built on an advertising campaign (it is not seen as a literary classic nowadays, and it is rarely read). An indication of Lobato's success is that his firm was selling an average of 4,000 books per month and by 1921 publishing a new book a week (Hallewell 329). Lobato had changed the publishing industry in Brazil almost overnight.

One further element needs to be mentioned and this is the culmination during this period of the process we have seen at work in the previous century, namely, the gradual professionalization of the literary career. Many of the best literary journals of this era were keen to set down markers describing the purview of their professional activity. The Argentinian journal, *Nosotros*, a jewel of its kind, is a case in point. Following the announcement of the winners of the annual national literary prizes of 1923, which were for literature and science combined, and given the substantial reward offered to the winners in each category (a first prize of 30,000 pesos, a second prize of 20,000 pesos, and a third prize of 10,000 pesos, with the first prize not far behind the Nobel Prize amount of the time), the editors at *Nosotros* called for a separation between the different fields, arguing: 'Las obras literarias sólo pueden juzgarlas con plena autoridad y dominio los profesionales de la literatura.'[1] The same point was made, with even more directness, two years later:

> no es suficiente haber sido hombre de gobierno, buen orador, persona culta y sagaz, para acertar a discernir cosa tan delicada como son los valores poéticos, de composición, de estímulo y todas las menudencias y exquisiteces del arte.[2]

---

[1] 'Los premios a las letras y las ciencias de 1923', *Nosotros* 187 (1924): 520–3 (at p. 522).
[2] 'Los premios nacionales de literatura de 1925', *Nosotros* 217 (1927): 449; 218 (1927): 593–5 (at pp. 594–5).

Both of these comments were predicated on an awareness of the increasing professionalization of the literary writer's craft during the 1920s, which strikes a vivid contrast with the ambiance only a generation before. The editors at *Nosotros* were finally recognised professionally; in the late 1920s they were the judges of the literary prizes, rather than commenting peevishly from the sidelines. A further boost was given to the institutionalisation of literary criticism by the Instituto de Filología in Buenos Aires, especially under the inspired leadership of Américo Castro in the 1920s and Amado Alonso in the 1930s and 1940s, which led to the creation of a new beast: the professional literary critic.

## Modernismo, Modernity and the Semana de Arte Moderna

Twentieth-century Latin American literature, especially its poetry, is defined by its sense of rupture from the past, its embracing of the modern world. For the inhabitants of the big cities of Latin America at the turn of the century, life began to change rapidly; industrialisation and technology were the main causes: the growth of mechanised labour, the expanding grip of communication (the telegraph, followed by telefax and telephone communication), the growth of the ease of travel, the growth of a new urban consciousness, as rural labourers flocked to the new jobs available in the cities where they could earn vast times more. Before long a poem dedicated to Helion seemed less relevant than a poem about the bright neon lights of the city. Brazil was in many ways the country most acutely conscious of the implications of this paradigm-shift. During the Modern Art Week which took place from 13 to 17 February 1922 in São Paolo, and which gave rise to Brazilian *Modernismo*, the poet Menotti del Pichia gave a sense of what had changed:

> We want light, air, ventilators, airplanes, workers' demands, idealism, motors, factory smokestacks, blood, speed, dream, in our Art. And may the chugging of an automobile on the track of two lines of verses, frighten away from poetry the last Homeric God who went on sleeping and dreaming of the flutes of Arcadian shepherds and the divine breasts of Helen, an anachronism in the era of the jazz band and the movie. (Bishop and Brasil xix)

The spell of Graeco-Roman culture – and particularly its association with ruralism (Vergil's *Georgics*) and the natural world iconically epitomised by the *topos* of the *locus amoenus* – had suddenly been broken. Menotti del Pichia balanced his rejection of the classical *topos* with the promotion of technology (ventilation, airplanes, motors, the chugging of an automobile) along with the inevitable results of industrialisation (workers' demands, factory smokestacks). This paradigm-shift did not in itself mean that this was a discourse without ideals, for Menotti del Pichia promotes 'idealism' and 'dream'. It is simply that the idealism of Helen's 'divine breasts' has been exchanged for an idealism based on 'blood, speed, dream'.

The metaphor Menotti del Pichia uses (the chugging of an automobile on the track of lines of verse) is eloquent in that it specifically refers to how the traditional symmetry of verse (as epitomised by the rhymed sonnet) has been displaced by the railway lines of modern industrialisation – yet note that there is also an element of the bizarre, the surreal, in the analogy, since it involves an automobile going along the train lines. This element of the unexpected – in the sense of the innovative juxtaposition of two elements not normally associated with each other (which would become one of the central tenets of Surrealism's creed) – would replace the safe complementarity implied by the use of rhyme in traditional poetry. The spark of the new image replaced the matching phonetic dualism of the rhyme.

Manuel Bandeira's poem, 'Poética' epitomises this impatience with the past:

> Estou farto do lirismo comedido
> Do lirismo bem compartado
> Do lirismo funcionário público com livro de ponto expediente protocolo e
>     manifestações de aprêço ao sr. Diretor
> Estou farto do lirismo que pára e vai averiguar no dicionário o cunho
>     vernáculo de um vocábulo
> Abaixo os puristas
> Tôdas as palavras sobretudo os barbarismos universais
> Tôdas as construções sobretudo as sintaxes de exceção
> Todos os ritmos sobretudo os inumeráveis. (Cândido, *Presença*, vol. 3, 38–9)

This poetics is a clear rejection of the Parnassians and the Symbolists with their purist attitude towards rhyme and language, and it is a clear rejection of the type of poet who combined poetry with a career in the civil service, perhaps as a diplomat. As such it voiced a notion of the artist as somebody totally committed to his art. What the Brazilian *Modernistas* rejected was the academic notion of the arts; instead they embraced art as part and parcel of real life. Such is the argument of Bandeira's 'O último poema':

> Assim eu quereria o meu último poema
> Que fôsse terno dizendo as coisas mais simples e menos intencionais
> Que fôsse ardente como um soluço sem lágrimas
> Que tivesse a beleza das flôres quase sem perfume
> A pureza da chama en que se consomem os diamantes mais límpidos
> A paixão dos suicidas que se matam sem explicação.
>                                    (Cândido, *Presença*, vol. 3, 43)

The important point about the various metaphors that Bandeira chooses is that they relate not to books or literary formulae but to the rawness of life itself, and also, perhaps more importantly, to the notion of the incomprehensibility of life ('sem explicação').

One of the key texts of Brazilian *Modernismo* is *Paulicéa Desvairada*

(1922) by Mário de Andrade (1893–1945). The prologue of this collection of poems, normally reserved as a space in which to thank one's masters, is instead a letter written on 14 December 1921 from one Mário de Andrade to one Mário de Andrade, and which begins:

> Mestre querido.
>
> Nas muitas horas breves me fizetes ganhar
> a vosso lado dizieis da vossa confiança pela arte
> livre e sincera. Não de mim, mas de vossa
> experiencia recebi a coragem da minha Verdade
> e o orgulho do meu ideal. (*Andrade: Poesias completas*)

Written in the style of the ephebe to the master, it upturns the system of patronage – whether commercial or artistic – by relating the source of inspiration firmly back to within the self. One of the aims of this work is to lay out a manifesto of what it means to create modern art. Andrade rejects the notion that simply mentioning icons of the modern world is the key to modern art: 'Escrever arte moderna não significa jamais / para mim representar a vida actual no que tem / de exterior: automovéis, cinema, asfalto. Si / estas palavras frequentam-me o livro não é porque pensei com / elas escrever moderno, mas / porque sendo meu libro moderno, elas têm nele / sua razão de ser' (*Andrade: Poesias completas* 28–9). He recognises furthermore that there are certain themes which transcend the modern and are, as it were, universal: 'Reconheço mais a existência de / temas eternos, passivéis de afeiçoar pela / modernidade: universo, pátria, amor e a / presença-dos-ausentes, ex-goso-amargo-de- / infelizes' (Andrade, *Poesias*, 29; for further discussion see Hart, 'Twilight').

An intrinsic part of the vitality of *Modernismo* had to do with its re-evaluation of Brazil's Amerindian cultural heritage. A key figure here was Oswald de Andrade (1890–1954). He published *Os Condenados* in 1922, a novel, and this was followed in 1925 by *Poema pau-brasil*, in which he published his famous 'Manifesto antropófago'. Beginning with a pun ('Tupi or not tupi, that is the question'), the poem – which is deliberately more of a running commentary on Brazilian culture and its place in the world, than a poem as traditionally understood – draws attention to the fear and horror experienced by Europeans when they encountered cannibalism in the New World, and then calls for 'a revolução Caraíba' (Cândido, *Presença*, vol. 3, 67), which will reject the Jesuits ('Contra o Padre Vieira', 68), and identify with cannibalism. Brazil has a 'Necessidade da vacina antropofágica' (68), in the sense that Brazilian culture, Oswald de Andrade argues, in what is essentially a post colonial move, needs to protect itself against European dominance by creating a cultural vaccine which would allow Brazil to achieve national identity. He gives an example of what this rejection of foreign influence might entail: 'Perguntei a um homen o que era o / Direito. Êle me respondeu que era a garantia do exercício da possibilidade. Êsse homen chamava-se Galli

Mathias. Comi-o' (Cândido, *Presença*, vol. 3, 70). Clearly a boutade in the avant-garde sense, the gesture of eating one's interlocutor had a specifically Brazilian flavour to it. The main problem, though, that the *Modernistas* in Brazil struggled with was how to find a form of expression which would be adequate to the task of returning to Brazil's cultural roots. As Mário de Andrade wrote in his essay, 'O Artista Moderno' in 1925: 'Somos na realidade uns primitivos. E como todos os primitivos realistas e estilizadores. A realização sincera da matéria afectiva e do subconsciente é nosso realismo' (Cândido, *Presença*, vol. 3, 88). The subconscious and the primitive – that was now Brazil's real.

The avant-garde in Spanish America was above all expressed in a cluster of poets flocking around a number of literary journals. Contacts between Spain and Spanish America intensified during the avant-garde period and poets such as the Chilean Vicente Huidobro (1893–1948) played a crucial role in introducing the avant-garde from France to Spain and thence to Spanish America; Jorge Luis Borges (1899–1986), the genius of his era, likewise, brought the energy of the new Spanish *ultraísta* movement back to Buenos Aires in 1921. The avant-garde had many diverse ramifications in Spanish America, ranging from the *ultraísta* group in Buenos Aires centring around the reviews *Prisma* (1921–22) and *Proa* (1922–23), both of which were founded by Borges, to the more politicized *estridentista* movement founded by Manuel Maples Arce (1898–1963) in Mexico City, of which the main reviews were *Actual: Hoja de vanguardia* and *Irradiador*. In all of the various journals that sprang up in the Americas as a result of this European influence (the *Revista de Avance* [1927–30] in Cuba, *Contemporáneos* [1928–31] in Mexico, and *Claridad* [1926–] in Argentina), one factor was constant: the use of new typography to open up the spatial depth of the printed word.

The key figure of the avant-garde movement in Spanish America is Huidobro. In a poem, 'Arte poética', from *Espejo del agua*, for example, Huidobro expounded his new poetic creed, which, given its reliance on the notion of creation, came to be known as *creacionismo*: 'Por qué cantáis la rosa, ¡oh, Poetas! / Hacedla florecer en el poema' (Huidobro 78). Two features of the poetry Huidobro wrote during this period in the avant-garde style ought to be emphasised. Firstly, and largely as a result of his enthusiasm for Marinetti's call for a new type of art inspired by the city, by its machines, its technology and its speed, Huidobro chose an urban, cosmopolitan environment as a backdrop to his poems. The first poem of his best collection of avant-garde poems, *Poemas árticos* (1918), for example, 'Exprés', mentions six European cities in the first four lines, London, Madrid, Paris, Rome, Naples and Zurich (Huidobro 211). The final section of *Ecuatorial* (1918), as another example, describes a breathtakingly fast train ride (Huidobro 250). The second feature of Huidobro's poetry which needs to be emphasised is his use of typographical spacing (evident in the passage of text quoted above). Often Huidobro used the white space on the page as a means of bodying forth a sense of nihilistic anguish. In the poem 'Universo' (Huidobro 232), for example, Huidobro is able to use the device of word spacing in order to enhance the meaning of the poem (which revolves around a sense of ontological lostness).

One poet whose work has some of the dislocated defamiliarisation we associate with the avant-garde is the Argentine poet Oliviero Girondo (1891–1967). In one poem Girondo takes the concept of sadness and crying, and by a process of repetition, empties it of meaning, making it absurd. The first stanza begins with a normal expression and gradually begins to tear it apart: 'Llorar a lágrima viva. Llorar a chorros. Llorar la digestión. Llorar el sueño. Llorar ante las puertas y los puertos. Llorar de amabilidad y de amarillo' (Caracciolo-Trejo 23). The reader is tempted to surmise that some of the associations have been created by phonetic coincidence more than the logic of cause and effect (namely, 'puertas/puertos' and 'amabilidad/amarillo'). This absurdity is pursued until it leads to deliberately non-logical associations: 'Asistir a los cursos de antropología, llorando. Festejar los cumpleaños familiares, llorando. Atravesar el África, llorando' (Caracciolo-Trejo 23). Girondo's poetry, like Huidobro's, is intended as a bracing shock to the bourgeois system of the reader, forcing him out of his complacency, allowing him to see the world anew.

## Poetry: From Avant-garde to Revolution

Unlike Huidobro who remained true to his avant-garde roots, a number of poets of this era began as poets of the vanguard but ended up in the revolution. Some, like César Vallejo and Pablo Neruda, turned to politics mid-way through their poetic careers. César Vallejo (1892–1938), was born in Santiago de Chuco, a tiny town in the Peruvian Andes, and ended his days in Paris. He is undoubtedly one of the finest, if not the finest, of all Spanish America's poets. While he wrote essays, short stories, a novel and some plays, he is mainly remembered for his poetry. His work is best understood if split into its five main stages which are: 1915–18 *modernismo*; 1919–26 the avant-garde; 1927–31 Marxist (Trotskyism gradually transformed into Stalinism); 1932–35 political disillusionment; 1936–38 Christian Marxism. Representative of the first phase is his collection of poems, *Los heraldos negros* (1918, though in circulation as of 1919) which shows clear signs of Vallejo's literary apprenticeship in *modernismo*, but also hints at a new poetic voice, one which eschews the Graeco-Roman world of mythology in favour of a mythology of the quotidian, and uses Christian symbolism in incongruous, disorientating contexts, such as in 'El pan nuestro'. Some poems openly question God's role in the universe ('Los dados eternos'), some demonstrate the stirrings of an Amerindian consciousness ('Huaco'), and others hint at the growth of social concern for the have-nots of the world ('El pan nuestro'). Poems such as 'A mi hermano Miguel' show Vallejo's skill in the use of colloquial language and everyday situations, tied to his ability to conjure up the world of the child, that would become the hallmark of his poetry. Some of these concerns would continue in his later collection of poems, *Trilce* (1922), published, not coincidentally it would seem, in the same year as Joyce's *Ulysses*, such as the poems dedicated to his immediate family, and poems which conjure up the lost magic of childhood. But there is also a palpable change in poetic diction and subject-matter. Some of the poems talk about the sexual act in a way that is remarkably explicit given the time they were published, while most of the poems demonstrate Vallejo's willingness to expand the resources of the Spanish language in order to create a new vision: neologism, provincialism, archaism, typographical innovation, letter spacing, calligrammatics, slang and legal language all find their way into his poetic armoury.

The work on which his reputation largely rests is his collection of *Poemas humanos*, written probably over a long period from 1927 until 1936, which show evidence of Vallejo's growing political commitment over those years (he was a frequent visitor to the bookstore of *L'Humanité*, the communist newspaper). The collection was published posthumously along with *Poemas en prosa* and *España, aparta de mí este cáliz*, by Vallejo's widow in 1939, the year after Vallejo's death. About one half of the poems of *Poemas humanos* take the collective as their point of departure; some such as 'Los mineros salieron de la mina' express enthusiasm for the collective ethos of communism, some express dismay at the exploitation and pain experienced by the proletariat ('Los desgraciados'), while others express disillusionment with politics and politicians ('Despedida recordando un adiós'). The recent discovery of the early autograph versions of many of Vallejo's posthumous poems reveal him to have been a poet who constantly reworked his poems (see Fló and Hart). *España, aparta de mí este cáliz*, written during the first two years of the Spanish Civil War (1936–38) which Vallejo did not live to see end, expresses a political faith in the Republican cause through the motif of Christian resurrection, a rather unusual choice given the proletarian and often anti-clerical bias of the Republicans, and especially the communists who supported the Republican war effort. The most famous poem of this collection is 'Masa' which uses the biblical parallel of Lazarus's resurrection to express the triumph of solidarity between all nations (Vallejo 300).

Pablo Neruda (1904–73), the Chilean poet who won the Nobel Prize in 1971, né Ricardo Nefaltí Reyes Basoalto, is along with Vallejo one of the best Spanish American poets of the twentieth century, and their poetry is similar in terms of its pursuit of truth (Vallejo once referred to his own work and Neruda's in terms of 'verdadismo'; see Stephen Hart, 'Pablo Neruda'). Neruda's early work, *Veinte poemas de amor y una canción desesperada* (1924) is Romantic, his first two collections of *Residencia en la tierra* (Part I, 1933; Part II, 1935) have striking similarities with Surrealism, while the poetry from *España en el corazón* (1937) onwards in the main is politically committed. *Veinte poemas de amor*, his most popular if not his best collection of poems, is addressed to two women who are given symbolic pseudonyms (Marisol from Temuco and Marisombra from Santiago) and typically expresses a view of love which is organicist, penetrative and phallic. The beloved is typically pictured as a bountiful and receptive earth, as in 'Cuerpo de mujer' (Neruda, *Twenty* 8). The poems of the second phase are more demanding and more intellectually rewarding. The main *topoi* of *Residencia en la tierra* are sex, death, and the decay of the universe. Often in these poems the reader becomes involved in the hermeneutic process itself, as if reliving the poetic subject's desperate groping for the meaning of the world, because of the stop-start nature of the syntax and the imagery. In 'Arte poética', for example, the poet's awareness of a 'confused name' (Neruda, *Residencia*, vol. 2, 40) is specifically related to his vision of the liquid drives which animate the human as well as the animal and plant kingdom; some poems specifically concentrate on thanatos ('Sólo la muerte') and eros ('Agua sexual'), while others concentrate on the elements of human life which repress those instincts, as in 'Ritual de mis piernas' where the accoutrements of civilisation (manufactured objects, and particularly shoes) cut the poetic subject off from direct contact with those terrestrial energies (Neruda, *Residencia*, vol. 2, 59).

The Spanish Civil War changed abruptly Neruda's preoccupation with the space of the personal. As a result of his first-hand experience of the atrocities of war (he was Chilean ambassador in Madrid at the time) he became a communist, and his work reflects this ideological upheaval. *España en el corazón*, which was written as a result and which is now included in *Tercera residencia* (1947), is a bitter attack on the Nationalists with their ecclesiastical and aristocratic allies; it has a section devoted to the three principal Nationalist generals, Sanjurjo, Mola and Franco (all of whom are treated to a vision of what it will be like when they are in hell) and it eulogises the Republican troops, hammering out in every stanza the natural, organic connection between them and the earth. *España en el corazón* is an angry, circumstantial poem in which Neruda honed his diatribic skills, skills which he would use to devastating effect in his monumental epic poem, *Canto general* (1950). This collection of poems relates in verse the history of the South-American peoples, from their genesis in the remote mists of time to present-day Chile (1950). Like the Old Testament it exudes a fascination with the genealogical along with the joy of new creation. The poet becomes the scribe of the limitless, unnamed reservoir of experience of the past (*Canto* I, xii; Neruda, *Canto* 38–9). Neruda writes the historical epic of the South-American peoples not from a Eurocentric point of view but rather from a worm's-eye view of the downtrodden Indians, the Negro slaves, the working masses, the communists. Neruda's is a defiantly oppositional writing of Latin American history. The political thematics of Neruda's work remained fairly constant in the poetry published after 1950 – his parting shot before he died was a short poetic diatribe entitled *Incitación al Nixoncidio y alabanza de la revolución chilena* (1973) in which he charged President Nixon with having conspired to bring about the downfall of Salvador Allende – although he did write some charming poems about the beauties of everyday life, particularly in his celebrated *Odas elementales* (1954).

One other major poet of this period is Nicolás Guillén (1902–89), Cuba's national poet and one who, in the words of one critic, 'for many years has preached the synthesis or the realisation of the universal man in an antiracist society where brotherhood rather than narrow racialism is sought' (Jackson, *Black Image* 125). Like Vallejo and Neruda, Guillén was marked by the wave of politicisation which swept through Latin America in the 1930s. His work may, roughly speaking, be divided into two periods, the pre-political era, including works such as *Motivos de son* (1930) and *Sóngoro cosongo* (1931), in which the *negrista* mode is dominant, and those works which are politicised in tone and subject matter, such as *West Indies Ltd* (1934), *Cantos para soldados y sones para turistas* (1937), *España (Poemas en cuatro angustias y una esperanza)* (1937), based specifically on his experience of the Spanish Civil War, *El son entero* (1947) and *La paloma de vuelo popular* (1958). Though we may plot different phases of his work, there is a sense in which they flow together, in that the *negrista* ideology of the earlier works leads naturally into the anti-imperialist stage of the later works. The early work is concerned essentially with expressing the black experience of the everyday Cuban. 'Búcate plata', for example, from *Motivos de son*, focuses on the 'incorrect' speech of a young woman telling her lover she will leave him if he doesn't earn more money: 'búcate plata, / búcate plata, / porque me voy a correr' (Chang-Rodríguez and Filer, 396). One of the most charming poems of the early work is 'Sensemayá (Canto para matar a una culebra)', from *Sóngora cosongo*, based on an African chant designed to hypnotise the snake allowing the singer to kill it. The poem uses a refrain throughout ('¡Mayombe-bombe-mayombe!') which, through its repetition of meaningless sounds (at least in Spanish), signals that the meaning of the poem centres around its use of musicality and rituality. Guillén's most powerful political poems are in *West Indies, Ltd* which homes in on the exploitation of Negroes in the sugar trade. Rather than overtly copy the language of the blacks and express sympathy linguistically (as was the case for example in the early works), now Guillén expresses solidarity in terms of the enunciation of political content. Guillén's work is varied. At its best it reveals a face of the Caribbean involving racism, and the ostracisation of the black Cuban from civil society, which many would have preferred not to see. In its honesty and integrity, Guillén achieves a voice of authenticity describing black experience which is unequalled in Spanish America.

## Two Poets in Counterpoint

Two poets who offer an interesting counterpoint to the notion of the avant-garde leading to the revolution are the Mexican Octavio Paz (1914–98) and the Cuban Regino Boti (1878–1958). Paz is often characterised as Latin America's Pope of Surrealism, such was the close relationship he established with André Breton. In his poem 'Esto y esto y esto' Paz describes Surrealism as a destructive as well as purificatory force:

> El surrealismo ha sido la manzana de fuego en el árbol de la sintáxis
> El surrealismo ha sido la camelia de ceniza entre los pechos de la adolescente poseída por el espectro de Orestes
> El surrealismo ha sido el plato de lentejas que la mirada del hijo pródigo transforma en festín humeante del rey caníbal.
> (Paz, *Collected Poems* 516–17)

In 'Cuarteto' he alludes to how 'Es frágil lo real y es inconstante / también, su ley el cambio, infatigable: / gira la rueda de las apariencias / sobre el eje del tiempo, su fijeza' (Paz, *Collected Poems*, 494–5). Providing a counterpoint to the poet's search for the 'fixed axis of time' beneath the sea of appearances is the sense that the centre (an image at once of knowledge and fixity) is always elusive. Man's meaning comes from elsewhere yet the key is not given. As we read in the poem 'Hermandad':

> Soy hombre: duro poco
> y es enorme la noche.
> Pero miro hacia arriba:
> las estrellas escriben.
> Sin entender comprendo:
> también soy escritura
> y en este mismo instante alguien me deletrea.
> (Paz, *Collected Poems* 508–9)

Caught on the knife-edge between knowing and unknowing (as suggested by the oxymoron 'Unknowing I understand') Paz's poetry searches out and also records the dizzying moment when opposites collide, and the impossible springs into being. As we read in 'Proema': 'A veces la poesía es el vértigo de los cuerpos y el vértigo de la dicha y el vértigo de la muerte: / el paseo con los ojos cerrados al borde del despeñadero y la verbena en los jardines submarinos' (Paz, *Collected Poems* 482–3). In two lines Paz juxtaposes height and depth – echoing Breton's sense that Surrealism attempts to identify that point in which height and depth are no longer contradictory terms – and this epiphany involves a coming-closer to the roots of language, to a point at which phenomenal world and language become as one: 'los sustantitvos óseos y llenos de raíces, plantados en las ondulaciones del lenguaje' (Paz, *Collected Poems* 482–3). As so often in his work the poet is caught, transfixed as it were between time and eternity, yet focused on the return to the birth of consciousness: 'nos bañamos en ríos de latidos, / volvemos al perpetuo recomienzo' (Paz, *Collected Poems* 608–9). It is at points like these that Paz allows an elemental, even Jungian, consciousness to surface within the language of his poetry.

Boti's poetry offers a similar trajectory to Paz's in that it explores the avant-garde as a vehicle through which an esoteric meaning to life's chaos could be glimpsed, though in Boti's case those deeper syntactic structures were often non-European, Afro-Cuban. He published five collections of poetry in his lifetime, *Arabescos mentales* (1913), *El mar y la montaña* (1921), *La torre del silencio* (1926), *Kodak-Ensueño* (1929) and *Kindergarten* (1930). In his *Arabescos mentales* Boti reveals himself to be clearly in tune with the *modernista* movement, and by and large this collection retains but transforms some common stanzaic structures of the time such as the sonnet form and the hendecasyllable, and shows the imprint of that gloomy Zeitgeist which permeated the work of the *modernistas*. In 'El puente' he asks: 'si todo ha de morir, ¿por qué edifico?' (l. 56; Boti, 48). From *El mar y la montaña* onwards, however, Boti – like many of his contemporaries – began to discard *modernista* rhetoric, a process which reaches its zenith in *Kodak-Ensueño* (1929); the primacy of the visual realm and the modern world is proclaimed in the double-barrelled title. It is in *Kindergarten* (1930), though, that we see a distinctively new poetic idiom emerging. Some of the poems are linguistically iconoclastic – note the deliberate Joycean-Vallejian mis-spellings and neologisms of 'Diálogo muy siglo 22', 'kolosal', 'Hominícaco', 'radiovitafónicas', and 'exámetros' (Boti 116) – while others such as 'Babul', for example, hint at the birth of a new Cuban poetics: 'Songo. Bilongo./ Repongo. Propongo./ Dispongo./ Tacatá, tacatá./ Tacatá, tacatá' (ll. 9–14; Boti 118–20).[3]

## Everyday Brazilian Poetry

After the heady rush of the Semana de Arte Moderna Brazilian poetry gradually settled down into what might be called the poetics of the everyday. The self-dramatisation, the grandeur of poetry, the love of the *grand récit* – traces of which, to be sure, underlay *Modernismo* – gradually seeped away as the century wore on. Carlos Drummond de Andrade (1902–87) was perhaps the poet *par excellence* of this new type of poetry, one which was able to use ordinary words to build up a picture of profound human significance. Drummond de Andrade's 'Procura da poesia', for example, is a masterfully ironic poem on the irrelevance of traditional *topoi* addressed to an imaginary up-and-coming poet. As the poem opens: 'Não faças versos sôbre acontecimentos./ Não há criação nem morte perante a poesia' (Caracciolo-Trejo 82). He is ironic about the Romantic emphasis on self-expression: 'Não me reveles teus sentimentos, / que se prevaleem do equívoco e tentam a longa viagem. O que pensas e sentes, isso ainda não é poesia' (83). Finally the poet is reminded not to dramatise his sentiments and ideas in the classical Narcissistic pose of the self-important poet: 'Não dramatizes, não invoques, / não indagues. Não percas tempo em mentir' (83). It is the realm of words, language itself, where poetry lies, waiting to be discovered: 'Penetra surdamente no reino das palavras./ Lá estão os poemas que esperam ser escritos' (83). His 'Viagem na família' describes a journey backwards into the past of his own family; it lists details about the life

---

[3] This section has necessarily had to sacrifice exhaustiveness in the interests of representativity; for an excellent selection of Mexican poetry of this period, for example see Paz et al., *Poesía en movimiento*.

of his ancestors in nouns which do not need adjectives to evoke a period of his family history:

> Pisando livros e cartas,
> viajamos na família.
> Casamentos; hipotecas;
> os primos tuberculosos; a tia louca; minha avó
> traída com as escravas. (Bishop and Brasil 58)

A poem to a friend who is suffering from a love affair, entitled 'Não se mate' tries to give some advice in unpretentious, unpoetic language:

> Carlos, sossegue, o amor,
> é isso que você está vendo: hoje beija, amanhã não beija,
> depois de amanhã é domingo
> e segunda-feira ninguém sabe
> o que será. (Bishop and Brasil 64)

'A mesa' and 'Infância' (Bishop and Brasil 86), though dealing with big issues such as love, death and fatherhood, keep the poem firmly within the realm of everyday activities such as eating, drinking, sitting, sewing. Yet, even when Drummond de Andrade uses everyday language this does not mean that the rhythm of speech or the sensitivity to poetic image are lost. 'A paixão medida' is a wonderfully witty comment on the interplay between love and poetry:

> Trocaica te amei, com ternura dáctila
> e gesto espondeu.
> Teus iambos aos meus com força entrelacei.
> Em dia alcmânico, o instinto ropálico
> rompeu, leonino, a porta pentâmetra.
> Gemido trilongo entre breves murmúrios.
> E que mais e que mais, no crepúsculo ecóico,
> senão a quebrada lembrança
> de latina, de grega, inumerável delícia? (Drummond de Andrade 27)

The lover's arms are turned into the poet's 'iambs', the briefness of the experience of love becomes the poem's 'breves' in a text which shows how language and life are inseparable within the context of human experience.

Named the 'most significant poet of the post-War War II generation in Brazil' by Djelal Kadir (Kadir ix) Carlos João Cabral de Melo Neto (1920–99) dominates the poetic landscape of contemporary Brazil. Though at first glance Cabral de Melo Neto's poetry appears easy to understand, it has a hermeneutical sting in its tail. Like a number of his contemporaries Cabral de Melo Neto uses a down-to-earth frame of reference rather than the *grand récit* of history and myth, though he typically focuses on the juxtaposition of simple words in order to create a sense of a more profound reality hovering behind that everyday reality. The first stanza of 'Espaço jornal', for example, uses images of everyday objects such as a shadow, an orange, a river, the sea, but – via a surprising set of juxtapositions – describes himself crying:

> No espaço jornal
> a sombra come a laranja
> a laranja se atira no rio,
> não é um rio, é o mar
> que trasborda de meu ôlho. (Bishop and Brasil 114)

Likewise, 'Poema' produces a jarring juxtaposition between the abstract (soul) and the concrete (telescope, street) in order to force the reader into a new awareness of their interplay: 'Meus olhos têm telescópios / espiando a rua, / espiando minha alma / longe de mim mil metros'; the poem ends by asserting that this soul, far from being his 'inner life', is in fact his 'inner death': 'Ficarei indefinidamente contemplando / meu retrato eu morto' (Bishop and Brasil 118). In 'A educação pela pedra' Cabral de Melo Neto explores the notion of the knowledge within stones in the Brazilian outback; while the stone is able to give lessons in morals, poetics and economics, 'No Sertão a pedra não sabe lecionar, e se lecionassse, não ensinaria nada: / lá não se aprende a pedra: lá a pedra, / uma pedra de nascença, entranha a alma' (Bishop and Brasil 148). Cabral de Melo Neto's vision is out of the ordinary (he sees knowledge within objects not normally associated with profundity), yet he is able to do so succinctly with everyday words and everyday concepts. In contrast to those stones which contain wisdom, man is full of emptiness, made of 'pieces of emptiness' and 'bits of nothingness, 'o vazio que inchou por estar vazio' ('Os vazios do homen', Bishop and Brasil 158). In his poem 'Poesia', for example, Cabral de Melo Neto emphasises how poetry alone is able to cause the meaning of the world to emerge, and it will do so within the 'supernatural atmosphere of poetry':

> Deixa falar todas as coisas visíveis
> Deixa falar a aparência das coisas que vivem no tempo
> Deixa, suas vozes seraõ abafadas.
> A voz imensa que dorme no mistério sufocara a todas.
> Deixa, que tudo só fructificará
> Na atmosfera sobrenatural da poesia. (Kadir, *Selected Poetry* 6)

One element which frequently allows Cabral de Melo Neto's poetry to acquire such depth is the way in which it introduces a self-conscious gaze into the space of the poem's enunciation, for example in 'Poema', where the sense of the way in which a street – which is before the poet – has been perceived by others, is turned into a theatrical as well as filmic performance.

> As estradas em *long-shot* todas
> se reuniram numa só Estrada

> que corria entre representações ideais
> e que ele descobriu estarem presentes
> na retina do primeiro homen
> quando ele foi ao teatro. (Kadir 8)

The writing of the poem thereby re-enacts a previous set of representations of the road in a highly self-conscious gesture. 'A lição de poesia' focuses likewise on the ways in which the phenomenal world is translated into the verbal reality of poetry – here epitomised as the 'twenty words of poetry':

> Vinte palavras sempre as mesmas
> de que conhece o funcionamento,
> a evaporação, a densidade
> menor que a do ar. (Kadir 28)

The words, now caught immobile on the page, the breath squeezed out of them, have a density less than the air's. For even as he uses everyday words ('household bees' as he calls them in another poem, 'Psicologia da composicação, V', Kadir 44), he turns the things to which the words refer into an inorganic, mineral substance ('Psicologia da composicação, VII', Kadir 48). Yet, even as he seems to empty those words of their life-blood, he is finding new life within life, finding – to use his own metaphor – 'an orchard in reverse' within the 'desert' ('Cultivar o deserto / como um pomar as avessas'; 'Psicologia da composicação, VIII', Kadir 50).

Cabral de Melo Neto's poetry has cast a long shadow in twentieth-century Brazilian poetry, and, thus, when the modern poet expresses a sense of existential lostness he will often do so with quotidian metaphors. Murilo Mendes's poem 'Mapa', for example, depicting the self as fluid; he is a mélange, 'um corpo desconjuntado', 'um fluido', not tied down by time or space (Bishop and Brasil 48), not subscribing to any theory (50):

> estou no ar,
> na alma dos criminosos, dos amantes desesperados,
> no meu quarto modesto da Praia de Botafogo,
> no pensamento dos homens que movem o mundo,
> nem triste nem alegre, chama como dois olhos andando,
> sempre em transformação. (Bishop and Brasil 52)

Even when invoking the agency of God within the world, Jorge de Lima's poetry uses a down-to-earth rhetorical vehicle to do so. In 'A mão enorme', for example, a ship sails through the night and, despite the darkness all around, it is protected by 'a mão eterna' of God (Bishop and Brasil 18). Ferreira Gullar's poetry runs along similar lines to that of Drummond de Andrade and Cabral de Melo Neto in that it focuses on everyday things such as 'A Casa' (Brasil and Smith 10–13) and 'Coisas da Terra', but with the injunction that the everyday contains a deeper, 'eternal' level. As the latter poem begins:

> Todas as coisas de que falo estão na cidade
> entre o céu e a terra.
> São todas elas coisas perecíveis
> e eternas como o teu riso
> a palavra solidária
> minha mão aberta. (Brasil and Smith 18)

Poetry is clearly associated with the deeper level of awareness since, as we learn towards the end of the same poem, these are

> Coisas,
> de que falam os jornais
> às vezes tão rudes
> às vezes tão escuras
> que mesmo a poesia as ilumina com dificuldade.
>
> (Brasil and Smith 18)

His poem 'Agosto 1964', written in the aftermath of the military coup which only four months before had deposed João Goulart, expresses his anger at this turn of events: 'Ao peso dos impostos, o verso sufoca, / a poesia agora responde a inquérito policial-militar' (Brasil and Smith 20). For poetry is seen as emerging from a realm of anarchic freedom, not weighed down by the laws of the state:

> A poesia
> quando chega
>           não respeita nada.
> Nem pai nem mãe.
>           Quando ela chega
> de qualquer de seus abismos
> desconhece o Estado e a Sociedade Civil
> desrespeita o Código de Águas. (Brasil and Smith 48)

A very significant Brazilian female poet of the twentieth century is Cecília Meireles (1901–64). One of her most famous poems is 'Balada das dez bailarinas do cassino' in which she attacks the merciless sexual exploitation of women within Brazil's casino culture. Despite their makeup, they are 'tão nuas se sentem que já vão cobertas / de imaginários, chorosos vestidos' and they carry their own bodies 'como quem leva para a terra um filho morto' (Bishop and Brasil 38). The (spiritual) death which they hold within their bodies – underlined by a series of images including 'anjos anêmicos' and 'múmias' – is distilled through the tears of the mothers who, the poem suggests, would weep if they saw their daughters exploited in this way: 'Dez mães chorariam, se vissem / as bailarinas de mãos dadas' (40).

Working seemingly in an opposite direction to the poetics of the quotidian is Concrete Poetry, for which – at least outside Brazil – Brazilian twentieth-century literature is famous. Three figures are normally associated with the movement Décio Pignatari (b. 1927), Augusto de Campos (b. 1931) and, arguably the key figure, Harold de Campos (1923–2003). In 'Servidão de passagem', for example, Harold de Campos explores the oppression of man caused by capitalism, but does so via a clever, self-referential exploration of the phonetic fibre of language. Naming is used to point to the hunger that capitalism serves up to the workers:

> poesia de dar o nome
> nomear e dar o nome
> nomeio o nome
> nomeio o homem
> no meio a fome
> nomeio a fome. (Brasil and Smith 53)

Naming, man and poetry, as a result of repetition of like-sounding words, are shown to have a necessary equivalence; their connectiveness is remotivated through word-play. Later on in the same poem phonetic overlap is used to produce new thought processes:

> e lucro a lucro
> logrado
> de lôgro a lôgro
> lucrado
> de lado a lado
> lanhado
> de lôdo a lôdo
> largado. (Brasil and Smith 54)

Once more human oppression is shown to be the inevitable corollary of any investigation of language. The poem, as Harold de Campos's notes reveal, is focused on the dilemma of whether poetry should be politically committed or 'pure', whether it should be 'poesia para' (literally 'poetry for') or 'poesia pura' (pure poetry, that is, devoid of any social or political significance). It could be argued that de Campos's poetry manages to combine the verbal sophistication we associate with 'poetry for poets' in the style of Stéphane Mallarmé, with a poetry which is committed to the cause of liberation. Certainly, word play is used to draw attention to oppression. Though not to everyone's taste – the influential cultural critic Roberto Schwarz launched a devastating attack on the movement in the 1980s, arguing that it was a symptom of the Brazilian malaise of the 'misplaced idea'; for further discussion see below pp.245–7 – Concrete Poetry is recognised as an important voice within the chorus of contemporary Brazilian poetry.

## The Novel 1900–30

In the first few decades of the twentieth century the novel in Latin America focused on two interrelated themes: the struggle over political space (that is, the identity of the nation), and the struggle over geographical space (namely, national territory). Though some would not see it as a novel, preferring to view it as an essay or at the very least a hybrid mix of novel and essay (for an excellent discussion see Souza Andrade 403–23), *Os Sertões* (1902) by Euclides da Cunha (1866–1909) is arguably the most important narrative text on Brazilian culture, geography and identity of the first half of the twentieth century. Neither an historical tract in the style of Edward Gibbon's *The History of the Decline and Fall of the Roman Empire* nor a novel in the Balzacian style, *Os Sertões* ranges widely, beginning with Brazil's geography, then turning to Brazilian 'man' as silhouetted against that landscape, who is first of all analysed in terms of the three races which are part of the Brazilian mix – the Indian, the African and the Portuguese – and subsequently in terms of types such as the *sertanejo* (inhabitant of the *sertões*, or backlands), the *gaúcho*, the *bandeirante*, and the *jagunço*. Finally the essay turns to an analysis of the life and deeds of one Antônio Vicente Mendes Maciel (which takes up the second half), called Antônio o Conselhiro by his followers. He led a messianic religious movement which grew in the backlands in the 1890s to such proportions that it became a grass-roots political attack on the legitimacy of the Republic. The movement was only finally vanquished as a result of a concerted military effort. Indeed, the second half of the book, in which the government campaign is meticulously recorded, is told with some verve (the first sally under the command of Lieutenant Manuel da Silva Pires Ferreira, was repulsed on 21 November 1896, the second expedition commanded by Major Febronio de Brito, turned back on 19 January 1897, the third under the command of General Moreira Cesar was forced to retreat on 3 March 1897, while the fourth and final expedition, under the command of General Arthur Oscar, set forth on 19 June 1897, and finally conquered the Canudos settlement on 5 October 1897, Antônio o Conselheiro having died on 24 September). It is clear early on in *Os Sertões* where da Cunha's allegiance lies – he refers to 'nossa gens, o portuguez' (da Cunha, *Os Sertões*, 66), he questions whether the African had any substantive role to play in the creation of Brazilian culture ('os africanos tiveram [...] uma função inferior' is his comment; 88), and he even describes the *sertanejo* as a 'Hercules-Quasimodo' type of person (114). In many respects, da Cunha holds views about race which were typical of an intellectual of his time; for him, thus, 'a mestiçagem extremada é um retrocesso' (108). For da Cunha the rebellion that Antonio o Conselhero orchestrated is important because it threw into very sharp focus the blindness which is at the core of Brazilian culture. As he puts it:

> Vivendo quatrocentos annos no littoral vastissimo, em que pallejam reflexos da vida civilizada, tivemos de improviso, como herança inesperada, a

Republica. Ascendemos, de chofre, arrebatados na caudal dos ideaes modernos, deixando na penumbra secular em que jazem, no amago do paiz, um terço da nossa gente. Illudidos por uma civilização de emprestimo; respigando, em faina cega de copistas, tudo o que de melhor existe nos codigos organicos de outras nações, tornamos, revolucionariarmente, fugindo ao transigir mais ligeiro com as exigencies da nossa propria nacionalidade, mais fundo o contraste entre o nosso modo de viver do que os immigrantes da Europa. (da Cunha, *Os Sertões*, 205)

As da Cunha puts it very succinctly, as a result of this distance between the city-dwellers and the *sertanejos*, the Canudos settlement became Brazil's Vendée (da Cunha, *Os Sertões*, 206); the comparison is apt given that the uprisings which occurred in the Vendée, an economically backward and fervently religious region of France, in 1793, were anti-statist and anti-republican and, as in Canudos, were eventually put down mercilessly. Perhaps most striking about *Os Sertões* is the way in which – as the narrative develops – it effects what is almost an ideological volte-face, for it eventually contrives to create a depth of sympathy, even admiration, for the inhabitants of the Canudos settlement, whereas early on in the essay da Cunha adopts a rather dismissive air towards the *sertanejos* on account of their backwardness, their lack of education, their medieval religious fervour, their anti-republicanism (Antônio o Conselheiro epitomises atavism, 149, and Canudos is the objectivisation of a tremendous insanity foisted upon it by him, 190–4). Pointing in a similar ideological direction da Cunha describes the battles from the technical point of view of a military strategist (he takes great delight in pointing out the various mistakes made: 'Reincidia-se num erro', 449) which in effect de-humanises the enemy. Yet, as the conclusion of the tale approaches, the tables are turned and his text becomes a 'grito de protesta' (571) against the barbarity of so-called civilisation, until – just before he describes the final stand of the *sertanejos* – da Cunha concludes: 'Atacava-se a fundo a rocha viva da nossa raça' (597). Da Cunha feels torn between the two sides of the battle, now siding with one, now with the other. He even seems to share the wonder of the government troops at the almost magical ease with which the inhabitants of the backlands could disappear and then re-appear seemingly at will, and, even after being shot, appeared to get up again, as if unharmed (271). The belief grew among the troops that the *sertanjeos* were superhuman, more like 'devils' and 'phantoms' than real men (283). Some of the government troops who had fought in previous campaigns, for example, were dumbfounded when they saw, resurrected in the flesh, two or three of the rebel leaders whom they believed had died in a previous campaign at Cambaio; to top it all, Antônio o Conselheiro appeared to have magical powers (177–80).

*Triste fim de Policarpo Quaresma* (1911) by Alfonso Henriques de Lima Barreto (1881–1922) is a powerful piece of fiction which expresses the despair of a social class set adrift by the perceived aimlessness of the Brazilian state. Similar in some key respects to *Memórias de um Sargento de Milícias* (see pp.84–6), it follows the trials and (mainly) tribulations of a single individual whose direct experience of a number of social apparatuses and life-styles – such as the civil service, the agrarian option, the army, – allows for the creation of great insight into the operations of the society of the time. In Barreto's novel that individual is Policarpo Quaresma, and we are first introduced to him when he is sub-secretary of the War Arsenal (Barreto 21). Well-read in the Brazilian literary canon, knowledgeable about the history, geography, flora and fauna of Brazil, a passable reader of French, English and German, he often finds himself in conflict with his peers, who see him as 'pedantic' (22). His erudition, as we soon learn, is coming to fruition in his fascination with the culture of the Tupi Indians (35), which leads him to send a letter to the government in which he argues that the Portuguese language has been foisted onto Brazil and that Tupi-Guarani 'é a única capaz de traduzir as nossas belezas, de pôr-nos em relação com a nossa natureza e adaptar-se perfeitamente aos nossos órgãos vocais e cerebrais' (61). He thereby exposes himself to public ridicule; to make matters worse he is sacked; as the Director says to him, simply because he has read a few novels ('por ter lido uns romances et saber um francesinho'; 70) does not justify his actions. As a result he sinks into a state of madness which is Quixotic in the sense that it sees through the absurdity of the laws which govern our social world. Quaresma is overwhelmed by a 'desesperadora compreensão inversa e absurda de nós mesmos, dos outros e do mundo. Cada louco traz em si o seu mundo e para êle não há mais semelhantes' (73). While many of his contemporaries are making their way in the world, getting married, building up successful careers, for Quaresma 'nada disso valia, nada disso tinha existência e importância' (74). He begins to drift, spends a period in a madhouse (85), recovers and then attempts to re-start his life as a farmer (Part II, chapter 4), though in this – the reader senses his demise is now inevitable – he fails miserably. This leads Quaresma, firstly, to experience a deep sense of pessimism about life and, secondly, a desire to retreat from this world to a state of ataraxia, in effect a re-enactment of Schopenhauer's philosophical meditations: 'Esta vida é absurda e ilógica; eu já tenho mêdo de viver [...] O melhor é não agir' (197). We find a similar structure of feeling at the heart of the novel, *El árbol y la ciencia* (1911), by the Spanish writer, Pío Baroja, though Barreto's novel has more of an ironic twist to it. Quaresma subsequently drowns his sorrows by enlisting in the national army and before long he is captured, imprisoned and sentenced to death, leading him to conclude that his life has been nothing other than 'um encadeamento de decepções'. The Brazil he fought for was just a figment of his imagination: 'A pátria que quisera ter era um mito; era um fantasma criado por êle no silêncio do seu gabinete. Nem a física, nem a moral, nem a intelectual, nem a política que julgava existir, havia' (Barreto 207). Barreto's novel is multi-layered, allowing interpretation on a variety of levels; it can, for example, be seen as a portrayal of the absurdity of life (a universalist reading), a depiction of the sense of political disenfranchisement felt by the more literary and aristocratic section of the upper class who felt overwhelmed by the advent of a ruthless grubby mercantilism which was booming in Brazil by the first decade of the twentieth century, or – perhaps more intriguingly – as a muted, displaced allegory of the oppression of the coloured class, to which Barreto belonged (he was a mulatto; see discussion below at p. 279).

The Mexican novelist, Mariano Azuela (1873–1952), offers an interesting counterpoint to the work of da Cunha and Lima Barreto given his interest in matters military. Azuela was born into a provincial, middle-class family (his father owned a local grocery store in Lagos de Moreno, a town in Eastern Jalisco). He qualified as a doctor and later became a supporter of Francisco Madero, who eventually dislodged Porfirio Díaz in the national elections held in 1912; Azuela was rewarded with the post of *Jefe político* in Lagos. Madero, however, was not to remain in power for long (he was murdered by his own Minister of War, Victoriano Huerta, in 1914) and, as Azuela supported Madero, it is no wonder that he saw the ensuing events of the Mexican Revolution (Huerta was succeeded by Carranza, who was in turn challenged by Zapata and Villa, who was vanquished by Obregón, all in rapid succession) as a process of mindless carnage (see Griffin, *Azuela* 9–25). He witnessed military action in 1914–15 when working as a surgeon in the army of Julián Medina, and then Pancho Villa. After the latter's División del Norte (Northern Division) was routed, Azuela crossed the US border in 1915 and took refuge in El Paso, Texas, where he completed the text which would make him famous. *Los de abajo*, as it came to be known, was published in a local Spanish-language newspaper, *El Paso del Norte*, in twenty-three weekly instalments from 27 October to 21 November 1915 (for which Azuela was paid $10 a week). Azuela brought out a revised, expanded version of the novel at his own expense in Mexico City in 1920 and, quite by chance, it caught the attention of the reading public in 1924, bringing him instant fame.

Azuela's detractors have argued that *Los de abajo* presents the events of the Mexican Revolution from too provincial a perspective and, furthermore, they charge its author with failing to understand (or reveal) the ideological causes of the Revolution. It is true that the Revolution as depicted in this novel is largely confined to Jalisco, Aguascalientes and Zacatecas (these were the areas in which Azuela witnessed the events of the Revolution), and that the actors in Azuela's version of the drama seem strikingly ignorant about the larger picture. The decisive battles of the Mexican Revolution, for example, occur off-stage in Azuela's novel; Demetrio and his followers, for example, only find out about the Battle of Celaya, which occurred in the spring of 1915 and in which Villa was decisively defeated by Obregón, when they question some soldiers whom they suspect of being deserters (Azuela 183). None of the various political manifestos which shaped the course of the Revolution – such as Madero's *Plan de San Luis Potosí* (1910), Zapata's *Plan de Ayala* (1911), and Carranza's *Plan de Guadalupe* (1913) – are even mentioned by the characters in the book. Pancracio manages to mispronounce Carranza's name, calling him Carranzo (Azuela 86), while Valderrama expresses lack of interest in either Villa, Obregón, or Carranza; they are simply meaningless names to him (186–7). But the geographical limitations of the novel are the judicious restraints of a seasoned artist rather than those of a timid one. Azuela pointed out, for example, in a speech given on 26 January 1950 when he was awarded the Premio Nacional de Ciencias y Artes, that he saw his role as one of describing rather than explaining events: 'Descubrir nuestros males y señalarlos ha sido mi tendencia como novelista; a otros corresponde la misión de buscarles remedio' (quoted in Richardson 48). Indeed, in his novel, Azuela homes in on the dangers involved in an idealised version of reality. The intellectual who accompanies Macías's army, Luis Cervantes, for instance, describes the Revolution as a time when the underdogs will finally be rewarded (Azuela 92), but his views are greeted scornfully by his companions and, indeed, he finally reveals himself to be a smooth-talking opportunist when he escapes to the US to avoid danger. Cervantes's name, given the obvious allusion to the author of Spain's literary masterpiece *Don Quixote*, is also meant to signal his lack of pragmatism. Even Solís, whom a number of critics have seen as a projection of Azuela himself, offers a pessimistic view of the Revolution: he refers to the 'psychology' of the Mexican people as summed up by two words: 'robar y matar' (135). These insights seem borne out by the various events described in the novel which involve violence, vengeance, rape and pillage. Life is cheap; one soldier boasts how he killed a man for giving him some currency printed by the enemy Huerta (140), another plays sadistically with one of his prisoners, threatening to kill him and then postponing the event until the following day (162–3). Culture is systematically destroyed; a typewriter is smashed on the rocks, and Dante's literary masterpiece, *The Divine Comedy*, is torn to shreds (128, 143). The ending of the novel seems to lend credence to the notion that the Revolution is presented as a vicious circle; we are left with an image of Macías fighting against impossible odds in exactly the same place that he started (197). Despite its pessimism, however, *Los de abajo* is unequalled in its vivid recreation of the daily events of the Revolution, its fast-moving narrative pace which cross-cuts from scene to scene, and its racy colloquial style.

The majority of the novels of the 1920s amplified the idiom of Realism which had characterised the nineteenth-century novel, without fundamentally invalidating it, the salient examples being *La vorágine* (1924) by José Eustasio Rivera (1889–1928), *Don Segundo Sombra* (1926) by Ricardo Güiraldes (1886–1927) and *Doña Bárbara* (1929) by Rómulo Gallegos (1884–1969). All three works, which are known as 'novelas de la tierra' (see Shaw, *Doña Bárbara*, 7), re-address an issue raised by Sarmiento some seventy years before in the context of Argentina's cultural spectrum: that of the struggle between civilisation and barbarism. For this reason, perhaps, the novels of this early period have a bilateral symmetry which seems crude when compared to the complex asymmetry of the Boom novels which followed. The best novel of this group was *Doña Bárbara* which centres around the conflict between barbarism and civilisation. The plot is relatively straightforward. Santos Luzardo, a young man fresh out of university studies in Caracas, goes back to his family's ranch, Altamira, set deep in the outback of the Venezuelan plains. He soon becomes locked in conflict with a woman, Doña Bárbara, whose own ranch, El Miedo, has steadily over the years been encroaching on Santos Luzardo's family's territory. The family strife began many years before, during the period immediately preceding the Spanish American war of 1898, when José de los Santos divided the Altamira ranch between his son José and his daughter, Panchita, who had married Sebastián Barquero. A lack of clarity in the title deed led to a dispute between José and Sebastián, which ended in the violent death of Sebastián at the hands of his brother-in-law. Later on José also killed his eldest son, Félix, with a spear (Part I, Chap. ii). The flaw of the action is thus set up in a way which is reminiscent of Aeschylus's *Oresteia* in which blood is spilled from generation to generation. When Santos Luzardo returns to Altamira, his first action is to pull the spear out of the wall, thus asserting his desire to break the cycle of violence and vengeance (Part I, Chap. v). In order to fight against Doña Bárbara's lawlessness, and to fix permanently the dividing line between the two properties, Santos Luzardo resorts to the law (what might be called the 'witchcraft' of Caracas). The conflict between Santos Luzardo and Doña Bárbara is not only a territorial dispute, it also becomes symbolic of a larger struggle between the forces of a traditional rural way of life and a new modern way of life based on law abidance, education, and urban democracy. Doña Bárbara, raped at a tender age and seemingly doomed to a life without love, is described at the beginning of the novel as a 'devoradora de hombres' and the reader expects Santos Luzardo to fall for her. Just the opposite happens and Doña Bárbara, for the first time in her life, falls under the spell of a man. But Santos Luzardo does not feel any emotion for her in return; instead he falls in love with Doña Bárbara's illegitimate daughter, Marisela, whom she had conceived, with a member of the Barquero family, Lorenzo. Marisela's gradual growth into the ideal wife for Santos Luzardo contains the kernel of the message of the novel which advocates a growth in urban democracy through the active co-option of the forces of the 'llano'. Doña Bárbara is associated with the Indian and with the land, and the book may be interpreted, through the image of Marisela, as the expression of a city-based creation of the Venezuelan nation via the co-option of subaltern elements in the society of the time (such as the Indian, and the inhabitants of the plains).

There were some experimental novels written in the 1920s. *Macunaíma o héroe sem nenhum carácter* (1925) by Mário de Andrade, one of the key figures of the Semana de Arte (discussed above, p. 142), is the novelistic *pièce-de-résistance* of *Modernismo*. Though it tells the life story of the protagonist, Macunaíma (his birth is recorded at the beginning of Chapter 1 (Andrade, *Macunaíma*, 13), his death described in the final chapter (155–59)), it does so in anything but a Realist style. A mythic-Surrealist novel, *Macunaíma* delves into Brazil's Amerindian past, recreating its horrors and grandeurs skilfully and playfully. Thus the cannibalism which filled the Jesuits with such Christian horror is represented in Chapter 2 in a grotesquely humorous scene in which the consumed human flesh is not yet dead: '– Carne de minha perna! carne de minha perna./ Lá de dentro da barriga do héroi a carne respondeu: / – Que foi?' (20). This is a world in which the Gods of Amerindia are alive, powerful, plotting against each other, such as Cio, the mother of the Mato forest, and other gods such as Maanape and Jigué. Andrade's gods are different from those portrayed in the work of an ethnographer such as Claude Lévi-Strauss in that Andrade's incarnations have a decidedly human side to them: Maanape likes coffee a great deal, and Jiguê insults other gods over the telephone (48–9). Though at first an incongruous mix of temporal spheres, this device allows Andrade to make some pointed references to the foibles of contemporary Brazil. He describes the enormous collection of artefacts held by a French woman (52) which amounts to an ironic, post-colonial point about the exploitation of Brazil's cultural wealth by Europeans – although there is a twist in this experimental novel since, as we subsequently learn, 'a francesa era Macunaíma' (52). He creates a hilarious send-up of the pretentious classicism and social snobbery of the upper-class women of São Paolo (71–81), with a sprinkling of slapstick humour ('já estamos em condições de citarmos no original latino muitas frases célebres dos filósofos e *os testículos* da Bíblia' (80; my emphasis). He makes some amusing comments about the indifference of the English to Brazilian poverty (96–7), as well as gentle mockery of those who attempt to affect a Portuguese accent in Brazil (72, 83–4), as well as describing the French novelist, Blaise Cendrars, dancing with Macunaíma. But, perhaps most important, this double vision – one eye on Amerindian culture, the other on *Modernismo* – allows Andrade to create some innovatory insights. For just as the human body is divided up, eaten, cannibalised, given a new form (Jiguê steals the *feiticeiro* Tzalo's head, 143; Carrapatu, another witch doctor, traps a man's soul in the body of a wolf, 139; Macunaíma himself is tricked by his arch-enemy, Vei, to have sex with a beautiful woman and, as a result, has one leg, his fingers, ears and nose eaten, 156), so the body of language, the signifier, becomes the engine behind the novel's forward propulsion, rather than, say, the plot. This emphasis upon the signifier is present not only in the various ritualistic songs which puncture the text ('ogoró! ogoró! ogoró!', 44; 'Bamba querê / Sai Arnuê / Mongi gongô / Sai Orobô', 60), but also the repetition of sounds which tends to break down the space of the signified, destroying its depth and reducing it to surface ('Vim buscar minha pacuera-cuera-cuera-cuera-cuera-cuera, de-lem', 136; 'Dormindo nada, então! Estava mas era negaceando um inanbuguaçu. Você fiz bulla, nhanbu escapuliu'; note the repetition of sounds here). This is, indeed, a characteristic of the novel. Even in those descriptions which appear to be referential, the repetition of sounds and the use of a string of nouns and adjectives give the sense that the words have been chosen for their rhetorical rather than strictly semantic force:

> Durante uma semana os três vararam o Brasil todo pelas restingas de areia marinha, pelas restingas de mato ralo, barrancas de paranãs, abertões, corredeira carrasco carracões e chavascais, coroas de vezante boqueirões mangas

e fundões que eram ninhos de geada, espraidoas pancadas pedrais funis bocaines barroqueiras rasouras. (108)

Notice the repetition of phrases ('pelas restingas'), the cumulative use of similar-sounding words ('carrasco carrascões', 'boqueirões ... bocaines barroqueiras') and the repetition of initial consonants ('fundões ... funis; pancadas perdais'). Indeed the above sentence is not untypical of many in this book. The at times feverish enhancement of phonic repetition lends a poetic air to *Macunaíma*, driving it relentlessly towards its mythic conclusion in which Macunaíma – though once a real person who danced a samba with Blaise Cendrars and wrote a biting letter of reproach to the women of São Paolo – is able, by the conclusion of the novel, to take leave of this world, and take his place in the heavens as the constellation of Ursa Maior (159).

Another experimental novel of the 1920s was *Las memorias de Mamá Blanca* (1926) by the Venezuelan novelist Teresa de la Parra (1889–1936). At first glance the novel seems traditional enough; it opens with the well-used introductory device, dating back at least to Benjamin Constant's *Adolphe*, of the author publishing the memoirs of another individual, in this case Mamá Blanca, a posthumous legacy. When the narrative proper begins it is that of the narrator Blanca Nieves, the third in a line of six daughters (called, excluding the narrator, Aurora, Violeta, Estrella, Rosalinda, and Aura Flor) who live with their parents in a big house on the plains of Venezuela called Piedra Azul. The plot is very thin; we learn about the daughters' idyllic childhood experience before this is wrenched from them when they have to move to Caracas, where they have money problems, they live in cramped conditions and are spurned by their elite neighbours. The first indication that there is more to *Las memorias de Mamá Blanca* than meets the eye occurs in the 'Advertencia' where the reader discovers that the text which we are now reading should not, in fact, have been published at all since Mamá Blanca asked the young girl – in effect, the editor and an alter ego of Teresa de la Parra – not to publish it. But she did. And not only that, she decided to edit it brutally, in the process cutting out all the beauty and spontaneity of the original; all the 'butterflies' as she calls them. The editor does not pass up the opportunity to mock her readership, those people who are used to 'stuffy' books, and would in any case be dreadfully bored with a text that was spontaneous. The prologue then alludes to how the text is a truncated version. She simply took, she says, the first 100 pages of Mamá Blanca's account. This could be seen as a recourse to the *deus ex machina* device, but it can be read alternatively as a metaphor of the ways in which women's lives are were (are) truncated in Latin America. As soon as the sisters leave the paradise of the sugar cane plantation, Piedra Azul, everything goes wrong: they have to deal with money, with real people, and their authority is questioned. We can legitimately interpret their arrival in Caracas as a re-writing of the Fall. Yet, because the novel ends before it has really started, this in effect throws the reader back on his own resources, forcing him to question the text he holds in his hands. There are, indeed, a number of subtle hints in the text which suggest that the various characters in the novel may be interpreted allegorically: Juan Manuel is associated with Simón Bolívar at the end of the first chapter ('no venía a ser más sensible a nuestras almas que la de aquel Bolívar militar'; Teresa de la Parra 328), Mamá Blanca is seen as similar to Napoleon (329), primo Juancho seems to symbolize the limp Liberal party, Evelyn, the English maid, is an image of the kindly but essentially ineffective role of the British during the nineteenth century, Vicente Cochocho is the jack of all trades *criollo*, and so on and so forth. If we use this allegorising reading (the novel is a *roman à clé* about the nation-building process), and apply it to the conclusion of the novel, we can interpret it as a veiled reference at once to the disintegration of the female world once it comes into contact with the male world of the city (in this case Caracas) but also as an allusion to the failure of patronymic politics, namely, men's failure to produce a national future. Silvia Molloy has argued convincingly that the novel evokes a forbidden lesbian love (Molloy, 'Disappearing Acts'), and this interpretation does not disqualify other readings of de la Parra's novel; indeed *Las memorias de Mamá Blanca* is a palimpsestic text with a number of levels of interpretation – each in their turn deconstructing the patriarchal code of verisimilitude (for further discussion see Hart, 'Some Notes on Teresa de la Parra').

## The Novel 1930–1960

It would be difficult to identify one overarching pattern characterising the Latin American novel from the 1930s until the end of the 1950s. During this period there were novels which stuck rather rigidly to the Realist formula (such as *Al filo del agua* [1947] by Agustin Yáñez), while others took a political line supporting the proletariat (such as *El Tungsteno* [1931] by César Vallejo [1892–1938]); there were novels which sought to identify with the indigenous world-view (the *indigenista* or neo-*indigenista* novel), while others were experimental and played with time, space and identity (such as *Hombres de maíz* or *Pedro Páramo*). The novels of this period do not evince an orderly sense of progression; they splay off in many different directions simultaneously. One of the best novels of this period was *Vidas secas* (1938) by Graciliano Ramos (1892–1953), a densely suggestive novel which – with hindsight – we can now plot as having premonitory parallels with Albert Camus's *L'Étranger* (1942) and Juan Rulfo's *Pedro Páramo* (1955). Ramos's novel has little plot. The novel begins with the description of a family on the road – Fabiano, his wife, Vitoria, their children – and progresses through a series of events that function more as vignettes than as elements of a plot (Fabiano is imprisoned for a night; the family visit a town during a festival; Fabiano kills the dog, Bateia; he has an argument about money with the landlord; finally the novel concludes with the family on the road again). It is tempting to view the novel as an allegory of the conflict between an illiterate individual and a literate society. Fabiano cannot read or write, and this disadvantage gets him into trouble when he agrees to play cards with a policeman (dressed in yellow), insults him, and then does not verbally defend himself when he ends up in a police cell later on: 'ouviu sem compreender uma acusação medonha e não se defendeu' (Ramos 31). He tries to sell a pig he has slaughtered in the city, but he is caught by the city council tax collector, and is unable to sell his goods (96). He has a furious argument with his landlord about his accounts, but when he is threatened with being ejected, he backs down: 'Se havia dito palavra à-toa, pedia desculpa. Era bruto, não fora ensinado' (94). His children, similarly illiterate, are bemused by the number of objects in the church and, in indirect free style, we hear their thoughts:

> Provavelmente aquelas coisas tinham nomes. O menino mais novo interrogou-o com os olhos. Sim, com certeza as preciosidades que se exhibiam nos altares da igreja e nas prateleirias das lojas tinham nomes. Puseram-se a discutir a questão intrincada. Como podiam os homens guardar tantas palavras? (Ramos 82)

There is thus clearly a level at which the novel can be understood as a record of the estrangement of the *sertanejo* within an urban, modern Brazil. But there are a number of factors which take this novel beyond a local context. Firstly there is a set of religious references placed strategically in the text which contrive to create an atmosphere of damnation. Fabiano calls his eldest son 'condenado do diabo' (9) because he will not walk any more, and calls him 'excomungado' (10) soon afterwards. The eldest son asks both of his parents what hell is, neither of them tells him, and the word 'inferno' is thereby allowed to hover over the text (55–6). The family's amazed reaction to the church they visit, and particularly Fabiano's sense of the hostility of the environment ('Fabiano sentia-se rodeado de inimgos', 75), as well as the unremitting heat of the sun in the opening chapters, all give a sense – very much like Rulfo's *Pedro Páramo* – of this being a hell on earth. There are other motifs within the novel which make it an allegory of man's existential plight. Similar in many ways to Mersault, the protagonist of Camus's *L'Étranger*, Fabiano spends a lot of his working hours unable to understand what is happening to him: 'Tudo na verdade era contra ele' (97). There is a sense equally that the cause of his *desgraça* is not only society – the police, the landlords, who exploit him – but also language itself from which he feels alienated: 'Na verdade falava pouco. Admirava as palavras compridas e difíceis da gente de cidade, tentava reproduzir algumas, em vão, mas sabia que elas eram inúteis e talvez perigosas' (20). Some of the laconicism finds its way into the narrative voice, not only when it is reporting Fabiano's thoughts (which we might expect in any case), as in the passage above, but also when the narrative describes the action sparsely, objectively: 'Alargou o passo, deixou a lama seca da beira do rio, chegou a ladeira que levava ao pátio' (21). Just as the linguistic unit of the sentences is shorn down to its lowest common denominator (there are only active, dynamic adjectives, and no poetic qualifiers for example), so the human mind is shorn down to its existential roots. While walking along the river bank, Fabiano shouts out to himself: 'Fabiano, você é um homem' (18), which he then corrects (in a whisper) to: 'Você é um bicho, Fabiano', before concluding 'Um bicho, Fabiano' (19). It is this sense of subtraction – understood in a linguistic as much as in an existential sense – that we find recurrently in Ramos's prose. It is not fortuitous, for example, that the longest passage of indirect free style in the novel should emanate from the dog Boteira, who is shot and left to die by Fabiano (87–91). None of the human beings in the novel, including the protagonist, Fabiano, is privileged with a stream of consciousness such as the dog enjoys. Similarly, the dog has a name, but the children do not; they are simply called 'O Menino Mais Novo' or 'O Menino Mais Velho'. The novel concludes on a pessimistic note. The family is caught in a vicious circle from which it is unable to escape. The *sertão* cannot sustain them, and the civilised world of Brazil and its cities will simply imprison them: 'Que iriam fazer? Retardaram-se, temerosos. Chegariam a uma terra desconhecida e civilizada, ficariam presos nela' (128). A haunting novel, *Vidas secas* allegorises the disorientation of the *sertanejo* in Brazil's modern concrete jungle as well as the lostness of modern man.

Similar in some important ways to the Realist novel (mainly in terms of its third-person objective style and its social message) was the *indigenista* novel which reached its peak impact during this period in a number of Andean works. At least three examples deserve special mention: *Huasipungo* (1934) by the Ecuadorian Jorge Icaza (1906–78), *El mundo es ancho y ajeno* (1940) by the Peruvian Ciro Alegría (1909–67), and the masterpiece of the genre, *Los ríos profundos* (1958) by the Peruvian José María Arguedas (1911–69).[4] Literary *indigenismo* is to be understood as a literary movement which asserts the need for the social recognition of the economic, political and cultural rights of the Indian population; unlike *indianismo*, which is utopian and unpoliticised since it offers an exoticised view of the Indian, *indigenismo* homes in on specific instances of oppression experienced by a particular local Indian community during the period the novel was published. Indeed, *indigenista* works are unlikely to be properly understood when removed from the particular historical circumstances which gave rise to the political dilemma which they describe. *Los ríos profundos* tells the story of the growth into adulthood of a young fourteen-year-old boy, Ernesto, his experience in a boarding school run by priests, his participation in a riot in which some salt is stolen, and his subsequent punishment. Ernesto's native language is Quechua, he feels in tune with

---

[4] Important precursory works were *Aves sin nido* (1889) by Clorinda Matto de Turner (1829–1909), discussed above in Chapter 4, and *Raza de bronce* (1919) by Alcides Arguedas (1878–1946) (see Rodríguez-Luis 17–87). Other works of this period by José María Arguedas can also be grouped under the rubric of *indigenismo* such as the short stories in *Agua* (1935), and the novels *Yawar fiesta* (1940), and *Todas las sangres* (1964). There were examples of the *indigenista* novel in Mexico, such as *El indio* (1935) by Gregorio López y Fuentes, and *El resplandor* (1937) by Mauricio Magdaleno (Rodríguez-Luis 252), but these are formula-driven rather than creative works of art.

Incan culture, and yet his final experience in the Peru of his day is that of an outsider. In this sense, the novel functions not only as the story of a young boy's growth into adulthood, but also that of Incan culture which achieves consciousness. The narrator becomes the focus of the resistance between the power of the oppressors and the resistance of the oppressed – which is epitomised by the *cholas* who take control of the town and reclaim the salt which they argue has been taken from them (the salt not only operates here in an empiric sense as an intrinsic part of their everyday livelihood, but also simultaneously alludes to the essence of life itself). The struggle within the seminary between the young boys and the priests is a microcosm of the struggle in the town for political power, which is expressed in clear-cut economic, cultural and linguistic lines. One of the first of its kind to see the world of the Indians from the inside, as it were, *Los ríos profundos* is a bilingual novel, in which Quechua is frequently alluded to – in the expression 'le dije en quechua' – or used in the text, frequently in the form of citation of oral poetry, which is then translated into Spanish. This provides the impression that the novel itself is evolving an act of transculturation, re-creating the Incan universe before the eyes of a Spanish-speaking audience. Through Ernesto's eyes, two institutions stand out as oppressive, the Church as symbolised by the director, and the army, as embodied by the soldiers who occupy Patibamba after the riot. Here, Arguedas is clearly making a post colonial point since the two forces which most clearly epitomised the Spanish conquest of the Incas were the Church and the army. Yet, it would be a mistake to see Arguedas's novel as simply an indictment of oppression, since it is skilful at capturing the essence of Incan culture, which is mainly engineered through the evocation of popular songs interspersed throughout the narrative; perhaps most emblematic is the 'huayno' which describes the way in which Doña Felipa, the ringleader of the *cholas*, outmastered her masters, which causes the singer to be arrested (Arguedas 195–201). *Los ríos profundos* marked a new departure in the evolution of the Spanish American novel, evoking with a freshness unequalled since its publication, the world of the Incas as it comes into contact with the world of the Spanish, mediated through the mind of an astute fourteen-year-old boy.

Apart from those novels which were characterised by some (perhaps unfairly) in terms of a *realismo trasnochado*, and the *indigenista* novels, there were others which experimented with the structure of the novel. This was due, in large measure, to the impact in Latin American literary circles of the experimental work of European writers such as Proust, Camus, Woolf, and Joyce and North American authors such as Steinbeck and Faulkner, particularly the latter's use of the stream-of-consciousness technique, free association, and the disruption of spatial and temporal parameters: internal logic rather than objective reality. *La última niebla* (1934) and *La amortajada* (1938), for example, by María Luisa Bombal (1910–80) are typical in this respect in that they demonstrate a readiness to experiment with the boundaries of what the novel can do. The latter novel, for example, in the manner of Zola's *La Terre*, recreates the thoughts of a woman as she lies in her coffin as if witnessing her relatives during the funeral wake (for further discussion of *La amortajada*, see Hart, *White Ink*, 37–45). *El túnel* (1948) by Ernesto Sábato (b. 1911), likewise, tends to focus on the paranormal and is an elegantly written novel about the growth of obsession and madness in the life of a young man. Related to the vogue of greater experimentalism was the search among the writers of this generation for what might be called cultural roots. In the work of Miguel Ángel Asturias and Alejo Carpentier, for example, the fragmented legacy of 'other' cultures – the Amerindian in the first and the African in the second – provides an image of a past of immanent meaning to which the alienated individual of the modern world feels drawn.

In Asturias's *Hombres de maíz* (1949), which is now considered the matrix text of magical realism, the fantastic and the originary are merged to create a world which is 'semisueño y semirrealidad' (Asturias 303). The novel homes in on a group of native Maya tribesmen led by Gaspar Ilóm who struggle in vain to protect their ancestral home in the highlands of Guatemala against the encroachment of the emerging capitalist, state-directed economy. The conflict is portrayed via frequent shifts between the discourse of the everyday (the whites burning down the Indians' trees for material profit) and the Jungian voices of the Indians; these latter voices do not belong to individuals but articulate a genetically inscribed memory. As one character says: 'Cuando uno cuenta lo que no se cuenta, dice uno, yo lo inventé, es mío. Pero lo que uno efectivamente está haciendo es recordar; vos recordaste en tu borrachera lo que la memoria de tus antepasados dejó en tu sangre' (Asturias 241). The governing principle of Asturias's novel is finally shown to be not the narrative action but the Amerindian world-view which weaves together the human, animal and vegetable kingdoms, making a man indistinguishable from maize, a postman merge with a coyote, and (echoing a Mayan trope) a man's thoughts turn into flowers.

Published in the same year as Asturias's *Hombres de maíz*, Carpentier's *Los pasos perdidos*, likewise, epitomizes the main thematic strands of the pre-Boom novel, namely (i) the fusion of national and personal narratives, (ii) the search for lost cultural origins (called in the novel 'ciertos modos de vivir que el hombre había perdido para siempre'; Carpentier 38), and (iii) the incorporation of myth. *Los pasos perdidos* tells the story of an individual bored with the Western paradigm of knowledge, who goes on a research trip to the Amazon to find himself; the journey becomes 'una suerte de retroceso del tiempo a los años de mi infancia' (Carpentier 79), and eventually leads to a passionate love affair with an earth mother type, Rosario, whom he loses tragically soon after finding her. The protagonist not only loses Rosario but also the musical work he composed while in the jungle entitled 'Trueno' – which manages to combine the sounds of nature with human music, and which fulfils the function of origin in the novel, now displaced. Some features of Carpentier's work were prescient about the direction the Spanish American novel would take; his sense of the coterminacy of the sexual and the ontological search would reappear later in Cortázar's fiction, and his sense of the interlocking nature of the fantastic and the real (which he dubbed 'lo real maravilloso') would find an echo in García Márquez's subsequent fiction.

*Pedro Páramo* (1955) by Juan Rulfo (1916–86), was the best example of the pre-Boom experimental novel. Set in a Mexican village, Comala, expanded to universalist proportions, the novel opens with the narrator searching for his father, Pedro Páramo. It gradually emerges that all the inhabitants of the village are dead, as is the narrator. Through the flashbacks which intersperse the narrative, we learn of the drama that reduced the inhabitants of Comala to their purgatorial predicament; it was the will of one man, Pedro Páramo, who acts in various roles as the cacique of the village and thereby claims rights over the villagers which are normally reserved for God. The flashbacks also give insight into Pedro Páramo's own desperate love; though he is the goal of others' search, he also is searching; the sense of an attainable origin is thus collapsed to produce a dizzying series of self-eliding substitute objects of desire. Rulfo's novel typifies a number of features of the pre-Boom novel; like *Los pasos perdidos* it emphasises the fusion of personal and national destinies (the narrator is at once an individual and an archetype of the search for Mexican identity), the importance of the search (even if frustrated, as here), and the free allusion to mythic texts. Thus, the narrator's quest echoes those quest-narratives of Greek mythology, such as Oedipus and Odysseus, although it is a truncated version in the sense that even the object of the quest is a shadowy figure, who disappears, true to the literal meaning of his name (Pedro is related to stone ['piedra'], while Páramo means 'wasteland'), into a pile of stones at the end of the novel. Perhaps most intriguing about Rulfo's novel is its ability to give a vision of an ultraterrene existence in a matter-of-fact way, an important characteristic of the magical-realist novel. In historico-political terms, *Pedro Páramo* expresses the angst of a rootless Mexican populace, displaced by the upheavals of the Revolution (1911–19), for whom the old certainties of previously-cherished ideologies – the landowning elite, the Church – have disappeared for ever, leaving for a number of years a political vacuum. These political uncertainties find expression as the elision of the difference between life and death, illusion and reality, and the distinctiveness of family roles (the narrator acts as brother, husband, son in quick succession to people he does not know) and gender. Political and historical uncertainty is thereby translated onto an ontological level.

Two Brazilian novels of the 1950s are so different from one other – João Guimarães Rosa's experimental, gender-bending *Grande sertão: Veredas* (1956) and Jorge Amado's Realist *Gabriela cravo e canela* (1959) – that they epitomise the difficulty in isolating an overarching pattern in Latin American fiction of this period. Guimarães Rosa's masterpiece manages to combine with great dexterity a knowledge derived from the Amerindian archive with a highly sophisticated use of the techniques associated with the modern novel. The subject matter is the hinterlands of Brazil, the very *sertão* which had formed the backbone of the classic work, *Os Sertões*, written over fifty years earlier (see above pp. 157–8), but Guimarães Rosa portrays that reality in a literary idiom which is recognisably modern, urbane, experimental. The novel is a long monologue directed by an inhabitant of the *sertão* at an unnamed interlocutor, who is educated ('Se vê que o senhor sabe muito, em idéia forme, além de ter cara de doutor' (Guimarães Rosa 41), but who does not respond. He wants to tell his mute interlocutor about the *sertão*, referring to incidents which happened, to the openness of the terrain and the wildness of its inhabitants: 'onde um pode torar dez, quinze léguas, sem topar com casa de morador; e onde criminoso vive seu cristo-jesus, arredado do arrôcho da autoridade' (24). He is intent on stressing the difference between the *sertanejos* and the city dwellers: 'sertão é onde o pensamento da gente se forma mais forte do que o poder do lugar. Viver é muito perigoso' (41). Since the *sertão* is being explained to 'o senhor', the novel is able to position itself as from within the *sertão*, thus going beyond that exoticist border between the city and the land drawn by Gallegos and others. The narrator strings together a number of stories of his life – a man called Aleixo who killed a man and whose three children went blind, whereupon he converted to Christianity (45–6), the story of Diadorim's desire for revenge (45–6), his meeting with a local prostitute, Ana Duzaza (49–50), his conversations with Diadorim who never knew his mother (57), the narrator who never knew his father (he is an 'orfão de conhecença e de papéis legais' (57). In between the description of events, the narrator gives his views about life, which are quite bleak: 'A gente viemos do inferno – nós todos' (64), and the killing he has seen, cutting off ears, cutting out tongues, burning people alive, as he asks: 'Esses não vieram do inferno'? (65). As in *Pedro Páramo* a picture of the *sertão* is built up of a place which is hell on earth. The reason why he has joined forces with Diadorim is that the *sertanejos* are being pursued by government troops: 'os soldados do Governo perseguiam a gente' (73). In this sense we can see Guimarães Rosa's novel as following in the line of Euclides da Cunha's novel, except that Guimarães Rosa attempts to tell the story of the struggle between *sertanejos* and government troops from within. The text is replete with references to the grotesque, barbaric events which happened in the past (first cousins who marry and have children with no arms and legs, 76; a priest who is castrated because he refuses to marry a mother and her son, 90), and which an educated person (i.e. the interlocutor, and by extension the reader) will not credit. As the narrator exclaims: 'A quanta coisa limpa verdadeira uma pessoa de alta instrução não concebe!' (101). Though the style is down-to-earth there is a self-consciousness within it which allies it with the Spanish American Boom novelists: 'De cada vivimento que eu real tive, de alegria forte ou pesar, cada vez daquela hoje vejo que eu era como se fosse diferente pessoa. Sucedido desgouvernado. Assim eu acho, assim é que eu conto!' (115). Deceptively simple, the narrative is highly wrought. The recollections have no chronological structure to speak of – thus we hear about the death of the narrator's mother and the protection offered him by her godfather, Selorico Mendes, some way into the narrative (126–31; although the latter may have been his father; see 138–9), before describing his life with various 'fazendas', and he is clearly involved in attempting to make sense of his life: 'a vida não é entendível' (150); 'esta vida é de cabeça – para-abaixo, ninguém pode medir suas pêrdas e colheitas' (161), which is no doubt why the author has not wished to impose an order on its events.

One intriguing aspect of the book is the way in which it describes the homoerotic feelings that the narrator feels for his male companion, Diadorim, who becomes furious when the narrator tells him about his affair with Otacília, Ana Duzaza's daughter, and also when he asks him to swear to a pact whereby neither of them will sleep with any women from that point onwards (207). Riobaldo's love for Diadorim grows: 'O nome de Diadorim, que eu tinha falado, permaneceu em mim. Me abracei como ele. Mal se sente é todo lambente – "Diadorim, meu amor..." Como era que eu podia dizer aquilo?' (307). As the narrative evolves it becomes less a war narrative and more an analysis of the mysterious otherness of life: 'mais temo o Outro: o figura, o morcegão, o tunes, o cramulhão, o dêbo, o carôcho, de pé-de-pato, o mal-encarado, aquele-o-que-não-existe!' (317). The *sertão* is no longer experienced as a landscape but as an innerness: 'Sertão: é dentro da gente' (325). The description of the horses which are attracted by the escaping prisoners is extraordinarily poetic (355–57), and leads to the question of God's existence, which is experienced in an un-theological but very direct way: 'O grande-sertão é a forte arma. Deus é um gatilho?' (359). The narrator is aware of his narrative as incomplete: 'A qualquer narração dessas depõe em falso, porque o extenso de todo sofrido se escapole da memória' (418). Even his own identity begins to be swallowed up by the *sertão*: 'Conforme eu pensava: tanta coisa já passada; e, que é que eu era?' (420). Diadorim says to the narrator how he would have liked Riobaldo to have been born as a relation of his (446), which is redolent of Rulfo's Pedro Páramo, suggesting the fluidity of family bonds in a world in which the family unit has begun to disintegrate. As he says later on: 'Falo por palavras tortas. Conto minha vida, que não entendi' (506). Towards the end of the novel, the narrator is surrounded by death, and he hears the voice of the blind man Borromeu, whom he mistakes for the *sertão*, but he does not understand his words (607). By the end of the novel we can say that the *sertão* has begun to speak through Riobaldo. A meandering though tightly-constructed novel, *Grande sertão: Veredas* manages to combine the stark world-view of a tough, murderous *sertanejo* with the flexible and experimental prose normally associated with Modernism, thereby bringing the mental deep structures of the *sertão* into being before our eyes.

Jorge Amado's *Gabriela cravo e canela* – winner of the first Jabuti prize awarded – appears, at first glance, to be very unadventurous when compared to *Grande sertão: Veredas*, yet Amado's novels will always win the popularity stakes; as late as 1995 Jorge Amado was voted their favourite writer by 67 per cent of Brazilian readers (Hallewell 716). True to the Realist formula, *Gabriela cravo e canela* focuses on a set of clearly-defined individuals (mainly Gabriela, the enticing Brazilian woman, happy-go-lucky, generous with her sexual favours, of uncertain roots, and Nacib, the restaurant owner of Syrian extraction who falls in love with her), with a verisimilar set of events occurring in a specific place (Ilhéus) at a specific time (1925–26). The characters of the novel are embedded within a societal continuum which is provided by the political struggles, vicissitudes and dramas which form a seamless backdrop for the novel. Indeed, the backdrop becomes almost a protagonist of this novel. Subtitled 'Crônica de uma cidade do interior', *Gabriela cravo e canela* is a novel about how the opposing forces of progress – understood as urbanity, banks, colleges, cabarets, cinemas – and the recent past of 'lutas e bandidos' (Amado 19) were played out in the tempestuous environment of Ilhéus, the capital of the sugar cane boom, in a period (the 1920s) of great social change. On the one hand are the landowners, such as Colonel Ramiro Bustos, who was part of the first generation of settlers who 'conquered' the land of Ilhéus, and turn their noses up at the mention of the recently founded Clube Progresso (63); on the other are capitalists such as Mundinho Falçao, who puts the money into the Clube Progresso, who invests in better infrastructure, who is involved in setting up a newspaper and likewise wants to have the harbour deepened to allow ships to berth, and thereby transport the area's local sugar cane directly to their clients in order to maximise profit. As the novel gradually unfolds it becomes clear that the ancien régime and the nouveaux riches are fighting their battles in the political arena, drumming up support via allegiances, then translating these allegiances into votes. Though Nacib is one among a number of the members of the social élite described in the opening chapters of the book – including, along with Colonel Ramiro Bustos and Mundinho Falçao, landowners such as João Fulgêncio, the Captain, the Doctor, Nhô-Galo and Ezequiel Prado – it soon becomes clear that this will be the story of Nacib's love-affair. All of these characters have an important role to play in the story, but their personalities as such do not develop; that is, they are simply foils against which the trials and tribulations of Nacib's life are delineated.

We are first introduced to Nacib in Chapter 4 entitled 'Don como Nacib despertou sem cozinheira' which then cuts to a number of scenes before taking up the story (rather like Dickens's *Tale of Two Cities*) from the perspective of a young woman, Gabriela, who is travelling to Ilhéus looking for work, accompanied by her lover, Clemente, and his friend, Fagundes (Amado 81–6). Her body exudes a fragrance, she is always smiling, and is an ardent lover:

> Mas quando a noite chegara, após ter cuidado do tio, vinha para o canto distante onde ele ia meter-se e deitava-se a seu lado, como se para outra cosa não houvesse vivido o dia inteiro. Se entregava toda abandonada nas mãos dele, morrendo em suspiros, gemendo e rindo. (Amado 84)

Soon after she arrives in Ilhéus she separates from Clemente, much to the latter's chagrin, and she is subsequently hired as a cook by Nacib. Once Gabriela is installed in his premises, the plot of the novel takes off: Nacib falls in love with Gabriela, marries her, discovers she is having an affair with his best friend, Tonico; then he throws her out, the marriage is declared null and void, and – in a final twist – he hires her back again to be the cook in his new restaurant.

The novel has a number of subplots which are used for different reasons. Thus the characters – in their desire to be part of modernity – discuss the events of the Semana de Arte Moderna (Amado 219), and since this was a real event which occurred in February 1922, this lends historical validity to the events of the novel. Secondly, the attempted assassination of Colonel Aristóteles Pires, which rocks the town, was carried out (as we later discover) by Fagundes, whom Gabriela had been on the road with earlier on (272–73). As a result of her quick-wittedness, Gabriela is able to save her life. Thirdly, narratalogical units in a subplot bring an idea into focus more clearly: Nacib, when discovering his best friend naked in his wife's bedroom, chooses not to kill either Gabriela or her lover (306), very much in contrast to the way the honour code would suggest things ought to be carried out, and indeed as implemented by Colonel Jesuíno who killed his wife, Sinazinha, and her lover, Doutor Osmundo (93–4); in this way Nacib's *modus operandi* is seen as an indication of a more civilised way of life. As Nhô-Galo says: 'Ilhéus possui, finalmente, um homem civilizado' (311). Indeed, the fact that his friend falls into disgrace as a result of his misdemeanour, and Nacib's success grows, seems to confirm this (in the sense that the novel's ideology of events supports modern rather than primitive behaviour). The vision of Brazil which emerges from *Gabriela cravo e canela* is that its success as a modern nation will be built on an alliance of resourceful capitalists (like Mundinho Falçao), hard-working immigrants who are committed to Brazil (such as Nacib), and beautiful women who captivate wherever they go (like Gabriela). The style of the novel is third-person realism, although description is kept to a minimum and the immediacy of the texts is ensured by reliance on the transcription of dialogue. When we hear the characters' thoughts, this often occurs via the technique of indirect free style, in the sense that we know of the thoughts without the need for quotation marks. There are very few poetic motifs used, the most obvious being the cinnamon used to describe Gabriela: 'Parecia feita de canto e dança, de sol e luar, era de cravo e canela' (355).

## The Short Story in Spanish America

The Spanish American short story came into its own during this period. One of the best *cuentistas* writing in the first decades of the century was Horacio Quiroga (1878–1937); his main short story collections are *Cuentos de amor de locura y de muerte* (1917), *Cuentos de la selva para niños* (1918), *El salvaje* (1919), and *Anaconda* (1921). The main theme of Quiroga's short stories is the struggle between man and his environment, in which, despite the dogged and sometimes heroic efforts of the (normally male) protagonist, he loses the battle and dies. In the typical short story by Quiroga, description is kept to a bare minimum and only used when it echoes the thrust of the main events.

Exploration of the inner psychology of the individual is kept to a bare minimum, which tends to reinforce Quiroga's essentially mechanistic and materialist view of humankind. 'El hombre muerto' is typical in this respect in that it has the stock ingredients of a bitter struggle of man against death told in stark, unencumbered prose. By the second paragraph of the story, the protagonist, simply called 'el hombre' as if to emphasize the generic nature of his plight, is already dead; he falls on his machete knife and kills himself (Horacio Quiroga 160). 'A la deriva' is similar. Again, the protagonist is nameless and, by the very first sentence of the story, he is doomed; he has trodden on a snake which bites him (156). He kills the snake, drinks some whisky, and then sets off on a boat journey along the Paraná river to seek medical help. As the title of the story already forewarns us, he is going nowhere. What is perhaps most interesting about Quiroga's short stories is their combination of the close attention to the here and now, described often with a scientific objectivity, with a hint of the supernatural, a device which Quiroga may well have learned from his master, Edgar Allan Poe, but which he transforms to produce a narrative unmatched in its use of suspense.

Another significant short-story writer of this period is the Mexican Juan José Arreola (1918–2001). His significance lies as much as in the tutelage he provided for an up-and-coming generation of Mexican writers as in his own literary output. In the 1950s he founded a book series, Los Presentes, which aimed to publish new Mexican writers, and with Juan Rulfo, under the auspices of the Centro Mexicano de Escritores in Mexico City, he taught a generation of writers how to write, including Homero Aridjis, Inés Arredondo, Emilio Carballido, Rosario Castellanos, Alí Chumacero, Fernando del Paso, Salvador Elizondo, Carlos Fuentes, Luisa Josefina Hernández, Jorge Ibargüengoitia, José Agustín, Vicente Leñero, Carlos Monsiváis, and Gustavo Sainz. Intriguingly, Arreola's literary output, compared to that of some of the writers he coached, is small. What is more, some of his stories are very small even by the standards of the genre (barely a page long). His most anthologised story, 'El guardagujas', is typical. It opens with an unnamed *forastero* who arrives at a railway station waiting for a train to take him to a place called T.; he engages in a conversation with a little old man (who is later revealed to be the switchman of the title), who advises him to forget about catching a train, but instead to look for lodging in the inn. The traveller is then regaled with a Kafkaesque description of how trains are very irregular, how they often do not go where they are meant to, and how the derailment of one train led to the foundation of a village. Finally, a whistle is heard in the distance and the train arrives. In this short story, Arreola manages to convert an everyday situation, waiting for a train, into an allegory of the Mexican nation (bureaucracy gone wild) as well as an existentialist tale of metaphysical aimlessness (the train, like life, leads nowhere).

One of the most distinctive short-story writers of this period is Juan Rulfo, whose novel *Pedro Páramo* has been discussed above (p. 170). Like Arreola, Rulfo was not a prolific writer. The seventeen short stories collected in *El llano en llamas* (1953) focus on themes which would also be present in his novel published two years later, such as existential lostness, the mythical search for ontological meaning, the inhospitability of climate (many of the stories take place against the backdrop of an arid, hot Mexican plain), an overpowering sense of guilt and a frustrated desire for redemption. There are, however, some leitmotifs which have a distinctive resonance in the short stories. Underlying the narrative of the typical short story is a murder in the past which erupts into the present, but which is remembered only fragmentarily or not at all by the perpetrator of the deed, who is often the narrator of the story itself, a device which raises the notion of the unreliable narrator to a new level. The narrator of 'El hombre', for example, does not recall committing the act of murder, but all the internal evidence points that way (Rulfo 22–8). The two best stories in *El llano en llamas* are 'Nos han dado la tierra' and 'Es que somos muy pobres'. The first is the story of four travellers, Melitón, Esteban, Faustino, and the narrator, who are walking to the arable land promised to them by the government authorities. The land is no more than a desert (4). The description of the journey, which comes to take on the ironically mythical proportions of a pilgrimage to the promised land, is interrupted by the memory of the conversation they had with a delegate who tells them not to be alarmed by having so much land (5), and, when they complain about its quality, tells them to put their complaint in writing, though he knows full well they cannot write ('Eso manifiéstalo por escrito'; 5). 'Es que somos muy pobres' is a tragic tale of a young girl, Tacha, whose cow, her only hope of a dowry, has been swept away by a river which has burst its banks, therefore in effect condemning her to a life of prostitution like her two older sisters. The last paragraph of the story, in describing Tacha's tears, manages to give an eerie sense of identity of inner and outer worlds, since her tears are like the swell of the river (17). Tacha's moral downfall is shown to be as inevitable as is the growth of her breasts. The short stories collected in *El llano en llamas* have a dramatic intensity which is redolent of Aeschylus in that they focus on the eternal cycle of murder and vengeance. But, perhaps most impressive about these stories is their laconic style. Description and dialogue are kept to a bare minimum, the external world is described at the expense of the portrayal of psychological reality, and the stories have a swiftness of pace which is well suited to the structure of the short story.

The master of the short story of this period was Jorge Luis Borges (1899–1986); who has already been discussed above as an avant-garde writer (see p. 145). The first edition of his masterpiece, *Ficciones*, was published in 1944, and the complete second edition in 1956. The main idea of this collection of short stories is, as the title suggests, fiction; here fiction is to be understood in the wider sense of the word to encompass cultural constructs such as society, mythology, metaphysics, religion. A recurring theme of *Ficciones* is the way in which mankind constructs fictions which envelop the individual like a labyrinth and in which he gets lost. The guiding archetype of the *Ficciones* is the futility of all human endeavour, especially when expressed as an intellectual desire for truth, coupled with a impish delight in intellectual conundrums. The reader is required to become the detective of the story and piece together the clues which, as he discovers on re-reading, never quite add up. The most important Borgesian metaphor, one which synthesises all the others, is the book; the indecipherable book, for example, a common enough stage prop in Borges's short stories, stands for the unknowable universe, the forever-out-of-reach objective of the quest-narrative of human existence. In 'Tlön, Uqbar, Orbis Tertius', for example, Borges goes to great lengths to provide a believable narrative which substantiates the account of an imaginary universe (described at the end of one version of *The Anglo-American Cyclopaedia* published in 1917, and confirmed by a book received in the mail in 1937 by a certain Englishman, Herbert Ashe, living in Argentina). Much of the text is taken up with a description of the laws of the planet Tlön, whose religion and metaphysics are idealist, whose languages have verbs but no nouns and whose inhabitants reject as contrary to common sense the notions of causal effect and temporal succession. The story concludes with a postscript which describes the irruption of this ideal universe into the everyday universe inhabited by the narrator (Tlön alphabetical characters appear on a compass and a cone of shining metal too heavy to be of this world surfaces) (Borges 35). Borges's *Ficciones*, as we can see, tend to undermine the hierarchy of different types of knowledge by suggesting that, because they are verbal, they are therefore also imaginary and fictitious. As the philosophers of Tlön argue, in a sentence that is typical of the world-view of the *Ficciones* as a whole, 'la metafísica es una rama de la literatura fantástica' (Borges 24).

Borges's short stories are concerned with mapping the quintessence of fictionality and demonstrating that the fictions in which man finds himself trapped are not externally created labyrinths but natural outgrowths of the human mind; 'to think is to abstract is to distort' could almost be a motto of these intriguing brain teasers. Borges's influence on his own and the succeeding generation of Spanish American writers was immense; the Boom writers, in particular García Márquez, Carlos Fuentes, Cortázar, all stressed the importance of his work. Although he would have been loath to admit it, Borges's work gained ground immensely during the 1960s when Latin American writers became all the rage in Europe and the United States. Given the early translation of his work into English and French, he soon achieved an international readership and, indeed, was one of the first Latin American writers to do so.

**The Short Story in Brazil**

The following brief overview is based on an analysis of the stories chosen to represent Brazilian short fiction in Italo Moriconi's *Os Cem Melhores Contos Brasileiros do Século* (2000). 'O bebê de tarlatana rosa' (Moriconi 28–33) by João do Rio is an intriguing story about a young man's adventures during carnival time in Rio. He meets the 'bebê de tarlatana rosa', they go off to have sex, but she refuses to take her mask off; when the narrator finally rips it off, he discovers she has no face, but simply a skull. A modern-day version of a medieval morality play, 'O bebê de tarlatana rosa' offers a critique of customs in contemporary Brazil. We find a similarly allegorical tone adopted in 'A nova Califórnia' (34–42) by Lima Barreto, which is a rather macabre tale about a chemist who believes that he has found a way of turning human bones into gold, leading to an epidemic of grave-diggers trying to find out his secret; Barreto's story is a grim parable about how the lust for money desacralises even death. Some of the stories of this period possess that trait we associate with the best type of short story, namely, the twist in the ending. 'A colha' (49–54) by Júlia Lopes de Almeida tells the story of a young boy who is teased mercilessly by his school-mates about this mother (she only has one eye), which leads him to resent her, until he discovers that he was the one who ruined her looks by stabbing her in the eye with a knife when he was a little boy. Some of the stories treat social inequality: 'Contrabandista' (72–7) by João Simões Lopes revolves around the attempt by a ninety-year-old smuggler to acquire a white wedding-dress for his daughter; his dead body is unceremoniously dumped in the house by the police who must have shot him, suspecting him of wrongdoing, raising in a vivid way the issue of impunity. A similar sense of social inequality forms the backbone of 'Negrinha' (78–84) by Monteiro Lobato, which describes the life of a little black orphan girl who is adopted, sees life on the other side of the tracks (her adopted parent's niece comes to stay bringing a beautiful doll), and, rather dramatically it must be said, dies of a broken heart, thereby making this tale an allegory of the legacy of slavery in modern-day Brazil. 'Galhina cega' (85–91) by João Alphonsus is about a man's irrational love for a blind hen which he cherishes and whose death drives him to distraction. Given the emphasis in the story of seeing the world from the hen's point of view, it is difficult not to see the hen's plight as an allegory of mankind, blind, defenceless in a cruel world, for whom the only remedy is death; Clarice Lispector would take up this motif, indeed, and transform it into a sharp-eyed critique of the plight of women in the modern world (see below, pp. 222–3).

During the 1940s and 1950s, as Italo Moriconi has pointed out, we witness the rural world of Brazil retreating from view, and, instead, personal relationships become the axis around which short story begins to turn (Moriconi 105). 'Viagem aos seios de Duília' (107–24) by Aníbal Machado described a young man's trip back to the past as he attempts to re-live the moment when his beloved unbosomed herself under a tree; unfortunately his hopes are dashed when he finally finds Duília with grey hair and rotten teeth (122). 'Nhola dos Anjos e a Cheia do Corumbá' (131–36) by Bernardo Élis focuses on the struggle for survival of a family caught in a natural disaster (a river has overflowed its banks). Because the tree they are clinging to cannot take their combined weight, in order to save the life of his son, a man kicks his mother in the face so that she falls into the water. This grim story of the survival of the fittest concludes with a powerful vision of the waters reflecting the sky 'cynically', and the turbulent waters full of ghosts and the cry of women. In 'Tangerine-Girl' (159–64) by Rachel de Queiroz, a young girl becomes fascinated by a US sailor she sees each day on the Zeppelin floating past her home, and she is overjoyed when the sailor drops a letter to her, inviting her to a dance. When she arrives at the dance, however, she realises she has been duped, since she is in effect just a tangerine girl to be played with at will by others. The story thereby becomes an allegory not only of the illusions of love, but also of the exploitation of the third world by the first world. 'As maõs de meu filho' (173–79) by Érico Verissimo takes place in the mind of a mother watching her son, a conductor, giving a brilliant rendition of Beethoven; she recalls the anguish of her life as she struggled to nurture her son's musical gift while dealing with her husband's drunkenness. Skilfully written, 'As maõs do meu filho' uses one event as a funnel with which to delve into a complex family history. 'Entre irmãos' (186–89) by José J. Veiga offers a grimly ironic view of how two brothers who do not get on are forced to make small talk while waiting outside the bedroom of their mother who is dying. Evoking a Sartrian sense of 'l'enfer c'est les autres', this story takes up a theme which is central to Brazilian literature, that of rivalry between two brothers, as in Machado de Assis's nineteenth-century masterpiece, *Isaú e Jacó* (see above, pp. 135–6), which would be taken up in Hatoum's twenty-first century novel about two brothers *Dois irmãos* (see below, p. 282).

**Theatre**

The difficulty in writing about the major dramatic works of the first half of the twentieth century is that there is little consensus about the canon. Three retrospective anthologies published in the early 1970s, for example, promote different writers as representatives of their nation's drama.[5] This period saw a number of independent theatrical groups spring up, such as the Teatro Experimental de la Universidad de Chile in 1941, and the Teatro Galpón (1949) in Uruguay under the direction of Atahualpa del Cioppo; in 1957 the First Festival de Teatro Libre was held in Buenos Aires. Given the great diversity of dramatic works during this period, I will focus on four geographic areas, the Southern Cone, Mexico, the Caribbean, and Brazil; as we shall see, plays from the Southern Cone were typically concerned with the tensions within the bourgeois institution

---

[5] An anthology of *El teatro actual latinoamericano* (1972), edited by Carlos Solórzano contains works by Carlos Gorostiza, Guillermo Francovich, Enrique Buenaventura, Daniel Gallegos, Antón Arrefat, Isidora Aguirre, and Demetrio Aguilera Malta. The works chosen in *Los clásicos del teatro hispanoamericano* (1975), edited by Luzuriaga and Reeve, to represent the same period, are works by Armando Moock, Samuel Eichelbaum, Xavier Villarrutia, Rodolfo Usigli, and Celestino Gorostiza. The works chosen in *The Modern Stage in Latin America: Six Plays* (1972), edited by George Woodward, are by René Marqués, Alfredo Dias Gomes, Osvaldo Dragún, Jorge Díaz, José Triana and Emilio Carballido. Since not one dramatist appears twice in any of these three anthologies, this suggests a lack of agreement about which the major works are.

of the family, theatre from Mexico and the Caribbean was preoccupied with the elusiveness of (national) identity, while Brazilian theatre often seeks to express the world-view of the subaltern.[6]

A number of the plays of this period from the Southern Cone centre almost obsessively on sexual relationships. *La serpiente* (1920) by the Chilean dramatist Armando Moock (1894–1942), for instance, focuses on the satanic attraction that women exert on men; its main thesis is that women ruin the artist's creative gift, and thus it is just in the nick of time that Pedro escapes the temptation of Luciana, the 'serpent'. Even in plays which ostensibly have other thematic purposes, this obsession emerges. *Un guapo del 900* (1940) by the Argentine writer Samuel Eichelbaum (1894–1969), for example, appears at first glance to be a play about the struggle for political power, since it tells the story of one Ecuménico who kills Clemente Ordóñez, the political rival to his own boss, Don Alejo. However, as the play unravels, it becomes transparently clear that the reason Ecuménico kills Ordóñez is because the latter had been having an affair with Don Alejo's wife. Anger about adultery, or the flouting of the institution of marriage, rather than the struggle for power, is shown to be the real reason for Ecuménico's rage. As he says at one point, he would have been unable to respect a man as his leader if he were known to be a cuckold (Luzuriaga and Reeve 652). *El pacto de Cristina* (1945) by Conrado Nalé Roxlo (1898–1971) is, on the surface, a reworking of Goethe's *Faust*; here it is a woman, Cristina, who sells her future son, rather than her soul, to the devil, in order to obtain by supernatural means a man's love. Though set in the Middle Ages, and appropriately couched in the language of romantic love, this play focuses on the problems inherent in sexual love, and, in effect, criminalises female sexual desire. Realising she has gone too far, Cristina commits suicide on her wedding night.

Plays written in Mexico and the Caribbean focus typically on the elusiveness of personal and national identity. Some plays raise this theme in the context of metaphysical unknowing. *Parece mentira* by the Mexican Xavier Villarrutia (1903–50), for example, is a Kafkaesque play in which a man visits a lawyer's office after receiving an anonymous note which suggests that he must do so in order to discover his wife's secret life; he then sees three identical women who walk across the stage and disappear mysteriously. As in the Theatre of the Absurd, an enigmatic situation is presented to the audience, but the spectators are no wiser about the meaning of the events they have witnessed when the curtain falls than when it rose. Other plays of this period address the issue of national identity more directly. *El color de nuestra piel* (1952) by Celestino Gorostiza (1904–67), for instance, treats the clash of ideologies within a family unit, as encapsulated, on the one hand, by the racist and pro-American father,

---

[6] This section deals in the main with plays understood in the conventional sense of the term. It could be argued, however, that Spanish America's most successful theatrical genre is *teatro breve* which, for reasons of space, it has not been possible to treat here; for an excellent anthology including work by the masters of this genre (Dragún, Solórzano and Garro), see *Teatro breve hispanoamericano contemporaneo*, ed. Carlos Solórzano.

Don Ricardo, who favours his white son, Héctor, and the mother, Beatriz, who is identified with Mexican *mestizo* identity. The father's option is shown ultimately to be erroneous for Mexico, since his favourite son is finally revealed to be the culprit behind the scandal at the family-owned laboratory; he was passing off old stock as new, and pocketing the proceeds.

The single most important drama of this period was *El gesticulador* (1937) by the Mexican Rodolfo Usigli (1905–80). This play tells the story of a disillusioned university professor, César Rubio, who has moved from Mexico City to a provincial town in north Mexico and who, quite by chance, meets a Harvard professor, Oliver Bolton. Rubio leads Bolton to believe, with spurious documentation, that he is a long-lost hero of the Mexican Revolution. As a result of this deception he is persuaded to stand in the elections for governor in his home state. Thus his political career begins until it is brought abruptly to a halt when he is murdered by a political opponent, Navarro. The reason why César decides to live the lie emerges in the agnorisis scene in Act III between César and Navarro when Navarro accuses him of being an imposter, to which César replies that Mexico is a country of imposters: '¿Quién es cada uno en México? Dondequiera encuentras impostores, impersonadores, simuladores' (Usigli 254). At this point perhaps the most intriguing insight of the play emerges, namely, not only that people are imposters but that they allow others to retain their façades since it is in their own interest to do so. Thus César uses his knowledge that Navarro killed César Rubio, the revolutionary, in order to blackmail Navarro into silence (256–58). César believes that this lying contract, by which we are given to understand society functions, justifies his new identity (260). Even after César is murdered by Navarro (although the latter does not of course admit to the deed in public), the social contract of deception is perpetuated in the relationship between Navarro and César's son, Miguel. For Miguel to point the finger at Navarro inevitably means exposing his father as an imposter and thereby endangering his mother's state pension. *El gesticulador*, thus, presents a grotesque version of deception in political office, which is maintained through the collusion and self-interest of others. Miguel, at the conclusion of the play, is left with this troubling knowledge (273). Usigli's play is technically innovative, particularly in its use of dramatic tension in the gradual unfolding of the truth, and of suspense, in the gap between the characters' and the audience's knowledge of events. Particularly skilful are the agnorisis scenes, such as between Bolton and César (Act I) and Navarro and César (Act III) in which the audience is kept in the dark about César's motives until the last moment.

*La muerte no entrará en palacio* (1957) by the Puerto Rican dramatist René Marqués (1919–79), like *El gesticulador*, focuses on the issue of an elusive national identity. It is a political drama in the sense that it is set at the time of the transition from colony to protectorate which occurred in Puerto Rico in 1952 when the island was given commonwealth status with the United States, a unique, hitherto unknown, political status. The ideology of the play clearly regrets this position and, indeed, presents this event as if it never took place;

Don José, Governor of the Isla (as it is elliptically referred to throughout the play), is shot by his daughter, Casandra, before he can sign the agreement with the United States ambassador. The ideal which the play supports is that embodied by Don Rodrigo, who fought for Puerto Rico's independence at Don José's side during their youth, for which he was imprisoned, unlike Don José, who turned his back on his rebellious past in order to pursue a political career. Rodrigo never makes an appearance on stage but his presence is assured through his son, Alberto, who works as a military aide in the Governor's palace but in whom Rodrigo's ideals burn brightly. Alberto could be seen as the main tragic figure in the play (*La muerte no entrará en palacio* was called a tragedy by its author), although the manner of his death (accidentally shot by his betrothed, Casandra) is melodramatic rather than tragic; Casandra could also be seen as a tragic figure since her political idealism obliges her to kill her political enemy, who happens to be her father, Don José.

Brazilian theatre of this period offers similar perspectives to those found in Spanish American drama (namely, in the sense of loss of identity), but also typically focuses on the world of the subaltern. *Vestido de Noiva* (1944) by Nelson Rodrigues (1912–80) is a complex play which uses a number of different spaces and levels on the stage in order to suggest the interweaving of the lives of different people, of the past, present and future, and finally of life and death. The space of the theatre is also expanded by an adroit use of an off-stage voice which further heightens the sense of a dramatic kaleidoscope. The audience is obliged to try to pull the various threads together and at one stage – as in a classic whodunnit – is deliberately misled in order to create suspense followed by a dramatic dénouement. The audience's initial impression is all wrong, as we later discover; we think that Alaíde, whom we meet early on as she is looking for the madame of a local brothel, Madame Clessi, is about to marry Pedro; her sister, Lúcia, is extremely jealous of her. A sub-plot is provided by the affair between Madame Clessi and a young man, Alfred. This would mean that much of what we see are memories being evoked before our eyes on one of the levels of the stage, but again this is misleading. The audience is also effectively tricked by one scene in which the murder of Pedro by Alaíde is re-enacted (Rodrigues, Act I, 31), and we are encouraged to dismiss it as paranoiac Alaíde's fears that Pedro and Lúcia are plotting to kill her (Act III, 38–9). But the anagnorisis turns everything upside-down since, in the final scene, it is Lúcia and Pedro who are getting married, and it is thus Alaída and Madame Clessi who are revealed to be nothing more than 'poéticos fantasmas' (Act III, 50). Indeed Alaída's death is shown to be the mirror image of her sister's wedding, since the two events are depicted simultaneously on opposite sides of the stage. Even the wedding music and the funeral music are, as the stage directions suggest, to be played in time (Act III, 50). This essentially means that the scene we witnessed in Act I in which Alaíde killed Pedro was nothing more than a confused imagining, and that what really happened – although it occurred off stage – is the opposite: Pedro killed Alaíde. Indeed he admits as much to Lúcia in the closing scene of the play: 'Ou você o ela tinhia que desaparecer. Preferi que fosse ela' (Act III, 48). It is likely that Pedro ran her over in the Glória district of Rio de Janeiro. Like Madame Clessi, who was the victim of an attack by her lover, Alberto, Alaíde was killed by someone she loved, and the appearance of both women throughout the three acts – often together – provides a poetic consistency to the play. Both are haunting the present; in a clever dramatic move, Rodrigues uses different levels on the stage to show how the dead invade the land of the living, just as the past – and indeed the future – haunts the present.

*Auto da Compadecida* (1955) by Ariano Suassuna (b. 1927), first staged on 11 September 1956 at the Teatro Santa Isabel in Recife, is a witty re-working of the medieval mystery play, now set within the contemporary context of the Brazilian outback. It is based, as the author himself has pointed out, on the ballads and popular tales of the north-east of rural Brazil (Suassuna 21). While the story, like the mystery plays, shows the actions of a number of characters followed by the judgment of those actions by God after death, it does so in a non-theological, earthy way. João Grilo has a grudge against the Padrão and his wife as a result of the way they treated him when he was ill, and he decides to pay a trick on them (he sells the wife a cat which 'excretes' money). He also tricks the local priest into performing the formal burial of a dog in Latin. A typical *maluco*, João Grilo is always getting himself out of one scrape only to find himself in another one. The humour does not stop even when the various characters are murdered by a ruthless bandit, Severino. João Grilo's first reaction, for example, when meeting Jesus in the afterlife is pithy: 'não è lhe faltando como o respeito não, mas eu pensava que o senhor era muito menos queimado' (148). The bishops, priest and sacristan are all about to be sentenced to hell while João Grilo has the idea of invoking the Virgin Mary, and she arrives and then 'pulls rank' on Jesus, allowing the men of the cloth to go to Purgatory instead and João Grilo to go back to earth. A work of sparkling, witty dialogue, based on the down-to-earth humour of the *sertanejo*, *Auto da Compadecida* is the work of a writer who is keenly aware of the importance of a fast-moving plot punctured by quick repartee.

*Navalha na Carne* (1967) by Plínio Marcos (b. 1935) is a play with a gritty feel to it. Vedo, a drug-taker, and Neusa Sueli, a prostitute, live together in a cramped, delapidated room. Realising some money has disappeared, they call in Veludo, and force her to admit to stealing the money, after Sueli threatens to slash her with a knife. She promises to pay it back, and then Vedo attempts to force her to take some drugs. Sueli complains about her life as a prostitute (Marcos 46), at which point Vedo accuses her of being an old whore who looks about fifty years old, whereupon Sueli flips and threatens him with a knife. Vedo runs off, never to return. The style of the language used in the play is colloquial, raw and vulgar. Though not a play in the dramatic sense of the word, *Navalha na Carne* is similar to a number of works in other genres such as the novel and the short story, in which there is a desire to express as realistically as possible the plight of the subaltern in Brazil.

## The Essay

One of the more colourful essayists of the early twentieth century was the Mexican José Vasconcelos (1882–1959). A lawyer who had supported Madero during the Mexican Revolution, he became Minister of Education in the post-Revolutionary government of Obregón (1920–24) and embarked on an ambitious social programme with the aim of bringing the education and the arts to the Mexican people. One of his most enduring contributions to Mexican culture was his enlightened commissioning of the work of muralists such as Diego Rivera, Siqueiros and Orozco. As a result of the Revolution the notion of race became a fiercely-debated topic; identification of race was no longer permitted to be part of the national census in Mexico. Artists, and particularly the muralists, began creating works which were sensitive to the Indian heritage of Mexico (Rivera and Vasconcelos, for example, visited Chichen Itza in the Yucatan together in 1921). It is perhaps not surprising, therefore, that Vasconcelos's *La raza cósmica* (1925) should be preoccupied with the notion of race, or even that it should use race as a means of understanding the cultural framework of post-Revolutionary Mexico. In this work, Vasconcelos proposes the notion of a 'cosmic' or 'fifth' race created in Latin America which will one day be the most powerful people on the earth. Two thinkers obviously influential in this formulation were the English naturalist, Charles Darwin (1809–82) and the Austrian naturalist, Gregor Mendel (1822–84); Vasconcelos emphasises the latter in favour of the former in order to propose miscegenation as the road to future genetic success. He splits the world into four races, the Negro, the Indian, the Mogul, and the white (Vasconcelos 16). He uses Spengler's theory of cultural decadence to argue that the white man's dominance will not last forever and thus the new *mestizo* race in Latin America will eventually prevail. Latin America has 'el tejido celular que ha de servir de carne y sostén a la nueva aparición biológica' (30). An important facet of Vasconcelos's thought is that it consistently views culture and race as indistinguishable; thus when stating the then common argument in intellectual circles that civilisations go through a process of birth, growth and decline, Vasconcelos substitutes race in the equation: 'Ninguna raza vuelve; cada una plantea su misión, la cumple y se va' (25). The eventual decline of the white man's power will lead to the third stage of humanity which Vasconcelos calls the spiritual-aesthetic stage (the previous two are the material-warlike and the intellectual-political stages, distinctions which, it must be said, do not bear much scrutiny, in spite of their Joachimite resonance). Even more impressionistically, Vasconcelos identifies the most appropriate territory for this new race to flourish as an area enclosing the whole of Brazil, plus Colombia, Venezuela, Ecuador, part of Peru, part of Bolivia, and the upper territories of Argentina (34). Thus: 'El mundo futuro será de quien conquiste la región amazónica. Cerca del gran río se levantará Universópolis' (35). The only danger, Vasconcelos hastily adds, is that this new city will be called Anglotown if it is colonised by the white man. The fact that Vasconcelos does not include his own country, Mexico, in this promised land is significant since it reveals Vasconcelos to be indulging in what might be called armchair colonialism.

José Carlos Mariátegui (1894–1930) is one of the most significant essay writers of twentieth-century Latin America. Like many Latin American intellectuals of his generation, he travelled to Europe (1919–23), spending most of his time in Italy, an experience which led him to embrace communism. On his return to Lima in 1923, Mariátegui became politically involved in his country's affairs, soon becoming a prominent spokesman of the Left. In 1928 his *Siete ensayos de interpretación de la realidad peruana* was published, on which his fame largely rests; he died of ill health at the tragically young age of thirty-six. Each of the seven essays has a specific theme (economic development, the Indian problem, the land problem, public education, religion, regionalism versus centralism, and literature), but one main theme threads its way through all of these essays and that is the coincidence between communism and the Incan system of government. As one would expect from a Marxist thinker, Mariátegui rejects the ideology of conquest and colonisation, and is caustic in his assessment of the continued existence of this mind-set in post-independence Peru. He argues forcefully for seeing the problem of the Indian in economic rather than racial or moral terms (Mariátegui 20–30). He shows that the lot of the Indian sub-class grew even worse in the Republic despite the rhetoric of liberation typical of the independence movement (31–67). He compares the colonial system instituted by the Spanish with that instituted in North America, and the former comes off worse in his estimation. He goes on to argue that the religion of the Incas was socio-political rather than theological and this was why it disappeared when confronted by Catholicism (105–10). Lastly, Mariátegui's essays on various Peruvian literary figures, ranging from Ricardo Palma to César Vallejo, are sensitive to racial, ethnic and historical variables in the literary works they treat. The most contentious and potentially intriguing element in Mariátegui's thesis was his view of the similarities between twentieth-century communism and pre-Columbian societies. While the truth value of Mariátegui's thesis with regard to this idea may be limited, it was clearly an important statement of his desire to ground the need for communism in twentieth-century Latin America in a prelapsarian space associated with the period before the Fall initiated by the conquest.

The political affiliation of *Radiografía de la pampa* (1933) by Ezequiel Martínez Estrada (1895–1964) could not be more different from Mariátegui's *Siete ensayos*. The aims of the two writers are similar – both set out to give a broad picture of the culture of their compatriots – but the results are diametrically opposed. Martínez Estrada's *Radiografía de la pampa*, unlike Mariátegui's work, pursues an anti-Indian thesis to its radical (and execrable) conclusion. Following the lead of Sarmiento's *Facundo* of the previous century (see pp. 101–2), Martínez Estrada attempts to map out the contours of the soul of Argentina, drawing much inspiration for this from the vast terrain of the pampa around Buenos Aires. *Radiografía de la pampa* has six parts, the first of which is broadly historical, while the subsequent parts address themes such as 'solitude', 'primitive forces', 'Buenos Aires', 'fear', and 'pseudo-structures', and attempt to re-create the distinctiveness of the life-experience of the so-called *homo pampaeus* (Martínez Estrada 146). The main focus of the work is man's endless struggle against adversity which is incarnated in a number of forms, such as nature, loneliness, the fear of the unknown, the Indian, and the void; sometimes these motifs are rolled indiscriminately into one to symbolise the enemy of (Caucasian) man.

Another significant essayist of the period was Gilberto Freyre (1900–87); his *Casa-Grande & Senzala* (1933) radically changed the conception of slavery in Brazil's history, and offered a completely new perspective on the way in which the races, and their cultures, had intermingled in the creation of contemporary Brazilian society. The Big House and the Slave Quarters in the title were not used in a strictly architectural sense but appeared in Freyre's masterpiece as symbolic of an entire social, political and economic system which divided the descendants of the Portuguese from the descendants of the slaves. The Big House of the plantation, a remarkably resilient institution during Brazil's colonial history, was 'a fortress, a bank, a cemetery, a hospital, a school, and a house of charity giving shelter to the aged, the widow, and the orphan' (Freyre, 'Preface', xxxiii). Starting its life as a master's thesis submitted in 1923 to the Faculty of Political and Social Sciences of Columbia University, Freyre's book is based on research culled from an extraordinarily broad set of documents, including not only the historical chronicles (the contents of some of which have been summarised in Chapters 1 and 2 above), but also the records kept by the Inquisition, registry-books of baptisms, court correspondence, royal decrees, the reports of hygiene committees, wills, family archives, manuscript archives held by prominent plantations, inventories, diaries, and letters. The picture that is thereby built up offers a highly convincing *tranche de vie* of the daily life of the nobility and the slaves – and all in between – in Brazil's colonial period. Freyre's research not only offered a paradigm-shift in terms of its meticulousness, it also transcended the rather deterministic understanding of race which was common in historical and sociological discourse in the early decades of the twentieth century, and departed from the discourse of vilification often applied to the subaltern. By promoting a more scientific understanding of the growth of culture, based on an analysis of a variety of factors including climate, feeding patterns, the flexibility of Catholicism, sexual mores, and the sadism prevalent in the master–slave relationship, Freyre was able to cut through the tired rhetoric which had obscured from view the material roots of Brazil's historical evolution. He proved, for example, that the native woman was much more knowledgeable about personal hygiene than 'o europeu porcalhão do seculo XVI' (Freyre, *Casa-Grande* 92). He argued against the idea that the Indians and the black slaves were prone to sexual indulgence, as Jesuits such as Father Nóbrega had argued, since the Portuguese was 'o mais libidinoso' (100). In a post-colonial frame of mind, he stated that 'A historia do contacto das raças chamadas "superiores" com as consideradas "inferiores" è sempre a mesma. Exterminio ou degradação' (113). His chapter on the

Portuguese colonizer seeks to puncture the latter's illusions of grandeur, calling him the 'o corruptor, e não a victima' (268). Thus he rejects the prolepsis underlying colonialist rhetoric: 'parece-nos absurdo julgar a moral do negro no Brasil pela sua influencia deleteria como escravo' (349). As he goes on to point out: 'Não ha escravidão sem depravação sexual' (324). It is as a result of his insistence on the detailed study of the material objects and activities of culture – dwellings, food, sexual habits, work – that Freyre was able to produce an authentically historicist reading of Brazil's history which finally laid to rest the universalist and transcendental myths produced by the coloniser's vivid imagination.

One essay of this period whose significance would only be fully grasped later was *Contrapunto cubano del tabaco y el azúcar* (1940) by the Cuban essayist and sociologist, Fernando Ortiz (1881–1969). In this essay Ortiz uses two Cuban products, tobacco and sugar, as a means of investigating the complex process whereby cultures intermingle and produce a new cultural reality. The study begins with a description of the physical appearance of the two plants which produced tobacco and sugar, their origins and cultural associations. Much is made in the opening section of the difference between the two, expressed in terms of gender: 'Si tabaco es varón, azucar es hembra' (Ortiz 20). Ortiz goes on to discuss the manufacturing process by which the refined products are made, its social implications, and its relationship with slavery and the growth of capital-based industrialisation in the nineteenth century. In order better to understand the complex historical process whereby products invade other cultures, Ortiz introduces the term 'transculturación', a neologism which he sees as more appropriate than its competitor term 'acculturation' (137). Transculturation is based on the insight that 'en todo abrazo de culturas sucede lo que en la cópula genética de los individuos: la criatura siempre es distinta de cada uno de los dos' (142). Ortiz subsequently conducts a fascinating and well-researched narrative of the use of tobacco and sugar and their transculturation when they traverse the Atlantic Ocean on their way to European society, as gleaned from an abundance of printed sources, which range from contemporary scientific studies (including medical reports positing a link between cigarette smoking and cancer) to the work of early chroniclers such as Fray Mendieta, Fernández de Oviedo and Bernal Díaz del Castillo.

Undoubtedly the most influential – and, in some, particularly feminist, quarters, most reviled – essay written during this period was Octavio Paz's *El laberinto de la soledad* (1950). Paz begins this essay with a discussion of the *pachucos* of Mexican descent who live in Los Angeles. The second chapter, 'Máscaras mexicanas', potentially the most interesting, discusses the role played by social masks in modern-day Mexico. Chapter 3 discusses the way in which festivals and social celebrations, such as the Día de Muertos, bring an element of participation into a life routine dominated by existential loneliness. In Chapter 4 Paz introduces one of the most contentious theses of his essay, that is, the origin of Mexican identity. Mexicans, he argues, are the children of La Malinche and Cortés, and, following the gender-specific lines already traced in

Chapter 2, he identifies Malinche as passive, raped ('chingada') and therefore 'open' (Paz, *Laberinto* 78). It is clear that Paz is conflating the Oedipal scene of the jealous son, taken from Freud's analysis of the development of the human personality, with the historical scene of the martial conquest by Spain of Mesoamerica, and thus interpreting one in terms of the other. Cortés's love-making with La Malinche, in effect, becomes the primal scene of Mexico's birth. Paz's choice of Cortés and La Malinche is highly symbolic, since they do not loom large in popular mythology. Though it might be criticized for 'racialising' the history of Mexico (namely, by seeing the creation of *mestizo* culture in post-Edenic terms as a fall from grace caused by the rape of one race by another), *El laberinto de la soledad* is an imaginative and insightful essay on the symbolism of Mexican nationhood.[7]

## The Multi-genre Writer

One of the most significant multi-genre writers of this era was the Mexican Rosario Castellanos (1925–74). University professor, ambassador, translator, essayist, short-story writer, novelist, dramatist and poet, Castellanos is now seen as a major literary figure of her time. Castellanos's poetry is conversational and focuses on cultural and gender oppression from a subjective angle. One of her most famous poems is 'Meditación en el umbral' which expresses disappointment at the roles traditionally allotted to women, which range from the literary stereotype (Tolstoy's Ana, Flaubert's Madame Bovary) to the literary writer (Santa Teresa, Sor Juana and Emily Dickinson), and leaves the reader at the threshold of 'another way of being' (Castellanos, *Meditation* 48). Some of Castellanos's best poems contemplate the dilemma at the intersection of gender and race. In 'Malinche', for example, Castellanos re-writes the narrative of La Malinche's life, diverging from the standard view of her as Cortés's interpreter-concubine who betrayed her native land for personal gain, as given by historians such as Díaz del Castillo (see 78–79), and instead focuses on her sorrow at being rejected by her mother. Castellanos thereby in effect writes herstory rather than history.

Castellanos's novel *Oficio de tinieblas* (1962) is set in a town called Ciudad Real – the connotations of royalty are not coincidental – and has as its theme the tragic conflict between the Indians and the *ladinos* (called *caxclanes* by the Indians) in that community. Much of the novel is concerned with tracing the gradual intensification of the conflict between the *caxlanes* and the Indians. The true depths of the horror of the social conflict are revealed on Good Friday when the Indian community sacrifice a young male child, Domingo, as a means of appropriating the cultural-religious dominance of the *ladinos*. Overall, the

---

[7] The popularity of this work is suggested by sales. From the second edition which came out in 1959 until 1984 there were thirteen reprints. In 1984 alone 50,000 copies of the book were printed in the Colección Popular series for the Fondo de Cultura Económica publishing house.

novel provides a pessimistic vision of the relationship between Indians and non-Indians in modern-day Mexico. The Indian population's re-appropriation of the symbolism of Christianity is, after all, grotesque in the extreme. Castellanos's short stories follow a similar theme and are the genre in which she excels. *Album de familia* (1971) contains four stories which focus on the emotional traumas which underlie everyday life in middle-class Mexican society. The masterpiece of this collection of short stories is 'Lección de cocina' which concentrates on the split between the role expected of Mexican women and the identity they wish to create for themselves. The action takes place in the mind of a woman preparing a meal for her husband who will shortly be returning from work, and it enacts a type of self-discovery. As the meat which she is preparing slowly disappears, so does her acceptance of patriarchy. In this short story, Castellanos adopts a mock-ignorant stance in order to give more urgency to her critique of the patriarchal institution of marriage. Her novella, *Balún-Canán* (1957), seen by many as her masterpiece, is set in an imaginary town, Balún-Canán in Chiapas, and presents some of the societal conflicts sketched in *Oficio de tinieblas*, but through the eyes of a child. Social conflict is expressed almost exclusively within the space of the local school – the Indians want their children to be educated (which is not unreasonable since this had become state policy in Cárdenas's post-Revolution Mexico) while the local oligarch, César, resists this development – and the children whose education is being denied are about the same age as the narrator, César's daughter (she is seven years old when the narrative begins). The build-up of political tension between the two social groups is presented suspensefully in the novel, beginning with the murder of one of the farm-hands who supports his political master rather than his fellow workers, leading through a series of visits from inspectors from the capital who attempt to enforce the establishment of a school, and climaxing with the arson attack on César's property and livestock after he closes the local school down and forces the workers to go back to work. The novel concludes on a pessimistic note with the death of the narrator's younger brother and the banishment of the nanny who had predicted that a tragedy of this kind would occur because of the father's actions. The strength of this novel lies not only in its use of the child narrator but its ability to merge seamlessly the language of the supernatural world with that of concrete societal conflict. The novel has, strikingly, taken on greater significance since the outbreak of political violence in the Chiapas region since 1994; the warring parties are, indeed, none other than those described in Castellanos's novel.

Castellanos's play *El eterno femenino* (1975), published posthumously, describes itself as a farce. The butt of its humour are the manifold versions of Mexican womanhood which are imposed on Mexican women; the critique of this practice is burlesque and light-hearted rather than serious and moralising. The play re-creates a number of scenes from the past – whether they be 'universal' history, or Mexican history – and provides a new, anti-patriarchal slant on those events. The Adam and Eve scene, for example, shows Eve running intellectual rings around Adam and even the serpent (Castellanos, *Eterno* 74–85). The scene in which Charlotte and Maximilian are discussing their options in nineteenth-century Mexico also reveals the familiar pattern of the woman as the active, intelligent party and the man as the unresourceful, slow agent in the relationship (120–27). Another scene – iconoclastically – shows Sor Juana reciting her love poems not to a man, but to another woman, Celia (106). The play concludes on a metatheatrical note. A number of women sit around having listened to the play, and proceed to castigate its author mercilessly, accusing her of attacking the sacred values of family, religion and motherland (181–94). The play thereby contains and, in effect, deflates by anticipation any conservative critique of its feminist message.

# 6
# Late Twentieth-Century Literature

Alan Sinfield has described effectively the change which occurred in the literary field in the 1960s.

> Literature since the 1960s has [...] looked increasingly like a commodity (with, for instance, a top ten like pop records). Books may be conceived not by authors, but by publishers who commission a work they believe they can sell. [...] The idea of literary quality is used as a manifest marketing ploy – in literary prizes such as the Booker (with the final announcement live on television), in the promotion of book clubs, and in the selling of films and television serials through their derivation from a literary classic – and then the book through its connections with the screen version. (Sinfield 291)

A similar type of commodification of literature began to emerge in Latin America. As Fernández Retamar recalls of the early 1970s: 'Grants proliferated, colloquiums flourished, chairs to study and dissect us sprouted like toadstools after a rainstorm. There was even talk, in the most wretched stock-market taste, of the Boom of the Latin American novel' (*Caliban Revisited* 48). These were new times in which Latin American writers, in direct contradistinction to a previous era, could gain substantial royalties for their work, win highly lucrative literary prizes and be lionised by the world press. The Boom – centring on writers such as Gabriel García Márquez, Julio Cortázar, Carlos Fuentes, and Mario Vargas Llosa – signalled the definitive birth of Spanish American literature, thrusting it to the centre of the world's literary stage (see, in particular, 'The Boom Novel', pp. 205–12 below).

The picture of the publishing industry in Brazil during this period is similar. By 1980, the Brazilian book market had grown by a ratio of almost 100, compared to its sales in 1917 (Hallewell 571). A number of factors had given rise to this expansion: the Globo booksellers, under the inspired leadership of Érico Verissimo, began to publish high-quality translations of foreign classics in the 1940s and 1950s (402); book clubs during the same period began to make the classics more widely available (297–8), as well as selling by instalments (528–31), the growth in co-editions particularly in the 1960s and 1970s (565–8), as well as the renaissance of interest in Brazilian writers by foreign publishers who commissioned translations of major works into English and Spanish (572–3), all contributed to a marked growth in the Brazilian book market during the twentieth century. In particular a quantum leap was evident in the late 1960s and early 1970s; While 4,169,466 books were published in Brazil in 1966, that figure had shot to 191,732,543 by 1974 (473).

## Poetry in Spanish America

The most significant poet of this period is Nicanor Parra (b. 1914). Born in Chillán, a small town 200 miles to the south of Santiago, Chile, he graduated in 1938 in mathematics and physics from the University of Chile in Santiago. There are three discernible stages in Parra's work which, excluding his juvenilia (1937–50), are 'antipoesía' (1954–67), poetry characterised by bitter social critique (1968–76), and poetry with a prophetic style (1977 to the present day). In the 1960s Parra created the 'antipoem' for which his work is famous, that is, the poem which rejects the artificial and high-flown language we normally associate with poetry and attempts to speak with a voice that is recognised by everybody and not just the elite. Thus, Parra rejects the conventions of poetry, seeing poems as mathematical theorems: Maximum content, minimum of words. [...] Economy of language, no metaphors, no literary tropes.' In 'La montaña rusa', from *Versos del salón*, for example, Parra shows how Mount Olympus, where traditionally the poets went to drink inspiration in the spring of Castalia, has given way to the roller-coaster. The thrill of Parra's poetry has more in common with the modern world; it is neither gentle nor soul-uplifting. It may even lead to a nose-bleed (Parra 42). During the 1970s, Parra expanded his poetic repertoire to include the merciless exposure of the ills of society. Parra rejects both communism and capitalism as being systems which are simply foisted on the common people. The United States is described as a place, 'Donde la libertad / es una estatua'. Cuba does not fare much better; parodying Fidel Castro's words, he writes:

> Si fuera justo Fidel
> debiera creer en mí
> tal como yo creo en él:
> la historia me absolverá. (Parra 114)

In his later poetry, Parra employs the Bible as ammunition for his social critique; in *Sermones y prédicas del Cristo de Elqui*, for example, Parra takes on the persona of an itinerant preacher, Domingo Zárate Vega, whom he had seen preaching in his childhood in Chile during the 1920s. Domingo Zárate Vega, who left his job as a construction foreman in order to preach to the masses on street corners, was known popularly as El Cristo de Elqui because he made no secret of his belief that he was the reincarnation of Christ. The Christ of Elqui in Parra's poetry, for example, starts off by giving his flock some advice of a 'practical nature', which includes 'get up early', 'don't wear tight shoes', and 'don't keep gas in your stomach'. In section XXIII he dares his audience to take communion without first making confession, use the Bible for toilet paper, and spit on the Chilean flag (Parra 124–40). Parra's poetry has not mellowed with age, as one might expect; his recent poetry is as iconoclastic as ever. He rejects rhetoric, lies and the rich, and stands for antipoetry, truth and the underdog.

'[U]ndoubtedly one of the most important Spanish American poets of the day' (Fernández Retamar, *Prologue* 103), the Nicaraguan Ernesto Cardenal (b. 1925) is a poet whose work skilfully combines interest in the political, the religious and the quotidian. A priest and one-time Minister of Culture for the Sandinistas in Nicaragua, Cardenal's work is well known both in Latin America and abroad and has an immediate relevance to the political situation of contemporary Latin America. More important in terms of the overall message of Cardenal's work is his religious calling. Cardenal's poetry is a poetry to be experienced aurally rather than a poetry to be pored over. Cardenal is at his best when he writes verse with a political-cum-religious resonance, the best example being the various psalms he wrote. The call for the enactment of God's justice in the here-and-now and for retribution on the enemies of Israel which resounds in the biblical Psalms is applied to the context of modern-day Latin America, and specifically Nicaragua with its dictators and henchmen. His version of Psalm 11 opens: 'Libértanos tú/ porque no nos libertarán sus partidos' (Cardenal 43). The favourite rhetorical trope in Cardenal's repertoire is that of recuperation, in the sense that classic texts are often used in his work as a backdrop against which the silhouette of modern-day events is displayed. This can take the form of a simple one-line quotation, as in 'De pronto suena en la noche una sirena', when Cardenal alludes to Bécquer's famous Rima X which concludes with 'Es el amor que pasa' in order to draw attention to the contrast between Bécquer's love and Somoza's hate:

> De pronto suena en la noche una sirena
> de alarma, larga, larga ...
> No es incendio ni muerte:
> Es Somoza que pasa. (Cardenal 11)

Or this intertextuality can take the form of an extended rewriting of other texts. His poem, 'Coplas a la muerte de Merton', for example, dedicated to Thomas Merton, begins with a rewriting of the famous lines of Jorge Manrique's 'Nuestras vidas son los ríos que van a la mar que es la muerte', which is transformed in order to imbue it with an ultramundane resonance: 'Nuestras vidas son los ríos / que van a dar a la muerte / que es la vida' (Cardenal 132). Cardenal's most famous poem is 'Oración por Marilyn Monroe' in which he skilfully interweaves the language of Christianity, with its emphasis upon sin, redemption and forgiveness, with that of Hollywood, with its espousal of physical beauty, money and pleasure. The poem has some striking contrasts; Cardenal imagines Monroe before God denuded of her make-up:

> ahora se presenta ante Ti sin ningún maquillaje
> sin su Agente de Prensa
> sin fotógrafos y sin firmar autógrafos
> sola como un astronauta frente a la noche espacial.

Mid-way through the poem, Cardenal asks God to forgive Monroe and, at its conclusion, in a scene reminiscent of a Hitchcock thriller, he imagines the Hollywood actress trying desperately to contact someone minutes before she would take her own life:

> Señor
> quienquiera que haya sido el que ella iba a llamar
> y no llamó (y tal vez no era nadie
> o era Alguien cuyo número no está en el Directorio de Los Angeles
> contesta Tú el teléfono. (Cardenal 42–3)

As this poem demonstrates, Cardenal is at his best when he combines the different languages of Christianity and popular culture, identifying coincidence where none was first divined.

A significant poet of the modern era is the Colombian Álvaro Mutis (b. 1923). His poetry typically rejects high-flown language (his preferred poetic form is the prose poem), is rooted in everyday reality, and favours the natural world as opposed to human artificiality. His 'Programa para una poesía' sets the tone for this and can be seen as an *ars poetica*. It describes a musical concert, followed by the (inane) comments of the spectators, and there then follows a picture of a new, more natural reality:

> A lo lejos comienza a oírse la bárbara música que se acerca. Del fondo más profundo de la noche surge este sonido planetario y rugiente que arranca de lo más hondo del alma las palpitantes raíces de pasiones olvidadas. Algo comienza. (Mutis 19)

Clearly taking a leaf out of Neruda's book, Mutis suggests that this music of the earth is more authentic than the concert music which preceded it. Much of Mutis's poetry can be viewed in these terms. His poem on death, for example, suggests that we must search for a truer more accepting vision of death: 'Desnudo el rostro, ceñida la piel a los huesos elementales que sostuvieron las facciones, la confianza en la muerte volverá para alegrar nuestros días' (Mutis 21). As this poem suggests Mutis often searches for a knowledge of the world which is contrary to common sense. Thus, his poem on hatred, 'El odio', sees it not, as it is traditionally seen, as a corrosive self-destructive emotion, but rather as a purifying element in human life which offers knowledge of human existence:

> No más falsificaciones del odio: el odio a la injusticia, el odio a los hombres, el odio a las formas, el odio a la libertad, no nos han dejado ver la gran

máscara purificadora del odio verdadero, del odio que sella los dientes y deja los ojos fijos en la nada, a donde iremos a perdernos algún día. El dará las mejores voces para el canto, las palabras que servirán para sostener en lo más alto su arquitectura permanente. (Mutis 22)

As the last sentence of this quotation suggests, Mutis also regards hatred as a reliable source of good poetry. This suggests that Mutis's view of human existence is negative or, at least, deflationary, and his poem 'El hombre' tends to corroborate this idea since it begins by giving a list of things and actions which should be the inspiration of poetry; they include man's 'torpeza esencial', his 'gestos vanos y gastados', his 'levantar los hombros como un simio hambriento', and, perhaps most tellingly, 'toda esta pequeña armonía de entrecasa' (Mutis 23); clearly, Mutis is concerned with the grind of everyday life, its repetitiveness and its futility. And he does not allow himself, as some poets have, to see the futility of everyday life somehow redeemed by a poetry that is able to express that sadness elegantly. For, as 'Cada poema' demonstrates, Mutis views poetry as itself gnawed from within by the futility of life. Each poem is 'un traje de la muerte / por las calles y plazas inundadas / en la cera letal de los vencidos' (83). The other images used to describe the poem are likewise deflationary and death-obsessed. The most telling of these images occurs midway through the poem when Mutis describes poetry as 'un lento naufragio del deseo, / un crujir de los mástiles y jarcias / que sostienen el peso de la vida' (83). Poetry, like life, is best described as a shipwreck, lost but searching for delivrance. If this can be assumed to be an authentic expression of the poet's views on matters such as life and poetry, then it is clear that these views are also expressed in the person of 'Maqroll el gaviero' who becomes his mouthpiece, and with whom he enacts a dialogue, very much in the vein of the Portuguese poet, Pessoa. Thus, Mutis will write a mock-ironic prayer for Maqroll which uses church litany ('Oración de Maqroll', Mutis 38–9), he writes of Maqroll's various illnesses, which Maqroll refers to as 'plagues' ('Las plagas de Maqroll', 117–18), he describes the various maps in Maqroll's possession ('El mapa', 119–22), and the various pictures which summarize – allusively and ambiguously – the history of the Americas ('La carreta', 128–9). Whether he uses Maqroll's voice or his own, Mutis seeks to undermine the conceptual structures used to understand and master the world. With a wry deflationary irony, he shows the inconsistencies in the values of our human society.

One of the more sophisticated poets of the modern era is the Peruvian Carlos Germán Belli (b. 1927). Author of a number of poetic collections ranging from his first work, *Poemas* (1958) to his most recent *En las hospitalarias estrofas* (2001), Belli's work is remarkably distinctive and stylistically consistent. A number of themes and techniques recur. Perhaps most characteristic of Belli's poetry is its Existentialism, that is, its expression of the notion that the body comes before the soul, food before thought, the material world before the world of the spirit. This idea is expressed explicitly in the last two lines of 'Cuando el espíritu no habla por la boca', for example, which run as follows: 'cuando el alma, ¡oh Dios!, por la boca no, / mas por el falo hablando eternamente' (Belli 175). This self-proclaimed materialism often leads Belli to praise the everyday at the expense of the pompous poetic language of the past, a gesture reminiscent of his Chilean contemporary, Nicanor Parra. His poem 'La canción inculta', for example, makes this point clearly:

> ¡ay Canción mía inculta!,
> que tras proclamar la beldad ayer,
> bien vale que la dulce
> lira por una vez siquiera hoy
> loe al porcino bolo alimenticio. (Belli 171)

Belli's argument is not a dogmatically materialist one, for his work calls precisely for a recognition of the material and does not necessarily reject the spiritual. The important image here is consubstantiality, for, as we read in 'Canción en alabanza del bolo alimenticio y en reprimenda del alma', it is as a result of feeding the body that 'eternal life' is glimpsed: 'y las grandes delicias / gozas entonces como eterna vida, / en virtud de tan sólo lo comido' (Belli 139). It is precisely this balance of the material and the spiritual that Belli's poetry strives to express. His 'Boda de la pluma y la letra', for example, skilfully deploys the contrast between antithetical imagery such as light versus darkness, life versus death, heaven versus earth, gold versus black, swan versus owl, elm versus ivy, in order finally to imagine the fusion of these opposites as encapsulated within a poetry which is able successfully to express the dialectical nature of life: 'y la áurea letra / escribirla al fin con la pluma negra' (117). To have one without the other will be detrimental to the poetic purpose. Indeed, an over-enthusiastic emphasis upon beauty, and, in particular, that expression of beauty in Golden Age pastoral poetry, is apt to bring a sardonic reaction from Belli's lips. In 'El jardín en casa', for example, begins with the supposition that Cloris, a typical name for the female beloved in Golden Age poetry, will be transmuted through the poet's word, into a flower. But, in the final stanza of the poem, this attempt is shown to be wrong-headed: 'En vano, Canción, estos pensamientos / del bosque en lo recóndito proclamas, / que allí la ninfa no se trueca en flor' (154). Though Belli's poetry strives to capture the fusion of 'heaven' and 'earth', to use his own imagery, it is only fair to point out that his poetry more typically stresses the ironic disjunction between these two universes. In 'Mis ajos', for example, he compares his poetry to garlic:

> Pero mal padre soy, varón tan loco,
> porque el jardín cercano de mis hijas,
> con malo olor de feos bulbos siempre
> infesto todo. (Belli 67)

Similarly, in 'Poema', the creation of a poem is compared to that of an unloved foetus (Belli 47). Typical of Belli's style in this poem is his use of images of light to signify the (unattainable) ideal, his use of material images to convey (such as the reference to a 'cloister' and a 'cistern' to describe the realm inhabited by Poetry), and, finally and most importantly, his allusion to physical deformity ('tartamudo o cojo o manco o bizco') which becomes a metaphor of the failures of everyday life. Distinctive to Belli's poetry is its expression of a sense of shame (see 'Segregación No. 1; 15–16; '¡Oh padres, sabedlo bien ...!' 33; 'Amanuense' 49; 'Mis ajos' 67–8; 'Sextina del mea culpa' 69–70). Shame is, after all, a much more down-to-earth, everyday emotion than love or ecstasy, though it is no less powerful.

Another arresting poet of this era is the Peruvian Antonio Cisneros (b. 1942). Perhaps most distinctive about his poetry is its ability to offer a poetic vision of everyday life with everyday language. Thus Cisneros's poetry appears deceptively simple, but this first impression soon dissolves after further study. The poetic stance typically adopted is that of an ironic, detached observer of everyday life. In 'Naturaleza muerta en Innsbrucker Strasse', for example, Cisneros projects himself in Baudelairean fashion, as an outsider surveying Western (capitalist) society:

> Ellos son (por excelencia) treintones y con fe en el futuro.
> Mucha fe.
> Al menos se deduce por sus compras (a crédito y costosas).
> Casaca de gamuza (natural), Mercedes deportivo color de oro.
> (Cisneros 186)

Cisneros projects himself as an unhealthy outsider looking in; a humorous detail is provided by the reference to the young German couple consuming everyone's oxygen in the district, including the poet's ('Cuando han consumido todo el oxígeno del barrio (el suyo y el mío)'). This self-deprecatory tone also applies to his status as a poet compared with the great poets of the past. His poem dedicated to Quevedo, for example, reveals him to be the typical epigonic artist of the post-Romantic era ('Y en verdad, don Antonio Cisneros vive seguro / De que sus versos no habrán de ser leídos por Quevedo / Aunque lo entierren en la tumba vecina'; Cisneros 65). Likewise his poem entitled 'Arte poética I' cocks a snook at the social prestige associated with official poetry, in a style of expression which is redolent of Parra's 'antipoesía': 'se come una bola de Caca / eructa / pluajj / un premio' (119). Intriguingly, even when his subject is transcendental, as for example in his religious verse, Cisneros still manages to bring a note of everyday realism into his poetry. Thus, in the poem 'Cuando librado del demonio, comulgué de manos del obispo', which celebrates his return to Christianity, Cisneros emphasises the quotidian aspects of his new-found faith rather than its transcendental side:

> Señor, siento tu sangre
> embravecer mis venas,
> lecho de hojas tu carne
> me conforta,

> es más dulce este amor
> de los rigores
> que ropajes ociosos
> y tabernas. (Cisneros 35–6)

Likewise, in 'Poema sobre Jonás y los desalienados', he uses the biblical story of Jonah and the whale, often used in New Testament theology as a forewarning of Christ's descent into hell before His resurrection, as a Swift-like parable wittily underlining the blindness of mankind:

> Si los hombres viven en la barriga de una ballena
> sólo pueden sentir frío y hablar
> de las manadas periódicas de peces y de murallas
> oscuras como una boca abierta. (Cisneros 93)[1]

Often, Cisneros's poems take the form of a micro-narrative; they tell a story drawn from everyday life and allow a message to emerge from that narrative. Typical of this feature of his verse is the poem 'Crónica de Lima' which combines a personal genealogy (the poem begins with the reference to his grandfather and his own son) with a chronicle of Lima's history (as expressed mainly through the architecture) and with a musical backdrop provided by the *criollo* waltz 'Hermelinda' which punctuates the narrative at various key junctures (Cisneros 73–5). One of the skilful features of Cisneros's poetry resides in its ability to allow a sense of history to permeate the poem, normally in the form of synecdochial allusions. In 'Kensington, primera crónica', for example, Cisneros refers to the Englishmen who died in the two world wars by describing how he is walking on their skulls ('alegre peatón sobre los cráneos de los ingleses muertos en la guerra'), and alludes to the bitterness engendered by Britain's colonial expansion in a surrealist description of the Queen being tortured by having lobsters inserted in her anus:

> Hombres de Australia, hombres del Canadá, hombres de Irlanda,
> todos los bárbaros
> metiendo lagartijas en el culo de la Reina, jubilosos
> y sin remordimiento. (Cisneros 82)

Through a dual-edged technique of 'ostranenie' (defamiliarization) as well as the use of synecdochial images, Cisneros is able to allow the historical past to permeate the vignette of everyday life with which he typically will open a poem. In this way, he is able to bring out the poetic in everyday life. Perhaps the best example of this is his poem dedicated to love, 'Tercer movimiento

---

[1] Cisneros's use of animals in his poetry has been noted by a number of critics. In a lecture he gave at the University of Kentucky on 19 March 1996, Cisneros referred to how he detested domestic animals, and often used animals as projections of the disagreeable side of human beings.

(affettuoso)' (Cisneros 54). What is most significant about this poem is the way it manages to take the topos of love and quotidianise it,[2] but without letting love slip into pornography (here I see pornography within the discourse of love, rather like Barthes sees wrestling within the discourse of struggle, that is, a realm where all is visible, and therefore obscene, and where symbolism is squeezed out of the picture).[3] It offers advice on lovemaking which includes the place (damp grass is better than yellow grass), the weather (the sky should be blue but not too sunny), the disposition of the lovers (open lungs) and important gestures (the lovers should use short sentences). An elegant poem (in this it is typical of Cisneros's work which is self-consciously erudite, self-consciously urbane), it teases the reader playfully, and is surely meant as the opening gambit of a seduction.[4]

It was in the 1970s that there emerged a new sense of the distinctiveness of women's writing in Spanish America, particularly in the genre of poetry, and largely as a result of the international impact of Anglo-Saxon and, particularly, French feminism. The important question to be addressed in this section is the extent to which women's writing of the contemporary period enunciates a vision of reality which is recognisably distinct from that of their male counterparts. In an article 'Is Women's Writing in Spanish America Gender-Specific?' I have argued that the difference between men's and women's writing only truly emerges after the 1960s (Hart, 'Women's Writing'), and that is the argument pursued in what follows. It is invidious to choose some figures over and above others, but the work of certain female poets does stand out, such as that of the Argentinian poet, Alejandra Pizarnik (1936–72) and of the Salvadorean, Claribel Alegría (b. 1924).

Alejandra Pizarnik's work is visionary and difficult and clearly shows the traces of the Surrealistic authors she studied and imitated. Like the Surrealists, Pizarnik's poems deal in apparently disconnected sets of images which operate in terms of emotional and visual impact; they deliberately lack a clear narrative. Often, Pizarnik's poems deal in liminality and imminence, portraying a psychical reality which typically does not happen and which then retreats from the poem's field of vision (Cobo Borda 95). 'Ojos primitivos', for example, indicates that Pizarnik's aim was to retrieve the visionary freshness of a prelapsarian view of the world, which is at once 'el silencio del mero estar' and 'la bella alegría animal' (Crow 46). Yet, one of the most disarming insights of Pizarnik's verse is the connection it elicits between poetic creativity and death. As many of her later poems suggest, it is only through death – whether expressed as emotional death, self-death, or suicide – that her poetic voice is able to flourish. Her

---

[2] For a related discussion on how Cisneros consistently demythifies social myth, see Higgins 65–88.

[3] As Barthes argues of wrestling, '[l]a vertu du catch, c'est d'être un spectacle excessif', and, later on, 'ici et là, une lumière sans ombre élabore une émotion sans repli' (Barthes 13).

[4] For reasons of space the work of some significant contemporary poets could not be discussed here; for an overview of poetry of this period see Quiroga, vol. 2, 303–64.

poem, 'Cantora nocturna', for instance, projects herself as already dead and singing (Crow 54). The colour blue appears here, as elsewhere in the later poetic works, to signify death, in contradistinction to the *modernistas* for whom blue stood for the ideal. One of Pizarnik's most haunting poems is 'El sueño de la muerte o el lugar de los cuerpos poéticos' from *Extracción de la piedra de locura*. This poem, which is written in prose and has strong parallels with *Les Chants de Maldoror*, explores the link between poetic creation and death. Here, as in *La condesa sangrienta* (1971), Pizarnik alludes to the sadistic practices of the Hungarian Countess Erzébet Báthory (born *c*. 1560) who was accused of the death by torture of over 600 girls between the ages of twelve and eighteen; she indulged in a programme of seduction, torment and murder of her victims (Foster 97). In her poem Pizarnik alludes to this story and places her poetic creation against that backdrop, as if to suggest that her poetry feeds on that image of death (*Extracción* 61). Our final impression of Pizarnik's work is one of a haunting, melancholic and at times unnerving poetic voice orientated towards the unconscious and death.

Born in Nicaragua in 1924, Claribel Alegría grew up in El Salvador, moved to the United States in 1943 and lived subsequently in Mexico, Chile, Uruguay and the Canary Isles. In 1978 her poetry won Cuba's prestigious Casa de las Américas prize. Alegría is renowned for the political bent of her poetry; an important theme is the concept of revolution understood as much in a natural sense as in a poetical sense (namely, the Izalco volcano which periodically erupts in modern times). Alegría's most significant poetic collection is *Flores del volcán* which is lyrical, politically committed and feminist. The style adopted throughout is prosaic, political and confrontational. In 'Flores del volcán', for example, Alegría compares the wanton killing of guerrillas in El Salvador during the civil war of the 1980s with the blood sacrifices of the Mayans who dedicated youths' hearts to the God of Rain, Chac (Claribel Alegría 46). This ancient world, however, seems to have been destroyed beneath the modern monster of United States capitalism, which is able to turn Central American food commodities such as coffee into gold (48). But, as the poem concludes, the modern calamities are due to Chac's desire for revenge (50).[5]

---

[5] Other significant female poets whose work is not discussed here are Ulalume González de León (b. 1932), Rita Geada (b. 1937), Delia Domínguez (b. 1934), Circe Maia (b. 1932), Violeta Parra (1917–67), María Mercedes Carranza (b. 1945), Nancy Morejón (b. 1944), Raquel Jodorowsky (b. 1927), Olga Orozco (b. 1920), and Carmen Ollé. For some discussion of their work, see Crow; Quiroga.

## Poetry in Brazil

Contemporary Brazilian poets return to some of the themes which had surfaced in the work of their predecessors – the search for an unencumbered, even prosaic poetic idiom – but their exploration of a new language to fit the postmodern world has led to a fixation with the tool of poetry itself, that is, language. It is almost as if the contemporary poet needs to check that language is in good working order before he feels confident about describing the world around him. As the second stanza of Cassiano Ricardo's 'Anoitecer' suggests, for example:

> Então, inventei as palavras. E as palavras pousaram gorjeando sôbre o rosto dos objetos.
> A realidade, assim, ficou com tantos rostos
> quantas são as palavras. (Bishop and Brasil 26)

Far from seeing language as simply a transparent vehicle which describes reality, the modern poet sees language as a creative tool, bringing new worlds into being. Mário Faustino's poem, 'Vida Toda Linguagem' offers an arresting sense of the vital interplay between life and language, which revolves around the central image of the foetus:

> Vida toda linguagem,
> feto sugando em língua compassiva
> o sangue que criança espalhará
> oh metáfora ativa!
> leite jorrado em fonte adolscente, sêmem de homens maduros, verbo, verbo.
> (Brasil and Smith 90)

Blood, milk, semen, language are mixed together in the liquid process of life. Indeed, if Michael Palmer's anthology, *Nothing the Sun Could Not Explain: 20 Contemporary Brazilian Poets* (1997), is anything to go by, there is clear evidence of a new paradigm-shift emerging, a sense of a new specifically linguistic self-reflexivity in the work of contemporary poets. 'Flor da Idade' by Francisco Alvim (b. 1938), for example, shows how far the contemporary poet is prepared to go in his search for linguistic simplicity:

> A tarde parou na janela
> úmida verde
> ela acabou de sair
> nos despedimos sem tristeza. (Palmer 100)

Also striking about the work of a number of contemporary poets is how 'un-Brazilian' it is. Gone are the reference-points we find so familiar in the work of the great Modernists: the streets of Rio and São Paolo, the allusions to Amerindian culture, the use of Brazilianisms. Régis Bonvicino (b. 1955) appears more interested in Picasso, Derain, Cézanne, Matisse, Seurat than in Brazilian autochthonous culture (see 'A disordem de', Palmer 182–5). Horácio Costa (b. 1954) writes an elegant poem about the Spanish Golden Age poet, Luis de Góngora ('O retrato de Dom Luis de Gôngora', 168). When a Brazilian landscape is invoked it is invariably in the context of the distanced rhetoric of European poetry. How, Carlos Ávila (b. 1955) asks, could Baudelaire's *Les Fleurs du Mal* survive in the *sertão*?:

> as flores do mal
> (descubro)
> não resistem à lenta
> violência do sol […]
> o que estaria baudelaire
> (em efigie gráfica)
> fazendo no sertão? (Palmer 174)

There is none of the attachment to Brazilian-ness we associate with the seers of Modernism in Ávila's poem. Typically the poet views himself as silhouetted against the backdrop of the universe, humanity taken as a whole. As one of the foremost poets of this generation, Torquato Neto (1944–72), suggests in the opening stanza of his poem, 'Cogito':

> eu sou como eu sou
> pronome
> pessoal intransferível
> do homen que iniciei
> na medida do impossível. (Palmer 38)

'Onde há fumaça' by Nelson Ascher (b. 1958) bears an epigraph penned by the German poet, Paul Celan, and has not one single image which could tie the poem to the Americas, let alone Brazil; it is rather a meditative poem about the ephemeral nature of human endeavour, how 'things' are lost in 'smoke' (though there could be a subtle reference to the Holocaust here) – even writing ('ink') is unable to leave a memory. The poem concludes rather enigmatically with the proposal that one should not ask about 'the deepest roots of smoke':

> não cabe perguntar
> acerca (onde há fumaça,
> há cinzas) das raízes
> mais fundas da fumaça. (Palmer 220)

Long gone are the diatribes against the injustice of military regimes, or capitalism, or US military interference. Far more pressing for this contemporary group of poets is their desire to capture in words the ineffable experience of otherness. Ana Cristina Cesar (1952–83), now recognised as one of the most expressive voices of her generation – though her potential was not fulfilled since she tragically took her own life while still young – captures the mystery of this idea effectively in her poem 'Nada, esta espuma':

> Por afrontamento do desejo
> insisto na maldade de escrever
> mas não sei se a deusa sobe à superficie
> ou apenas me castiga com seus uivos.
> Da amurada deste barco
> quero tanto os seios da sereia. (Palmer 54)

Is the desire mentioned in the first line of the poem a desire to express (the poem) or a (sexual?) desire for the 'goddess'? In what sense are the goddess's howls a punishment for the poet? Do they fill her with remorse? Is the poet's desire for the 'mermaid's breasts' an image of poetic ineffability, a figure to represent the Freudian unconscious, or an expression of lesbian libido? It is no doubt acceptable to take one's pick from one of the above, or even see the poem as a mixture of these and even other levels of association, but the imagery of the poem is, surely, designed to leave the expression of the emotion at the threshold of ambiguity. At times this leads this group of poets to an emotionally intense focus on the dividing-line between reality and language. 'O bicho alfabeto' by Paolo Leminski (1945–89), of all the contemporary poets the most visionary, switches their attributes, thereby turning language into a living beast:

> O bicho alfabeto
> tem vinte e três patas
> ou quase
>
> por onde ele passa
> nascem palavras
> e frases
>
> como frases
> se fazem asas
> palavras
> o vento leve
>
> o bicho alfabeto
> passa
> fica o que não se escreve. (Palmer 68)

Deliberately subverting the instrumentalist view of language which sees human speech as simply an advanced tool which we use in order to exploit our environment, Leminski's poem suggests that language has a life of its own (since, by passing by us, it gives rise to words and phrases) and, even more, that it gives rise to ideas over which human agency has no jurisdiction since they are not even written down ('o que não se escreve'). The poem leaves us with a sense of language as a quasi-magical arena, something which possesses an agency of its own which is beyond human understanding. This notion of language as animate reappears in Leminski's humorous poem about his former grammar teacher, a 'pleonasm', as 'possessive as a pronoun', who was denied entry to the United States because an 'indefinite article' was found in his luggage, and whom Leminski finally killed off by hitting him on the head with a 'direct object' ('O assassino era o escriba', Palmer 72). Other poets have homed in on the interplay between reality and language. Waly Salomão (b. 1944) has a powerful poem about the indifference of the wind (here to be read as a metaphor, perhaps, of phenomenal reality in a broader sense) towards the naming process whereby summer is differentiated from spring:

> Vento bêbado de amnésia e desmemória,
> incapaz de verão ou outono ter por nome próprio,
> trafega indiferente a nossa tradição ibérica
> que exige para tudo registro o certidão. ('Meia-estação', Palmer 132)

Often the contemporary Brazilian poet strives to capture reality before the process of expression in language has taken hold but, as Júlio Castañon Guimarães (b. 1951) finds out, once 'representation' is subtracted, there is not much left:

> quando, desfeitos os
> nós da representação
> contra si a imagem
> investe, pouco resta
> além da indagação
> cínica ou retórca.
>      ('Sem título, óleo sobre tela, 70 × 50 cm', Palmer 146)

We find a similar quasi-philosophical desire to get round the back of language and representation in Horácio Costa's evocative poem, 'História natural', in which the poet is portrayed as a taxidermist trying to get under his own skin:

> Detrás do taxidermista, há a palha,
> detrás do rinoceronte, a savana,
> detrás desta escritura só a noite,
> a noite que galopa até o fronte. (Palmer 170)

Yet all he finds behind his writing is 'the night', the black hole of meaning which frustrates the semantic inquiry underlying scientism. Pointing in a similar direction, 'Teatro ambulante' (Palmer 122–3) by Duda Machado (b. 1944), which tells the story of the members of a theatrical troupe who take their play to the provinces only to panic when they find that they have started to improvise so much during performances that the words of the play are beginning to become 'strange' and 'unrecognisable', can be read as an allegory of the poet who is confronted by a language he has created but which has taken on a separate life of its own – a prototype, indeed, of the linguistic conundrum encountered by a significant number of contemporary Brazilian poets, as we have seen. It is this linguistic-existential alterity which is at the matrix of some of this generation's best poems. 'As pedras' by Arnaldo Antunes (b. 1960), for example, is a deceptively simple poem which goes to the heart of the matter. Beginning with sentences which appear to be self-evident such as 'As pedras são muito mais lentas do que os animais' and 'As plantas exalam mais cheiro quando a chuva cai', it then graduates to sentences which hint at the complexity of life ('Palavaras podem ser usadas de muitas maneiras'), others which suggest its strangeness ('As baleias vivem na água mas não são peixes'), even its absurdity ('Cabelos quando ficam velhos ficam brancos'), before concluding that we do not have all the answers: 'Crianças gostam de fazer perguntas sobre tudo. Nem todas as respostas cabem num adulto' (Palmer 256).

## The Boom Novel

The novels which are traditionally included in the generic title of the Boom novel are: *Rayuela* (1963) by Julio Cortázar (1914–84), *La muerte de Artemio Cruz* (1962) and *Cambio de piel* (1967) by Carlos Fuentes (b. 1928), *La ciudad y los perros* (1962) and *La casa verde* (1966) by Mario Vargas Llosa (b. 1936), and *Cien años de soledad* (1967) by Gabriel García Márquez (b. 1928). My intention here has not been to narrow the Boom down to only a few novels. Indeed, a significant number of novels were published during the 1960s which are not normally included in the generic title of the Boom novel. Some of these were written by authors who had established their reputation in an earlier generation, such as Sábato's *Sobre héroes y tumbas*, and Carpentier's *El siglo de las luces*, both of 1962; others are by writers whose work was not caught up in the mass publicisation that authors such as Fuentes, Cortázar, García Márquez and Vargas Llosa enjoyed, such as *Los recuerdos del porvenir* (1962) by Elena Garro. However, for the purposes of clarity I shall be discussing in this section only those works which are unmistakably associated with the Boom novel.

José Donoso provides a clear description of the Boom in his *Historia personal del 'Boom'* (1972). In that work he describes how the Boom suddenly internationalised Latin American novelists; the pre-Boom literary generation espoused a nationalist regionalist ethos (*Historia* 24–5). Donoso recalls how Jorge Edwards caused a scandal when he stated that he was more interested in foreign than Chilean literature (24). Linked to this internationalism was a new sense of Latin American political identity produced by widespread support for the Cuban Revolution, expressed, as Donoso remembers, during a conference held at the Universidad de Concepción in Chile in 1962, which was attended by a number of prominent writers of the day (Pablo Neruda, José María Arguedas, Augusto Roa Bastos, Carlos Fuentes, Claribel Alegría, Alejo Carpentier; *Historia* 34–6). The bubble of support for Cuba, however, burst in 1971 when the scandal of the Padilla affair broke the ranks of the Latin American intelligentsia. Like other communists such as Jean-Paul Sartre and Hans Magnus Enzensberger, many of the Boom writers (and, in particular, Vargas Llosa) turned away from Cuba as a source of political inspiration.

An important indication of the difference between the pre-Boom and the Boom novel appears in their respective circulation figures. Donoso's *Veraneo* (1955), published in the pre-Boom era, came out in a print-run of 1,000, of which Donoso had himself to sell 900 (*Historia* 26–7). The Boom, however, changed all that, and literature became a lucrative industry. As is well known, the Boom novel came about as the result of a felicitous mix of a far-sighted editor, the Spaniard Carlos Barral, editor of Seix Barral of Barcelona, and a new type of writing from Latin America which caught his attention. Cortázar's *Rayuela*, for example, began with a print-run of 4,000 in 1963, shot to 10,000 for 1966 and 1967, and then rocketed to 26,000 and 25,000 for the years 1968 and 1969 respectively. The novel which fundamentally changed the paradigm was García Márquez's *Cien años de soledad* which had an initial print-run of 25,000 in the year of publication (1967), and from 1968 onwards sold about 100,000 copies per year (Rama, *Crítica* 291–92). Perhaps inevitably, since the Boom novel threw a new generation of Latin American writers into the international limelight in an unprecedented way, the movement had its detractors. Miguel Angel Asturias, for example, accused the Boom novels of being 'meros productos de la publicidad' (quoted in Donoso, *Historia* 15). However one views the Boom novelists, they were the first generation of Spanish American writers who were able to live from the labour of their pens; in effect, they brought Latin American literature from the backwaters to the centre-stage of the literary world.

*La muerte de Artemio Cruz* (1962) by Carlos Fuentes, winner of the Príncipe de Asturias prize in 1994, is one of the first major Boom novels, and demonstrates the main characteristics of the genre. Its narrative concerns the life story of Artemio Cruz, born on 9 April 1889, an individual who fought in and survived the Mexican Revolution, got involved in the reconstruction programme afterwards (specifically attracting and overseeing United States investment), married Catalina, the daughter of Don Gamaliel Bernal, a wealthy landowner, and died on 10 April 1959, surrounded by friends and relatives. The novel is essentially the testimony of his life and is meant also to be representative of the history of Mexico. The most striking innovation of the novel is its use of tense and person. Whereas the Realist novel usually employs the grammatical person in the following way (I-narrator, present tense; you-reader, present tense; (s)he-protagonist, past tense), *La muerte de Artemio Cruz* employs the following innovative format: I-Artemio Cruz, present tense; you-Artemio Cruz, future tense; (s)he-Artemio Cruz, past tense. The novel is divided up between these three voices, the 'él' section taking up two-thirds of the available space, with the 'yo' and the 'tú' sections taking up roughly one-sixth each. Of the three sections the 'él' passages, given their use of dates and the third-person narrator, approximate more to the expectations of traditional Realism. The 'tú' section, though expressed in the future, gives the impression of being an omniscient conscience which knows Artemio Cruz's destiny and unpacks it before his, and indeed our, eyes. The 'yo' passages, according to the novel's logic narrated on the day of Artemio's death (10 April 1959), are very body-orientated and home in obsessively on corporeal sensation. As the above suggests, *La muerte de Artemio Cruz* is an experiment in the intercrossings of tense and person and, by implication, time, space and identity. But it is also specifically a novel about the genesis of Mexican identity. In a section roughly mid-way through the novel, Paz's notion of Mexicans as 'hijos de la chingada' is taken up and exploited in a meandering, taboo-breaking passage: 'eres hijo de los hijos de la chingada; serás padre de más hijos de la chingada: nuestra palabra, detrás de cada rostro, de cada signo, de cada peperada: pinga de la chingada, verga de la chingada, culo de la chingada' (Fuentes, *Muerte* 145). In a gesture typical of the Boom novel, Fuentes casts fear of taboo to one side and, indeed, exploits the resonance of dirty words to reach a deeper level of understanding of existence (the quest pursued by the protagonists of his novels, though it breaks down taboo, is always mythical, always Jungian).

One of the foundational Boom novels was *La ciudad y los perros* (1963) by Mario Vargas Llosa, which tells the story of the murder of a fourth-year intern at the Leoncio Prado Military Academy in Lima because he had blown the whistle on his friends about cheating for a chemistry exam. The novel is based on Vargas Llosa's own experience at the Academy from 1950 to 1952, and is, at the most fundamental level, a record of his personal perception of the spiritual sterility and moral corruption produced by military life. Though not as formally innovative as some of the other Boom novels, *La ciudad y los perros* is superb in bringing to life the world of the adolescent trapped within the straitjacket of social institutions, and struggling to find and achieve an authentic identity. The world of the adolescents is shown to be a cruel and brutalising one: in the Leoncio Prado Military Academy the interns are treated barbarically by their military overseers and even worse by their peers. The important metaphor is, as the title suggests, animality and its juxtaposition with the apparently civilised world of the city outside. The structure of the novel is rather like Dickens's *Tale of Two Cities* in that it begins by showing two worlds as separate, and then gradually shows how they are interconnected. The animality of the cadets' behaviour – they are given nicknames such as Boa and Jaguar which they thoroughly deserve, and the nickname for first-year cadets is 'los perros' – is underlined through juxtaposition with the dog, La Malpapeada, which is treated lovingly by its owner, and therefore appears to be more 'human' than the humans. When Ricardo Arana, nicknamed Esclavo, is found badly injured on the ground during a military manoeuvre, at the conclusion of Part I, the linearity of the novel is thenceforth disrupted, as if to emphasise the temporal centrality of that discovery; Part II opens with the narrative delving into the past. Though the world of the adolescents is cruel, that of the 'adult world' is worse, since it is governed by the laws of collusion and corruption. A great deal of pressure is brought to bear on the officer, Gamboa, to prevent him from officially transmitting a deposition in which he records his suspicion that Arana was murdered (which, in the epilogue to the novel is shown to be true). For his temerity in fighting against the system he is banished to an out-of-the-way military post in the jungle. Alberto, in many ways a projection of the author Vargas Llosa himself, is forced to retract his accusation when the Colonel shows him the pornographic novels he has been writing for his peers. The most intriguing feature of *La ciudad y los perros* is the status that literature plays within the novel. Alberto, nicknamed 'el poeta', emerges as the hero of the piece in that he is prepared, against all the odds, to denounce the crime which Arana suffered, and yet, when he does so, his action is seen as reprehensible and novelistic. Thus, literature finally reveals the truth about social institutions such as the military academy and marriage (both as seen through Alberto's wise eyes) that society is determined not to reveal. Perhaps most interesting about *La ciudad y los perros* is the fact that it so incensed the authorities of the Leoncio Prado Military Academy that they attempted to discredit Vargas Llosa publicly by publishing details of his poor academic record while at the Academy, and by incinerating 1,000 copies of the book in the parade ground outside the Academy shortly after the book was published, thereby, unwittingly, ensuring its fame for years to come.

*Rayuela* (1963) by Julio Cortázar (1914–84) is the most intellectually sophisticated novel of the Boom, describing the search for ontological meaning of Oliveira, a young Argentine man, in Paris and later in Buenos Aires. The novel has three parts: the first is set in Paris ('del lado de allá'), the second in Buenos Aires ('del lado de acá'), and in concludes with a theory-of-the-novel section in which a novelist, Morelli, rejects the old Galdosian format and proposes a self-reflexive, open work of art ('de otros lados'). Oliveira is involved in a search for transcendental meaning, and much of his search is predicated on the rejection of Western categories of thought, including the two large Kantian categories of time and space; the form and technique of the novel echo his search. *Rayuela* deconstructs time in the sense that there are at least two ways of reading the novel, one of which is a linear reading beginning at Chapter 1 and ending at Chapter 56, the second of which is the hopscotch version as described in the 'Tablero de dirección'. Space is deconstructed in the novel in the sense of the moving backwards and forwards in the hopscotch reading process, and also in the sense that the two main spaces of the novel, Paris and Buenos Aires, are shown to be interlinked to such an extent that one can talk of a Paris in Buenos Aires and a Buenos Aires in Paris. Given this desconstruction of the spatio-temporal continuum, it is understandable that *Rayuela* has three possible endings: (i) Oliveira goes mad, (ii) he commits suicide by throwing himself out of the window of the lunatic asylum, or (iii) he plans to go and see a film with his girlfriend, Gekrepten (Boldy 89). A more radical deconstructive move in the novel is its dismantling of language. This process is evident in a number of ways but all point to the fundamental desire to open language up to new expressive possibilities. Thus Cortázar employs a number of languages in the novel, (self-consciously Argentine) Spanish, French, Latin, Italian, French, German, English, and even *glíglico*, the nonsense language Oliveira's girlfriend, La Maga, uses to talk about sex (Cortázar, *Rayuela* 104–5). In Joycean fashion, Cortázar invents portmanteau words by running them together ('corriócomounreguerodepólvora' or splitting them up ('se-re-tor-cía-las-manos'), or misspelling them for comic effect (492, 379). This demanding artistic form requires active participation on the part of the reader, for whom Morelli invents the distinction of 'lector-cómplice', in opposition to the reader (in a slight which feminists have never allowed him to forget) who is passive and inactive, called 'el lector-hembra' (453, 508).

*La casa verde* (1966) by Vargas Llosa is a novel which has two basic narrative strands: one is the events occurring in a brothel called La Casa Verde, which is based on an actual brothel of that name which had fascinated the author as a young man living in Piura, and the other is a *tranche de vie* of a number of individuals living in the Amazon region, which was likewise based on the author's experience (he visited the Upper Marañón region in 1958 with the Mexican anthropologist, Juan Comas; Vargas Llosa, *La historia secreta*). But more important than the biographical sources of the novel is the artistry with which the various strands of the lives of the characters are woven together. Like *La ciudad y los perros*, *La casa verde* employs the Faulknerian technique of cutting unexpectedly from one scene to another and from one set of characters to another, and typically oscillates between the objective transcription of dialogue and the third-person description of events or places or objects. The main structure of the novel is provided not by the unity of the characters' lives – the disconnected narrative style works against that – but rather through the patterning of oppositions throughout the novel, which range from jungle (Santa María Nieves in Marañón) versus aridity (Piura), repression (La Misión) versus lust (La Casa Verde), barbarism (the lowlife *inconquistables*) versus civilisation (Padre García). On one level, these oppositions are reinforced as the novel progresses; thus, in the last chapter of the novel, Padre García and Lituma, one of the *inconquistables*, trade insults, as if to underline that the worlds for which they stand will never see eye to eye. But there is a deeper sense in which these apparently different worlds are connected, and Bonifacia is crucial in this context. The fact that she moves from one world to the next – from the nunnery to the brothel – serves to underline how deception, corruption and exploitation are at the root of human life. There is, after all, hardly a character who does not become victim of his or her circumstances; Fuschía, the Japanese smuggler, contracts leprosy and is left to die in a leper colony, Padre García is victimised by the *inconquistables*, the *inconquistables* are oppressed by the law, and Don Anselmo, the owner of the Casa Verde, is ostracised by the town (the brothel is burnt down) when his wrongdoing is discovered (he seduced a blind girl and, when she died in childbirth, had her secretly buried). Rather than conferring a sense of ethical justification on the rewards meted out to his characters, Vargas

Llosa presents a gripping vision of dog-eat-dog materialism in which the struggle to survive seemingly renders moral criteria irrelevant.

*Cambio de piel* (1967), by Carlos Fuentes, follows the Boom formula in that it is technically innovative and strives to weave together mythic and quotidian levels. Fuentes's novel takes its point of departure from the daily lives of four people, Elizabeth and Javier, Isabel and Franz, travelling from Mexico City to Veracruz; their lives are informed, we find out as the novel progresses, by the historical neuroses of the cultures to which they belong. A common technique, for example, is for the narrative to cut suddenly from the present to Cortés's conquest of Amerindia or the concentration camps of World War II. One other important motif of the text is the primacy given to the sexual act, which is understood as an archetypal return to all sexual encounters: hence the slippage between cultures. The panculturalism of the narrative is echoed by the many languages used in the narrative: Spanish, French, English, German, Latin, Portuguese. The title 'cambio de piel' is a reference to the Aztec God, Xipe Totec, who is able to change his skin and take on a different human form. The novel climaxes in the third chapter, which is set in the chambers beneath the Pyramid of Cholula. Given that we witness what appears to be Franz's body being carried out of the chambers, we might at first assume that the chapter is concerned with the details of and motives for a vengeful murder. But, the chapter is more interested in the archetypal nature of human passion, the truth of creation (Fuentes, *Cambio* 479), and projects orgasm as one of the pointers to that truth. *Cambio de piel* is a complex novel, more complex than a few lines about it can suggest, and epitomises the mythicist, sexological and panculturalist side of the Boom novel. Its bewildering range of cultural and literary reference is suggested by the fact that it even has a reference to Cortázar's *Rayuela*, which is referred to as being used as a pillow (431).

Gabriel García Márquez's novel, *Cien años de soledad* (1967) is now universally seen as a classic, 'the Latin American Don Quixote' as one critic called it. It established García Márquez's fame overnight (it sold 50,000 copies in two weeks in Buenos Aires alone soon after publication). It tells the story of the five generations of the Buendía family, beginning with the patriarchal figure José Arcadio Buendía and ending with the child Aureliano who is born with a pig's tail, in the mythical town of Macondo over a period of 100 years (the number is meant to be reminiscent of the 100-year period in the fairy-tale world of *Sleeping Beauty*). The lives of the Buendía men are shown to be nothing more than a repetition of the lives of their forebears; their options seem to be either war (as happens most notably in the case of Colonel Aureliano Buendía who organized thirty-two armed uprisings, although he lost all of them; García Márquez, *Cien años* 88), or alchemy/science – the study to which the Colonel as well as his nephew, José Arcadio Segundo, later retreat. Without exception they suffer the temptation of incest which becomes fatal in the fourth generation when Aureliano has a child with his sister Amaranta Ursula. By contrast, the women who marry the Buendía men, of whom Ursula Iguarán is the most representative example, remain within the domestic sphere and are presented as more level-headed than the menfolk; they also live longer – Ursula sees four generations come and go. *Cien años de soledad* has twenty (un-numbered) chapters which, given the repeated references to how the characters will meet their death as well as the demise of Macondo, give the text a sense of foreboding reminiscent of the Maya Quiché *Popol Vuh*; the number system of the Mayas was, we may recall, duodecimal. Certainly the end of the novel in which Aureliano deciphers the destruction of Macondo and his own death is as final as the last sentence of the Maya Quiché text (García Márquez, *Cien años*, 334; see above, Chapter 1, pp. 3–4).

Despite the lack of temporal co-ordinates in the novel (one is given the day or the month but never the date or the year of occurrences), one can devise an historical narrative underlying the events depicted (though they are subject to irony). Chapters 1–5, in their references to the founding of Macondo, church-building, and the amnesia plague brought on by Rebeca the Indian girl, narrativise the discovery of the New World, the foundation of the Christian church there, and the concomitant destruction of the Amerindian cultures; seemingly random references to a fifteenth-century suit of armour, a Spanish galleon, Sir Francis Drake and an effeminate Italian piano-tuner, help to fill out the European historical context. Chapters 6–9 possess their own backdrop, namely the struggle between liberals and conservatives in nineteenth-century Colombia following independence; the Buendía family are inveterate liberals. Chapters 10–14 are set against the period of export–import growth characteristic of the late nineteenth and early twentieth centuries in Latin America, the emphasis here being on the banana fever which emerged during this period as a result of United States investment. Chapters 15–20 begin with the description of a strike initiated by José Arcadio Segundo (based on the strike which took place in Ciénaga, Colombia, in 1928), the first step of a phase of gradual economic deterioration in Macondo leading to its destruction by a biblical hurricane at the conclusion of the novel.

Despite the recognisable historical phases implicit in the novel (though interestingly the great figures of independence, Simón Bolívar and José de San Martín, are conspicuously absent even in displaced form), *Cien años de soledad* cannot be seen as an historical novel in any empiric sense. It strives rather to blur the dividing-line between reality and fantasy, but not simply in the manner of the Surrealists for whom the two terms were meant to be interchangeable, but rather in a cultural-political sense. A leitmotif of the novel is the sense in which occurrences seen as supernatural in the First World (such as ghostly apparitions, human beings with the ability to fly, levitate, disappear or increase their weight at will) are presented as natural from a Third-World perspective, while occurrences seen as normal in the First World (magnets, science, ice, railway trains, the movies, phonographs) are presented as supernatural from the point of view of an inhabitant of the Caribbean. García Márquez's playing with the distinction between fantasy and fact – his recourse to what is commonly termed magical realism – does, indeed, have a political edge since one of the episodes on which there is the least agreement is the alleged murder and disposal of the 3,000 banana plantation workers described by José Arcadio Segundo in Chapter 15, but not credited by the authorities (García Márquez, *Cien años* 236–52). *Cien años de soledad* therefore not only confronts the reader with the question of what the real is but also forces him to reconsider the boundaries of that (unconsciously politicised) ideology which informs the structure of his mental universe.

A further twist is given to the reality/fiction interface at the end of the novel. In Chapter 18 Aureliano, the daughter of Meme and Mauricio Babilonia, discovers that the text which the gypsy, Melquíades, left in the workshop and which the Buendía descendants successively attempt to decipher, is written in Sanskrit; two chapters later, he cracks the code in which it is written. (The code – a typically magical-realist detail – is written in a combination of the private cipher of the Emperor Augustus and a Lacedemonian military code; García Márquez, *Cien años* 333.) The last two pages of the novel describe Aureliano deciphering the history of Macondo – the very story we have been reading for 300 pages – until the point at which he reads about himself reading the text (334), when the text ends. The implication of this clever device is that the text gives the impression – via reference to Melquíades's authorship of the text we hold in our hands – of having written itself. The empiric author of the text, Gabriel García Márquez, as if to confirm this impression, is found in the text in two distinct projections, one as the liberal military leader who shares the destiny of Colonel Aureliano Buendía, namely, Colonel Gerineldo Márquez, and the other Gabriel, as one of the four literary bohemians who appear in Macondo in Chapters 19–20 and who divide their time between literary pursuits and whorehouses. (The reference to the 'sabio catalán' in the same chapter, it should be added, is also highly autobiographical; 320–23.) In this final image of the novel as it were disappearing into itself, we have a concrete linguistic embodiment of the incestuous desire which has haunted every male member of the Buendía lineage. In its use of myth – and principally in Lévi-Strauss's theory of the prohibition of incest as the corner-stone of culture which figures strongly in García Márquez's novel – its disruption of linear temporality, and the use of individual history to signify the national narrative, *Cien años de soledad* was to become famous as the prototype of the Boom novel.

## Spanish American Novels Contemporary with the Boom

There were a number of Spanish American novels which, though significant and published at the same time as the Boom, have received less critical attention. A selection of these novels is discussed in this section. *Los recuerdos del porvenir* (1963) by Elena Garro (b. 1920) is ostensibly about the ravages caused by the Mexican Revolution; the poor are duped and eventually find themselves in a prison of their own making, the *cristero* revolution leaves everyone as badly off as before, and absolute power is held by the *caciques* who do what they want with their subalterns (i.e. General Rosas). There is, however, a sub-plot which, sometimes interweaves with the macro-plot and sometimes contrasts with it, an inner history to which women have privileged access. Garro's novel seems to change place, time and mood in a way that can be disconcerting. In the passage which concludes the first part of the novel, for example, the scene in which Francisco Rosas is waiting for Hurtado to emerge, suddenly time stops ('pero entonces sucedió lo que nunca antes me había sucedido; el tiempo se detuvo en seco'; Garro 144), and a parallel emerges with the 100-year sleep of the characters in the fairy-tale *Sleeping Beauty*. Just as it dislocates the linear nature of time and space (as underlined by its title), so *Los recuerdos del porvenir* dislocates one other important paradigm, that of gender. On a superficial level, the boundaries between the sexes seem permanently fixed; the men are all-powerful and the women submissive. But a sub-plot gradually asserts itself, mainly through the person of Isabel, who questions patriarchal law and promotes the primacy of the imagination:

> A Isabel le disgustaba que estableciera diferencia entre ella y sus hermanos. [...] Le humillaba la idea de que el único futuro para las mujeres fuera el matrimonio. Hablar de matrimonio como de una solución la dejaba reducida a una mercancía a la que había que dar salida a cualquier precio. (Garro 22)

Tyranny, presented as a phallocentric law, must be fought, the logic of the novel suggests, by the imagination: 'La vida en aquellos días se empañaba y nadie vivía sino a través del general y su querida. Habíamos renunciado a la ilusión' (Garro 116). The play which Hurtado brings to Ixtepec amid the carnage of war, is an example of this 'ilusión' for which the novel stands. *Los recuerdos del porvenir* celebrates the 'sorpresa infinita de encontrarse en el mundo' (Garro 31–2) which tyranny wishes to suppress but which imagination, to which womanhood has privileged access, strives to bring to fruition. The plot of the individual struggling to keep his identity intact in contrast to the master narrative of history and politics, a story which has been around since Rousseau's times, is feminised in *Los recuerdos del porvenir* to produce a contestatory narrative in which the subject is feminine and society is male.

Another significant novelist of this period is the Uruguayan Juan Carlos Onetti (1909–94). *Juntacadáveres* (1964) is a strange, morbid novel which describes the life of a small provincial town in Uruguay, Santa María, during a summer of discontent. The underlying motif of the novel, expressed in different ways, is prostitution. On the literal level, we have the story of Larsen, whose nickname ('Juntacadáveres', bodysnatcher) provides the title for the novel, who attempts to establish a whorehouse in the town. This project is defeated when Father Bergner, a lugubrious, fire-and-brimstone priest, begins fulminating against the whorehouse in his sermons, and when the young ladies from the Catholic League band together and start sending out anonymous letters to the next of kin of those known to frequent the bordello. A more metaphoric level of prostitution is explored in the person of the narrator, Jorge Malabia.

He returns to Santa María to visit his sister-in-law, Julita, whose husband, Federico, has recently died. In a sequence of events which emphasizes the etymological meaning of prostitution (Latin 'to stand in for'), Julita sleeps with Jorge in substitution for his brother. In a sordid end to a sordid novel, Julita hangs herself (Chap. XXXIII). (The other bombshell of the novel is that the priest's nephew, Marcos Bergner, is caught visiting the brothel.) Most impressive about Onetti's novel is not the story – a thin plot, to be sure – but the dry, Faulkneresque manner in which it is told. Like Faulkner, Onetti records with little commentary visual reality (things, people) and aural reality (sounds, conversations). There is no overarching teleology to the events being described; Father Bergner, of all people, captures this at one point when the thought passes through his mind that 'la miseria del hombre llega hasta quitar grandeza a las desgracias que debe atravesar, a convertir en anécdotas los símbolos trágicos' (Chap. XXVIII; Onetti 241). Occasionally, Onetti will deliberately show us the points at which reality is attempting to transform itself into symbol but, with an impish sense of delight, will not allow this to happen, as in, for example, the following description of the bar scene in Chap. XXX:

> Ahora, de pronto, aprovechando un silencio, la tarde reveló que pasaba, que no había prometido eternizarse en el salón del hotel ni eternizar la penumbra cálida [...] vidrios y fichas que sonaban en el mostrador, falazmente lejanos, ilusoriamente comprometidos en la corroboración de un símbolo. (Onetti 252)

Onetti's prose, as its best, as here, is studded with awkward metaphors which hold up the onward propulsion of the prose, and thereby add to the sense of oppression, as if the very forward movement of time were a burden. It would be tempting to see the narrator as a thinly disguised projection of Onetti's alter ego; this may be true, but there is also a sense in which his authorial identity is projected in the anonymous letters. Though they were sent, most plausibly, by the girls of the Catholic League or, possibly, by an embittered, solitary old woman, at one point the narrator also imagines them being written by 'un ángel gigantesco [...], contra el techo de la sacristía por los rezos del cura Bergner (arrodillado y prescindente), iluminado con el oro de su cabeza redonda y caída el retrato del Papa en el muro' (Chap. XXI; Onetti 258), as if to suggest that writing, like the world it describes, has no identifiable origin. The final point to be made is that prostitution is also evoked on a social level as political defeatism. As Marcos Bergner says: 'En este país no se puede hacer nada. Todo está sucio y gastado' (Chap. XXIX; 244). Despite this apparent pessimism and apparent dismantling of any teleology, the reader is left with an impression of a deeper level of meaning to life, even if it is ungraspable, rather like the portrait on Father Bergner's wall which the latter suspects 'un significado inasible, un valor secreto y fabuloso' (Chap. XXVIII; 240).

A significant experimental novel written during this period but not always included within the Boom is *Tres tristes tigres* (1965) by G. Cabrera Infante

(1929–2005). A playful novel, it provides a phantasmagorical, nocturnal and Bacchic view of pre-revolutionary Cuba. The novel opens with the word 'Showtime!', the beginning of an introductory presentation by a compère in a Cuban nightclub (full of hype, repetition and bad grammar), and the reference to showtime sets the tone for the rest of the novel. There are characters who people its pages, but more important is the re-creation of their reality through language. Rather than having a plot, the novel has a series of episodes, ranging from the death of a budding writer who is shot by an editor he goes to see (the reason for this is left unexplained), to the description of the protagonist's visit to a nightclub and his mesmerised description of the gyrating hips of the dancer, La Estrella. A section entitled 'Visitantes' regales the reader with a version of a visit to Havana by a certain Mr Campbell, followed by a revised version based on the comments and criticisms made by Mrs Campbell. The section 'Rompecabeza' takes the verbal pyrotechnics of the novel to their logical limit; here the plot breaks down completely to reveal nothing more than a Joycean play on words. Thus, *Alice in Wonderland* is turned on its head: 'Alicia en el mar de villas, Alicia en el País que Más Brilla, Alicia en el Cine Maravillas, Avaricia en el País de las Malavillas' (Cabrera Infante 209). The subsequent section provides, rather like the French Surrealist writer Raymond Queneau's *Exercices de style*, different versions of the death of Leon Trotsky (who was killed in Mexico City in 1940) according to the style of a number of Cuban writers, ranging from José Martí to Alejo Carpentier. The final section, 'Bachata', is the most Realist in the novel, and concentrates on the lives of Silvestre, Cué and Bustrófedon. Yet, even here, much of the action centres around the verbal jousting of the characters. *Tres tristes tigres* is, with the possible exception of Cortázar's *Rayuela*, probably one of the most lexically inventive novels written in Spanish America. As such it deserves to be remembered as a significant novel of its time.

*Gazapo* (1965) by the Mexican Gustavo Sainz (b. 1940), as Raymond Williams suggests, 'was a notable innovation for the Mexican postmodern: it brought the young language of adolescents into the Mexican novel, as well as the new technologies of communicating by means of tape recorders and other media' (Raymond Williams 26). It did have some roots in the past, however; like the Boom novel, Sainz's novel strove to undermine the structured nature of chronological time. The novel starts *in medias res* and seems to end there as well; it tells the story of group of a adolescent boys living in Mexico City who share their tales of sexual and criminal exploits with each other, even going to the extreme of recording each others' stories with a tape-recorder, to such an extent that it becomes difficult to separate the fact from the fiction. At this point *Gazapo* becomes decidedly postmodern in that it focuses on the play-acting involved in their stories, how the telling of the stories is more important than the events which they supposedly relate, and how the stories live each time they are related, with no version having more validity than any other. Apart from the main narrative of the boys' exploits, there are no real other subtexts, apart from the medieval texts which interrupt the narrative towards the end of the novel, and the snatches of the Catechism. Both are meant to throw an ironic light on the gang's deeds. But, perhaps more important, the text is interrupted by snatches of the narrator's diary and his tape-recorded narratives, all of which give the novel a play-back feel.

One writer who has a special relationship with the Boom novelists is the Chilean José Donoso (b. 1924). His masterpiece is *El obsceno pájaro de la noche* (1970), described by one critic as 'one of the most complex novels ever published by a Chilean writer' (Raymond Williams 72). The action is centred on the events occurring in two houses, the Casa de Ejercicios Espirituales de la Encarnación at La Chimba, and La Rinconada. In the Casa de Ejercicios Espirituales live thirty-seven female inmates, five orphans and a nun, Mother Benita, who looks after them. One of the young orphans, a fifteen-year-old girl called Iris Mateluna, falls pregnant, and the old women in the Casa become obsessed with the idea that her pregnancy was caused by an immaculate conception. Halfway through the novel, Inés Azcoitía, the wife of Jerónimo, arrives to stay at the Casa. As a result of a trip to Rome on which she had unsuccessfully attempted to persuade the bishops that one of her eighteenth-century ancestors should be canonised, she had retreated, half-crazy, to a Swiss sanatorium and then come to stay in the Casa in order to look for the bones of her ancestor, which have never been found and, legend had it, are hidden somewhere in the Casa. While she has been in Europe, Jerónimo has decided to sell the Casa, which has been a family possession for generations. Inés stops the sale of the Casa, but finally goes mad and has to leave. Mother Benita subsequently has a nervous breakdown, at which point, the inhabitants of the Casa are moved out by Father Azócar. These are the objective components of the first plot. But a degree of mystery is added to this story by the narrator, a diffuse, osmotic consciousness who appears to have several simultaneous identities, Mudito, Humberto, the Seventh Witch, Iris Mateluna's unnamed child, Iris Mateluna's dog, and even a stain on the wall. Mudito is the mute child who lives in the Casa and observes everything. Humberto is Jerónimo's secretary and is intensely jealous of his employer. The narrative voice switches disconcertingly between these identities.

The second parallel plot takes place in La Rinconada. Jerónimo's son has been born a deformed monster, and is so ugly as to be simply named Boy. Jerónimo has taken the bizarre decision to have his son brought up in a place in which he would never become aware of his deformities and has therefore hired a woman, Emperatriz, to scour the city and find the most deformed people (grotesquely obese people, hunchbacks and dwarves) to live in a special residence for Jerónimo's son, La Rinconada. Humberto has been hired to be secretary to Jerónimo and specifically to write an account of Boy's life, but he has proved unequal to the task. But Boy escapes from La Rinconada, is ridiculed by normal people in the outside world, and decides to take his revenge on the world. He invites his father to stay with him in La Rinconada and eventually Jerónimo goes mad, and is found drowned in the lake in the gardens, to the consternation of the general public, who are now without a senator. It is difficult to know whether Boy and the inhabitants of La Rinconada deliberately bring about Jerónimo's downfall, or whether the latter simply goes mad through living too long within the walls of La Rinconada.

A clue to the meaning of the novel appears in the epitaph which is a passage from a letter by the North American novelist, Henry James to his sons Henry and James in which the following sentence appears: 'The natural inheritance of everyone who is capable of spiritual life is an unsubdued forest where the wolf howls and the obscene bird of night chatters.' The aim of Donoso's novel is to chart precisely that territory. And in exploring the depths of the human mind, one important insight is revealed: human beings disguise from themselves the true reality of things because of its painful nature, just as Jerónimo tries to shield his son from the reality of his ugliness. Since *El obsceno pájaro de la noche* focuses on the world of the unconscious mind, Donoso deliberately chose to divest his narrative of linear sequentiality and thereby produced a flexible text in which the narrative voice darts quickly and unannounced from the mind of one character to that of another. Typical of the Boom novel, the narrative swerves unexpectedly, as if it were a dream-sequence. A good example of Donoso's use of dream sequence narrative occurs in the last series of events of the novel in Part II, Chapter 30. Here we, as readers, appear to be listening to the thoughts of someone being put into a sack and covered with layers and layers of jute. Every time the narrator tries to get out the sack, some hand outside sews up the hole again. Then, suddenly, the narrative swerves and we are presented with the description of a female person who takes a sack out of the house, down to the river and then proceeds to burn it. At this point, we are forced to reread the previous scene and reinterpret it: the unnamed female person who burns the sack is actually burning the person inside the sack who had been expressing his thoughts to us only a few paragraphs before. As to the identity of the female person (we only know of her gender because the adjectives give her away), we cannot know for certain, but it is likely to be Peta, the old witch woman who has grown to hate Humberto. And the consciousness in the sack is again likely to be an amalgamation of the persons of the Seventh Witch, Mudito, Humberto, and the illegitimate baby of Iris Mateluna, which has now been turned into an *imbunche* which, according to witchcraft legend, is what witches do with children they steal (they sew up all their orifices).[6] The last image of the novel, the *imbunche*, is an ironic and inverse image of the birth of Christ, since the *imbunche* is wrapped in a material similar to the swaddling clothes in which Christ was wrapped. Fittingly, the narrative consciousness is destroyed as we reach the last page of the book. The novel thereby turns in on itself and destroys itself.

*Maitreya* (1978) by Severo Sarduy (b. 1939) is a complex *Tel Quel*-inspired novel in which conventional plot is sacrificed in favour of linguistic virtuosity

---

[6] Donoso is here referring to the beliefs of the Araucanian Indians, the original inhabitants of Chile. For them, the *imbuches*, or *ivunches*, were evil spirits and/or man-animals which 'at night were changed into ravenous birds' and 'launched attacks from the air' (Lancaster 20).

and the portrayal of character is superseded by an obsession with certain key themes such as ritual and sex. Though not devoid of plot (each section of the novel, for example, depicts an event, the first section 'En la muerte del Maestro' describes the Lama's dying hours followed by his death (Sarduy 15–26), while 'El Instructor' (27–33) focuses on the funeral arrangements), these events become the surface into which an extraordinary linguistic-cum-spiritual journey is meticulously woven. The novel describes a journey to nirvana ('Este es la última vez que nazco. No volveré más', 'but all pure, I shall go from here, to Nirvana', 32), echoing the Upanishads which describe how the aim of the soul is to escape reincarnation, which is complemented by the pursuit of sexual ecstasy. Thus Iluminada Leng has a vision in a temple of a couple making love ('ay qué rico, métemela más, en sánscrito oral o en tibetano antiguo', 46); 'El Doble' (85–97), which portrays the life of Siameses twins joined since birth, concludes with a description of how Leng manage to pleasure both of them simultaneously (96–7). It also describes Leng's sexual orgy with two Chinese women (117–19), as well as the sexual antics of La Tremenda with the driver while a dwarf is watching the proceedings with his cymbals ready (175–79). Though explicit, these scenes could not be called pornographic, since they use a highly stylised, Baroque set of images to describe sex (Luis Leng's penis becomes a 'cetro de jade' [118], for example, thereby redolent of the imagery common in Chinese erotic fiction). And yet this novel is not simply a Chinese calque for the metaphorical language applied to sex is extended to form a complex web of imagery. Sex and religious ritual are shrouded in mystery (the novel abounds in imagery of veils and concealment) and this sense of mystery is also carried over into the world of language, for the novel is like a semantic striptease which, refusing to reveal its meaning first time, does so gradually, teasingly.

One of the masterpieces of the Golden Age of the Spanish American novel was undoubtedly *Yo el Supremo* (1974) by the Paraguayan Augusto Roa Bastos (1917–2005). An intricate, multi-layered novel, it creates in imaginative form the thoughts of a dictator, whose generic name is contained in the title, as they are dictated to his secretary-cum-scribe, Patiño. Given his name 'el Supremo', the novel is self-evidently based on Dr José Gaspar Rodríguez de Francia (1776–1840), a creole lawyer and philosopher, who was appointed Supreme Dictator of Paraguay for life by a congress in 1816, and who ruled his country with an iron fist until his death; his regime was particularly harsh after he discovered and quashed a conspiracy in 1820, whereupon he instituted a reign of terror, 'executing, imprisoning, banishing', as one critic has it (Lynch 667).

While the dialogue between the Dictator and Patiño is the backbone of the novel, there are a number of other sections which make the novel polyphonic rather than strictly dialogic. These are the extracts from the 'cuaderno privado', the Dictator's personal diary and from his 'Circular perpetua', which are intended to give an historical account of the events of the independence movement of the River Plate region in the early years of the nineteenth century and which the Dictator, in a footnote, bids the reader to pay special attention (Roa Bastos 114); the marginal notes in italic which describe the state of the document being transcribed (its quality, legibility, etc., an example being the reference to a 'letra desconocida', 45) and which introduce a note of indeterminacy into the novel since the identity of the editor is not clarified; and, finally, the footnotes which are superficially intended to provide historical references for events referred to in the narrative proper. These various voices introduce a level of ambiguity into the text, and specifically undermine the sense of semantic stability attached to the Dictator's voice. In one of the sections of his private notebook, for example, the Dictator describes his notes as straightforward fact ('Nada de historias fingidas para diversión de lectores [...] Esto es un Balance de Cuentas'; 53), yet the rest of the novel shows this not be the case. There is discontinuity, first of all, between the Dictator and his scribe; at one point in the narrative, he complains to Patiño about distortion during transcription: 'eres mi fide-indigno secretario. No sabes secretar lo que digo. Tuerces retuerces mis palabras' (64). Here Roa Bastos employs word-play with the adjective 'fide-indigno' which turns the word for reliable ('fidedigno') inside-out and creates a new word within it ('indigno') to underline the scribe's unworthiness. Perhaps more subtle is the play on the sense of 'secreto' contained within 'secretar'; in stating that the scribe does not know how to 'secretarialise' his words, the Dictator also unwittingly betrays the sense of secrecy surrounding his inner thoughts.

The slippery nature of language and referentiality is also suggested by the interface between the footnotes and the narrative proper. While most of the footnotes are intended to substantiate the events described in the text (the best example being the letter that Bolívar wrote in October 1823 to Francia about his friend, Bonpland, who had been imprisoned by the Paraguayan Dictator), at other times Roa Bastos takes great liberties with historical reality. Thus, at various stages of the narrative Julius Caesar's military *Commentaries* are referred to in the context of the wars in Paraguay (Roa Bastos 175, 206, 211, 263). Likewise the adventures of the brothers Robertson – who managed to visit Paraguay despite the economic and commercial blockade erected at Paraguay's borders by Francia, and about which they later wrote *Letters on Paraguay* (1838) – provide Roa Bastos with the historical framework around which he weaves a fantastic story of, among other things, a passionate love-affair between John Robertson and an eighty-four-year-old woman (Roa Bastos 138–58). The important point here, however, is not the historical grounding of the novel, since the success of *Yo el Supremo* resides in its ability to produce an imaginative re-creation of the mind-universe of an excessively neurotic, cruel and power-hungry nineteenth-century dictator.

The style of the novel is characterised by the stream-of-consciousness technique perfected by James Joyce and Virginia Woolf in which the resonance of events in the mind is registered rather than their empirical, objective description simply being recorded. Not only is the dialogue polyphonic in *Yo el Supremo* but the words are too. Taking a leaf out of Cortázar's book, Roa

Bastos creates a novelistic language which is flexible and neologistic; the most common technique used by Roa Bastos is parataxis, as in 'Soplo-mancha-mujer rápidamente saliendo, lentamente siendo otra vez la juncal Andaluza' (Roa Bastos 59; my emphasis). It is precisely as a result of the slippery nature of language and referentiality that the Dictator's main aim is to impose his voice over and above that of everyone else and, at one point, this is expressed in terms of his vision of a country of speechless subjects: 'Deslenguar a los hablantes. Volverlos a poner en cuatro patas. Petrificarlos en el límite de la degradación más extrema, de donde ya no se puede volver. Monolitos de vaga forma human. Sembrados en un carrascal. Jeroglíficos, ellos mismos' (60). Yet, there is also one other very important consequence of Roa Bastos's technique of unsettling the historical moorings of his narrative and this concerns its meaning for Paraguay in the 1970s. General Alfredo Stroessner was at the time the Dictator of Paraguay; though the Dictator in *Yo el Supremo* is based on Francia, his name is never given. The reference to Stroessner was transparent and the point was not lost on Stroessner himself who, when Roa Bastos returned to Paraguay in 1982 after many years of exile, expelled him from his homeland for life, a point which serves to remind us that creative literary writing has a social and political impact which is all too easily forgotten.

## The Brazilian New Novel

Judith A. Payne and Earl E. Fitz have argued that contemporary Brazilian literature has always 'seemed "different" from Spanish American literature' in that it has been blessed with 'a surprisingly large number of women writers' (Payne and Fitz 3), including Clarice Lispector (1925–77), Nélida Piñon (b. 1935), and Lygia Fagundes Telles (b. 1923). In even a brief survey of Brazilian fiction from the 1960s until the present day, it is clear that women's fiction plays a foundational and intrinsic role. *A Paixão Segundo G.H.* (1964) by Clarice Lispector is one of the classics of contemporary Brazilian literature. A resolutely modernist text, *A Paixão* has a minimal plot in the conventional sense (it describes the thoughts of a woman who finds herself in her apartment, looking at the objects around her, thinking about her maid, noticing a cockroach), yet these events lead to an extraordinary *tour de force* in which the mind is caught as it is beginning to think, and language is caught as it is beginning to express. The first two sentences of the novel set the tone: '– estou procurando, estou produrando. Estou tentando entender' (Lispector, *A Paixão*, 11). While attempting to understand the life that she perceives all round her, she encounters language as a barrier: 'não tenho uma palavra a dizer' (20). At every turn her consciousness is turned back in on herself so that she attempts to capture the life force within her, a force which is as pre-linguistic as it is pre-conscious, an inner self, whose name mutates as the text develops; at one time it is imaged as 'a incógnita e anónima' (28), and at another as 'água fervendo' (28), Clearly elusive, this life force emerges in different images. Emotions arise within her consciousness. She recalls that the maid, Janair, hates her (42), yet even while the narrator delves into her emotions she thinks about them, intellectualises them, moving from the level of brute emotivity to abstract intellectuality within an instant. The sight of a cockroach leads to an extraordinary set of thoughts on her connectiveness with 'os primeiros bichos da Terra' (48). Overcome with fear she attempts to kill the cockroach but, squeezing it in the wardrobe door, she only manages to half-kill it, and it is at that point that the narrator begins to sympathise, identify and finally almost become the cockroach, via its blood: 'Pois o sangue que eu via fora de mim, aquele sangue eu o estranhava como atracao: ele era meu' (59). The cockroach's blood becomes hers. And via that identification with the insectile, the prehistoric, she approaches nothingness, which she also experiences as a life force (61), and as a 'silence' (66), and subsequently as 'alegria' (73), something which is pre-human' ('ainda anterior ao humano', 84).

This movement back in time, this communion with a timeless reality via the cockroach also leads, rather paradoxically, to a direct experience of God ('qualquer um têm medo de ver o que é Deus' *A Paixão* 97), since it is the pre-human aspect of the cockroach which offers a conduit to God: 'A vida prehumana divina é de uma atualidade que queima' (101). This reality is also pre-linguistic, and one which is difficult for human consciousness to countenance or to accept: 'aquilo era inegávelmente uma verdade anterior a nossas palavras, aquilo era inegávelmente a vida que até então eu não quisera' (119). This realm which the narrator reaches is as much hell as it is heaven, and yet she feels that she is before God (138), before a God who is 'tão grande e vital' (147). In the closing pages of the novel it becomes clear that a parallel is being woven between the dying moments of the cockroach and the transcendent reality of God; at the point at which the cockroach is consumed God's immanence is imbibed, and Christ's passion is invoked: 'A condição humana é a paixão de Cristo' (175). Bringing together heaven and hell, cockroach and God, self and other, *A Paixão Segundo G.H.* is an extraordinary, complex and sensitive text which is able to explore the subconscious mind in a way rarely achieved before – or indeed since – in the Brazilian novel.

*As Meninas* (1973), by Lygia Fagundes Telles, a novel awarded the Coelho Neto prize, focuses, like Lispector's novel, on feminine experience but from a very different perspective. It describes the lives of a set of young women, their inner lives, their thoughts, their conversations. Fitting broadly within the Modernist-Joyce-Woolf-stream-of-consciousness tradition, the novel declines to tell a story in the Realist manner. Rather the dynamism of the plot (a set of closely related actions) is transferred to the thoughts which are running through their minds. Sex looms large – thoughts about it, rather than descriptions – particularly the (possibly imaginary) affair Lorena is having with a married man, M.N. The cultural context in which these thoughts emerge – either through first-person narration or dialogue, third-person narrative being reduced to a minimum – is internationalist rather than nationalist, cosmopolitan rather than Brazilian. The range of literary and historical references is broad, ranging from Che Guevara (Fagundes Telles 3), to Santa Teresa (12, 16, 48), Jimi Hendrix (5–6, 16, 48), Marx (49), Wagner (48), James Bond (59), Bach (65), Chopin (67), Mozart (67), Renoir (82), Simone de Beauvoir (101), André Maurois (112), Rosa Luxembourg (115), Rita Hayworth (124), Marc Chagall (93), Federico García Lorca (230): world culture rather than Brazilian culture. There are descriptions of heterosexual sexual encounters (99), masturbation (14–15), lesbian sex (113–14). Despite its desire to confront issues of sexual intimacy, the novel is muted on the issue of politics; thus a description of torture is followed by the words 'etc., etc.' (132), thereby appearing to denigrate the political in favour of the personal. The narrative moves from scene to scene in such a way as to offer a sense of the world as a collage. *As Meninas* thereby adopts the internationalist idiom central to Modernism in a way which is redolent of the Spanish American Boom novel, as suggested by José Donoso (see discussion above, p. 205–6). In its use of the stream-of-consciousness as applied to the 'female mind', and particularly in terms of its frank treatment of sex, *As Meninas* broke important new ground in the Brazilian novel of the 1970s.

Lispector's *A hora da estrela* (1977) is nothing short of a masterpiece. One one level it can be seen as the story of a rather uncouth young girl called Macabéa from the north-east who comes to work as a typist in Rio for Raimundo Silveira; we learn about her early life in the north-east, her current problems at work, her love affair with Olímpico, her friendship with Glória, her visit to Carlota the fortune-teller, and her death when knocked over by a yellow Mercedes. Her life is summed up in three attributes: she is a typist and a virgin, and she likes Coca Cola (Lispector, *A hora da estrela* 44), yet, despite her anonymity, she becomes an icon of the world's silent poor: 'Embora a moça anônima da história seja tão antiga que podia ser uma figura bíblica' (38). She accepts her lot without complaint: 'Nunca se queixava de nada, sabia que as coisas são assim mesmo e – quem organizou a terra dos homens?' (43). Macabéa is something of a contradiction in that while, on the one hand, she seems empty (her inner life is 'uma longa meditação sobre o nada'; 47), yet she is embarked on a path to stardom: 'Pois na hora da morte a pessoa se torna brilhante estrela de cinema, e o instante de glória de cada um é quando como no canto coral se ouvem agudos silbantes' (36).

More important than the details of her life, though, is the telling of her life – for her life is narrated by an unnamed male narrator, and the novel begins to develop into an intense dialogue between Macabéa and that narrator. Appalled by the squalor of her life (she comes from a dysfunctional, poverty-stricken family, lives in Rio in the red-light district, has a mundane job), the narrator – who is clearly bourgeois (he is able to pay for his electricity, gas and telephone bills) – begins gradually to feel diminished by her presence: 'Mas eu, que não chego a ser ela, sinto que vivo para nada' (Lispector, *A hora da estrela* 40). The narrator is inspired to think about his craft as a writer as a result of the minimalism of his subject: would he improve his story if he used some literary techniques? he wonders. His conclusion: 'esta história não tem nenhuma técnica, nem de estilo, ela é ao deus-dará' (45). The writing process itself gradually impinges on the narration, such as when the narrator describes how he had to rewrite three pages thrown away by the cleaner (52). Macabéa's inability to understand words such as 'álgebra' (which she pronounces as 'élgebra'), 'culture' and 'electronic' (61) suggests her intellectual vacuousness, but also refers back to the writing process, since the text – as so often in Lispector's work – is involved in a process of paring back words as well as peeling off the outer wrappings of things in order to get back to the ontological source of reality. Likewise the mention of the difficulty she experiences when trying to think ('Pensar era tão difícil, ela não sabia de que jeito se pensava'; 65) has a deeper level since it not only refers to Macabéa's lack of sophistication but also operates simultaneously as an indication of the narrator's linguistic-metaphysical quest. When Macabéa refers to a word she heard on the radio that she only half-understands but finds exquisite ('mimetismo'; 67) this term inevitably works from its utterance by her lips outwards into the text with which the narrator is 'surrounding' her, for *his* text 'mimics' *her* reality. A level of self-reflexivity is thereby introduced into Lispector's text. Macabéa's statement ('Mas nao sei o que está dentro do meu nome'; 68) operates not only as a comment made by an idiot (as Olímpico sees it) but also as a philosophical reflection (as the narrator, and by extension, the reader view it). This is the beauty of Lispector's text: it can operate simultaneously on two levels. This self-reflexivity grows as the text moves towards its climax; the narrator says that he is writing simply because he has nothing else to do, and then refers to how he had to stop writing for three days (84–5). Then, when Macabéa's death finally occurs, the narrator is forced to accept his own mortality: 'Meu Deus, só agora me lembrei que a gente morre. Mas – mas eu também?!' (104). Beneath its deceptively simply façade, *A hora da estrela* leads the reader on a complex journey of ontological and linguistic self-discovery which – given that the novel is written by a woman who adopts the position of a male narrator in order to study a female narratee – reveals itself to be as much about reflecting on the function of fiction as about thinking about a woman called Macabéa.

*Mulher no Espelho* (1983) by Helena Parente Cunha is a complex, experimental novel about the doubleness of women. As the novel informs us on the first page: 'Não, não vou escrever minhas memórias nem meu retrato, nem minha biografia. Sou uma personagem de ficção. Só existo na minha imaginação e na imaginação de quem me lê. E, naturalmente, para a mulher que me escreve' (Parente Cunha 3). As the novel begins to evolve it is clear that it is a dialogue between different images of what it means to be a woman, and the text often refers to the 'woman who writes me' as the counterbalance to the image of womanhood which the narrator proper is bringing into being before our eyes. The narrator begins to question the submissive role she plays in her marriage (11), as well as the frustration she feels in bringing up her children (19), and the anger her father and brother arouse in her (33). Despite how alienated she feels at the Carnival celebrations (70–71), she has an affair with 'o rapaz que me sorri' (71) and later experiences deep happiness in the 'entrega a um homem que não é bufalo, nem sua, nem baba no orgasmo' (87), at which point her alter ego appears to desert her, then feels jealous of her (103). She expresses a deep affinity with Afro-Brazilian culture as epitomised by Xangô, the African God of thunder (115), and the novel ends, appropriately enough, with an image of a storm which is brewing (132). Redolent in different respects of the fiction of Virginia Woolf, Clarice Lispector and Hélène Cixous, Parente Cunha's fiction strives to create a new sense of the world by exploring its significance from the vantage-point offered by the female body, producing an intricate and linguistically self-reflective discourse between the inner self which strives to break free, and the social self which attempts to stifle that self. In its emphasis upon fluidity it recalls Cixous's poetics, and in its allusiveness to the mirror, Lacan's theory of the mirror stage is brought delicately into the frame. We recall that for Lacan the mirror image is the metaphor of a false self created by society and its tool, language, and Parente Cunha is clearly, in *Mulher no Espelho*, striving to break down that fallacious unity in order to body forth a fluid and vital sense of the female self centred on the body.

*A República dos Sonhos* (1984) by Nélida Piñon (b. 1937), winner in 2005 of the prestigious Príncipe Asturias prize, is one of the classics of contemporary Brazilian fiction. Opening at the point when the matriarch, Eulália, has begun to die, Piñon's novel traces the history of a family who left Galicia in the nineteenth century, for Brazil, the 'Republic of Dreams' of the title, where they and three subsequent generations of descendants settled (in this the novel has an autobiographical flavour, given the proximity of the plot to Piñon's own family story). Yet *A República dos Sonhos* is anything but a straight, historical narrative; the novel darts back and forth between different historical eras, sometimes fusing them in the reader's mind, and it up-ends linear temporality, for example, by having characters refer to the death of Eulália, and her daughter, Esperança, only to have them appear later on in the novel as if they were still alive. In a deliberately postmodern gesture, the creation of the past – rather than its mere recording – is imbued with intrinsic value in that Grandfather Xan's obsession that his story-telling prowess should be a living legacy for the family, in effect, becomes a central leitmotif of the novel. The 'I' of the narrator glides seamlessly and without warning between different characters in the story, thereby deliberately 'jamming' the fixity of vision we associate with the traditional Realist novel. The novel cocks a snook at historicity in its metafictional finale – Breta decides to write a novel about the history of the emigration of Madruga's family to the New World, that is, the novel we have just read.

*A República dos Sonhos* has to some extent a feminist axe to grind in that it highlights – and makes us hate in the process – the bullying patriarchalism of Eulália's husband, Madruga, who attempts to dominate friends, business partners, his wife and his children. At one juncture in the novel, Esperança comes to the pointed realisation that, as a result of being female, she automatically loses entitlement to one half of her attainments. At another point the reader is led to experience great sympathy for Sílvia when she stumbles across her husband having sex with her friend, Irene. Indeed this novel paints a stark picture of the human heart – within every human being there is an animal aggressivity ready to pounce and tear to pieces the fragile veneer of social etiquette. The instincts of jealousy, hatred, lust, and rivalry are played out unremittingly within the family unit – thus we see son (Miguel) fight against father (Madruga); wife (Eulália, Sílvia) fighting against husband (Madruga, Miguel); brother (Miguel) pitted against sister (Esperança) – as well as in the work place (González and Madruga are business partners at each other's throats). This predatory instinct appears even in the metaphors; for example one character is described as eating dinner as if dissecting a human member with a fork, and another nibbles delicately at her food as if, unlike other mortals, she had never had human flesh between her teeth.

Offsetting to some degree the starkness of its vision of dangerous liaisons, *A República dos Sonhos* is intent on reviving a collective, national unconscious and has recourse to a choral, epic and vibrantly poetic rhetoric in order to do so. Galicia is portrayed as a repository of 'hungry' myths – a land which obtains energy from its own enigma, where people are condemned by fate to truths they do not understand, where they cultivate their gods, take them into their houses like domestic animals, licking them, stroking them – functioning as the bedrock from which the dreams which lie behind the creation of the New World (ranging from the Quixotic idealism of the Jesuits, to economic migrants such as Madruga, even the desperate imagination of the social subaltern) drew their inspiration. In its focus on a myth rooted in the Spanish-speaking world from the perspective of the Portuguese language Piñon's novel offers a reverse-image of Vargas Llosa's *La guerra del fin del mundo*, which homes in on a Brazilian myth from the perspective of the Spanish-speaking world (see discussion below, pp. 228–9). A postmodern epic of the Brazilian nation narrated via a collage of voices criss-crossing the death-bed of a moribund matriarch, *A República dos Sonhos* portrays 'our corporality, which is capable of crushing and dreaming at the same time' (Piñon, 'Acceptance speech').

The Brazilian novel took an unexpected turn in the 1980s, one which would not have been easy to predict given the evolution to that point of a solid tradition of complex, experimental fiction, as epitomised by Lispector's work. Many Latin American countries witnessed in the 1980s the birth of a hybrid, middle-brow type of fiction which was more accessible than the Boom and more salesworthy as a result – Isabel Allende's fiction is a good example from Chile (for further discussion see Hart, 'House of the Spirits') – but it was in Brazil that this new form of fiction took off. The matrix text was Paulo Coelho's *O Alquimista* (1988) which proved to be one of the best-selling novels of all time, having sold twelve million copies in Portuguese to date (Mooney 8). Coelho's fiction, which is nowadays more routinely sold in the New Age Philosophy or Mind, Body, Soul sections in bookshops, has been translated into fifty-one languages and its world sales are estimated as at between 70 and 90 million copies (Mullan 2). His book-signing sessions are more akin to the arrival of a nineteenth-century monarch than a literary event, as occurred in Russia in May 2006 (see Mullan 3). It is difficult to pinpoint one single cause of his success; Coelho's view is that he uses a type of language which speaks to all mankind:

> My idea is to share the symbolic language of mankind – like angels and devils, dark forest, high mountains and wolves, gold and buried treasure. There is a part of everyone, whatever their cultural background, that connects with symbols and omens [...] it is an alphabet you develop to talk to the soul of the world. (Mooney 8)

Coelho writes regularly for the Brazilian newspaper, *O Globo*, and he regularly includes a horoscope column; in some ways his novels could be described as animated horoscopes. This, indeed, is one of the reasons why Coelho's work has not always endeared itself to some readers for whom it is 'New Ageish, self-help tosh' (Mooney 8). *O Alquimista* describes a young Spanish shepherd's search for buried treasure; Santiago has various adventures on his way across the deserts of northern Africa, following the advice of the Alchemist, risking life and limb, on his way to Egypt where he discovers that the treasure he was looking for was – all the time – under the sycamore tree in the abandoned church in Andalusia where he used to tend his flock. By his own admission Coelho has been influenced by Jorge Amado and Jorge Luis Borges (Mooney 9), and certainly a number of stock techniques drawn – via these two writers perhaps – from the repertoire of fables, myths and fairy tales are in evidence in *O Alquimista*: the search for buried treasure, the use of omens, the sense of life as a pilgrimage, the importance of listening to the advice of an individual who is blessed with superhuman knowledge, a seer, a prophet or, as in this novel, an alchemist. Coelho's fiction promotes the idea that each of us has a magical answer to life's secret buried deep down within us, and that it is up to us to search the reality around us until we finally discover what it is (for further discussion see Hart, 'Cultural Hybridity').

The Brazilian novel of the 1990s proved itself adept at exploring this populist vein. *A Mão Esquerda* (1995) by Fausto Woolf (b. 1940, though this is a *nom de plume*), for example, is a mock-autobiographical account provided by the Narrador of the lives of his various ancestors and contemporary family members. Each individual, including the narrator, is given a chapter for the account of the most crucial events of their lives, and each chapter is provided with a name and a date, the earliest being the chapters written by 'O Bobo' in 1594 (Chaps. XXII, XXXIII, XLIII) though he also has chapters dedicated to 1689 (Chap. L) and 1824 (Chap. LV); the most recent being those written by the narrator which range from 1969 to 1995 (the time the novel is being composed). Various other people from the narrator's immediate family, including his brother, father, mother, and grandparents, enter the narrative with their versions of events given in the first person, and the narrative flows from the present to the past and back to the present, thereby evolving a complex synchronic and diachronic interweaving of life stories. The novel is made up of three types of narrative strand: objective historical events (the Thirty Years War in Europe, Chap. L, Woolf 413;

President Colhor's impeachment, Chap. LI, 427), and real people (such as Christian IV of Denmark [1577–1648], Chap. XXII, 137), along with events within the narrator's family history (it is likely given the way the memoirs read that they are based in part on the lives of the author's close family, including for example, the history of how his Polish-German family left Europe in the mid-nineteenth century in order to emigrate to Brazil (Chap. V, 31), though, for reasons of discretion, Fausto Wolff, as Luiz Lisboa points out, 'é o pseudônimo de um autor que acolhe bem a fama mas recusa falar de sua vida e dar seu nome verdadeiro' (Lisboa 145). But the novel does have a number of highly imaginary events, one example being the humorous episode when the Fool captures William Shakespeare, who is on his way to Denmark, takes him to visit Henrique Julius in Traurigzeit, an episode which is then seen to provide Shakespeare with the material which would inspire the creation of Hamlet (Chaps. XXII, XLIII). The novel plays with narrational time as much as it does with historical time. Occasionally this derives from the context of authorial omniscience, such as when the Narrator in 1980 discovers 'a crônica de uma morte anunciada que García Márquez ainda não havia escrito' (Chap. LVI, 484), a humorous reference to the Colombian's novel, *Crónica de una muerte anunciada*, which would be published the following year (1981); or when the various narrators refer to the events which will occur in the future (Chap. V, 32). At times the novel adopts a playfully postmodern stance towards the narrative proces itself. Thus Hermano Molokinsky at one point addresses his readers: 'Embora vocês estejam lendo o que digo em português, estou mesmo falando en alemão' (Chap. V, 30), though the trick behind the transcription is not explained. The novel indeed ends with a Cervantine irony to its genesis, since the narrator's mother in 1905 refers to the novel which the narrator is writing (or, more correctly, will be writing) under the incorrect title of *Mão Esquerda de Deus* (Chap. VIII, 42), and we later find out that a reward has been offered by the police for information leading to his arrest (Chap. LVII, 509), for the murder of a bishop – thereby introducing a ludic, self-reflexive level into the novel.

*A Casa dos Budas Ditosos* (1999) by João Ubaldo Ribeiro is typical of a marked strain within Brazilian narrative (long and short), namely, the frank if not pornographic treatment of sexual life. It is a racy description of the sexual awakening of a young girl from Outeirão in Bahia. The prologue explains the memoir was left at the offices where Ubaldo Ribeiro works as a journalist and that 'sua autora é uma mulher de 68 anos, nascida na Bahia e residente no Rio de Janeiro' (Ubaldo Ribeiro 10). The author refuses to give the name of the author of the memoirs and – no doubt to add a touch of authenticity – comments on the problems of transcription he encountered in preparing the text for publication (11). The book is named, as the account informs us, after the House of the Blissful Buddhists, where those who were about to wed went in order to familiarise themselves with sexual practices which would be useful for the future (14). As in Li Yu's *The Carnal Prayer Mat* (1634), the bliss sought in Ubaldo Ribeiro's novel is earthy rather than spiritual. The narrator describes her first sexual experience in a church (29–30), her early friendship with Norma

Lucia in which she swapped tips on the best seduction techniques, the seduction of her teacher, José Luís, with whom she loses her virginity (77–9), her reading of the *History of O* (82), her seduction by her uncle, Afonso Pedro (83–5), her sexual antics with her brother (93–5), her open relationship with Rodolfo with whom she shares various partners (wife-swapping and group sex), the time they studied together at a US university, and their subsequent return to Rio. The description of sexual performances are detailed and explicit and some readers will find the novel pornographic, but the narrator argues that the account of her sexual experiences is designed to attack hypocrisy: 'Vão à merda, vocês todos mentirosos, todos mentirosos, mentirosos, a esmagadora maioria hipócrita e santarrona' (149). As she suggests: 'A vida é foder, em último análise' (140).

## Two Late Boom Masterpieces

It would be wrong to give the impression that, once the zenith of the Boom receded from public perception, the Boom novelists themselves also retired from the business of writing novels. There are two novels in particular which demonstrate this to be far from the truth, and they are Vargas Llosa's *La guerra del fin del mundo* (1981) and García Márquez's *El amor en los tiempos del cólera* (1985). *La guerra del fin del mundo* is an extraordinarily well-written novel which is based on the events that took place in the backlands of the Brazilian state of Bahia in 1897 when successive waves of Brazilian soldiers arrived in Canudos to put down a rebellion headed by a religious fanatic who had mobilised the impoverished and credulous masses against the republic and all it stood for. It is a reworking of Euclides Da Cunha's classic novel, *Os Sertões* (1902), which has been discussed above (see pp. 157–8). Vargas Llosa's novel analyses the complex ways in which modernity and mythology clash in Latin American society. Modernity is epitomised by the various armies which are sent from the capital to attempt to quash the rebellion, the railways used to transport the soldiers, the various reports which need to be written about the rebellion, the officialdom of the state and the Church. In contrast to the republic we find a tightly packed array of dissident social elements, ranging from the Counsellor, a Messianic figure who speaks to the people in parables and warns them to have no truck with the republic since it is the Anti-Christ, a hermit woman who lives in the hills, a brutal, sadistic outlaw called Satan João who subsequently becomes a saint and changes his name to Abbot João, and the common rabble. The Catholic Church, needless to say, is appalled by accounts it receives of the Counsellor's words, regarding him as a rabble-rouser and a heretic. The narrative voice specifically draws attention to this contrast between the two warring worlds, with Canudos standing for religion and the Brazilian state standing for science. Taking a leaf out of da Cunha's book, but exploiting its power of suggestion more effectively, Vargas Llosa focuses on the enigmatic figure of the Counsellor who appears to have almost supernatural powers of persuasion over the people. A foreign observer in Brazil, the Scot Galileo Gall (the reference to the scientific spirit in the Scot's name is tongue-in-cheek), points out the role of the marvellous in what is happening all around him, which he can scarcely believe (Vargas Llosa, *La guerra* 53–7). The novel is self-consciously written in an objective, Realist style in order to draw a contrast with the 'irreality' of the events being described. The structure of the novel echoes this cultural contrast in that it is antiphonal, moving alternately from the world of the cities (the government officials, the members of the clergy, the generals and the newspaper editors) to the world of the backlands (hermits, bandits, the common people, the poor and infirm). A common motif in the novel is how the authorities are mystified by the people's actions, and this magic-realist element is brought to a head at the conclusion of the novel when a military official asks an old woman what happened to João Abbot and she replies: 'lo subieron al cielo algunos arcángeles. [...] Yo los vi' (531).

*El amor en los tiempos del cólera*, as Márquez has pointed out, is based on the accounts given to him by his parents about their rather extravagant love affair (Simons). It is thence transmuted into the story of the love between Florentino Ariza and Fermina Daza, which is postponed for more than a half a century, because of the latter's marriage to Juvenal Urbino. Perhaps more important than its sources, though, is the novel's structure, which is rather like that of a picaresque novel. After each episode, the frame, as it were, freezes, and then the life of another individual takes off. This is clear if we consider the opening scenes of the novel. We are introduced at great length to the life (and death) of Jeremiah de Saint-Amour only to discover that he is no longer to figure in the story. Here García Márquez is surely cocking a snook at the reader, because Jeremiah de Saint-Amour is dead, and therefore, to follow the logic of life rather than the logic of the novelist's world, he appears no more. For it is the individual who discovers him – namely, his friend, Juvenal Urbino – whose life we subsequently hear about. The novel is also picaresque in that there are a number of scenes which follow each other episodically, and are there, seemingly, for the joy of narration rather than as parts of a precise architectural framework. This is most evident in the description of the minute details of each of Florentino's love affairs (including Ausencia Santander, Leona Cassiani, Sara Noriega, Olimpia Zuleta, Prudencia Pitre, and América Vicuña). For all this, though, the novel is not told chronologically. Instead the episodes are contained within the two defining moments in Florentino's existence: when he is rejected by the love of his life, Fermina Daza and the day, fifty-three days, seven months, and eleven days and nights later, when they sail off into the sunset together. True to Márquez's style, the novel glides easily between different slices of lived time. For example, we witness Juvenal Urbino's rather comic death (he falls off a ladder while trying to retrieve his parrot from a tree) early on in the novel, and we hear the bells tolling for his funeral via Florentino's much later in the novel, when Florentino is making love to América Vicuña. The novel follows the logic of its own association rather than the chronology of everyday time. There is an important connection established throughout the novel between disease and love (an idea which dates back at least to medieval times), which is given a new vibrancy in García Márquez's hands, such that Florentino's mother does not know whether her son is suffering from cholera or from love since the physical symptoms are identical. The theme is resolved at the conclusion of the novel when the captain agrees to allow Florentino and Fermina to be his special guests of honour and, so they can carry on their secret tryst, raises the yellow flag of cholera, thereby establishing a direct causal link between love and cholera.

### The Short Story in Spanish America[7]

One of the most significant short-story writers of this period is Julio Cortázar (1914–84) whose work has already been reviewed in the section on the novel. Though his novels have received rave reviews, his short stories are probably better. Similar to his novels, Cortázar's short stories are centred on an unsolvable mystery. 'Cartas de mamá', for example, tells the story of Luis and Laura who have run away from Argentina to Paris after a shotgun wedding. One day Laura's mother in a letter mentions that Nico has been asking after them, and this is taken by Luis to be a sign of senility since Nico was Luis's brother from whom Luis effectively stole Laura (they were engaged) and who subsequently died. The story gradually builds up the tension until, finally, Luis 'becomes' Nico, or so we are led to believe by the concluding comments of the story. The realm of the strange and the terrifying has broken into the world of the quotidian. 'Los buenos servicios' is likewise a bizarre story which centres on the perception of a widow, Madame Francinet, of a rich household which she visits on two occasions to fulfil domestic tasks. She is later asked to attend the funeral of Monsieur Bébé and pretend that she is his mother; through naivety and greed (Monsieur Rosay offers her a considerable sum of money for the task) she agrees to do so; in effect, we are none the wiser at the end of the story as to the manner of Monsieur Bébé's death (Susana Jakfalvi suggests there is a homosexual sub-plot; Cortázar, *Ediciones* 41). 'Las babas del diablo', like the other stories, takes a mundane context – a young photographer, Michel, takes a photograph of a man and woman talking to each other by the Seine –

---

[7] One genre which has not been discussed in this work is the novella. An argument could be made for there being a separate category reserved for the Spanish American novella, seen as a shrunk novel rather than an extended short story, but in length somewhere in between. Examples of the Spanish American novella would be María Luisa Bombal's *La última niebla* (1935), Juan Carlos Onetti's *El pozo* (1939), Adolfo Bioy Casares's *La invención de Morel* (1940), Ernesto Sábato's *El túnel* (1948), Gabriel García Márquez's *El coronel no tiene quien le escriba* (1958), discussed in this chapter as a short story, Carlos Fuentes's *Aura* (1962), Mario Vargas Llosa's *Los cachorros* (1967), finally leading to a rapid growth of the genre in the 1980s with works such as Mempo Giardinelli's *Luna caliente* (1983), discussed in chapter 7, and Álvaro Mutis's *La última escala del Tramp Steamer* (1988). The kernel of this argument is found in a doctoral dissertation which uses the term 'nouvelle' rather than novella; see Cardona-López 63–7, *passim*.

and converts it into a mystery since something very untoward occurs when the photographs are developed (the narrator is turned into a still while the photographed couple seem to take on a life of their own [138]. The final paragraph of the story, with its references to passing clouds, the occasional falling of rain, and birds flying by, reinforces the eerie impression that the narrator has now been confined for eternity in the eye of the camera. 'El perseguidor', a short story in which the narrator, Bruno, describes his relationship with a jazz musician, Johnny Carter, allows Cortázar once more to focus on the elusive interface between art and life, literature and reality, since Bruno is Johnny's biographer as well as his friend. Johnny Carter, like the real person on whom his character is based (the celebrated American saxophonist, Charlie Parker [1920–55]), is a wild man, prone to outbursts of temper, bouts of insanity and suicidal clinical depression, but those around him recognise his musical gift to be something special which separates him from other men. This becomes evident particularly during the conversation in which Johnny explains to Bruno that he is able to experience time in a more inward way, as if he were entering a different time dimension, an experience which overtakes him on the Métro in Paris; '¿Cómo se puede pensar un cuarto de hora en un minuto y medio?' (*Ediciones* 153). The mystery underlying this experience is enhanced towards the end of the story in a conversation that Bruno has with Johnny shortly before the latter's death; Johnny angrily rejects Bruno's biography as a charade, in particular the latter's notion of God (196). This conversation between Johnny and Bruno, which leads to an intellectual impasse, builds on one of the main tropes of Cortázar's fiction: the intellectual comprehension of life destroys its beauty. It is not coincidental, thus, that, after Johnny's death, Bruno seems relatively unconcerned; he simply refers to how well his biography of Bruno is selling, and that there are plans for a new translation. The narrator is finally revealed to be an integral part of the stultifying intellectualism which ruins the elusive and mysterious beauty of life. Finally 'Las armas secretas' is about the mystery of bodily possession. Pierre and Michèle are two lovers in Paris; Michèle is hesitant to make love to Pierre because of a previous experience (she was raped by a German during the occupation). But finally she invites Pierre to her home, only to stop him when the look in his eyes reminds her of the German; Pierre leaves, Michèle calls her friend, Babette, asking her to come and see her, and at this point the mystery begins. While driving through the woods where the German was killed in retaliation, Pierre suddenly swerves the car round and returns to the house, we presume, in order to re-enact the rape. Cortázar manages to create tension and mystery in this short story by leaving the door open for reincarnation as a possibility; thus Pierre had always imagined in the most vivid terms what Michèle's house would look like, he is obsessed with possessing her physically, and he has the odd habit of humming German songs. A change in Pierre's identity is suggested by the dog, Bobby, who seems to recognise him, accept him, but then barks at him later on. Perhaps the most intriguing detail of all is that Michèle's friends, Roland and Babette, who discovered and killed the German, have been alerted and are depicted as driving to the house when the narrative ends; it is likely, therefore, that not only will Michèle's rape be re-enacted, but also the murder of the rapist as well, who this time will be a Frenchman, Pierre. In this Cortázar is similar to other Spanish American writers such as Borges and Fuentes; he is obsessed with the coincidence between the plot worked out between individuals in the past, and its re-enactment in the present. Cortázar's trump card is his use of suspense, at which he is an unrivalled master.

Equally important to mention here are the short stories of Gabriel García Márquez, whose novels have been discussed above. *Los funerales de la mamá grande* epitomises some of the strengths of García Márquez's narrative skill. Each of the eight short stories in this collection focuses on a number of scenes taken from everyday life in order to address larger more problematic patterns of cultural life. 'La siesta del martes', for example, only allows the reader to know the purpose of the events being described (a woman and her daughter are taking a train ride to another village in order to visit the son's grave) halfway through the story. The reason why they wish to visit the cemetery where the thief is buried is presented laconically to the priest: 'Yo soy su madre' (*Funerales* 16). Often in these stories García Márquez will use an everyday scene in order to address a political issue. Thus in 'Un día de éstos' a visit by the mayor to the dentist allegorises the struggle between the power of the state and the people's resistance. As the dentist remarks when he pulls out the mayor's tooth: 'Aquí nos paga veinte muertos, teniente' (García Márquez, *Funerales*, 25). This story, like the others, works by innuendo and understatement; García Márquez leaves the reader to draw conclusions and authorial intervention is kept to a minimum. He uses the apparently trivial theft of three billiard balls in 'En este pueblo no hay ladrones' to portray the limited nature of people's lives (now the billiard balls have gone, the owner has to close down his establishment, and all social activity ceases). The short story which gives its title to this collection is different from the others in that it gives us an early indication of the style for which García Márquez would become famous, namely, the dead-pan description of fantastic events, or magical realism. The short stories in *Funerales de la mamá grande* are visually orientated, deliberately do not provide exact temporal or spatial parameters for the setting of the action, use dialogue at the expense of third-person description, and derive their power mainly through a clever balance of humour and suspense. Indeed, they are like snapshots whose significance is gradually unravelled before the reader's eyes.

García Márquez's best short story is *El coronel no tiene quien le escriba*. Filmic and objectivist, this short story manages within a hundred pages or so to conjure up the political atmosphere of Colombia in the 1950s. The plot is so simple as to be almost non-existent. A man, called the Colonel, has been waiting for fifteen years for a letter which he believes to be imminent, in which he will receive news of his military pension. Much of the novel is taken up with the description of the various things he and his wife – simply called 'la mujer' – do in order to survive, while retaining their dignity. It takes place in a short period of time from October to December in an unspecified year in the 1950s (although it is probably 1956 since this was the year of the Suez crisis, which is mentioned twice in the narrative; García Márquez, *Coronel*, 25, 41). No details are provided by an omniscient third-person narrator; instead we are seduced into constructing the outline of the characters' lives based on a number of asides which we, as readers, overhear. As we soon find out, the Colonel and his wife are severely affected by the loss of their son, Agustín, who, it gradually emerges, was clearly involved in anti-government activities, for which he paid with his life. (He probably died in the period of political violence which occurred after the assassination of the leftist politician, Jorge Eliécer Gaitán in 1948.) This, and a number of other clues, point to a sense of society as characterised by an overwhelming political oppression. The Colonel mentions that the person being buried at the time the novel opens is the first who has died a natural death in years (11), the assumption being that everybody else in recent years has died a violent death caused by political motives. The local priest rings the church bell a certain number of times to indicate whether the movie currently being shown in the local cinema is appropriate; for the last year no film has passed muster (25). Another example of social control occurs during the scene when the funeral cortege is prohibited from passing in front of the police barracks (16). There is frequent mention of press censorship, and in one scene the Colonel reads a sign which says: 'Prohibido hablar de política' (64). Nothing is stated in an obvious manner; this elliptic quality is also evident in the dialogues which often consist of one or two words (66). Often the narrative eye of the work stays locked onto the surface of things, refusing to penetrate into the mind of the characters; thus, typically, the characters' thoughts are transcribed as if they were spoken sentences. The most elusive part of this short story concerns not the letter which appears in the title, but the cockerel which the Colonel refuses to sell, even though he and his wife are practically starving to death. It comes to have a symbolic value, being associated with leftist ideology, with the couple's dead son (it once belonged to Agustín), with the people's hope for a brighter future (the 'ilusión' mentioned towards the end of the novel; 70), as well as (rather ominously) with death (71). Thus, the cock comes to stand for the people's determination to survive even in the face of the most abject political oppression. On a number of occasions, the Colonel's anguish is so great that he feels as if his body is excessive; political oppression is thus experienced in a physical, bodily sense by him. After the Colonel reads the sign that forbids political discussion, the immediately following sentence reads (with a Sartrian flavour): 'El coronel sintió que le sobraba el cuerpo' (64). *El coronel no tiene quien le escriba* is a *tour de force* which manages to combine the allegorical portrayal of the destiny of a nation within the apparently small frame of the everyday life of an ageing couple.

In the short stories of the brilliant Argentine writer Luisa Valenzuela (b. 1938) the notion of gender-specific writing is championed. In her well-known essay 'Mis brujas favoritas', for example, Valenzuela forcefully rejects the apartheid suffered by women, their bodies and their writing, and proposes a 'lenguaje hémbrico' to counter the hegemony of patronymic discourse (Valenzuela, 'Brujas', 91). The question to be raised here is to what extent this women's language is in evidence in her creative writing. *Cambio de armas* (1982), a collection of stories and Valenzuela's most impressive work, addresses the notion of 'lenguaje hémbrico' in a complex manner. All of the five short stories follow the pattern of a birthing of feminine consciousness which typically takes on a linguistic metaphor. This motif is most clearly expressed in 'La palabra asesino' in which the act of pronouncing the word 'asesino' is a moment of liberation through knowledge for the female protagonist. Likewise, in 'Cambio de armas', it is not fortuitous that the point at which Laura reaches self-knowledge at the dénouement of the story is when she understands for herself the workings of the phenomenal universe indicated by the world of language; she points the revolver at the Colonel's back and (presumably) fires. The birthing of the feminine consciousness is predicated on a linguistic dynamic. Clearly the most important story in the context of 'lenguaje hémbrico' is 'Cuarta versión'. This particular story, the most metatextual of the collection, focusses on the *guerra sucia* in Argentina during the 1970s and early 1980s through three conflicting narrative perspectives. On the one hand we have the perspective of Bella, the beautiful actress who is having an affair with Pedro the ambassador; secondly, we have the perspective provided by the 'narradora anónima' who relates Bella's story, and thirdly we have the perspective of the transcriber/narrator whose comments on the narrative proper are printed in italic script, and are more in evidence at the beginning of the story. These three levels are, however, not distinct; in this Chinese-box-like configuration of narrative levels there is a good deal of overlapping. We are never sure when Bella is narrating or when she is being narrated by the 'narradora anónima'. The reader is therefore only half-prepared for the conclusion of the story in which Bella is the only target who is shot at and killed ('se oyó un único disparo'; Valenzuela, *Cambio* 63), from which we must conclude that she is the most subversive of the group. This leads the reader to re-examine the previous events of the story. What is intriguing is that Bella's perspective seems to emphasise the personal dimension of her love for Pedro the ambassador. Bella never once appears to focus her action in political terms, which means that there is a disjunction between the way she is perceived, according to the internal evidence of the narrative and her actions as perceived by extra-narrational elements (in this case, the secret police or the ambassadorial guards who kill her). The point of revelation, in 'Cuarta versión' as in the other stories, coincides with a linguistic birthing in that the text which we have just read, in a Borgesian sleight of hand which defies verisimilitude, is narrated by Pedro to Bella while she falls dying to the floor. It is between the official story of Bella's life given by the transcriber/narrator and the personal story of her life that the space of feminine consciousness lies. The linguistic mediation to which her story is subjugated may make it ultimately indecipherable. But what finally emerges from 'Cuarta versión', as in Valenzuela's fiction taken as whole, is that there is not only a difference between men's and women's writing but that the parameters of the latter must be actively explored.

One of the best short stories of this period by a female writer is *La muñeca menor* (1976) by the Puerto Rican short-story writer, Rosario Ferré (b. 1938). It describes the strange Gothic horror tale of a young girl who is bitten by a *chágara* while in the water which then inserts itself in her leg and begins to live there. The local doctor is unable to do anything, or so it appears, until we discover later on in the story that he had deliberately not cured the young girl's illness in order to collect enough dues to put his son through college. The story ends with a gruesome twist. The aunt is an expert in making porcelain dolls which are exact replicas of her nieces. When the doctor's son falls in love with the youngest niece, the scene is set for the aunt's gruesome revenge. The doctor's son marries the youngest daughter and they go off to live in the provinces and, suddenly, the doll disappears. When the doctor checks on his wife, the following episode occurs:

> Una noche decidió entrar en su habitación para observarla durmiendo. Notó que su pecho no se movía. Colocó delicadamente el estetoscopio sobre su corazón y oyó un lejano rumor de agua. Entonces la muñeca levantó los párpados y por las cuencas vacías de los ojos comenzaron a salir las antenas furibundas de las chágaras. (Chang Rodríguez and Filer 524)

The story is not only a horror story in the style of Hitchcock's *The Body Snatchers*, with its symbolism of the body being destroyed from within by an alien force, it is an acerbic critique of a patriarchal ideology which turns women's bodies into objects designed for men's pleasure, and which is prepared to make a profit out of suffering. The story is thus not only feminist but also anti-capitalist. This is clear given the symbolism surrounding the fact that the son, like his father, becomes very rich as a result of his trade and thus does not have time to notice the gradual transformation of his wife into a porcelain doll. There are a few details which point to a distrust of male sexuality; the fact that the *chágara* is described as emitting sperm ('aquella inmensa vejiga abotagada que manaba una esperma perfumada'; Chang Rodríguez and Filer 523), and that it is contained within a perpetually-open wound, suggests that the *chágara* is a symbol of the penis within the vagina. A powerful story, *La muñeca menor* is able to combine a radical feminist message with a magical-realist style in a unique unforgettable way.

Another intriguing short story of this period by a female writer is *Encancaranublado* (1983) by Ferré's compatriot, Ana Lydia Vega (b. 1946). It is set on a small boat stranded in the Caribbean, whose owner, the Haitian Antenor, is attempting to reach Miami in the hope of making a fresh start in life. On the way, he picks up a Dominican, Diógenes, and then a Cuban, Carmelo, all intent on the same plan. They begin to squabble over the provisions and the water bottle, and then proceed to insult each others' countries, unaware of the storm which is brewing all around them. Luckily saved by a passing American ship they are sent down to the hold; the moral of this humorous tale is that, despite their 'pursuit of happiness' in the United States, each of these representatives of a Caribbean country, the Haitian, the Dominican, and the Cuban, is about to have his dreams rudely shattered; the Puerto Rican already knows what to expect. The subaltern status of each of the representatives of a Caribbean nation is neatly expressed by their position below deck in the American ship, this being the symbol of their so-called economic salvation.[8]

## The Short Story in Brazil

The 1960s in Brazil were dominated by the short stories of Clarice Lispector and Rubem Fonseca. The latter's 'A Colera do Cão' (1965), one of the classics of the decade, tells the story of the murder of a prominent individual, Claudinior. The police commissioner, Vilela, begins an enquiry and discovers that the hit was carried out by a ruthless gang led by Mabbaia. A squad of six policemen is set to arrest Bambaia, but the mission fails and a policeman, João, is shot and dies. The story switches to a dramatic format in the closing scene in which Vilela tells his wife that João has died. The directness of the narrative style, the rapidity with which the narrative moves along, and the skilful delineation of character all contrive to produce a powerful piece of writing. The lack of over-sentimentalisation, the refusal to judge the characters' actions, the clipped, matter-of-fact description of events is in direct contrast to the hysterical, overdramatic tone of the newspaper article which reports on the murder, and tells untruths about it. While the reader knows that Vilela investigates the murder immediately, the newspaper embellishes the facts (see esp. Fonseca 233). As a result of its laconic, pithy style, this story is able to underscore points such as Vilela's 'A pobreza e pior do que a morte' (260). Fonseca's 'A força humana' likewise focuses on the subaltern, allowing the reader into the world of a muscle-builder, beginning with his chance encounter with a young man, Waterloo, who is dancing on the street and whom he invites to his gym, and concluding with a description of his love-making with the Leninha who works as a prostitute (Moriconi 195–211). The style is concise, pared and muscular. The description of objects and people is kept to a minimum, and often simply kept for the dialogue.

Lispector's fiction, by contrast, though less gripping, was more sophisticated, more measured. Her *Uma galhina* (Moriconi 258–60), for example, is a story about a hen which, about to become lunch, escapes, is caught and promptly lays an egg, prolonging its life a few years. That with this story Lispector is creating a metaphor of women's life is hinted at in a subtle way. Even in her freedom she is 'stupid' and 'timid':

---

[8] One of the most interesting developments in contemporary short-story writing is the ascendancy of the female writer; for a good selection (in English), see Ross and Miller.

Não vitorioso como seria um galho em fuga. Que é que havia nas suas
vísceras que fazia dela um ser? A galhina é um ser. É verdade que não se
poderia contar com ela para nada. Nem ela própria contava consigo, como
o galo era na sua crista. (Moriconi 259)

The references later on in the story to her desire for freedom, the 'resquícios
da grande fuga' (Moriconi 260) suggest that this story also operates as an
allegory of the dilemma of women in the 1960s, trapped by circumstance and
desiring to break free.

Other stories of this period focused on the quotidian. 'O homem nu' by
Fernando Sabino (Moriconi 249–51), for example, is a short, humorous piece
about a man who hasn't the money to pay for the TV rental, so he persuades
the wife not to answer the door. While putting the rubbish out, he gets locked
out, then trapped in the lift, causing a scandal with the next-door neighbour,
and finally ends up answering the door to the TV man; the story in effect
becomes an allegory of the entrapment of man within the system of modern
urban life. 'O Vampiro de Curitiba' by Dalton Trevisan (Moriconi 252–55)
suggests that in every young man there is a vampire lurking, while 'Toda
família tem uma virgem abrasada no quarto' (254).

In the 1970s short narrative in Brazil turned in on itself as well as towards
the darker side of life. *A morte de D. J. em Paris* by Roberto Drummond,
ostensibly written as the account of a trial in which a man called called D. J. is
judged according to a number of pieces of evidence which are compared and
evaluated, turns out to be a postmodern piece of fiction in which notions of
truth, causality and motive are turned on their heads to produce a collage of
inconsistent narratives about D. J.; this is a short story in which all is 'invenção'
(309). 'Correspondência completa' by Ana Cristina Cesar (Moriconi 341–49),
expressed as a letter to an addressee simply called 'My dear' offers an ironic
comment on communication. The reader is placed in the position of someone
eavesdropping on a monologue in which the main referents (people referred
to, events referred to) have been removed, thus transforming the story into a
set of 'Notícias imprecisas' (341), in which certain statements (such as 'what
are men for?' 342) become enigmatic. The very title of the story, 'Complete
Correspondence', is revealed as deeply ironic. 'A balada do falso Messias' by
Moacyr Scliar (Moriconi 352–57) is similarly ironic; set in 1906, it describes
the forced exile of Russian Jews, and a family's belief that the Messiah is a
Palestinian, Shabatai Zvi. As the story concludes, we find out that the reason
for this belief is that he can change wine into water (357). Other works of this
period demonstrate a similar sense of the absurd. The morbidly absorbing story
'O arquivo' by Victor Guidice, for example, describes the working career of a
young man who, after one years's service, has his salary reduced by 15 per
cent, two years later by 17 per cent, after another four years by 16 per cent,
at which point he is demoted, until after 40 years service, his salary is elimi-
nated and he is obliged to clean the toilets. Each of these cuts is greeted by
congratulations on the part of his friends, and finally João dies, and turns into

a metal filing cabinet. An allegory of Third World debt, this story uses the discourse of the Absurd to make a powerful political point. 'O Guardador' by João Antônio (Moriconi 385–90) offers a similar vision of Brazil though from an everyday perspective; it shows us beggars, rich tourists, and the workers of the big cities who are struggling to make a crust.

One of the more postmodern collections of short stories was *O banquete* (1970) by Silviano Santiago; as the author's prologue and artistic credo included in the volume suggests, the latter half of the volume constitutes a mirror image of the first half, that is, a mirror image which deconstructs the Realist first half. Thus: 'O retrato do conto tradicional formado pela estructura de "Mosquitos", "Praia do Flamengo", "O piano", e "O jantar" è desmembrado nos contos seguintes, onde o questionamento da representação atua como objeto do discurso' (Santiago 4). 'Mosquitos', for example, tells the story of a young boy's fascination with capturing mosquitoes, along with his growing awareness of sex (which alarms his parents), while 'Praia do Flamengo' recounts a young boy's awareness of his mother's adultery which leads to the murder (presumably by the father) of her German-Brazilian lover. We inevitably fill in the gaps (presuming, for instance, the father to have committed the murder out of revenge), but rereading the stories in the light of the later ones produces discrepancies. The concluding short story of the collection, 'O banquete', for example, begins by complaining about the complexity of André Gide's stories, which hide ideas behind characters in such a way – the story tells us – as to trick the reader:

> Cria um personagem, mas tem de escondê-lo por detrás de uma idéia – acaba é a idéia ficando escondida por detrás do personagem. Quando se vai agarrar um, se agarra o outro; e no final, fica-se insatisfeito porque não se tem nas mãos nem o personagem nem a idéia. (Santiago, *O banquete* 92)

In that way we can understand the bite of the mosquito of the first story as similar to the invasion of one body by another in the sexual act (which we are, indeed, encouraged to do via a discussion in the eighth story of the collection, 'Perigo no uso de recursos não-científicos na Labiologia'; see esp. Santiago, *O banquete* 73), but rereading the first story leads the reader to see that the metaphor is not actually resolved by the conclusion of the story, which leaves the reader hanging in the air. Similarly the notion of the narrator's unreliability allows us to reread the story and question whether the narrator's statement: 'Foi ele, só pode ter sido ele' (36) is really true, since all we have is the description of the dead body found on the beach, and indeed we recall that the narrator stayed out of the house in the time between the point of discovery (he sees his mother in bed with another man) and the news about the man's murder. A profoundly postmodern text, *O Banquete* deconstructs the Realist postulates on which, at first glance, it appears to have been built. Just as important, the collection of stories uses Paul Valéry's notion that 'um leão è feito de carneiros digeridos' (94) in order to construct a vision of Brazilian literature and culture as a mosaic of living tissue extracted from other cultures (European, African, Amerindian) in which the writer is himself intimately involved. A truly creative reading will be one in which the reader is involved in re-ingesting those digested elements, and creating a new work of art: 'os verdadeiros banqueteadores são o autor e o leitor. E, sendo esperto o leitor, é ele que acaba traçando o romancista' (94).

Brazilian short fiction of the 1980s broke new ground, pushing still further the limits in its exploration of the world of the subaltern, while tapping into the hitherto unexplored realm of homosexual love. 'Alguma coisa urgentemente' (1980) by João Gilberto Noll (b. 1946) is a brutal, arresting account of the hopeless life of a young boy whose father is a jailbird (Moriconi 418–22). Having served his prison sentence the father returns, ostensibly to care for his son – who has been forced through poverty to become a rent-boy – but actually to die before his son's very eyes. The story ends with a bang – as Noll's fiction often does (see Alencar Brayner's study) – since the words with which the story concludes and which are used for the story's title indicate ironically that, despite the widespread crime and poverty in Brazil, nothing can or will be done. 'Aquiles dois' (1982) by Caio Fernando Abreu (1948–96) is a painful story about a young man who goes off women, discovers his gay self, but realises that Brazilian society will never accept him, concluding with the sense that he and his friends will be forever 'infelizes' (Moriconi 439–46; 446). 'Intimidade' by Edla Van Steen treats a similar theme, that of the growing love between two women, which is allied to the sense of being able to fly (Moriconi 450), thereby alluding to a code word used by French feminist critics such as Hélène Cixous to delineate feminine experience. 'I love my husband' (1980) by Nélida Piñon (b. 1938) is a subtle piece of fiction, pointing to the unexpressed longings of a heterosexual woman who repeats the idea that she loves her husband so much that we know that her reference to 'nossa maravilhosa paz conjugal' (Moriconi 453) is nothing more than self-deceit. Typical of the unsettling irony of the fiction of this era, in which there are no longer any sacred cows, 'O santo que não acreditava em Deus' (1981) by João Ubaldo Ribeiro (b. 1940) is a rather odd tale about a fisherman who picks up God in his fishing boat in order to take him to see a hermit, Quinca, whom God tries to persuade to become a saint (Moriconi 478–87); Quinca tells God to get lost, and the fisherman has to take God back again, feeling rather sorry for him. A rather quirky tale, 'O santo que não acreditava em Deus' has some clear links with the magical realism more readily associated with Spanish America.

Brazilian fiction in the 1990s has a rather desperate feel to it. 'O anti-Nadal de 1951' (1996) by Carlos Sussekind (b. 1937) is a Kafkaesque story about Brazilian bureacracy. The narrator is informed by letter that he has been granted a free return trip with his son to São Paulo. Yet when he attempts to claim his tickets he is first told that he should have claimed them three days before making the trip, then that no seats are specified in the letter so he must buy the 'seats' even though the journey is 'free', and that he cannot have seats in the shade. The narrator feels impelled to fall back on God's mercy, but given that he will have to travel on Christmas Eve, his journey is in effect an 'anti-Christmas' as the title suggests. The power of this story lies in the fact that neither the reasons why bureaucracy has treated him in this way nor why he wants to make the journey in the first place are ever explained. 'Dois corpos que caem' (1997) by João Silverio Trevisan (b. 1944) likewise focuses on an enigma. Two men, João and Antônio, meet by chance at the top of the tallest building in Sao Pãolo, both intent on committing suicide, João because his lover has left him for a man with blue eyes. As they jump Antônio asks João if he likes his blue eyes, which allows the story to be read as a tragic story of two men who are in love with the same woman, but ultimately the reader is none the wiser at the end of the story; we are left guessing. 'O importado vermelho de Noé' (1999) by André Sant'Anna (b. 1964) describes the desperate thoughts going through the mind of a driver who is stuck in traffic in a yellow imported car, and slowly being engulfed by a rising tide of excrement-filled flood water (Moriconi 596–603). By endlessly repeating a set stock of phrases (the excrement is caused by the blacks, his car was imported from Germany, and he wants to go to New York where it is raining money), the stream-of-consciousness eventually becomes itself an allusive marker of Third-World psychosis.

## Theatre

One of the distinguishing features of Latin American theatre during this period is the Nuevo Teatro movement which arose at the end of the 1950s and spread, mainly in the 1960s and 1970s, thoroughout the sub-continent. It was galvanised by the creation of a number of independent theatrical groups such as El Teatro Libre in Argentina (1969), the Grupo Aleph in Chile (1969), the Teatro Escambray in Cuba (1971), the Cuatrotablas group in Peru (1971), and the Rajatabla group in Venezuela (1971). Nuevo Teatro is characterized by (i) the desire to speak on behalf of the *pueblo*, (ii) the espousal of the notion of collective authorship, (iii) an emphasis on everyday life and historical themes, and (iv) the Brechtian distancing-effect (*Verfremdungseffekt*) whereby actors – and audience – do not empathise with the characters portrayed. Latin American collective theatre also has similarities with United States and European 'hippie' theatre and living theatre. Its most important characteristic, though, is its break with the notion of authorial ownership. As the Colombian dramatist, Enrique Buenaventura, put it memorably: 'El teatro ha cambiado de proprietario' (Reyes 77). Often the practitioners of Nuevo Teatro will take an historical event in which the have-nots were pitted against the rich and use it for the political purpose of attacking a regime currently in power. Staging and acting are improvised; and the important part is the message rather than the style or artistry of the performance. Predictably, the Nuevo Teatro movement often found itself in conflict with the society it attempted to depict. In Argentina, a week after the Teatro Abierto '81 event in which more than 200 authors, directors and actors put on their work in the Teatro del Picadero in Buenos Aires, the theatre suffered an arson attack which completely destroyed its premises.

One of the most successful theatrical enterprises, and the prototype for the Nuevo Teatro, is Enrique Buenaventura's Teatro Experimental de Cali, whose origins can be traced back to 1955 when Buenaventura took over the directorship of the Teatro Escuela in Cali. This company has put on over a hundred plays, has shown its work in thirty-seven European cities, seven United States cities, and twenty-three Latin American cities. The first work put on was a *Misterio de adoración de los Reyes Magos* in which the Sacred Family was turned into an allegory of the Colombian people, with Herod as a dictator (Jaramillo 140–42). Fame arrived with the production of *A la diestra del Dios padre* (1958); this play is based on the Faustus theme and, more concretely, on a short story of the same title by Tomás Carrasquilla. It has five versions which were elaborated over the period 1958–84 (156). One of the aims of Buenaventura's theatre is not simply to entertain his audience but to construct culture: 'consideramos nuestros espectáculos aportes discutibles y discutidos a la construcción de una cultura de liberación y de divulgación' (quoted in Jaramillo 144). Very much following in the Nuevo Teatro tradition founded by Buenaventura, there are at the present time a great number of contemporary theatrical groups in Colombia; Jaramillo lists twenty-five (289–335). An example of outdoor theatre is TECAL (Teatro Estudio Calará) of Bogotá. Its *Preludio para andantes o Fuga eterna* (1990) is a fast-moving piece based on the life of a musician which delights in quick, ironic repartee, and is reminiscent of Beckett's theatre of the absurd and, particularly, *En attendant Godot*.

If one were to identify one feature of Latin American theatre of the 1960s to the present which differentiates it from the work of the preceding generation, it would be its new awareness of, and expression of, the voice of the lower classes.[9] *El menú* by Enrique Buenaventura is typical in this respect. It describes the world of those preparing the meal for a VIP who is about to be initiated into membership of the 'Círculo Cerrado'. The language used by the characters, who range from the cook, to a man/woman figure, to various types of beggars and hired assassins, is humorous, sparkling with slang and, at times, vulgar. When the candidate finally arrives, they force him to eat so much that, when he is about to give his speech, he vomits and falls over. *El menú* provides great opportunity for slapstick, and is a satire against the rich who feed on fine French food, while the poor and destitute starve around them. *Los papeleros* (1964),

---

[9] It is important to recognise the Manichean split within contemporary Spanish American drama. While it is undeniable that the works mentioned above project the voice of the lower classes, there are a number of works which have gained some notoriety but which do not do so. Examples are Carlos Fuentes's *Todos los gatos son pardos* (1970), a play recreating the drama of the Conquest (for more discussion, see Hart, *Other* 29–35), and Vargas Llosa's *Kathie y el hipopótamo* (1983), the latter of which was staged very successfully in English translation in London in the mid-1980s (for more discussion see Gerdes 530). These works, and others like them, should be seen as 'overflow' works from another genre rather than works central to the contemporary dramatic canon.

by the Chilean dramatist Isidora Aguirre (b. 1928), likewise focuses on the trials and tribulations of the lower classes. It describes the growing politicisation of garbage collectors, and the language of the characters, like that of *El menú*, is down-to-earth and vivid. There is some mention of the significant role that women play in civil rights movements (Solórzano, *El teatro actual* 272), and it is not by accident that the most authentic voice of the oppressed is a woman, Romelia, who is accused in the last scene of being 'mad'; her final words, before being led off, convey that the world has been turned upside-down: '¡este es el mundo al revés!' (Solórzano, *El teatro actual* 288). Following the Brechtian model, the audience is called upon in the closing scene of the play to reflect upon what they have seen, rather than drowning all critical analysis in an Aristotelian emotional involvement:

> El teatro cuenta los hechos
> tan absurdos como son
> a vosotros corresponde
> ¡pensar en la solución! (Solórzano, *El teatro actual*, 290)

One of the more artistically sophisticated plays written in this vein is *Los invasores* by Egon Wolff, which was first staged in 1963 in the Teatro Antonio Vares by the Instituto de la Universidad de Chile, and directed by Víctor Jara. It expresses the polarisation at that time between the haves and the have-nots of Chilean society. More than anything it is a household drama since everything takes place within four walls. The husband and wife, Meyer and Pietá, and their children, Marcela and Bobby, are presented as a stable, upper-middle-class family whose world is suddenly invaded by the poor, spearheaded by their ringleaders, China and Alí Baba, who live on the other side of the river in the town which is almost certainly Santiago. The play begins realistically enough with a typical domestic setting, although the wife, Pietá, is feeling apprehensive about something she cannot define. That night, however, an intruder breaks in and, from that point on, the play becomes gradually more unrealistic and even absurd. Meyer refuses to stop the invaders from taking over his home, and even turns a blind eye when one of them strikes his daughter (Act I, Scene ii; Wolff 162). The process described in the play, as Bobby lucidly points out, is '[e]l ocaso de la propiedad privada' (Act I, Scene ii; 176). Other elements underline the supernatural nature of the events described; thus, the individuals who torment Marcela at the beginning of Act II (Toletole, Alí Baba, and el Cojo) entered the bedroom by going through the wall, as Toletole explains (Act II; 186). Furthermore, these intruders know too much about Meyer's life to be accidental thieves. China, for example, knows enough about Meyer's life to wheedle the truth out of him about an unsavoury event committed by him in the past (Meyer murdered a business partner in order to get the insurance; 156, 205). Given this uncanny knowledge on the part of the intruders, it comes therefore as no surprise to the audience when we discover, after Meyer's screaming fit, that the play has been nothing more than a dream; the characters are projections of Meyer's guilty imagination. But *Los invasores* has a final twist. Just when the audience is letting its defence down, Bobby mentions that one of the events described in the dream actually happened (the Gran Jefe Blanco who burns all the students' coats for warmth). At that moment a window shatters downstairs, conveying that Meyer's dream is about to be enacted for real. The conclusion of the play is convincing in that it confirms the previous actions as subconsciously valid (that is in Meyer's dream world), while introducing the possibility that it was also for real. The inner and outer worlds are finally revealed to be identical.

Contemporary Brazilian theatre offers some intriguing points of overlap with Spanish American drama particularly in terms of its portrayal of a 'normal' world, which is subsequently shown to have been false. A number of plays use the past or foreign countries as a means of placing present-day Brazil under the microscope. *As pulgas* by Cunha de Leiradella, premiered in 1989, won first prize in the National Competition of Belo Horizonte, and subsequently transferred to Lisbon from 1990 until 1992 (Hamden, vol. 2, 149). Similar in some ways to Ionesco's *La Cantatrice chauve*, Leiradella's play homes in on the niceties of parlour talk in an upper-class setting, which are revealed by circumstances to be hollow, even farcical, such as when Monsieur explains tautologically to his daughter, Mademoiselle, that the only city in the world which has a tower like the Tower of London is London (Hamden, vol. 2, 101)! A witty piece of work, the English and their love of formality provide a set of gags which allows the script to evolve effortlessly in its descent into meaningless: 'Infelizmente, hoje já não se fazem mais antigüidades como antigamente. Nem na própria Inglaterra' (141).

*O homem imortal* (1990) by Luis Alberto de Abreu, uses the 1930 Revolution, its hopes and its fears, as a means of focusing on the challenges faced by Brazil at the close of the twentieth century. That history is seen as crucial for an understanding of the present; as Isidro suggests in the last act of the play: 'Eu conto e reconto pra lembrar, è lembrando, continuo vivo. Morrer é só perder lembrança' (Hamden, vol. 3, 76). *A lei e a rei* (1995) by Teresa Frota was very successful when it premiered in Rio in 1995, and it remained on the stage continuously for a year (Hamden, vol. 2, 46). With characters who have names such as Rei Mássimo and Hediondo, Lindomais and Belamenos, this is a light-hearted piece which describes the antics of a king who is intent on making absurd new laws such as that he must have a birthday every day and thus receive presents from his people, and that there must be cartoons on TV all day (12). As the critics were quick to point out, the play uses Brazil's colonial past in order to satirise all that is lacking in contemporary Brazil (corruption, nepotism, *plus ça change*; 46). *Salve amizade* (1997) by Flávio Marinho premiered at the Teatro Vanucci in Rio on 2 October 1997; it revolves around a get-together of some forty-year-olds who reminisce about their college days in the 1970s. Like *Bolo de nozes* (see below), *Salve amizade* offers a reflection on Brazil's turbulent political past, concluding with the idea that the only thing that can be truthfully said about human nature is that it changes (207). Lea and Ritinha are shocked to find that the inflamatory, left-wing student leader of their youth, Nandinho do Topete, has turned into an unscrupulous businessman with a penchant for young models in their twenties, while the stud of their college days, Pedro Cabeleira, turns out to have been gay. A tight script is complemented by shrewd character portrayals, offering a convincing portrait of the conflict between the two Brazils – the idealistic, Romantic Brazil of the 1970s versus the plastic-surgery-fixated, capitalist and egotistic Brazil of the 1990s.

Other plays of this period focus on the private space of the individual as a means of unlocking notions about human personality. *Aniversário de casamento* (1996) by Sergio Abritta, for example, looks at the ways in which individuals are involved in and create social rituals (wedding anniversary parties, sports events, watching films) in order to produce an elusive meaning to their lives, while *Vida privada* (1998) by Mara Carvalho records the conversation between two lovers who are intent on finding out the details of their sex lives with previous partners as a means of delving into the mechanics of social interaction in Brazilian society. *Bolo de nozes* (1998) by Edla Van Steen uses three slices of the past, 1 May 1968, 18 May 1973, followed by 1987, in order to trace the lives of Theo, a professor, his wife Nin, and her two younger sisters, Lili and Carlota, who live with them. A gripping, fast-moving drama, Van Steen's play looks at the difficulties of a loveless middle-class marriage set against the backdrop of stressful work environments. Theo has been demoted at work because the military dictatorship found his ideas too dangerous, and Nina has taken on the family business, having hardly a minute to herself. The mix is complicated by two love triangles: Theo is sleeping with his sister-in-law, Carlota, and Nina is having an affair with a man called Raul who is also sleeping with Lili. As the moment arrives for the final outing of truths at Theo's fiftieth birthday party, it is even worse than expected; Nina gets a phone-call informing her that the family business is burning down, and Lili shoots herself. A quick-paced drama with a lively script, *Bolo de nozes* offers a compelling snapshot of the malaise at the centre of contemporary Brazilian society.

**The Essay**

A great deal of contemporary essay writing in Latin America addresses the problem of identity, ethnicity and origins. One of the more searching examples of this line of enquiry is Roberto Fernández Retamar's *Calibán* (1971), which Fredric Jameson calls 'the Latin American equivalent of Said's *Orientalism*' (Jameson viii). It begins with the question put to Fernández Retamar by a European journalist ('Does a Latin American culture exist?'), and uses this as a spring-board to dismantle the premises underpinning such a question. The Cuban critic then takes the figure of Caliban from Shakespeare's *The Tempest*, and homes in on his rebuke to Prospero: 'You taught me language, and my profit on't / Is. I know how to curse. The red plague rid you / For learning me your language' (Act I, Scene ii; ll. 362–64). Fernández Retamar compares this situation to that of the Latin American who, unlike the inhabitants of other post colonial nations, still speaks Spanish, the language of his conqueror. In particular, he sees Shakespeare's vision of Caliban as specifically Caribbean-centred since Caliban is Shakespeare's anagram for 'cannibal', by which term the Carib Indians were known. He argues that the notion of an 'anthropophagus' is a fiction produced by a vigorous emerging bourgeoisie, as likely, he says, as 'one-eyed men'. In effect, Fernández Retamar rejects Enrique Rodó's defence of Ariel (see above pp. 129–30) (for whom it symbolised the spiritual, Hispanic heritage of America) and instead proposes Caliban as the symbol for the people of Latin America who were enslaved and taught a foreign tongue by their conquerors. Using Martí as a yardstick, and specifically his notion that 'Nuestra Grecia es preferible a la Grecia que no es nuestra', Fernández Retamar then goes on to berate those writers and intellectuals who, in his view, have sold out to the forces of imperialism, among them Borges. Fernández Retamar concludes by rejecting the pro-Western and overtly racist stance underlying Sarmiento's *Facundo* and Martínez Estrada's *Radiografía de la pampa*. By untying the barbarism/civilisation binary opposition promoted by Sarmiento, *Calibán* in effect becomes a defiant re-writing of the First-World mythology which excludes the Third World from the arena of culture. The space inhabitated by Caliban becomes the authentic ground in which popular, revolutionary culture can grow.

A specifically Marxist interpretation of Latin American culture is found in *La ciudad letrada* (1984) by the Uruguayan essayist Ángel Rama (1926–83). Unlike Fernández Retamar, who pursues a synchronic reading, Rama's approach is diachronic. In the first three chapters of *La ciudad letrada* Rama focuses on the ordering principles animating the culture which was built in the New World, the first on the city as the site of civilisation, as opposed to the barbarism of Amerindia, the second and third on the lettered elites whose writings 'planned' the cities in which they lived; roughly speaking, these chapters concentrate on the early years of the conquest and the colonial period. The last three chapters turn their attention to the modern period from 1870 to the present day, the emphasis here being the modernisation process, the growth of the economy, the formation of new social classes, the politicisation of the masses and the revolutions which shook the sub-continent after 1911. Rama's approach is vigorously eclectic, but it often takes the form of setting the historical scene (main historical events, ideologies, etc.), and discussing the literature as mediating those historical processes, and his insights are new and original. Rama's discussion of the literature of orality has opened up new avenues of research (Rama, *Ciudad* 86–8). Fundamental to his approach, and in this his work echoes Foucault's, is that different types of writing, ranging from legal documents to poetry, are social discourse. His historicist re-readings of literary works have proved to be highly influential (see Hart and Young; Golnick; Moraña; Del Sarto et al.).

As a result of the publication in 1977 of two seminal works, *Ao vencedor as batatas* and *O pai de família*, Roberto Schwarz (b. 1938) soon established himself as one of Brazil's foremost contemporary cultural critics. In these works Schwarz sought to produce a 'second-degree reading' (the term is Schwarz's; 66) of the work of major literary figures (such as Machado de Assis), or major historical events (such as the 1964 military coup and its aftermath), or significant films (such as Rui Guerra's *Os fuzis*), or important literary movements (such as Modernism or concrete poetry), by analysing their formal arrangement (if it happened to be a novel for example) and demonstrating how this structure was predicated on structural patterns within the society which produced it. Perhaps his most fortunate coining, Schwarz applied the notion of 'as idéias fora do lugar' (misplaced ideas), originally appearing as the title of an essay published in the journal *Estudos Cebrap* in 1973, to his sense of the distinctiveness of Brazilian culture. Starting from the notion that Brazilians, like other Latin Americans, often experience cultural life as something artificial and imitative (1), Schwarz went on to argue that the technique of imitation – including literary works which copy European models, politicians who ape foreign models, the electric guitar in the land of samba – is not so much a national characteristic as a malaise of the dominant class (15). Particularly in his brilliant studies of literary masterpieces Schwarz was able to show how the technical solutions proposed by the authors grew out of an awareness of the *aporia* which undermined the society. He argued, for example, that the ideology of scepticism which is at the heart of Machado de Assis's nineteenth-century novels reflects an awareness of the impossible (and indeed embarrassing) situation in which the Brazilian intelligentsia found itself, for 'liberal ideas could not be put into practice, and yet they could not be discarded' (28). It is within the Brazilian Realist novel that the drama and movement of world history, and particularly the economic dependency and parasitism of Brazil – rather than simply its localised result – is enacted (30). It is this unwrapping of the larger ideological backdrop underlying the specific features of a particular work of art that marks Schwarz's critique off from that of his contemporaries. Often the kernel of an idea is expressed as a paradox. While discussing the negative effects that external influence plays in an underdeveloped culture, he is also quick to point out that 'external influence is indispensable to progress, at the same time as it subordinates us and gets in the way of that same progress' (35). In his discussion of José de Alencar's fiction (see the discussion of his novel *Iracema* above, pp. 86–8) Schwartz recognises the 'flawed' and 'inconsistent' nature of Brazilian Realism, but turns the argument on its head by suggesting that that very 'inconsistency' is not a weakness but is rather an 'essential aspect of that reality' (66). In his extraordinary analysis of Machado de Assis's fiction he shows how the narrator's position echoes the 'ideological discomfort' of the elite in Brazilian society at the turn of the twentieth century (84–92). Schwarz points out how the clash of bourgeois and pre-bourgeois elements in the poems of the Modernists becomes an allegory of the country as a whole (esp. 110), how the clash of the modern and the archaic in the political culture which grew out of the 1964 military coup and its aftermath led to some misplaced allegiances (126–59), and how the classic films of Cinema Novo fail because, as he argues in a memorable phrase, 'I witness suffering, but I am not guilty' (Schwarz). He delivers a devastating attack on the myths which underpin the notion of a Third-World aesthetic; the 'charm' that 'backwardness' may have for someone who does not suffer is another of the myths which masks the fact that the Third World is an 'organic part' of the 'organisation' and 'iniquitous nature' of the world in which we live (174). In spreading his net widely across various types of cultural expression Schwarz's essays throw up intellectually arresting coincidences between popular and elite culture, between official and non-official culture, between Brazil and the world.

It was mainly as a result of the publication of a collection of his essays under the title *Uma literatura nos trópicos* (1978), and particularly the application of the concept of 'o entre-lugar' (in-betweenness) to Latin American discourse that Silviano Santiago (b. 1936) made his name as a significant contemporary literary and cultural critic. In 'O entre-lugar do discurso latino-americano', Santiago examines critically the neo-colonialist prejudice which sees the Latin American writer as perpetually consigned to the role of imitator and debtor, arguing instead that the main contribution of Latin America to western culture has been its systematic destruction of the concepts of unity and purity (Santiago, *The Space In-Between* 30). By giving a specifically Brazilian/ cannibalistic tone to Paul Valéry's notion that the lion is made up of 'digested sheep', Santiago argues that Latin American discourse is characterised by a dissenting and anthropophagous assimilationism, based on a strategy of learning the language of the metropolis, so better to be able to combat its elusive power (32–3). The Latin American writer is a 'devourer' of books, and yet even as – apparently like a parasite – he consumes the original text, he also creates within that text a new 'invisible work', a 'second text', similar in many ways to the way in which Pierre Menard produces a copy of Cervantes's original in Borges's famous short story, 'Pierre Menard, autor del Quijote' (1944) (Santiago, *The Space In-Between* 36). This new space created within the original text relates specifically to the cultural, social and political situation in which the Latin American writer is located, and has the effect of producing a 'rupture' between model and copy. It is anything but a facile reading of European culture; it has nothing to do with an exoticist interpretation of the Other, a type of approach that Santiago dismisses bitterly as a 'smiling carnival' or a 'fiesta-filled holiday haven for cultural tourism' (38). For it is its 'in-betweenness' that characterises the gaze which underlines Latin American discourse:

> Somewhere between sacrifice and playfulness, prison and transgression, submission to the code and aggression, obedience and rebellion, assimilation and expression – there, in this apparently empty space, its temple and its clandestinity, is where the anthropophagous ritual of Latin American discourse is constructed. (Santiago, *The Space In-Between* 38)

Santiago pushes the paradox underlying Borges's brilliant little story even further, allowing it to become a metaphor of the cultural transactions between

Europe and Latin America. In his essay, 'Eça, autor de *Madame Bovary*', Santiago begins with an empiric event – the accusation that Eça de Queiroz plagiarised the work of novelists such as Zola – in order to construct a theory of art as inevitably trapped by its own condition of rewriting the work of others. Thus, 'the work of art is organized by an artist's silent and treacherous meditation, which is designed to surprise the original in its very limitations' (Santiago, *The Space In-Between* 46). This means that the decolonised text is often richer than the original text since it has two levels of meaning, containing within itself 'a representation of the dominant text and a response to that representation within its very fabrication' (63). In a brilliant reading of the master text of the nineteenth century, *Dom Casmurro*, Santiago shows how Machado de Assis deconstructs the either/or of Capitu or Bentinho, the either/or of truth or verisimilitude, the either/or of imagination or memory, thereby producing an exposure of the two 'flaws' of Brazilian culture, its lawyers and its Jesuits (73). When turning his attention to the interface between the sociological and the cultural, Santiago's critique is no less perceptive; he draws attention to the inanity of the Modernists attempting to write for the people ('what efficacy can it have?' he asks; 92), as well as the irony of the use of government censorship of the arts in the 1970s in a country like Brazil when the readership at that time numbered 60,000 out of a total population of 110,000,000 (79; 111–18). He goes on to question the relevance of literature in modern times; literature, he suggests, is 'functionally untimely' in our cinematic era (131), though he does leave open the intriguing possibility that literature is able to create a dialogue with the future in order to be able to speak about the present and the past: 'Literature offers through the future reader of the work a present vision of the past and a past vision of the present' (132).

It is difficult to identify one all-embracing trend within the contemporary essay in Latin America, but it is clear that a number of concepts have provided fresh new perspectives on Latin American culture and literature. Beatriz Sarlo's ground-breaking study in intellectual history, *Una modernidad periférica: Buenos Aires 1920 y 1930* (1988), ranges widely over various fields, from tango to poetry, novels to architecture, and uses the notion of the periphery to characterise Argentina's evolution into a modern nation at the beginning of the twentieth century, a concept which has proved to be influential (see, for example, Herlinghaus and Walter's 1994 collection of essays, *Posmodernidad en la periferia*). Néstor García Canclini's introduction of the term 'hybridity' into the discussion of Latin American culture in his major essay, *Culturas híbridas* (1989; English translation 1995), particularly in terms of the asymmetrical balance of the traditional/rural and the modern/urban, has given rise to a more nuanced understanding of the interplay of these factors in modern and popular Latin American cultures; later works such as *Latinoamericanos buscando lugar en este siglo* (2002) have also proved to be highly influential. In his trail-blazing work, *Escribir en el aire: ensayo sobre la heterogeneidad socio-cultural en las literatuas andinas* (1994), Antonio Cornejo Polar has used the notion of 'heterogeneity' as a key to unlock the cultural discourse in the Andes; he has demonstrated that – from the works of El Inca Garcilaso de la Vega right up to the present day – culture has never been unitary and has always been based on a conflict between different languages – Spanish and Quechua – and between different discursive modes – typically the oral versus the scriptural (see Higgins). The Latin American essay genre continues its intellectual vibrancy into the twenty-first century. In *Mexican Postcards* (1997) and *Aires de familia: cultura y sociedad* (2000), for example, Carlos Monsiváis interrogates the emergence of modernity and the creation of cultural identity via TV and popular culture, while Nelly Richard has explored the applicability of metaphors such as 'collage' and 'residue' to our understanding of Latin American culture (see her essay 'Latinoamérica y la post modernidad', as well as the collection of essays, *Cultural Residues* [2004]).

# 7
# Some Postmodern Developments

These final remarks on some postmodern developments are intended as a postscript to the previous chapters. They concentrate on a number of new developments in contemporary Latin American literature and analyse a representative sample of works from those new genres. As we saw in Chapter 6, the decade of the 1960s witnessed a boom of Spanish American literature such as had never been seen before. As a result of a number of developments – among which should be mentioned political events such as the Cuban Revolution, economic events such as the commodification of literature, and cultural events such as the growth of the New Latin American Cinema – there emerged a new sense of a common cultural voice in Latin America. Paradoxically enough, following close on the heels of the creation of a new Latin American literary canon in the 1960s, new dissident voices became audible. The canon became gradually more diversified, the old hegemony of white, male, middle-class literature came more and more to be questioned, until, certainly by the 1980s, it became difficult to talk of a single canon. New canons, such as women's writing, Afro-Hispanic writing, Latino and Brazuca literature, gay literature and *testimonio*, to give a few examples, began to emerge and claim space exclusively for themselves.

## The Post-Boom Novel

While there is much debate about the difference between the Boom and the post-Boom novel (some critics have even gone as far as to deny that there is any difference), it is clear that the progression from Boom to post-Boom constitutes a change of paradigm. As Philip Swanson has suggested:

> [F]rom, roughly, the late sixties/early seventies, the Latin American novel began to experience a shift away from complex, even tortuous narrative forms towards more popular forms, often (though not always) relatively straightforward and sometimes, too, more directly political: a shift from the Boom to the post-Boom. The new novel had acquired an official air, lapsing into stereotype and a kind of heavy neo-classicism. The re-evaluation of popular culture (meaning, again, broadly speaking, mass culture rather than a form of indigenism) [...] brought a wind of change. (Swanson 161)

It is also important to note that the post-Boom novel differs from the Boom novel in terms of the gender of the author; the Spanish American new novel, as has been suggested, 'was a male-dominated affair' (Payne and Fitz 15), while there are a significant number of female authors of post-Boom novels, including, *inter alia*, Isabel Allende, Marta Traba, Carmen Peri Rossi, and Laura Esquivel.[1]

## The Men of the Post-Boom

*La guaracha del Macho Camacho* (1976), by the Puerto Rican Luis Rafael Sánchez (b. 1936), is typical of the post-Boom novel in its playful eroticism and its allusiveness to popular culture, since it effectively novelises the 'popular culture of Caribbean music and American television' (Raymond Williams 102). The title of the novel is based on a pop song and is the refrain which laces together a number of otherwise disconnected *tranches de vie* of various stereotypical individuals from Puerto Rico, including a senator and his critics with a clandestine lover, a playboy who is addicted to his Ferrari and masturbation, and a high-class woman interested in art and the psychoanalyst's couch. The narrative switches easily and unexpectedly between scenes in the lives of these and other people, often in mid-sentence. A demeaning view is taken of human activity; social culture is reduced to copulation (a recurrent metaphor of the novel), eructation, vomiting and spitting. In this postmodern world, all is levelled and a pop song is neither more nor less significant than the foundation

---

[1] It is worthy of note that, during the period in which a new genre, the post-Boom novel, began to assert its dominance in the literary landscape of the 1980s and 1990s, the Boom novelists continued to write, and, in some cases, went on to write some of their best works. What is striking, however, is that the narrative of the Boom novelists typically alternated between two poles, that of the traditional Boom format, and a new style of writing in which some postmodern trends were assimilated. García Márquez, for example, continued to write novels in the traditional 'mythical' style of the Boom novel, such as his complex Dictator novel, *El otoño del patriarca* (1975), arguably his most sophisticated work, while at the same time writing works with a more postmodern feel, such as *Crónica de una muerte anunciada* (1981), which incorporates typical post-Boom features such as the detective-novel style and the 'reportaje' format (Hart, *García Márquez* 17) and *El amor en los tiempos del cólera* (discussed above at pp. 229–30). The focus of Vargas Llosa's novels has shifted noticeably. His best work, *La guerra del fin del mundo* (1981; discussed above at pp. 228–9) follows the established format of the Boom novel. But some of his later works, such as *Historia de Mayta* (1984) and *¿Quién mató a Palomino Molero?* (1986), show him experimenting with postmodern techniques such as rapportage and the detective novel formula. Cortázar's work in the 1970s continued exploring the Boom blueprint he created with *Rayuela* (*Libro de Manuel* [1973] being a good example of this) but in some works, particularly *Fantomas contra los vampiros multinacionales* (1975), Cortázar attempted to integrate popular culture into his work. Even Carlos Fuentes, of all the novelists the most impervious to the techniques of postmodernism (his masterpiece, *Terra Nostra* [1975], is a grandiose novel reminiscent of the epic and totalising scale of the Boom formula) approaches the Realism of the post-Boom novel in his more recent novel, *Gringo viejo* (1985), which has been made into a successful movie.

of the United States. Culture is not only interchangeable, it is also repeatable; thus, scenes from the novel are repeated verbatim (Sánchez 103, 149–50). As the narrator suggests at one point: 'el misterio del mundo es un mundo de misterio: cita citable' (77). The notion of a quotable quote is repeated throughout the novel emphasising an epistemological strategy in which culture is experienced by the individual as a repeatable, interchangeable and empty reality, in which 'el aquí es esta desamparada isla de cemento nombrada Puerto Rico' (34). In contradistinction to the lyrics of the pop song, according to which 'la vida es una cosa fenomemal', life is shown to be trite, nasty and pointless.

*Respiración artificial* (1980) by Ricardo Piglia (b. 1940) is one of the classics of the contemporary Latin American novel. A sophisticated Borgesian novel, it opens with the narrator, Emilio Renzi, explaining the circumstances whereby he wrote his first novel, *La prolijidad de lo real* (Piglia 16) which was published in April 1976 (13), and which was based on the strange story of how Emilio's uncle had stolen the savings of Emilio's mother (Esperancita) and eloped with a cabaret dancer called Coca, for which – once apprehended – he had been tried and imprisoned (13–15). All we get of the novel is the first, rather long sentence (15–16), and this then becomes the launch-pad for an exchange of letters between the narrator, Emilio, and Professor Marcelo Maggi Pophan, who describes himself as an educator and a radical (18) who lives in Concordia, a province of Entre Ríos (24). Not only is the novel alluded to but not reproduced, but some of the later letters also are not quoted literally but only summarised, since 'No tiene sentido que se reproduzca todas esas cartas' (23). This leads to a sense of reality experienced as if at one step removed. Producing an even more elusive sense of reality is the fact that Marcelo is writing (without much success) a biography of Enrique Ossorio, a prominent man of letters of the nineteenth century (26–7). The novel soon reveals itself to be not only a set of self-reflecting mirrors (since Enrique Ossorio happens to be Esperancita's grandfather; 31), but also metatextual, since at one point the virtues and vices of the genre of the epistolary novel (which is what the novel appears to be) are discussed (33), as well as the impossibility of actually describing reality through the written word since writing itself presupposes invention:

> Una historia o una serie de historias inventadas que al final son lo único que realmente hemos vivido. Historias que uno mismo se cuenta para imaginarse que tiene experiencas o que en la vida nos ha sucedido algo que tiene sentido. (Piglia 35)

Chapter II opens with the monologue of an individual who calls himself 'el Senador', and who is speaking to an interlocutor who does not respond, but whom we soon deduce (Piglia 47) to be the same person as Don Luciano described earlier (21), and indeed is revealed to be Marcelo's father (50). The novel thereby gives the impression of developing in the manner of Cubism in the sense that various facets of individuals are revealed, and only later are the links revealed. The link between the various characters – Marcelo, his father Senator Luciano, and his mother's grandfather, Enrique Ossorio – is that they are all involved in sending and receiving messages, which they often find difficult to decipher (indeed, some are coded). A nod in the direction of postmodern play, the status of these missives is often in doubt; as Senator Luciano says: 'Fragmentos de esas cartas cifradas que recibo o sueño o que imagino recibir o que yo mismo dicto porque no puedo escribir' (62). Chapter III is principally written from the perspective of Enrique Ossorio during his stay in New York in the 1850s (bar the sporadic appearance of voices such as Marcelo's). Enrique Ossorio is sifting through various documents while writing his autobiography. But his imagination looks towards the future and he imagines what Argentina will be like in 1979 (83), and the visions of the future seen by his female companion, Echevarne Angélica Inés, in which she sees so much pain that she cannot bear it anymore (81), become transparent upon the torture of the Dirty War of 1975–83. This is an effectively poignant device since Inés, as a nineteenth-century seer, does not understand what she sees. Chapter IV is a literary-philosophical theory behind-the-scenes discussion of the novel (in the form of dialogue mainly between Renzi and Tardewski) which is reminiscent of the Morelli–Oliveira discussion in Cortázar's *Rayuela* (see discussion above, pp. 208–9). Like the 'capítulos precindibles' of Cortázar's novel, the discussion ranges widely over a number of fields including Wittgenstein, Borges (especially his famous short story, *Pierre Menard, autor del Quijote*), the classics of Argentine literature, the social role played by literature, Ortega y Gasset (who does not get a good press; 167), Kafka, Descartes, Hitler, Valéry, Joyce. The connections between these rather different writers and themes are drawn out in an erudite, rather Borgesian way. The 'artificial breathing' of the title is revealed in the last analysis to be breath of textual life – constituted variously as (reported) speech, letters, autobiography or novels – which binds together different members of Argentina's literary 'family' otherwise divided by time and space.

*Luna caliente* (1983), by the Argentine novelist Mempo Giardinelli (b. 1947), epitomises the demythifying ethos of pastiche. It tells the story of a young man, Ramiro Bermúdez, recently returned to Buenos Aires from Paris, who has a distinguished career before him, but whose life swiftly disintegrates once he becomes fascinated with Araceli, the thirteen-year-old daughter of a doctor friend, Braulio Tennembaum. He rapes and kills Araceli, or at least so he thinks, and, as a result, decides to kill Braulio when they are out driving. Ramiro returns to Buenos Aires only to find that Araceli did not die after all. At this point, the narrative becomes gradually more fantastic; Ramiro is apprehended by the police but they are unable to press charges against him when Araceli provides him with an alibi. Later on, Ramiro, in a fit of rage inspired by Araceli's sexuality, kills her, and then flees to Paraguay. The novel ends with a twist. Waiting in a run-down hotel in Asunción, Ramiro is awakened by the porter's phone call informing him: 'Que lo busca una señorita, señor, casi una niña' (Giardinelli 158). At this point, it becomes clear that Araceli is a supernatural being who is able to return from the dead. *Luna caliente* basically derives from three sources. The most important of these is the *novela negra* (or hard-boiled crime novel) which centres on the discovery of the identity of the murderer, although here the narrative is written in the first person. The second is the Gothic novel, above all in its combination of mystery and horror. The third is the political thriller, expressed mainly in the murky business in Chapter XVI when Ramiro is informed by the Chief of Police that he will be looked after if he admits to having committed the murder and agrees to collaborate on the police side against the subversives (the novel is set during the 'Guerra sucia'). The confluence of these three sources contrives to produce a text which has a rapidly moving plot, and a clear sense of time and place as in the Realist novel, combined with a Cortazarian sense of the uncanny which unexpectedly explodes that world from within. Intriguingly, the appearance of the Chief of Police is as uncanny and unexplained as is Araceli's presence in the novel, which suggests the extent to which the political plot is a micro-narrative contained within the overarching paradigm of the mystery thriller. Though almost devoid of literary references in the first part of the book, literary allusions abound in the final chapter of the novel. Ramiro compares his love of Araceli to the ill-starred love of Paolo and Francesca in Dante's *Inferno*, as well as to that of Vergil's Dido and Homer's Helen (156–57). His final thought, just before Araceli returns to him, is to compare himself to a prisoner of Dante's seventh circle of Hell (157). *Luna caliente*, in its use of devices such as melodrama, coincidence, suspense and the supernatural derived from narratives of popular culture, is a good example of the more immediate appeal of the post-Boom novel as distinct from its rather erudite forebear, the Boom novel.

*Ardiente paciencia* (1983) by the Chilean Antonio Skármeta (b. 1940), like *Luna caliente*, has a number of post-Boom features, in particular, its demythifying allusiveness to the *petite histoire* of popular culture. The plot centres around the love affair and eventual marriage of Mario Jiménez and Beatriz González. In order to win Beatriz's heart, Mario seeks the help of Pablo Neruda, for whom he works as the postman; given his fame and the quantity of letters he receives, Neruda has to have a postman all to himself to deliver his mail to his house in Isla Negra in southern Chile. While the novel does focus to some extent on the turbulent political landscape of the late 1960s and early 1970s in Chile (references are made to Neruda's political involvement, to Salvador Allende's election in 1970 and the *coup d'état* which unseated him in 1973 and ushered in Pinochet's dictatorship), the emphasis is much more on the texture of everyday life; this is the Neruda of *Odas elementales* rather than *Canto general*. Thus, in one of the most successful scenes of the novel, we see Neruda explaining to his postman what a metaphor is, only to find himself put in his place afterwards: '– ¿Y por qué si es una cosa tan fácil, se llama tan complicado?' (Skármeta 11). As this passage makes quite clear, one of the most important techniques of the novel is humour. Nothing is spared, including romantic love (after one graphic sexual scene when Beatriz has an orgasm, she says: 'Me hiciste acabar, tonto'; 63) and the mother-in-law (Antonio is described as coming a cropper against 'una institución temible en Chile: las suegras'; 36). The novel is also very amusing in its use of repartee; the following exchange between Mario and Neruda just before his death is typical: '– ¿Cómo se siente, don Pablo? – Moribundo. Aparte de eso nada grave' (112). Another feature of the novel which suggests its post-Boom pedigree is the way in which it blends different cultural codes. Like *Luna caliente*, *Ardiente paciencia* contains allusions to literary masterpieces, such as Shakespeare's play, *Hamlet* (112), and to Dante (Beatriz's name is an overt reference to Dante's beloved), but it also has many references to popular culture, such as the Peruvian soap-opera, *Simplemente María* (it is referred to in the novel as Mexican, but this is a slip of the pen; 71), popular songs such as 'no me digas que Merluza no, Maripusa, que yo sí como merluza' (85), classic movies such as *West Side Story* (5), and the Beatles' song 'The Postman' (51). The allusions to popular culture are not surprising given that, strictly speaking, *Ardiente paciencia* is not a novel but, rather, a film-script; it won prizes at the Biarritz and the Huelva film festivals and has recently led to a very successful Italian film version. Nevertheless, it is typical of the post-Boom novel's fondness for the language of film. A good example of this occurs when Mario uses a filmic metaphor to express the plenitude of sexual love: 'Las escenas vividas en el rústico lecho de Beatriz durante los meses siguientes hicieron sentir a Mario que todo lo gozado hasta entonces eran una pálida sinopsis del film que ahora se ofrecía en la pantalla oficial en Cinerama y technicolor' (67). Literature is explored in this novel not as a high-brow intellectual activity but as a cultural reservoir which, especially in its refinement of the language of love, plays a direct formative role in the everyday lives of ordinary people.

One author who has managed to burst into the bestseller market with his novels is Luis Sepúlveda (b. 1949), whose *Un viejo que leía novelas de amor* (1993), in the space of ten years (from February 1993 until February 2003), managed to achieve fifty-nine impressions. It is easy to see why. A charming tale, *Un viejo que leía novelas de amor* tells the story of Antonio José Bolívar Proaño, a kind of Lone Ranger figure, except that his hunting territory is the jungle rather than the Wild West. Despite his masculine toughness, he has a weakness for love stories, especially those with 'sufrimientos, amores desdichados y finales felices' (Sepúlveda 32), a bundle of which he receives every six months or so from the local dentist. Antonio José is given the mission of tracking down a tiger which is causing havoc around El Idilio. As he and the local Shua Indians who accompany him get closer to the tiger they find the various dead bodies of its prey. The decaying bodies are described in a matter-of-fact way; the plot is quick-paced, the description of the environment is concise, the portrayal of the various individuals on the hunt dynamic (indeed, in this sense Sepúlveda sees his novels as distinct from the Boom novel with its Baroque plot and its 'large impenetrable tomes plagued by obstacles'; see

Lindsay 73). Once he finds the tiger – it happens to be a tigress – it becomes clear that the two strands of the novel, the love stories and the hunting narrative, have been brought together for the tigress is mourning her dying mate. As Antonio José cries out to her when he discovers this: '– ¿Eso buscabas? ¿Que le diera el tiro de gracia? – gritó el Viejo hacia la altura, y la hembra se ocultó entre las plantas' (Sepúlveda 130). He decides on a mercy killing, muttering to himself: 'Lo siento, compañero. Ese gringo hijo de puta nos jodió la vida a todos. – Y disparó' (131), revealing himself to be more in tune with nature, with the animal world, with the Shua Indians. Even when he finally kills the tigress as she leaps at him, the novel becomes almost an elegy to a way of life which is being destroyed by a modern world which has no time for the Amazon, the Indians, the animals or, indeed, for true love.

There were some indications by the mid-1990s that the Boom novel formula – particularly in its magical realism incarnation – was meeting energetic resistance. In 1996 *McOndo* – a collection of works by Latin Americans born after 1960 – was published (edited by Alberto Fuguet [b. 1964] and Sergio Gómez [b. 1962]), which sought specifically to distance the new generation from what they saw as the tired rhetoric of magical realism, what Julian Barnes once satirised as 'the spread of package-tour baroque and heavy irony. Ah, the propinquity of cheap life and expensive principles, of religion and banditry, or surprising honour and random cruelty' (Barnes 104). Pointing in a similar anti-magical-realist direction is the new 'Generación del Crack', epitomized by *En busca del Klingsor* (1999) by Jorge Volpi (b. 1968), a sophisticated novel which won the prestigious Biblioteca Breve prize, and which steers clear of the awe of the supernatural so often associated with novelists such as García Márquez and Isabel Allende, choosing instead to tell a story about the search for the mastermind of Hitler's atomic research programme (code-named 'Klingsor') during the final years of the World War II. A lieutenant called Francis Bacon and a mathematician called Gustav Links are leading the hunt, while a number of real scientists – such as Max Planck, Albert Einstein and Werner Heisenberg – are given walk-on parts. The style of the novel is deliberately historical (or mock-historical, if one accepts that though some characters are real people such as Hitler, the conversations they have and actions they carry out are scripted), such that actions are placed within real environments, happen on specific days, and are described by an objective narrator. The most distinctive fiction of *En busca del Klingsor*, though, is the imaginative use of scientific concepts such as relativity and the uncertainty principle which are discussed by the protagonists and then neatly incorporated into the syntax of the plot; at times this is humorous as when a chapter on the attraction of bodies turns into the description of scientists having an orgy. As one might expect – given the rather Borgesian feel of the novel – Gustav Links is no nearer to Klingsor at the conclusion of the novel than he was at the beginning, and the underlying message of the tale is the moral aimlessness of the present generation. One of the characters baldly states that 'la asociación entre ciencia y crimen me parece natural' (Volpi 404) and it becomes clear that Volpi's novel

## The Women of the Post-Boom

is as much about the ethical issues surrounding science in the modern world as about what was happening in the Third Reich in the mid-1940s.

## The Women of the Post-Boom

*Conversación al sur* (1981) by Marta Traba (1930–83) centres on the memories of two women, Dolores and Irene, who were involved in the revolutionary movement in the Southern Cone during the 1970s; as a result, both suffer mental and physical torture and lose their loved ones. Traba's presentation of the political conflict is gendered in that it projects femaleness and political insurgency as indivisible notions. Thus the political reality of oppression is experienced by one sex in particular (women); men are depicted in *Conversación al sur* as associated with the Right (if they are Leftist they are ineffectual, such as Andrés and Enrique). The women, however, as typified by Dolores and Irene, direct and sustain political insurgency. One of the most important rhetorical strategies of this novel is synecdoche; thus, the visible reality drawn in Traba's text alludes to the invisible reality which the reader is forced to reconstruct (the latter being the systematic abduction and torture of political subversives by the Argentine armed forces of which no empiric details are given in the text). The objective facts are reduced to tantalising allusions, the metaphor shorn from its concrete referent. As Dolores says to Victoria at one stage: 'Peor es imaginarse las cosas' (Traba 123). Not surprisingly, fear pervades Dolores's whole existence; she becomes paranoid, at one point suspecting the bus-driver of informing on her (155). Despite the pain which is inflicted on the subversives' minds and particularly their bodies, they are able, through political solidarity, to achieve a new identity. This is most evident during the description of the women who congregate every Thursday in the Plaza de Mayo to protest the disappearance of their loved ones, a voice that one day would be heard. Thus, although *Conversación al sur* has a pessimistic level, since it seems to accept defeat as inevitable and ends with a scene in which Irene and Dolores are about to meet their doom, it also has a positive message in that the sense of solidarity shared by the women points the way forward to the path of social justice (Hart, *White Ink* 99–107).

*La casa de los espíritus* (1982) by Isabel Allende (b. 1942), published a year after *Conversación al sur*, is typical of a certain type of women's writing of the 1980s which flies in the face of the notion of the woman writer as interested only in the space of the home and the emotions (and especially love), since it addresses political issues directly. The novel traces, through the vicissitudes of three generations of women – Clara, Blanca and Alba – the political struggle in twentieth-century Chile between the Left (symbolised by Pedro García, his son Pedro Segundo and grandson Pedro Tercero) and the Right (personified by Esteban Trueba). The women of the family are consistently portrayed as the mediators in this political struggle; thus Blanca, though Esteban Trueba's daughter, falls in love with Pedro Segundo, and Alba falls for a revolutionary by the name of Miguel. Whereas the Left is presented in terms of continuity through family lineage, the Right is shown finally to be issueless since Esteban Trueba's sons either become Marxists (Jaime) or dropouts (Nicolás) and his daughters fall in love with revolutionaries. The exception to this rule is Esteban García, the second-generation illegitimate son of Esteban Trueba and Pancha García (Pedro García's sister); he ends up being a colonel in the police force and takes terrible revenge on Alba for the wrong he sees his unacknowledged grandfather as having committed to him. By these means Allende presents the military who took over power in Chile in the 1973 coup as a bastard breed of the landed classes (Esteban Trueba) and the unlanded (Pedro García); the insult could not be more carefully chosen. This sardonic depiction of the military class in the person of Esteban García is made all the more striking since, as the last chapter informs us, the text we have before us is the result of the collaborative effort of the Conservative Right (Esteban Trueba) and the Left (Alba). Indeed, it is only in the last chapter that we discover why Esteban Trueba's mini-memoirs are recorded in the text. As the collaboration between Esteban Trueba and Alba in the epilogue demonstrates, *La casa de los espíritus* traverses class as well as gender boundaries (landed/unlanded, male/female), despite the often stereotyped portrayal of identity in gendered terms (Hart, *White Ink* 91–9). Even though the reader is not spared some of the more gruesome details of tyranny, political oppression and sadism in the prison camps of Pinochet's Chile, Allende's novel is ultimately a positive affirmation of the value of solidarity in the face of evil and political oppression.

*Como agua para chocolate* (1989) by the Mexican novelist Laura Esquivel (b. 1950) is best seen in terms of its quotidianisation of the value of love; it merges high and low culture (ranging from motifs from Mexican soap opera to recipes), gives high priority to the mass-media notion of love as an all-consuming passion and, most importantly, lends itself well to the language of film; a very successful film version was released in 1985, and broke box-office records. The book is set up like a *folletín* (its subtitle is 'Novela de entregas mensuales'), and it is redolent of the *telenovela* (a great favourite in Mexico, where there are many television channels which exclusively play soaps back to back all day long) in its reference to the next episode once one has finished ('Continuará'). *Como agua para chocolate* is, in essence, a feminine counter-version of the Mexican Revolution, offering a kitchen-eye's view of those turbulent years, which is at odds with the masculinist rhetoric of the history books with their emphasis on battles and the struggle for civic power. The most striking characteristic of the novel, as its title suggests, is the use of food as a metaphor for the human emotions. There are various examples of this; Tita's tears which drop into the cake being prepared for Rosaura and Pedro's wedding meal produce a fit of vomiting in the guests (Esquivel 44–5), and Tita's blood mixed up with rose petals, when added to the quails, produces an aphrodisiac reaction in those who consume it (Esquivel 54–61), an idea which is repeated in the last chapter of the novel when Tita makes *chile en nogada* and unleashes an orgy of the senses (240–2). While the link between food and sex is a traditional one, *Como agua para chocolate* manages to extend this association in unexpected ways. Perhaps the best illustration of this occurs when Tita has to sing to the *frijoles* to make them cook; in a house where there have been arguments, so popular knowledge suggests, the food is 'annoyed' and therefore will not cook (218). Most intriguing of all is the way in which the emotions are depicted as emanating from the body like a cloud, influencing everything in their path. Such is the cloud of rose perfume which emanates from Gertrudis's body and attracts Juan, the *villista*, to her, at which point, following a Romantic stereotype, they ride off into the sunset on a horse, copulating as they go (56–60); another example is the anger which invades Tita when she has a tiff with Pedro (154). Alongside its sensitivity to the ways of the flesh, the novel is also alert to the realm of the spirit; Tita sees John Brown's Indian grandmother, *la kikapú*, when recovering from an illness, and she is haunted by the spirit of her mother, Mamá Elena (115–18, 177, 200–1). These events, and here Esquivel shows her roots in the magical-realist tradition, are presented as if they were part of everyday life, as are other fantastic occurrences, which include those already mentioned, such as tears in food producing botulism, or food producing sexual frenzy, or others such as Tita suddenly lactating and therefore being able to feed her nephew (82), and people dying of love (this is essentially what happened to Nacha [45], as well as Tita and Pedro [243–44]). With its roots so firmly in popular culture, it is not surprising that *Como agua para chocolate* should have only one reference to high culture, namely, the comparison between Tita and Ceres, the Roman goddess of fertility (82), or that it deals in stereotypes, a good example being the difference between the Anglo-Saxon male, John Brown, and the Hispanic male, Pedro. Written from a feminine perspective – its thesis is essentially that women are closer to food, love and life – *Como agua para chocolate* is one of the best of the novels to emerge in the post-Boom era. Its humour (a good example being when Tita explains, in the presence of John Brown's deaf aunt, that she does not love him; 220–22), and metaphoric flair are carried over successfully into the movie version.

Set in Colombia in the first half of the twentieth century, *La novia oscura* (1999) by Laura Restrepo (b. 1950) is a well-written novel about a prostitute, La Sayonera, who captivates men, and particularly the men who work for the Tropical Oil Company. At first glance this novel has a Zolaesque air about it, given its focus on the plight of fallen women, the awesome nature of machines epitomised by the oil company's enormous drills, the objective style of the narrative and its stark though epic vision of human endeavour. There are some Zolaesque moments too, such as when La Sayonera blithely tells her lover, Payanés, who is shocked to see some dead bodies floating in a nearby river: 'Hay que comer y hay que vivir aunque los demás se hayan muerto' (Restrepo 155). Yet *La novia oscura* ultimately transcends the straitjacket of Naturalism, for not only does it seek to recuperate herstory rather than just history by focusing on the prostitutes' perspective (for them prostitution is a work contract rather than a sin) as well as their political activism (they decide to join the oil workers' strike; 298) but it also manages to introduce a level of self-reflexivity about the difficulties involved in reconstructing the past: 'Escribir esta historia se me ha convertido en una carrera perdida de antemano contra el tiempo y la desmemoria, que son dos hermanos gemelos de dedos largos que todo lo tocan' (229). La Sayonera's decision to leave the brothel for a new life comes as a result of her experience of what might be called a collectivist epiphany when she feels the dead brushing past her legs in the Magdalena River, after which she becomes 'serena, y como Moisés, salvada de las aguas: vencedora de sus propios fantasmas' (325). Conquering her own ghosts means not only turning from prostitution to love (the personal) but also communing with those people assassinated as a result of La Violencia (the political). As she says: 'Yo soy yo y mis muertos' (324); she marries Sacramento and 'becomes' Amanda Monteverde (330). Yet the novel ends with a recognition of the splitness of human identity: 'La Nina, la Sayonara y Amanda: he sido testigo de tres personas distintas y no he logrado conciliarlas del todo en una identidad verdadera' (376). A complex novel, *La novia oscura* expresses a gendered, politicised vision of the trauma of Colombia's recent historical past which is as engaging as it is convincing.

## Testimonio

*Testimonio*, or testimony (the word in Spanish suggests the act of testifying or giving witness in a legal or religious sense) refers to a new type of autobiography in Spanish America which denounces political injustice. On the one hand, there are those works which are pure autobiographies, that is, they are narratives in which the teller is/was also the actor. Some of the more gripping examples are autobiographies by *guerrilleros*, such as the Argentine Ernesto Che Guevara's *Paisajes de la guerra revolucionaria* (1969). Beside these autobiographical narratives are those *testimonios* in which the teller is not also the actor. These are potentially the more interesting since they combine the artistry of a good novelist with the freshness of the account of an action-packed life (novelists are, after all, not always the people who lead exciting lives). A good early example of this was the series of articles written for *El Espectador* by García Márquez, about the experiences of a shipwreck, which was put together in book form subsequently; it has an extraordinarily long title: *Relato de un náufrago que estuvo diez días a la deriva en una balsa sin comer ni beber, que fue proclamado héroe de la patria, besado por las reinas de la belleza y hecho rico por la publicidad, y luego aborrecido por el gobierno y olvidado para siempre* (1970). The beauty of the account, the irony of its title, are due to García Márquez's story-telling ability; it is easy to imagine that the shipwreck's story would have been distinctly unmemorable were it not for García Márquez's role in the process. The best example of the *testimonio* occurs when at least two factors are present; firstly, as in García Márquez's narrative, there is a split between the actor and the teller, and, secondly, when the story speaks on behalf not of one individual, but of a social group, or a nation. This occurred in the case of *Biografía de un cimarrón* (1966), the matrix text of the *testimonio* genre.

*Biografía de un cimarrón* is based on the life of Esteban Montejo, and particularly his experiences as a runaway slave in late nineteenth-century Cuba, and it is recounted by the university ethnologist, Miguel Barnet. This text is the classic of the genre since it combines the two levels of quotidian personal narrative and ethnographic epic (González Echeverría 117–18). It allows a vision of the life of a slave 'from the inside', as it were, and gains authenticity as a result of there being two hands in the work, compiler and author. The narrative describes the life of Esteban Montejo, who was born on 26 December 1860 and became a Maroon living in the *monte* soon afterwards (and therefore did not know his parents). It describes how he managed to survive while there (eating patterns, etc.), then portrays his life as a wage-earner in the sugar plantations immediately after the abolition of slavery (the main freedom he appreciated in the post-slavery world seems to have been that of pursuing women), as well as his role in the militias during the War of Independence. The description of his life – the vicissitudes of everyday life, the subversion of official culture as expressed by the work ethic, the institution of the family, and adherence to Christianity – is a useful corrective to the versions of slaves' lives which appear in other nineteenth-century texts, such as Gómez de Avellaneda's *Sab*. *Biografía de un cimarrón*; it has an air of authenticity even when the account of Montejo's everyday life is bizarre. The predominance of the African religion in Cuba ('los dioses más fuertes son los de África'; Barnet 18), the horrors of war and guerrilla warfare, especially the use of the machete by the Cubans (167–70), the scarcity of women and the use of hand-picked slaves for breeding purposes (42–4), the use of witchcraft if a slave-owner punished a slave (31), the horrors of punishment (43–4), the temptations offered by running away from the slave plantation (49–63), the gruelling work regime (69–70), the description of visions of ghosts, *güijes* (supernatural beings that live in rivers), mermaids and (most bizarre of all) witches which fly in seconds from the Canary Islands to Cuba (124–6), all contrive to produce a gruesomely verisimilar *tranche de vie* of life in pre- and post-independence Cuba. Though based on Montejo's personal life, it speaks on behalf of a people denied access to the fruits of this earth, and therefore stands as a testimony to the injustice of colonialist political systems.

One other extremely important *testimonio* of this period is Rigoberta Menchú's autobiography, which, like *Biografía de un cimarrón*, is at once personal testimony and ethnobiography. A book of thirty-four carefully organised chapters, *Me llamo Rigoberta Menchú y así me nació la conciencia* (1983) tells the story of her life, beginning with her childhood lived in Chimel, a small village in the *altiplano* in Guatemala near San Miguel de Uspantán, which is the capital of the north-western province of Quiché. We learn of how, as a young girl, she was forced, like the rest of her family, to work at the *finca* in the lowlands in subhuman conditions at the hands of the *mestizo ladinos*, of how landowners referred to as the Garcías, the Brols and the Martínez, and soldiers gradually destroyed the Indian community, and of how the Indians decided to resist – with force if necessary – the unlawful expropriation of their lands. Rigoberta Menchú describes the role played by her father, Vicente Menchú, in this consciousness-raising process in which he networks with unions and other Indian communities and then joins the Comité de Unidad Campesina, an organisation defending peasants' rights, for which he suffered imprisonment and torture, as did Rigoberta's brother and mother. (A revolutionary christian group was formed bearing Vicente Menchú's name, after his death by burning in the Spanish Embassy in Guatemala on 31 January 1980.) Rigoberta also describes her own role as a catalyst in enabling surrounding Indian communities to defend themselves, for which she used her previous experience as a catechist. The narrative shows how this conflict between the peasants and the military gradually takes on political connotations, suggested by the later use of the word *compañero/compañera* to indicate 'comrade'. *Me llamo Rigoberta Menchú* concludes with a description of the forced exile from Guatemala of its author. What is remarkable about this autobiography is that it is, like no other text published to date, an authentic example of the vision of life for a Quiché community harassed by an enemy that, literally and linguistically, it does not understand. Rigoberta Menchú herself, though clearly one of the most adept communicators in her community (in this she followed in her father's footsteps) only learned Spanish some three years before she began telling her story, sitting in Paris with an interviewer and a tape-recorder, at the age of twenty-three. It is not a text for the fainthearted as the 'horror movie' description of the torture and public burning of the so-called subversives, including Rigoberta's brother, in Chajul on 24 September 1979 in Chapter XXIV makes quite clear. An important statement on the injustice suffered by the Amerindian population of Central America, *Me llamo Rigoberta Menchú* was awarded the Nobel Peace Prize in 1992; the medal is on display in the Museum of the Templo Mayor in Mexico City until democracy returns to Guatemala. Menchú's notoriety grew exponentially when some of the claims she made in her book were publicly denounced by a US academic, David Stoll, who spent some time in Guatemala researching her story; his book, *Rigoberta Menchú and the Story of All Poor Guatemalans* (1999), unleashed a storm of protest, and the debate about who is telling the truth rages to this day.

Of all the Latin American countries Brazil is the one with arguably the most vibrant and varied tradition of orature. From the *literatura de cordel* (particularly the popular legends about the *cangaçeiros* of Limpião in the 1920s and 1930s printed in pamphlets; see *Literatura de cordel: antologia*, and Curran) to the *romance-reportagem* (see Simpson; Johnson; Craig-Odders et al.) to the more recent *favela*-narratives, Brazil has given birth to a wealth of texts which could be incorporated within the broader parameters of what is known in the Spanish American countries as *testimonio*. Undoubtedly the most significant

Brazilian text to express an authentically popular structure of feeling is Paulo Lins's *Cidade de Deus* (1997), which very quickly became an international bestseller, translated into six languages, a process accelerated by the release in 2002 of the Oscar-winning blockbuster film of the same title, directed by Fernando Meirelles and Katia Lund (for more on the film see Hart, '*Cidade de Deus*'). Lins's text describes the everyday lives of a group of gangsters – including, inter alia, Busca-Pé, Barbantinho, Acerola, Inferninho, Tutuca, Martelo, Carlinho Pretinho, Pelé, Pará, and Manguinha – as they struggle to survive in the dog-eat-dog environment of the *favelas*. Though Lins's *Cidade de Deus* is referred to as a 'romance' (novel) in its published title, it is based on empiric research carried out by the author in the housing project, Cidade de Deus, one of the *favelas* on the outskirts of Rio de Janeiro where Paulo Lins grew up (his family moved there when he was seven years old). The events depicted in this text – the drug trafficking and gang warfare which characterised the neighbourhood in the 1960s, 1970s and 1980s – are rooted in fact. As Lins has pointed out, the characters depicted are 'based on real people' who 'had already gained public visibility in the Brazilian press by the time the researched facts surfaced' (Lins, 'Cities of God' 129). Especially as a result of the massive media coverage which followed the screening of the film version, a number of dissenting voices emerged, arguing that the book – like the film – was not telling the truth about life in the *favela* and, furthermore, was exploiting that reality for personal gain. As M. V. Bill, the self-appointed spokesman of the *favelas*, put it in an open message: 'They turned our people into stereotypes, and they have given them nothing in exchange. Even worse, they stereotyped them as fiction and sold it as if it were true' (Bill 123). Lins responded to this charge by pointing to the research which he had carried out in order to create the novel, and stuck to his contention that the book – like the film – 'is true to the reality of the large Brazilian cities' (Lins, 'Cities of God' 127, 128). Ultimately, though, he went on to argue, the book is art and therefore must be allowed some poetic licence:

> Any schoolboy knows that poetic license is used to give the work rhythm, to elaborate the narrative, to create the plot and the suspense, to establish the difference between an account and art, finally to thrill the reader. Both in the film and in the book, this poetic license was used in order to achieve such artistic goals. (Lins, 'Cities of God' 128)

Examination of Lins's *Cidade de Deus* certainly bears this out; more significant than its putative realism is its extraordinary expressive power, its 'poetic charge', which makes it very different from the typical Spanish American *testimonio*. In an interview for *El País* Lins stated that his use of poetic imagery was quite deliberate: 'I thought that if I didn't put a poetic charge into the work nobody would be able to read such horror' (Arias). Indeed, as Lúcia Nagib has pointed out, the first ten pages of the book are 'written in a deliberately poetic way, full of alliterations, rhymes and figures of speech' (Nagib

33); in this way we 'witness the evolution of a language that, through onomatopoeia, synthesis and aggression, attempts to materialise gunshots, the cut and death' (34). The poetry is normally reserved in Lins's text for the short, sharp descriptions of the material setting of the favela:

> Ainde hoje, o céu azula e estrelece o mundo, as matas enverdecem a terra, as nuvens clareiam as vistas e o homen inova avermelhando o rio. Aqui agora uma favela, a neofavela de cimento, armada de becos-bocas, sinistros-silêncios, com gritos-desesperos no correr das vielas e na indecisão das encruzilhadas. (Lins, *Cidade de Deus* 16)

Onomatopoeia ('becos-bocas'), Joycean portmanteau constructions ('sinistros-silêncios' 'gritos-desesperos'), semantic ambiguity (How does man innovate the river? Why does he redden the river? Is it with his blood? If so, why would death necessarily imply innovation?) – all these techniques contrive to produce a powerfully poetic expression. The aim behind this use of poetic imagery is to illuminate the harshness of the environment of the *favela*: 'Poesia, minha tia, illumine as certezas dos homens e os tons de minhas palavras. É que arrisco a prosa mesmo com balas atravessando os fonemas' (Lins, *Cidade de Deus* 21). In an extraordinarily condensed metaphor Lins is able to combine the idea of the illumination of the *favelas* with, on the one hand, the image of gunfire lighting up the darkness and, on the other, the spark of poetry which weaves its way through the phonemes of his words. This poetic use of language is thrown into relief in the clinical, almost Hemingwayesque way in which the gruesome events of the *favela* are described, such as when Inferninho kills Francisco for being a grass (54), or when Pelé and Pará shoot people to death in the hotel room (66), or a gangster slowly cuts his girlfriend's baby to pieces (69), or the husband who cuts his wife's lover's head off and throws it into his wife's lap (70–1). The description of violent actions is, indeed, typically kept low-key and factual, as if to suggest that their significance cannot be enhanced by the use of adjectives or metaphors. There is no remorse, no psychology, no sense of innerness. As Roberto Schwarz suggests: 'Choreographic exactitude fuses with a blurring of good and evil' (Schwarz, 'Paulo Lins's Novel' 6). Sometimes bullets speak louder than words; as what might be described as the leitmotif of the text puts it, in notably onomatopoeic terms: 'Falha a fala. Fala a bala' (Lins, *Cidade de Deus* 21). Lins's *Cidade de Deus* irrevocably transformed the paradigm of the Latin American *testimonio* by introducing a level of vibrant poeticity into a genre which, until then, had been characterised by a conventional diet of verisimilitude, realism and historicity.

## Latino/a and *Brazuca* Literature

In this period a new genre, or sub-genre, emerged within the Latin American literary canon, Latino/a literature, which may be defined as literature written in Spanish, Portuguese, English, or a mixture of these languages such as Spanglish, by authors of Hispanic or Brazilian descent who presently reside in the United States on a permanent basis, and/or which has a Hispanic or Brazilian focus. Certainly some important examples of Latino literature were published in the 1940s, and according to some critics a long time before that, but the crescendo of its popularity may be located in the period stretching from the 1970s until the present day.[2] During the 1970s Latino/a writers were mainly published by Latino presses such as Bilingual Review and Arte Público Press, but since the 1980s they have branched out into the major publishing houses: Julia Alvarez (Alonquin Books), Ana Castillo (Norton), Sandra Cisneros (Random House), Dagoberto Glib (Grove Press), Cristina García (Knopf), and Helena Viramontes (Dutton) (Torres, 'US Latino/a Literature', 1). Latino/a literature has some way to go before it is officially canonised in the university curriculum. In the words of Lourdes Torres, '[a]s a stepchild of both English and Spanish departments it participates in the literary canons of neither' (2).

One of the classics of Latino literature is *Mi querido Rafa* (1981) by Rolando Hinojosa (b. 1929). Set in Klail City, it tells the story of Jehú, a Chicano loan officer, who works in a local bank, and uses his position there to back the political campaign of Ira Escobar, who won the Democratic primary while running against the incumbent candidate, Roger Terry; Ira is outwitted by Terry, however, when the latter decides to run as an independent and gets the coveted seat in Washington. As the complicated plot unfolds, it becomes clear that Jehú has been set up by Noddy, his boss, and the story ends with a scene in which he is asked to resign. The intriguing thing about the novel is its structure and its language. The first half of the novel consists of twenty-two letters from Jehú to his cousin, Rafa, which show how Jehú gets caught up in the muddy waters of politics, unbeknownst to him; the second half incorporates a series of testimonies of people who knew Jehú during the period in which he supported Ira Escobar's election campaign. The language is a delicious blend of Spanglish; it interjects Spanish words in English sentences, and vice versa, and thereby sustains a credible code-switching linguistic environment. A very subtle novel, *Mi querido Rafa* has established Hinojosa as one of the most important Chicano writers of his time; this was confirmed when he was awarded the Casa de las Américas Prize.

Latino literature is often commonly interpreted to mean literature written in English by writers of Hispanic descent; one of the best known Latino writers

---

[2] A critic such as Luis Leal, for example, traces Latino literature back to the seventeenth century, his definition of the genre being literature written in Spanish which focuses on the land now known as the United States. Thus, the chronicle *Historia de la Nueva México, 1610* by Gaspar Pérez de Villagrá (1555–1620) is included as an early example of Chicano literature (Arias and Gonzales-Berry 654), but it is preferable to retain the term for late twentieth-century literature, when it achieved canonic status. The desire to rewrite the canon of Spanish American literature from the vantage-point of Latino literature is not uncommon, as the recent *Masterpieces of Latino Literature*, ed. Frank Magill, suggests; this anthology contains sections on writers such as Cortázar and Manuel Puig whose connections with what is normally known as Latino literature are sketchy, to say the least.

within this vein is Oscar Hijuelos whose novel, *The Mambo Kings Sing of Love* (1989), won the Pulitzer Prize in 1990. In some senses like a *Bildungsroman*, the novel describes the adventures of a group of Cuban musicians, with a particular focus on the Castillo brothers, Cesar and Nestor, who arrived in New York in 1949, hoping to make their fame as musicians. A raunchy and raw novel, *The Mambo Kings Sing of Love* is not for the puritanical reader. Unlike the classic formation-novel *The Mambo Kings Sing of Love* does not describe a learning curve in the mind of the main protagonist, Cesar; his life is described as a seemingly endless procession from one woman's body to another and bears more traces of a Maroon biography than that of a classic *Bildungsroman*. When Cesar lies dying at the end of the novel, for example (he is suffering from kidney failure because of his excessive drinking), his life is not provided with a perspective produced by hindsight; rather he simply longingly recalls the many women he has slept with. Perhaps the most skilful aspect of the novel is the underlining of the interplay between the life of the lover described in their songs, and the life the singers lead: during the short period of happiness before his demise as a result of kidney failure, Cesar becomes '[l]ike a character in a happy habanera' (Hijuelos 368).

One genre in which there has been an effective presence of Latino/a writers has been the short story. The *Cuentos Chicanos* anthology, edited by Rudolfo Anaya and Antonio Márquez, gives a good indication of the dominant themes within short Chicano fiction. In general, the stories in this collection are witness to a people in transition, struggling to cling on and assert its identity, caught in a no-man's-land between two cultures. Thus, some of the stories have an epic quality about them. 'The Migrant', by Mario Suarez, for example, tells the story of a young man, Teofilo, who tries to keep mind and soul together as a migrant worker; his story of attempting to bring up a family despite a hostile economic environment, though personalised, is meant as an ethno-history of a displaced people. Not surprisingly, given their ethnographic bent, a number of the stories use allegory to convey their message. Ana Castillo's 'Ghost Talk', for example, tells the story of a young girl whose Mexican mother was seduced by her Anglo work supervisor and made pregnant. The story describes how the young girl enacts her revenge and is meant to be understood as an allegory of the clash of Hispanic and Anglo cultures, since it essentially re-writes the trauma of the conquest in a new geographical context. Denise Chávez's 'Willow Game' re-enacts, through the allegory of an uprooted willow tree, the pain felt by women from male violence. Not all the stories are ethnographic – Rudolfo Anaya's 'B. Traven is Alive and Well in Cuernavaca' and Juan Bruce-Novoa's 'The Manuscript' defiantly focus on the process of their own telling – but the majority of them use the narrative of an individual's biography as a vehicle with which to express a community's experience of political disempowerment.

Also important within this genre is literature written by Latinas. As Lourdes Torres has pointed out, Latina writers such as Cherríe Moraga, Aurora Levins Morales, Rosario Morales, and Gloria Anzaldúa, 'subvert both Anglo and

Latino patriarchal definitions of culture', thereby appropriating a new space which 'seeks to integrate ethnicity, class, gender, sexuality, and language' (Torres, 'Construction', 272). Indeed, Cherríe Moraga's work expresses a triple disenfranchisement, that of being Latino/a in an Anglo society, that of being female in a macho society, and that of being gay in a heterosexual society. A poet, playwright and essayist, Moraga uses each of these genres to express this disenfranchisement, sometimes in a vituperative manner. What is fascinating about Moraga's work is the way she works through cultural symbols, feminising them and lesbianising them; in the primal scene of the birth of the New World, she identifies not with Cortés nor La Malinche, nor with Christ nor Moctezuma, but with Coyolxauhqui, the daughter of Coatlicue, the principal female Aztec goddess, who is murdered by her brother, Huizilopotchli, the God of War ('El mito azteca', *Last Generation*, 73–6). Her utopia is a place she calls Queer Aztlán, a nation in which Latino/a culture is respected, gays are free, and the environment is respected (145–74); in a sense, one could argue that her work is an attempt to body that land into existence.

One of the most significant of the Latina writers is Helena Maria Viramontes (b. 1954) who has published a number of collections of short stories, including *The Moths and Other Stories* (1985) and *Under the Feet of Jesus*. Two main themes emerge within her work: family relationships and the female body, evident in stories such as 'Growing', 'Birthday', and 'The Cariboo Cafe'. The experience of womanhood is positivised, and that of masculinity negativised. The universe of the male is typified by the Church which is presented in Viramontes's short stories as a social institution which alienates women. It is perhaps not surprising to discover that murder by women of their male tormentors is presented as a comprehensible outcome in stories such as 'The Broken Web' and 'Neighbors'. Viramontes's most anthologised short story, 'Moths', focuses on the bonding between a miscreant fourteen-year-old girl and her grandmother. When the narrator works in the garden she feels a oneness with the universe, which is noticeably absent from her experience of the chapel in Jay's Market (Viramontes 25). Perhaps most distinctive about this story, and not a common technique in her work, is the note of magical realism which occurs in the final paragraphs of the story. The protagonist and her *abuelita*, now deceased, are in a bath: 'Then the moths came. Small, gray ones that came from her soul and out through her mouth fluttering to light, circling the single dull light bulb of the bathroom' (28). Viramontes's fiction, as 'The Moths' suggests, is complex and sophisticated, and evokes with great poignancy the 'feminine' within the universe.

The other main chord within the symphony of contemporary Latino/a writing, although some would dispute the validity of its presence in this section, includes those Spanish American writers who were born in Latin America but who now reside in the United States, and who write in Spanish. Unlike Latino/a authors who write in English and whose audience is located within the United States, these writers are writing for an audience which is Spanish-speaking. Typically, this genre is created by writers who also teach at university level in the United

States. Examples are Eduardo Espina, born in Uruguay, Carlota Caulfield and Jesús Barquet, born in Cuba, José Antonio Mazzotti and Miguel Angel Zapata, born in Peru, and Armando Romero, born in Colombia. Their work might be characterised in terms of a letter sent home to their compatriots. Like the writing more traditionally associated with Latino/a literature, it focuses on the experience of life in the United States. Since, unlike other Latino/a writers, they tend to write in Spanish even though they inhabit an Anglophone environment, it could be argued that they are self-consciously using their literature in order to create a 'magic capsule' of Spanish which separates them from the language-world they inhabit on a day-to-day basis (Hart, 'La cápsula mágica').

A relative latecomer on the scene of Latino literature is Brazilian-American, or *Brazuca* as it is commonly known, literature. There is a long tradition of autobiographies by Portuguese immigrants in the United States (Francisco Cota Fagundes lists twelve of them, beginning with *The Autobiography of Charles Peter*; see Cota Fagundes 702–3), but it is only in the last three decades that Brazilian emigration to the US has been demographically noteworthy, and only in the last decade or so that *Brazuca* literature has become a significant strand within Latin America's emigré literature. There have been plays (such as Edel Holz's *Meu Brasil é Aqui* performed in South Boston in September 2004), and poetry (such as Angela Bretas's anthology, *Brava Gente Brasileira* [2004]), but the favoured genre has been the novel. Important *Brazuca* novelists of the 1980s include José Victor Bicalho and Silvano Santiago, and of the 1990s, Tereza Albues, Júlio Bráz, Angela Bretas, Norma Guimarães and Luiz Alberto Scotto (for discussion of the latter's novel *46th Street: o Caminho Americano* [1993], see Franconi). Bretas's *Sonho Americano* (1997) is paradigmatic of *Brazuca* literature in a number of key respects; an indication of the breadth of its impact is suggested that the first edition – in the US in 1997 – was followed by a Brazilian second edition (São Paolo, 2003). This novel offers a sense of balance about the immigrant experience in the US, contrasting the benefits of working within a more efficient economy with the downside of a society overrun by rules; as one of the characters of *Sonho Americano* says, after looking at all the regulations on a notice-board at a camping-site: 'Isso é camping ou campo de concentração?' (Bretas 79). In America, self-reliance is key ('aqui na América é cada um por si e Deus por todos'; 722), and this leads to some problems of adjustment for the *Brazucas* (for further discussion see Andrade Tosta, 'American Dream').

## The Gay/Lesbian Novel

Gay and lesbian writing has only recently been co-opted into the Latin American literary canon, and that largely as a result of the 1991 study by David William Foster, *Gay and Lesbian Themes in Latin American Writing*. Most of the works he studies come from Argentina and Mexico, countries with historically active gay communities; the main authors he studies are Reinaldo Arenas, Isaac Chocrón, Sylvia Molloy, and Luis Zapata.[3] In this section I have decided to focus on six novels, two by Hispanic men (Puig and Arenas), two by Brazilian men (Santiago and Noll) and two by women (Peri Rossi and Molloy), and concentrate on their literary qualities rather than their gayness. This is an appropriate approach, since in none of these works is there an explicit campness, or, indeed, a revelation-scene in which the protagonist suddenly realises who (s)he is. The insights in these writers' novels echo those in the work of critical theorists such as Paul Julian Smith, Eve Kosofsky Sedgwick and Jonathan Dollimore, who problematise the notion that homosexuality is a discrete or essentialist identity, and instead see it as a discursive construct.[4] In the case of Manuel Puig, as we shall see, the discursive construct of homosexuality is seen to be predicated upon the performativity of art.

The most significant Hispanic gay writer, and indeed, post-Boom writer, is the Argentine Manuel Puig (1932–89), whose best work, arguably, is *El beso de la mujer araña* (1973). The sixteen chapters of this novel focus on the relationship in a prison cell between Valentín, a revolutionary subversive convicted of terrorist activites, and Luis Alberto Molina, a gay man convicted of corrupting a minor. Puig's novel includes a number of different discourses: (i) the colloquial conversations between Valentín and Molina about their everyday life in the prison cell (food, excrement, etc.), (ii) the Hollywood films Molina lovingly recounts to Valentín, (iii) discussions between Molina and the Prison Inspector, and (iv) the footnotes which give scientific psychoanalytic information about the 'perverse' nature of homosexuality. An important aspect of this novel is its willingness to address the issue of gender difference; in Puig's novel this takes the form of reference to Molina's homosexuality and paedophilia (since the latter crime is the reason for his imprisonment). The relationship between Valentín and Molina eventually becomes homoerotic and, in telescoped form, the novel alludes to male–male sex (Puig 265–66). It is difficult to extract the precise nature of the relationship and, indeed, if Molina actually did betray Valentín to the authorities; chapter 14 ends with Molina asking for the sensitive information Valentín wants to relay to the outside world, and chapter 15 is based on a police report describing Molina's movements once released from jail and his eventual murder, by parties presumably close to Valentín in retaliation for (actual or presumed) betrayal (Puig 279). In an about-turn of roles, Molina dies as a martyr for a cause in which he is not immediately involved. The final message of Puig's novel is fundamentally ambiguous in that it relates the dissidence of perverse sexual behaviour to political dissidence in such a way that the parallels sought between the sex and politics, the personal

---

[3] An important and theoretically sophisticated analysis of gay culture appears in Paul Julian Smith's work, *Laws of Desire*. A good gay reading of modern narrative by Hispanic women, including discussion of Peri Rossi and Sylvia Molloy, appears in Pertusa Seva's dissertation, 'Escribiendo entre corrientes: Carmen Riera, Esther Tusquets, Cristina Peri Rossi y Sylvia Molloy'.

[4] See Smith; Kosofsky Sedgwick; and Dollimore.

and the public are ambivalent. And yet, finally, despite the seriousness of the themes treated (political versus sexual deviance, the law and the penal system, the normal and the dysfunctional) Puig's novel ultimately reduces the various functions of the characters to the performance of roles: since Molina performs as a martyr for the cause, does that make him a communist? Since Valentín performs sexually with a homosexual, does that make him gay? The fact that both Molina and Valentín do something out of character questions the notion of the character as a self-coherent identity understood in an Aristotelian sense. *El beso de la mujer araña*, thus, emphasises the ontological falseness but unavoidability of roles; in Oscar Wildesque fashion Puig suggests that human beings simply play different roles (bourgeois, woman, man, etc.) and are in essence nothing more than masks. In this resides the most subversive point of Puig's text. Since the various footnotes which periodically punctuate the text lead to no conclusion about homosexuality that is not subversive, and, since they simply expose the lack of validity of societal, cultural and, indeed psychoanalytic systems used to interpret homosexuality, we must see them as acting, not as a true subconscious, which we might expect, given the Freudian references, but as an inappropriate hermeneutic taxonomy having no power to judge the relationship between Molina and Valentín. Indeed, the footnotes simply constitute a misreading of a sexuality which remains undefined and indefinable throughout the novel; the nearest approximation we have to the riddle of sexuality is the suspension points which punctuate the description of the sexual relationship between Molina and Valentín (Puig 266–67). Sexuality becomes an ambiguous trace in the novel's structure; once more Puig's text underlines the notion of the performance of roles rather than the discovery of an authentic, self-identical self.

An important writer of the post-Boom novel is the gay Cuban novelist, Reinaldo Arenas (1943–92). One of his best novels, *Otra vez el mar* (1982), treats themes which are common in his work: desire, love, the individual pitted against society. Part I of the novel is written from the perspective of a young Cuban wife married to Héctor, a dreamy young man who finds it difficult to keep down a job, while they are spending a holiday at the beach in September 1969, with their small child. There is a type of plot; a woman and her son move into the cabin next door to Héctor and his wife, and the son is found later that evening dead on the beach, although the cause of his death remains a mystery. More important than the plot, however, is the novel's Joycean rejection of the limitations of Euclidean space and time. At various points the narrative is punctuated, without any warning, by scenes from the past (as when Héctor goes off to become a revolutionary in the mountains before the 1959 Revolution, and they witness a death by murder squad in Havana soon after the Revolution), as well as dream scenes (such as the scene early on in which the Trojan war over Helen is enacted on a beach with the soldiers using their penises for swords, or when the Virgin Mary and God appear, accompanied by angels who walk across the ocean and then fly off in an aeroplane, or when a food line in Havana is merged with a Nazi concentration camp in which individuals are burnt alive on the slightest pretext). The main aim of Part I of the novel is to assert a new type of language in contradistinction to the language of state power, one which rejects the dictates of time (as encapsulated by the government slogan of 'ten million tons of sugar by next year, 1970!'; Arenas 52) and, indeed, space (since the time of the Trojan war is shown to be porous with that of present-day Cuba), in order to pursue a vision of life which privileges desire over all else. This defiance of the official version of Castro's Cuba (Arenas was persecuted and imprisoned by Castro for being a homosexual), submerged in Part I, emerges openly in Part II, an angry set of free-verse poems, prose passages, timid first encounter conversations between gays on the beach, gay love scenes, and exposure of the hypocrisy of the Castro regime. The criticism of the regime meant, of course, that *Otra vez el mar* could not be published in Cuba; Canto IV has a section which ironically describes the business of officially sponsored literary publication as a monster whose anus exhales the perfume of odes and whose mouth disgorges vomit 'in its moments of greatest orgy' (294). Arenas's work is significant not only in terms of its expression of the gay's right to free speech in Spanish America but also because of its lyric search for a world as yet untouched by human hypocrisy.

*La nave de los locos* (1984) by Cristina Peri Rossi (b. 1941) is a playfully postmodern gay text which rewrites the alphabet of Christian culture. It describes the misadventures of a character whose name is simply a letter of the alphabet, Equis (that is, 'X'), in a variety of urban settings; the novel includes episodes describing sordid sexual encounters, far-fetched dream-sequences, and Equis's philosophising about life and the universe with his companions, Vercingetorix and Graciela. The novel has little narrative structure and is furthermore punctuated by a backdrop-discourse which describes in meticulous detail the celebrated eleventh-century tapestry depicting the creation of the world which is held in Gerona Cathedral, Spain. Peri Rossi's text declares its own epigonic status to a variety of other texts such as Sebastian Brandt's *Narrenschift* (1494), Pío Baroja's *La nave de los locos* (1925), and Katherine Anne Porter's *Ship of Fools* (1959). All of these works ultimately derive inspiration from the historical practice common in Europe, and especially Germany, in the first half of the fifteenth century, when ships were loaded with mad people and sent downstream in order to drop their human cargo off at another unsuspecting town; though rooted in a particular historical practice, the *navis stultiferum* soon became a literary *topos* emblematizing the uncertainties of man's life. This notion is used in Peri Rossi's text to undercut ironically the androcentric narrative of the Creation, as symbolised by the tapestry of the Creation; in effect her novel strives to deconstruct the patriarchal notion of Godhead, which itself is the madness of the world. Thus, the bathetic vicissitudes of the life of Equis, and his friends are interspersed with grandiose, eloquent descriptions of the cathedral tapestry (see Hart, *White Ink* 124–31). *La nave de los locos* is a playful feminocentric text which contrasts the macro-narrative of the Creation story with the micro-narrative of the sordid antics of three individuals caught in the trap of modern urban life.

A significant gay novel of the post-Boom is Sylvia Molloy's *En breve cárcel* (1981) which, as the title of its translation into English suggests (*Certificate of Absence*, published in 1989), is a textual memory which focuses on absence, in this case, that of the narrator's previous lovers, Vera and Renata. Described by one critic as 'a self-conscious feminist text that defends its marginality and refuses to comply with many of the expectations traditional readers may have of masculine texts' (Raymond Williams 88), this novel possesses a strikingly intra-feminine quality. There are men in the narrative, and the plot concerns the triangular (and troublesome) relationship between the three female protagonists. The second chapter of the novel focuses on the narrator's memory of her sister, how they were bathed together and used each other as mirrors of being, and Part II, Chap. 7, concludes with a jubilant sense of the unity between the women in her life: 'yo quería – madre, hermana, amante – que estuvieran conmigo, yo vivo sino por ustedes' (Molloy, *En breve cárcel*, 147). *En breve cárcel* is at the furthest remove from the action-packed magical-realist novel format; it concentrates on the details of everyday life, social etiquette, meeting people, eating meals, and so forth, at times in a disorientatingly perceptive way. Molloy's novel is being written in the room in which the narrator had an affair with Vera, and is an attempt to remember that relationship and salvage it from the ravages of time. Each detail, even the most trivial, is lovingly and painfully recorded, and becomes obsessive in a way which is redolent of Proust. One striking metaphor, which occurs twice, is the connection between bones and text (which are negativised) and skin and voice (which are valorised); the important thing is to record the past before it fades, the voice before it turns into text, and the skin before it turns into bones (122; see also 38). Despite this loving attention to detail, there is a sense throughout the novel that the true meaning of the events lies in an elsewhere which is unrecorded, but which nevertheless gives rise to the events narrated, as when the narrator speaks of 'Conversaciones [...] alrededor de algo que no se nombra' (54). The effect of distance with regard to 'something unnamed' is retextualised in the novel through the distance created by the reported speech mode of the novel. *En breve cárcel* alludes to its own genesis, particularly in the detailed description of the room in which the narrator is sitting. *En breve cárcel* is also intertextual in that it defiantly alludes to other literary texts: to Proust in its anguished, recording mode, and to Shakespeare, specifically Desdemona, from *Othello*, whose cruel death at the hand of her husband is used as a metaphor to describe the relationship between the narrator and Vera in Part II, Chap. 5. And yet, just as the text is gradually consumed by its literariness – this story is also the story of growing into literature – so a sense of otherness creeps into the text. And since the body and writing are seen as mutually dependent – '[p]ero hoy escribe, y quería escribirse y leerese en un cuerpo: está ahora sola con el suyo, también con la imagen de la que escribe, de la que lee' (107) – the alienation produced by writing also leads to an alienation of the body: 'El cuerpo – su cuerpo – es de otro. Desconocimiento del cuerpo, contacto con el cuerpo, placer a violencia, no importa: el cuerpo es de otro' (31). In this sense, the act of writing is built on an attempt to find a space in which to reside, specifically within the house of language, to use Heidegger's favourite metaphor. Words and the phenomenal world fuse, for example, in a remarkable descriptive passage in Part I, Chap. 5: 'Ve que las palabras se levantan una vez más, como se levanta ella, agradece la letra ondulante que la enlaza, reconoce las cicatrices de un cuerpo que acaricia' (67). While *En breve cárcel* ends on a pessimistic note – a nihilism predicated on the title, taken from one of Quevedo's gloomy death-inspired poems to Lisi – there is also a sense, hinted at in the above passage, that language offers a home.

Authored by a writer who has been described as 'openly gay', Silviano Santiago's *Stella Manhattan* (1985) is anything but a trawl through the vicissitudes of gay experience in Brazil. In Borgesian fashion, Santiago's novel sequentially builds up pictures of reality – it consists of three parts and eleven separate though interlocking sections – in order then to dismantle them all one by one. The opening pages of the novel give a foretaste of what lies ahead; a setting is provided (Manhattan Island, New York, 18 October 1969) in which a young woman, Stella Manhattan, is greeting another beautiful day in America (*Stella Manhattan* 11). But then we discover that Stella Manhattan is the alias of Eduardo de Costa e Silva, a young Brazilian man who is working at the Brazilian Consulate in the Rockefeller Center. As the chapter unfolds it becomes clear the protagonist is sometimes Stella and sometimes Eduardo – the reason behind this dual identity is not at first explained to the reader. Eduardo's gayness is introduced obliquely via his developing relationship with Paco, a gay Cuban who lives in a nearby apartment (29–37), as well as his friendship with Vianna, who confesses his true sexual identity to Eduardo in gay code: 'Também sou entendido' (52). Just as the reader is growing accustomed to the development of a set of interlocking life-stories, however, the carpet is pulled from beneath him with the introduction of a section called 'Começo: o narrador' (67) in which the narrative consciousness suddenly splits into two; in the interior monologue which follows – 'Você volta ao escritório e recomeça a escrever pedindo a minha ajuda' (73) – it may be the narrator and the writer who are being alluded to, though it is difficult to be sure, and the hermeneutic difficulty of the text is compounded by the inclusion immediately afterwards of a rather quirky theoretical discussion of the conflicts between Christianity and Judaism, and between capitalism and communism (81–4). From this point onwards the novel jumps into a highly experimental gear, becoming almost a sequence of set pieces exposing different ways of conjuring up reality in a novel, ranging from quick-paced dialogue (III, 93–117), to the use of italics to indicate the unspoken level of a conversation (in this case between Marcelo and his self-important US professor, Aníbal; IV, 121–37), an exercise in punctuation-free, flowing prose (this time between Aníbal and his resentful wife, Leila; V, 139–46), the use of a sequence of short narrative fragments in order to create a sense of the disconnectedness underlying reality (VI, 147–65), even a deliberate parody of the stilted prose style of a nineteenth-century Realist novel (VII, 167–85). It is in Part III that the various threads of the novel are (at least on one level) drawn together as the novel apes the idiom of a detective novel; Eduardo is being interrogated by the FBI about the political credentials of his Cuban friend, Paco (207–22), as well as being suspected himself of being a Brazilian terrorist (254). But there is anything but a clean ending to this novel. Eduardo and Paco are arrested in the street late one evening, kept in a cell with other inmates for the night, after which Paco is found to have committed suicide and, perhaps, suffered rape before he did so; though Eduardo is a prime suspect for this crime, there is a cover-up and he is not charged (258–60). That his detective-novelesque mystery is left unsolved ultimately exposes *Stella Manhattan* as a Borgesian send-up of a spy thriller-cum-gay murder mystery.

*A céu aberto* (1996) by João Gilberto Noll (b. 1946) can be described accurately as a gay novel though, like Santiago's *Stella Manhattan*, it is not a thesis-novel about gay rights in Brazil. The plot is very sketchy, describing the (seemingly random) events which happen to an unnamed narrator, which include going with his brother to ask for the help of their father who is fighting on an unnamed battle front, then enlisting himself in the war, getting seduced by a paedophile called Arthur (one of the few people with a name in the novel), deserting, marrying a woman who may or may not be an incarnation of his brother, going to Stockholm with Arthur's son, with whom he has a fling, strangling his wife, becoming a sex slave on a ship, escaping and then being arrested on terrorism charges; the novel ends with the narrator being seduced by a prostitute in his hotel room. The impression of dizziness that the average reader will experience when reading this novel is compounded by its lack of spatial and temporal co-ordinates, the absence of names for the main characters (apart from Arthur as already mentioned), as well as the lack of any sense of causal structure to the events described. Emotionally the text is drawn to the orgasmic nature of sexual excitement, and describes – in rapid succession – various sexual acts, mainly homosexual but also heterosexual and *ménage-à-trois*. Women are strikingly absent from the novel, with the exception of the narrator's wife, although she is presented as simply a body ready for procreation and is swiftly killed off (not that the narrator feels particularly worried about this fact). Gay sex is typically presented in terms of the brutal exercise of power, as when a military officer, without any warning, forces the narrator to fellate him (Noll, *A céu aberto* 53), or when the narrator sodomises Arthur's son after which he discovers he is splattered in blood (105), or when he is kept for months as a sex slave below deck on a refugee boat and raped repeatedly by a sweaty, toothless fifty-year-old sailor who has terrible BO (141–58). The style of the novel is flowing, breathless, phantasmagoric, and offers an important prop at once for the existential questioning which punctures the text at crucial intervals ('eu era ainda o mesmo homem?', 145), as well as a linguistic echo of the non-causal succession of incarnations of the narrator's identity: 'resurgir a primeira manhã dentro de uma nova cápsula de vida como por exemplo un ente escuro da floresta, inominado, fugaz, inapreensível para a percepção alheia' (158). In Noll's *A céu aberto* a straight, omniscient vantage-point is meticulously deconstructed in order to produce a fluid, gay consciousness in which outer and inner worlds merge, 'uma consciência extremada de como as coisas se mostravam no espaço mas ao mesmo tempo me sentia flutuar' (164).

## Afro/a/-Hispanic and Afro/a/-Brazilian Literature

Like Latino/a literature and Spanish American women's writing, Afro/a/-Hispanic literature, that is literature written by Spanish American writers of African descent, has created space for itself in the new Spanish American canon, especially since the 1970s, as Richard Jackson has pointed out ('Emergence' 4). The term Afro/a/-Hispanic literature covers work produced by a multitude of writers ranging from Nicolás Guillén, the national poet of Cuba, to Leoncio Evita (b. 1929), a novelist of Spanish Guinea. The main aim of many of the writers included for discussion here is that of formulating an authentic vision of the life and identity of blacks living in Hispanic America, as expressed from the inside by writers of African descent, rather than by *criollo* writers (the classic case being Gómez de Avellaneda's nineteenth-century novel *Sab* which spilt 'crocodile tears' for the negro). Often the Afro/a/-Hispanic is portrayed as an individual who has suffered political, economic, and emotional oppression by the culture in which (s)he has lived. The work of the Afro/a/-Hispanic writers discussed here constitutes a means whereby the political powerlessness of their race is given voice. What Jean-Paul Sartre said in his now famous essay, *Orphée Noir*, which served as an introduction to an anthology of African and West Indian poets published in 1948, is emblematic of these writers: 'These black men are addressing themselves to black men about black men; their poetry is neither satiric nor imprecatory: it is an awakening to consciousness' (Sartre 16).

An important poet whose work emblematises this 'awakening to consciousness' is the Dominican Blas Jiménez (b. 1949). His poem 'Diálogo negro', from *Exigencias de un cimarrón (en sueños)* (1987), for example, dramatises the poet's discovery of blackness:

> Vino un negro y me dijo
> que el viejo del tío Tom
> era un negrito creado
> por la discriminación. (Watson Miller 73)

As the poem concludes, the 'negro' who brings knowledge of cultural oppression is actually the poet himself. Based on the idea of self-discovery in the mirror, this poem is also meant to be understood as a rallying-cry for all blacks imprisoned by what Jiménez calls the 'white imagination'. A similar type of consciousness-raising occurs in the work of the Ecuadorian poet Adalberto Ortiz (b. 1914). Like Nicolás Guillén, Ortiz evokes the nuances of black-

Hispanic speech in his poetry. His poem 'Yo no sé', for example, though based on apparent unknowing, evokes the injustice of social oppression. As the poem opens:

> ¿Po qué será,
> me pregunto yo,
> que casi todo lo negro
> tan pobre son
> como yo soy?
> Yo no lo sé.
> Ni yo ni Uté. (Watson Miller 99)

Likewise his poem 'Contribución' speaks of the need for the sounds of African music to 'shake up' the whites; as the poem concludes, the Hispanic African symbolises not only the sweetness of sugar cane, but also the 'fire' of revenge:

> porque el alma, la del Africa
> que encadenada llegó
> a esta tierra de América
> canela y candela dio. (Watson Miller 100)

One of the best contemporary Afro-Hispanic short-story writers is Carlos Guillermo Wilson, aka 'Cubena', who was born in Panama City. His short stories are intentionally shocking, and, given their political message, it is perhaps not surprising that they have been censored in Panama. 'El niño de harina', for example, from *Cuentos del negro Cubena* (1971), describes the strange behaviour of a young boy living in the San Miguel district of Panama who persists in pouring flour on himself at night. At first interpreted as a childhood aberration similar to bed-wetting, the last sentence of the story, however, shows the motive for this behaviour to be a profoundly cultural one: 'El niño de harina era negro' (Watson Miller 83). Other works offer a vision of the dispossessed of this earth. The moving tale, 'Una carta', from *Una canción en la madrugada* (1970) by Quince Duncan (b. 1940), for example, presents the world-view of an older woman whose son has left her with eight children to look after (each by a different woman); the son follows the *cimarrón* prototype so common in Duncan's fiction (Smart 156). While the mother refuses to hear any wrong said about her son, the anger associated with this injustice is expressed – poetically – by the image of boiling water which opens the tale and concludes it: 'Afuera, todavía hervía el agua en las venas de la tierra' (Watson Miller 91).

Aida Cartagena Portalatín (1918–94) is one of the few Afra-Hispanic writers known outside her country of origin; she was born in Moca, Dominican Republic. Her work, which spans the genres of poetry, novel and short story, focuses on the dilemma of black identity in Hispanic culture. Her short story, 'La llamaban Aurora (Pasión por Donna Summer)', is written from the 'innocent' perspective of a young black girl who is unable to work out the contradiction between white people's love of Donna Summer's music, and the violent political discrimination that blacks suffer around the globe (Watson Miller 70). The reader is asked to focus on this cultural inconsistency, and invited to conclude that white culture's love of Donna Summer's music is merely another form of cultural oppression.[5]

The work of two Hispanic writers of African descent deserves special mention, and they are the Peruvian Nicomedes Santa Cruz (1925–82) and the Colombian Manuel Zapata Olivella (b. 1920). Nicomedes Santa Cruz is best known for his *décimas*, a traditional poetic form dating from the seventeenth century which he has Africanised. Perhaps the single most famous poem by an African-Hispanic writer is 'Ritmos negros del Perú' by Santa Cruz, which is to be understood as a cultural memorial of the history of his race:

> De Africa llegó mi abuela
> vestida con caracoles,
> la trajeron lo' españoles
> en un barco carabela. (Watson Miller 103)

His poem 'De ser como soy, me alegro' in a straightforward manner speaks on behalf of a non-racialist society:

> Muy claramente se explica
> que, viviendo con honor,
> nacer de cualquier color
> eso a nadie perjudica. (Watson Miller 106)

His work has its roots in the oral tradition of poetic repartee; his poem 'Si tú eres cantor completo', for example, in which he manages to use every letter of the alphabet in four rhymed *décimas*, clearly grows out of this tradition (for further discussion of his work see Ojeda).

Zapata Olivella's masterpiece is *Changó, el gran putas* (1983), which takes as its theme 'the psychical and physical liberation of an entire ethnic group in its confrontation, as African prisoners, with Western culture' (Lewis 112). The novel has five parts, each of which has as its theme a defining moment of history for the peoples of African descent; the first on the slave trade in the early sixteenth century, the second on the early colonial days in the New World, the third on the slave rebellions in the last decade of the eighteenth century in the Caribbean which led to a black republic in Haiti, the fourth on the fight for independence in the sub-continent, and the fifth on the struggle against racism in the United States as seen particularly through the perspective of

---

[5] It is important to note that a new canon has begun to emerge within Afro-Hispanic literature: Afra-Hispanic literature, that is, literature written by Spanish American women of African descent. Portalatín is part of this new canon; see DeCosta and Feal for some discussion of the themes and theorisation of this canon.

Malcolm X's life. Given its broad panoramic focus, *Changó, el gran putas* can legitimately be seen as the epic of the Afro/a/-Hispanic peoples. The most striking feature about the form of the novel is the narrative voice which is transferred from person to person without warning. This technique – which is now part of the narratological repertoire of the modern novel since Faulkner first introduced it in *The Sound and the Fury* in 1929 – is utilised in *Changó, el gran putas* for a specific reason, namely, that of stressing the symmetry between the different lives described, a pattern which is woven round the 'Fall' of the African peoples, their banishment from Africa by Shango, the Yoruba God of thunder and lightning, and their subsequent experience of the diaspora. Olivella's novel is Afrocentric in one other important way, and that is its skill in presenting the historical events of this world from the perspective of the world of the spirit as inhabited by the African gods. In the stomach-churning description of life on the slave-ships in the first part of the novel, for example, Zapata Olivella focuses on the ways in which the African gods accompanied their people on their transatlantic journey to be sure that they were present if they died during the voyage. Similarly, the slave rebellion led by Toussaint L'Ouverture in the French colony of Haiti in 1791 is portrayed through the lens of voodoo. These various themes are brought triumphantly together in the very last paragraph of the novel when the dead are addressed by their ancestors and their actions are placed in the larger, teleological context of Last Things (Olivella 511). This makes it quite clear that Olivella's novel is meant to be understood as transcending the three-dimensional limitations of literature in order to enter the fourth dimension of politics; the last sentence of this 'self-consciously-liberationist' novel, as one critic puts it (Smart 115), functions as a wake-up call for all Americans of African descent to take up the fight for the right to own their own culture.

Though not as clearly demarcated as Afro-Hispanic literature, Afro-Brazilian literature runs a course through Brazilian literature which is parallel to that of its Hispanic cousin, building from rather timid eddies of discontent in the nineteenth century to forthright denunciation of racism in the late twentieth. One of the most famous early examples of Afro-Brazilian angst occurs in Castro Alves's striking poem, 'O navio negreiro' (1868), discussed above in the context of Brazilian Romantic literature (see p. 72), which denounces the inhumanity of life on the slavers; the slaves 'nem são livres p'ra morrer'. The issue of African ethnicity emerges in the Brazilian nineteenth-century novel in ways which echo that of the Spanish American novel; there are a number of skeletons in the cupboard. Aluísio de Azevedo's *O mulato* (1881), for example, paints a powerful picture of the racial prejudice prevalent at the time in northern Brazil, while Adolfo Caminha's *Bom Crioulo* (1895), in Piers Armstrong's words, 'openly addresses interracial homosexual relations' (Armstrong 107). Even a canonised writer such as Machado de Assis is vulnerable to an Afrocentric reading; in a powerful interpretation of his work, Roberto Schwarz, as we have seen, has pointed to a connection between the great writer's parodic, distanced style and his straddling of two different worlds, understood as marked not only by class but also by race (see Schwarz, *A Master*, and discussion above, pp. 245–6). João da Cruz e Souza (1861–98) was the son of slaves, suffered prejudice as a result and edited an abolitionist journal, *Tribuna Popular*. There is something odd, even disturbing, about his Symbolist poems, and their obsession with whiteness (see discussion of his work as a Symbolist above, pp. 115–6). Lima Barreto (1881–1922), son of a (mad) Portuguese father and a black slave, allowed some of his personal experience of racial prejudice to filter into his uneven novel, *Triste fim de Policarpo Quaresma* (1911) (see pp.158–60) One of the most important contemporary Afra-Brazilian writers is Maria da Conceição Evaristo (b. 1946), the author of poetry and short stories which have been published and of a novel which has not (see Aparecida Andrade Salgueiro 121). Her short story *Maria* (1991), published originally in *Cadernos Negros* 14 (1991), and then in English translation in *Callaloo* 18.4 (Fall 1995), translated by Carolyn Richardson Durham, is brutal in its simplicity; the protagonist, Maria, a poor black, is seen talking on a bus to man – her son's father – who is identified as an assailant. She is subsequently attacked by a crowd and loses her life (for fuller discussion, see Aparecida Andrade Salgueiro 126–8).

## The Latin American Novel of the New Millennium

It is difficult to characterise the novel of the new millennium for it has departed at once in several directions, but a few themes and obsessions appear to be making their mark. The brash simplicity of earlier decades, which was often accompanied by a political provocativeness, appears to have been replaced by a more reflective tone. Some novels are profitably viewed as forging new directions in already well-worn territory. Mario Vargas Llosa's *La fiesta del chivo* (2000), for example, on one level is clearly a descendant of a long tradition in Latin American creative writing, the Dictator novel, epitomised by Augusto Roa Bastos's *Yo, el Supremo* and García Márquez's *El otoño del patriarca*. It tells the story of the horrifying excesses of the thirty-one-year dictatorship of the Dominican Republic's General Trujillo, the cruelty with which he had his enemies killed off – often throwing them to the sharks – his enjoyment in publicly humiliating those who worked for him, by raping their wives and daughters – and it offers a vivid picture of the torture cells which are set up by the Trujillo camp in order to find out who killed the benefactor. The details are not for the weak-hearted; the detainees have their eyes gouged out, they suffer repeated electric shocks on the 'Throne', one prisoner is castrated and forced to eat his own testicles while his jailers snigger. All of this offers a recognisable continuity with the Latin American novelistic tradition, of which Vargas Llosa – since the heady days of the Boom – is very much part. There are also elements which mark *La fiesta del chivo* off as a novel very much in the Vargas Llosa mould, including the use of unexpected shifts from one set of events to another (so that we alternately follow the life of a young woman called Urania as well as the events of Trujillo's life, his assassination and the bloody aftermath), which can be traced back to *La ciudad y los perros*, the use of an objectivist, Realist narrative style, and the obsession with violence. But there are also elements in this novel which show a new direction emerging in Vargas Llosa's fiction: the two narratives – Trujillo's life and death on the one hand and Urania's return to her native Dominican Republic after an absence of many years – are brought together in the unexpected denouement (Trujillo 'raped' Urania when she was a fourteen-year-old girl, which led to her rapid departure for the United States since Trujillo was unable to get an erection) which shows Urania's return to be a result of resentment towards her (now invalid) father who sent her knowingly into the Goat's bedroom. The sub-plot – Urania's return – is thus shown to be more important than the grand historical narrative of Trujillo's demise; Urania's life has been emptied of meaning since her 'rape' at the hands of the Goat, and this emptying-out of meaning, the 'desert' which Urania now feels in her soul, comes to stand as a symbol of the destruction of everyman at the hands of political evil.

*El sueño de la historia* (2000) by Jorge Edwards (b. 1931) is redolent in a number of keys respects of the New Historical Novel which has been a popular sub-genre in Latin American literature for a number of decades now, in that it uses historical research to develop a convincing picture of past (for further discussion of the genre see Menton) but it develops the genre in an innovative way. It tells the story of a left-wing emigré, Ignacio Medio, known as 'el Narrador' in the text, who returns to Chile after a long exile abroad during the twilight years of Pinochet's dictatorship, in order to research the lives of an Italian architect, Joaquín Toesca, who was commissioned in the 1780s to complete the palace La Moneda in Santiago, Chile, and his wayward wife, Manuela Fernández. The novel, rather like Dickens's *Tale of Two Cities*, moves alternately between the two life-stories, and, gradually as the novel develops, a number of similarities begin to emerge between the lives of the two men. The Narrator and Joaquin Toesca both have troubled marriages, and their professional life in each case is marked by failure (the Narrator had to leave Chile immediately after Pinochet's coup in 1973, thereby truncating his career, and Toesca's work on La Moneda is littered with difficulties). Yet, perhaps the element which most crucially joins them is that they both live in the aftermath of a failed revolution; the Narrator, 'en su condición de intelectual y de hombre de tendencias de izquierda' (Edwards 245) is intellectually wedded to Salvador Allende's experiment in revolution (1970–73), while Toesca, as an architect, is associated with the sceptical and scientific frame of mind associated with the Enlightenment. At one point the text explicitly questions whether the lives of both men overlap:

> Nosotros, desde nuestro limbo, nos preguntamos si los sentimientos de Toesca al besar a Manuelita, después de saber que había pasado horas encerrada con Juan Josef Goycoolea en la habitación del fondo, no eran similares? ¿Pueden existir sentimientos similares, o por lo menos comparables, a dos siglos de distancia? El hombre es historia, es memoria, y es, a la vez, como se sabe,

desmemoria. Hay una dosis saludable de olvido, ya que la memoria perfecta, la de Funes el Memorioso, nos agobiaría y al fin nos destruiría. (Edwards 87)

At this point the text speculates as to whether the two men would have exchanged notes and found points of similarity (in their experience of marriage, for example). The reference to Borges's famous story, *Funes el Memorioso*, the man who could never forget anything, is apt, given that Edwards's novel focuses on the paradox of the intrinsic importance of memory to the conservation of human culture (the Left's view of Pinochet's dictatorship is that it carried out a deliberate process of *desmemoria* in order to destroy Allende's legacy) versus the necessity of forgetfulness (since if we do not forget at least some of what we experience our minds will be overloaded and unable to function). The metaphor also has a consciously self-reflexive side to it. There are points in the narrative when we hear the 'author' commenting on the Narrator's life; indeed the quote just provided does this – the author is included in the reference to 'Nosotros – desde nuestro limbo'. At other points, the crisscrossing between the past and the present is more subtle, as when the Narrator thinks that it is likely that Manuelita's 'calesa prebenida' may well have gone past the very spot where Pinochet's torture chambers were set up: 'quizás por el mismo lugar donde se había abierto alrededor de dos siglos después los subterráneos de tortura' (Edwards 250). And this image of torture is enlivened by the creation of a set of self-resonant references: the portrayal of Manuelita's imprisonment in the convent by her husband because of her licentiousness is followed by a description of the torture chambers used in the 1970s – a subliminal connection between the two rather different events is thereby made. At other times the text appears to slip effortlessly between past and present, while emphasising – in a postmodern way – the existence of the act of writing itself: '¿Quién sería, se pregunta el Narrador, sentado ahora en la sala de lectura del Archivo Nacional, rodeado de enormes expedientes encuadernados, esta Xavierita ...?' (237–8). We look over the Narrator's shoulder at the world ('El Narrador (y nosotros con él, a pocos centímetros de distancia, mirando por encima de su hombro'; 303) The weaving between the two epochs reaches a dizzying crescendo in the repetition of names, for the Narrator is called Ignacio, his son – who is on the run for undisclosed political activities – is called Ignacio chico, the Narrator's father is also called Ignacio, and – to cap it all – the man that Manuelita marries after her husband dies is also called Ignacio (364). As an unnamed individual points out to the Narrator, the days of the fall of the viceroyalty and of Pinochet's last days are uncannily similar: 'Somos del país del no drama, del conflicto no formulado, del cadáver escondido en el fondo del armario' (346). Edwards's *El sueño de la historia*, in its balancing act between the historical and the postmodern send-up of the very notion of the historical, offers a powerful picture of Chile's ideological stagnation, of the 'sustained grey' ('sostenido gris'; 346) which binds together its colonial past with its post-Allende blues.

Pitted against these historicist narrative voices, the silhouette of other types of narrative adventure are beginning to emerge. Undoubtedly one of the freshest novels of the new millennium was Milton Hatoum's *Dois Irmãos* (2000), which won Brazil's prestigious Jabuti prize and has been translated into English, French, German, Dutch and Arabic; it is an extraordinarily powerful novel about the rivalry between two brothers growing up in a Brazilian-Lebanese family in Manaus in the mid-twentieth century. *Dois Irmãos* catches the reader by surprise since its opening gambit focuses on the local, but, as the novel progresses, the lens gradually widens until it becomes rather a parable of man's struggle for life, with deliberate and apposite references to the biblical story of Cain and Abel. Though they look similar, the two twins around whom the plot wraps itself, Yaqub the older and Omar the younger, are diametrically opposed. Yaqub is shy, studious, a brilliant mathematician and a successful engineer who marries well; Omar is a carousing, extrovert womaniser with a violent streak who cannot get a steady job and who will not commit to marriage. Yaqub is favoured by his father, Halim, while Omar is idolised by his mother, Zana. Because of jealousy over a woman, the brothers come to blows, and Omar attacks his brother with a bottle, producing an unsightly scar on his right cheek. In an attempt to defuse the tension, Yaqub is sent to his father's native Lebanon, but this only drives the brothers further apart. The novel climaxes with Yaqub's persecution of his brother, which he pursues with almost mathematical precision once the main obstacle, Zana, is out of the way. The precise details are difficult to pin down – this is a book which works in innuendo rather than direct statement – but it is likely that Yaqub made a deal with the Indian businessman, Rochiram, which he knew would go wrong, cause the family home to be sold and, in the process, wreak a terrible revenge on his mother as well as his twin brother (who is imprisoned as a result of his anti-government leanings). The novel is narrated – with a deftness which recalls L. P. Hartley's innocent narrator in *The Go-Between* – by Nael, the illegitimate son of the maid, Domingas, who was raped by Omar. The fact that Nael, like his mother, favours Yaqub colours the narrative, but it is sufficiently objective to allow the reader to draw his own conclusions about which of the brothers is most to blame for the biblical scene which is re-created before our eyes. The novel can be interpreted on a number of levels – as the story of a family feud, as an allegory of the split produced within the Brazilian nation as a result of the military coup which ousted President João Goulart in April 1964 and brought General Castello Branco to power (Yaqub is associated with the military, having served in the army, and Omar is the disciple of Antenor Laval, the left-wing French teacher whose murder in the first week of April 1964 is described in Chapter 7), and as a compelling fable about the inhumanity which is at the root of humanity.

Some novels of the new millennium seem downright quirky. César Aira's *La Villa* (2001) is a case in point. Typical of much of Aira's fiction it begins in a rather odd way, and then gets increasingly stranger as it progresses. We begin with Maxi, a twenty-year-old young man, the son of a wealthy businessman, who keeps himself fit and then decides (we never really get to the bottom of this) to help out all the rag-and-bone men who wander the streets, picking up what they can, before returning to La Villa, their slum on the outskirts of Buenos Aires. Superficially this is a novel about the way that crime and drug-trafficking destroy innocent lives – such as that of the fifteen-year-old girl, Cynthia – as well as dragging leading upright members of the community, such as the Pastor, and the inspector, Ignacio Cabezas, down into the infernal depths of corruption, for which they are both 'punished' (both are shot to death). But this is only as far as the novel can be assimilated with the detective novel genre. There are lots of things that do not add up. Firstly, Maxi, while he is gradually being pulled into a murky world of crime, and drug-trafficking in La Villa, seems strangely unaware of what he is witnessing, even to the point of not recognising his sister's friend, Jessica, when he finds her unconscious in the gymnasium: 'tu hermano no se ha dado cuenta de que soy yo. Es un marciano' (Aira, *La Villa* 115). The narrative consciousness, indeed, at times is redolent of the style of Mark Haddon's *The Curious Incident of the Dog in The Night-Time* (2003). Much the same might be said of all of the characters – they are like Martians. The individual referred to as Pastor appears to be a totally incongruous mixture of a religious proselytiser and a drug-peddlar, although his mother, la Jueza, appears on TV at the conclusion of the novel, and 'reveals' that he was an undercover agent fighting corruption (140). Though it is never explained how she came to know this, she reveals who the murderer was – Cabezas the corrupt inspector – and does this dramatically in a TV interview. She subsequently leads him into a trap in La Villa, which becomes like a Borgesian labyrinth, and has him shot. To compound things further, the novel does not solve the enigma as to whether Cabezas is or is not the father of Cynthia, the murdered girl. He is referred to as such by the other characters of the novel but when we 'hear' his thoughts, we simply learn of the 'casualidad verdaderamente asombrosa' that there was another man who lived in his district with exactly the same name as him (42). As Jessica says at one point: 'Es como si uno viviera en un laberinto al que siempre le están haciendo reformas. Es increíble lo que uno puede llegar a ignorar. Todo' (106). Jessica's sense of bewilderment echoes the reader's; finishing the novel leaves you deeper inside the maze than when you began.

Alfredo Bryce Echenique's *El huerto de mi amada* (2002), awarded the Premio Planeta, and with a very respectable initial print-run of 210,000 copies, is a charming story about a scandalous love affair between a sixteen-year-old young man, Carlitos Alegre, and a thirty-three-year old married, aristocratic and totally irresistible *femme fatale*, Natalia de Larrea. Succumbing to an overpowering *coup de foudre* when they meet at a posh soirée in a discreet suburb of Lima, Carlitos is subsequently challenged by Natalia's husband, comes off the worst for wear after some fisticuffs, at which point the lovers elope to Natalia's country mansion, the 'huerto de mi amada' of the title. Just as important as the love affair, though, is the delicate delineation of the social world in which the characters live, their obsession with social appearances: Natalia's circle is mortified, Carlitos's father is worried his business may be adversely affected by the rumours, and a humorous foil to this bourgeois anxiety about 'el que dirán' is provided by the gauche social antics of the two twins, Arturo and Raúl Céspedes Salinas, who are always trying to ingratiate themselves with their social superiors. As with all of Bryce Echenique's love stories this one ends badly, with Natalia callously betraying Carlitos for a younger man, and getting Carlitos beaten up in the process (Bryce Echenique 282–3), but this rather pessimistic *desenlace* does not ultimately detract from the versatile narrative touch which characterises *El huerto de mi amada*. In what is effectively an inventive rewriting of Flaubert's 'style indirect libre' the third-person narrative of the standard Realist novel is suddenly broken down mid-sentence, allowing us to enter into the mind of the characters whose thoughts we now hear in the first person (24). In an intriguing revamping of Virginia Woolf's stream-of-consciousness technique the narrative voice is rendered malleable enough in order to allow it to incorporate the subtleties of quotidian, earthy, sardonic *limeño* speech. This linguistic playfulness also extends into the description of sex, for linguistic playfulness is consistently allied in the novel to sexual teasing: 'Y éste era, precisamente, el dominio del amor en el que, sin darse cuenta, siquiera, mientras jugueteaban con un par de palabras, y con la imaginación y el deseo, habían ingresado Natalia y Carlitos' (80). Natalia effectively admits that she is seduced not by his physique but by the way in which Carlitos speaks: 'deliciosamente' (83). Similarly, the Peruvian novelist has no qualms in disrupting novelistic conventions; in order, for example, to underline the theatricality of the gestures of love portrayed, the novel – out of the blue – breaks into a stagescript featuring the same characters (60–1, 64–8). The humour of social interaction is highlighted by the gradually more outlandish circumlocutions the *arriviste* twins use in a vain attempt to impress their hosts:

> – ¿Y la mantequilla? – les preguntó Carlitos […].
> – Muy agradable también, sí.
> – De mi entero agrado, también, sí.
> – ¿Y la mermelada?
> – Sumamente agradable, Carlitos.
> – Me sumo al agrado, Carlitos. (Bryce Echenique 207)

Though concluding in the guise of a doomed sexual relationship, there is a sense in which *El huerto de mi amada* also functions as a light-hearted elegy to the beauty, fun and humour that is at the heart of true sexual passion, and this is likely to be why it has proved itself to be so popular with readers.

*Budapeste* (2003) by Chico Buarque de Hollanda (b. 1944), winner of the 2004 Jabuti prize, a bestseller with more than a quarter of a million copies alone sold in Brazil, sold in over fifteen countries, tells the story of a ghost-writer, José Costa, living in Rio, who makes his money working for A Cunha & Costa Agência Cultural, by penning articles, speeches and novels anonymously for others. He is married to a news presenter, Vanda, and they have a child. Costa's domestic life is turned upside-down when he ends up, as a result of a mix-up in his flight plans, in Budapest, as well as a result of his attendance at (a curious notion) the Annual Meeting of Anonymous Writers in Melbourne (Buarque 18). At this point there begins a breathtaking toing and froing between Rio and Budapest; the plot moves so rapidly that there is no time for verisimilitude (Costa seems to be able to stay in a hotel in Rio for 100 days without being asked for the bill; after walking out on his Hungarian girl-friend, Kriska, he checks into a hotel which happens to have a room waiting for him; though starting at zero he appears to have reached such proficiency in Hungarian that he is able to correct the Hungarian of the most prestigious contemporary writers of Budapest; he is about to be beaten up by a skin-head covered with tattoos in the street but discovers he is his long-lost son). Character development too is limited (Vanda and Kriska seem surprisingly flat considering they are Costa's lovers). Though *Budapeste* is a page-turner, it deserves to be read slowly, for – in a rather unusual way – it seems to go backwards as much as forwards. There are some interesting parallelisms: the novel ends and begins with the narrator's attendance as the Annual Meeting of Anonymous Writers; just as José Costa, as a ghost-writer, has his life stolen from him in Rio (in that he writes a novel, *O Ginógrafo*, for a German, Kaspar Krabbe, who then robs him not only of his fame but also his wife, Vanda) so, as Zsose Kósta, in the last chapter of the novel, he steals fame from the author of the novel called *Budapeste* which he believes he did not write but for which he becomes famous (167–74). This device is constructed in some respects as an allusion to the famous ending of García Márquez's *Cien años de soledad* in which the last descendant of the Buendía reads about himself reading the novel he is holding (as Zsose Kósta suggests: 'agora eu lia o livro ao mismo tempo que o livro acontecia'; 174) but this novel offers more interest in terms of its ingenious treatment of the interplay of cultures, here embodied through a witty, occasionally extravagant running commentary about the overlay between Hungarian and Portuguese. As Costa at one point says:

> Talvez fosse possível substituir na cabeça uma língua por outra, paulatinamente, descartando uma palavra a cada palavra adquirida. Durante algum tempo minha cabeça será assim como uma casa em obras, com palavras novas subindo por um ouvido e o entulho descendo por outro. (Buarque 120–1)

*Budapeste* has a sensitivity to the phonetic fibre of language (unsurprisingly since Buarque is also a famous song-writer and singer) as well as a fast-moving plot, and its mix of the high and the low brow is original and compelling.

*Lorde* (2004) by João Gilberto Noll (b. 1946) is typical of Noll's work in that it focuses on the inner thoughts of an individual who wanders apparently aimlessly through an anodyne urban landscape. The plotless narrative is occasionally punctured by descriptions of (often homosexual) sexual activity. Though cut from the same cloth as many of Noll's other novels, *Lorde* offers the rather intriguing difference that it is based in some measure on his experience at King's College London as the writer-in-residence in 1998. It begins with the description of his being picked up at Heathrow, taken to his lodgings in Hackney, his various wanderings around central London, followed by a visit to Liverpool, the description of a sexual experience there, and concluding with the description of his trip to the local cemetery where the novel, rather abruptly, ends. The narrative consciousness is absorbed completely within the narrator's mind so that the various other characters are always secondary and their voices are reported rather than heard. The initial greeting between the narrator and the King's professor (based on David Treece) who comes to pick him up is typical in this respect:

> Olhamos-nos. Um falou o nome do outro. Como se isso fosse necessário para acentuarmos nossas presenças. Asseguramo-nos definitivamente delas. Demos-nos as mãos. A dele estava fria, não tanto como o telefone. Fazia frio em Londres, ele disse. Tinha nevado um dia antes. (Noll, *Lorde* 12)

The first third of the novel is taken up by the narrator's obsessive self-questioning in that he cannot understand why an English university should pay him. As the narrative develops – and we catch glimpses of his wanderings around the ethnic neighbourhoods of Hackney, his travels to Bloomsbury on the 55 bus, his visits to the British Museum – the narrator, far from becoming more accustomed to his environment, becomes gradually more estranged from the people and things around him. As he comments at one point: 'Lá jaz um pedaço de mim que parou, sem pensamento para controlar o mundo nem o que vai dentro dele, pedra à pedra' (Noll, *Lorde* 39). In a way which is vaguely reminiscent of Lispector's style the narrator analyses his sensorial sensations minutely and intelligently. Noll clearly delights in teasing the reader. Just when we thought this was a psychological novel based on real events, the narrator describes his visit to the home of Mark, a professor of Latin American Studies at Empire's University; although they have never met before, Mark gets into the bath, sings a few 1950s songs, invites the narrator into the bath with him, at which point the narrator bursts into tears, and then they kiss passionately (47–9). In the second half of the novel, the narrator appears to become more and more frustrated with his visit to London, seeing himself as a 'prisoner' (65) under military guard; at the same time the other characters in the story become more and more ghostlike – even George, with whom he makes love in Liverpool (a reference to George Harrison of the Beatles perhaps?; 107) – until he escapes to a graveyard where he wants to see 'se sonharia o sonho do outro de quem jurava ter ainda sobras do sêmen na mão' (111), a phantasmagoric ending which, in keeping with the rest of the novel, leaves the reader hanging in the air.

It is clear that the modern Latin American novel has no need to stay geographically tied to Latin America. A surprisingly unexotic, Eastern feel, for example, is present in *Una novela china* (2004) by César Aira (b. 1949) which tells the story of Lu Hsin, a Chinese intellectual who lives on the outskirts of a remote province, Hosa-Chen. In its description of Ls Hsin's everyday life – his philosophical discussions over tea with his friends, the conflict with his helper, Kiu, the article he published renouncing Marxism – the novel provides an arresting sense of the mood of an era (the novel is set in the twenty or so years before the Long March and the Cultural Revolution). Echoing the slow deliberateness with which these events are described is the love motif. Lu Hsin decides to adopt Hin, the daughter of a peasant woman, and he looks after her until, one day, he is overcome with love:

> Por un azar, de su disposición, la luna daba en los dos rostros. [...] Y fue entonces, no antes, cuando Lu Hsin, que se había equivocado tanto, supo qué era el amor. Su vida entera se borró súbitamente en el resplandor discreto de la luna. (Aira, *Una novela china* 174)

A subtle and understated novel, *Una novela china* is effective at drawing the reader into a meticulously drawn and fundamentally exotic world.

Milton Hatoum's third novel, *Cinzas do norte* (2005), winner of the Jabuti literary prize, tells the story of two boys, Lavo, the narrator, and his best friend, Mundo. Set in Manaus (the author's home town), in the 1950s and 1960s, this novel plumbs the internal depths of a subject on which he is now acknowledged as a master – interfamilial warfare. Whereas *Dois irmãos* had focused on the fraught relationship between two brothers, here the focus is on the violent relationship between father (Jano) and son (Mundo) as seen through Lavo's eyes. The father's full name, Trajano, recalls the ferocity of the Roman emperor after whom he is named. He resents particularly the bohemian activities of his son who loves art, despises discipline and rebels against his school and the army – he ends up expelled from both – just, it appears, in order to spite his father; as he writes in a letter to Lavo, 'Ou a obediência estúpida, ou a revolta' (Hatoum, *Cinzas* 10). Yet this is not simply the story of the breakdown of a family relationship, for this novel has a skeleton in the cupboard; the secret – which is only incontrovertibly confirmed on the penultimate page of the novel (310) – is that Mundo is not Jano's son, but in fact the son of Alícia's lover, Ranulfo, a bohemian, art-loving, promiscuous drifter who cannot keep a job down. There are a number of junctures in the novel when Mundo's true identity is hinted at – particularly in Lavo's italicised soliloquies directed towards Mundo which tell him about how he first met and fell in love with the latter's mother – though the main emotional dilemma of the novel centres around the titanic struggle between father and son. Mundo confesses at one point that it will lead to 'o fim da vida ... da minha ou da dele' (123), and it in fact leads to the death of both: after Mundo disappears without trace (he has 'buried' himself with Ranulfo), Jano takes to his bed and dies, and this inspires Mundo, now that he is free from his father's influence, to go to London, where he lives as a bohemian and starves to death. There are a number of loose ends in this novel – What status do the italicised soliloquies have? Were they actual or imagined conversations between Ranulfo and Mundo? Why did Alícia destroy her son's work? Why is the narrator, an orphan, so like Jano, i.e. by becoming a lawyer? Could he be Jano's son? – that it is tempting to see *Cinzas do Norte* as a twenty-first-century novel in the style of Machado de Assis. Whatever the answer to these and other questions – and they may be unanswerable – it is clear that Hatoum's vision of human society is that it is inevitably grounded in acute suffering, for the closest relationships (namely the sexual love between man and woman, or the love between parent and child) are the ones which cause the deepest pain.

# Postlude

> Cada estado social trae su expresión a la literatura, de tal modo, que por las diversas fases de ella pudiera contarse la historia de los pueblos con más verdad que por sus cronicones y sus décadas. (Martí, *Prosas* 98)

Analysing the evolution of Latin American literature in its Portuguese- as well as Spanish-language manifestations is often like watching a three-legged race – two individuals more or less moving in the same direction but often tugging against each other. In this study we have seen many cases of intellectual coincidence, that is, when a Spaniard and a Portuguese were writing about the world around them in complete isolation from each other, yet the ideas inspired by that reality seem – with the benefit of hindsight – remarkably similar, almost if they were penned by the same mind: such is the case with Columbus's and Vaz de Caminha's discovery-letters. Likewise religious men such as Motolinía and Fray Diego de Landa writing in Mexico, and José de Anchieta and Manoel da Nóbrega writing in Brazil, reached very similar conclusions about the Indians and Amerindian culture. Caviedes in the colonial era wrote satiric verse in Peru which – we can now see – overlapped in specific ways with Matos de Guerra's in Brazil, and José de Alencar wrote a Romantic novel in Brazil, *Iracema*, which is strikingly similar to Jorge Isaacs's Colombian masterpiece, *María*, though each of these writers was working independently of the other. Sometimes the writers from the two colonies knew of each other; yet here again the result was not always predictable; New Spain's Sor Juana de la Cruz, for example, fought tooth and nail against Brazil's Antônio Vieira, unleashing a theological-cum-political storm which would lead eventually to her untimely death. At other times Spanish American and Brazilian literature seemed to be pulling in different directions; Lispector's fiction is as brilliant as García Márquez's but its agenda is very different, and it would be misleading to place Lispector *post facto* in the Boom. Indeed, even when Brazilian and Spanish American writers were pulling in the same direction – as occurred with the avant-garde, for there are specific similarities between the work of César Vallejo and Mário de Andrade – nevertheless the Brazilians were using a term *Modernismo* to describe the avant-garde which had already been used to mean something quite different in Spanish America at the end of the previous century (*fin-de-siècle* aestheticism). Occasionally the interface between the two literatures has been dense and textured, as occurred in Mario Vargas Llosa's extraordinary rewriting of Da Cunha's *Os Sertões* in his novel *La Guerra del fin del mundo* (1981). One of the aims of this book has been to draw attention to the convergences as well as the divergences between Spanish American and Brazilian literature.

Despite their differences there are a number of concrete features common to both the Portuguese and the Spanish flanks of the Latin American literary canon. The press, and its product the printed word, functioned as the common denominator binding together, in different ways over time, the complex and variable relationship between the writer, the reader and the state. Latin American literature passed through a number of phases from its humble beginnings in the sixteenth century until the present day, and the notion of literature and the social role of the writer changed substantially during this period. Three defining moments are evident. From the conquest until the independence movements which occurred at the beginning of the nineteenth century, literature was subject to the Maecenal law of literary production, and its source of support was often the Spanish or Portuguese monarch, or the Church. The advent of serialised printing during the era of independence, however, dealt the final blow to this mode of literary production. Brazil gained a royal (subsequently an independent) press in 1822, and the newly independent Spanish American republics, as they split off from the viceroyalties, used print to proclaim their freedom. Print technology continued to improve through the remainder of the nineteenth century and, by the end of that century, many writers in Rio de Janeiro as much as in Buenos Aires were beginning to live off their pens as journalists and serial novelists. The growth of print-runs and sales of literary works continued apace in the first half of the twentieth century, and then in the 1960s writers such as Clarice Lispector in Brazil and García Márquez in Colombia suddenly burst onto the world stage. A stream of new writers – some of them part of the Boom, some of them post-Boom – began to make inroads into the hallowed halls of world literature. Latin American literature had finally arrived.

# Suggestions for Further Reading

These suggestions for further reading are arranged by the chapter sequence in the text, which necessarily leads to overlap in coverage; some suggestions listed in the general section are also relevant for other chapters. The titles were chosen to provide an indication of further profitable reading in Latin American literature. In most cases these texts have been tried and tested in the classroom environment. Readers who want greater detail will find a wealth of leads in the books suggested. The best detailed introduction to Latin American literature is provided by the three volumes of *The Cambridge History of Latin American Literature*, edited by Enrique Pupo-Walker and Roberto González Echeverría, and published in 1995. Though the volume is not uniform in approach to the different areas and there is a degree of unevenness in the contributions, it is nevertheless the necessary first stepping-stone in any analysis of Latin American literature. For a broader approach, the *Encyclopedia of Latin American Literature*, edited by Verity Smith and published in 1997, is invaluable; not only does it cover canonical literary authors as well as providing helpful separate short commentaries on their main works, but it also introduces new topics such as 'Resistance Literature in Spanish America', and 'Popular Culture' into the canon. Jean Franco's *An Introduction to Spanish American Literature*, and José Miguel Oviedo's two-volume *Historia de la literatura hispanoamericana* offer the best in balanced appraisals and continuous narratives, and are highly recommended. Also worth mentioning are Jacques Joset's *La literatura hispanoamericana* which, not surprisingly, given its length (155 pages), is unable to give even the major works more than a cursory glance; and José Juan Arrom's *Esquema generacional de las letras hispanoamericanas: ensayo de un método*. The drawback of this latter work, despite the wisdom of the judgements on individual works, is that Arrom splits the literature from the conquest to 1983 into seventeen thirty-year periods, which is too tidy to be believable.

For a traditional approach to the authors of the canon which has the advantage of a uniform format, see *Latin American Writers*, edited by Carlos A. Solé and Maria Isabel Abreu in three volumes; the quality of the contributions, though, is variable. Though the present study reads against the grain of a nationalist approach, for an introduction to the literature of the sub-continent which is country-based, see David William Foster's edition of a *Handbook of Latin American Literature*. This handbook has the advantage of offering separate sections on Latino literature, paraliterature and film. A representative sample of the best of the criticism on the main authors of the canon is to be found in *Spanish American Literature: A Collection of Essays*, edited by David William Foster and Daniel Altamiranda, and published in five volumes. Volume 1 treats theoretical debates such as post colonialism, postmodernism, and ethnicity; volume 2 colonial literature; volume 3 nineteenth-century literature; volume 4 literature from 1900 to 1960, while volume 5 concludes with a selection of essays on authors published after the 1960s. A collection of the main canonic texts, ranging from Bartolomé de las Casas to Rigoberta Menchú, is provided in Foster's *Literatura hispanoamericana: una antología*. Also helpful is Chang-Rodríguez and Filer's annotated anthology *Voces de Hispanoamérica*.

There are a number of general works on Brazilian literature which are worth consulting, including Érico Verissimo's *Brazilian Literature: an Outline* and Afrânio Coutinho's *An Introduction to Literature in Brazil*. Very helpful reference works are the two-volume *Pequeno dicionário da literatura brasileira*, Graça Coutinho's two-volume *Enciclopédia da literatura brasileira*, and Paul Teysseier's *Dicionário da literatura brasileira*. José de Nicola's *Literatura brasileira das origens aos nossos dias* provides basic information. Offering a slightly more humorous tone to the construction of the Brazilian literary canon is Luis Carlos Lisboa's *Tudo que você precisa ler sem ser um rato de biblioteca: guia do melhor da literatura brasileira*. Laurence Hallewell's *O livro no Brasil* is excellent on the history of the book in Brazil. E. Bradford Burns, *Perspectives on Brazilian History* offers an excellent account of early Brazilian historiography, including discussion of the major Jesuit historians and essayists. A good overall introduction to Brazilian theatre is provided by J. Galanta de Sousa's *O teatro no Brasil*. An important interdisciplinary study of the novel is Judith A. Payne and Earl E. Fitz's *Ambiguity and Gender in the New Novel of Brazil and Spanish America*, which looks at the main Spanish American novels of the Boom and the main contemporary Brazilian novels, and analyses overlaps and differences; well documented and well argued. Michael Palmer (ed.), *Nothing the Sun Could Not Explain: 20 Contemporary Brazilian Poets* is a good selection of contemporary Brazilian poetry. Ítalo Morioni's edition of *Os Cem Melhores Contos Brasileiros do Século* is an excellent selection of twentieth-century short stories. For a good sample of contemporary Brazilian theatre the reader is referred to Soraya Hamden's three-volume *Coleção Teatro Brasileiro*.

A number of excellent books on Latin American literature have appeared since the first edition of this book was published. Aníbal González's *Killer Books: Writing, Violence and Ethics in Modern Spanish American Narrative* offers excellent readings of texts by Manuel Gutiérrez Nájera, Teresa de la Parra, Borges, Carpentier and Cortázar. Donald L. Shaw has published an authoritative study of twentieth-century Spanish American fiction: *A Companion to Modern Spanish American Fiction*; essential reading. Roberto Ignacio Díaz's *Unhomely Rooms: Foreign Tongues and Spanish American Literature* studies, inter alia, the Comtesse Merlin's *La Havane*, Bombal's *House of Mist*, Cabrera Infante's *Holy Smoke* and Fuentes's *Una familia lejana*. Herbert E. Craig studies

Proust's influence on the Spanish American novel, *Marcel Proust and Spanish America*. Philip Swanson (ed.), *The Companion to Latin American Studies* contains essays on Latin American literature and US Latino literature. The same author's *Latin American Fiction: A Short Introduction* is a lucid and insightful introduction to nineteenth- and twentieth-century fiction. John King's *The Cambridge Companion to Modern Latin American Culture* includes three very helpful overview-type essays on Spanish American narrative from 1810 until 1920, from 1920 until 1970, and from 1970 to the present day, a very good essay on Brazilian narrative, and two authoritative essays on Latin American poetry and theatre; essential reading. Efraín Kristal's *The Cambridge Companion to the Latin American Novel* offers an excellent selection of essays including sections on the nineteenth-century novel, the Boom and post-Boom, as well as an excellent essay on the Brazilian novel (105–24), one on the lesbian and gay novel, and separate essays on *Dom Casmurro, Pedro Páramo, The Passion According to G.H., One Hundred Years of Solitude, The House of the Spirits* and *The War of the End of the World*; highly recommended. Stephen M. Hart and Wen-chin Ouyang's *A Companion to Magical Realism* contains essays with discussion of the work of Borges, García Márquez, Carpentier, Asturias, Bombal, Rulfo, Rivera, Montero, Allende and Esquivel. Julio Ortega's *Translantic Translations* offers a well-informed overview of some of the salient landmarks of Spanish American literature from Columbus to García Márquez. The best way to research recent criticism on Latin American authors is to use a combination of the following three methods: (i) conduct a PMLA on-line search giving the author as subject, (ii) consult the appropriate years of the *Year's Work in Modern Language Studies*, and (iii) consult the online HAPI database, which gives an up-to-date list of journal articles published on the Latin American canon.

## Chapter 1

John E. Kicza's *Resilient Cultures: America's Native Peoples Confront European Civilization, 1500–1800* offers a coherent historical account of the European conquest of the Americas. For an excellent introduction to Amerindian culture, see Gordon Brotherston's *Book of the Fourth World*, and for more on the *Chilam Balam*, consult Munro S. Edmonson's *Heaven Born*. Regina Harrison's *Signs, Songs and Memory in the Andes* is an authoritative introduction to Quechua culture. Edmundo Bendezú Aybar's *Literatura quechua* provides an excellent selection of Quechua literature. Miguel León-Portilla is the best critic on Aztec literature and culture of Mexico; his *The Broken Spears* and *Fifteen Poets of the Aztec World* are highly recommended. There are also excellent introductory surveys of Aztec, Maya and Quechua literature in Verity Smith's *Encyclopedia of Latin American Literature*. Particularly good on the issue of transculturation is Elizabeth Boone and Walter D. Mignolo's *Writing Without Words*. On the conquest, see Tzvetan Todorov's *La conquista de América*,

George Baudot's *Utopía e historia en México*, and Antonello Gerbi's *La naturaleza de las Indias Nuevas*. A good overview of Cortés's work is provided in Marcel Bataillon's *Hernán Cortés*; see also Inga Clendinnen's 'Cortés, Signs and the Conquest of Mexico'. For an insightful introduction to the literature of conquest and discovery, see Beatriz Pastor, *Discursos narrativos*; Rolena Adorno, 'Cultures in Contact: Mesoamerica, the Andes, and the European Written Tradition'; Stephanie Merrim, 'The First Fifty Years of Hispanic New World Historiography: The Caribbean, Mexico and Central America'; Kathleen Ross, 'Historians of the Conquest and Colonization of the New World: 1550–1620'; and Stephen Greenblatt's *Marvelous Possessions*. James Murray's *Spanish Chronicles of the Indies* is a clear, no-nonsense introduction to the *crónicas*. A competent overview of the main writers of this period is provided by Mario Hernández Sánchez-Barba in his *Historia y literatura en Hispanoamérica (1492–1820)*. David Foster and Daniel Altamiranda's *Spanish American Literature: A Collection of Essays*, vol. 2, has accurate introductory essays on authors of this period, such as Bartolomé de las Casas, Alvar Núñez Cabeza de la Vega, Bernal Díaz del Castillo, El Inca Garcilaso de la Vega, Alonso de Ercilla y Zúñiga, and others such as Sor Juana Inés de la Casa, Juan del Valle y Caviedes, and Alonso Carrió de la Vandera. Susan Castillo's *Colonial Encounters in New World Writing, 1500–1700: Performing America* is a wide-ranging and enlightening study which juxtaposes Spanish, English and French colonial texts. For an authoritative introduction to El Inca Garcilaso's work, see Margarita Zamora's *Language, Authority and Indigenous History*. Serafim Leite, *Novas páginas de história do Brasil* is an excellent overview of the Jesuits in Brazil. For a discussion of religious thought among the Jesuits and beyond, see João Camilo de Oliveira Tôrres, *História dos idéais religiosos no Brasil*. S. Buarque de Holanda's *Antologia dos poetas brasileiros da fase colonial* offers a good selection of the work of Brazil's colonial poets.

## Chapter 2

Students wishing to flesh out the historical background of the viceroyalty of Peru should consult Kenneth Andrien's excellent *Crisis and Decline: The Viceroyalty of Peru in the Seventeenth Century*. For a detailed overview of the culture of this period, see Asunción Lavrín, 'Viceregal Culture'; and Karen Stolley, 'The Eighteenth Century: Narrative Forms, Scholarship and Learning'. For a well-written overview of colonial literature full of original insight, see René Prieto, *The Identity of Hispanoamerica*. Essential background reading are John Lanning's *Academic Culture in the Spanish Colonies* and Irving Leonard's *Books of the Brave*. For a balanced appraisal of the poets in particular, see Roberto González Echeverría, 'Colonial Lyric'. A good selection of colonial poets is provided in Campa and Chang-Rodríguez's edition of *Poesía hispanoamericana colonial*. James Nicolopulos's *The Poetics of Empire in the Indies* is excellent on *La Araucana*. For an introduction to the theatre, see Frederick

Luciani, 'Spanish American Theatre of the Colonial Period'. A selection of theatrical works is found in Luzuriaga and Reeve's *Los clásicos del teatro hispanoamericano*, which should be complemented with José Rojas Garcidueñas and José Juan Arrom's *Tres piezas del virreinato*. A good sampling of essays by established scholars on the main authors of the colonial period may be found in *Historia de la literatura hispanoamericana. Vol. 1, Época colonial*, edited by Luis Íñigo Madrigal; it contains separate essays on, inter alia, Sor Juana Inés de la Cruz, Juan del Valle y Caviedes, and colonial theatre; highly recommended. An anthology which is still worth consulting is Ángel Flores and Helene Anderson's *Masterpieces of Spanish American Literature: The Colonial Period to the Beginnings of Modernism*. David Bradley provides a wonderful overview of the main thinkers of New Spain in his study, *The First America*. Mark Burkholder's *Politics of a Colonial Career* fleshes out the backdrop on the role of the writer/politician in the Spanish colonies. Julie Greer Johnson's *Satire in Colonial Spanish America* also functions as an authoritative overview of the main writers of this period.

The best overall introduction to the history of the press during this period is S. H. Steinberg's fascinating *Five Hundred Years of Printing*. Clive Griffin's study of *The Crombergers of Seville* is the definitive study of print culture of the time. Also helpful are Vicente Quesada's *The History of Printing and Early Publications in the Spanish American Colonies* and Lawrence Thompson's *Printing in Colonial Spanish America*. D. W. Cruickshank's article, 'Literature and the Book Trade in Golden-Age Spain' is excellent. Essential readings on Sor Juana Inés de la Cruz are Stephanie Merrim, *Feminist Perspectives on Sor Juana Inés de la Cruz*; Ludwig Pfandl, *Sor Juana Inés de la Cruz*; Octavio Paz, *Sor Juana Inés de la Cruz o las trampas de la fe*; and Georgina Sabat de Rivers, *El 'sueño' de Sor Juana Inés de la Cruz*. Dauril Alden's *Royal Government in Colonial Brazil* offers an engaging analysis of the evolution of the viceroyalty in Brazil. José Aderaldo Castello's *Manifestações literárias do período colonial* is an excellent overview of Brazilian colonial literature. Ivan Teixeira's *Mercenato pombalino e poesia neoclásica* offers wonderful insight into Brazil's literary culture in the colonial period. The best study of colonial and nineteenth-century Brazilian literature is Antônio Cândido's two-volume *Formação da literatura brasileira (momentos decisivos)*, 2nd edn; the first volume covers the period 1750–1836, the second 1836–80. Thomas M. Cohen, *The Fire of Tongues: Antônio Vieira and the Missionary Church in Brazil and Portugal* is an excellent study of Vieira's life and work. Marcelo Baches's edition of Vieira's best sermons, *Os melhores sermões*, is a good selection.

## Chapter 3

For overviews of the emancipation movements in Latin America see William Pilling's *The Emancipation of South America*, Robert Harvey's *Liberators: Latin America's Struggle for Independence, 1810–1830*, Kirsteen Schultz's

*Tropical Versailles*, Leslie Bethell's *The Abolition of the Brazilian Slave Trade*, and David Baronov's *The Abolition of Slavery in Brazil*. For a selection of criticism on the main authors of the nineteenth century, see David William Foster and Daniel Altamiranda, *Spanish American Literature: A Collection of Essays*, vol. 3. A helpful overview of the novel is found in Antonio Benítez-Rojo, 'The Nineteenth-Century Spanish American Novel'. The classic study of Realism is Erich Auerbach's *Mimesis*, which should be complemented with Ian Watt's study, *The Rise of the Novel*. The best study of the nineteenth-century Spanish American novel is Doris Sommer's *Foundational Fictions*. For the background on drama of this period, see Frank Dauster, 'The Spanish American Theatre of the Nineteenth Century'; and for an overview of the essay during this period, consult Nicholas Schumway, 'The Essay in Spanish America: 1800 to Modernismo'; and Martin S. Stubb, 'The Essay of Nineteenth-Century Mexico, Central America, and the Caribbean'. Benedict Anderson's *Imagined Communities* is essential reading on the interface between print and nationalism in the nineteenth century. An excellent overview of the press in Spanish America is provided by Antonio Checa Godoy in his *Historia de la prensa en Iberoamérica*. The best introduction to Spanish American Romanticism is Emilio Carilla's *El romanticismo en la América Hispánica*. For an overview of the main themes and motifs of the Romantic movement Mario Praz's *The Romantic Agony* should be consulted. Manuel Bandeira's *Antologia dos poetas brasileiros: fase romântica* offers a good selection of Brazil's Romantic poets. For more on Bello, see Rafael Caldera, *Andrés Bello*. Antonio Cussen, *Poetry and Politics in the Spanish American Revolution* is excellent on Bello and Bolívar. For a good overview study which places Echeverría's work in a cultural context, see William H. Katra, *The Argentine Generation of 1837*. A review of Fernández de Lizardi's work which has stood the test of time is Jefferson Rea Spell's *The Life and Works of José Joaquín Fernández de Lizardi*. For excellent, probing discussions of Sarmiento's work, see Noé Jitrik's *Muerte y resurreción de Facundo* and Enrique Anderson-Imbert's *Genio y figura de Sarmiento*. For a good overview of Isaacs's work see Susana Zanetti's *Jorge Isaacs*. Vera Kutzinski's *Sugar's Secrets* has thought-provoking chapters on Plácido and Villaverde. For a competent overview of Avellaneda's work, see Hugh H. Harter, *Gertrudis Gómez de Avellaneda*. Susan Kirkpatrick, *Las Románticas*, has a good chapter on Avellaneda.

## Chapter 4

For a good introduction to *modernismo*, Cathy L. Jrade, 'Modernist Poetry'; and Aníbal González, 'Modernist Prose', should be consulted. A judicious selection of *modernista* poetry may be consulted in Ivan Schulman and Evelyn Picón Garfield's *Poesía modernista hispanoamericana y española*. Given that the notions of imitation and originality became crucial for the *modernistas*, Harold Bloom's study, *The Anxiety of Influence*, provides a good context with which to analyse the movement. Since the *modernistas* experimented so much with rhyme schemes, Tomás Navarro Tomás's *Métrica española* should be consulted; also helpful is Antonio Quilis's *Métrica española*. For an excellent discussion of Darío's work, see Angel Rama, *Rubén Darío y el modernismo*. Gwen Kirkpatrick's *The Dissonant Legacy of 'Modernismo'* is cogent on Herrera y Reissig and Lugones. There is some excellent discussion of the postmodernist poets, including Agustini, in Emir Rodríguez Monegal, *Sexo y poesía en el 900 uruguayo*. A good overview of Mistral's work is Fernando Alegría, *Genio y figura de Gabriela Mistral*, and a good overview of Storni's work is provided by Rachel Phillips in her *Alfonsina Storni: From Poetess to Poet*. For a good introduction to Ibarbourou's work, see Jorge Arbeleche, *Juana de Ibarbourou*. Excellent background information on the prose of this era is available in Aníbal González's *Journalism and the Development of Spanish American Narrative*; this study also has a good chapter on Palma's *Tradiciones*. For information on *costumbrismo*, see Enrique Pupo-Walker, 'The Brief Narrative in Spanish America: 1835–1915'. A good clear introduction to José Hernández's work is provided by, Roque Raúl Aragón and J. Calcetti in their *Genio y figura de José Hernández*. For more on the backdrop to the literature inspired by the *gaucho*, see Josefina Ludmer, 'The Gaucho Genre'. William Rowe and Vivian Schelling's *Memory and Modernity* also has some good discussion of the *gaucho*. Lafleur's study of literary magazines of this period, *Las revistas literarias argentinas 1893–1967*, is indispensable. For an introduction to Villaverde's work, see Imeldo Alvarez García, *La obra narrativa de Cirilo Villaverde*. There are good chapters on *Aves sin nido* in John Brushwood, *Genteel Barbarism*; Efraín Kristal, *The Andes Viewed from the City*; and Francine Masiello, *Between Civilization and Barbarism*. An absorbing selection of women writers' essays of this period appears in Doris Meyer's *Rereading the Spanish American Essay*. Doris Sommer's *Foundational Fictions* contains discussion of *Iracema* and *O Guaraní*. For the theatre, Judith Weiss's *Latin American Popular Theatre* is the definitive study. For new readings of Rodó's work, see Gustavo San Román (ed.), *This America We Dream Of*. For a challenging reading of Martí's work, see Blanca Rivera-Meléndez, *Poetry and the Machinery of Illusions*. Important studies of Machado de Assis's fiction include Helen Caldwell, *Machado de Assis: The Brazilian Master and his Novels*; John Gledson, *The Deceptive Realism of Machado de Assis*; Earl Fitz, *Machado de Assis*; José Raimundo Maia Neto, *Machado de Assis, The Brazilian Pyrrhonian*; and essays by Schwarz and Santiago which are discussed in chapter 6. There is also the indispensable *Dicionário de Machado de Assis* by Francisco Pati. Other important studies include *The Author as Plagiarist – The Case of Machado de Assis, Portuguese Literary & Cultural Studies*, 13–14 (2004–2005); a special number on all aspects of Machado de Assis's work.

## Chapter 5

Gilberto Mendonça Teles, *Vanguarda europea e modernismo,* sets Brazil's *Modernismo* within a broader context, and John Nist, *The Modernist Movement in Brazil: A Literary Study* is a helpful introduction. Robert Havard's *A Companion to Spanish Surrealism* contains an excellent essay by Jason Wilson on surrealism in Spanish America. For an excellent overview of the poetry of this period, see Gordon Brotherston, *Latin American Poetry.* For the main outlines of the avant-garde, see Hugo J. Verani, 'The Vanguardia and its Implications'. For an excellent, theoretical analysis of Brazilian as well as the Spanish American avant-garde (including Andrade's *Macunaíma*), see Fernado J. Rosenberg's *The Avant-Garde and Geopolitics in Latin America.* For a good discussion of Huidobro's work, see René de Costa, *Vicente Huidobro: The Careers of a Poet.* On Vallejo, see Jean Franco, *Poetry and Silence.* On Paz, see John M. Fein, *Octavio Paz*; and on Nicolás Guillén, see Lorna Williams, *Self and Society in the Poetry of Nicolás Guillén.* Olímpio de Souza Andrade, *História e interpretação de 'Os Sertões'* is an excellent study of Da Cunha's novel. An excellent study on Lima Barreto's fiction set against the backdrop of Realism is provided by R. J. Oakley, *The Case of Lima Barreto and Realism in the Brazilian 'Belle Epoque'.* René Prieto's 'The Literature of *Indigenismo'*, provides a competent overview of *indigenismo*, which should be complemented with Manuel Aquézolo Castro's edition, *La polémica del indigenismo*, which is a judicious selection. Also worth consulting are Luis Alberto Sánchez, *Indianismo e indigenismo en la literatura peruana*, and Julio Rodríguez-Luis, *Hermenéutica y praxis del indigenismo*. On Arguedas, see William Rowe, *Mito e ideología en la obra de José María Arguedas* and Antonio Cornejo Polar, *Los universos narrativos de José María Arguedas.* For the background to the *novela de la tierra*, see Carlos J. Alonso, 'The *Criollista* Novel', as well as his *The Spanish American Regional Novel.* For more on *Los de abajo*, see John Rutherford, 'The Novel of the Mexican Revolution'; and Verity Smith, *Encyclopedia*, 91–2. For good preliminary discussions of Ricardo Güiraldes's *Don Segundo Sombra* and Teresa de la Parra's *Las memorias de la Mamá Blanca*, see Verity Smith, *Encyclopedia*, 403–4, 631–32. *Spanish American Literature: A Collection of Essays*, edited by David William Foster and Daniel Altamiranda, vol. 4, provides excellent overview essays on Quiroga, Mistral, Vallejo, Huidobro, Asturias, Borges, Guillén, Neruda, and Carpentier. For a discussion of two of Carpentier's novels not treated here (*El reino de este mundo* and *El siglo de las luces*), see Verity Smith, *Encyclopedia*, 171–74. For a succinct analysis of Asturias's *El Señor Presidente*, see Verity Smith, *Encyclopedia*, 79–81. Frank Dauster, *Historia del teatro hispanoamericano*, is a magisterial introduction to the theatre of this period; also worth consulting is Diana Taylor's *Theatre of Crisis.* For a good selection of plays consult Carlos Solórzano's edition of *El teatro actual latinoamericano*, as well as his edition of *Teatro breve hispanoamericano.* For some probing analyses of women writers of this period, see Francine Masiello's *Between Civilization and*

*Barbarism*. A good overview of Rulfo's work is found in Luis Leal, *Juan Rulfo*. On Quiroga, see Peter R. Beardsell, *Quiroga. Cuentos de amor, de locura y de muerte*, and Emir Rodríguez Monegal, *Genio y figura de Horacio Quiroga*. On Borges, see Harold Bloom's collection of essays, *Jorge Luis Borges*; Donald Shaw, *Borges' Narrative Strategy*; Sylvia Molloy, *Signs of Borges*; Ronald Christ, *The Narrow Act*; and John Sturrock, *Paper Tigers*. Efraín Kristal's *Invisible Work: Borges and Translation* and Jason Wilson's *Jorge Luis Borges* are excellent new studies of Borges's genius. The best introduction to Usigli is Peter Beardsell, *A Theatre for Cannibals*; for more on René Marqués, see Bonnie Hildebrand Reynolds, *Space, Time and Crisis*. For an imaginative discussion of Mariátegui's work, see Roland Forgues, *Mariátegui: la utopía realizable*. There are excellent chapters on Castellanos in Debra Castillo, *Talking Back*, and Naomi Lindstrom, *Women's Voices in Latin American Literature*.

## Chapter 6

José Quiroga, 'Spanish American Poetry from 1922 to 1975', offers background information on the poetry of this period. For a good poetic anthology, see José Olivio Jiménez's *Antología de la poesía contemporánea*. The best study of Parra's work is Edith Grossman, *The Antipoetry of Nicanor Parra*, and the best study of Cardenal's work is Paul W. Borgeson, Jr., *Hacia el hombre nuevo*. The definitive overview of Pizarnik's work is Cristina Piña, *Alejandra Pizarnik*; for a good selection of essays on Claribel Alegría, see Boschetto-Sandoval and Phillips McGowan's *Claribel Alegría and Central American Literature*. The first port of call for the Boom novel is Randolph D. Pope, 'The Spanish American Novel from 1950 to 1975'; also indispensable are José Donoso's *Historia personal del 'Boom'*, Carlos Fuentes's *La nueva novela hispanoamericana*, Luis Harss's *Into the Mainstream*, Gerald Martin's *Journeys Through the Labyrinth*, and Ángel Rama's *La ciudad letrada*. There are some good authoritative essays on the Boom writers in John King's *Modern Latin American Fiction: A Survey*. For discussion of Fuentes's novellas, see Verity Smith, *Encyclopedia*, 330–33, and of his *La muerte de Artemio Cruz*, see Harold Bloom (ed.), *Carlos Fuentes, 'The Death of Artemio Cruz'*. For excellent studies on Cortázar's novels, see Steven Boldy, *The Novels of Julio Cortázar*, and Carmen Ortiz, *Julio Cortázar*. Santiago Juan-Navarro's *Archival Reflections* includes analysis of novels by Fuentes and Cortázar. Wendy Faris, *Ordinary Enchantments* contains analysis of the fiction of García Márquez and Isabel Allende. For a brief analysis of Donoso's *Casa de campo*, Onetti's *El astillero*, and Vargas Llosa's *Histora de Mayta*, none of which are treated in this study, see Verity Smith, *Encyclopedia*, 269–70, 598–99, 833–34. For Sabato's *Abaddón el exterminador*, and *El túnel*, see Verity Smith, *Encyclopedia*, 739–42. Succinct and insightful discussions of two of García Márquez's important novels not discussed here, *El otoño del patriarca* and *El general en su laberinto*, are to be found in Verity Smith, *Encyclopedia*, 350–51, and 353–54. Daniel Balderston, 'The Twentieth-Century Short Story in Spanish America', is a thematic analysis. For an overview of Cortázar's short stories, see Ilan Stavans, *Julio Cortázar*. José Miguel Oviedo, 'The Modern Essay in Spanish America', is a well thought-out piece on the essay. For a competent overview of the theatre, Sandra M. Cypess, 'Spanish American Theatre in the Twentieth Century', should be consulted. Beatriz Rizk's *El nuevo teatro latinoamericano* is authoritative. Ángel Flores, *Spanish American Authors: The Twentieth Century*, is an excellent reference manual; it has hard facts, critical judgements and impressive bibliographies. Also useful is *Masterpieces of Latino Literature*, edited by Frank N. Magill, which contains biographies of the main writers of the Latin American as well as the Latino literary canon, along with separate sections on their key works. The intriguing feature of this volume is that it allows Latin American writers and Latino writers to rub shoulders indiscriminately. Two excellent dictionaries edited by Peter Standish, *Hispanic Culture of South America*, and *Hispanic Culture of Mexico, Central America, and the Caribbean*, place contemporary literature within the context of other cultural expressions such as music, dance and film. A canon-creating anthology of women poets of this era is provided by Mary Crow in her excellent *Woman Who Has Sprouted Wings*. Julio Ortega's *Reapropiaciones* has two excellent essays on Ferré's fiction; Margarite Fernández Olmos judiciously compares the short stories of Ferré and Ana Lydia Vega in her *Contemporary Women Authors of Latin America*. Important studies of Lispector's fiction include Earl E. Fitz, *Clarice Lispector*, Solange Ribeiro de Oliveira and Judith Still, *Brazilian Feminisms*, and Cláudia Pazos Alonso and Claire Williams, *Closer to the Wild Heart: Essays on Clarice Lispector*. Neil Larsen, *Reading North by South* has compelling things to say about a number of Latin American essayists including Roberto Schwarz.

## Chapter 7

For an authoritative introduction to postmodernism, see Lyotard's *The Postmodern Condition*; also worth consulting are Jameson's *Postmodernism, or the Cultural Logic of Late Capitalism*, Steven Best and Douglas Kellner's *Postmodern Theory*, and Steven Connor's *Postmodernist Culture*. For some canonical essays on the Latin-American post-modern, see David Foster and Daniel Altamiranda's *Spanish American Literature: A Collection of Essays*, vol. 1, 205–98. Raymond Williams, *The Postmodern Novel in Latin America*, offers a detailed account of postmodernism in the novel. For an insightful discussion of the post-Boom in Spanish America, see Gustavo Pellón, 'The Spanish American Novel: Recent Developments, 1975 to 1990'; also indispensable are Philip Swanson's *The New Novel in Latin America*, Judith Payne and Earl Fitz's *Ambiguity and Gender in the New Novel of Brazil and Spanish America*, and Donald Shaw's *The Post-Boom in Spanish American Fiction*. The best introduction to Luis Rafael Sánchez's work is Efraín Barrandas, *Para leer en puertorriqueño*. Karl Kohut is the editor of a good selection of essays on Giardinelli, *Un universo cargado de violencia*. The best study of Skármeta's work is Donald Shaw, *Antonio Skármeta and the Post Boom*. There is some good discussion of Traba's work in Elia G. Kantaris, *The Subversive Psyche*. The best introduction to Isabel Allende's work is Patricia Hart's *Narrative Magic in the Fiction of Isabel Allende*. For some indication of the debate currently raging on the *testimonio*, see Foster and Altamiranda's *Spanish American Literature: A Collection of Essays*, vol. 1, 99–153. John Beverley's *Against Literature* also has some important essays on this topic. Roberto González Echeverría's *The Voice of the Masters* has a good chapter on Miguel Barnet's *Biografía de un cimarrón*. Else R. P. Vieira, *City of God in Several Voices*, has some excellent essays on Lins's *Cidade de Deus*. For a good introduction to Chicano literature, consult Charles Tatum, *Chicano Literature*, as well as Luis Leal and Manuel M. Martín-Rodríguez, 'Chicano Literature'. For competent discussions of Latino literature, see William Luis, 'Latin American (Hispanic Caribbean) Literature Written in the United States'. For a good selection of Chicano short stories, see Rodolfo Anaya and Antonio Marquéz's edition of *Cuentos chicanos*. Carlota Caulfield and Darién J. Davis (eds), *A Companion to US Latino Literatures* offers an excellent survey of Latino literature, and includes an informative essay on *Brazuca* literature. The best introduction to Latin-American gay literature is David William Foster's *Gay and Lesbian Themes in Latin American Writing*. Indispensable studies on Puig's work are Pamela Bacarisse, *The Necessary Dream*, and Lucille Kerr, *Suspended Fictions*. Julio Hernández-Miyares and Perla Rozencvaig have edited a collection of essays on Reinaldo Arenas entitled *Reinaldo Arenas: alucinaciones, fantasías y realidad*. Amy Kandinsky has an excellent discussion on Peri Rossi's work in her *Reading the Body Politic*. For the backdrop to Afro-Hispanic literature the reader is advised to consult Vera M. Kutzinski, 'Afro-Hispanic American Literature', as well as Richard Jackson's *The Black Image in Latin American Literature*. Also important is the same author's more recent *Black Writers and the Hispanic Canon* which has discussion of the work of Blas Jiménez, Carlos Guillermo Wilson, Nicomedes Santa Cruz, and Manuel Zapata Olivella. An excellent anthology is provided by Ingrid Watson Miller in her *Afro-Hispanic Literature*, and a canon-defining essay on Afra-Hispanic literature appears in the guise of Miriam DeCosta's 'Afra-Hispanic Writers and Feminist Discourse'; see also Flora González Mandri's *Guarding Cultural Memory: Afro-Cuban Women in Literature and the Arts*. For Afro-Brazilian literature see Roger Bastide's *Estudos Afro-Brasileiros*, and Maria Nazareth Soares Fonseca's *Brasil Afro-Brasileiro*. Maria Aparecida Andrade Salgueiro, *Escritoras negras contemporáneas* compares Afro-Brazilian with Afro-American writing in an insightful way. For individual essays on Puig, Luis Rafael Sánchez, Luisa Valenzuela, Isabel Allende, Reinaldo Arenas, and Rigoberta Menchú, see Foster and Altamiranda, *Spanish American Literature: A Collection of Essays*, vol. 5.

# BIBLIOGRAPHY

Acosta, José de, *Obras del P. José de Acosta*, ed. P. Francisco Mateos. Madrid: Atlas, 1954.
Aderaldo Castello, José, *Manifestações literárias do período colonial*. São Paolo: Cultrix, 1981.
Adorno, Rolena, 'Cultures in Contact: Mesoamerica, the Andes, and the European Written Tradition', in *The Cambridge History of Latin American Literature*, ed. Enrique Pupo-Walker and Roberto González Echeverría. Cambridge: Cambridge University Press, 1996, vol. 1, 33–57.
Agustini, Delmira, *Poesías completas*, ed. Alberto Zum Felde. 4th ed. Buenos Aires: Losada, 1971.
Ahern, Maureen, 'The Cross and the Gourd: The Appropriation of Ritual Signs in the *Relaciones* of Alvar Núñez Cabeza de Vaca and Fray Marcos de Niza', in *Early Images of the Americas: Transfer and Invention*, ed. Jerry M. Williams and Robert E. Lewis. Tucson and London: University of Arizona Press, 1993, 215–44.
Aira, César, *La Villa*. Buenos Aires: Emecé, 2001.
——, *Una novela china*. Barcelona: Mondatori, 2004.
Aldens, Dauril, *Royal Government in Colonial Brazil*. Berkeley: University of California Press, 1968.
Alegría, Ciro, *El mundo es ancho y ajeno*. Madrid: Alianza, 1993.
Alegría, Claribel, *Flowers from the Volcano*, trans. Carolyn Forché. Pittsburgh: University of Pittsburgh Press, 1982.
Alegría, Fernando, *Genio y figura de Gabriela Mistral*. Buenos Aires: Editorial Universitaria, 1966.
Alencar, José de, *Verso e Reverso*, 2nd ed. Rio de Janeiro: B. L. Garnier, 1869.
——, *Iracema*. 3rd ed. São Paulo: Edições "O Livreiro" Ltda, 1945.
——, *Iracema*, trans. Clifford E. Landers. Oxford: Oxford University Press, 2000.
Alencar Brayner, Aquiles, 'Body, Corporeal Perception and Aesthetic Experience in the Work of João Gilberto Noll', unpublished PhD thesis, King's College London, 2006.
Almeida, Manuel Antonio de, *Memórias de um Sargento de Milícias*, ed. Mamede Mustafa Jarouche. Coitia: Atelie Editorial, 2000.
Alonso, Carlos J., *The Spanish American Regional Novel*. Cambridge: Cambridge University Press, 1990.
——, 'The *Criollista* Novel', in *The Cambridge History of Latin American Literature*, ed. Enrique Pupo-Walker and Roberto González Echeverría. Cambridge: Cambridge University Press, 1996, vol. 2, 95–212.

Alvarez García, Imeldo, *La obra narrativa de Cirilo Villaverde*. Havana: Letras Cubanas, 1984.
Amado, Jorge, *Gabriela cravo e canela*. São Paulo: Martins Editora, 1966.
Anaya, Rodolfo A., and Antonio Márquez (eds), *Cuentos Chicanos: A Short Story Anthology*. Albuquerque: University of New Mexico Press, 1984.
Anchieta, José de, *Arte de Grammatica da lingoa mais usada na costa do Brasil. Feyta pelo padre Joseph de Anchieta de Capanhia de IESV*. Coimbra, 1595. 59 pp. Biblioteca Nacional, Rio de Janeiro, Obras Raras, Cofre 2, 19, ex 1-OR–02.
——, *Cartas, informacões, fragmentos históricos e Sermões de Pedro Joseph de Anchieta SJ*. Rio de Janeiro: Civilização Brasileira, 1933.
Anderson, Benedict, *Imagined Communities: Reflections on the Origin and Spread of Nationalism*. London: Verso, 4th impression, 1987 [1983].
Anderson-Imbert, Enrique, *Genio y figura de Sarmiento*. Buenos Aires: Editorial Universitaria, 1967.
——, *Spanish-American Literature. A History*, trans. John V. Falconieri. 2 vols. Detroit: Wayne State University Press, 1969.
Andrade, Mário de, *Poesias completas*. São Paolo: Livraria Martins Editora, 1966.
——, *Macunaíma o héroe sem nenhum carácter*. Belo Horizonte: Livraria Garnier, 2005.
Andrade Tosta, Antonio Luciano de, 'Between Heaven and Hell: Perceptions of Brazil and the United States in Brazuca Literature', *Hispania* (Washington) 88.4 (2005): 713–25.
——, 'American Dream, Brasileiro Jeitinho: On the Crossroads of Cultural Identities in Brazilian-American Literature', in *A Companion to US Latino Literature*, eds Carlota Caulfield and Darién J. Davis. Ipswich: Boydell and Brewer, 2006, 140–57.
Andrien, Kenneth J., *Crisis and Decline: The Viceroyalty of Peru in the Seventeenth Century*. Albuquerque: University of New Mexico Press, 1985.
Aparecida Andrade Salgueiro, Maria, *Escritoras negras contemporánas: Estudos de narrativas. Estados Unidos e Brasil*. Rio de Janeiro: Caetés, 2004.
Aquézolo Castro, Manuel (ed.), *La polémica del indigenismo*. Prólogo y notas de Luis Alberto Sánchez. Lima: Mosca Azul, 1976.
Aragón, Roque Raúl, and J. Calcetti. *Genio y figura de José Hernández*. Buenos Aires: Editorial Universitaria, 1972.
Arbeleche, Jorge, *Juana de Ibarbourou*. Montevideo: Editorial Técnica, 1978.
Arenas, Reinaldo, *Farewell to the Sea: A Novel of Cuba*, trans. Andrew Hurley. New York: Viking, 1986.
Arguedas, José María, *Los ríos profundos*. Lima: Editorial Horizonte, 1993.
Arias, Juan, 'Paulo Lins: "la poesía da miedo a los adultos por su carga de verdad"', *El País* (26 July 2003): 2.
Arias, Santa, and Erlinda Gonzales-Berry, 'Latino Writing in the United States', in *Handbook of Latin American Literature*, ed. David William Foster. New York and London: Garland, 1992, 649–85.
Armstrong, Piers, 'The Brazilian Novel', in *The Cambridge Companion to the Latin American Novel*, ed. Efraín Kristal. Cambridge: Cambridge University Press, 2005, 105–24.
Arrom, Juan José, *Esquema generacional de las letras hispanoamericanas: ensayo de un método*. 2nd ed. Bogotá: Caro y Cuervo, 1977.

Arzáns de Orsúa y Vela, Bartolomé, *Tales of Potosí*, ed. R. C. Padden, trans. Frances M. López-Morillas. Providence, RI: Brown University Press, 1975.
Asturias, Miguel Angel, *Hombres de maíz*. 3rd ed. Madrid: Alianza, 1979.
Audiencia de Lima, *Correspondencia de Presidentes y Oidores. Documentos del Archivo de Indias. 1549–1564*, ed. Roberto Levillier. Vol. 1. Madrid: Juan Pueyo, 1922.
Auerbach, Erich, *Mimesis. Dargestelle Wirklichkeit in der Abländischen Literatur*. Bern, 1946.
Aybar, Edmundo Bendezú, *Literatura quechua*. Caracas: Ayacucho, 1980.
Azuela, Mariano, *Los de abajo*, ed. W. A. R. Richardson. London: Harrap, 1980.
Bacarisse, Pamela, *The Necessary Dream: A Study of the Novels of Manuel Puig*. Cardiff: University of Wales Press, 1988.
Balderston, Daniel, 'The Twentieth-Century Short Story in Spanish America', *The Cambridge History of Latin American Literature*, ed. Enrique Pupo-Walker and Roberto González Echeverría. Cambridge: Cambridge University Press, 1996, vol. 2, 465–96.
Bandeira, Manuel (ed.), *Antologia dos poetas brasileiros: fase romântica*. Rio de Janeiro: Editôra Nova Fronteira, 1996.
Baranov, David, *The Abolition of Slavery in Brazil*. Westport, CT: Greenwood Press, 2000.
Barnes, Julian, *Flaubert's Parrot*. New York: McGraw Hill, 1984.
Barnet, Miguel, *Biografía de un cimarrón*. Havana: Editorial Letras Cubanas, 1980.
Barradas, Efraín, *Para leer en puertorriqueño: acercamiento a la obra de Luis Rafael Sánchez*. Río Piedras, PR: Cultural 1981.
Barreto, Alfonso Henriques de Lima, *Triste fim de Policarpo Quaresma*. 11th ed. São Paulo: Editôra Brasiliense, 1974.
Barthes, Roland, 'Le monde où l'on catche', in *Mythologies*. Paris: Seuil, 1957, 13–24.
Bastide, Roger, *Estudos Afro-Brasileiros*. São Paulo: Editôra Perspectiva, 1973.
Bataillon, Marcel, *Hernán Cortés: autor prohibido*. Mexico: UNAM, 1956.
Batres Montúfar, José, *Poesías*. Guatemala: Tipografía nacional, 1944.
Baudot, Georges, *Utopía e historia en Mexico: las primeras cronistas de la civilización mexicana (1520–1569)*. Madrid: Espasa Calpe, 1983.
Bautista Avalle-Arce, Juan, 'El poeta en sus poemas: el caso Ercilla', in *Historia y crítica de la literatura hispanoamericana*, ed. Cedomil Goic. Vol. 1. Barcelona: Editorial Crítica, 1988, 220–6.
Beardsell, Peter R., *Quiroga. Cuentos de amor, de locura y de muerte*. London: Grant and Cutler, 1986.
———, *A Theatre for Cannibals. Rodoflo Usigli and the Mexican Stage*. London: Associated University Presses, 1992.
Belli, Carlos Germán, *Boda de la pluma y la letra*. Madrid: Ediciones Cultura Hispánica, 1985.
Bello, Andrés, *Obra literaria*, eds, Pedro Grases and Oscar Samrano Urdaneta. 2nd ed. Caracas: Biblioteca Ayacucho. 1985 [1979].
Benítez-Rojo, Antonio, 'The Nineteenth-Century Spanish American Novel', in *The Cambridge History of Latin American Literature*, ed. Enrique Pupo-Walker and Roberto González Echeverría. Cambridge: Cambridge University Press, 1996, vol. 1, 417–89.

Berdan, Frances F. and Patricia Rieff Anawalt, *Codex Mendoza*. 4 vols. Berkeley, Los Angeles and Oxford: University of California Press, 1992.
Best, Steven, & Douglas Kellner, *Postmodern Theory: Critical Interrogations*. New York: The Guilford Press, 1991.
Bethell, Leslie, *The Abolition of the Brazilian Slave Trade*. Cambridge: Cambridge University Press, 1970.
Beverley, John, *Against Literature*. Minneapolis: University of Minneapolis Press, 1993.
Bill, M. V., '*Cidade de Deus*: History's Silent Protagonist', in *City of God in Several Voices: Brazilian Social Cinema as Action*, ed. Else Vieira. Nottingham: Critical, Cultural and Communications Press, 2005, 121–6.
Bishop, Elizabeth, and Emanuel Brasil (eds), *An Anthology of Twentieth-Century Brazilian Poetry*. Middletown, CT: Wesleyan University Press, 1972.
Bloom, Harold, *The Anxiety of Influence. A Theory of Poetry*. New York: Oxford University Press, 1973.
—— (ed.), *Jorge Luis Borges*. New York: Chelsea House, 1986.
—— (ed.), *Carlos Fuentes*. New York: Chelsea House, 2006.
Boldy, Steven, *The Novels of Julio Cortázar*. Cambridge: Cambridge University Press, 1980.
Bolívar, Simón, *Documentos*, ed. Manuel Galich. Cuba: Casa de las Américas, 1964.
——, *Obras completas*, ed. Vicente Lecuna. La Habana: Lexis, 1950. 3 vols.
Boone, Elizabeth and Walter D. Mignolo (eds), *Writing Without Words: Alternative Literacies in Mesoamerica and the Andes*. Durham, NC: Duke University Press, 1994.
Borgeson, Jr., Paul W., *Hacia el hombre nuevo: poesía y pensamiento de Ernesto Cardenal*. London: Tamesis, 1984.
Boschetto-Sandoval, Sandra M. and Marcia Phillips McGowan, *Claribel Alegría and Central American Literature: Critical Essays*. Athens: Ohio University Center for European Studies, 1994.
Botelho de Oliveira, Manuel, *Hay Amigo Para Amigo*, ed. Felinto Rodrigues Neto. Rio de Janeiro: Ministério de Educação e Cultura, 1973.
Boti, Regino, *Kindred Spirits*, ed. Stephen Hart. London: Mango Press, 2005.
Bougainville, Luis Antoine de, 'The Expulsion of the Jesuits from Paraguay as Recounted by Louis Antoine de Bougainville', in *Colonial Travelers in Latin America*, ed. Irving A. Leonard. New York: Alfred A. Knopf, 1972, 183–91.
Boxer, C. R., *A Great Luso-Brazilian Figure Padre Antônio Vieira, SJ, 1608–1697: The Fourth Canning House Annual Lecture delivered at Canning House 6 February 1957*. London: Canning House, 1957.
Bradley, D. A., *The First America: The Spanish Monarchy, Creole Patriots, and the Liberal State 1492–1867*. Cambridge: Cambridge University Press, 1991.
Brasil, Emanuel, and William Jay Smith (eds), *Brazilian Poetry (1950–1980)*. Middletown, CT: Wesleyan University Press, 1983.
Bretas, Angela, *Sonho Americano*. São Paolo: Scortecci, 2003.
Brotherston, Gordon, *Latin American Poetry: Origins and Presence*. Cambridge: Cambridge University Press, 1976.
——, *Book of the Fourth World: Reading the Native American Through their Literature*. Cambridge: Cambridge University Press, 1992.
——, *Mexican Painted Books: Originals in the United Kingdom and the World They Represent*. Colchester: University of Essex Press, 1992.

Brushwood, John, *Genteel Barbarism: Experiments in the Analysis of Nineteenth-Century Spanish American Novels*. Lincoln: University of Nebraska Press, 1981.
Bryce Echenique, Alfredo, *El huerto de mi amada*. Barcelona: Planeta, 2002.
Buarque de Holanda S. *Antologia dos poetas brasileiros da fase colonial*. São Paulo: Instituto Nacional do Livro, 1953.
Buarque de Hollanda, Francisco 'Chico', *Budapeste*. Rio de Janeiro: Companhia das Letras, 2003.
Burkholder, Mark A., *Politics of a Colonial Career: José Baquíjano and the Audiencia of Lima*. Albuquerque: University of New Mexico Press, 1980.
Burns, E. Bradford, *Perspectives on Brazilian History*. New York: Columbia University Press, 1967.
Cabrera Infante, Guillermo, *Tres tristes tigres*. Barcelona: Seix Barral. 1965.
Caldera, Rafael, *Andrés Bello: Philosopher, Poet, Philologist, Educator, Legislator, Statesman*, trans. John Street. London: Allen and Unwin, 1977.
Caldwell, Helen, *Machado de Assis: The Brazilian Master and his Novels*. Berkeley: University of California Press, 1970.
Camarinha da Silva, Mario, 'Apresentação', in *Basílio da Gama: O Uraguai*. Rio de Janeiro: Agir, 1964, 5–18.
Campa, Antonio R. de la, and Raquel Chang-Rodríguez (eds), *Poesía hispanoamericana colonial: antología*. Madrid: Alhambra, 1985.
Campbell, Joe R., and Frances Kartunnen, *Foundation Course in Nahuatl Grammar*. Austin: Institute of Latin American Studies, University of Texas at Austin, 1989. 2 vols.
Cândido, Antônio, *Formação da literatura brasileira (Momentos Decisivos)*. 2 vols, 2nd ed. São Paulo: Livraria Martins Editôra, 1964.
——, *Presença de literatura brasileira (Historia e Antologia)*. 3 vols. São Paulo: Difusão Européia do Livro, 1964.
Caracciolo-Trejo E. (ed.). *The Penguin Book of Latin American Verse*. Harmondsworth: Penguin, 1971.
Cardenal, Ernesto, *Poesía escogida*. Barcelona: Barral, 1975.
Cardim, Fernão, *Tratados da terra e gente do Brasil*, ed Batista Caetano, Capistrano de Abreu and Rodolofo Garcia, 3rd ed. São Paulo: Companhia Editora Nacional, 1978.
Cardona-López, José, 'La *nouvelle* hispanoamericana reciente', Dissertation, University of Kentucky, 1996.
Carilla, Emilio, *El romanticismo en la América Hispánica*. 2 vols. 2nd ed. Madrid: Gredos, 1967.
Carlyle, Thomas, *On Heroes, Hero-Worship and the Heroic in History*. Philadelphia PA: Henry Altemus, 1894.
Carpentier, Alejo, *Los pasos perdidos*. Barcelona: Barral, 1974.
Carrió de la Vandera, Alonso, *El lazarillo de ciegos caminantes*. Caracas: Biblioteca Ayacucho, 1985.
Casas, Bartolomé de las Casas, *Breuissima relacion de la destruycion de las Indias colegida por el Obispo do fray Bartolome de las Casas* (1552). Cambridge University Library, Microfiche 163.
Caso, Fernando, *Explicación del reverso del Codex Vindobonensis*. Mexico: Colegio Nacional, 1950.

Castellanos, Rosario, *Oficio de tinieblas*. 2nd ed. Mexico: Joaquín Mortiz, 1966 [1962].
——, *Album de familia*. Mexico: Joaquín Mortiz, 1985.
——, *Balún-Canán*. 14th printing. Mexico: Fondo de Cultura Económica, 1987 [1957].
——, *Meditation on the Threshold*. New York: Bilingual Press, 1988.
——, *El eterno femenino*. 7th printing. Mexico: Fondo de Cultura Económica, 1990 [1975].
Castillo, Debra, *Talking Back: Toward a Latin American Feminist Criticism*. Ithaca, NY: Cornell University Press, 1992.
Castillo, Sor Francisca Josefa de la Concepción de, *Análisis crítico de los 'Afectos espirituales' de Sor Francisca Josefa de la Concepción de Castillo*, ed. Darío Acury Valenzuela. Bogotá: Imprenta Nacional, 1962.
Castillo, Susan, *Colonial Encounters in New World Writing, 1500–1700: Performing America*. London: Routledge, 2006.
Caulfield, Carlota, and Darién J. Davis (eds), *A Companion to US Latino Literatures*. Woodbridge: Tamesis, 2006.
Cervantes, Miguel de, *El Ingenioso Hidalgo Don Quijote de la Mancha*, ed. John Jay Allen. 2 vols. Madrid: Cátedra, 1977. 2 vols.
Chang-Rodríguez, Raquel, and Malva E. Filer, *Voces de Hispanoamérica: antología literaria*. Boston: Heinle & Heinle, 1988.
Charno, Steven M., *Latin American Newspapers in United States Libraries: A Union List*. Austin and London: University of Texas Press, 1968.
Chávez Orozco, Luis, *Códice Osuna: reproducción facsimilar de la obra del mismo título, editada en Madrid, 1878. Acompañada de 158 páginas inéditas encontradas en le Archivo General de la Nación (México)*. Mexico: Ediciones del Instituto Indigenista Interamericano, 1947.
Checa Godoy, Antonio, *Historia de la prensa en Iberoamérica*. Seville: Alfar, 1993.
Christ, Ronald J., *The Narrow Act: Borges's Art of Allusion*. New York: New York University Press, 1969.
Cieza de León, Pedro, *La Chronica del Perv, nvevamente escrita, por Cieça de Leon, vezino de Sevilla*. Antwerp: Martin Nucio, 1554. Sala de Investigaciones, Biblioteca Nacional, Lima. X985.0092.
Cisneros, Antonio, *Propios como ajenos: antología personal Poesía 1962–1969*. 2nd ed. Lima: Peisa, 1991.
Clendinnen, Inga, 'Cortés, Signs, and the Conquest of Mexico', in *The Transmission of Culture in Early Modern Europe*, eds Anthony Grafton and Ann Blair. Philadelphia: University of Pennsylvania Press, 1990, 87–130.
Cobo Borda, Juan Gustavo, *Usos de la imaginación*. Buenos Aires: El Imaginario, 1984.
*Codex Dresden. Commentary on the Maya Manuscript in the Royal Public Library of Dresden*, by Ernst Förstemann, trans. Selma Wesselhoeft and A. M. Parker, Cambridge, MA: Peabody Museum of American Archeology and Ethnology, 1906.
*Codex Kingsbrough. Códice Kingsborough. Memorial de los indios de Tepetlaoztoc al monarca español contra los encomenderos del pueblo*, ed. Francisco del Paso y Troncoso. Madrid: Hauser y Memet, 1912.
*Codex Mendoza. Códice Mendocino. Documento mexicano del siglo XVI que se*

*conserva en la biblioteca bodleiana de Oxford, Inglaterra*. Facsímile fototípico dispuesto por don Francisco del Paso y Troncoso. Mexico: Museo Nacional de Arqueología, Historia y Etnografía, 1925.
*Codex Perez, The, and the Book of Chilam Balam of Maní*, trans. Eugene R. Craine and Reginald C. Reindorp. Norman: University of Oklahoma Press, 1979.
*Codex Tro-Cortesianus (Codex Madrid). Museo de América, Madrid*. Introduction and summary F. Anders. Graz: Akademische Druck und Verlagsanstalt, 1967.
*Códice de 1576 (Códice Aubin). Historia de la nación mexicana*, ed. Charles E. Dibble. Madrid: Ediciones José Porrúa Turanzas, 1963.
Cohen, Thomas M., *The Fire of Tongues: Antônio Vieira and the Missionary Church in Brazil and Portugal*. Stanford, CA: Stanford University Press, 1998.
Columbus, Christopher, *Journal of the First Voyage (Diario del primer viaje)*, ed. and trans. B. W. Ife, with an essay on Columbus's language by R. J. Penny. Warminster: Aris & Phillips Ltd., 1990.
Connor, Steven, *Postmodernist Culture: An Introduction to Theories of the Contemporary*. Oxford: Basil Blackwell, 1989.
Cornejo Polar, Antonio, *Los universos narrativos de José María Arguedas*. Buenos Aires: Losada, 1973.
——, *Escribir en el aire: ensayo sobre la heterogeneidad socio-cultural en las literaturas andinas*. Lima: Editorial Horizonte, 1994.
Corominas, Joan, and J. A. Pascual, *Diccionario crítico etimológico hispánico*. 5 vols. Madrid: Gredos, 1980.
Cortázar, Julio, *Rayuela*. 21st ed. Buenos Aires: Editorial Sudamericana, 1977 [1963].
——, *Las ediciones secretas*, ed. Susana Jakfalvi. Madrid: Cátedra, 1979.
Cortés, Hernán, *Cartas de relación*. Mexico: Editorial Porrúa, 1960.
Costa, René de, *Vicente Huidobro: The Careers of a Poet*. Oxford: Clarendon Press, 1984.
Cota Fagundes, Francisco, 'Portuguese Immigrant Experience in America in Autobiography', *Hispania* (Washington) 88.4 (2005): 701–12.
Coutinho, Afrânio, *An Introduction to Literature in Brazil*. New York: Columbia University Press, 1969.
Coutinho, Graça (ed.), *Enciclopédia da Literatura Brasileira*. 2 vols. São Paolo: Global Editôra, 2001.
Craig, Herbert E., *Marcel Proust and Spanish América: From Critical Response to Narrative Dialogue*. Lewisburg PA: Bucknell University Press, 2002.
Craig-Odders, Renée W., Jacky Collins and Glen S. Close (eds), *Hispanic and Luso-Brazilian Fiction: Essays on the 'Género Negro' Tradition*. Jefferson, NC: McFarland & Co., 2006.
Craine, Eugene R. and Reginald C. Reindorp, 'Preface', *The Codex Pérez and the Book of Chilam Balam of Maní*. Norman: University of Oklahoma Press, 1979, xiii–xviii.
Crow, Mary (ed.), *Woman Who Has Sprouted Wings: Poems by Contemporary Latin American Poets*. 2nd ed. Pittsburgh: Latin American Literary Review Press, 1987.
Cruickshank, D. W., 'Literature and the Book Trade in Golden-Age Spain', *MLR* 73 (1978): 799–824.
Cruz, Sor Juana Inés de la, *Obras completas. Lírica personal*, vol. 1, ed. Alfonso Méndez Plancarte. Mexico: Fondo de Cultural Económica, 1951.

——, *Obras completas*, vol. 4, ed. Alberto G. Salceda. Mexico City: Fondo de Cultura Económica, 1957.
Curran, Mark J., *A literatura de cordel*. Recife: Universidade Federal de Pernambuco, 1973.
Cussen, Antonio, *Poetry and Politics in the Spanish American Revolution: Bello, Bolívar and the Classical Tradition*. Cambridge: Cambridge University Press, 1991.
Cypess, Sandra M., 'Spanish American Theatre in the Twentieth Century', in *The Cambridge History of Latin American Literature*, ed. Enrique Pupo-Walker and Roberto González Echeverría. Cambridge: Cambridge University Press, 1996, vol. 2, 497–525.
Da Cunha, Euclides, *Os Sertões (Campanha de Canudos)*, 12th ed. Rio de Janeiro: Paulo de Azevedo & C., 1933.
——, *Rebellion in the Backlands, Translated from* Os Sertões *by Euclides da Cunha*, with introduction and notes by Samuel Putham. Chicago: University of Chicago Press, 1944.
Da Gama, Basílio, *O Uraguai*. Rio de Janeiro: Agir, 1964.
Darío, Rubén, *Poesías completas*, ed. Alfonso Méndez Plancarte. Madrid: Aguilar, 1968.
Dauster, Frank N., *Historia del teatro hispanoamericano. Siglos XIX y XX*. Mexico: De Andrea, 1973.
——, 'The Spanish American Theatre of the Nineteenth Century', in *The Cambridge History of Latin American Literature*, ed. Enrique Pupo-Walker and Roberto González Echeverría. Cambridge: Cambridge University Press, 1996, vol. 1, 536–55.
DeCosta, Miriam, 'Afra-Hispanic Writers and Feminist Discourse', *NWSA Journal* 5 (1993): 204–17.
Del Sarto, Ana, Alicia Ríos, and Abril Trigo (eds), *The Latin American Cultural Studies Reader*. Durham, NC: Duke University Press, 2004.
Díaz, Roberto Ignacio, *Unhomely Rooms: Foreign Tongues and Spanish American Literature*. Lewisburg PA: Bucknell University Press, 2002.
Díaz del Castillo, Bernal, *Historia verdadera de la conquista de la Nueva España*, ed. Miguel León-Portilla. 2 vols. Madrid: Historia 16, 1984.
*Diccionario de la lengua española*, Madrid: Espasa-Calpe, 1992.
Diego de Landa, Fray, *Relación de las cosas de Yucatán*. Mérida: Editorial San Fernando, 1992.
Dollimore, Jonathan, *Sexual Dissidence: Augustine to Wilde, Freud to Foucault*. Oxford: Oxford University Press, 1991.
Donoso, José, *El obsceno pájaro de la noche*. Barcelona: Seix Barral, 1970.
——, *The Boom in Spanish American Literature: A Personal History*, trans. Gregory Kolovakos. New York: Columbia University Press, 1977.
——, *Historia personal del 'Boom'*. 2nd ed. Barcelona: Seix Barral, 1983.
Drummond de Andrade, Carlos, *A paixão medida*. Rio de Janeiro: Editôra Record, 2002.
Eagleton, Terry, *Literary Theory: An Introduction*. Minneapolis: University of Minnesota Press, 1985.
Echeverría, Esteban, *Obras completas*, ed. Juan María Gutiérrez. Buenos Aires: Ediciones Antonio Zamora, 1951.

Edmonson, Munro S. (ed.), *Heaven Born. Mérida and its Destiny: The Book of Chilam Balam of Chumayal*. Austin: University of Texas Press, 1986.
Edwards, Jorge, *El sueño de la historia*. 3rd ed. Barcelona: Tusquets, 2000.
Eiró, Paulo, *Sangue limpo*, ed. Jamil Almanour Haddad. São Paulo: Departamento de Cultura, Divisão do Arquivo Histórico, 1949.
*Enciclopedia Universal Ilustrada Europea-Americana*. vol. XXX. Barcelona. Hijos de J. Espasa, Editora. n.d.
*Encyclopedia Britannica*, 15th ed. Chicago: Encyclopedia Britannica Inc., 1995.
Espinosa Pólit, Aurelio, '*La victoria de Junín* de José Joaquín de Olmedo', in *Historia y crítica de la literatura hispanoamericana*, ed. Cedomil Goic. Barcelona: Editorial Crítica, 1988, vol. 1, 536–41.
Esquivel, Laura, *Como agua para chocolate*. 17th reprint. Mexico: Editorial Planeta Mexicana, 1992 [1989].
Fagundes Telles, Lydia, *As Meninas*. 8th ed. Rio de Janeiro: José Olympio Editôra, 1976.
Faris, Wendy, *Ordinary Enchantments: Magical Realism and the Remystification of Narrative*. Nashville TN: Vanderbilt University Press, 2004.
Feal, Rosemary G., 'Reflections in the Obsidian Mirror: The Poetics of Afro-Hispanic Identity and the Gendered Body', *Afro-Hispanic Review* (1995): 26–32.
Fein, John M., *Octavio Paz: A Reading of his Major Poems, 1957–1976*. Lexington: Kentucky University Press, 1986.
Fernandes Brandão, Ambrósio, *Diálogos das Grandezas do Brasil*, ed. Afrânio Peixoto, J. Capistrano de Abreu and Rodolfo Garcia. Rio de Janeiro: Edicões de Ouro, 1968.
Fernández de Lizardi, José Joaquín, *El Periquillo Sarniento*. Mexico: Porrúa, 1984.
Fernández Olmos, Margarite, *Contemporary Women Authors of Latin America*. Brooklyn, NY: Brooklyn College Press, 1983.
Fernández de Oviedo, Gonzalo, *De la natural historia de las Indias (Sumario de historia natural de las Indias)*, ed. Enrique Alvarez López. Madrid: Summa, 1942.
Fernández Retamar, Roberto, *Caliban and Other Essays*, trans. Edward Baker. Minneapolis: Minnesota University Press, 1989.
——, 'Prologue to Ernesto Cardenal', in *Caliban and Other Essays*, trans. Edward Baker. Minneapolis: Minnesota University Press, 1989, 100–10.
Fitz, Earl E. *Clarice Lispector*. Boston: Twayne, 1985.
——, *Machado de Assis*. Boston: Twayne, 1989.
Fló, Juan, and Stephen Hart (eds), *César Vallejo: autógrafos olvidados*. London and Lima: Tamesis-La Católica, 2003.
Flores, Angel, *Spanish American Authors: The Twentieth Century*
——, and Helene M. Anderson (eds), *Masterpieces of Spanish American Literature. The Colonial Period to the Beginnings of Modernism*. Vol. 1. New York: Macmillan, 1974.
*Juan del Valle Caviedes. Obra completa*, ed. Daniel R. Reedy. Caracas: Biblioteca Ayacucho, 1984.
Fonseca, Rubem, 'A Colera do Cão', in *A Colera do Cão*. Rio de Janeiro: Edicões GRD, 1965, 205-60.

Foreno Benavides, Abelardo, *Impresión y represión de los derechos del hombre.* Bogotá: Universidad de los Andes, 1967.
Forgues, Roland, *Mariátegui: la utopía realizable.* Lima: Amauta, 1995.
Foster, David William, *Gay and Lesbian Themes in Latin American Writing.* Austin: University of Texas Press, 1991.
—— (ed.), *Handbook of Latin American Literature.* 2nd ed. New York and London: Garland, 1992.
—— (ed.), *Literatura hispanoamericana: una antología.* New York and London: Garland, 1994.
——, and Daniel Altamiranda (eds), *Spanish American Literature: A Collection of Essays.* 5 vols. New York and London: Garland, 1997.
Foucault, Michel, *The Order of Things: An Archaeology of the Human Sciences.* New York: Pantheon, 1970.
Franco, Jean, *An Introduction to Spanish-American Literature.* Cambridge: Cambridge University Press, 1969.
Franconi, Rodolfo A., 'Between Brazilian in the States: Between Fiction and Reality', *Hispania* (Washington) 88.4 (2005): 726–32.
Freyre, Gilberto, *Casa-Grande & Senzala: Formação da família brasileira sob o regimen de economia patriarchal.* Rio de Janeiro: Maia & Schmidt, 1933.
——, 'Preface to the Second English-Language Edition'. *The Masters and the Slaves: A Study in the Development of Brazilian Civilization,* trans. Samuel Putnam. New York: Alfred A. Knopf, 1970. xviii-lxx.
——, *La nueva novela hispanoamericana.* Mexico: Joaquín Mortiz, 1972.
——, *Cambio de piel.* 2nd ed. Barcelona: Seix Barral, 1980 [1967].
Fuentes, Carlos, *La muerte de Artemio Cruz.* Mexico: Fondo de Cultura Económica, 1962.
Galante de Sousa, J., *O teatro no Brasil.* Rio de Janeiro: Gráfica, 1968.
Gândavo, Pêro de Magalhães de, *Tratado da Terra do Brasil, no qual se contém a informação das cousas que há nestas partes; feito por Pêro de Magalhães.* Lisboa: Academia das Sciencias, 1826. Book IV in the Colleção de noticias para a historia e geografia das nações ultramarinas.
García Canclini, Néstor, *Culturas híbridas: estrategias para entrar y salir de la modernidad.* México: Grijalbo, 1989.
——, *Latinoamericanos buscando lugar en este siglo.* Buenos Aires: Paidos, 2002.
García Goyena, Rafael, *Fábulas,* ed. Carlos Samayoa Chinchilla. Guatemala: Ediciones del Gobierno de Guatemala, 1950.
García Márquez, Gabriel, *Los funerales de la mamá grande.* Buenos Aires: Editorial Sudamericana, 1977.
——, *El coronel no tiene quien le escriba.* 6th ed. Barcelona: Plaza & Janés, 1979.
——, *Cien años de soledad.* Barcelona: Argos Vergara, 1980.
——, *El amor en los tiempos del cólera.* 5th ed. Barcelona: Plaza & Janés, 1998.
Garcidueñas, José Rojas, and José Juan Arrom (eds), *Tres piezas teatrales del virreinato.* Mexico: Universidad Nacional Autónoma de México, 1976.
Garro, Elena, *Los recuerdos del porvenir.* Mexico: Joaquín Mortiz, 1963.
Gerbi, Antonello, *La naturaleza de las Indias Nuevas: De Cristóbal Colón a Gonzalo Fernández de Oviedo.* Mexico: Fondo de Cultura Económica, 1978.

Gerdes, Dick, 'Peru', in *Handbook of Latin American Literature*, ed. David William Foster. 2nd ed. New York and London: Garland, 1992, 493–553.
Giardinelli, Mempo, *Luna caliente*. Buenos Aires: Planeta Argentina, 1995.
Gledson, John, *The Deceptive Realism of Machado de Assis: A Dissenting Interpretation of Dom Casmurro*. Liverpool: Francis Cairns, 1984.
Goic, Cedomil (ed.), *Historia y crítica de la literatura hispanoamericana*. Vol. 1. Barcelona: Editorial Crítica, 1988.
Gollnick, Brian, 'Approaches to Latin American Literature', in *The Companion to Latin American Studies*, ed. Philip Swanson. London: Arnold, 2003, 107–21.
Gomes, Eugênio, 'O testamento estético de Machado de Assis', in *Esaú e Jacó*, ed. Eugênio Gomes. Rio de Janeiro: José Aguilar Editôra, 1973, 13–43.
Gómez de Avellaneda, Gertrudis, *Antología poética*. Havana: Editorial Letras Cubanas, 1983.
Gonçalves Dias, *Teatro Completo*, ed. Marlene de Castro Correia. Rio de Janeiro: Ministério de Educação e Cultura, 1979.
González, Aníbal, *Journalism and the Development of Spanish American Narrative*. Cambridge: Cambridge University Press, 1993.
——, 'Crónica y cuento en el modernismo', *El cuento hispanoamericano*, ed. Enrique Pupo-Walker. Madrid: Castalia, 1995, 155–70.
——, 'Modernist Prose', *The Cambridge History of Latin American Literature*, ed. Enrique Pupo-Walker and Roberto González Echeverría. Cambridge: Cambridge University Press, 1996, vol. 2, 69–113.
——, *Killer Books: Writing, Violence and Ethics in Modern Spanish American Narrative*. Austin, TX: University of Texas Press, 2001.
González Echeverría, Roberto, *The Voice of the Masters: Writing and Authority in Modern Latin American Literature*. Austin: University of Texas Press, 1985.
——, 'Colonial Lyric', *The Cambridge History of Latin American Literature*, ed. Enrique Pupo-Walker and Roberto González Echeverría. Cambridge: Cambridge University Press, 1996, vol. 1, 191–259.
Gonzalez Mandri, Flora, *Guarding Cultural Memory: Afro-Cuban Women in Literature and the Arts*. Charlottesville: University of Virginia Press, 2006.
Greenblatt, Stephen, *Marvelous Possessions: The Wonder of the New World*. Chicago: University of Chicago Press, 1991.
Greer Johnson, Julie, *Satire in Colonial Spanish America: Turning the New World Upside Down*. Foreword by Daniel R. Reedy. Austin: University of Texas Press, 1993.
Griffin, Clive, *The Crombergers of Seville. The History of a Printing and Merchant Dynasty*. Oxford: Clarendon, 1988.
——, *Azuela: Los de abajo*. London: Grant & Cutler, 1993.
Grossman, Edith, *The Antipoetry of Nicanor Parra*. New York: New York University Press, 1975.
Guaman Poma de Ayala, Felipe, *Nueva corónica y buen gobierno*, ed. Franklin Pease. 2 vols. Caracas: Biblioteca Ayacucho, 1980.
Guerra, Alvaro, *Gregório de Matos: sua vida e suas obras*, 2nd ed. São Paulo: Edições Melhoramentos, 1942.
Guimarães, Bernardo. *A escrava Isaura*. São Paolo: Editôra Atica, 1992.
Guimarães Rosa, João, *Grande sertão: Veredas*, ed. Paula Rónai. 19th ed. Rio de Janeiro: Nova Fronteira, 2001.
Güiraldes, Ricardo, *Don Segundo Sombra*. 30th ed. Buenos Aires: Losada, 1971.

Gutiérrez, Eduardo, *Juan Moreira*. Buenos Aires: La Patria Argentina, 1879.
Haberly, David T., 'Bernardo Guimarães', in *Encyclopedia of Latin American Literature*, ed. Verity Smith. Chicago: Dearborn, 1997, 395–6.
Hallewell, Laurence, *O livro no Brasil*, 2nd ed. São Paulo: Editôra da Universidade de São Paulo, 2005.
Hamden, Soraya (ed.), *Coleção Teatro Brasileiro*. Vols 2 and 3. Belo Horizonte: Hamden Editores, 1998.
Harrison, Regina, *Signs, Songs and Memory in the Andes: Translating Quechua Language and Culture*. Austin: University of Texas Press, 1989.
Harss, Luis, *Into the Mainstream. Conversations with Latin-American Writers*. New York: Harper & Row, 1969.
Hart, Patricia, *Narrative Magic in the Fiction of Isabel Allende*. Rutherford, NJ: Fairleigh Dickinson University Press, 1989.
Hart, Stephen M., *The Other Scene: Psychoanalytic Readings in Modern Spanish and Latin-American Literature*. Boulder, CO: SSASS, 1992.
——, *White Ink: Essays on Twentieth-century Feminine Fiction in Spain and Latin America*. London: Tamesis, 1993.
——, 'Some Reflections on the Spanish American Literary Canon', *Siglo XX/20th Century* 1 (1994): 145–55.
——, *García Márquez: 'Crónica de una muerte anunciada'*. London: Grant & Cutler, 2005.
——, 'Is Women's Writing in Spanish America Gender-Specific?' *MLN* 110 (1995): 335–52.
——, 'La cápsula mágica: los poetas latinoamericanos que viven en los Estados Unidos y su Público', *The Seventeenth Louisiana Conference on Hispanic Languages and Literatures. Louisiana State University, Baton Rouge, 1996*, ed. Jesús Torrecilla et al. Baton Rouge, LA: Department of Foreign Language and Literatures, 1996: 3–10.
——, '"La boca asfixiada": Literary Projections of the Italian in Argentina 1870–1900', *Studi Ispanici* III (1997–1998): 191–202.
——, 'Literary Print Culture in Spanish America 1880–1910', *Anales de la literatura española contemporánea* 23.1–2 (1998): 165–80.
——, '"El oficio de escribir": Some Notes on Literary Print Culture in Spanish America in the Twentieth Century', *Neophilologus* 83 (1999): 387–409.
——, 'Public Execution and the Body Politic in the Work of the Argentine *Folletinista* Eduardo Gutiérrez', *Bulletin of Hispanic Studies* 76 (1999): 673–90.
——, 'Literary Print Culture in the Spanish Colonies', *Forum for Modern Language Studies* 36.1 (2000): 92–107.
——, 'Pablo Neruda and "Verdadismo"', *Hispanic Research Journal* 5.3 (2004): 255–64.
——, 'Cultural Hybridity, Magical Realism, and the Language of Magic in Paulo Coelho's *The Alchemist*', *Romance Quarterly* 51.4 (2004): 304–12.
——, '*Cidade de Deus*', *Companion to Latin American Film*. Woodbridge: Tamesis, 2004, 205–10.
——, 'Four Stomachs and a Brain: An Interpretation of Esaú e Jacó', *Portuguese Literary & Cultural Studies* 13–14 (Fall 2004–Spring 2005): 317–31. Special number 'The Author as Plagiarist – The Case of Machado de Assis'.

——, 'Some Notes on Teresa de la Parra's *Las memorias de Mamá Blanca*', *Revista Brasileira do Caribe* 2.11 (July–December 2005): 185–94.
——, 'The House of the Spirits by Isabel Allende', in *The Cambridge Companion to the Latin American Novel*, ed. Efraín Kristal. Cambridge: Cambridge University Press, 2005, 270–82.
——, 'The Twilight of the Idols in Modernism's 1922', in *Modernisms and Modernities: Studies in Honour of Donald L. Shaw*, ed. Susan de Carvalho. Newark, DE: Juan de la Cuesta, 2006, 175–99.
——, and Wen-chin Ouyang (eds), *A Companion to Magical Realism* (Woodbridge: Tamesis, 2005.
——, 'Blood, Ink and Pigment: Simón Bolívar as Proteus', in *Studies in Modern Hispanic Literatures in Honour of Donald L. Shaw*, ed. Robin W. Fiddian and C. Alex Longhurst, *Bulletin of Spanish Studies* 82.3–4 (2005): 335–52.
——, and Richard Young (eds), *Contemporary Latin American Cultural Studies*. London: Arnold, 2003.
Harter, Hugh A., *Gertrudis Gómez de Avellaneda*. Boston: Twayne, 1981.
Harvey, Robert, *Liberators: Latin America's Struggle for Independence, 1810–1830*. London: John Murray, 2000.
Hatoum, Milton, *Dois Irmãos*. São Paulo: Companhia das Letras, 2000. (Published in English as *The Brothers* trans. John Gledson. London: Bloomsbury, 2003.)
——, *Cinzas do norte*. Rio de Janeiro: Companhia das Letras, 2005.
Havard, Robert (ed.), *A Companion to Spanish Surrealism*. Woodbridge: Boydell and Brewer, 2004.
Hellenbeck, Cleve, *Alvar Núñez Cabeza de Vaca. The Journey and Route of the First European to Cross the Continent of North America 1534–1536*. Port Washington, NY: Kennikat Press, 1971.
Herlinghaus, Hermann, and Manika Walter, *Posmodernidad en la periferia: enfoques latinoamericanos de la nueva teoría cultural*. Berlin: Astrid Langer Verlag, 1994.
Hernández-Miyares, Julio and Perla Rozencvaig (eds), *Reinaldo Arenas: alucinaciones, fantasías y realidad*. Glenview, IL: Scott Foresman Montesinos, 1990.
Hernández Sánchez-Barba, Mario, *Historia y literatura en hispano-américa (1492–1820)*. Madrid: Castalia, 1978.
Higgins, James, *The Poet in Peru*. Liverpool: Francis Cairns, 1982.
—— (ed.), *Heterogeneidad y literatura en el Perú*. Lima: Centro de Estudios Literarios Antonio Cornejo Polar, 2003.
Hijuelos, Oscar, *The Mambo Kings Sing of Love*. London: Hamish Hamilton, 1990 [1989].
Hinojosa, Rolando, *Mi querido Rafa*. Houston, TX: Arte Público Press, 1981.
Huidobro, Vicente, *Poesía y prosa de Vicente Huidobro*, ed. Antonio de Undurranga. Madrid: Aguilar, 1957.
Jackson, Richard, *The Black Image in Latin American Literature*. Albuquerque: University of New Mexico Press, 1976.
——, 'The Emergence of Afro-Hispanic Literature', *Afro-Hispanic Review* 10 (1991): 4–10.
——, *Black Writers and the Hispanic Canon*. Boston: Twayne, 1997.
Jameson, Fredric, *Postmodernism, or the Cultural Logic of Late Capitalism*. Durham, NC: Duke University Press, 1991.

Jaramillo, María Mercedes, *El nuevo teatro colombiano: arte y política*. Medellín: Editorial Universidad de Antioquia, 1992.
Jarouche, Mamede M., 'Introdução', in Manuel Antonio de Almeida, *Memórias de um Sargento de Milícias*, ed. Mamede Mustafa Jarouche. Coitia: Atelie Editorial, 2000, 13–59.
Jiménez, José Olivio (ed.), *Antología de la poesía hispanoamericana contemporánea: 1914–1987*. 3rd ed. Madrid: Alianza, 1988.
Jitrik, Noé, *Muerte y resurección de Facundo*. Buenos Aires: Centro Editor de América Latina, 1968.
Johnson, Randal, 'The *Romance-Reportagem* and the Cinema: Babenco's *Lúcio Flávio* and *Pixote*', *Luso-Brazilian Review* 24.2 (1987): 35–48.
Joset, Jacques, *La literatura hispanoamericana*. Barcelona: Ockros-Tau Ediciones, 1974.
Jrade, Cathy L., 'Modernist Poetry', in *The Cambridge History of Latin American Literature*, ed. Enrique Pupo-Walker and Roberto González Echeverría. Cambridge: Cambridge University Press, 1996, vol. 2, 7–68.
Juan-Navarro, Santiago, *Archival Reflections: Postmodern Fiction of the Americas (Self-Reflexivity, Historical Revisionism, Utopia)*. Lewisburg, PA: Bucknell University Press, 2000.
Judson, C. Fred, 'Continuity and Evolution of Revolutionary Symbolism in *Verde Olivo*', in *Cuba: Twenty-Five Years of Revolution, 1959–1984*, ed. Sandor Halesbsky and John M. Kirk. New York: Praeger, 1985, 233–50.
Kadir, Djelal, *João Cabral de Melo Neto: Selected Poetry 1937–1990*. Hanover, NH: Wesleyan University Press, 1994.
Kaminsky, Amy, *Reading the Body Politic: Feminist Criticism and Latin American Women Writers*. Minneapolis: University of Minnesota Press, 1993.
Kantaris, Elia G., *The Subversive Psyche. Contemporary Women's Narrative from Argentina and Uruguay*. Oxford: Oxford University Press, 1996.
Katra, William H., *The Argentine Generation of 1837: Echeverría, Sarmiento, Alberdi, Mitre*. Rutherford, NJ: Fairleigh Dickinson University Press, 1996.
Kerr, Lucille, *Suspended Fictions: Reading Novels by Manuel Puig*. Urbana: University of Illinois Press, 1987.
Kettle, M., 'The Most Famous Names in History', *The Guardian* (13 September 1999).
Kicza, John E., *Resilient Cultures: America's Native Peoples Confront European Civilization, 1500–1800*. Upper Saddle River, NJ: Prentice Hall, 2003.
King, John (ed.), *Modern Latin American Literature: A Survey*. London: Faber and Faber, 1987.
—— (ed.), *The Cambridge Companion to Modern Latin American Culture*. Cambridge: Cambridge University Press, 2004.
Kirkpatrick, Gwen, *The Dissonant Legacy of 'Modernismo': Lugones, Herrera y Reissig, and the Voices of Modern Spanish American Poetry*. Berkeley: University of California Press, 1989.
Kirkpatrick, Susan, *Las Románticas: Women Writers and Subjectivity in Spain, 1835–1850*. Berkeley: University of California Press, 1989.
Kohut, Karl (ed.), *Un universo cargado de violencia: presentación, aproximación y documentación de la obra de Mempo Giardinelli*. Frankfurt: Vervuert Verlag, 1990.

Kristal, Efraín, *The Andes Viewed from the City: Literary and Political Discourse on the Indian in Peru 1848–1930*. New York: Peter Lang, 1987.
——, *Invisible Work: Borges and Translation*. Nashville, TN: Vanderbilt University Press, 2002.
—— (ed.), *The Cambridge Companion to the Latin American Novel*. Cambridge: Cambridge University Press, 2005.
Kutzinski, Vera M., *Sugar's Secrets. Race and the Erotics of Cuban Nationalism*. Charlottesville: University of Virginia Press, 1993.
——, 'Afro-Hispanic American Literature', in *The Cambridge History of Latin American Literature*, ed. Enrique Pupo-Walker and Roberto González Echeverría. Cambridge: Cambridge University Press, 1996, vol. 2, 164–94.
Lafleur, Héctor René, Sergio D. Provenzano and Fernando P. Alonso, *Las revistas literarias argentinas 1893–1967*. Buenos Aires: Centro Editor de América Latina, 1962.
Lagmanovich, David, 'Para una caracterización de *Infortunios de Alonso Ramírez*', in *Historia y crítica de la literatura hispanoamericana*, ed. Cedomil Goic. Barcelona: Editorial Crítica, 1988. vol. 1. 411–16.
Lanning, John Tate, *Academic Culture in the Spanish Colonies*. Oxford: Oxford University Press, 1940.
Larsen, Neil, *Reading North by South: On Latin American Literature, Culture and Politics*. Minneapolis: University of Minnesota Press, 1995.
Lavrín, Asunción, 'Viceregal Culture', in *The Cambridge History of Latin American Literature*, ed. Enrique Pupo-Walker and Roberto González Echeverría. Cambridge: Cambridge University Press, 1996, vol. 1, 286–335.
Leal, Luis, *Juan Rulfo*. Boston: Twayne, 1983.
——, and Manuel M. Martín-Rodríguez, 'Chicano Literature', in *The Cambridge History of Latin American Literature*, ed. Enrique Pupo-Walker and Roberto González Echeverría. Cambridge: Cambridge University Press, 1996, vol. 2, 357–86.
Leite, Serafim, *Novas páginas de história do Brasil*. São Paolo: Companhia Editôra Nacional, 1965.
Leonard, Irving A., *Books of the Brave: Being an Account of Books and of Men in the Spanish Conquest and Settlement of the Sixteenth-Century New World*. Cambridge, MA: Harvard University Press, 1949.
——, *Baroque Times in Old Mexico: Seventeenth-Century Persons, Places and Practices*. Ann Arbor: The University of Michigan Press, 1959.
—— (ed.), *Colonial Travelers in Latin America*. New York: Alfred A. Knopf, 1972.
León-Portilla, Miguel, 'Teatro náhuatl prehispánico', *La Palabra y el Hombre* (Mexico City) 9 (1959): 13–35.
—— (ed.), *The Broken Spears: The Aztec Account of the Conquest of Mexico*. Boston: Beacon Press, 1992.
——, *Fifteen Poets of the Aztec World*. Norman and London: University of Oklahoma Press, 1992.
Lewis, Marvin, *Treading the Ebony Path: Ideology and Violence in Contemporary Afro-Colombian Prose Fiction*. Columbia: University of Missouri Press, 1987.
Lindsay, Claire, 'Luis Sepúlveda, Bruce Chatwin and the Global Travel Writing Circuit', *Comparative Literature Studies* 43.1–2 (2006): 57–78.

Lindstrom, Naomi, *Women's Voices in Latin American Literature*. Washington, DC: Three Continents Press, 1989.
Lins, Paolo, *Cidade de Deus*. 2nd ed., 5th impression. Rio de Janeiro: Companhia das Letras, 2002. (Published in English as *City of God*, trans. Alison Entrekin. London: Bloomsbury, 2006.)
——, 'Cities of God and Social Mobilisation', in *City of God in Several Voices: Brazilian Social Cinema as Action*, ed. Else Vieira. Nottingham: Critical, Cultural and Communications Press, 2005, 127–31.
Lisboa, Luis Carlos, *Tudo que você precisa ler sem ser um rato de biblioteca: guia do melhor da literatura brasileira*. 6th ed. São Paolo: Editoria Papagaio, 2001.
Lispector, Clarice, *A hora da estrela*. Rio de Janeiro: Livraria José Olympio Editora, 1977.
——, *A Paixão Segundo G.H.* Rio de Janeiro: Editôra Rocco, 2001 [1964].
*Literatura de cordel: antologia*. São Paolo: Global, 1976.
Lívio Ferreira, Tito, *Nóbrega e Anchieta em São Paulo de Piratininga*. São Paolo: Conselho Estadual de Cultura, 1970.
Lloyd, David, *Anomalous States: Irish Writing and the Post-Colonial Moment*. Durham, NC: Duke University Press, 1993.
Lopes de Souza, Pêro, *Diário da navegação da armada, que foi à terra de Brasil em 1530 sob a capitania-mor de Martin Affonso de Souza, escripto por seu irmão Pêro Lopes de Souza*. Lisbon: Sociedade de Propagadora de Conhecimentos Uteis, 1839. Biblioteca Nacional, Rio de Janeiro. Obras raras. 981.01.
López de Gómara, Francisco, *Historia general de las Indias y Vida de Hernán Cortés*, ed. Jorge Gurria Lacroix. Caracas: Ayacucho, 1979.
Lorente Medina, Antonio, 'Introducción', in Alonso Carrió de la Vandera, *El lazarillo de ciegos caminantes*. Caracas: Biblioteca Ayacucho, 1985, ix–xxxv.
Luciani, Frederick, 'Spanish American Theatre of the Colonial Period', in *The Cambridge History of Latin American Literature*, ed. Enrique Pupo-Walker and Roberto González Echeverría. Cambridge: Cambridge University Press, 1996, vol. 1, 260–85.
Ludmer, Josefina, 'The Gaucho Genre', in *The Cambridge History of Latin American Literature*, ed. Enrique Pupo-Walker and Roberto González Echeverría. Cambridge: Cambridge University Press, 1996, vol. 1, 608–31.
Luis, William, 'Latin American (Hispanic Caribbean) Literature Written in the United States', in *The Cambridge History of Latin American Literature*, ed. Enrique Pupo-Walker and Roberto González Echeverría. Cambridge: Cambridge University Press, 1996, vol. 2, 526–56.
Luzuriaga, Gerardo, and Richard Reeve (eds), *Los clásicos del teatro hispanoamericano*. Mexico: Fondo de Cultura Económica, 1975.
Lynch, John, 'The River Plate Republics from Independence to the Paraguayan War', in *Cambridge History of Latin America*. Vol. III. *From Independence to c. 1870*, ed. Leslie Bethell. Cambridge: Cambridge University Press, 1985, 615–76.
Lyotard, Jean François, *The Postmodern Condition: A Report on Knowledge*, trans. Geoff Bennington and Brian Massumi. Minneapolis: University of Minnesota, 1984.
Machado de Assis, Joaquim Maria, *Desencantos: Phantasia Dramatica*. Rio de Janeiro: Paulo Brito, 1861.

———, *Os deuses de Casaca*. Rio de Janeiro: Tipographia do Imperial Instituto Artistico, 1886. BN, Rio de Janeiro. Obras raras, 80,1,6.
———, *Obra completa*, ed. Afrânio Coutinho. 2 vols. Rio de Janeiro, José Aguilar, 1959.
———, *Esaú e Jacó*, ed. Eugênio Gomes. Rio de Janeiro: José Aguilar Editôra, 1973.
———, *Dom Casmurro*. Lisbon: Publicacões Europa-America, 1998.
———, *Contos Fluminenses*, ed. Antonio Arnoni Prado. São Paulo: Ática, 2000.
———, *Antologia Machadiana: Memórias Póstumas de Brás Cúbas*. Rio de Janeiro: Lia Editora, n.d.
Madrigal, Luis Iñigo (ed.), *Historia de la literatura hispanoamericana*. 2 vols. Madrid: Cátedra, 1982, 1987.
Magill, Frank N. (ed.), *Masterpieces of Latino Literature*. New York: HarperCollins, 1995.
Maia Neto, José Raimundo, *Machado de Assis: The Brazilian Pyrrhonian*. Lafayette, IN: Purdue University Press, 1994.
Mallarmé, Stéphane, *Igitur. Divagations. Un Coup de dés*. Paris: Gallimard, 1976.
Marcos, Plínio, *Navalha na carne: Quando as maquinas param*. São Paulo: Círculo do Livro, 1978, 7–53.
Mariátegui, José Carlos, *Siete ensayos de interpretación de la realidad peruana*, ed. Aníbal Quijano and Elizabeth Garrels. Caracas: Ayacucho, 1979.
Martí, José, *Prosas*, ed. Andrés Iduarte. Mexico: Unión Panamericana, 1950.
———, *Versos libres*, ed. Ivan A. Schulman. Barcelona: Editorial Labor, 1970.
———, *Prosa escogida*, ed. José Olivio Jiménez. Madrid: Editorial Magisterio Español, 1975.
Martin, Gerald, *Journeys Through the Labyrinth: Latin American Fiction in the Twentieth Century*. London: Routledge, 1989.
Martinengo, Alessandro, 'La cultura literaria de Juan Rodríguez Freyle', in *Historia y crítica de la literatura hispanoamericana*, ed. Cedomil Goic. Barcelona: Editorial Crítica, 1988, vol. 1, 147–52.
Martins, Paula (ed.), *José de Anchieta, S.: Poesias: manuscrito do séc XVI, em português, castelhano, latim e tupi*. São Paulo: Comissão do IV Centenário da Cidade de São Paolo, Serviço de Comemorações Culturais, 1954.
Masiello, Francine, *Between Civilization and Barbarism: Women, Nation, and Literary Culture in Modern Argentina*. Lincoln and London: University of Nebraska Press, 1992.
Melgar, Mariano, *Antología*, ed. Edmundo Cornejo. 2nd ed. U. Lima: Ediciones Populares, 1972.
Mendieta, Fray Jerónimo de, *Historia eclesiástica indiana*, ed. Francisco Solano y Pérez-Lila. 2 vols. Madrid: Atlas, 1973. 'Biblioteca de Autores Españoles' Series, nos. 260 and 261.
Mendonça Teles, Gilberto, *Vanguarda europea e modernismo*. São Paolo: Vozes, 1982.
Menéndez Pidal, Ramón, *Colección de incunables americanos*. Madrid: Ediciones Cultura Hispánica, 1944.
Menezes, Armando (ed.) in *A Carta de Pêro Vaz de Caminha: edição comemorativa dos 500 anos de Brasil*. Mariaus: Academia Amazonense de Letras, 2000.
Menton, Seymour, *La nueva novela histórica*. Mexico City: FCE, 1993.

Merrim, Stephanie (ed.), *Feminist Perspectives on Sor Juana Inés de la Cruz*. Detroit: Wayne State University Press, 1991.

——, 'The First Fifty Years of Hispanic New World Historiography: The Caribbean, Mexico and Central America', in *The Cambridge History of Latin American Literature*, ed. Enrique Pupo-Walker and Roberto González Echeverría. Cambridge: Cambridge University Press, 1996, vol. 1, 58–100.

Meyer, Antonio, 'Introdução Geral', in *Antologia Machadiana: Memórias Póstumas de Brás Cúbas*. Rio de Janeiro: Lia Editôra, n.d., 7–31.

Meyer, Doris (ed.), *Rereading the Spanish American Essay: Translation of 19th and 20th Century Women's Essays*. Austin: University of Texas Press, 1995.

Mignolo, Walter, 'Cartas, crónicas y relaciones del descubrimiento y la conquista', in *Historia de la literatura hispanoamericana: época colonial*, ed. Luis Iñigo Madrigal. Madrid: Cátedra, 1982. vol. 1, 57–116.

Moliner, Israel M. (ed.), *Obras de Juan Francisco Manzano*. Havana: Instituto del Libro Cubano, 1972.

Molloy, Sylvia, *En breve cárcel*. Barcelona: Seix Barral, 1981.

——, *Signs of Borges*. Durham, NC: Duke University Press, 1994.

——, 'Disappearing Acts: Reading Lesbian in Teresa de la Parra', in *¿Entiendes? Queer Readings, Hispanic Writings*, ed. Emilie Bergmann and Paul Julian Smith. Durham, NC: Duke University Press, 2003.

Monsiváis, Carlos, *Mexican Postcards*, trans. by John Kraniauskas. London: Verso, 1997.

——, *Aires de familia: cultura y sociedad*. Barcelona: Anagrama, 2000.

Montalvo, Juan, 'La República de América', in *La literatura de ideas en América Latina*, ed. Lucila Pagliai. Buenos Aires: Ediciones Colihue, 1987, 51–5.

Mooney, Bel, 'Paulo's Conversion', *The Times (Review Books)* (11 June 2005): 8–9.

Moraga, Cherríe, *Loving in the War Years: lo que nunca pasó por sus labios*. Boston, MA: South End Press, 1983.

——, *The Last Generation: Prose and Poetry by Cherríe Moraga*. Boston, MA: South End Press, 1993.

Moraña, Mabel, *Crítica impura*. Frankfurt: Iberoamericana/Vervuert, 2004.

Moriconi, Italo (ed.), *Os Cem Melhores Contos Brasileiros do Século*. Rio: Editôra Objetiva, 2000.

Motolonía, aka R. P. Fr. Toribio de Benavente, *Historia de los indios de la Nueva España*. Barcelona: Herederos de Juan Gili, Editores, 1914.

Mullan, John, 'The Mysterious Alchemy of Paulo Coelho', *The Guardian*. G2 (24 May 2006): 2–3.

Murilo Leal, Cláudio, 'The Poetry of Machado de Assis', *Portuguese Literary & Cultural Studies*, 13–14 (Fall 2004-Spring 2005): 585–98. Special number 'The Author as Plagiarist – The Case of Machado de Assis'.

Murray, James C., *Spanish Chronicles of the Indies: Sixteenth Century*. Boston: Twayne, 1994.

Mutis, Álvaro, *Summa de Maqroll el gaviero (Poesía 1947–1970)*. Bogotá: Editorial La Oveja Negra.

Nagib, Lúcia, 'Talking Bullets: The Language of Violence in *City of God*', in *City of God in Several Voices: Brazilian Social Cinema as Action*, ed. Else Vieira. Nottingham: Critical, Cultural and Communications Press, 2005, 32–43.

*Naufragio que passou Jorge de Albuquerque Coelho Vindo do Brazil para este*

*Reyno no anno de 1565. Escrito por Bento Teixeira Pinto que se achou no ditto naufragio*. Lisboa: Antonio Alvarez, 1601. 59 pp. Obras raras, BN, Rio, 36,4,21.
Navarro Tomás, T., *Métrica española: reseña histórica y descriptiva*. 3rd ed. Madrid: Guadarrama, 1972.
Nebrija, Antonio, *Gramática castellana*, ed. Pascual Galindo Romeo. Madrid: Junta del Centenario, 1965.
Neruda, Pablo, *Twenty Love Poems and a Song of Despair*, trans. W. S. Merwin. London: Jonathan Cape, 1975.
Nicola, José de, *Literatura brasileira das origens aos nossos dias*. São Paolo: Editôra Scipione, 1989.
Nicolopulos, James, *The Poetics of Empire in the Indies: Prophecy and Imitation in 'La Araucana' and 'Os Lusíadas'*. University Park: Pennsylvania State University Press, 2000.
Nist, John, *The Modernist Movement in Brazil: A Literary Study*. Austin: University of Texas Press, 1967.
Nóbrega, Manoel da, *Cartas do Brasil*, ed. P. Antonio Franco. São Paolo: Editoria da Universidade de São Paolo, 1988.
Noll, João Gilberto, *A céu aberto*. Rio de Janeiro: Companhia das Letras, 1996.
——, *Lorde*. São Paolo: Francis, 2004.
Núñez, Estuardo, 'Notas a la obra y vida de Don Pedro de Peralta', *Homenaje a Peralta*. Lima: Universidad Nacional Mayor de San Marcos, n.d., 21–33.
Oakley, R. J., *The Case of Lima Barreto and Realism in the Brazilian 'Belle Epoque'*. Lampeter: The Edwin Mellen Press, 1998.
Ojeda, Martha, *Nicomedes Santa Cruz: Ecos de África en Perú*. London: Tamesis, 2003.
Olavide, Pablo de, *Obras dramáticas desconocidas*, ed. Estuardo Núñez. Lima: Biblioteca Nacional del Perú, 1971.
——, *El desertor (Teatro)*, ed. Trinidad Barrera and Piedad Bolaños. Seville: Imprenta Escandón, 1987.
Oliveira Tôrres, João Camilo de, *História das idéiais religiosas no Brasil*. São Paulo: Grijalbo, 1968.
Olivio Jiménez, José (ed.), *Antología de la poesía hispanoamericana contemporánea: 1914–1987*. Madrid: Alianza, 1988.
Ollé, Carmen, *Noches de adrenalina*. Lima: Lluvia Editores, 1992 [1981].
Olmedo, José Joaquín de, *Poesías completas*, ed. Aurelio Espinosa Pólit. Mexico: Fondo de Cultura Económica, 1947.
Onetti, Juan Carlos, *Juntacadáveres*. Montevideo: Alfa, 1964.
Ortega, Julio, *Reapropiaciones: culturas y nueva escritura en Puerto Rico*. Río Piedras, PR: Universidad de Puerto Rico, 1991.
——, *Transatlantic Translations: Dialogues in Latin American Literature*, trans. Philip Derbyshire. London: Reaktion, 2006.
Ortiz, Carmen, *Julio Cortázar: una estética de la búsqueda*. Buenos Aires: Almageste, 1994.
Oviedo, José Miguel, *Historia de la literatura hispanoamericana*. 2 vols. Madrid: Alianza, 1995.
——, 'The Modern Essay in Spanish America', in *The Cambridge History of Latin American Literature*, ed. Enrique Pupo-Walker and Roberto González Echeverría. Cambridge: Cambridge University Press, 1996, vol. 2, 365–424.

*Oxford English Dictionary*, 20 vols. 2nd ed. Oxford: Clarendon, 1989.
Pace, David, *Claude Lévi-Strauss: The Bearer of Ashes*. London: Routledge, 1986.
Palma, Ricardo, *Tradiciones peruanas*. 2 vols. Lima: Editorial Universo. 1980.
Palmer, Michael, et al. (eds), *Nothing the Sun Could Not Explain: 20 Contemporary Brazilian Poets*. Los Angeles: Sun & Moon Press, 1997.
Pardo Y Aliaga, Felipe, *Teatro: (selección). 'Frutos de la educación' & 'Una huérfana en chorrillos'*. Lima: Editorial Universo, 1977.
Parente Cunha, Helena, *Mulher no Espelho*. Florianópolis: Fundação Catarinenes de Cultura, 1983.
Parker, Alexander A., 'The Calderonian Sources of *El Divino Narciso* de Sor Juana Inés de la Cruz', *Romantisches Jarbuch* 19 (1968): 257–74; Spanish translation in Cedomil Goic (ed.), *Historia y crítica de la literatura hispanoamericana: 1: Epoca colonial*. Barcelona: Editorial Crítica, 1988, 360–65.
Parra, Nicanor, *Antipoems: New and Selected*, ed. David Unger. New York: New Directions, 1985.
Parra, Teresa de la, *Obras completas*. Caracas: Editorial Arte, 1965.
——, *Obra: narrativa, ensayos, cartas*, ed. Velia Bosch and Julieta Fombona, Caracas: Ayacucho, 1982.
Pastor, Beatriz, *Discursos narrativos de la conquista: mitificación y emergencia*. Hanover, NH: Ediciones del Norte, 1983.
Pati, Francisco, *Dicionário de Machado de Assis*. São Paolo: Rêde Latina Editôra, 1958.
Payne, Judith A., and Earl E. Fitz, *Ambiguity and Gender in the New Novel of Brazil and Spanish America: A Comparative Assessment*. Iowa City: University of Iowa Press, 1993.
Paz, Octavio, *Corriente alterna*. Mexico: Siglo Veintiuno Editores, 1967.
——, *Conjunciones y disyunciones*. Mexico: Joaquín Mortiz, 1969.
——, *In/mediaciones*. Barcelona: Seix Barral, 1979.
——, *Poesía en movimiento: México 1915–1966*. 13th ed. Mexico: Siglo XXI, 1979.
——, *Puerta al campo*. Barcelona: Biblioteca Breve de Bolsillo, 1981 [1966].
——, *Sor Juana Inés de la Cruz o las trampas de la fe*. Barcelona: Seix Barral, 1982.
——, *El laberinto de la soledad*. Mexico: Fondo de Cultura Económica, 1984 [1959].
——, *The Collected Poems 1957–1987*, ed. Eliot Weinberger. Manchester: Carcanet, 1988.
——, *Obras completas*. 14 vols. Mexico City: Fondo de Cultura Económica, 1993.
——, Alí Chumacero, José Emilio Pacheco and Homero Aridjis (eds), *Poesía en movimiento: México 1915–1966*. 13th ed. Mexico: Siglo XXI Editores, 1979.
Pazos Alonso, Cláudia, and Claire Williams (eds), *Closer to the Wild Heart: Essays on Clarice Lispector*. Oxford: European Humanities Research Centre, 2002.
Peixoto, Afrânio, 'Introdução', in *Cartas, informacões, fragmentos históricos e Sermões de Pedro Joseph de Anchieta SJ*. Rio de Janeiro: Civilização Brasileira, 1933, 29–38.
Pellón, Gustavo, 'The Spanish American Novel: Recent Developments, 1975 to 1990', in *The Cambridge History of Latin American Literature*, ed. Enrique

Pupo-Walker and Roberto González Echeverría. Cambridge: Cambridge University Press, 1996, vol. 2, 274–302.
*Pequeno Dicionário da Literatura Brasileira*. 2 vols. São Paolo: Editora Cultrix, 1971.
Peri Rossi, Cristina, *La nave de los locos*. Barcelona: Seix Barral, 1989.
Pertusa, Inmaculada, 'Escribiendo entre corrientes: Carmen Riera, Esther Tusquets, Cristina Peri Rossi y Sylvia Molloy', Ph.D. dissertation. University of Colorado, 1995.
Pfandl, Ludwig, *Sor Juana Inés de la Cruz: la décima musa de México*. Mexico: UNAM, 1963.
Phillips, Rachel, *Alfonsina Storni: From Poetess to Poet*. London: Tamesis, 1975.
Piedra, José, 'Literary Whiteness and Afro-Hispanic Difference', in *The Bounds of Race: Perspectives on Hegemony and Resistance*, ed. Dominick LaCapra. Ithaca, NY: Cornell University Press, 1991, 278–310.
Pierce, Frank (ed.), *The Heroic Poem of the Spanish Golden Age: Selections*. Oxford: Dolphin, 1947.
Pierce, Robert N. and Kurt Kent, 'Newspapers', in *Handbook of Latin American Popular Culture*, ed. Harold E. Hinds, Jr. and Charles M. Tatum. Westport, CT: Greenwood Press, 1985. 230–50.
Piglia, Ricardo, *Respiración artificial*. Barcelona: Seix Barral, 1994.
Pilling, William, *The Emancipation of South America*. New York: Cooper Square Publishers, 1969.
Piña, Cristina, *Alejandra Pizarnik*. Buenos Aires: Planeta, 1991.
Piñon, Nélida, *A República dos Sonhos*. Rio de Janeiro: Livraria Francisco Alves, 1984.
——, 'Acceptance speech: 2005: Príncipe de Asturias', http://www.fundacionprincipedeasturias.org/ing/o4/premiados/discursos, consulted 1 December 2006.
'Plácido', Gabriel de la Concepción Valdés. *Los poemas más representativos de Plácido*, ed. Frederick S. Stimpson and Humberto E. Robles. Chapel Hill, NC: University of North Carolina Press and Castalia, 1976.
Pope, Randolph D., 'The Spanish American Novel from 1950 to 1975', in *The Cambridge History of Latin American Literature*, ed. Enrique Pupo-Walker and Roberto González Echeverría. Cambridge: Cambridge University Press, 1996, vol. 2, 226–78.
*Popol Vuh. The Sacred Book of the Ancient Quiché Maya*. English version by Delia Goetz and Sylvanus G. Morley from the translation of Adrián Recinos. Norman: University of Oklahoma Press, 1950.
Praz, Mario, *The Romantic Agony*. London: Oxford University Press, 1970.
Prieto, René, 'The Literature of *Indigenismo*', in *The Cambridge History of Latin American Literature*, ed. Enrique Pupo-Walker and Roberto González Echeverría. Cambridge: Cambridge University Press, 1996, vol. 2, 69–113.
Promis, José, *The Identity of Hispanoamerica: An Interpretation of Colonial Literature*, trans. Alita Kelley and Alec E. Kelley. Tucson: University of Arizona Press, 1991.
Puig, Manuel, *El beso de la mujer araña*. 8th ed. Barcelona: Seix Barral, 1988.
Pupo-Walker, Enrique, 'El relato virreinal', in *El cuento hispanoamericano*, ed. Enrique Pupo-Walker. Madrid: Castalia, 1995, 55–78.
——, 'El relato costumbrista', in *El cuento hispanoamericano*, ed. Enrique Pupo-Walker. Madrid: Castalia, 1995, 79–110.

——, 'The Brief Narrative in Spanish America: 1835–1915', in *The Cambridge History of Latin American Literature*, ed. Enrique Pupo-Walker and Roberto González Echeverría. Cambridge: Cambridge University Press, 1996, vol. 1, 490–535.

——, and Roberto González Echeverría, *The Cambridge History of Latin American Literature*, 3 vols. Cambridge: Cambridge University Press, 1996.

Quesada, Vicente G., *The History of Printing and Early Publications in the Spanish American Colonies*, trans. Gustavo E. Archilla. New York: Columbia University Press, 1938. (Translated as a report on Project 465–97–3–81 under the auspices of the Works Progress Administration and the Department of Social Science, Columbia University)

Quilis, Antonio, *Métrica española*. 3rd ed. Barcelona: Ariel, 1989.

Quiroga, Horacio, *Cuentos escogidos*, ed. Jean Franco. Oxford: Pergamon, 1968.

Quiroga, José, 'Spanish American Poetry from 1922 to 1975', in *The Cambridge History of Latin American Literature*, ed. Enrique Pupo-Walker and Roberto González Echeverría. Cambridge: Cambridge University Press, 1996, vol. 2, 303–64.

Rama, Ángel, *Rubén Darío y el modernismo*. Caracas: Biblioteca de la Universidad Central de Venezuela, 1970.

——, *La ciudad letrada*. Hanover, NH: Ediciones del Norte, 1984.

——, *La crítica de la cultura en América Latina*, ed. Saúl Sosnowski and Tomás Eloy Martínez. Caracas: Ayacucho, 1985.

Ramos, Graciliano, *Vidas secas*. 98th ed. Rio de Janeiro: Editoria Record, 2005.

Restrepo, Laura, *La novia oscura*. Bogotá: Editorial Norma, 1999.

Reyes, Carlos José, 'La creación colectiva: una nueva organización interna del trabajo teatral', in *El teatro latinoamericano de creación colectiva*, ed. Marina García. Havana: Casa de las Américas, 1978, 75–107.

Reynolds, Bonnie Hildebrand, *Space, Time, and Crisis: The Theatre of René Marqués*. York, SC: Spanish Literature, 1988.

Ribeiro de Oliveira, Solange, and Judith Still, *Brazilian Feminisms*. Nottingham: University of Nottingham Press, 1999.

Ricard, Robert, *Antônio Vieira et Sor Juana Inés de la Cruz*. Coimbra: University of Coimbra, 1948.

Richard, Nelly, 'Latinomérica y la posmodernidad', in Hermann, Herlinghaus and Manika Walter (eds), *Posmodernidad en la periferia: enfoques latinoamericanos de la nueva teoría cultural*. Berlin: Astrid Langer Verlag, 1994, 210–22.

——, *Culture Residues: Chile in Transition*, trans. Alan West-Durán and Theodore Quester. Minneapolis: University of Minnesota Press, 2004.

Richardson, W. A. R., 'Introduction', in Mariano Azuela, *Los de abajo*. London: Harrap, 1980, 9–62.

Rivera, José Eustasio, *La vorágine*. Barcelona: Planeta, 1975.

Rivera-Meléndez, Blanca, *Poetry and the Machinery of Illusion: José Martí and the Poetics of Machinery*. Ithaca, NY: Cornell University Press, 1992.

Rizk, Beatriz J., *El nuevo teatro latinoamericano: una lectura histórica*. Minneapolis, MN: I&L, 1987.

Roa Bastos, Augusto, *Yo, el Supremo*. 6th ed. Mexico: Siglo Veintiuno Editores, 1976.

Rodó, José Enrique, *Ariel*. 3rd ed. Montevideo: Claudio García & compañía, n.d.

Rodrigues, Nelson, *Vestido de Noiva*. Rio de Janeiro: Ministério de Educação e Cultura, 1973

Rodríguez-Luis, Julio, *Hermenéutica y praxis del indigenismo: la novela indigenista de Clorinda Matto de Turner a José María Arguedas*. Mexico: Fondo de Cultura Económica, 1980.
Rodríguez Freyle, Juan, *El Carnero*, ed. Dario Achury Valenzuela. Caracas: Ayacucho, 1979.
Rodríguez Monegal, Emir, *Genio y figura de Horacio Quiroga*. Buenos Aires: Editorial Universitaria, 1967.
——, *Sexo y poesía en el 900 uruguayo*. Montevideo: Alfa, 1969.
Rodríguez Torres, Alvaro, 'Reseña histórica de la Biblioteca Nacional de Colombia', *Biblioteca Nacional de Colombia* (1994): 1–18.
Rosas y Oquendo, Mateo, *Sátira hecha por Mateo Rosas de Oquendo a las cosas que pasan en el Pirú, año de 1598*, ed. Pedro Lasarte. Madison, WI: The Hispanic Seminary of Medieval Studies, 1990.
Rosenberg, Fernando J., *The Avant-Garde and Geopolitics in Latin America*. Pittsburgh, PA: University of Pittsburgh Press, 2006.
Ross, Kathleen, 'Historians of the Conquest and Colonization of the New World: 1550–1620', in *The Cambridge History of Latin American Literature*, ed. Enrique Pupo-Walker and Roberto González Echeverría. Cambridge: Cambridge University Press, 1996, vol. 1, 101–90.
——, and Yvette E. Miller, *Scents of Wood and Silence: Short Stories by Latin American Women Writers*. Pittsburgh: Latin American Literary Review Press, 1991.
Rowe, William, *Mito e ideología en la obra de José María Arguedas*. Lima: Instituto Nacional de Cultura, 1979.
——, and Vivian Schelling, *Memory and Modernity: Popular Culture in Latin American*. London: Verso, 1991.
Rulfo, Juan, *Obra completa: 'El llano en llamas'/'Pedro Páramo'/Otros textos*, ed. Jorge Ruffinelli. Caracas: Ayacucho, 1985.
Rutherford, John, 'The Novel of the Mexican Revolution', in *The Cambridge History of Latin American Literature*, ed. Enrique Pupo-Walker and Roberto González Echeverría. Cambridge: Cambridge University Press, 1996, vol. 2, 213–25.
Sabat de Rivers, Georgina, *El 'Sueño' de Sor Juana Inés de la Cruz: tradiciones literarias y originalidad*. London: Tamesis, 1976.
Sahagún, Bernardino de, *A History of Ancient Mexico*, trans. Fanny R. Bandelier. Nashville, TN: Fish University Press, 1932.
——, *Historia general de las cosas de Nueva España. Códice florentino*. Facsimile ed. Mexico: Secretaría de Gobernación, 1979.
Sainz, Gustavo, *Gazapo*. Mexico: Grijalbo, 1975.
San Román, Gustavo (ed.), *This America We Dream Of: Rodó and* Ariel *One Hundred Years On*. London: Institute of Latin American Studies, 2001.
Sánchez, Luis Alberto, *Indianismo e indigenismo en la literatura peruana*. Lima: Mosca Azul, 1981.
Sánchez, Luis Rafael, *La guaracha del Macho Camacho*. Barcelona: Argos Vergara, 1982.
Santa Cruz y Espejo, Eugenio de, *Obra educativa*, ed. Philip L. Astuto. Caracas: Ayacucho, 1981.
Santa Rita Durão, José de, *Caramuru: poema épico do descobrimento da Bahia*, ed. Ronald Polioto. São Paolo: Martins Fontes, 2001.

Santiago, Silviano, *O banquete*. São Paolo: Atica, 1977.
——, *Stella Manhattan*. Rio de Janeiro: Editôra Nova Fronteira, 1985.
——, *The Space In-Between: Essays on Brazilian Culture*, ed. Ana Lúcia Gazzola. Durham, NC: Duke University Press, 2001.
Sarduy, Severo, *Maitreya*. 2nd ed. Barcelona: Seix Barral, 1981.
Sarlo, Beatriz, *Una modernidad periférica: Buenos Aires, 1920 y 1930*. Buenos Aires, Ediciones Nueva Visión, 1988.
Sarmiento, Domingo Faustino, *Facundo*. Madrid: Biblioteca Edad, 1969.
Sartre, Jean-Paul, 'Black Orpheus', *The Massachusetts Review* 6:1 (1964–65): 13–52.
Schulman, Ivan A., and Evelyn Picón Garfield (eds), *Poesía modernista hispanoamericana y española (Antología)*. Madrid: Taurus, 1986.
Schultz, Kirsteen, *Tropical Versailles: Empire, Monarchy and the Portuguese Royal Court in Rio de Janeiro, 1808–1821*. London: Routledge, 2001.
Schumway, Nicholas, 'The Essay in Spanish America: 1800 to Modernismo', in *The Cambridge History of Latin American Literature*, ed. Enrique Pupo-Walker and Roberto González Echeverría. Cambridge: Cambridge University Press, 1996, vol. 1, 556–89.
Schwarz, Roberto, *Misplaced Ideas: Essays on Brazilian Culture*, trans. John Gledson. London: Verso, 1992.
——, *A Master on the Periphery of Capitalism: Machado de Assis*, trans. John Gledson. Durham, NC: Duke University Press, 2001.
——, 'Paulo Lins's Novel *City of God*', *City of God in Several Voices: Brazilian Social Cinema as Action*, ed. Else Vieira. Nottingham: Critical, Cultural and Communications Press, 2005, 32–43.
Sedgwick, Eve Kosofsky, *Epistemology of the Closet*. Berkeley: University of California Press, 1991.
Seed, Patricia, 'Taking Possession and Reading Texts: Establishing the Authority of Overseas Empires', in *Early Images of the Americas: Transfer and Invention*, ed. Jerry M. Williams and Robert E. Lewis. Tucson & London: University of Arizona Press, 1993, 111–47.
Sepúlveda, Luis, *Un viejo que leía novelas de amor*. 59th impression. Barcelona: Tusquets, 2003.
Shaw, Donald L., *Gallegos: Doña Bárbara*. London: Grant & Cutler, 1972.
——, *Borges' Narrative Strategy*. Liverpool: Cairns, 1992.
——, *Antonio Skármeta and the Post Boom*. Hanover, NH: Ediciones del Norte, 1994.
——, *The Post-Boom in Spanish American Fiction*. Ithaca, NY: State University of New York Press, 1997.
——, *A Companion to Modern Spanish American Fiction*. Woodbridge: Boydell and Brewer, 2002.
Silva, José Asunción, *Poesía y prosa*, ed. Eduardo Camacho Guizado. Bogotá: El Ancora Editores, 1993.
Silva, José Bonifácio de Andrade e, *Memórias Sobre a Escravidão*, ed. João Severiano Maciel da Costa. Rio de Janeiro: Arquivo Nacional, 1988.
——, *Projetos para o Brasil*, ed. Miriam Dolhnikoff. São Paolo: Companhia das Letras, 2005.
Simons, Marlise, 'The Best Years of His Life: An Interview with Gabriel García Márquez', *New York Times Book Review* (10 April 1988): 48.

Simpson, Amelia S., *Detective Fiction from Latin America*. Madison, NJ: Fairleigh Dickinson University Press, 1990.
Sinfield, Alan, *Literature, Politics, and Culture in Postwar Britain*. Berkeley and Los Angeles: University of California Press, 1989.
Skidmore, Thomas E., and Peter H. Smith, *Modern Latin America*. 3rd ed. New York: Oxford University Press, 1992.
Smart, Ian Isidore, *Amazing Connections: Kemet to Hispanophone Africana Literature*. Washington DC and Port-of-Spain: Original World Press, 1996.
Smith, Paul Julian, *Laws of Desire*. Oxford: Oxford University Press, 1994.
Smith, Verity (ed.), *Encyclopedia of Latin American Literature*. London: Fitzroy Dearborn, 1997.
Soares de Sousa, Gabriel, *Tratado descritivo do Brasil em 1587*, ed. Leonardo Dantas Silva. Recife: Editôra Messangana, 2000.
Soares Fonseca, Maria Nazareth, *Brasil Afro-Brasileiro*. Belo Horizonte: Autêntica, 2000.
Solé, Carlos and Maria Isabel Abreu (eds), *Latin American Writers*,
Soley, Lawrence C., & John S. Nichols, *Clandestine Radio Broadcasting: A Study of Revolutionary and Counterrevolutionary Electronic Communication*. New York: Praeger, 1987.
Solís Alcalá, Emilio (trans. and intro.), *Códice Pérez*. Mérida, Yucatán: Imprenta Oronte, 1944.
Solórzano, Carlos (ed.), *Teatro breve hispanoamericano contemporáneo*. Madrid: Aguilar, 1970.
—— (ed.), *El teatro actual latinoamericano*. Mexico: Ediciones de Andrea, 1972.
Sommer, Doris, *Foundational Fictions: The National Romances of Latin America*. Berkeley: University of California Press, 1991.
Sousa Meneses, Agrário de, *Os Miseravéis*. Rio de Janeiro: Poggetti, 1863.
Souza Andrade, Olímpio de, *História e interpretação de 'Os Sertões'*, 4th ed. Rio de Janeiro: Acadêmia Brasileira das Letras, 2002.
Spell, Jefferson Rea, *The Life and Works of José Joaquín Fernández de Lizardi*. Philadelphia: University of Pennsylvania Press, 1931.
Standish, Peter, *Hispanic Culture of South America* New York: Manly, 1995.
——, *Hispanic Culture of Mexico, Central America and the Caribbean* New York: Manly, 1996.
Stavans, Ilan, *Julio Cortázar: A Study of the Short Fiction*. Boston: Twayne, 1996.
Steinberg, S. H., *Five Hundred Years of Printing*. 2nd ed. Harmondsworth: Penguin, 1966.
Stoll, David, *Rigoberta Menchú and the story of all poor Guatemalans*. Boulder CO and Oxford: Westview Press, 1999.
Stolley, Karen, 'The Eighteenth Century: Narrative Forms, Scholarship and Learning', in *The Cambridge History of Latin American Literature*, ed. Enrique Pupo-Walker and Roberto González Echeverría. Cambridge: Cambridge University Press, 1996, vol. 1, 336–74.
Stubb, Martin S., 'The Essay of Nineteenth-Century Mexico, Central America, and the Caribbean', in *The Cambridge History of Latin American Literature*, ed. Enrique Pupo-Walker and Roberto González Echeverría. Cambridge: Cambridge University Press, 1996, vol. 1, 590–607.

Sturrock, John, *Paper Tigers: the Ideal Fictions of Borges*. Oxford: Clarendon Press, 1977.
Suassuna, Ariano, *Auto da Compadecida*. Rio de Janeiro: Agir Editôra, 1970.
Swanson, Philip, *The New Novel in Latin America: Politics and Popular Culture After the Boom*. Manchester: Manchester University Press, 1995.
—— (ed.), *The Companion to Latin American Studies*. London: Arnold, 2003.
——, *Latin American Fiction: A Short Introduction*. Oxford: Blackwell, 2005.
Tamayo Vargas, Augusto, 'Obras menores en el teatro de Peralta', in *Homenaje a Peralta*. Lima: Universidad Nacional Mayor de San Marcos, n.d., 5–20.
Tanner, Tony, *Adultery in the Novel: Contract and Transgression*. Baltimore, MD: Johns Hopkins University Press, 1979.
Tatum, Charles, *Chicano Literature*. Boston: Twayne, 1982.
Taylor, Diana, *Theatre of Crisis: Drama and Politics in Latin America*. Lexington: The University Press of Kentucky, 1991.
Teixeira, Bento, *Prosopopéia*, ed. Celso Cunha and Carlos Durval. 9th ed. São Paulo: Instituto Nacional do Livro, 1977.
Teixeira, Ivan, *Mercenato Pombalino e Poesia Neoclássica*. São Paolo: Universidad de São Paolo, 1999.
Teysseier, Paul, *Dicionário da literatura brasileira*. São Paulo: Martins Fontes Editoria, 2003.
Thomas, H., *Short-Title Catalogues of Portuguese Books and of Spanish-American Books Printed Before 1601 now in the British Museum*. London: Bernard Quaritch Ltd., 1926.
Thompson, Lawrence S., *Printing in Colonial Spanish America*. Hamden, CT: The Shoe String Press, 1962.
Todorov, Tzvetan, *La conquista de América, la cuestión del otro*. Mexico: Siglo XXI, 1987.
Torres, Lourdes, 'The Construction of the Self in US Latina Autobiographies', in *Third World Women and the Politics of Feminism*, ed. Chandra Mohanty, Ann Russo and Lourdes Torres. Bloomington: Indiana University Press, 1991.
——, 'US Latino/a Literature: Re-creating America', *ANQ* 10.3 (1997): 47–50.
Traba, Marta, *Conversación al sur*. 3rd ed. Mexico: Siglo Veintiuno Editores, 1988.
Ubaldo Ribeiro, João, *A Casa dos Budas Ditosos*. Rio de Janeiro: Editôra Objetiva, 1999.
Valenzuela, Luisa, *Cambio de armas*. Hanover, NH: Ediciones del Norte, 1980.
——, 'Mis brujas favoritas', in *Theory and Practice of Feminist Literary Criticism*, ed. Gabriela Mora and Karen S. Van Hooft. Ypsilanti, MI: Bilingual Press, 1982, 88–95.
Valle Cabral, Alfredo do (ed.), *Obras poeticas de Gregório de Mattos publicadas por Alfredo do Valle Cabral*. Rio de Janeiro: Typographica Nacional, 1881. 224 pp. BN, Rio, Sala João Antônio Marquês, 90,1,28.
Vallejo, César, *Obra poética completa*, ed. Américo Ferrari. Madrid: Alianza, 1983.
Vargas Llosa, Mario, *La orgía perpetua: Flaubert y 'Madame Bovary'*. Barcelona: Seix Barral, 1975.
——, *La casa verde*. 18th ed. Barcelona: Seix Barral, 1978.
——, *La ciudad y los perros*. 19th ed. Barcelona: Seix Barral, 1981.
——, *La guerra del fin del mundo*. Barcelona: Seix Barral, 1981.

———, *La historia secreta de una novela*. Barcelona: Tusquets Editor, 1981.
Vasconcelos, José. *La raza cósmica*. 11th ed. México: Espasa-Calpe Mexicana, 1986.
Vega, Ana Lydia, *Encancaranublado y otros cuentos de naufragio*. Río Piedra, PR: Editorial Antillana, 1983.
Verani, Hugo J., 'The Vanguardia and its Implications', in *The Cambridge History of Latin American Literature*, ed. Enrique Pupo-Walker and Roberto González Echeverría. Cambridge: Cambridge University Press, 1996, vol. 2, 114–37.
Verissimo, Erico, *Brazilian Literature: an Outline*. New York: Greenwood, 1969.
Vieira, Father Antônio, *Os melhores sermões*, ed. Marcelo Baches. Porto Alegre: Mercado Aberto, 1999.
Vieira, Else P. (ed.), *City of God in Several Voices: Brazilian Social Cinema as Action*, Nottingham: Cultural and Communications Press, 2005.
Viramontes, Helena Maria, *The Moths and Other Stories*. Houston, TX: Arte Publico Press, 1985.
Volpi, Jorge, *En busca de Klingsor*. Barcelona: Seix Barral. 1999.
Watson Miller, Ingrid (ed.), *Afro-Hispanic Literature: An Anthology of Hispanic Writers of African Ancestry*. Miami, FL: Ediciones Universal, 1991.
Watt, Ian, *The Rise of the Novel. Studies in Defoe, Richardson and Fielding*. Berkeley and Los Angeles: University of California Press, 1957.
Weiss, Judith A., *Latin American Popular Theatre: The First Five Centuries*. Albuquerque: University of New Mexico Press, 1993.
Wellek, René, 'The Concept of Realism in Literary Scholarship', in *Concepts of Criticism*. New Haven, CT: Yale University Press, 1963, 222–55.
Williams, Lorna, *Self and Society in the Poetry of Nicolás Guillén*. Baltimore: Johns Hopkins University Press, 1982.
Williams, Raymond Leslie, *The Postmodern Novel in Latin America: Politics, Culture, and the Crisis of Truth*. New York: St Martin's Press, 1995.
Wilson, Jason, *Jorge Luis Borges*. London: Reaktion Books, 2006.
Wold, Ruth, *El diario de México, primer cotidiano de Nueva España*. Madrid: Gredos, 1970.
Wolff, Egon, *Los invasores. Teatro chileno contemporáneo*, ed. J. Duran-Cerda. Mexico: Aguilar, 1970, 131–209.
Woodward, George (ed.), *The Modern Stage in Latin America: Six Plays*. New York: E. P. Dutton, 1971.
Woolf, Fausto, *A Mão Esquerda*. Rio de Janeiro: Bertrand Brasil, 1995.
Zamora, Margarita, *Language, Authority, and Indigenous History in the 'Comentarios Reales de los Incas'*. Cambridge: Cambridge University Press, 1988.
Zanetti, Susana, *Jorge Isaacs*. Buenos Aires: Centro Editor de América Latina, 1967.

# Index

Abreu, Caio Fernando   239
Abreu, Luis Alberto de   243
Abritta, Sergio   244
Acosta, José de   18–19
Aeschylus   108, 166, 176
Aguilera Malta, Demetrio   179 n.5
Aguirre, Isidora   179 n.5, 242
Aguirre, Juan Bautista   46 n.5
Agustín, José   175
Agustini, Delmira   112–13
Aira, César   282–3, 286–7
Alarcón, Juan Ruiz de   56
Alberdi, Juan Bautista   70, 129
Alegría, Ciro   167
Alegría, Claribel   199, 200, 206
Alemán, Mateo   36
Alencar, José de   86–8, 97, 289
Allende, Isabel   257–8
Almagro, Diego de   15
Almeida, Manuel Antônio de   69, 84–6
Alphonsus, João   178
Altamirano, Ignacio Manuel   83 n.7, 106
Alvar Ixtilxochitl, Fernando de   26
Alvarado Tezozomac, Fernando   26
Álvares Cabral, Pedro   1, 13
Alvares de Azevedo, Manuel   71
Alvarez, Julia   265
Alvim, Francisco   201
Amado, Jorge   170, 172–4
Amaral, José Maria do   71
Anaya, Rodolfo   266
Anchieta, José de   19–20, 32–4, 37, 60
Andrade, Mário de   28, 144–5, 162–4
Andrade, Oswald de   144–5

Antunes, Arnaldo   205
Anzaldúa, Gloria   266
Arenas, Reinaldo   269–71
Arguedas, Alcides   167 n.4
Arguedas, José María   167–8, 206
Aridjis, Homero   175
Ariosto, Ludovico   39
Aristophanes   108
Arredondo, Inés   175
Arrefát, Antón   179 n.5
Arreola, Juan José   175
Arzáns de Orsúa y Vela, Bartolomé   51
Ascensio Segura, Manuel   93, 95–6, 126
Ascher, Nelson   207
Asturias, Miguel Ángel   28, 164, 206
Asunción Silva, José   109–9
Ávila, Carlos   207
Axayacotl   9
Azuela, Mariano   160–1

Balbuena, Bernardo de   36, 38, 41–2, 56
Balzac, Honoré de   82, 132
Bandeira, Manuel   143
Barnet, Miguel   261
Barquet, Jesús   268
Barros Grez, Daniel   126
Batres Montúfar, José   80–1
Belli, Carlos Germán   195–7
Bello, Andrés   72, 74–5
Benavente, Fray Toribio de Paredes o   18–19
Bilac, Olivo   113–15
Bioy Casares, Adolfo   230 n.7
Blest Gana, Alberto   83 n.7, 120
Bocanegra, Mathias de   57

Bolívar, Simón  67–8, 72–3, 98–9, 128, 165
Bombal, María Luisa  168, 230 n. 7
Bonifácio de Andrade e Silva, José  99–101
Bonvicino, Régis  201–2
Borges, Jorge Luis  131, 145, 176–7, 247, 253, 279, 281
Boscán, Juan  39
Botelho de Oliveira, Manuel  59
Boti, Regino  150–1
Brasseur de Bourbourg, Abbé  29
Bravo, Francisco  36
Bretas, Angela  268
Bretón de los Herreros  93
Bruce-Novoa, Juan  266
Bry, Theodor de  ix
Bryce Echenique, Alfredo  283–4
Buarque de Hollanda, Chico  284–5
Buenaventura, Enrique  179 n. 5, 240–1
Byron, Lord (George Gordon)  70, 123

Cabral de Melo Neto, Carlos João  152–4
Cabrera Infante, Guillermo  214–15
Calderón de la Barca, Pedro  56, 60, 65, 97
Camões, Luis de  41, 49, 136–7
Campos, Augusto de  156
Campos, Harold de  156
Camus, Albert  165–6, 168
Carballido, Emilio  175, 179 n. 5
Cardenal, Ernesto  193–4
Cardim, Fernão  10, 21–2
Carlyle, Thomas  69, 129
Carpentier, Alejo  169–70, 206
Carranza, María Mercedes  200 n. 5
Carrió de la Vandera, Alonso  54–5
Carvalho, Mara  244
Casal, Julián del  106, 108–9
Casas, Bartolomé de las  19, 36
Castanon Guimarães, Júlio  204
Castellanos, Rosario  175, 188–90
Castillo, Ana  265–6
Castillo, Francisca Josefa de la Concepción de  53–4
Castro, Fidel  130, 134

Castro Alves, Antônio de  71–2, 278
Caulfield, Carlota  268
Caviedes, Juan del Valle y  44–6, 78, 289
Centeno de Osma, Gabriel  58–9
Cervantes, Miguel de  88, 130–1
Cervantes de Salazar, Francisco  36
Cesar, Ana Cristina  202–3, 237
Chateaubriand, François-August-René, Viscount  70, 89
Chávez, Denise  266
Che Guevara, Ernesto  260
Chekhov, Anton (Pavlovich)  177
Chocrón, Isaac  268
Chumacero, Alí  175
Cicero  37
Cieza de León, Pedro  17–18
Cisneros, Antonio  197–9
Cisneros, Sandra  265
Codices  4–6
Coelho, Paulo  225–6
Columbus, Christopher  ix, 1, 13, 15, 289
Compte, Auguste  129
Concolorcorvo  54–5
Cornejo Polar, Antonio  248
Correia, Raimundo  114
Cortázar, Julio  177, 191, 205, 208–9, 225 n. 1, 230–2, 253
Cortés, Hernán  14–15, 28
Costa, Horácio  202, 204
Cromberger, Juan  35
Cruz, Sor Juana Inés de la  60–6, 188, 289
Cruz e Sousa, João  114–16

Da Costa Guimarães, Afonso Henriques  114–15
Da Cunha, Euclides  157–60, 228, 290
Da Gama, Basílio  48–9
Dante (Alighieri)  134, 161, 255
Darío, Rubén  107, 109–10
Descartes, René  55, 253
Dias Gomes, Alfredo  179 n. 5
Díaz, Jorge  179 n. 5
Díaz del Castillo, Bernal  17, 28, 187–8

Díaz Mirón, Salvador   108
Dickens, Charles   82, 173, 280
Domínguez, Delia   200 n. 5
Donoso, José   205, 216–17, 222
Dragún, Osvaldo   179 n. 5
Drummond, Roberto   237
Drummond de Andrade, Carlos   151–2
Ducange   93
Dumas, Alexandre   93
Duncan, Quince   275
Durán, Diego de   26
Dutra e Melo, Antônio Francisco   71

Echeverría, Esteban   70, 84, 91–3, 119
Edwards, Jorge   280–1
Eichelbaum, Samuel   179 n. 5, 180
Eiró, Samuel   97–8
Elizondo, José F.   128
Elizondo, Salvador   175
Ercilla y Zúñiga, Alonso de   31, 38–40, 42–3
Espina, Eduardo   268
Espronceda, José de   70
Esquivel, Laura   258–9
Evaristo, Maria da Conceição   279
Evita, Leoncio   275

Fagundes Telles, Lygia   220–2
Faulkner, William   168, 278
Feijóo, Fray Benito Jerónimo   55
Fernandes Brandão, Ambrosio   22, 24–5
Fernández de Lizardi, José Joaquín   69, 82–3
Fernández de Oviedo y Valdés, Gonzalo   15–16, 187
Fernández Retamar, Roberto   71, 129, 191, 193, 244–5
Ferré, Rosario   235
Ferreira Gullar   154–5
Fidel López, Vicente   119
Fonseca, Rubem   236
Francovich, Guillermo   179 n. 5
Freyre, Gilberto   186–7
Frota, Teresa   243
Fuentes, Carlos   175, 177, 191, 205–7, 210, 230 n. 7, 251 n. 1
Fuguet, Alberto   256

Gallegos, Rómulo   161–2
Ganivet, Angel   129
García, Cristina   265
García Canclini, Néstor   248
García de Palacio, Diego   36
García Goyena, Rafael   78–81
García Gutiérrez, Antonio   93
García Márquez, Gabriel   177, 191, 205–6, 210–12, 229, 230, 230 n. 7, 232–3, 251 n. 1, 260, 279, 289–90
Garro, Elena   205, 212–13
Gautier, Théophile   114
Geada, Rita   200 n. 5
Giardinelli, Mempo   230 n. 7, 253–4
Gide, André   238
Girondo, Oliviero   146
Glib, Dagoberto   265
Gómez de Avellaneda, Gertrudis   91, 102–5, 275
Gonçalves de Magalhães, Domingos José   70–1
Gonçalves Dias, Antônio   71, 96–7
Góngora, Luis de   52, 65, 202
González de Eslava, Fernán   43
González de León, Ululame   200 n. 5
González Martínez, Enrique   111
Gorostiza, Carlos   179 n. 5
Gorostiza, Celestino   179 n. 5, 180
Gorostiza, Manuel Eduardo de   93–4
Guaman Poma de Ayala, Felipe   19
Guidice, Victor   237
Guillén, Nicolás   148–9, 275
Guimarães, Bernardo   71, 106, 118–19
Guimarães Rosa, João   170–2
Güiraldes, Ricardo   161
Gutenberg, Johann   ix
Gutiérrez, Eduardo   106, 120–1, 125
Gutiérrez Nájera, Manuel   108

Hartzenbusch, Juan Eugenio   93
Hatoum, Milton   179, 282, 287–8
Heredia, José María   72, 75–7
Hernández, José   106, 116–17, 126
Hernández, Luisa Josefina   175
Herrera y Reissig, Julio   111
Hijuelos, Oscar   266

Hinojosa, Rolando 265
Hojeda, Diego de 39, 42–3
Horace 37
Hostos, Eugenio María de 127–8
Hugo, Victor 30, 93
Huidobro, Vicente 145–6

Ibarbourou, Juana 112
Ibargüengoitia, Jorge 175
Icaza, Jorge 167
Isaacs, Jorge 88–90, 289

Jaimes Freyre, Ricardo 110
Jiménez, Blas 275
Jodorowsky, Raquel 200 n. 5
Joyce, James 132, 168, 221, 253

Kafka, Franz 132, 175, 239, 253

Landa, Diego de 2, 10, 18–19
Lanuchi, Vincencio 31
Larra, Mariano José de 70, 93
Leiradella, Cunha de 243
Leminski, Paolo 203–4
Leñero, Vicente 175
Lévi-Strauss, Claude 11, 212
Levins-Morales, Aurora 266
Lima, Jorge do 154
Lima Barreto, Alfonso Henriques de 158–60, 178, 279
Lins, Paolo 263–4
Lispector, Clarice 178, 220–3, 236–7, 289–90
Lopes de Almeida, Júlia 178
Lopes de Souza, Pêro 16–17
López de Gómara, Francisco 17
López de Gómara, Justo 125
López y Fuentes, Gregorio 167 n. 4
Lucan, Marcus Annaeus 37
Lugones, Leopoldo 111–12

Machado, Aníbal 178
Machado, Duda 204
Machado de Assis, Joaquim Maria 70, 117, 119, 127, 130–7, 179, 278
Magalhães de Gândavo, Pêro de 22–3
Magdalena, Mauricio 167 n. 4

Maia, Circe 200 n. 5
Mallarmé, Stéphane 115, 156
Manrique, Jorge 37
Manzano, Juan Francisco 90–1
Maples Arce, Manuel 145
Marcos, Plínio 183
Mariátegui, José Carlos 185
Marinho, Flávio 243
Mármol, José 84
Marqués, René 179 n. 5, 181–2
Martí, José 130, 137–9, 289
Martial, Marcus Valerius 37
Martínez de la Rosa, Francisco 93
Martínez Estrada, Ezequiel 185–6
Martins Pena, Luis Carlos 96
Matos Guerra, Gregório de 46–7, 59, 289
Matto de Turner, Clorinda 122–4, 167 n. 4
Mazzotti, José Antonio 268
Meireles, Cecília 155
Melgar, Mariano 76–7
Menchú, Rigoberta 28, 261–2
Mendes, Murilo 154
Mendieta, Jerónimo de 30–1, 187
Menotti del Pichia 142
Mistral, Gabriela 112–13
Mitre, Bartolomé 119
Molina, Alonso de 36
Molloy, Sylvia 269, 272–3
Monsiváis, Carlos 175, 249
Montaigne, Michel de 11
Montalvo, Juan 127–8
Monteiro Lobato, José Bento 140–1, 178
Moock, Armando 179 n. 5, 180
Moraga, Cherríe 266–7
Morales, Rosario 266
Moratín, Leandro Fernández 93
Morejón, Nancy 200 n. 5
Morelli de Castelnovo, João 37
Muñoz Camargo, Diego 26, 28
Mutis, Alvaro 194–5, 230 n. 7

Nalé Roxló, Conrado 180
Nariño, Antonio 69
Nebrija, Antonio 12, 37
Neruda, Pablo 147–8, 206, 254–5
Nervo, Amado 110

Neto, Torquato 202
Newton, Isaac 55
Nóbrega, Manoel da 10–11, 20–1, 60
Noll, João Gilberto 239, 269, 274–5, 285–6
Núñez Cabeza de Vaca, Alvar 16, 53, 117
Núñez de Pineda y Bascuñán, Francisco 52

Ocampo, Miguel 125
Olavide y Jáuregui, Pablo 57–8
Ollé, Carmen 200 n.5
Oliveira, Alberto de 114
Olmedo, José Joaquín de 72–4
Oña, Pedro de 40
Onetti, Juan Carlos 213–14, 230 n.7
Orozco, Olga 200 n.5
Ortiz, Adalberto 275
Ortiz, Fernando 187
Ovid 37

Pablos, Juan 35–6
Palma, Ricardo 124–5
Pardo y Aliaga, Felipe 93–5
Parente Cunha, Helena 223–4
Parra, Nicanor 192–3, 197
Parra, Teresa de la 164–5
Parra, Violeta 200 n.5
Paso, Fernando del 175
Paz, Octavio 149–50, 187–8
Pentateuch 12
Peralta y Barnuevo, Pedro de 57
Pérez de Montalbán 56
Pérez de Villagrá, Gaspar 265 n.2
Pérez Galdós, Benito 132, 137
Peri Rossi, Carmen 269, 271–2
Pessoa, Fernado 60
Petronius 111
Piglia, Ricardo 252–3
Pignatari, Décio 156
Piñon, Nélida 220, 224–5, 239
Pío Pérez, Juan 10
Pizarnik, Alejandra 199–200
Pizarro, Francisco 30
'Plácido' 76–8
Podestá, José J. 125
Pombal, Marquis 48

Portalatín, Aida Cartagena 276–7
Porteiro, Samuel 12
Proust, Marcel 168
Puig, Manuel 269–70

Queroz, Rachel de 179
Quiroga, Horacio 174–5

Racine, Jean 58
Rama, Angel 69, 245
Ramos, Graciliano 165–7
Renan, Ernest 119, 129
Restrepo, Laura 259–60
Reynoso, Diego 3
Ricardo, Cassiano 201
Richard, Nelly 249
Rio, João do 177–8
Rivas, Duque de (Don Angel de Saavedra) 93
Rivera, José Eustasio 161
Roa Bastos, Augusto 218–20, 279
Rodó, Enrique 128–30
Rodrigues, Nelson 182–3
Rodríguez Freile, Juan 50–1
Romero, Armando 268
Rosado de Lunha, Luis Antonio 37
Rosas de Oquendo, Mateo 44–5
Rousseau, Jean-Jacques 74
Rulfo, Juan 165–6, 170, 175–6
Runasimi 6–8

Sábato, Ernesto 169, 205
Sabino, Fernando 237
Sahagún, Bernadino de 2, 8, 25–8
Sainz, Gustavo 175, 215–16
Salomão, Waly 204
San Anton Munon Chimalpain Cuauhtelhuanitzin, Domingo Francisco de 26
Sánchez, Florencio 126–7
Sánchez, Luis Rafael 251–2
Sánchez Baquero, Juan 31
Sant'Anna, André 240
Santa Cruz y Espejo, Javier Eugenio de 24, 55–6
Santa Cruz, Nicomedes 277
Santa Rita Durão, José de 49–50
Santiago, Silviano 238–9, 247–8, 269, 273–4

Santillana, Marqués de  37
Sarduy, Severo  217–18
Sarlo, Beatriz  248
Sarmiento, Domingo Faustino  70, 101–2, 116, 119, 185
Sartre, Jean-Paul  179, 206, 275
Schiller, Herbert I.  93
Schwarz, Roberto  156, 245–7, 264, 278–9
Scliar, Moacyr  237
Scott, Sir Walter  70
Seneca, Lucius Annaeus  31, 37
Sepúlveda, Luis  255–6
Shakespeare, William  93, 128–9, 227, 244, 255
Sigüenza y Góngora, Carlos de  52–3, 117
Silverio Trevisan, João  240
Simões Lopes, João  178
Skármeta, Antonio  254–5
Soares de Souza, Gabriel  22–4
Steinbeck, John  168
Stendhal (Henri Beyle)  82
Storni, Alfonsina  112–13
Suarez, Mario  266
Suassuma, Ariano  183
Suetonius, Tranquillus  37
Sussekind, Carlos  239

Taine, Hippolyte  129
Teixeira, Bento  37–8, 40–1, 48
Terence  37
Terrazas, Francisco de  43
Tezozomac  27
Tibullus  108
Tolstoy, Count Leo Nikolayevich  82, 188
Traba, Marta  257
Trevisan, Dalton  237
Triana, José  179 n. 5

Ubaldo Ribeiro, João  227–8, 239
Usigli, Rodolfo  179 n. 5, 181

Valencia, Guillermo  110–11
Valenzuela, Luisa  233–5
Valera, Juan  109
Valéry, Paul  238, 253
Vallejo, César  146–7, 165, 289
Van Steen, Edla  239, 244
Vargas Llosa, Mario  191, 205, 207–10, 225, 228–9, 230 n. 7, 251 n. 1, 279, 289
Vasconcelos, José  112, 184–5
Vaz de Caminha, Pêro  1, 12–15, 289
Vega, Ana Lydia  235–6
Vega, Garcilaso de la  6, 18, 249
Veiga, José J.  179
Ventura de la Vega  93
Vera Cruz, Fray Alonso de la  36
Vergil  37–8, 142
Verissimo, Érico  179, 191
Verlaine, Paul  109
Verney, Luís Antônio  48
Vieira, Antônio  11, 37, 60–2, 144, 289
Villarroel, Gaspar  52
Villarrutia, Xavier  179 n. 5, 180
Villaverde, Cirilo  121–2
Viracocha  7, 10
Viramontes, Helena  265, 267
Volpi, Jorge  256–7
Voltaire, François-Marie Arouet  58

Wilson, Carlos Guillermo  275
Wolff, Egon  242–3
Woolf, Fausto  226–7
Woolf, Virginia  168, 221

Yáñez, Agustín  165

Zapata, Luis  269
Zapata, Miguel Angel  268
Zapata Olivella, Manuel  277–8
Zola, Emile  168, 248
Zorrilla, José  93, 105, 132
Zumárraga,  Bishop 36

www.ingramcontent.com/pod-product-compliance
Lightning Source LLC
Chambersburg PA
CBHW071228230426
43668CB00011B/1351